Peugeot 305
Owners
Workshop
Manual

RGO Hawes

Models covered
Peugeot 305 GL, GR, GLS, S, SR, GT, GTX & Automatic
Saloon, Estate and Van
1290 cc, 1472 cc, 1580 cc & 1905 cc petrol engines

Does not cover Diesel engine

ISBN 1 85010 510 3

© Haynes Publishing Group 1981, 1985, 1987, 1988, 1989
Printed in England *(538-3R4)*

ABCD

Haynes Publishing Group
Sparkford Nr Yeovil
Somerset BA22 7JJ England

Haynes Publications, Inc
861 Lawrence Drive
Newbury Park
California 91320 USA

British Library Cataloguing in Publication Data

Hawes, R. G. O.
  Peugeot 305 owners workshop manual.
  1. Cars. Maintenance & repair – Amateurs' manuals
  I. Title   II. Series
  629.28'722
  ISBN 1-85010-510-3

Acknowledgements

No work of this sort is achieved by one person. This Owner's Workshop Manual is no exception, being the work of many to whom credit is due.

In particular, thanks are due to Peugeot Automobiles UK Limited for their important assistance with technical information and for the supply of certain illustrations. Duckhams Oils supplied lubrication data and the Champion Sparking Plug Company supplied the illustrations showing the different spark plug conditions.

Our special thanks go to Mr. N. J. Tucker who made his car available for use in our workshops.

About this manual

Its aim

The aim of this manual is to help you get the best value from your car. It can do so in several ways. It can help you decide what work must be done (even should you choose to get it done by a garage), provide information on routine maintenance and servicing, and give a logical course of action and diagnosis when random faults occur. However, it is hoped that you will use the manual by tackling the work yourself. On simpler jobs it may even be quicker than booking the car into a garage and going there twice to leave and collect it. Perhaps most important, a lot of money can be saved by avoiding the costs the garage must charge to cover its labour and overheads.

The manual has drawings and descriptions to show the function of the various components so that their layout can be understood. Then the tasks are described and photographed in a step-by-step sequence so that even a novice can do the work.

Its arrangement

The manual is divided into Chapters. The Chapters are each divided into Sections, numbered with single figures, eg 6; and the Sections into paragraphs (or sub-sections), with decimal numbers following on from the Section they are in, eg 5.1, 5.2, 5.3 etc.

It is freely illustrated, especially in those parts where there is a detailed sequence of operations to be carried out. There are two forms of illustration: figures and photographs. The figures are numbered in sequence with decimal numbers, according to their position in the Chapter – eg Fig. 6.4 is the fourth drawing/illustration in Chapter 6. Photographs carry the same number (either individually or in related groups) as the Section or sub-section to which they relate.

There is an alphabetical Index at the back of the manual as well as a contents list at the front. Each Chapter is also preceded by its own individual contents list.

References to the 'left' or 'right' of the vehicle are in the sense of a person in the driver's seat facing forwards.

Vehicle manufacturers continually make changes to specifications and recommendations, and these, when notified, are incorporated into our manuals at the earliest opportunity.

Unless otherwise stated, nuts and bolts are removed by turning anti-clockwise, and tightened by turning clockwise.

Whilst every care is taken to ensure that the information in this manual is correct, no liability can be accepted by the authors or publishers for loss, damage or injury caused by any errors in, or omissions from the information given.

Introduction to the Peugeot 305

Introduced in France in November 1977, the Peugeot 305 was launched in the UK in May 1978. Originally the range consisted of the GL and GR with a 1290 cc petrol engine and the SR with a 1472 cc petrol engine. In May 1979 a diesel-engined version of the GR was introduced as the GRD with a light alloy 1548 cc diesel engine (this model is not covered in this manual) and in April 1980 the GLS with a 1472 cc petrol engine was introduced, aimed at the fleet-sales market.

All models have four doors, a transversely mounted engine driving the front wheels, a gearbox with four forward all synchro gears plus reverse, and servo-assisted dual circuit braking with front discs and rear drums.

The GL is the basic model and the GR is similar, with a lockable glovebox, a clock, side fresh air vents, and pockets on the backs of the front seats. The SR has, in addition to the larger engine, a tachometer, front seat head restraints, a central armrest in the rear seat and a wider range of optional extras such as a laminated windscreen, tinted glass, electrically operated front windows, etc.

Models added to the range for the 1981 model year include the GL, GLS and SR Estates, and the sporty and well-equipped S Saloon. All models benefited from a face-lift and suspension improvements at the beginning of 1983; later that year a new 1580 cc engine and a new gearbox appeared in the GT Saloon and Estate. Details of the 1905 cc GTX models, and of automatic versions with the GT engine, are given in Chapter 12.

As with other current Peugeot cars, the 305 does present some problems for the DIY mechanic. Some of these are due to the design of the engine/transmission assembly with its wet, removable cylinder liners; others are due to the extensive use of special tools, in the absence of which some tasks are much more difficult, if not impossible. However, most of the basic routine maintenance tasks can be easily accomplished given a reasonably good tool kit. It is always advisable when doing a job for the first time to read through the Sections concerned before starting, to assess the problems and the need for any special tools or other unusual requirements.

Contents

Peugeot 305 SR Saloon

Dimensions, weights and capacities

For information applicable to later models, see Supplement at end of manual

Overall dimensions
Length .... 4.237 m (13 ft 10.8 in)
Width:
    GL and GR .... 1.630 m (5 ft 4.2 in)
    SR .... 1.642 m (5 ft 4.6 in)
Height (at kerb weight):
    GL .... 1.405 m (4 ft 7.3 in)
    GR .... 1.402 m (4 ft 7.2 in)
    SR .... 1.400 m (4 ft 7.1 in)
Height (laden):
    GL .... 1.327 m (4 ft 4.2 in)
    GR .... 1.324 m (4 ft 4.1 in)
    SR .... 1.323 m (4 ft 4.1 in)
Wheelbase .... 2.62 m (8 ft 7.1 in)
Overhang:
    Front .... 0.727 m (2 ft 4.6 in)
    Rear .... 0.89 m (2 ft 11 in)
Track:
    Front .... 1.37 m (4 ft 5.9 in)
    Rear .... 1.322 m (4 ft 4 in)

Weights
Maximum permissible laden weight (MLW)*:
    GL and GR .... 1340 kg (2954 lb)
    SR .... 1355 kg (2987 lb)
Maximum permissible rolling weight (MLW plus weight of trailer)*:
    GL and GR .... 2290 kg (5049 lb)
    SR .... 2305 kg (5082 lb)
Maximum towing capacity*:
    Trailer without brakes:
        GL and GR .... 460 kg (1014 lb)
        SR .... 470 kg (1036 lb)
    Trailer with brakes (within MRW limit):
        All models .... 1000 kg (2205 lb)
French legal limits

Capacities
Engine and transmission oil .... 4 litres (7.04 pints)
Cooling system .... 5.8 litres (10.2 pints)
Fuel tank .... 43 litres (9.46 gal)
Screen washer reservoir (may vary on some models) .... 1.5 litres (2.64 pints)

Tyre pressures
Front:
    145 x 14 .... 1.8 bars (26 lbf/in^2)
    155 x 14 .... 1.9 bars (27.6 lbf/in^2)
Rear:
    145 x 14 .... 2.1 bars (30.5 lbf/in^2)
    155 x 14 .... 2.1 bars (30.5 lbf/in^2)

Buying spare parts
and vehicle identification numbers

For information applicable to later models, see Supplement at end of manual

Buying spare parts

Spare parts are available from many sources. Peugeot have many dealers throughout the UK, and other dealers, accessory stores and motor factors will also stock some spare parts suitable for Peugeot cars.

Our advice regarding spare part sources is as follows:

Officially appointed vehicle main dealers – This is the best source of parts which are peculiar to your vehicle and are otherwise not generally available (eg complete cylinder heads, internal transmission components, badges, interior trim etc). It is also the only place at which you should buy parts if your vehicle is still under warranty. To be sure of obtaining the correct parts it will always be necessary to give the storeman your vehicle's engine and chassis number, and if possible, to take the 'old' part along for positive identification. Remember that many parts are available on a factory exchange scheme – any parts returned should always be clean! It obviously makes good sense to go straight to the specialists on your vehicle for this type of part, for they are best equipped to supply you.

Other dealers and auto accessory stores – These are often very good places to buy materials and components needed for the maintenance of your vehicle (eg oil filters, spark plugs, bulbs, fanbelts, oils and greases, touch-up paint, filler paste etc). They also sell general accessories, usually have convenient opening hours, charge lower prices and can often be found not far from home.

Motor factors – Good factors will stock all of the more important components which wear out relatively quickly (eg clutch components, pistons, valves, exhaust systems, brake cylinders/pipes/hoses/seals/ shoes and pads etc). Motor factors will often provide new or reconditioned components on a part exhange basis – this can save a considerable amount of money.

Vehicle identification numbers

Modifications are a continuing and unpublicised process in vehicle manufacture. Spare parts manuals and lists are compiled on a numerical basis, the individual vehicle numbers being essential to identify correctly the component required.

The engine number is located on the top of the flange joining the cylinder block to the transmission just to the right of the coil bracket on the back of the engine (photo).

The engine type is identified by two letters stamped on the front right-hand side of the cylinder block. Their significance is:

SB – XL5 (118) with 8.8:1 compression ratio
ZB – XL5 (118) with 7.6:1 compression ratio
SF – XR5 (142) with 9.2:1 compression ratio
ZC – XR5 (142) with 8:1 compression ratio

The vehicle type and serial number is stamped on an identification plate riveted to the top of the front right-hand wheel valance under the bonnet (photo). The car serial number is also marked on the engine, if it is the original installed on production, on a printed label stuck on the side face of the timing case.

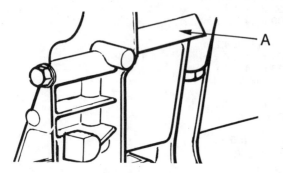

Engine type identification letters (A) are stamped on the right-hand side of the cylinder block

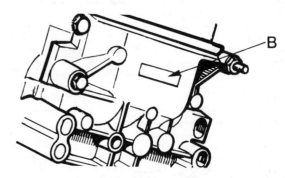

Vehicle serial number (B) is printed on a label stuck to the timing case

The engine number is located to the right of the coil bracket

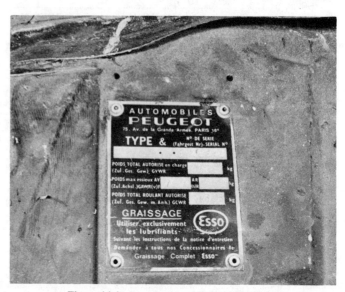

The vehicle type and serial number plate

Tools and working facilities

Introduction

A selection of good tools is a fundamental requirement for anyone contemplating the maintenance and repair of a motor vehicle. For the owner who does not possess any, their purchase will prove a considerable expense, offsetting some of the savings made by doing-it-yourself. However, provided that the tools purchased are of good quality, they will last for many years and prove an extremely worthwhile investment.

To help the average owner to decide which tools are needed to carry out the various tasks detailed in this manual, we have compiled three lists of tools under the following headings: *Maintenance and minor repair*, *Repair and overhaul*, and *Special*. The newcomer to practical mechanics should start off with the *Maintenance and minor repair* tool kit and confine himself to the simpler jobs around the vehicle. Then, as his confidence and experience grows, he can undertake more difficult tasks, buying extra tools as, and when, they are needed. In this way, a *Maintenance and minor repair* tool kit can be built-up into a *Repair and overhaul* tool kit over a considerable period of time without any major cash outlays. The experienced do-it-yourselfer will have a tool kit good enough for most repair and overhaul procedures and will add tools from the *Special* category when he feels the expense is justified by the amount of use these tools will be put to.

It is obviously not possible to cover the subject of tools fully here. For those who wish to learn more about tools and their use there is a book entitled *How to Choose and Use Car Tools* available from the publishers of this manual.

Maintenance and minor repair tool kit

The tools given in this list should be considered as a minimum requirement if routine maintenance, servicing and minor repair operations are to be undertaken. We recommend the purchase of combination spanners (ring one end, open-ended the other); although more expensive than open-ended ones, they do give the advantages of both types of spanner.

Combination spanners - 10, 11, 12, 13, 14 & 17 mm
Adjustable spanner - 9 inch
Engine sump/transmission drain plug key
Spark plug spanner – use special Peugeot spanner (see Chapter 4)
Spark plug gap adjustment tool
Set of feeler gauges
Brake bleed nipple spanner
Screwdriver - 4 in long x $\frac{1}{4}$ in dia (flat blade)
Screwdriver - 4 in long x $\frac{1}{4}$ in dia (cross blade)
Combination pliers - 6 inch
Hacksaw, junior
Tyre pump
Tyre pressure gauge
'Mole' wrench – 8 inch
Oil can
Fine emery cloth (1 sheet)
Wire brush (small)
Funnel (medium size)

Repair and overhaul tool kit

These tools are virtually essential for anyone undertaking any major repairs to a motor vehicle, and are additional to those given in the *Maintenance and minor repair* list. Included in this list is a comprehensive set of sockets. Although these are expensive they will be found invaluable as they are so versatile - particularly if various drives are included in the set. We recommend the $\frac{1}{2}$ in square-drive

type, as this can be used with most proprietary torque spanners. If you cannot afford a socket set, even bought piecemeal, then inexpensive tubular box wrenches are a useful alternative.

The tools in this list will occasionally need to be supplemented by tools from the *Special* list.

Sockets (or box spanners) to cover range in previous list
Reversible ratchet drive (for use with sockets)
Extension piece, 10 inch (for use with sockets)
Universal joint (for use with sockets)
Torque wrench (for use with sockets)
Ball pein hammer
Soft-faced hammer, plastic or rubber
Screwdriver - 6 in long x $\frac{5}{16}$ in dia (flat blade)
Screwdriver - 2 in long x $\frac{5}{16}$ in square (flat blade)
Screwdriver - 1$\frac{1}{2}$ in long x $\frac{1}{4}$ in dia (cross blade)
Screwdriver - 3 in long x $\frac{1}{8}$ in dia (electricians)
Pliers - electricians side cutters
Pliers - needle nosed
Pliers - circlip (internal and external)
Cold chisel - $\frac{1}{2}$ inch
Scriber (this can be made by grinding the end of a broken hacksaw blade)
Scraper (this can be made by flattening and sharpening one end of a piece of copper pipe)
Centre punch
Pin punch
Hacksaw
Valve grinding tool
Steel rule/straight edge
Allen keys
Selection of files
Wire brush (large)
Axle-stands
Jack (strong scissor or hydraulic type)

Special tools

The tools in this list are those which are not used regularly, are expensive to buy, or which need to be used in accordance with their manufacturers' instructions. Unless relatively difficult mechanical jobs are undertaken frequently, it will not be economic to buy many of these tools. Where this is the case, you could consider clubbing together with friends (or a motorists' club) to make a joint purchase, or borrowing the tools against a deposit from a local garage or tool hire specialist.

The following list contains only those tools and instruments freely available to the public, and not those special tools produced by the vehicle manufacturer specifically for its dealer network. You will find occasional references to these manufacturer's special tools in the text of this manual. Generally, an alternative method of doing the job without the vehicle manufacturer's special tool is given. However, sometimes, there is no alternative to using them. Where this is the case and the relevant tool cannot be bought or borrowed you will have to entrust the work to a franchised garage.

Valve spring compressor (where applicable)
Piston ring compressor
Balljoint separator
Universal hub/bearing puller
Impact screwdriver
Micrometer and/or vernier gauge
Dial gauge
Stroboscopic timing light

Dwell angle meter/tachometer
Universal electrical multi-meter
Cylinder compression gauge
Lifting tackle
Trolley jack
Light with extension lead

Buying tools

For practically all tools, a tool dealer is the best source since he will have a very comprehensive range compared with the average garage or accessory shop. Having said that, accessory shops often offer excellent quality tools at discount prices, so it pays to shop around.

Remember, you don't have to buy the most expensive items on the shelf, but it is always advisable to steer clear of the very cheap tools. There are plenty of good tools around at reasonable prices, so ask the proprietor or manager of the shop for advice before making a purchase.

Care and maintenance of tools

Having purchased a reasonable tool kit, it is necessary to keep the tools in a clean serviceable condition. After use, always wipe off any dirt, grease and metal particles using a clean, dry cloth, before putting the tools away. Never leave them lying around after they have been used. A simple tool rack on the garage or workshop wall, for items such as screwdrivers and pliers is a good idea. Store all normal spanners and sockets in a metal box. Any measuring instruments, gauges, meters, etc, must be carefully stored where they cannot be damaged or become rusty.

Take a little care when tools are used. Hammer heads inevitably become marked and screwdrivers lose the keen edge on their blades from time to time. A little timely attention with emery cloth or a file will soon restore items like this to a good serviceable finish.

Working facilities

Not to be forgotten when discussing tools, is the workshop itself. If anything more than routine maintenance is to be carried out, some form of suitable working area becomes essential.

It is appreciated that many an owner mechanic is forced by circumstances to remove an engine or similar item, without the benefit of a garage or workshop. Having done this, any repairs should always be done under the cover of a roof.

Wherever possible, any dismantling should be done on a clean flat workbench or table at a suitable working height.

Any workbench needs a vice: one with a jaw opening of 4 in (100 mm) is suitable for most jobs. As mentioned previously, some clean dry storage space is also required for tools, as well as the lubricants, cleaning fluids, touch-up paints and so on which become necessary.

Another item which may be required, and which has a much more general usage, is an electric drill with a chuck capacity of at least $\frac{5}{16}$ in (8 mm). This, together with a good range of twist drills, is virtually essential for fitting accessories such as wing mirrors and reversing lights.

Last, but not least, always keep a supply of old newspapers and clean, lint-free rags available, and try to keep any working area as clean as possible.

Spanner jaw gap comparison table

Jaw gap (in)	Spanner size
0.250	$\frac{1}{4}$ in AF
0.276	7 mm
0.313	$\frac{5}{16}$ in AF
0.315	8 mm
0.344	$\frac{11}{32}$ in AF; $\frac{1}{8}$ in Whitworth
0.354	9 mm
0.375	$\frac{3}{8}$ in AF
0.394	10 mm
0.433	11 mm
0.438	$\frac{7}{16}$ in AF
0.445	$\frac{3}{16}$ in Whitworth; $\frac{1}{4}$ in BSF
0.472	12 mm
0.500	$\frac{1}{2}$ in AF
0.512	13 mm
0.525	$\frac{1}{4}$ in Whitworth; $\frac{5}{16}$ in BSF
0.551	14 mm
0.562	$\frac{9}{16}$ in AF
0.591	15 mm
0.600	$\frac{5}{16}$ in Whitworth; $\frac{3}{8}$ in BSF
0.625	$\frac{5}{8}$ in AF
0.630	16 mm
0.669	17 mm
0.686	$\frac{11}{16}$ in AF
0.709	18 mm
0.710	$\frac{3}{8}$ in Whitworth, $\frac{7}{16}$ in BSF
0.748	19 mm
0.750	$\frac{3}{4}$ in AF
0.813	$\frac{13}{16}$ in AF
0.820	$\frac{7}{16}$ in Whitworth; $\frac{1}{2}$ in BSF
0.866	22 mm
0.875	$\frac{7}{8}$ in AF
0.920	$\frac{1}{2}$ in Whitworth; $\frac{9}{16}$ in BSF
0.937	$\frac{15}{16}$ in AF
0.945	24 mm
1.000	1 in AF
1.010	$\frac{9}{16}$ in Whitworth; $\frac{5}{8}$ in BSF
1.024	26 mm
1.063	$1\frac{1}{16}$ in AF; 27 mm
1.100	$\frac{5}{8}$ in Whitworth; $\frac{11}{16}$ in BSF
1.125	$1\frac{1}{8}$ in AF
1.181	30 mm
1.200	$\frac{11}{16}$ in Whitworth; $\frac{3}{4}$ in BSF
1.250	$1\frac{1}{4}$ in AF
1.260	32 mm
1.300	$\frac{3}{4}$ in Whitworth; $\frac{7}{8}$ in BSF
1.313	$1\frac{5}{16}$ in AF
1.390	$\frac{13}{16}$ in Whitworth; $\frac{15}{16}$ in BSF
1.417	36 mm
1.438	$1\frac{7}{16}$ in AF
1.480	$\frac{7}{8}$ in Whitworth; 1 in BSF
1.500	$1\frac{1}{2}$ in AF
1.575	40 mm; $\frac{15}{16}$ in Whitworth
1.614	41 mm
1.625	$1\frac{5}{8}$ in AF
1.670	1 in Whitworth; $1\frac{1}{8}$ in BSF
1.688	$1\frac{11}{16}$ in AF
1.811	46 mm
1.813	$1\frac{13}{16}$ in AF
1.860	$1\frac{1}{8}$ in Whitworth; $1\frac{1}{4}$ in BSF
1.875	$1\frac{7}{8}$ in AF
1.969	50 mm
2.000	2 in AF
2.050	$1\frac{1}{4}$ in Whitworth; $1\frac{3}{8}$ in BSF
2.165	55 mm
2.362	60 mm

Jacking and towing

A pantograph type of jack is supplied with the car but this is only suitable for changing a wheel in an emergency. Under no circumstances work under the car when it is only supported on this jack; additional support is essential and the car should have axle stands or substantial blocks located under the sub-frames whenever it is necessary for you to get underneath.

When using the wheel-changing jack on Saloon models, position it under the jacking point adjacent to the wheel to be changed with the screw spindle pointing towards the diagonally opposite wheel (photo). This will allow the jack to tilt safely as the car lifts through an arc as it is jacked up. On Estate models there is only one jacking point on each side, as shown in the illustration. On all models, engage first or reverse gear (or 'P' on automatics), apply the handbrake and chock the wheel diagonally opposite the one to be removed.

Front and rear anchorage points are provided for tying the vehicle down when being transported. These can be used for towing or being towed in an emergency (photos). Certain precautions must be observed when towing a vehicle equipped with automatic transmission – see Chapter 12, Section 14.

Provision has been made to install a tow-bar at the rear of the car without the need for drilling holes, and an approved towing attachment is available through Peugeot agents.

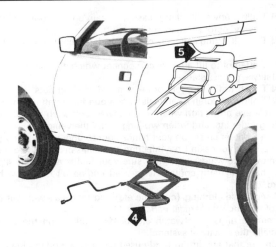

Jack (4) and jacking point (5) – Estate models

The wheel-changing jack in use

The front ...

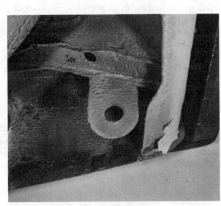

... and rear tie-down points can be used for emergency towing

Safety first!

Professional motor mechanics are trained in safe working procedures. However enthusiastic you may be about getting on with the job in hand, do take the time to ensure that your safety is not put at risk. A moment's lack of attention can result in an accident, as can failure to observe certain elementary precautions.

There will always be new ways of having accidents, and the following points do not pretend to be a comprehensive list of all dangers; they are intended rather to make you aware of the risks and to encourage a safety-conscious approach to all work you carry out on your vehicle.

Essential DOs and DON'Ts

DON'T rely on a single jack when working underneath the vehicle. Always use reliable additional means of support, such as axle stands, securely placed under a part of the vehicle that you know will not give way.

DON'T attempt to loosen or tighten high-torque nuts (e.g. wheel hub nuts) while the vehicle is on a jack; it may be pulled off.

DON'T start the engine without first ascertaining that the transmission is in neutral (or 'Park' where applicable) and the parking brake applied.

DON'T suddenly remove the filler cap from a hot cooling system – cover it with a cloth and release the pressure gradually first, or you may get scalded by escaping coolant.

DON'T attempt to drain oil until you are sure it has cooled sufficiently to avoid scalding you.

DON'T grasp any part of the engine, exhaust or catalytic converter without first ascertaining that it is sufficiently cool to avoid burning you.

DON'T allow brake fluid or antifreeze to contact vehicle paintwork.

DON'T syphon toxic liquids such as fuel, brake fluid or antifreeze by mouth, or allow them to remain on your skin.

DON'T inhale dust – it may be injurious to health (see *Asbestos* below).

DON'T allow any spilt oil or grease to remain on the floor – wipe it up straight away, before someone slips on it.

DON'T use ill-fitting spanners or other tools which may slip and cause injury.

DON'T attempt to lift a heavy component which may be beyond your capability – get assistance.

DON'T rush to finish a job, or take unverified short cuts.

DON'T allow children or animals in or around an unattended vehicle.

DO wear eye protection when using power tools such as drill, sander, bench grinder etc, and when working under the vehicle.

DO use a barrier cream on your hands prior to undertaking dirty jobs – it will protect your skin from infection as well as making the dirt easier to remove afterwards; but make sure your hands aren't left slippery. Note that long-term contact with used engine oil can be a health hazard.

DO keep loose clothing (cuffs, tie etc) and long hair well out of the way of moving mechanical parts.

DO remove rings, wristwatch etc, before working on the vehicle – especially the electrical system.

DO ensure that any lifting tackle used has a safe working load rating adequate for the job.

DO keep your work area tidy – it is only too easy to fall over articles left lying around.

DO get someone to check periodically that all is well, when working alone on the vehicle.

DO carry out work in a logical sequence and check that everything is correctly assembled and tightened afterwards.

DO remember that your vehicle's safety affects that of yourself and others. If in doubt on any point, get specialist advice.

IF, in spite of following these precautions, you are unfortunate enough to injure yourself, seek medical attention as soon as possible.

Asbestos

Certain friction, insulating, sealing, and other products – such as brake linings, brake bands, clutch linings, torque converters, gaskets, etc – contain asbestos. *Extreme care must be taken to avoid inhalation of dust from such products since it is hazardous to health.* If in doubt, assume that they *do* contain asbestos.

Fire

Remember at all times that petrol (gasoline) is highly flammable. Never smoke, or have any kind of naked flame around, when working on the vehicle. But the risk does not end there – a spark caused by an electrical short-circuit, by two metal surfaces contacting each other, by careless use of tools, or even by static electricity built up in your body under certain conditions, can ignite petrol vapour, which in a confined space is highly explosive.

Always disconnect the battery earth (ground) terminal before working on any part of the fuel or electrical system, and never risk spilling fuel on to a hot engine or exhaust.

It is recommended that a fire extinguisher of a type suitable for fuel and electrical fires is kept handy in the garage or workplace at all times. Never try to extinguish a fuel or electrical fire with water.

Note: *Any reference to a 'torch' appearing in this manual should always be taken to mean a hand-held battery-operated electric lamp or flashlight. It does NOT mean a welding/gas torch or blowlamp.*

Fumes

Certain fumes are highly toxic and can quickly cause unconsciousness and even death if inhaled to any extent. Petrol (gasoline) vapour comes into this category, as do the vapours from certain solvents such as trichloroethylene. Any draining or pouring of such volatile fluids should be done in a well ventilated area.

When using cleaning fluids and solvents, read the instructions carefully. Never use materials from unmarked containers – they may give off poisonous vapours.

Never run the engine of a motor vehicle in an enclosed space such as a garage. Exhaust fumes contain carbon monoxide which is extremely poisonous; if you need to run the engine, always do so in the open air or at least have the rear of the vehicle outside the workplace.

If you are fortunate enough to have the use of an inspection pit, never drain or pour petrol, and never run the engine, while the vehicle is standing over it; the fumes, being heavier than air, will concentrate in the pit with possibly lethal results.

The battery

Never cause a spark, or allow a naked light, near the vehicle's battery. It will normally be giving off a certain amount of hydrogen gas, which is highly explosive.

Always disconnect the battery earth (ground) terminal before working on the fuel or electrical systems.

If possible, loosen the filler plugs or cover when charging the battery from an external source. Do not charge at an excessive rate or the battery may burst.

Take care when topping up and when carrying the battery. The acid electrolyte, even when diluted, is very corrosive and should not be allowed to contact the eyes or skin.

If you ever need to prepare electrolyte yourself, always add the acid slowly to the water, and never the other way round. Protect against splashes by wearing rubber gloves and goggles.

When jump starting a car using a booster battery, for negative earth (ground) vehicles, connect the jump leads in the following sequence: First connect one jump lead between the positive (+) terminals of the two batteries. Then connect the other jump lead first to the negative (–) terminal of the booster battery, and then to a good earthing (ground) point on the vehicle to be started, at least 18 in (45 cm) from the battery if possible. Ensure that hands and jump leads are clear of any moving parts, and that the two vehicles do not touch. Disconnect the leads in the reverse order.

Mains electricity

When using an electric power tool, inspection light etc, which works from the mains, always ensure that the appliance is correctly connected to its plug and that, where necessary, it is properly earthed (grounded). Do not use such appliances in damp conditions and, again, beware of creating a spark or applying excessive heat in the vicinity of fuel or fuel vapour.

Ignition HT voltage

A severe electric shock can result from touching certain parts of the ignition system, such as the HT leads, when the engine is running or being cranked, particularly if components are damp or the insulation is defective. Where an electronic ignition system is fitted, the HT voltage is much higher and could prove fatal.

Routine maintenance

For information applicable to later models, see Supplement at end of manual

Maintenance is essential both for safety and for obtaining the best in terms of performance and economy from your vehicle. Over the years, the need for periodic lubrication — oiling, greasing, and so on — has been drastically reduced, and this has led some owners to think that the various components either no longer exist or will last forever. This is a serious delusion. It follows, therefore, that the largest initial element of maintenance is visual examination.

The following routine maintenance summary is based on the manufacturer's recommendation, but is supplemented by certain checks which we think will add up to improved reliability and an increase of component life.

Every 250 miles/400 km, weekly, or before a long journey

Engine

Check the engine oil level with the car standing on level ground and, if necessary, top up to the upper mark on the dipstick (photos)

Cooling system

Check the coolant level in the radiator. The level should be within 5 cm (2 in) of the filler orifice.

Check for leaks if the level is low (photo).

Brakes

Check the reservoir fluid level. If it requires topping up use an approved fluid and examine the brake pipes and hoses for fluid leaks (photo).
Check the effectiveness of the brakes including the handbrake.

Steering and suspension

Check the tyre pressures, including the spare, and adjust them as necessary.
Examine the tyres for wear and damage.
Check the steering for smooth and accurate response.

Electrical system

Check battery electrolyte level and top up with purified water if necessary (photo).
Check the operation of all the lights, the wipers (wet the screen first), the horns, instruments and gauges.
Check the windscreen washer reservoir fluid level and top up as required (photo).

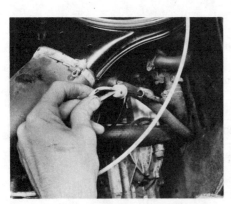
Removing the oil level dipstick

Topping up the engine oil

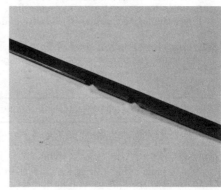
Upper and lower marks on the oil level dipstick

Topping up the coolant level

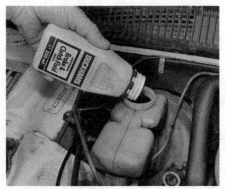
Topping up the brake fluid level

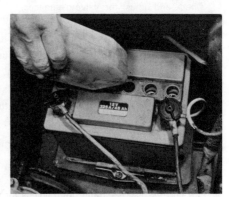
Topping up the battery electrolyte

Checking the windscreen washer fluid level

Fitting a new oil filter cartridge

Every 5000 miles/7500 km, or six months

In addition to the work listed for the weekly servicing

Engine

Drain the engine oil when hot. If this is the first 5000 miles/7500 km servicing, renew the oil filter cartridge. Refill wth fresh oil.
Clean and adjust the spark plugs.
Check, clean and adjust the contact breaker points.
Wipe clean the distributor cap, coil and HT leads.
Examine for oil, coolant or fuel leaks.
Check the exhaust system for damage and security

Steering, suspension, and driveshafts

Inspect all rubber gaiters for leaks, damage and deterioration.

Every 10 000 miles/15 000 km, or annually

In addition to the work listed for the six-monthly servicing

Engine

Renew the oil filter cartridge on draining the engine oil (photo).
Renew the spark plugs and the contact breaker points.
Lubricate the distributor
Check and adjust the ignition timing
Check and adjust the carburettor idle setting.
Check and adjust the valve clearances.
Check and adjust the fanbelt and the alternator belt.
Change the air cleaner filter if the car is used in dusty conditions.
Clean the fuel pump and filter.
Check all nuts and bolts for tightness, but don't exceed torque loads where these are specified.

Electrical

Clean the battery, its stowage and the battery terminals.

Cooling system

Check the radiator, heater and carburettor hoses for deterioration and tightness of their clips.

Brakes

Inspect the disc pads and drum linings for wear.
Check the clearance of the foot pedal when the brakes are applied.

Suspension and steering

Inspect all the joints for excessive play and the rubber bushes for wear.
Check the shock absorber struts for security and fluid leaks.
Check the steering rack for security.
Inspect the condition of the steering column flexible coupling.

Clutch

Check and adjust the clutch cable

Lights

Check and adjust the headlamp beam alignment.

Bodywork

Lubricate all door locks and hinges including the bonnet and boot.
Check the seat belts for security and wear.

Every 20 000 miles/30 000 km, or two years

In addition to the work listed for the annual servicing

Engine

Drain and flush the cooling system, and refill with fresh antifreeze mixture.
Change the air cleaner filter.

Brakes

Clean out the rear brakes, removing all dust, but take care not to inhale it.

Hubs

Check the front and rear wheel hub bearings, clean and regrease them (see Chapter 7).

Every 30 000 miles/45 000 km or two years

In addition to the work listed for the annual or two-yearly servicing, as applicable

Brakes

Drain and renew the hydraulic fluid.

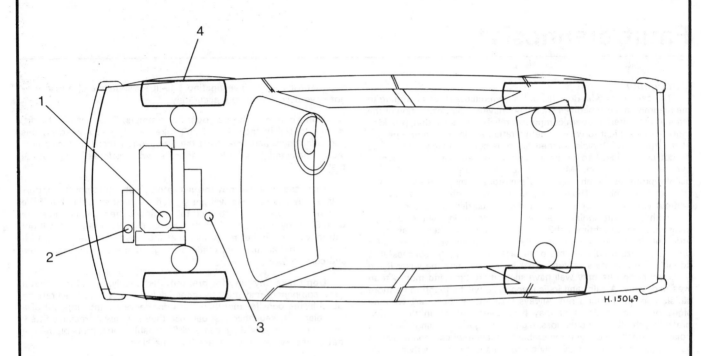

Recommended lubricants and fluids

Component or system	Lubricant type/specification	Duckhams recommendation
1 Engine	Multigrade engine oil, viscosity SAE 10W/40 to API SF/CC	Duckhams QXR, Hypergrade, or 10W/40 Motor Oil
Manual transmission BB8 (406) BE1 (up to 1986) BE1 (1987 on)	Shares engine lubricant Multigrade engine oil, viscosity SAE 10W/40, to API SF/CC Gear oil, viscosity SAE 75W/80	Duckhams QXR, Hypergrade, or 10W/40 Motor Oil Duckhams Hypoid PT 75W/80W
Automatic transmission	Dexron II type ATF	Duckhams D-Matic
2 Cooling system	Antifreeze to BS 3151, 3152 or 6580	Duckhams Universal Antifreeze and Summer Coolant
3 Brake fluid reservoir	Hydraulic fluid to SAE J1703	Duckhams Universal Brake and Clutch Fluid
4 Wheel hub bearings	Multi-purpose lithium-based grease	Duckhams LB 10
Gearchange balljoints	Kluber Proba 270 Altemp grease	
Power-assisted steering	Dexron II type ATF	Duckhams D-Matic

Fault diagnosis

Introduction

The car owner who does his or her own maintenance according to the recommended schedules should not have to use this section of the manual very often. Modern component reliability is such that, provided those items subject to wear or deterioration are inspected or renewed at the specified intervals, sudden failure is comparatively rare. Faults do not usually just happen as a result of sudden failure, but develop over a period of time. Major mechanical failures in particular are usually preceded by characteristic symptoms over hundreds or even thousands of miles. Those components which do occasionally fail without warning are often small and easily carried in the car.

With any fault finding, the first step is to decide where to begin investigations. Sometimes this is obvious, but on other occasions a little detective work will be necessary. The owner who makes half a dozen haphazard adjustments or replacements may be successful in curing a fault (or its symptoms), but he will be none the wiser if the fault recurs and he may well have spent more time and money than was necessary. A calm and logical approach will be found to be more satisfactory in the long run. Always take into account any warning signs or abnormalities that may have been noticed in the period preceding the fault – power loss, high or low gauge readings, unusual noises or smells, etc – and remember that failure of components such as fuses or spark plugs may only be pointers to some underlying fault.

The pages which follow here are intended to help in cases of failure to start or breakdown on the road. There is also a Fault Diagnosis Section at the end of each Chapter which should be consulted if the preliminary checks prove unfruitful. Whatever the fault, certain basic principles apply. These are as follows:

Verify the fault. This is simply a matter of being sure that you know what the symptoms are before starting work. This is particularly important if you are investigating a fault for someone else who may not have described it very accurately.

Don't overlook the obvious: For example, if the car won't start, is there petrol in the tank? (Don't take anyone else's word on this particular point, and don't trust the fuel gauge either!) If an electrical fault is indicated, look for loose or broken wires before digging out the test gear.

Cure the disease, not the symptom. Substituting a flat battery with a fully charged one will get you off the hard shoulder, but if the underlying cause is not attended to, the new battery will go the same way. Similarly, changing oil-fouled spark plugs for a new set will get you moving again, but remember that the reason for the fouling (if it wasn't simply an incorrect grade of plug) will have to be established and corrected.

Don't take anything for granted. Particularly, don't forget that a 'new' component may itself be defective (especially if it's been rattling round in the boot for months), and don't leave components out of a fault diagnosis sequence just because they are new or recently fitted. When you do finally diagnose a difficult fault, you'll probably realise that all the evidence was there from the start.

Electrical faults

Electrical faults can be more puzzling than straightforward mechanical failures, but they are no less susceptible to logical analysis if the basic principles of operation are understood. Car electrical wiring exists in extremely unfavourable conditions – heat, vibration and chemical attack – and the first things to look for are loose or corroded connections, and broken or chafed wires, especially where the wires

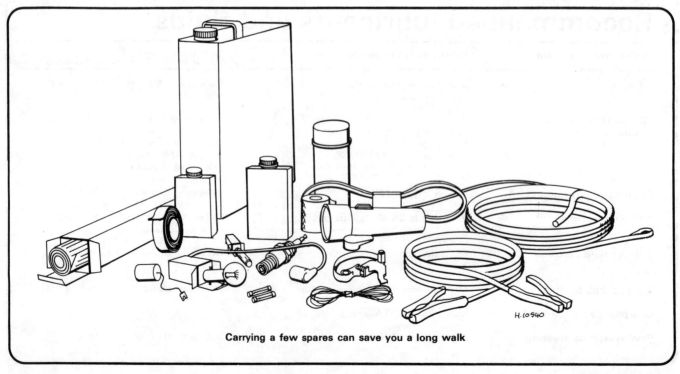

H.10540

Carrying a few spares can save you a long walk

pass through holes in the bodywork or are subject to vibration.

All metal-bodied cars in current production have one pole of the battery 'earthed', ie connected to the car bodywork, and in nearly all modern cars it is the negative (–) terminal. The various electrical components – motors, bulb holders etc – are also connected to earth, either by means of a lead or directly by their mountings. Electric current flows through the component and then back to the battery via the car bodywork. If the component mounting is loose or corroded, or if a good path back to the battery is not available, the circuit will be incomplete and malfunction will result. The engine and/or gearbox are also earthed by means of flexible metal straps to the body or subframe; if these straps are loose or missing, starter motor, generator and ignition trouble may result.

Assuming the earth return to be satisfactory, electrical faults will be due either to component malfunction or to defects in the current supply. Individual components are dealt with in Chapter 10. If supply wires are broken or cracked internally this results in an open-circuit, and the easiest way to check for this is to bypass the suspect wire temporarily with a length of wire having a crocodile clip or suitable connector at each end. Alternatively, a 12V test lamp can be used to verify the presence of supply voltage at various points along the wire and the break can be thus isolated.

If a bare portion of a live wire touches the car bodywork or other earthed metal part the electricity will take the low-resistance path thus formed back to the battery: this is known as a short-circuit. Hopefully, a short-circuit will blow a fuse, but otherwise it may cause burning of the insulation (and possibly further short-circuits) or even a fire. This is why it is inadvisable to bypass persistently blowing fuses with silver foil or wire.

Spares and tool kit

Most cars are only supplied with sufficient tools for wheel changing; the *Maintenance and minor repair* tool kit detailed in *Tools and working facilities*, with the addition of a hammer, is probably sufficient for those repairs that most motorists would consider attempting at the roadside. In addition, a few items which can be fitted without too much trouble in the event of breakdown should be carried. Experience and available space will modify the list below, but the following may save having to call on professional assistance:

Spark plugs, clean and correctly gapped
HT lead and plug cap – long enough to reach the plug furthest from the distributor
Distributor rotor, condenser and contact breaker points
Drivebelt(s) – emergency type may suffice
Spare fuses
Set of principal light bulbs
Tin of radiator sealer and hose bandage
Exhaust bandage
Roll of insulating tape
Length of soft iron wire
Length of electrical flex
Torch or inspection lamp (can double as test lamp)
Battery jump leads
Tow-rope
Ignition waterproofing aerosol
Litre of engine oil
Sealed can of hydraulic fluid
Emergency windscreen
Worm drive hose clips
Tube of filler paste

If spare fuel is carried, a can designed for the purpose should be used to minimise risks of leakage and collision damage. A first aid kit and a warning triangle, whilst not at present compulsory in the UK, are obviously sensible items to carry in addition to the above.

When touring abroad, it may be advisable to carry additional spares which, even if you cannot fit them yourself, could save having to wait while parts are obtained. The items below may be worth considering:

Clutch and throttle cables
Cylinder head gasket
Alternator brushes
Fuel pump repair kit (if available)
Tyre valve core

One of the motoring organisations will be able to advise on availability of fuel etc in foreign countries.

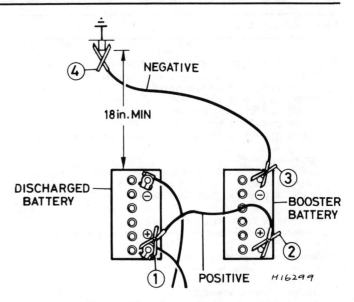

Jump start lead connections for negative earth vehicles – connect leads in order shown

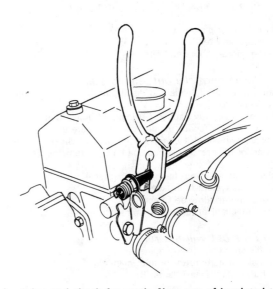

Crank engine and check for spark. Note use of insulated tool to hold plug lead

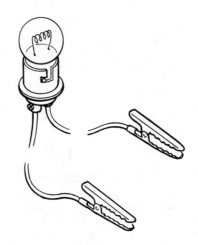

A simple test lamp is useful for tracing electrical faults

Engine will not start

Engine fails to turn when starter operated
　　Flat battery (recharge, use jump leads, or push start)
　　Battery terminals loose or corroded
　　Battery earth to body defective
　　Engine earth strap loose or broken
　　Starter motor (or solenoid) wiring loose or broken
　　Automatic transmission selector in wrong position, or inhibitor switch faulty
　　Ignition/starter switch faulty
　　Major mechanical failure (seizure) or long disuse (piston rings rusted to bores)
　　Starter or solenoid internal fault (see Chapter 10)

Starter motor turns engine slowly
　　Partially discharged battery (recharge, use jump leads, or push start)
　　Battery terminals loose or corroded
　　Battery earth to body defective
　　Engine earth strap loose
　　Starter motor (or solenoid) wiring loose
　　Starter motor internal fault (see Chapter 10)

Starter motor spins without turning engine
　　Flat battery
　　Starter motor pinion sticking on sleeve
　　Flywheel gear teeth damaged or worn
　　Starter motor mounting bolts loose

Engine turns normally but fails to start
　　Damp or dirty HT leads and distributor cap (crank engine and check for spark)
　　Dirty or incorrectly gapped CB joints (if applicable)
　　No fuel in tank (check for delivery at carburettor)
　　Excessive choke (hot engine) or insufficient choke (cold engine)
　　Fouled or incorrectly gapped spark plugs (remove, clean and regap)
　　Other ignition system fault (see Chapter 4)
　　Other fuel system fault (see Chapter 3)
　　Poor compression (see Chapter 1)
　　Major mechanical failure (eg camshaft drive)

Engine fires but will not run
　　Insufficient choke (cold engine)
　　Air leaks at carburettor or inlet manifold
　　Fuel starvation (see Chapter 3)

Other ignition fault (see Chapter 4)

Engine cuts out and will not restart

Engine cuts out suddenly – ignition fault
　　Loose or disconnected LT wires
　　Wet HT leads or distributor cap (after traversing water splash)
　　Coil or condenser failure (check for spark)
　　Other ignition fault (see Chapter 4)

Engine misfires before cutting out – fuel fault
　　Fuel tank empty
　　Fuel pump defective or filter blocked (check for delivery)
　　Fuel tank filler vent block (suction will be evident on releasing cap)
　　Carburettor needle valve sticking
　　Carburettor jets blocked (fuel contaminated)
　　Other fuel system fault (see Chapter 3)

Engine cuts out – other causes
　　Serious overheating
　　Major mechanical failure (eg camshaft drive)

Engine overheats

　　Slack or broken drivebelt (photo) – retension or renew (Chapter 2)
　　Coolant loss due to internal or external leakage (see Chapter 2)
　　Thermostat defective
　　Low oil level
　　Brakes binding
　　Radiator clogged externally or internally
　　Electric cooling fan not operating correctly
　　Engine waterways clogged
　　Ignition timing incorrect or automatic advance malfunctioning
　　Mixture too weak
Note: *Do not add cold water to an overheated engine or damage may result*

Low engine oil pressure

Gauge reads low or warning light illuminated with engine running
　　Oil level low or incorrect grade
　　Defective gauge or sender unit

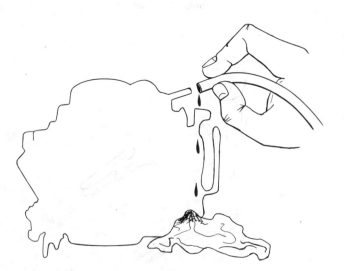

Remove pipe from carburettor and check for fuel delivery

A slack or broken drivebelt can cause overheating

Wire to sender unit earthed
Engine overheating
Oil filter clogged or bypass valve defective
Oil pressure relief valve defective
Oil pick-up strainer clogged
Oil pump worn or mountings loose
Worn main or big-end bearings

Note: *Low oil pressure in a high-mileage engine at tickover is not necessarily a cause for concern. Sudden pressure loss at speed is far more significant. In any event, check the gauge or warning light sender before condemning the engine!*

Engine noises

Pre-ignition (pinking) on acceleration

Incorrect grade of fuel
Ignition timing incorrect
Distributor faulty or worn
Worn or maladjusted carburettor
Excessive carbon build-up in engine

Whistling or wheezing noises

Leaking vacuum hose
Leaking carburettor or manifold gasket
Blowing head gasket

Tapping or rattling

Incorrect valve clearances
Worn valve gear
Worn timing chain or belt
Broken piston ring (ticking noise)

Knocking or thumping

Unintentional mechanical contact (eg fan blades)
Worn fanbelt
Peripheral component fault (generator, water pump etc)
Worn big-end bearings (regular heavy knocking, perhaps less under load)
Worn main bearing (rumbling and knocking, perhaps worsening under load)
Piston slap (most noticeable when cold)

Chapter 1 Engine

For modifications, and information applicable to later models, see Supplement at end of manual

Contents

Specifications

General

Engine type	Four-cylinder, in-line, ohc, water-cooled, transverse mounting
Engine type reference:	
GL and GR models	XL5 (118)
SR models	XR5 (142)
Bore (all models)	78 mm (3.071 in)
Stroke:	
XL5	67.5 mm (2.657 in)
XR5	77 mm (3.031 in)
Cubic capacity:	
XL5	1290 cc
XR5	1472 cc
Compression ratio:	
XL5	8.8 : 1
XR5	9.2 : 1
Compression pressure (on starter, with spark plugs removed):	
XL5	11 kgf/cm^2 (157 lbf/in^2)
XR5	11.5 kgf/cm^2 (166 lbf/in^2)
Maximum power (DIN):	
XL5:	
Fan disengaged	65 bhp at 6000 rpm
Fan engaged	59.5 bhp at 5750 rpm
XR5:	
Fan disengaged	74 bhp at 6000 rpm
Fan engaged	67 bhp at 5700 rpm
Maximum Torque (DIN):	
XL5:	
Fan disengaged	9.6 kgf m (69.4 lbf ft) at 3750 rpm
Fan engaged	9.4 kgf m (67.99 lbf ft) at 3750 rpm
XR5:	
Fan disengaged	11.8 kgf m (85.3 lbf ft) at 3000 rpm
Fan engaged	11.5 kgf m (83.2 lbf ft) at 3000 rpm
Location of No 1 cylinder	At clutch end of block
Firing order	1 – 3 – 4 – 2
Direction of rotation	Clockwise viewed from pulley end

Camshaft

Camshaft drive	Chain and sprockets
Identification (see Section 35):	
XL5 – earlier	Green paint dab near centre journal
XL5 – later	Blue paint dab near centre journal
XR5 – earlier	White paint dab near centre journal
XR5 – later	Yellow paint dab near centre journal
Camshaft bearings	5, plain, unlined, in cylinder head
Camshaft journal diameters:	
1 (Clutch end)	40.03 to 40.05 mm (1.5760 to 1.5768 in)
2	40.43 to 40.45 mm (1.5917 to 1.5925 in)
3	40.83 to 40.85 mm (1.6075 to 1.6083 in)
4	41.23 to 41.25 mm (1.6232 to 1.6240 in)
5 (sprocket end)	41.63 to 41.65 mm (1.6390 to 1.6398 in)
Maximum ovality of end journals	0.02 mm (0.0008 in)
Running clearance	0.05 to 0.11 mm (0.002 to 0.004 in)
Endfloat	0.04 to 0.15 mm (0.002 to 0.006 in)
Camlift	4.972 mm (0.1957 in)

Connecting rods

Type	H section, steel forging
Length between centres:	
XL5	132.7 mm (5.2244 in)
XR5	126.8 mm (4.9921 in)
Big-end bearings	Steel back, faced with aluminium and 20% tin alloy
Big-end bearing thickness:	
New	1.817 mm (0.0715 in)
Repair	1.967 mm (0.0774 in)
Big-end bearing diameter	48.655 to 48.671 mm (1.9155 to 1.9162 in)
Small-end bearing diameter	20.465 to 20.478 mm (0.8057 to 0.8062 in)
Maximum permissible weight difference in set of 4 connecting rods	3g (0.1058 oz)

Crankshaft and main bearings

Number of bearings	5
Main journal diameter:	
New	53.027 to 53.046 mm (2.0877 to 2.0884 in)
Regrind 0.30 mm (0.0118 in)	52.727 to 52.746 mm (2.0759 to 2.0766 in)
Crankpin diameter:	
New	44.991 to 44.980 mm (1.7713 to 1.7709 in)
Regrind 0.30 mm (0.0118 in)	44.691 to 44.680 mm (1.7595 to 1.7591 in)
Crankpin throw:	
XL5	67.5 mm (2.6575 in)
XR5	77.0 mm (3.0315 in)
Main journal running clearance	0.016 to 0.066 mm (0.0006 to 0.0026 in)
Crankpin running clearance	0.024 to 0.063 mm (0.0009 to 0.0025 in)
Crankshaft diameter at input bearing location	41.980 to 41.991 mm (1.6528 to 1.6532 in)
Crankshaft endfloat	0.07 to 0.27 mm (0.0028 to 0.0106 in)
Thrust washers:	
Material:	
Series 1 engines	Steel backed, tin/aluminium/lead alloy faced
Series 2 engines	Steel backed, aluminium/lead alloy faced
Number fitted:	
Series 1 engines	2, in cylinder block, No 2 bearing
Series 2 engines	2, in cylinder block, No 2 bearing, and 2 on No 2 bearing cap
Thicknesses available	2.30, 2.40, 2.45 and 2.50 mm (0.0906, 0.0949. 0.0965 and 0.0984 in)

Note: *Series 1 thrust washers can be fitted to Series 2 engines but the reverse is not permissible*

Main bearing thickness:	
New	1.874 to 1.880 mm (0.0738 to 0.0740 in)
Repair	2.024 to 2.030 mm (0.0797 to 0.0799 in)
Bearing cap shells	Plain
Cylinder block shells	Grooved

Cylinder block

Type and material	Cylinder block integral with top half of crankcase, pressure die-cast in aluminium alloy with cast iron bearing blocks for crankshaft

Liners

Length, overall	133 mm (5.236 in)
Identification	1 to 4 lines on upper edge
Bore:	
1 line	78.0 to 78.01 mm (3.0709 to 3.0713 in)
2 lines	78.01 to 78.02 mm (3.0713 to 3.0717 in)
3 lines	78.02 to 78.03 mm (3.0717 to 3.0720 in)
4 lines	78.03 to 78.04 mm (3.0720 to 3.0724 in)

Liner protrusion on assembly:
    Relative to cylinder block joint face .... 0.11 to 0.21 mm with 0.14 mm as ideal (0.0043 to 0.0083 in with 0.0055 in as ideal)
    Relative to adjacent liner(s) .... 0.04 mm (0.0016 in) max
Maximum out-of-squareness .... 0.02 mm (0.0008 in)
Liner gasket thicknesses:
    Blue .... 0.087 mm (0.0034 in)
    White .... 0.102 mm (0.0040 in)
    Red .... 0.122 mm (0.0048 in)
    Yellow .... 0.147 mm (0.0058 in)

Pistons

Type .... Aluminium alloy with two compression and one oil control ring. Gudgeon pin free to rotate in piston – press fit in connecting rod
Identification .... Letter A, B, C or D and number 1, 2 or 3 on piston crown
Diameter:
    A .... 77.920 to 77.931 mm (3.0677 to 3.0681 in)
    B .... 77.931 to 77.942 mm (3.0681 to 3.0686 in)
    C .... 77.942 to 77.953 mm (3.0686 to 3.0690 in)
    D .... 77.953 to 77.964 mm (3.0690 to 3.0694 in)
Note: *A grade A diameter piston must be used in a liner with 1 line marked, grade B in a liner with 2 lines and so on*
Gudgeon pin bore diameter .... 20.506 to 20.515 mm (0.8073 to 0.8077 in)
Ring thicknesses:
    Upper compression .... 1.73 to 1.72 mm (0.0681 to 0.0677 in)
    Lower compression .... 1.98 to 1.99 mm (0.0780 to 0.0783 in)
    Oil scraper .... 4.011 mm (0.1579 in)
Gudgeon pin:
    Length .... 68 mm (2.6772 in)
    Diameter grades:
        Blue .... 20.500 to 20.497 mm (0.8071 to 0.8070 in)
        White .... 20.497 to 20.494 mm (0.8070 to 0.8069 in)
        Red .... 20.494 to 20.491 mm (0.8069 to 0.8067 in)
Note: *A blue grade pin must be used in a piston marked 1, white grade in 2 and red grade in 3*

Cylinder head

Type .... Pressure die-cast aluminium alloy, bi-spherical combustion chambers, offset valves, taper seats for spark plugs and five bearings for camshaft
Camshaft bearing diameters:
    1 (clutch end) .... 40.1 to 40.139 mm (1.5787 to 1.5803 in)
    2 .... 40.5 to 40.539 mm (1.5945 to 1.5960 in)
    3 .... 40.9 to 40.939 mm (1.6102 to 1.6118 in)
    4 .... 41.3 to 41.339 mm (1.6260 to 1.6276 in)
    5 (timing end) .... 41.7 to 41.739 mm (1.6417 to 1.6433 in)
Maximum distortion or out-of-flat on joint face .... 0.05 mm (0.002 in)

Valves

Head diameter:
    Inlet .... 39.5 mm (1.5551 in)
    Exhaust .... 32.5 mm (1.2795 in)
Seat angle:
    Inlet .... 120° to 120° 25′
    Exhaust .... 90° to 90° 25′
Stem diameter:
    Inlet:
        Bottom .... 7.97 to 7.98 mm (0.3138 to 0.3142 in)
        Top .... 7.98 to 7.99 mm (0.3142 to 0.3146 in)
    Exhaust:
        XL5 – Bottom .... 7.95 to 7.96 mm (0.3130 to 0.3134 in)
        XL5 – Top .... 7.97 to 7.98 mm (0.3138 to 0.3142 in)
        XR5 – Bottom .... 7.945 to 7.96 mm (0.3128 to 0.3134 in)
        XR5 – Top .... 7.956 to 7.966 mm (0.3133 to 0.3136 in)
Valve seat width:
    Inlet .... 2.3 mm (0.0906 in)
    Exhaust .... 2.8 mm (0.1102 in)

Valve springs

Type .... Single coil spring
Free length (approximately) .... 47.2 mm (1.858 in)
Height:
    Valve open .... 32.2 mm at 54.9 to 57.9 kg load (1.2678 in at 121.0 to 127.6 lbs load)
    Valve closed .... 40.0 mm at 23.8 to 27.4 kg load (1.5748 in at 52.5 to 60.4 lbs load)
Fitting direction .... Joined spiral towards head

Valve guides
Length .... 51 mm (2.0079 in)
Internal bore diameter .... 8.02 to 8.04 mm (0.3157 to 0.3165 in)

Valve clearances (cold)
Inlet .... 0.10 mm (0.004 in)
Exhaust .... 0.25 mm (0.010 in)

Valve timing

	XL5	XR5
Inlet valve:		
Opens	6° BTDC	3° BTDC
Closes	38° ABDC	41° ABDC
Exhaust valve:		
Opens	45° BBDC	42° BBDC
Closes	1° ATDC	2° BTDC

Lubrication system
Type .... Wet sump – pressure and spray
Oil filter:
    Type .... Full flow, renewable cartridge
Lubricant type/specification .... Multigrade engine oil, viscosity SAE 10W/40, to API SF/CC
(Duckhams QXR, Hypergrade, or 10W/40 Motor Oil)
System capacity .... 4 litres (7 pints) approx
Oil pump type .... Eccentric bi-rotor
Oil pressure .... 4 bars (58 lbf/in²)
Low pressure warning .... 0.6 bars (8.7 lbf/in²)

Torque wrench settings

	lbf ft	kgf m
Cylinder head bolts (10):		
Stage 1	32.5	4.5
Stage 2, early engines*	43.4	6.0
Stage 2, later engines*	54.2	7.5
*Important: See explanation in paragraph 6, Section 35		
Camshaft sprocket bolts (3)	14.5	2.0
Timing case bolts (17)	10.8	1.5
Engine mountings:		
Bolts (4) in timing case	12.7	1.75
Upper bolts (4) in engine	10.8	1.5
Upper nuts (3) in RH mounting	12.7	1.75
Lower bolts and nut (3)	13.0	1.8
Main bearing cap bolts (10)	38.0	5.25
Big-end bearing cap nuts (8)	27.1	3.75
Sump filter gauze bolts (3)	4.3	0.6
Sump cover bolts (13)	7.2	1.0
Sump drain plug (1)	19.9	2.75
Crankshaft sprocket and gear bolt (1)	79.6	11.0
Timing chain tensioner blade pivot (1)	9.4	1.3
Timing chain tensioner bolts (2)	4.3	0.6
Oil gallery cover plate bolts (5)	9.0	1.25
Exhaust manifold nuts (8)	10.8	1.5
Gear selection rod front bolt (1)	13.0	1.8
Starter motor bolts (3)	25.3	3.5
Crankshaft pulley bolt	65.1	9.0
Spark plugs	13.0	1.75

1 General description

A four-cylinder, in-line overhead camshaft engine is fitted to the Peugeot 305. There are two versions: the XL5 (118) engine of 1290 cc is used in GL and GR models and the XR5 (142) engine of 1472 cc in SR models. The smaller engine was previously used in Peugeot 304 cars; the larger engine is a more recent version of that engine having a longer stroke. The engine is mounted transversely in an upright position to drive the front wheels.

A manual gearbox is bolted to the bottom of the engine and uses a common oil system. The final drive to the roadwheels is via a differential unit on the front of the gearbox. Drive to the gearbox is via conventional clutch on the left-hand side of the engine, through an input pinion free-running on the crankshaft and located between the clutch and the engine block.

All the major casings and housings are manufactured from pressure die-cast aluminium alloy. The cylinder block has removable wet cylinder liners which are centrifugally cast from special iron alloy and the main bearing caps are made of cast iron. The cylinder head has bi-spherical squish effect combustion chambers each having one exhaust valve, one inlet valve, and a taper seated spark plug location. Single springs are fitted to the valves which are operated by rockers each incorporating an adjustable screw and locknut for valve clearance setting.

The aluminium alloy pistons are fitted with three rings, two compression and one 'perfect circle' scraper. The pistons are assembled to the forged steel connecting rods by a gudgeon pin which is a force fit in the connecting rod small-end.

The crankshaft is carried in five main bearings and has a polygon taper (with three faces) at the left-hand end on which the clutch and flywheel assembly is mounted. The other end is keyed to drive the camshaft chain sprocket and also a shaft by which the oil pump, fuel pump and distributor are driven. A twin pulley is bolted to the clutch end of the crankshaft to drive the coolant pump/fan assembly and the alternator via separate drivebelts.

The power unit is suspended on two rubber cushioned mountings attached at each end of the cylinder head. A third rubber cushioned mounting is attached to the right-hand side of the transmission unit.

Special notes

Because of the unusual layout of the engine and transmission systems, extra care and attention are necessary during maintenance and overhaul procedures which, in many instances, differ from more conventional systems.

Read through the various Sections concerned before tackling any job, to analyse the instructions and so that any snags or possible difficulties can be noted in advance. Because the sub-assembly castings are made from aluminium alloy, it is of utmost importance that, where specified, all fastenings are tightened to the correct torque and, in some instances, in the correct sequence.

You will probably already be aware that accessibility can be very difficult, especially for the distributor, fuel pump and starter motor. This difficulty arises principally as a result of the move on right-hand drive cars of the brake master cylinder from the left to the right side of the bulkhead. Frequently, work involves the disturbance of unrelated components or assemblies. However, quite a lot of work can be done with the power unit installed, but this often required the use of special tools.

2 Major operations possible with engine installed

The following operations are possible with the engine in the car:

(a)* *Removal and refitting of the clutch unit*
(b)* *Removal and refitting of the input pinion and oil seals*
(c)* *Removal and refitting of the cylinder head*
(d) *Removal and refitting of the timing case*
(e) *Removal of the engine mountings*

The tasks can only be achieved with the use of special Peugeot tools.

Fig. 1.1 The engine assembly, front right-hand view (Sec 1)

3 Major operations requiring engine removal

The engine must be removed for the following operations:

(a) Removal and refitting of the transmission unit
(b) Removal and refitting of the crankshaft and main bearings
(c) Removal and refitting of the piston and connecting rod assemblies
(d) Renewal of the big-end bearings

4 Engine and transmission unit – removal

1   The engine and transmission unit must be removed as a complete assembly and cannot be separated until removed. The combined weight of the two components is not great due to the extensive use of aluminium alloy, but certain operations are awkward and care must be taken not to damage adjacent components in the engine compartment, especially during removal, as space is limited in which to manoeuvre the assembly out. It therefore pays to have an assistant on hand whenever possible.

2   To disconnect the driveshafts from the final drive the manufacturer recommends that the right-hand front suspension be dismantled to allow the strut to be moved out sideways and permit the right-hand driveshaft's withdrawal. However, in the Haynes workshop it was found that, with the engine hanging free on the hoist, the driveshafts could be disconnected without disturbing the front suspension. An SR model was used for the exercise and it might be necessary to disconnect the suspension on the other models, although this is doubtful. It would be worth having a try at removing the engine and transmission assembly before the suspension is disturbed. If unsuccessful, refer to Chapter 9 and disconnect the right suspension in order to withdraw the right-hand driveshaft.

3   Position the car with the engine under the lifting tackle location and make sure that there is sufficient room around the car to work comfortably. With a mobile hoist the engine assembly can obviously be wheeled away after removal, but if the hoist location is fixed then ensure that there is room for the car to be moved back after lifting the engine out.

4   Chock the rear wheels and apply the handbrake.

5   Raise and support the bonnet. Mark the position of the hinge brackets on the bonnet so that they can be reassembled in the same position. Support the bonnet and remove the retaining bolts in the

Fig. 1.2 The engine assembly, rear left-hand view (Sec 1)

hinge brackets and support strut. Lift the bonnet clear and remove it to a safe place.

6   Disconnect and remove the battery as described in Chapter 10.

7   Refer to Chapter 2 and drain the cooling system. Also drain the engine oil and refit the plug.

8   Refer to Chapter 2 and remove the radiator.

9   Refer to Chapter 3 and remove the air cleaner and air intake.

10   Disconnect the hoses from the engine such as the brake servo hose on the manifold, heater hoses and so on. When disconnecting the fuel feed hose, plug it temporarily to prevent fuel loss and dirt ingress.

11   Detach the HT leads from the spark plugs, remove the distributor cap and remove the assembly from the engine.

12   Take careful note of their positions and disconnect the following electrical connections:

  (a)   Coolant temperature sender
  (b)   Oil pressure switch
  (c)   Coil
  (d)   Radiator temperature sender (fan switch)
  (e)   Starter solenoid
  (f)   Earth wire from top of timing case
  (g)   Reversing light switch

13   Don't disconnect the electrical wires on the alternator but remove the alternator, referring to Chapter 10 if necessary, and swing it to one side away from the engine. Similarly, leave the voltage regulator connections done up but unbolt it from the inside wall of the left-hand front wheel arch and swing it out of the engine bay to provide more room to move the engine when it is free.

14   Disconnect the throttle cable and the choke control cable from the carburettor.

15   Disconnect the exhaust pipe from its connection with the manifold on the front of the engine.

16   Disconnect the gearchange linkage. You may find that you can improve access by first removing the intake manifold support strut. Prise off the balljoint female half on the end of the gear engagement rod and similarly the balljoint female half on the selection link; then remove the bolt securing the gear selection rod balljoint to the selector mechanism cover assembly, see Fig. 1.3.

17   Jack up the front of the car and support it on axle stands positioned under the front subframe assembly; alternatively put ramps under the front wheels.

18   Remove the front section of the exhaust pipe from the engine assembly.

19   Disconnect the clutch control cable, referring to Chapter 5 for details.

20   Remove the three bolts in the bottom engine mounting – two are in the front face and the other is at the back (photo).

21   Connect the lifting tackle to the two lugs on the back of the cylinder head and take the load of the engine assembly without lifting it.

22   Undo the top engine mountings and remove the brackets from the engine to give more clearance when the engine is free.

23   Lift the engine enough to clear the bottom mounting and at the same time pull it forwards so as to keep the rear edge of the transmission case clear of the steering mechanism.

24   Loosen the locknut, remove the retaining screw and pull the speedometer drive cable out of its location in the transmission unit.

25   Check all round the engine assembly to make sure that is completely disconnected from the car.

26   Move one of the front wheels on to full steering lock to retract its driveshaft. Then by gently lifting and manoeuvring the engine forward and over to the opposite side, disconnect that shaft from the final drive. This needs care as there is very little room in which to move the assembly and it is easy to damage something if it is allowed to swing out of control. With care the shaft can be extracted and then the other driveshaft can be withdrawn in a similar manner. Rest the two shafts on the subframe and carefully lift the engine unit out of the car. Wheel the car back if necessary so that the engine unit can be lowered and removed to a workbench or work area.

5   Engine dismantling – general

1   A good size clean work area will be required, preferably on a bench. Before moving the engine and transmission assembly to the work area it should be cleaned to remove road dirt, oil and grease.

2   During the dismantling process care should be taken to avoid contaminating the exposed internal parts with dirt. Although everything will be cleaned separately before reassembly, road dirt or grit can cause damage to parts during dismantling and could also affect inspection and checks.

3   A good proprietary grease solvent will make the job of engine/transmission cleaning much easier but if this is not available use paraffin. With a solvent the usual procedure is to apply it to the contaminated surfaces and, after a suitable soaking period has elapsed, to wash it off with a jet of water. Where the grease or oil and dirt mixture is encrusted the solvent should be worked in using a stiff brush.

4   After rinsing off the solvent and dirt, wipe down the exterior of the assembly and then, only when it is clean and dry, the dismantling process can be started.

5   As the unit is stripped, the individual parts should be examined before being washed in a bath of paraffin and wiped dry. The examination need only be cursory at this stage but it is sometimess helpful as the cleaning procedure might wash away useful evidence of running conditions. Avoid immersing parts with internal oil passages, such as the crankshaft and the timing case, in paraffin. To clean such parts use a paraffin-damped rag and clean out the oilways with wire. If an air supply is available the oilways can be blown through to clear them.

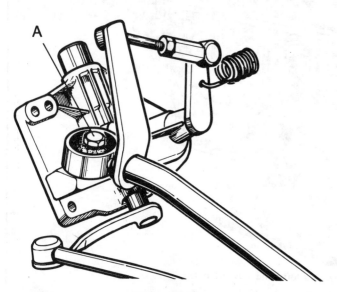

Fig. 1.3 The gear selection rod retaining bolt, A (Sec 4)

4.20 The two bolts (arrowed) on the front of the bottom mounting

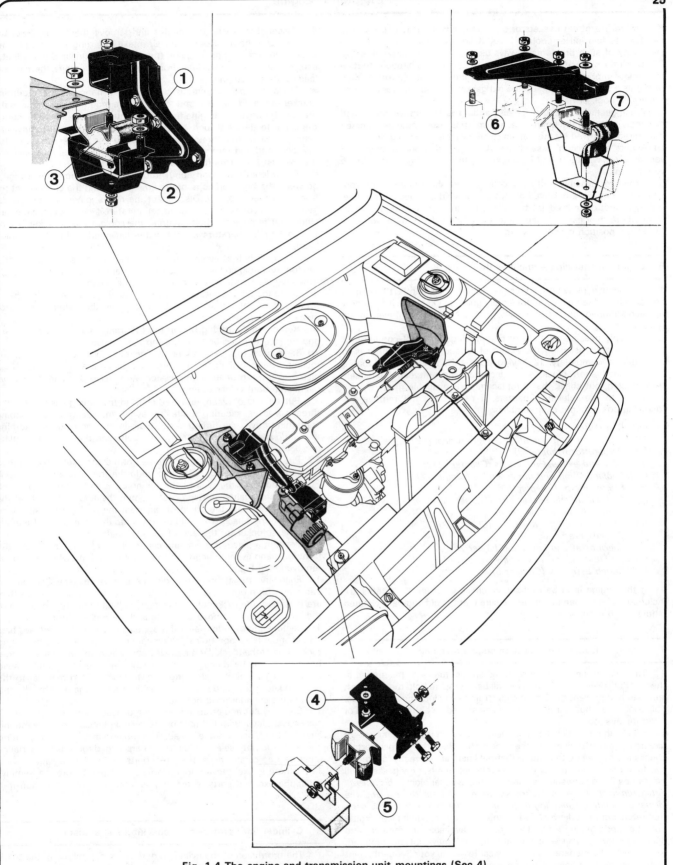

Fig. 1.4 The engine and transmission unit mountings (Sec 4)

1 Upper right-hand engine bracket
   (early models pattern)
2 Upper right-hand chassis bracket

3 Flexible mounting
4 Bottom transmission unit bracket
5 Flexible mounting

6 Upper left-hand engine bracket
7 Flexible mounting

6   The re-use of old gaskets or old oil seals is a false economy and can lead to fuel, oil or coolant leaks, if nothing worse. To avoid the possibility of such problems, always use new gaskets throughout.

7   Don't throw away the old gaskets as it sometimes happens that an immediate replacement is not available and the old gasket is then useful as a template. Hang up the old gaskets as they are removed on a suitable hook or nail.

8   A suggested procedure for dismantling is to remove the clutch assembly and then the timing mechanism (this order could be reversed if required) followed by the transmission, cylinder head and finally the crankshaft and piston assemblies. A supply of wooden blocks of varying sizes will be useful in supporting the assembly as it is being worked on.

9   Wherever possible refit nuts, bolts, and washers finger tight from wherever they were removed as this helps avoid later loss or muddle. If they cannot be refitted, lay them out in such a fashion that it is clear from where they came. Make sketches or notes if you think you may forget the position of washers etc.

6   Engine dismantling – ancillary items

1   Irrespective of whether you are going to dismantle the engine completely and rebuild it, or are simply going to exchange it for a new or reconditioned unit, the ancillary components will have to be removed.

2   The only possible method of determining the exact condition of the engine and assessing the extent of reconditioning required is to dismantle it completely. If, having done this, it is decided that a reconditioned short block is needed then the unit can be loosely reassembled, but check that a replacement is available first.

3   Refer to the relevant Chapters, if necessary, and remove the following components or assemblies:

   (a) Distributor (Chapter 4)
   (b) Fuel pump and operating plunger (Chapter 3)
   (c) Carburettor (Chapter 3)
   (d) Inlet and exhaust manifolds (Chapter 3)
   (e) Coolant pump and fan assembly (Chapter 2)
   (f) Starter motor (Chapter 10)
   (g) Coil, diagnostic socket and TDC sensor complete with connecting harness (Chapter 4)
   (h) Coolant temperature sender (Chapter 2)
   (j) Oil pressure sender
   (k) Thermostat and housing (Chapter 2)
   (l) Oil filter and dipstick tube
   (m) Clutch assembly (Chapter 5)

4   If the engine is to be exchanged, check what ancillary items are included in the exchange unit. Make sure that the old engine is cleaned before being exchanged.

7   Cylinder head – removal with engine installed

1   The cylinder head can be removed and refitted with the engine in the car, but a Peugeot special tool will be needed to hold the camshaft sprocket and prevent the timing chain from falling into the timing case. This tool is part number 8.0140 and one should be either borrowed or hired for this job.

2   When the cylinder head is being removed there is a risk of disturbing the wet liners in their locations. Because of this certain checks are necessary to confirm that the liners are correctly located. If it is found that they are not within permissible limits, new gaskets will have to be fitted between the liners and the cylinder block. *This job will entail removal of the engine/transmission unit from the car and the virtual complete dismantling of the unit on the bench.* It can be seen that removing the cylinder head on this engine, when installed, should only be undertaken if full facilities are available to remove and dismantle the engine – even though they may not be required. Alternatively, be prepared to have the car towed to your Peugeot agent if the liner gaskets have to be renewed.

3   First drain the cooling system, referring to Chapter 2 for details if necessary. Apply the handbrake and locate a jack under the engine bottom mounting at the right-hand end of the transmission unit. Undo the bolts connecting the exhaust pipe brackets to the bottom of the transmission unit.

4   Disconnect the battery cables and remove the battery from the car. Remove the air cleaner and air intake, referring to Chapter 3 for details. Pull the ignition leads off the spark plugs, unclip the distributor cap, disconnect the HT lead from the coil and remove the cap and leads from the engine.

5   Undo the bolts securing the top right-hand engine mounting bracket to the timing case and to the engine mounting and remove the bracket. Remove the engine flexible mounting. Undo the nut securing the cable to the earth bolt on the transmission case and remove the cable. Remove the three screws securing the rocker cover to the cylinder head and remove the cover. Remove the three nuts securing the exhaust heater muff and remove the muff.

6   Cut a length of wood about a foot long (300 mm) and wedge it between the front top edge of the timing case and the cross rail at the front of the engine bay. Disconnect the hoses joined to the cylinder head and disconnect the coolant temperature sender electrical cable. Undo and remove the bolt securing the coolant pipe bracket behind the coolant temperature sender in the left-hand end of the cylinder head.

7   Undo the bolt attaching the inlet manifold bracket and disconnect the four manifold connections to the cylinder head; move the manifold assembly rearwards away from the cylinder head.

8   Undo the nuts securing the exhaust manifold to the cylinder head, retrieve the heater muff backplate and move the manifold forwards away from the cylinder head.

9   Remove the earthing bolt in the top front hole in the timing case and remove the two bolts in the top rear holes.

10 Bend back the tabs of the locking plate behind the three bolts retaining the camshaft timing sprocket. Turn the engine to get No 2 piston at the top of the compression stroke (No 3 cylinder on valve overlap, ie both valves open).

11 Put a piece of clean, fluff-free cloth in the timing case below the three sprocket securing bolts to avoid the danger of dropping something down the timing case. Restrain the sprocket from turning and undo the three bolts; remove the bolts and the old locking plate but don't disturb the sprocket.

12 Put a new locking plate on the pad of the sprocket retaining tool, Peugeot part number 8.0140, and undo the thumbscrew in the tool. Put the tool over the wall of the timing case and, with the pad and locking plate against the sprocket, tighten the two bolts to hold the sprocket. Withdraw the piece of rag from the timing case and hand tighten the thumbscrew to hold the tool onto the timing case. Carefully slide the sprocket off the end of the camshaft.

13 Position a piece of modelling clay or similar compound under the front left-hand cylinder head nut to keep it in position when the bolt is removed, see Fig. 1.6.

14 Following the tightening sequence in reverse, (see Section 35, paragraph 5), progressively loosen the 10 cylinder head bolts; as they are loosened, the rocker shaft assembly will lift under the influence of the valve springs. Remove the bolts and the rocker shaft assembly.

15 Remove the cylinder head. If it appears to be stuck insert two bars into cylinder head bolt holes, taking care not to damage the head, and rock it free of the block. Don't, on any account, hammer on the cylinder head as it can be damaged very easily. Remove the cylinder head gasket. Fit temporary restraining straps made of strip material to the block to keep the cylinder liners in position; secure them with bolts and nuts in the cylinder head bolt holes.

16 Carefully cut and remove the upper, exposed portion of the timing case gasket level with the face of the cylinder block. Clean the mating faces of the block, cylinder head, and timing case free of all jointing materials. Do not use emery cloth or sharp-edged tools as the surfaces must be free of all traces of scores, burrs, or impact damage.

17 If there is likely to an appreciable time lapse before reassembly, cover the exposed parts of the engine internals with clean, fluff-free rag.

8   Cylinder liner protrusion – checking and adjusting

1   The protrusion of the cylinder liners when assembled to the block must be within prescribed limits so that a gastight seal can be achieved when the head is bolted on. One liner protruding too much or not enough will, despite the cylinder head gasket, make it impossible to secure a gas or watertight joint.

2   First check the squareness of each liner in the block. This is done using a dial test indicator (clock gauge) based on the cylinder head

Fig. 1.5 Using the Peugeot special tool, 8.0140, to hold
the camshaft sprocket (Sec 7)

1   A new locking plate fitted before installation
2   The pad of the tool bolted to the sprocket

mating face on the cylinder block. Gauge the top face of the liner at
four equi-spaced points to measure parallelity of the liner face with the
block face. The faces must be parallel within 0.02 mm (0.0008 in) of
each other. Repeat the check on all four liners.

3   Next check the protrusion of each liner above the face of the block.
This is most easily checked with an accurate straight-edge and a set
of feeler gauges. Lay the straight-edge across the liner in a fore and aft
direction (right-angles to the crankshaft) and measure the gap between the straight-edge and the block face. If this check is being done
after fitting new liner gaskets, press down on the liner to compress the
gasket when using the feeler gauges. Measure the front and back
clearances; they should be within the limits given in the Specifications.
Repeat the check on the other three cylinders. It is permissible to tap
all around the top of a liner after new gaskets have been fitted so as
to seat it fully. The check must be repeated after doing this.

4   Finally check the difference in height between adjacent liners. Use
the dial test indicator to measure the difference in height, if any,
between adjacent liners at a point on each lying along the centre axis
parallel with the crankshaft on the top face. Each difference in level
must not exceed the maximum specified.

5   The three separate checks of squareness, protrusion and height
difference are sequential and each must be correct before proceeding
to the next. If, for example, the first check shows a liner to be out of
square beyond the permissible limit the cause must be found and
eliminated. It could be due to a gauging error so check the measuring
equipment for cleanliness and accuracy. It could also be due to a
distorted liner (if you are doing a check with the engine installed this

Fig. 1.6 The cylinder head front left-hand nut retained by
modelling clay, 1 (Sec 7)

Fig. 1.7 Using two bars to rock the cylinder head off
(Sec 7)

is more likely) or there could be foreign matter between the liner and the block (more likely if you are doing the check on reassembly after complete dismantling.

6 If the checks reveal a discrepancy on an installed engine it will be necessary to renew the liner gaskets or even one or more liners. In either case the engine/transmission unit will have to be removed for dismantling.

7 Once the checks have shown the liners to be within limits of protrusion and squareness reassembling can continue or, if appropriate, temporary retainer straps should be fitted to hold them in position. *Don't turn the crankshaft if the liners are not restrained from movement.* Cover the exposed engine internal parts if there is likely to be a delay before completing reassembly.

9 Cylinder head – refitting with engine installed

1 Make sure that all mating faces are clean, that the cylinder liner protrusion and squareness checks have been done with satisfactory results and that a new cylinder head gasket, a new timing case gasket, a new rocker cover gasket and new exhaust manifold gaskets etc are available.

2 Measure a distance of 125 mm (4.92 in) from the top of the new timing case gasket down each side and cut off the top portion using a razor blade to get a clean cut. Stick this new gasket to the timing case exposed face (the gasket will extend above the timing case), using jointing compound and fill the two unused holes at the bottom of the gasket.

3 Lightly lubricate the walls of the 4 liners using clean engine oil and, if necessary and if liner retaining straps are fitted, turn the crankshaft to position Nos 2 and 3 pistons at TDC (top of compression stroke No 2). In this position check that the distributor rotor arm is pointing out towards the right wing – if not rotate the crankshaft a full revolution – and align the timing marks on the pulley and timing plate (see Chapter 4 if in doubt).

4 Remove the liner retainer straps and clean off any excess jointing compound in the corners between the timing case face and the cylinder head face.

5 Wipe the mating faces of the cylinder head and block clean and fit a new, dry cylinder head gasket to the block.

6 Clean the threads on the cylinder head bolts and in the nuts. Oil the bolt threads and under the bolt heads.

7 Turn the camshaft to the position shown in Fig. 1.8 which is the position when both valves are open on number 3 cylinder, piston at TDC. If this is not done there may be trouble with valves contacting pistons, and it will be impossible to fit the camshaft sprocket.

8 Wipe the rocker arm faces clean and lightly spray them with Molykote 321 R or equivalent.

9 Carefully lower the cylinder head into position on the block and then fit the rocker assembly into position on the cylinder head. Fit the 10 cylinder head bolts and nuts but leave them untightened for the moment.

10 Refit the earthing bolt at the top front hole in the timing case and the two bolts in the top rear holes. On some models the lower of the

two top rear bolts will be covered by the early type of engine mounting bracket. In such cases the lower bolt should be tightened now to the specified torque. Refit the engine mounting bracket but first coat the bottom bolt in the bracket with thread locking compound. Tighten the bolts lightly to 3 or 4 lbf ft (0.5 kgf m); they will need to be fully tightened after the cylinder head bolts are tightened.

11 Refer to Section 35 and, following the sequence shown, tighten the cylinder head bolts. Two stages of tightening are necessary. Go right round all bolts and tighten to the Stage 1 torque quoted in the Specifications and then go round again tightening to the Stage 2 specified torque.

12 The bolts in the timing case can now be fully tightened to the specified torque, as can the four bolts securing the engine mounting bracket.

13 Push a piece of fluff-free rag into the timing case under the sprocket holding tool to prevent anything falling down into the case. Fit one sprocket retaining bolt to the hole not covered by the special tool (but don't tighten it yet) and locate the sprocket on the camshaft; the sprocket should fit without having to force it. Remove the piece of rag and check that the timing chain is properly located on the tensioner rubbing plate and then put the rag back into place.

14 Undo the two bolts in the sprocket holding tool, remove the bolts and the special tool. Then fit the remaining two bolts in the camshaft sprocket and tighten all three bolts to the specified torque. Bend up the locking plate to lock each bolt and then remove the piece of rag from the timing case.

15 The timing chain tension must now be checked. A long hooked tool is required; this could be made up from a piece of strong fence wire or similar. The procedure is to reach down into the timing case with the tool and hook it into the fifth free link below the sprocket in the rear leg of the chain (the front leg runs down onto the tensioner rubbing plate). Exert a strong pull on the hook to deflect the chain. When released the stretch of chain should remain untensioned. If this is not so, the timing case will have to be removed (refer to Section 10) and the tensioner slackened off (Fig. 1.10).

16 Carefully cut off the surplus part of the timing case gasket flush with the rocker cover mounting face.

17 Adjust the inlet and exhaust valve clearances; refer to Section 39 for this procedure.

18 Refitting of all the removed components now follows. It is broadly a reversal of the removal procedure but take note of the following points:

(a) Tighten fasteners to the correct torque where these are listed in the Specifications

(b) Fit new gaskets to the exhaust manifold and check that the crimped side of the gasket is against the manifold not the cylinder head

(c) Make a thorough check that no loose articles are left on the rocker mechanism before refitting the rocker cover, especially check that the piece of rag is removed from the timing case. Fit a new gasket to the cover

(d) Refill the cooling system and check the engine oil level before starting the engine

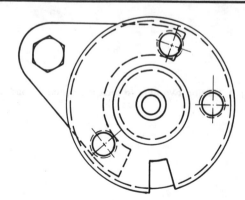

Fig. 1.8 Align the camshaft in this position before refitting the cylinder head (Sec 9)

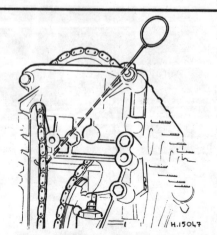

Fig. 1.9 Checking the timing chain tension (Sec 9)

19 After starting the engine, check for leaks and then run it until the electro-magnetic fan engages. Stop the engine and when it is cool top up the cooling system.

20 After the engine has been allowed to cool for at least two hours the cylinder head bolts must be retightened. First remove the rocker cover and, following the sequence in Fig. 1.19, slacken the first bolt and then retighten it to the Stage 2 specified torque. Then slacken the second bolt and retighten it, and so on until all bolts have been separately retightened.

21 Following the retightening of the cylinder head bolts the inlet and exhaust valve clearances must be reset.

22 Finally, after the car has travelled between 1000 and 1500 miles (1500 and 2500 km), the cylinder head bolts must again be slackened and retightened and the valve clearances again reset.

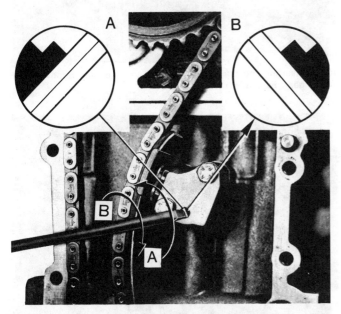

Fig. 1.10 Turn the tensioner ratchet lock anti-clockwise (A) to slacken the tensioner and then clockwise (B) to re-lock it (Sec 9)

10 Timing case – removal and refitting with engine installed

1 To remove the timing case from an installed engine, first drain the engine oil into a clean container and, using a new washer, refit the drain plug and tighten it to its specified torque.

2 Disconnect the battery cables and remove the battery from the car.

3 Disconnect the wires on the earth bolt at the top front position on the timing case and disconnect the oil pressure switch connection.

4 Remove the air cleaner and intake pipe; remove the rocker cover.

5 Unclip the distributor cap and remove the distributor by loosening the clamp bolt and lifting the assembly out of the timing case.

6 Disconnect the fuel inlet and outlet pipes from the fuel pump. Temporarily plug the pipes to prevent fuel loss and dirt ingress. For the same reason, cover the pump apertures.

7 Cut a piece of wood about a foot long (say 300 mm) and wedge it between the cylinder head and the cross rail at the front of the engine compartment.

8 Undo the retaining bolts and remove the engine mounting bracket from the transmission case and the flexible mounting.

9 Loosen the right-hand track control arm pivot bolt nut and remove the bolt and washer securing the safety stop plate. Tilt the stop plate away from the timing case.

10 Undo and remove the 17 bolts securing the timing case to the engine. There are five different sized bolts in this collection and their disposition is shown in Fig. 1.13.

11 Carefully remove the timing case. If it is stuck, check that all the bolts have been removed, then gently break the joint by tapping with a soft-faced hammer, but don't use excessive force as the light alloy casting can be easily damaged. Remove the old gasket.

12 Clean off all traces of old gasket and any sealer, but don't use emery cloth or hard metallic scrapers. The mating surfaces must be free from all traces of scoring, burrs, impact dents and other damage. If the oil filter is not removed from the timing case it need not be renewed, unless of course it is due for renewal with an oil change. However, if it is removed a new one must be fitted on reassembly.

13 Before starting to refit the timing case make sure that you have a complete set of seals and gaskets that will be needed. If the fuel pump was removed a new gasket will also be needed for that on reassembly.

14 Check that the two locating dowels are in position in the joint face on the engine. Fit a new O-ring to the oil transfer spigot in the front joint face, and fit the new gasket.

15 Using a spanner on the crankshaft pulley bolt, turn the engine to position No 2 piston at TDC on the compression stroke. To do this an alignment rod is required. It should be 8 mm (0.315 in) diameter and at least 100 mm (4 in) long. Make sure that the rod is clean and insert it in the hole just above the crankshaft in the block wall. Turn the

Fig. 1.11 Wedge the cylinder head with a piece of wood before removing the mounting bracket (Sec 10)

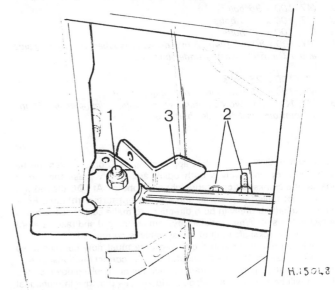

Fig. 1.12 The right-hand track control arm pivot bolt nut (1) and the bolt and washer (2) securing the safety stop plate (3) (Sec 10)

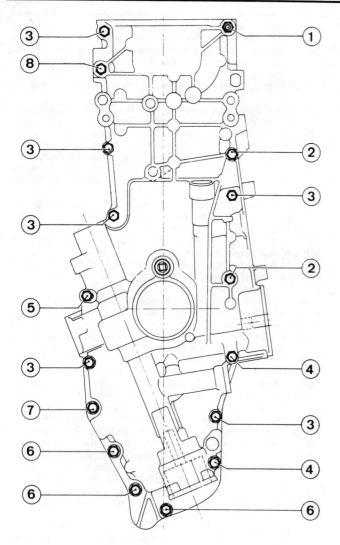

Fig. 1.13 The timing case securing bolts (Sec 10)

1   Earth bolt
2   M7, 100 x 95 bolts
3   M7, 100 x 51.5 bolts
4   M7, 100 x 80 bolts
5   M7, 100 x 80 bolt (two 16 mm dia wave washers timing case side
     and 13 mm dia washer under bolt head)

6   M7, 100 x 25 bolts
7   M7, 100 x 25 bolt, spring retaining bracket
8   M7, 100 x 75 (two 16 mm dia wavy washers timing case side and
     13 mm dia washer under bolt head)

10.15 Inserting the crankshaft alignment rod (engine removed and timing gear dismantled)

10.16 The distributor drive dog slot (arrowed) before installing the timing case and ...

10.17 ... after installing the timing case

crankshaft until No 2 piston is approaching TDC on compression (ie with No 3 cylinder valves both open) and gently press the rod in against the crankshaft counterweight web (photo). At TDC the rod will enter a slot milled in the web and will prevent further rotation. Rock the crankshaft carefully in both directions to make sure that the rod is in fact in the slot. When satisfactory, remove the rod and take care not to turn the crankshaft until after assembly is completed.

16 The distributor drive in the timing case must now be aligned so that, when assembled, the distributor is in the correct relationship with the crankshaft to permit accurate ignition timing. Looking down on the drive it will be seen that a horizontal slot divides the drive into unequal parts. Turn the drive so that the smaller part is on the outside of the drive housing and the slot is in an east-west alignment, that is, parallel with the crankshaft axis (photo).

17 Carefully refit the timing case to the engine. As the driveshaft

wheel meshes with the worm on the crankshaft the shaft will turn slightly. If the mesh is correct it will have moved the slot in the drive slightly clockwise as shown (photo). If the drive slot is in any other position, remove the timing case and make another attempt at aligning the driveshaft so that, on assembly, it finishes up in the correct position.

18 Fit the seventeen retaining bolts in their correct positions, referring to Fig. 1.13 if necessary, with a wavy washer under each bolt head, but don't tighten any until they are all located. Then they can be tightened to the specified torque.

19 Refit the engine mounting bracket and flexible mounting. Where the timing case bolts do not locate in the joint flange they should have thread sealer applied to their threads. Tighten all engine mounting bolts to the specified torque.

20 Carefully trim off the surplus part of the gasket protruding above the rocker cover face. Take care not to damage the joint face.

21 Refit the distributor, referring to Chapter 4 for detailed instructions.

22 The rest of the reassembly follows the reverse of the removal procedure. Don't forget to refit the safety stop plate at the right-hand track control arm, and tighten the pivot bolt nut to its specified torque. When all is reassembled replenish the sump with engine oil, run the engine and adjust the ignition timing as described in Chapter 4. If necessary adjust the idling speed as described in Chapter 3.

11 Clutch and housing – removal

1 The clutch can be removed with the engine installed in the car or with the engine/transmission on the bench. Refer to Chapter 5 for details of the procedure and special tools required, disregarding references to the engine being in the car if appropriate.

12 Timing mechanism – removal

1 If not already removed, undo the two bolts securing the fuel pump to the rear of the timing case, remove the pump and gasket and withdraw the pump plunger.

2 Undo the single bolt in the distributor clamp plate and remove the distributor and clamp plate complete.

3 Undo and remove the seventeen bolts securing the timing case to the engine and carefully remove the timing case. Tap it gently with a soft-faced hammer if it sticks, but don't use excessive force.

4 Note that if the crankshaft is rotated after the timing chain is removed, there is a danger of piston/valve contact. The same applies if the camshaft is rotated with the timing chain removed and any pistons at TDC. The following dismantling sequence is therefore recommended. If it is only wished to renew the timing chain, however, there is no need to remove the sprockets.

5 Undo and remove the bolt in the end of the crankshaft. Lock the crankshaft if necessary by inserting an 8 mm (0.315 in) dia rod in the hole just above the crankshaft and engaging the rod with the slot milled in the web. (Pistons 2 and 3 are at TDC when the rod is engaged.) Remove the locking rod.

6 Bend back the locking tabs on the three bolts in the camshaft sprocket. Slacken, but do not remove, the bolts.

7 Unlock the timing chain tensioner and release the tension in the chain, refer to Fig. 1.10 for details if necessary. Undo the two bolts retaining the tensioner and remove the bolts and tensioner. Undo the bolt at the bottom of the chain rubbing plate and remove the plate from the block. Retrieve the fine mesh filter from the tensioner location on the block.

8 Remove the timing chain from the crankshaft and camshaft timing sprockets.

9 Slide the sprocket, wormwheel and spacers off the crankshaft, noting the order in which they were assembled and also the way round each was fitted.

10 Remove the camshaft sprocket bolts, the locking plate and the sprocket. Discard the locking plate.

13 Engine and transmission – separation

1 With the timing mechanism and the clutch and housing removed, only the bolts in the front and rear joint flanges hold the engine and

transmission together.

2 Position the assembly under a hoist, or the hoist over the assembly if possible, and progressively loosen the bolts in the two joint flanges. Take the weight on the hoist and remove the bolts. Lift the engine assembly off the transmission unit and lower it onto the workbench.

14 Cylinder head – removal with engine on bench

1 Support the engine with wooden blocks and then, referring to Section 35, progressively loosen the ten cylinder head bolts in the reverse sequence to that for tightening. As the bolts are undone the rocker assembly will lift off the head due to the pressure of the valve springs and cams. Remove the bolts and retrieve the nuts from the webs in the block.

2 Lift the rocker assembly off the cylinder head.

3 Remove the cylinder head from the block. If necessary insert a couple of rods in bolt holes in the head and rock the head off the block. Don't hammer the head to free it and don't insert a wedge such as a screwdriver to lever the head off – this will damage the joint faces. Remove the cylinder head gasket.

4 Fit a restraining strap, or straps, to the block to keep the cylinder liners in position if it is not intended to proceed with further dismantling. The strap(s) should be bolted to the block utilising the cylinder head bolt holes and can be made up from any available strip material, requiring only bolt holes to be drilled, spaced to suit the holes in the block. Remove any burrs before fitting to avoid damaging the head joint face.

15 Pistons, connecting rods, and crankshaft – removal

1 The pistons, connecting rods and crankshaft can only be removed from the engine with the engine removed from the car and with the timing case, clutch, transmission and cylinder head removed from the engine.

2 Inspect the big-end assemblies and ensure that the connecting rods and caps are marked to identify their location and orientation. If necessary use a file or centre punch, applied lightly, to mark them.

3 Turn the crankshaft to position two of the pistons at TDC and two at BDC and, on the two at BDC, undo the nuts holding the bearing caps. Work on one assembly at a time and, after removing the nuts, remove the bearing cap and bearing shell. You may have to prise the cap and shell off, but be careful not to damage them as they may be fit for re-use. If you intend to remove the liners the liner and piston assembly can be removed complete from the block after first removing the restrainer and rocking the liner to ease it out of the bottom joint. Alternatively, keep the liner held in position and, using a hammer shaft, push the piston and connecting rod up out of the liner. Temporarily refit the bearing shell, bearing cap and nuts to the connecting rod, observing correct orientation. Watch out for the upper half bearing shell sticking to the crankshaft – if it does, remove it and replace it in the connecting rod to keep it safe.

4 Repeat the piston removal procedure on the remaining assemblies.

5 Note that the piston crowns are marked to show which liner they fit and also which way round they fit. The arrow and the word DIST point to the timing chain end of the engine. It is important to fit the piston correctly on reassembly as the gudgeon pin bore is slightly off centre.

6 Don't attempt to separate the piston from its connecting rod. Not only is it necessary to renew the piston if this is done but a heating process involving the use of a special jig is essential for reassembly. Your Peugeot agent should be consulted if you have to fit new pistons, gudgeon pins or connecting rods.

7 Note that the five caps for the crankshaft main bearings are numbered 1 to 5 on the timing side face. Undo the ten bolts retaining the caps.

8 Remove the main bearing caps, keeping the plain half bearing shells with their relative caps.

9 Lift the crankshaft out of the upper half bearings. These shells are grooved and they should be removed and stored with their relative lower shells and bearing caps. Remove the two half thrust washers from the No 2 bearing, noting that their grooved faces are towards the crankshaft web, mark them so that they can be reassembled correctly, but not on the bearing face. Later models have two half thrust washers in addition in the bearing cap.

16 Piston rings – removal

1   To remove the piston rings, slide them carefully over the top of the piston, taking care not to scratch the aluminium alloy. Never slide them off the bottom of the piston skirt. It is very easy to break the iron piston rings if they are pulled off roughly so this operation should be done with extreme caution. It is useful to employ three strips of thin metal or feeler gauges to act as guides to assist the rings to pass over the empty grooves and to prevent them from dropping in.
2   Lift one end of the piston ring to be removed out of its groove and insert the end of the feeler gauge under it.
3   Turn the feeler gauge slowly round the piston and as the ring comes out of its groove apply slight upward pressure so that it rests in the land above. It can then be eased off the piston.

17 Camshaft – removal

1   If the engine is installed in the car the cylinder head will have to be removed before it is possible to remove the camshaft. If the engine is on the bench the timing case and mechanism will need removing and the top end will need dismantling as far as the removal of the rocker shaft assembly and, as the head will not be retained, temporary bolts should be fitted while the camshaft is removed. Alternatively the camshaft can be removed after the head has been removed from the engine.
2   With the rocker assembly and timing sprocket removed, undo the

camshaft retaining plate bolt and remove the bolt and plate.
3   Carefully slide the camshaft out of its bearings in the cylinder head towards the timing end. Take special care not to damage the bearing surfaces with the sharp edges on the cam profiles.

18 Lubrication system – description

A pressure feed system of lubrication is fitted, with oil being circulated round the engine by a pump which draws oil from the sump below the transmission unit.

The high output rotary pump is located in the bottom of the timing case and it is driven by a shaft and skew gear off the crankshaft. Oil is drawn through a strainer in the sump and delivered to a filter cartridge mounted on the front of the timing case. A relief valve operates to prevent excessive pressure when approximately 58 lbf/in^2 (4 bars) is reached.

On leaving the cartridge filter the oil is ducted by a gallery to the crankshaft main bearings and by an external pipe to the transmission bearings. An internal duct conducts oil up to the camshaft and it is distributed to the camshaft bearings and rocker mechanism through the hollow rocker shaft. The big-end bearings are supplied with oil through drillings in the crankshaft.

After lubricating the bearing surfaces to which it is ducted the oil leaks into the engine interior where, as spray or mist, it lubricates the other bearing surfaces such as cylinder walls, small-ends, gears and so on. The oil then drains down into the sump to repeat the cycle.

A pressure switch located in the filter outlet duct will light the oil

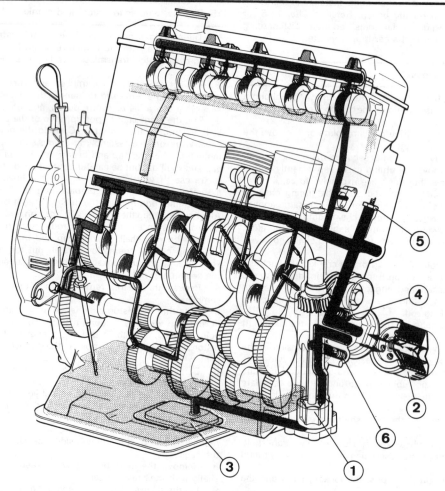

Fig. 1.14 The engine and transmission lubrication system (Sec 18)

1 Oil pump	3 Sump strainer screen	5 Oil pressure sender switch
2 Oil filter cartridge	4 Safety by-pass valve	6 Oil pressure relief valve

pressure warning light in the instrument panel if the pressure falls below 8.7 lbf/in^2 (0.6 bars) with the ignition switched on. In the event of the cartridge filter becoming clogged a safety bypass valve located in the filter mounting will open to prevent oil starvation. Unfiltered oil is then supplied to the bearings.

19 Oil filter – removal and refitting

1   A full-flow type oil filter is fitted to the front of the timing case on the right-hand side of the engine.
2   This is a renewable cartridge type filter which screws directly on to a threaded spigot in the timing case.
3   Before unscrewing the oil filter cartridge, locate a suitable receptacle underneath in which to catch any oil spillage. The best tool to undo the cartridge is a strap or chain spanner but a large hose clip (of the worm screw variety), or two small ones joined together, when tightened round the case will provide a good purchase by which to unscrew the filter.
4   Wipe the filter location on the timing case clean and lubricate the new cartridge seal with clean oil before fitting it to the cartridge. Fit the cartridge to its spigot and hand tighten only until the mating surfaces meet. Then give the cartridge a further $\frac{3}{4}$ turn to correctly tighten it.
5   When possible run the engine and check for leaks; then stop the engine and top up the oil to the full mark on the dipstick.

20 Cylinder head – dismantling, inspection and renovation

1   Having removed the cylinder head, place it onto a clean work-bench or work area where it can be dismantled and examined. Remember that it is made of light alloy and must be treated carefully to avoid damage.
2   Remove each valve and spring assembly using a valve spring compressor. Extract the split collets from between the spring retaining cup washer and the valve stem.
3   Progressively release the tension of the compressor until it can be removed, the spring and retainer withdrawn, and the valve extracted from the guide. Remove the old seals from the guides.
4   As the valves are removed keep them in order by inserting them in a piece of cardboard having suitable holes punched in it, numbered 1 to 8. Keep the spring, retainer and split collets together with their original valve.
5   Wash the cylinder head clean in paraffin and carefully scrape away the carbon build-up in the combustion chambers and exhaust ports. Use a scraper which will not damage the surfaces to be cleaned and be especially careful with the cylinder head joint face. Dry the head thoroughly after cleaning.
6   Wash the valves, springs, retainers and collets in paraffin and scrape off all deposits on the valves. The heads can be cleaned with emery cloth but don't use this on the bearing surfaces or the stems. Wipe all parts clean and dry after washing.
7   After cleaning the cylinder head examine it for cracks or damage. In particular inspect the valve seat areas for signs of hairline cracks, pitting or burning. Check the head mating surfaces for distortion and flatness using an accurate straight-edge and feeler gauges. The maximum permissible distortion or out-of-flat is 0.05 mm (0.002 in). Minor bruises can be carefully blended out but retain the original flatness. Note that resurfacing of the cylinder head on the Peugeot 305 engine is strictly forbidden.
8   Minor surface wear and pitting of the valve seats can probably be rectified when the valves are reground. Serious wear, ridges or burnt areas should be shown to your Peugeot dealer or a competent automotive engineer who will advise you on the action necessary.
9   Carefully inspect the valves, in particular the exhaust valves. Check that the stems are not bent or bowed and that no wear ridges are visible. The valve seat faces must be in reasonable condition and if they have covered a high mileage they will probably need to be refaced on a valve grinding machine. This work can be done by your Peugeot agent or a suitably equipped garage. If the valves have been refaced previously they will probably need renewal if their seat faces are in poor condition.
10   Insert each valve into its respective guide and check for wear. Worn valve guides and/or stems allow oil to be drawn past the inlet valve stem causing a smoky (blue-white) exhaust and high oil

consumption, while exhaust gas leakage past the exhaust valve stems can overheat the guides and stems causing sticking valves and heavy carbon deposits.
11   If the valve guides need renewing this will have to be done by your Peugeot agent as they are an interference fit in the head and specialist equipment is necessary.
12   Assuming that the valves and seats are in reasonable condition, or that new valves are being fitted, they must be ground in using valve grinding paste to produce a gastight joint when the valves are closed.
13   The carborundum paste used for this job can be obtained in a double-ended tin with coarse paste at one and fine at the other. The coarse paste is used only if the condition of the valve face and seat needs it but, if used, regrinding must be done afterwards using the fine paste. The fine paste is always used to get the correct finish. A suction tool will be needed to rotate and lift the valve during the grinding process. To grind in a valve, first smear a trace of paste onto the seat face and fit the suction tool to the valve head. Fit the valve to its guide and with a semi-rotary motion grind the valve face onto its seat, lifting and repositioning the valve occasionally to redistribute the grinding paste. When a dull matt continous line has been produced on both the valve seat and the valve then the paste can be wiped off. If coarse paste was used repeat using the fine grinding paste. A light spring fitted under the valve head to hold the head up when the pressure of the grinding tool is released will help speed up the job. If a continous matt seat cannot be achieved by grinding, or if it is apparent that the valve seat shows signs of excessive grinding or ridges are visible, it probably means that the seat needs refacing or, in extreme cases, renewing altogether. In either case your Peugeot agent should be consulted as specialist equipment is necessary.
14   Consideration should be given to renewing all the valve springs at this stage. However, if they meet the Specifications regarding free length and compressed heights they can be refitted. Obviously any broken springs must be renewed together with any that show distortion or other signs of distress.
15   Before starting reassembly, clean the cylinder head thoroughly free of all traces of grinding paste. Be very meticulous over this because any trace left in will be spread through the engine and lead to very expensive repair bills. Fit new oil seals to the valve guides, then lubricate the valve stems and guides with clean engine oil and refit the valves following the reverse of the removal procedure. Make sure that original parts are fitted to their original locations. Note that the valve springs have a closed coil at one end and an open coil at the other; the closed coil should be fitted towards the cylinder head on assembly (photos).
16   After fitting the valve, springs, etc the camshaft can be fitted. Make sure that it is clean and that the bearing surfaces are freely lubricated with clean engine oil. Take care not to damage the bearings as the shaft is slid home and secure it with the retaining plate, bolt and lockwasher. Cover the assembly to keep it clean until required for fitting to the engine (photos).

21 Crankshaft – examination and renovation

1   Carefully examine the crankpin and main journal bearing surfaces for signs of scoring or scratches and check the ovality of each bearing surface. Use a micrometer to measure the diameter of each bearing in turn at a number of positions. The discrepancy between the various measurements on a single bearing surface indicates the degree of wear and if a journal or pin is more than 0.001 in (0.02 mm) out-of-round the shaft will have to be reground. Where there are scores, grooves or scratches don't bother to measure the bearing surfaces as regrinding will be necessary in any case.
2   Crankshaft regrinding will have to be done by your Peugeot agent or by a specialist workshop. The regrind will remove 0.30 mm (0.0118 in) from the diameter of each journal and crankpin and of course new, undersize bearing shells will be needed.
3   If the crankshaft is found to be in good condition and regrinding is not required, new bearing shells of the original size should be fitted on reassembly.

22 Big-end and main bearings – examination and renovation

1   The bearing surface on the bearing shells is highly polished when new but becomes a matt grey after use; there should be no sign of pitting, ridging, grooving or picking up. Even if the bearing shells

20.15a Fit a new valve stem seal and ...

20.15b ... then fit the valve

20.15c Fit the spring seat washer and ...

20.15d ... then fit the spring and spring retainer followed by ...

20.15e ... the split collets (note spring compressor)

20.16a Installing the camshaft and ...

20.16b ... its retaining plate

24.8 The rings fitted to the piston

26.6 Check that the oil jet (arrowed) in each rocker arm is clear

appear to be in good condition it is still worthwhile renewing them if you have gone to the trouble of removing the crankshaft, particularly if the engine has had extensive use. Of course renewal is essential if there is any sign of damage or if the crankshaft has been reground.

2   If you have found the crankshaft to be in good condition and intend only to fit new bearing shells, check whether or not the crankshaft has been reground before. This will be indicated by the bearing shells that were fitted; the new set should have the same part number as those removed during dismantling.

3   The big-end bearings are subject to wear at a greater rate than the crankshaft main bearings. Big-end failure is accompanied by a knocking from the crankcase and a slight drop in oil pressure. Main bearing failure is accompanied by vibration which can be quite severe as the engine speed is increased. At the outset of either of these conditions the engine should be switched off as any further running will only make matters worse very quickly.

23 Cylinder liner bores – examination and renovation

1   The liner bores may be examined for wear either in or out of the engine block; the cylinder head must, of course, be removed in either case. If the liners are still in the block the retaining strap(s) should be kept in place where possible to avoid having to relocate the liners in their beds. However if the engine is dismantled to the point of piston removal it is better to remove the liners for inspection.

2   The top edge of each liner carries a marking of one to four lines indicating the size grade of the bore. The grade is an average of the diameters measured at six points and is used to match the liner to the piston which is similarly graded but which is marked with a letter. The four grades of piston are identified by the letters A to D inclusive and a grade A piston must be used in a liner with a grade mark on one line. Similarly a grade B piston must be used in a liner with a grade mark

of two lines and so on. The grade sizes of the liners and pistons are listed in the Specifications.

3 The liner bores must be examined for taper, ovality, scoring and scratches. Start by inspecting the top of the bores. If they are worn, a slight ridge will be found on the piston thrust side. This marks the top limit of the piston ring travel. You will probably have a good indication of the bore wear prior to dismantling the engine or removing the cylinder head. Excessive oil consumption accompanied by blue exhaust smoke is a sure sign of worn liner bores and piston rings.

4 Measure the bore diameter just under the ridge with an internal micrometer and compare it with the diameter at the bottom of the bore which is much less prone to wear. Also make comparative measurements of the liner diameter parallel with the gudgeon pin and at right-angles to it to determine the extent of ovality. Taper and ovality will decrease from the top of the liner down to the bore. If a micrometer is not available comparative measurements can be made with a set of feeler gauges and a pair of internal calipers but considerable care is needed to get good results.

5 As a general guide it may be assumed that any variations more than 0.010 inch (0.25 mm) indicate that the liners should be renewed. Provided that all variations are less than this it is likely that the fitting of new rings to the pistons will rectify excessive piston-to-bore clearance. If the liner has a top ridge a special stepped piston ring can be fitted which will clear the ridge. Alternatively the ridge can be removed by stoning with a carborundum stone. Where new liners are fitted, new pistons and rings will also be required.

24 Connecting rods, pistons and piston rings – examination and renovation

1 With the piston and connecting rod assemblies removed from the liners, give them a thorough cleaning using paraffin. Scrape the carbon deposit off the piston heads but avoid damaging them. Remove the old rings carefully, keeping them in their assembled sequence and orientation. Clean out the ring grooves in the piston using an old hacksaw blade or a piece of broken ring, taking care not to score or widen the grooves. Protect your fingers if using a piece of piston ring – the edges can be sharp.

2 The top ring groove is likely to have worn the most. After the groove has been cleaned out put the top ring into the groove and check the fit with a feeler gauge.

3 Examine each piston carefully for wear or damage; especially look for hair cracks around each gudgeon pin area.

4 If any of the pistons are obviously badly worn, cracked, burnt or otherwise defective, new ones must be fitted. A badly worn top ring groove in an otherwise satisfactory piston can be machined out to take a thicker ring. If necessary this can be a stepped ring having a step on its outer face to clear the ridge in the liner resulting from previous use. New pistons must be matched by grade with their liners (see the previous Section). Removal from and assembly to the connecting rods will have to be done by your Peugeot agent as the gudgeon pin is an interference fit in the rod little end.

5 Providing that the engine has not seized or suffered any other serious damage, the connecting rods should require no attention other than cleaning and a check for obvious defects. If damage has occurred or if there is evidence of irregular wear in the pistons, liners or bearings it is advisable to have the connecting rod alignment checked. This requires specialist tools and should be left to your Peugeot agent or a suitably equipped engineering workshop.

6 Before fitting new rings to the pistons each should have the gap checked. Peugeot supply the rings pre-gapped but, if there is any doubt, insert a ring halfway down the liner bore, making sure that it is square in the liner, and measure the end gap with feeler gauges. A gap of between 0.010 and 0.040 in (0.254 and 1.016 mm) will be satisfactory.

7 When fitting new pistons and rings to new liners the ring gaps can be measured, if required, at the top of the bore as the bore will not now taper.

8 Fit the three-piece scraper ring to the piston first, followed by the middle, compression, ring. This middle ring has a taper on the face which contacts the liner bore and, as a result, the ring must be fitted the right way up. A mark on the top face of the ring must be towards the piston crown. The next ring, the top one, has a slight curve on the bore contacting face but the ring can be fitted either way up. Fit the rings in the reverse way they were removed, but exercise care as the

two top ones are very brittle and easily broken (photo).

25 Timing chain and sprockets – examination and renovation

1 Examine the teeth of both sprockets for wear. Each tooth on a sprocket is an inverted V-shape and wear becomes apparent when one side of the tooth appears more concave in shape than the other. When badly worn the teeth become hook-shaped and the sprockets must be renewed.

2 If the sprockets need renewing then the chain will have worn as well and should be renewed. If the sprockets are satisfactory examine the chain and look for play between the links. When the chain is held horizontally with the link pins vertical it should not bend appreciably – the greater the amount of bending in this position the more the chain is worn. A chain is a relatively cheap item and it is well worthwhile fitting a new one if you have dismantled the engine.

3 Check the condition of the chain tensioner blade for grooving by the timing chain; if this is pronounced renew the blade. It is recommended that the tensioner unit is not dismantled as reassembly is difficult.

26 Camshaft and rocker assembly – examination and renovation

1 The camshaft lobes should be examined for signs of flats or scoring or any other form of wear and damage. At the same time the rocker arms should be examined, particularly on the faces which bear on the cam lobes, for signs of wear. If the case-hardened faces of the rocker arms or the surfaces of the cam lobes have been penetrated it will be quite obvious as there will be a darker, rough pitted appearance to the surface in question. In such cases the parts concerned must be renewed. Where the cam or rocker arm surfaces are still bright and clean, although showing slight signs of wear, they are best left alone. Any attempt to reface either will only result in the case-hardened surface being reduced in thickness with the possibility of subsequent rapid and extreme wear.

2 The camshaft bearing journals should be in good condition and show little signs of wear as they are relatively free from stress.

3 If the bearing surfaces are found to be discoloured, or wear is evident, it is possible that the camshaft is not running true and, in this case, it will have to be renewed. For an accurate check get your Peugeot agent to inspect both the camshaft and the cylinder head.

4 The rocker assembly can be dismantled after removing the setscrew in the mounting block furthest from the timing sprocket end. When removing the various components from the shaft, take careful note of the sequence in which they are removed. Refer to Fig. 1.15 and note the differences between the mounting blocks. Keep the components in order as they are removed for cleaning and inspection.

5 Check the rocker shaft for signs of wear, and check it for straightness by rolling it on a flat surface. It is unlikely to be bent but if this is the case it must be carefully straightened, if possible, or renewed. The shaft surface should be free of wear ridges caused by the rocker arms. Inspect the oil feed holes and clear them out if blocked.

6 Check each rocker arm for bearing wear by sliding it on to an unworn part of the shaft. Inspect the oil jet (photo) and make sure that it is clear. Inspect the end of the valve clearance adjusting screw for signs of cracks or serious wear that may have penetrated the case-hardening. If present the screw must be renewed.

7 Reassemble the rocker assembly in the reverse order to dismantling. Lubricate all bearing surfaces with clean engine oil, except the rocker pads which should have Molykote applied when installed on the cylinder head, and make sure that all components are the right way round and in the correct sequence.

27 Starter ring gear – examination and renovation

1 Examine the starter ring gear on the flywheel for signs of obvious damage such as worn, chipped or broken gear teeth. If several of the teeth are broken or missing or the front edges of all teeth are obviously badly worn then it would be advisable to fit a new gear ring. The ring is shrunk onto the flywheel after being heated and, apart from the friction plate, it is the only renewable part in the flywheel/clutch assembly. The assembly is balanced on production and must otherwise be renewed complete when defective.

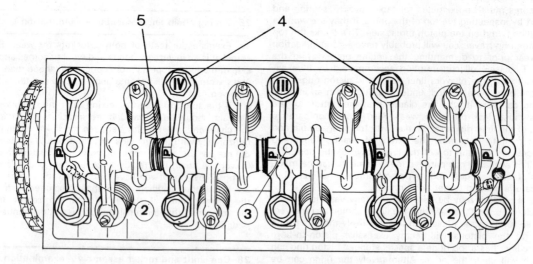

Fig. 1.15 Rocker shaft bearing blocks identification (Sec 26)

1   Screw seating on block I
2   Locating dowels on blocks I and V
3   Tapped hole for rocker cover bolt in block III

4   Blocks II and IV are identical
5   Letter P on all blocks must be towards sprocket

2   Renewing the ring gear is a job best left to a suitably equipped garage or workshop as the difficulty of heating the gear without overdoing it and thereby adversely affecting its hard wearing properties is usually beyond the ability of the average home mechanic. However, the procedure is straightforward given the right facilities.

3   The old ring gear can be removed by cutting a slot between two gear teeth, using a hacksaw, and then splitting it with a cold chisel. Note that one side of the gear teeth has a lead for the starter pinion and the ring must be fitted the right way round.

4   To fit a new ring gear requires it to be heated to about 200°C (say 400°F) but no more. Ideally this should be done in a temperature controlled oil bath (don't use a naked flame), but a makeshift method can be adopted using a blowlamp or welding torch if either is available. Polish four equally spaced areas on the gear ring upper face and support the ring on suitable heat resisting material such as firebricks. Apply heat evenly all round the ring until the polished areas start to turn a light yellow colour. This colour is an oxide film which gives some indication of temperature. The important thing is to heat the ring evenly and not to exceed the specified temperature.

5   When the ring is hot enough, fit it to the flywheel and tap it into position all round its periphery – get it on the right way round! Let it cool down naturally without quenching.

28 Oil pump – examination and renovation

1   The oil pump is located in the bottom of the timing case and it is driven by a shaft from a skew gear on the crankshaft. It is an eccentric rotor type pump and access can be gained by a cover bolted on the bottom of the pump housing.

2   Undo the four bolts retaining the cover and remove the cover and its gasket. The rotors can then be withdrawn as the inner rotor has a sliding keyway to mate with the key in the shaft. Wash the rotors in paraffin and wipe dry with fluff-free rag. Clean the pump housing with a paraffin-damped rag and wipe dry with fluff-free rag.

3   Inspect the pump rotors and housing for damage, scores or obvious signs of wear. Normally this type of pump has a long life but wear will eventually occur resulting in reduced output. If the components are defective or the pump output is suspect after prolonged use a new pair of matched rotors should be fitted but, as wear is also likely to have occurred in the pump housing on an old engine, a new timing case might be required, in addition, to effect a complete cure.

4   Reassembly is the reverse of the removal procedure, but lubricate the moving parts liberally with clean engine oil and use a new cover gasket (photos).

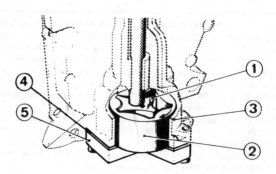

Fig. 1.16 The oil pump (Sec 28)

1   Inner rotor
2   Outer rotor
3   Timing case

4   Pump cover gasket
5   Pump cover

29 Inlet and exhaust manifolds – examination

1   The inlet manifold is connected to the cylinder head by four short lengths of flexible housing and it is worth renewing these when overhauling the engine. The hose clips must be in good condition; if in doubt, renew them to avoid the possibility of weak mixture problems. Check the carburettor mating face for flatness and freedom from damage. Finally flush the coolant passages in the manifold with clean water.

2   Examine the exhaust manifold for cracks and obvious damage. Use a straight-edge to check the faces mating with the cylinder head for flatness and lack of distortion. If there should be any sign of pitting or distortion in the mating faces it might be possible to have the defects removed by refacing at a suitably equipped workshop but if this is not possible, or if the problem is too severe for this remedy, a new manifold will be needed. Any accumulations of carbon in the exhaust manifold can be removed using a flexible wire brush or a scraper.

30 Engine mountings – inspection

The engine mounting rubbers are often ignored simply because

28.4a Fit the key to the driveshaft keyway

28.4b Fitting the outer rotor followed by ...

28.4c ... the inner rotor and finally ...

28.4d ... the cover with a new gasket

33.2 Installing the crankshaft upper half bearing shells

33.3 Fitting a half thrust washer

they do not normally present any problems. If they show signs of deterioration due to oil impregnation, heat or simply age, they should be renewed. Mountings that have lost their resilience and are unable to resist shock will result in engine/transmission vibration and will increase the risk of failure in other components and cause fatigue for the driver and passengers.

31 Engine reassembly – general

1   In the course of reassembling the engine, one or two basic principles must be observed to ensure a long, trouble free life subsequently.
2   Paramount is the need for absolute cleanliness. The working area, the engine components, the tools and hands of those working on the engine must be completely free of grime, grit and any other foreign matter. One speck of carborundum dust, or a small piece of swarf for instance, can ruin a bearing very quickly and undo all your efforts.
3   Always use new gaskets, locking tabs, seals, self-locking nuts etc. It is pointless to spend considerable time and money overhauling an engine only to have it fail as a result of, say, a defective re-used circlip. If necessary delay the rebuilding.
4   Don't rush the job. Anyone, however skilled and experienced, can make a mistake if he is trying to beat the clock.
5   Check that all nuts and bolts are clean and in good condition and, ideally, renew all spring washers, tab washers and similar locking devices as a matter of course.
6   In addition to most of the tools used during dismantling you will need a supply of clean engine oil, clean fluff-free cloths (domestic kitchen paper is a good alternative) and a torque wrench.
7   The torque wrench is really essential for this engine and, if you haven't got one try to borrow or hire one. The need arises because so much of the engine and transmission is made of light alloy which, although it has the advantage of low weight, is easily distorted by abnormal loads. The various fastenings must be torque loaded, where specified, to avoid such distortion while being tight enough to perform their intended task. Cracked or distorted casings are expensive to renew, so beware.

32 Engine – preparation for reassembly

1   Assuming that the engine has been completely stripped for overhaul and that the block is now bare, before any reassembly takes place it must be thoroughly cleaned both inside and out. If it has not already been removed, undo the five bolts retaining the oil gallery cover along the side of the block, remove the bolts and cover and discard the old gasket. Also remove the old O-ring located on the spigot in the block/transmission face at the clutch end.
2   The easiest way to clean the block is to immerse it in a garage's cleaning tank and leave it to soak before getting to work on it with a stiff brush and a selection of scrapers and probes. Clean out all the crevices but be careful not to scratch mating faces. Sediment collects round the liner seatings so check for this and clean it out.
3   Hose down the block with a garden hose and if an air supply is available use it to blow off surplus liquid. Dry and thoroughly clean the block with lint-free rags.
4   Oilways should be cleaned out using a thin bottle-brush, pipe cleaners and similar implements. Again, blow them through with compressed air if a supply is available. Squirt clean engine oil through to check that the oilways are clear.

33 Crankshaft – refitting

1   Ensure that the crankcase/ cylinder block is thoroughly clean, if necessary refer to the previous Section. Position the casing with the cylinder head joint face downwards on the bench.
2   Install the five bearing upper half shells in their locations after wiping the locations clean and dry. These shells have an oil groove (as opposed to the half shells in the caps which are plain) and the locating tongues should be fitted snugly in their slots in the case. If you are reusing the original bearings make sure that they are fitted in their original locations. After installation oil the shells freely with clean engine oil (photo).
3   Fit the half thrust washers in the No 2 bearing block with their grooves facing towards the crankshaft (photo).

4   Check that the crankshaft is perfectly clean and carefully lower it into the main bearings in the case (photos).

5   Check that each main bearing cap is clean and fit the plain lower half bearing shells (photo). Again if the original shells are being refitted make sure that each is in its correct cap. On Series II engines another two half thrust washers must be fitted to the No 2 main bearing cap, again with the grooves facing the crankshaft.

6   Check that all the main bearing cap locating spigots are present in the case. Oil the bearings then fit the caps to their respective bearings – each cap is numbered, No 1 being at the clutch end (photos).

7   Fit new plain washers to the ten cap retaining bolts. If the crankcase has bolt holes that are not blind, ie the hole goes right through, apply thread locking compound to the bolt threads. If the bolt holes are blind do not use thread locking compound. Fit the bolts and tighten them to the specified torque (photo).

8   The crankshaft endfloat must now be checked. In fact this check could be done before fitting the bearing caps on Series I engines which have 2 half thrust washers in the case only. On the Series II engines,

4 half thrust washers are fitted and all should be in position to check the endfloat. Push the crankshaft axially in one direction to its limit and using feeler gauges measure the clearance between the thrust washers and the crankshaft face (photo). The endfloat should be within the tolerance quoted in the Specifications. If it is not, new thrust washers should be selected from the range available which will produce the correct endfloat. Note that the washers must all be the same thickness on the engine. After adjusting the endfloat, or if it is found to be within tolerance, rotate the crankshaft and make sure that it turns smoothly without binding and without tight spots.

34 Pistons, connecting rods and liners – refitting

1   First the liners must be fitted to the block and checks made to ensure that each liner is square. Liner protrusion above the cylinder head joint face and protrusion relative to the adjacent liner(s) must be within tolerance.

33.4a Fitting the crankshaft

33.4b Note the milled slot in the crankshaft web which is used for setting TDC accurately

33.5 Fitting the lower half bearing shell to a main bearing cap. Note that the shell has no groove

33.6a Lubricate moving parts, in this case the main bearings, on assembly

33.6b No 2 main bearing cap with thrust washers (Series II engine) being fitted

33.7 Tightening the main bearing cap bolts with a torque wrench

33.8 Using feeler gauges to measure crankshaft endfloat

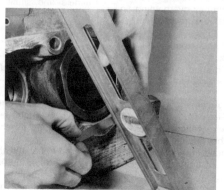
34.3a Using a straight-edge and feelers to check liner protrusion

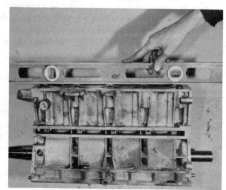
34.3b ... and relative difference in protrusion of adjacent liners

2   Turn the cylinder block upright and make sure that the seat for each liner is meticulously clean. This is very important because the slightest trace of dirt here could cause eventual cylinder head gasket leaks. Where original liners are being re-used they must locate in their original positions and the marks made during dismantling should be used for this purpose. Check that each liner is clean and that its bottom joint face is perfectly free of any old joint material, dirt, etc.

3   Insert the liners into their locations without base gaskets and, preferably using a dial test indicator (clock gauge), measure the protrusion of each liner relative to the cylinder block top face. Make four measurements on each liner at 90° intervals and note the readings. In the absence of a dial test indicator, a straight-edge and feeler gauges can be used, but care is needed to produce accurate results (photos).

4   Study the protrusion readings obtained for each liner. All four readings should be identical on each liner; if they vary by more than 0.02 mm (0.0008 in) on the same liner, the liner is not squarely located.

5   Select the appropriate gasket for each liner which will produce the specified protrusion without exceeding the maximum relative liner difference. One gasket only must be fitted to each liner. Where difficulty arises check that there is no dirt between the liner and the block and that your measuring equipment is accurate. New liners can be exchanged with others in the block. If the required result still cannot be obtained it is possible that the liners are distorted and you should have them professionally checked.

6   Fit the selected gasket to each liner, assembly the liners into the block and make a check of the protrusions and squareness again to confirm that all is well. Refer to Section 8 if necessary. This repeat check is worth doing as a leaking cylinder head gasket can prove to be an expensive fault.

7   Where the original pistons are being used, identify them with their liners using the marks made during dismantling. Before fitting each piston to its liner the ring gaps must be positioned correctly. The expander in the bottom composite scraper should have the gap located directly over the axis of the gudgeon pin and the gaps in the thin scraper rings should be within 20 to 50 mm (0.79 to 1.96 in) to each side of the expander gap (see Fig. 1.17). The tapered face compression ring gap and the top, curved face compression ring gaps should be located at 120° on opposite sides away from the expander gap. Lubricate the rings and pistons with clean engine oil.

8   Fit the upper half shells to the big-ends after wiping their locations clean and dry (photo). Lubricate each liner bore with clean engine oil and, using a suitable ring compressing tool, insert the piston and connecting rod into the liner (photo). Make sure that the liner gasket is snugly fitted and insert the liner into the block guiding the connecting rod onto the crankpin (photos). Make sure also that the liner is fitted the right way round in the block and the piston is the right way round in the liner. Previously used components should have the marks made during dismantling correctly aligned. Mark new liners to identify their location.

9   When all the liner and piston assemblies are fitted, install the liner retaining strap(s) to keep them in position while the big-end caps are being fitted (photo). Wipe each cap clean and dry and fit the lower half bearing shells. Identify each cap with its correct connecting rod and, after well lubricating the crankpin and bearing shells with clean engine oil, fit the caps (photo). Make sure that the locating tabs on the bearing shells butt each other on the same side. Fit and tighten the cap retaining nuts to the specified torque (photo).

10   Check that the crankshaft is still free to rotate without tight spots.

35 Cylinder head – refitting with engine on bench

1   Assuming that the cylinder head assembly has been overhauled as described in Section 20 and the cylinder block assembled to the stage reached in the last Section, temporarily fit the timing sprocket and key to the crankshaft and turn the crankshaft so that the marked tooth on the sprocket is aligned with the left-hand joint faces of the adjacent main bearing cap and cylinder block. This will position all the pistons at mid-stroke. Remember not to turn the crankshaft after fitting the cylinder head until after the timing chain has been fitted otherwise damage might result from the pistons contacting the valve heads.

2   Remove the liner retaining strap(s) and make sure that the cylinder block mating face is thoroughly clean. Check for any burrs or other accidental damage in the face and then position a new gasket on the head. Do not use any jointing compound.

3   Give the cylinder head a last check for cleanliness and lack of damage to the joint face and then lower the head carefully onto the cylinder head gasket on the block. Turn the camshaft so that its drive end is positioned as shown in Fig. 1.18.

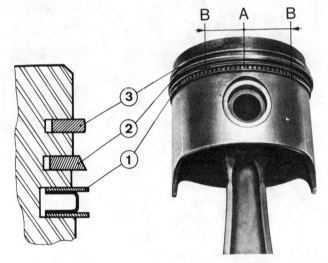

Fig. 1.17 Positioning the piston ring gaps on assembly (Sec 34)

1   Scraper ring
  (a) Expander gap on axis of gudgeon pin hole
  (b) Scraper rings gaps on alternate sides of gudgeon pin axis within 20 to 50 mm (0.79 to 1.96 in)
2   Tapered face ring gap 120° from gudgeon pin axis
3   Curved face ring gap 120° from gudgeon pin axis in opposite direction

34.8a Fitting a big-end upper half bearing shell

34.8b Inserting a piston into a liner using a ring compressor

34.8c Make sure that the liner gasket is fitted carefully with its inner lugs in the liner groove

34.8d Inserting a piston and liner assembly into the block

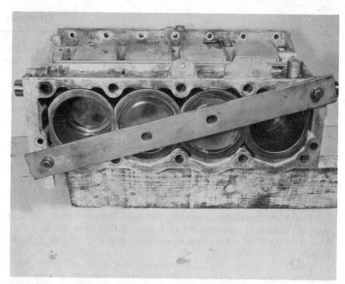

34.9a A piece of steel bar being used as a liner retainer strap

34.9b Fit a big-end bearing cap, then ...

34.9c ... fit and tighten the retaining nuts

Fig. 1.18 Align the camshaft in this position before installing the cylinder head (Sec 35)

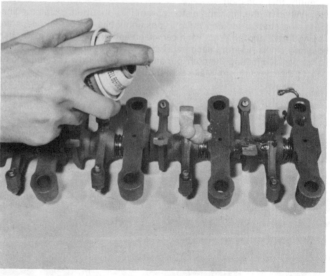

35.4a Spray the rocker pads with Molykote before ...

4   Give the rocker assembly a check to see that all is well and spray the rocker arm cam pads with Molykote 321 R or a suitable alternative (photo). Lower the assembly on to the cylinder head, engaging the locating dowels in the two end bearing blocks in their holes in the head (photo).

5   Oil the threads of the ten cylinder head bolts and also under their heads. Fit the bolts and nuts but don't use any washers. Refer to Fig. 1.19 and, following the sequence shown, tighten the bolts to the Stage 1 torque quoted in the Specifications (photo). Then go round again in the same sequence tightening to the Stage 2 torque.

6   In June 1980 Peugeot introduced an increased torque for the cylinder head bolts and, at the same time, a modified camshaft and stronger cylinder head bolts. *It is absolutely forbidden to use the higher torque on earlier engines* unless the new camshaft and new bolts are fitted in place of the originals. The camshafts can be identified by a coloured paint dab adjacent to the centre bearing journal and the bolts by numbers on the heads of the bolts as follows:

	Old	New
XL5 (118) camshaft	*Green*	*Blue*
XR5 (142) camshaft	*White*	*Yellow*
Cylinder head bolts (all engines)	*8.8*	*10.9*

36 Engine and transmission – reassembly

1   Refer to Chapter 6, Section 6 and reassemble the transmission unit to the engine.

2   If the transmission unit has not been dismantled it is advisable to remove the bottom cover plate and then remove the oil pump suction filter gauze, retained by three bolts. Clean the filter gauze thoroughly in paraffin and, if available, dry with compressed air. Refit the filter gauze using a new rubber seal and tighten the three bolts to the specified torque. Then refit the bottom cover using a new gasket and tighten the thirteen bolts to the specified torque. This additional chore is well worth while, ensuring that any sludge or particles trapped in the filter gauze or sump will not be circulated around the rebuilt engine.

37 Timing sprocket and chain – reassembly

1   Make sure that the keyways in the end of the crankshaft are clean and fit the keys. Refer to Fig. 1.20 and note the sequence of assembly of the various parts.

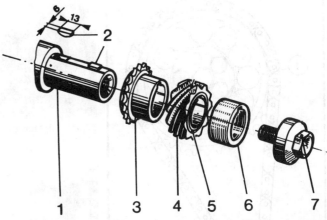

Fig. 1.20 Sequence of assembly of crankshaft drive components (Sec 37)

1   *Crankshaft*
2   *Keys*
3   *Timing chain sprocket, teeth towards engine*
4   *Oil pump/distributor driveshaft driving gear*
5   *Boss on gear away from engine*
6   *Spacer*
7   *Washer and bolt*

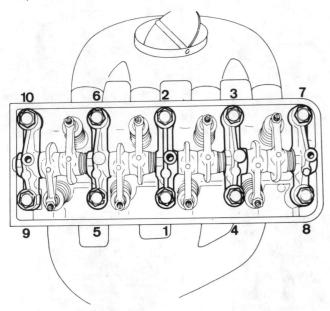

Fig. 1.19 Cylinder head bolts tightening sequence (Sec 35)

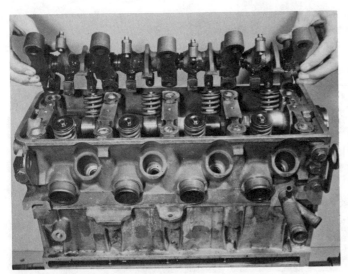

35.4b ... lowering the rocker assembly onto the cylinder head

35.5 Tightening the cylinder head bolts

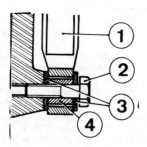

Fig. 1.21 Sequence of assembly of tension plate pivot (Sec 37)

1 Chain tensioner rubbing plate
2 Pivot bolt
3 Washers
4 Spacer

Fig. 1.22 Assembling the timing chain to the sprockets (Sec 37)

1 Camshaft sprocket timing mark
2 Crankshaft sprocket timing mark

37.2 The marked tooth should be aligned with the mating face joint

37.4a Fit the camshaft sprocket then ...

37.4b ... tighten the bolts and ...

37.4c ... bend up the locking washer. Note the marked tooth at 9 o'clock

37.6a Fit the chain tensioner oil filter

37.6b The tensioner shoe in the retracted position. Note the position of the lock ratchet

37.6c After fitting the tensioner ...

37.6d ... arm it by turning the lock ratchet clockwise

2   Assemble the sprocket, teeth towards the block, followed by the skew gear and spacer. Then fit the retaining bolts and washer but do not tighten yet. The marked sprocket tooth should be aligned with the main bearing cap/cylinder block mating faces if the crankshaft was positioned as described in Section 35, paragraph 1 (photo)
3   Assemble the chain tensioner rubbing plate pivot bolt, spacer and washers as shown in Fig. 1.21 and coat the bolt thread with thread locking compound. Fit the assembly to the block and tighten the bolt to its specified torque. Check that the plate moves freely.
4   Fit the camshaft sprocket to the shaft (photo), then fit the locking plate and the three retaining bolts. Tighten the bolts to the specified torque and bend up the locking plate to lock the bolts (photo). Align the marked sprocket teeth at the nine o'clock position when looking at the sprocket (photo).
5   The timing chain has three links marked white to facilitate correct valve timing. If these are not visible mark the links by first putting a mark on an outer link plate as a starting point. Count off 16 outer link plates, including the one just marked, and mark the 16th and 17th links. Fit the chain to the sprockets with the single marked link aligned with the marked tooth on the crankshaft sprocket and the twin marked links each side of the mark on the camshaft sprocket (Fig. 1.22). If necessary slightly adjust the camshaft position to fit the chain.
6   Refit the chain tensioner filter in its recess in the block. Check that the tensioner shoe is locked in the retracted position and assemble the two retaining bolts and locking washers, the joint gasket and the spacer plate to the tensioner. Fit the tensioner to the block and tighten the two bolts to their specified torque. Arm the tensioner by turning the lock ratchet in a clockwise direction and allow the tensioner to automatically take up the chain tension; don't assist the action of the tensioner (photos).
7   The crankshaft sprocket retaining bolt can now be tightened to the specified torque. Lock the crankshaft if necessary as described in Section 12, paragraph 5.

38 Timing case – reassembly and refitting

1   Fit the combined skew gear and fuel pump cam into its location in the timing case, slide the driveshaft into position and engage the drive dogs (photos). Lubricate the mechanism with clean engine oil.
2   Reassemble the oil pump components, referring to Section 28 for details if necessary.
3   Check that the oil pressure relief valve, spring and cap are perfectly clean, lubricate them with clean engine oil and fit them to their location adjacent to the filter mounting (photos), using a new sealing washer.
4   Fit the oil pressure sender to its location using a new sealing washer (photo).
5   Fit the distributor clamp plate and secure it with the single retaining bolt and lockwasher.
6   Install a new O-ring on the oil transfer spigot in the block joint face near the chain tensioner plate (photo).
7   Position a new timing case joint gasket on the block face using sealing compound to hold it in position (photo).
8   Refer to Section 10 and follow the procedure described in paragraphs 15 to 18 inclusive for fitting the timing case to the engine. When fitted, carefully trim off the surplus part of the joint gasket which protrudes above the rocker cover face (photos).

39 Valve rocker clearances – checking and adjusting

1   This operation is the same whether carried out with the engine installed or on the bench. If installed it must only be done when the engine is cold. The importance of correct rocker arm clearances cannot be overstressed as they vitally affect the performance of the engine. If the clearances are too big, engine efficiency is reduced as the valves open too late and close too early. On the other hand inadequate

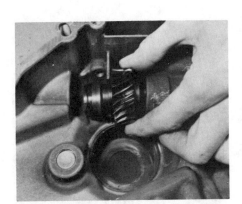

38.1a Fit the skew gear to the timing case and ...

38.1b ... slide the driveshaft into position ...

38.1c ... making sure that the drive dogs are engaged

38.3a Fit the oil pressure relief valve and spring, then ...

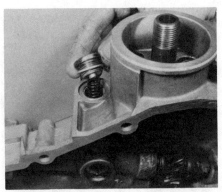

38.3b ... fit the retaining cap using a new sealing washer

38.4 The oil pressure sender being fitted

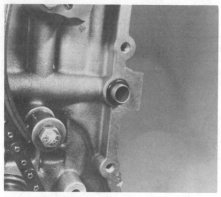
38.6 A new O-ring fitted to the oil transfer spigot

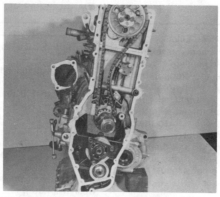
38.7 Fit a new timing case joint gasket

38.8a Fitting the timing case and ...

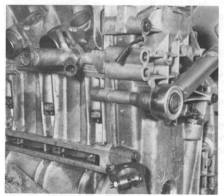
38.8b ... tightening the bolts

38.8c Trimming off the surplus part of the joint gasket

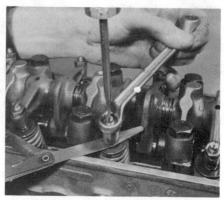
39.4 Adjusting the valve clearances

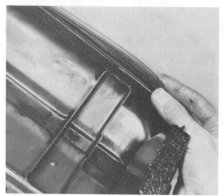
39.6a Check the rocker cover seal and ...

39.6b ... fit the cover to the cylinder head ...

39.6c ... using new sealing washers under the bolts

41.2 Refitting the oil gallery cover plate

41.3a The thermostat housing being refitted

41.3b Refitting the exhaust damper

clearances may prevent the valves closing when the engine is warmed up, resulting in burnt valve seats and possible warping.

2   If the engine is installed, remove the air cleaner and the rocker cover.

3   It is important that the clearance is set only when the rocker of the valve being adjusted rests on the heel of the cam, that is directly opposite the peak of the cam. This can be ensured by carrying out the adjustments in the following sequence, which also avoids turning the engine more than necessary:

Valve fully open	Adjust valve numbers
1 exhaust	3 inlet and 4 exhaust
3 exhaust	4 inlet and 2 exhaust
4 exhaust	2 inlet and 1 exhaust
2 exhaust	1 inlet and 3 exhaust

The correct clearances are listed in the Specifications. The engine can be turned with a spanner on the pulley retaining bolt; removal of the plugs will make the job easier. Exhaust valves are at the front of the engine (when installed in the car), inlet valves at the rear.

4   Set the clearances by positioning a valve fully open and inserting a feeler gauge in the gap between the tappet and valve stem of the appropriate valve. Loosen the locknut with a spanner and turn the adjuster screw with a screwdriver (photo). Adjust the screw so that the feeler gauge slides in the gap with a slight drag. Tighten the locknut, recheck the clearance and readjust if necessary. Repeat until all clearances have been set.

5   Checking and setting the valve clearances must always be carried out after removing and refitting the cylinder head and also whenever the cylinder head bolts are retightened following overhaul (see Section 9).

6   Check that the rocker cover seal is in good condition, renewing it if in doubt, and refit the cover (photos). Fit new sealing washers under the retaining bolts and tighten the bolts. Refit the air cleaner on an installed engine.

40 Clutch – refitting

1   Refer to Chapter 5, Section 7, paragraph 5 et seq for the refitting procedure of the clutch assembly, making due allowance for the fact that the description applies to an installed engine.

41 Engine reassembly – final stages

1   Having reassembled the major engine components, the various ancillary components and minor fittings can be re-installed. It is best to reassemble as much as possible before installing the engine/transmission in the car. If you elect to defer refitting some components until after installation be certain that it is in fact possible to refit them then.

2   Use a new gasket and, after checking that all is perfectly clean, refit the oil gallery cover plate (photo). Tighten the five bolts to the specified torque with new copper washers under their heads.

3   Refit the following components, referring to other Chapters if necessary:

   (a) Thermostat (Chapter 2) (photo)
   (b) Coolant pump and fan (Chapter 2)
   (c) Exhaust manifold and damper (Chapter 3) (photo)
   (d) Fuel pump (Chapter 3)
   (e) Starter (Chapter 10)
   (f) Distributor and coil (Chapter 4)

Leave the inlet manifold and carburettor until the engine is installed as it will then be easier to get to the gearchange mechanism and the fuel pump inlet pipe to reconnect them. Fit the pump outlet pipe now if not already fitted.

4   Finally check the complete engine/transmission unit to make sure that nothing is missing unless it is being deliberately deferred until after the unit it installed.

42 Engine and transmission unit refitting – general

1   Before refitting the power unit give the bay a good clean out. A thick poultice of dirt and oil tends to accumulate round the bottom end which should be removed with a proprietary solvent and washed off. Make a general inspection for frayed and damaged wires, corrosion, cracks and so on. If appropriate, touch up the underbody protection wherever required in the engine bay. Make sure that the driveshaft splined ends are clean and lubricated with clean engine oil.

2   Although it is feasible for the engine unit to be refitted by one person using a suitable hoist, it is much easier for two people to work together so that the upper and lower parts of the assembly can be attended to whilst the unit is being manoeuvred into position, especially in view of the limited accessibility.

3   Check that new seals have been fitted to the differential final drives and that the space between the two lips in each seal has been filled with grease.

43 Engine and transmission unit – refitting

1   Generally speaking the installation of the engine/transmission unit is the reverse of the removal procedure. First check that the lifting arrangements and sling are adequate for the job and securely attached to the lifting lugs on the engine.

2   Before lowering check that all loose wires, hoses and components in the engine bay are moved back out of the way. Apply a few drops of thread locking compound in the hole in the gear selector cover which accommodate the vertical bolt in the front end of the gear selection rod. Unscrew the threaded stud and locknut in the speedometer drive adaptor to permit entry of the speedometer drive cable end fitting.

3   Carefully lower the assembly into the bay. Keep the assembly moving slightly to confirm that it is not caught up as it is being lowered, and manoeuvre it over to one side of the bay. As soon as the unit is low enough engage the first driveshaft in the final drive, taking great care not to damage the oil seal in the drive. Move the engine assembly over towards the engaged shaft and turn the other front wheel outwards at the front to provide more room. Engage the second driveshaft. It might help in cases of difficulty to rock the car slightly and thereby alter the relationship between the shaft and final drive to permit engagement. Again be very careful not to damage the oil seal in the drive (photos).

4   After engaging both shafts, fit the speedometer cable end fitting in the drive adaptor. Fit the retaining screw and locknut, tightening them both in that order.

5   Move the assembly and lower it slowly to position the transmission rear edge under the steering box and locate the bottom right-hand mounting (photo).

6   If they have not yet been fitted, install the two upper mounting brackets on the engine and lower the engine into final position. Fit and tighten all upper mounting nuts and bolts to the specified torque (photos). Fit and tighten the lower mounting bolts to the specified torque. Unhook and remove the lifting tackle.

7   Clean the thread on the gear selection rod front bolt and lubricate the balljoint fittings with the specified grease. Reconnect the balljoints and fit the bolt, tightening it to the specified torque (photo).

8   If the starter motor is not already fitted refer to Chapter 10, for details and refit it. Reconnect the electrical connections and tighten the nuts.

9   Refer to Chapter 5 and refit the clutch control cable, adjusting it as described.

10   Reconnect the electrical connections to the coil and distributor.

11   Fit the inlet manifold and carburettor, making sure that all eight hose clips are in good condition and done up tightly. Fit the manifold support bracket, tightening the bolt in the engine/transmission joint face to its specified torque. Reconnect the coolant hoses to the carburettors and to the inlet manifold. Reconnect the fuel supply pipe and the vacuum advance pipe to the carburettor and the brake servo pipe to the manifold.

12   Refer to Chapter 10 and refit the alternator, then tension the drivebelt. Refit the voltage controller to its location on the left wheel bay wall.

13   Refer to Chapter 3 and refit the exhaust system piping. Make sure that there is at least 1.3 in (35 mm) clearance between the pipe and the rear subframe behind the sump.

14   Refer to Chapter 2 and refit the radiator. It would be worthwhile fitting new coolant hoses to and from the radiator if the originals have seen much service. With the radiator fitted the air baffles in front of it can be refitted followed by the front grille.

43.3a Lowering the engine/transmission assembly into the car

43.3b Engaging the right-hand driveshaft

43.5 The bottom right-hand mounting being engaged

43.6a Fitting the top right-hand mounting bracket ...

43.6b ... and the top left-hand bracket

43.6c The top right-hand bracket located on its mounting

43.7 Tighten the gearchange linkage bolt (arrowed)

15 Reconnect the remaining coolant hoses and after a check to make sure that the system is complete, refill the system with new antifreeze mixture. Refer to Chapter 2 for details.
16 Reconnect the electrical harness connectors and any loose wires that remain. Make sure that the distributor rotor is fitted, then fit the cap and ignition harness. Fit a set of new spark plugs after checking their gaps and connect the ignition leads. Note that the plugs must be tightened to the correct torque on this engine as explained in Chapter 4.
17 Refer to Chapter 3 and reconnect the choke and accelerator controls. Leave the air filter until after the engine has been given its initial run.
18 Refill the sump with the correct grade of engine oil up to the full mark on the dipstick.
19 Go carefully round the engine to make sure that all reconnections have been made. Especially check that the electrical earth connections are made, the drivebelts are correctly tensioned, the carburettor controls are connected and that there are no apparent oil or coolant

leaks. Remove all loose tools, rags, etc.
20 Refit the battery and secure with its clamp plate. Reconnect the battery leads and check the operation of the electrical circuits.
21 If the suspension was disconnected to remove the engine/transmission unit, refer to Chapter 9 and reconnect it.
22 The engine is now ready for its initial run which is dealt with in the next Section.

44 Engine – initial start-up after overhaul

1   Make sure that the battery is fully charged, that fuel is in the tank and that coolant and lubricants are topped up.
2   It will require several revolutions of the engine on the starter motor to pump fuel up to the carburettor and fill it.
3   As soon as the engine fires and runs, keep it going at a fast tickover only (no faster) and bring it up to normal working temperature as indicated by the fan engaging.

4 As the engine warms up there will be unusual smells and perhaps some smoke as parts get hot and burn off oil deposits. Examine all systems closely for signs of leaks of coolant, oil or fuel. In addition check the exhaust manifold and connections in the exhaust system for leaks as these usually settle down after being heated and vibrated. When the engine is stopped these connections will need retightening.

5 If necessary a temporary adjustment of the carburettor idle setting can be made but final adjustment will be needed later with the air intake cleaner fitted.

6 When satisfactory running is achieved with no leaks, no tell-tale warning lights alight and no abnormal indications, accelerate the engine over its speed range but don't race it unnecessarily.

7 Stop the engine and check again for leaks. When cool enough, retighten the exhaust pipe connections and manifold nuts.

8 Allow at least two hours for the engine to cool down and then remove the rocker cover and retighten the cylinder head bolts as explained in Section 9, paragraph 20. Following this reset the valve clearances as explained in Section 39. Refit the rocker cover and fit the air cleaner as described in Chapter 3. Retighten the crankshaft pulley bolt to its specified torque. Refit the bonnet using the marks made on the hinges to ensure a good fit. Top up the oil and coolant to the full level.

9 Restart the engine and, if necessary, trim the carburettor idle setting. Road test the car to check that the timing is correct and that the engine is giving the necessary smoothness and power. Don't race the engine – if new bearings and/or pistons have been fitted treat it as new and run it in at reduced speed, avoiding harsh acceleration, and using the gearbox to avoid loading the engine at low rpm.

10 After the car has travelled between 1000 and 1500 miles (1500 and 2500 km) the cylinder head bolts must again be retightened and the valve clearances reset.

45 Fault diagnosis – engine

Symptom	Reason(s)
Engine fails to turn when starter switch operated	Battery discharged Battery connections loose or corroded Starter connection, or engine or battery earth straps, loose or broken Starter motor or solenoid fault (see Chapter 10) Ignition/starter switch fault Major mechanical failure (seizure) Piston rings rusted to bores (after long disuse)
Starter motor turns engine slowly	Battery discharged Battery connections loose or corroded Starter connections, or engine or battery earth straps, loose Incorrect grade of oil in use Starter motor fault (see Chapter 10)
Starter motor turns engine normally but engine fails to start	HT leads damp or dirty Contact breaker points fouled or incorrectly gapped Spark plugs fouled or incorrectly gapped Loose or broken ignition connection Other ignition fault (see Chapter 4) Fuel tank empty, or pump defective Excessive/insufficient choke Choke linkage incorrectly adjusted Air cleaner clogged Carburettor jet(s) blocked Other fuel system fault (see Chapter 3) Valve clearances incorrect Incorrect valve timing (after rebuild) Poor compression
Engine fires but will not run	Loose ignition connection or internal fracture in wire Air leak at inlet manifold or carburettor joint face Fuel pump defective Other fuel system fault (see Chapter 3)
Engine idles erratically	Carburettor maladjustment or blockage (see Chapter 3) Ignition timing incorrect (see Chapter 4) Valve clearances incorrect Air leak at inlet manifold or carburettor joint face Air cleaner element clogged Uneven compression due to wear or leakage Worn distributor Worn timing components or valve gear

Symptom	Reason(s)
Engine misfires	Spark plugs fouled or incorrectly gapped HT leads damp or dirty, or cracked internally Contact breaker points fouled or incorrectly gapped Other ignition system fault (see Chapter 4) Air leaks at carburettor or inlet manifold Carburettor maladjustment or jet(s) blocked Fuel contaminated Other fuel system fault (see Chapter 3) Valve clearances incorrect Valve(s) sticking, incorrectly seated or burnt Valve spring(s) broken Uneven compression due to wear or leakage
Engine lacks power	Ignition timing incorrect Air cleaner clogged Overheating (see Chapter 2) Carburettor maladjustment or jet(s) blocked Valve clearances incorrect Distributor malfunctioning (automatic advance/retard inoperative) Brakes binding Excessive carbon build-up in cylinder head Poor compression Incorrect valve timing (after rebuild)
Pinking or knocking on acceleration	Incorrect grade of fuel in use Ignition timing over-advanced or automatic advance/retard defective Carburettor maladjustment Overheating (see Chapter 2) Excessive carbon build-up in cylinder head Valve timing incorrect (after rebuild)
Unusual noise from engine	Unintentional mechanical contact (eg fan blades) Worn drivebelt Peripheral component fault (eg water pump or alternator) Excessive valve clearances (tapping noise) Worn timing chain or sprockets Broken piston ring(s) (ticking noise) Big-end bearings worn (knocking noise, perhaps lessening under load) Main bearings worn (rumbling or thumping, perhaps worsening under load)

Chapter 2 Cooling system

For modifications, and information applicable to later models, see Supplement at end of manual

Contents

Specifications

General
System type	Pressurised, assisted by pump and fan
System capacity (with heater)	5.8 litres (10.2 pints)
Coolant type/specification	Antifreeze to BS 3151, 3152 or 6580 (Duckhams Universal Antifreeze and Summer Coolant)

Thermostat
Type	Wax capsule
Location	Top left of cylinder head
Opening temperature	80° to 83°C (176° to 181°F)
Temperature at which valve is open by 7.5 mm (0.3 in)	95°C (203°F)

Radiator
Cap pressure rating	0.8 bar (11.6 lbf/in^2)
Radiator test pressure	0.8 bar (11.6 lbf/in^2)

Coolant pump and fan
Pump type	Centrifugal impeller
Fan hub to pump pulley clearance	0.35 mm (0.014 in)
Fan drive	Electro-magnetic
Fan engages	87° to 89.5°C (189° to 193°F)
Fan disengages	77.5° to 81°C (171° to 178°F)
Electro-magnet winding current at 12V	0.7 to 0.9 amps
Drivebelt free play	1.5 to 2% or 0.5 in (13 mm)

Torque wrench settings
	lbf ft	kgf m
Jockey pulley M7 bolts	9.4	1.3
Lower jockey pulley pivot bolt	39.7	5.5
Temperature sender (taper seat – no sealing washer)	20	2.75

1 General description

The cooling system is of the pump-assisted thermal syphon type and is pressurised by means of a pressure valve filler cap. The main components of the system are the radiator, the coolant pump, the thermostat, the cooling fan, the heater and the connecting hoses. The system operates as follows.

Cold coolant from the bottom of the radiator is pumped into the coolant passages of the engine cylinder block and cylinder head. Heat from the combustion chambers and moving parts of the engine is absorbed by the coolant which is then directed to the upper section of the radiator. The passage of air through the radiator (due to the action of the cooling fan, when engaged, and to the forward movement of the car) cools the coolant as it passes down through the radiator matrix and the cycle is then repeated.

To accelerate the warming-up process when starting the engine, and thereafter to maintain the correct operating temperature, a thermostat is fitted in the coolant outlet from the engine to the radiator top hose. When the coolant is cold the thermostat is closed and circulation is limited to the engine coolant passages by means of a bypass route. As coolant temperature rises, the thermostat opens to allow coolant to flow through the radiator.

The system is pressurised to raise the boiling point of the coolant. This allows the engine to achieve its most efficient operating temperature as well as reducing the amount of coolant needed. It also brings the risk of scalding if the cap is removed whilst the system is pressurised.

Hot coolant is tapped from the system to supply the heater matrix for car interior heater and also to supply heat to the carburettor and inlet manifold to improve fuel vaporisation (photo).

The fan pulley incorporates an electro-magnetic drive which is only energised when the coolant is hot. By this means the fan is only driven when it is really needed, with a consequent reduction in noise and power consumption.

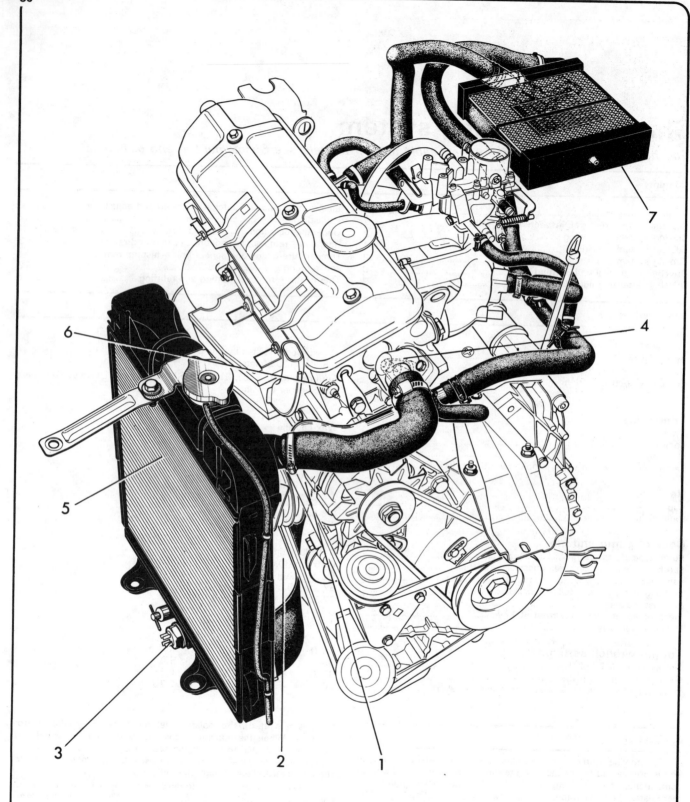

Fig. 2.1 The cooling system (Sec 1)

1   Coolant circulating pump
2   Fan with electro-magnetic clutch
3   Electro-magnetic clutch switch
4   Thermostat
5   Radiator
6   Coolant temperature sender
7   Heater matrix

1.0 Coolant is ducted to the carburettor and inlet manifold

2 Cooling system – draining

1   If the engine is cold, remove the filler cap from the radiator by turning the cap anti-clockwise. If the engine is hot, then turn the filler cap very slightly until pressure in the system has had time to be released. Use a rag over the cap to protect your hand from escaping steam. If, with the engine very hot, the cap is released suddenly, the drop in pressure can result in the water boiling. With the pressure released the cap can be removed.

2   If antifreeze is used in the cooling system, drain into a bowl having a capacity of at least 12 pints (nearly 7 litres) for re-use if appropriate.

3   Open the drain tap, located at the front bottom face of the radiator (photo). Move the heater control knob on the facia to full heat.

4   When the coolant has finished draining, probe the drain cock with a piece of wire to dislodge any particles of rust or sediment which may cause blockage.

5   Remember that, without dismantling, it is impossible to drain the system dry as some coolant will be retained in the heater matrix. If there is no antifreeze in the system, frost damage is still possible in winter even through the system is 'drained'.

6   If you intend to re-use the coolant, cover it to prevent dust or other contaminants from affecting it.

2.3 The radiator drain tap (arrowed). Fan thermal switch is on right

3 Cooling system – flushing

1   Every two years the cooling system should be drained, thoroughly flushed and refilled with fresh coolant. This is necessary because sediment, rust and scale will have accumulated in the system and, if not removed, could lead to overheating. In addition, the corrosion inhibitors in the antifreeze fluid deteriorate with time and, to restore protection, the antifreeze mixture must be periodically renewed. The procedure is covered in Section 11 but it is convenient to combine the two operations.

2   Drain the system as described in the previous Section and remove the drain tap from the radiator. Cover the engine and all electrical circuits with a sheet of plastic to stop water getting on them, as you are bound to cause some splashing. Insert a hose in the radiator filler neck and flush the system with fresh water for ten to fifteen minutes.

3   In extreme cases of sediment formation it may be necessary to use a proprietary chemical cleaner and/or to reverse flush the system. In the latter case disconnect the bottom hose from the radiator and remove the thermostat (Section 6). Direct the hose into the thermostat housing so that water is forced through the engine coolant passages and out of the bottom hose. To reverse flush the radiator it is advisable to remove it as described in Section 5 and invert it whilst flushing.

4   Flushing should be continued until the water runs clear and you are satisfied that the system is clean; then close the drain tap and refit any components which were removed.

4 Cooling system – filling

1   Check the condition and security of all cooling system hoses and connections, and ensure that the drain tap is firmly closed and that the heater temperature control is in the 'hot' position.

2   Fill the system slowly, using antifreeze mixture, until the level approaches the radiator filler neck. Carefully compress the top and bottom hoses with the hand to remove any air locks from the system, then continue filling until the level is within 2 in (50 mm) of the bottom of the filler neck.

3   Firmly refit the radiator filler cap and then start the engine and let it idle until the coolant is just warm. At this stage accelerate the engine several times to a fast speed to help move any air locks, then switch it off.

4   Carefully remove the filler cap and top up the coolant level as described in paragraph 2, then refit the cap.

5   If the original antifreeze is being re-used, remember that topping it up with plain water will dilute the mixture and weaken its properties; therefore it is best to use an antifreeze mixture for topping up.

6   Finally run the engine again and check the system for any leaks.

5 Radiator – removal, inspection cleaning and refitting

1   Drain the cooling system as described in Section 2.

2   Loosen the clips securing the top and bottom hoses to the radiator and carefully ease the hoses off the connecting tubes (photos).

3   Undo the fasteners securing the baffles on the front of the radiator which direct the airflow into the matrix. The fasteners can be prised loose if they are the button type or, alternatively, remove the securing nuts (photo).

4   Disconnect the electrical leads from the fan thermal switch located at the bottom front of the radiator.

5   Undo and remove the two bottom securing nuts in the radiator brackets and retrieve the rubber mounting washers. Undo the top securing bolt and carefully remove the radiator (photos).

6   Radiator repairs are best left to a specialist as without the relevant equipment it is quite easy to make matters worse, although minor repairs can be tackled with a proprietary compound. The radiator matrix, header and bottom tanks should be thoroughly examined for signs of damage, deterioration and leakage; very often a rusty sediment will have been deposited where a leak has occurred.

7   After inspection, the radiator should be flushed as described in Section 3 and the matrix and exterior cleaned of dirt and dead flies with a strong jet of water.

8   Refitting the radiator is a reversal of the removal procedure but the

5.2a The radiator top hose ...

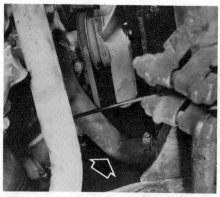

5.2b ... and the bottom hose (arrowed)

5.3 Undo the nuts (arrowed) to remove the radiator baffles

5.5a Undo the bottom securing nuts (arrowed) ...

5.5b ... and the top securing bolt to remove the radiator

5.8 Fit new rubber washers if necessary

6.5a Undo the two bolts (arrowed) and remove the outlet ...

6.5b ... to gain access to the thermostat. Note the position of the vent pin (arrowed)

6.7 When renewing a thermostat check that the new one is similar by its markings

Fig. 2.2 Testing a thermostat (Sec 6)

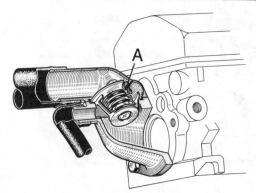

Fig. 2.3 Make sure that the vent pin (A) is uppermost on installation of the thermostat (Sec 6)

following additional points should be noted:

    (a) *Examine and renew any clips, hoses and rubber mounting washers which have deteriorated (photo).*

    (b) *Refill the cooling system as described in Section 4*

9 Peugeot have fitted at least five different types of radiator to the 305 and, if you have to renew a radiator, you may find that the new radiator is different from the old one. In some cases alterations to the bodywork may be necessary and your local Peugeot dealer should be consulted for details as their scope is outside the range of this manual.

6 Thermostat – removal, testing and refitting

1 The function of the thermostat is to enable the engine to reach its most efficient operating temperature in the shortest time, and this is accomplished by restricting the circulation of coolant to the engine during warming up; after reaching the operating temperature the thermostat opens and allows the coolant to circulate through the radiator.

2 A faulty thermostat can cause overheating or slow engine warm-up as well as affecting performance of the heater.

3 The thermostat is located at the engine end of the radiator top hose under a cover secured to the cylinder head adaptor by two bolts.

4 To remove the thermostat, first partially drain the cooling system (Section 2) and then disconnect the top hose from the thermostat housing outlet.

5 Unscrew and remove the two retaining bolts and carefully lift the coolant outlet away from the cylinder head adaptor (photos).

6 Extract the thermostat from its recess and remove the old gasket. Clean the faces of the cylinder head adaptor and the mating thermostat cover free of all traces of gasket and sealer.

7 To test whether the thermostat is serviceable, suspend it by a piece of string in a pan of water, which is then heated but make sure that it does not touch the pan. Use a similarly suspended thermometer to check the operating temperatures of the thermostat with reference to the information given in the Specifications. If the thermostat is faulty it must be renewed (photo).

8 Refitting the thermostat is a reversal of the removal procedure, but it will be necessary to use a new gasket, and the cooling system must be refilled as described in Section 4. To prevent leaks, the mating surfaces of the water outlet and head or manifold must be clean and free of excessive corrosion. When refitting the thermostat make sure that the vent pin is positioned upwards to allow air to escape from the system.

7 Coolant pump – removal, inspection and refitting

1 An impeller-type pump is located behind the radiator fan. The pump case is bolted to the front of the cylinder block by four bolts. The seal between the pump case and the cylinder block is a rubber O-ring fitted into a square recess. The pump is belt-driven from a pulley on the crankshaft. The belt is made to change direction through 90° on two jockey pulleys, one of which is adjustable to permit adjustment of the belt tension.

2 Before removing the coolant pump, disconnect the battery earth lead. Refer to Section 2 and drain the cooling system. Refer to Section 5 and remove the radiator.

3 Undo the three nuts securing the fan to the electro-magnetic clutch and remove the fan assembly. Do not disturb the three adjusting studs.

4 Release the wire clip retaining the electrical brush in its housing on the magnetic clutch and carefully remove the brush, ensuring that it is not damaged.

5 Slacken the belt tension adjuster on the lower jockey puller bracket and slacken the pulley pivot nut and bolt. Remove the drivebelt.

6 Undo and remove the four bolts securing the pump case to the cylinder block. Carefully remove the pump from the block; you might need to use a wooden lever to free the pump. Remove the old O-ring seal from the groove in the cylinder block.

7 Once the pump is on the bench, clean the exterior thoroughly. Undo the five bolts securing the front half of the pump to the rear half and separate the two halves. Clean off all traces of the old gasket and sealer from the two halves and also clean the interior passages and the impeller.

8 Check the pump spindle for smooth rotation in its bearing and for freedom from sideways play. A small amount of endplay may be tolerated but if it is excessive and if there is an appreciable amount of sideways play the bearing is worn and the pump will need renewing.

9 Check that the fan hub revolves freely on its bearings on the pump spindle. Only a small degree of play is tolerable here. The gap between the fan hub and the pump pulley is adjustable and should be checked and, if necessary, adjusted as explained in Section 8.

10 The electro-magnet in the fan clutch should also be checked as explained in Section 8.

11 Reassembling and refitting the coolant pump, hub and fan assembly are essentially the reverse of the removal and dismantling sequences. Use a new gasket and sealer when reassembling the pump and a new O-ring in the cylinder block groove when refitting the pump. If wished, the pump case may be fitted to the block first, followed by the body of the pump (photos).

12 Retension the drivebelt on completion as described in Section 9.

8 Electro-magnetic fan clutch – checking and adjustment

1 The electro-magnetic fan clutch ensures that the fan is only driven when the temperature of the coolant is high enough to require assisted airflow through the radiator – when the car is moving slowly in traffic on a hot day, for example. As the fan can absorb as much as seven horsepower when engaged at high engine rpm, clearly a useful saving on fuel is achieved by restricting its operation to those periods when it is needed. A temperature switch in the bottom of the radiator closes when the coolant is hot, and electric current is directed to the clutch magnetic coil by a carbon brush located behind the fan. The clutch, being part of the coolant pump, is always rotating when the engine is running. When energised, the fan is driven to assist radiator airflow. When de-energised, the fan spins freely if the car is in motion.

2 To check the operation of the fan clutch, disconnect the electrical leads from the radiator temperature switch and, with the ignition

7.11a When refitting the coolant pump fit a new seal to the block before ...

7.11b ... fitting the pump case ...

7.11c ... and use a new gasket when fitting the pump

switched on, short out the two connectors in the lead with a piece of wire. You should hear the electro-magnet click as the connectors are short-circuited.

3   If there is no noise of the electric-magnetic clutch being energised, examine the contact brush. Release the wire clip retaining the brush and carefully remove the brush from its housing. Examine for wear or contamination with dirt, grease, etc, and check that it moves easily in its housing. Reassemble the brush and check that it is in contact with the collector ring on the clutch body.

4   To check the winding of the electro-magnet in the fan pulley. connect a 12 volt battery and ammeter in series with the clutch but to avoid dismantling put the carbon brush back in the holder temporarily and connect the lead from the positive terminal of the battery to the brush. **Do not** attempt to push a wire or prod through the brush holder direct onto the slip ring. You may scratch or burn it. Compare the ammeter reading with those listed in the Specifications. A high reading indicates a partial or complete short-circuit whilst a lower or zero reading denotes a break in the winding. In either case, or if the collector ring is scratched or damaged, the electro-magnet/pulley assembly will need renewing.

5   The gap between the fan assembly and the electro-magnet/pulley assembly is critical for the correct operation of the clutch. With the ignition switched off, that is with the clutch de-energised, measure the gap, using feeler gauges, at three points adjacent to the three adjusting studs in the fan (photo). Compare the gap with that listed in the Specifications. To adjust the gap, loosen the locknut and turn the adjusting stud in or out as required. Tighten the locknut before re-checking the gap and repeat the procedure on the other two adjusting studs.

6   The coolant temperature switch is a simple thermal switch which closes two contacts at a given temperature and opens them on cooling. If you have a thermometer you can check its operation by first connecting a 12V bulb to the switch in place of the lead to the electro-magnetic clutch and to earth. Run the engine and monitor the temperature of the coolant in the radiator with the thermometer, noting when the light comes on and when it goes out. The correct temperatures are listed in the Specifications. A more accurate test could be made by immersing the threaded part of the switch in water with a lamp wired in series with a 12V battery and checking the light operation with a thermometer in the water as it is heated. However, this procedure would entail removal of the switch from the radiator which in turn would require the system to be drained.

9 Drivebelt – tension adjustment

1   Correct tensioning of the drivebelt will ensure that it has a long life. If the belt is loose, pump and fan functioning will be adversely affected and if it is too tight it will cause unnecessary bearing wear. Either way the belt itself will suffer.

2   The drivebelt is tensioned by moving the lower of the two jockey pulleys. If you are reassembling the engine make sure that the alternator drivebelt is in position on the crankshaft inner pulley, although it need not be tensioned, before adjusting the tension of the water pump drivebelt, as you cannot fit the alternator drivebelt with the pump drivebelt already fitted.

3   To tension the drivebelt first ensure that the lower jockey pulley pivot pin nut and pin are slightly loosened, that the belt is snugly fitted on all four pulleys, and that maximum twist is 90° on each leg between pulleys. With the belt slack make two marks on the belt 100 mm apart (work in metric units for this adjustment). Tighten the lower jockey pulley adjusting bolt to tension the belt so that the marks open up to 101.5 to 102 mm. Alternatively, tighten the adjuster until the belt has 0.5 in (13 mm) play when deflected by thumb pressure at a point mid-way between pulleys. Tighten the jockey pulley pivot pin and nut to the specified torque (photos).

4   If you have fitted a new belt and tensioned it, run the engine briefly and then readjust the tension. Check the tension again after about 500 miles (800 km) as some belts tend to stretch initially.

5   For the procedure for tensioning the alternator drivebelt refer to Chapter 10, Section 10.

10 Drivebelt – removal and refitting

1   If the drivebelt is worn, frayed or unduly stretched it should be

8.5 Measuring the fan-to-clutch clearance. Arrow shows one of the three adjusting studs

renewed. However, the most common reason for renewing a belt is that the original has broken, and it is therefore advisable to carry a replacement in the car for such an occurrence. The same reasoning applies to the alternator drivebelt.

2   To remove the belt, first loosen the nut under the lower jockey pulley pivot pin and losen the pivot pin. Screw back the adjuster bolt in the pulley bracket until the belt can be lifted out of a jockey pulley groove. Slip the belt out of the crankshaft and pump pulleys and lift it over the fan blades, turning the fan to help removal of the belt.

3   Fit a new belt on the pulleys and make sure that the maximum twist is 90° between pulleys. Tension the belt as described in the previous Section.

4   Refer to Chapter 10 for the procedure for changing the alternator drivebelt.

11 Antifreeze mixture

1   In weather conditions where the ambient temperature is likely to drop below freezing point it is essential to use an antifreeze solution in the cooling system; if the coolant is allowed to freeze in the engine or radiator, serious damage can result which could be very expensive to repair. A further consideration is the need for anti-corrosive protection, especially in modern alloy engines. As approved antifreeze fluids containing anti-corrosive additives are available it is recommended that antifreeze mixture is used all the year round for double protection.

2   Peugeot recommend that a 40% mixture of antifreeze and clean (preferably rain) water is used in the 305. The system holds a total of 10.2 pints (5.8 litres) and to mix a 40% solution, 4.1 pints (2.3 litres) of antifreeze will be needed.

3   Before filling with fresh antifreeze mixture, drain and flush the system as described in Sections 2 and 3. The easiest way to make the mixture is to put two or three pints of water into the system, add the correct amount of antifreeze and top up with water. Follow the full filling procedure described in Section 4.

4   Antifreeze mixture can remain in the system for up to two years when it should then be renewed. It is a sensible precaution to have the strength of the mixture checked periodically, especially at the onset of winter, and adjusted as required. Special antifreeze hydrometers are now available in motor accessory shops and are simple to use, following the maker's instructions. Alternatively your local garage will make the check for you.

5   Renew any hoses or clips whose condition is doubtful before adding fresh antifreeze mixture to the system.

12 Temperature gauge and sender unit – testing, removal and refitting

1   If the temperature gauge is faulty and gives an incorrect reading,

9.3A Lower jockey pulley removed from engine, showing adjuster and pivot pin nut

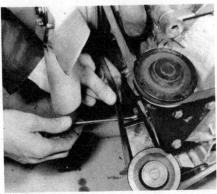

9.3B Adjusting drivebelt tension (engine removed)

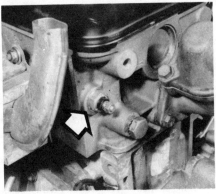

12.4 The temperature gauge sender unit (arrowed) (engine partly dismantled)

either the sender unit, the gauge, the wiring or the connections are responsible.

2   First check that all the wiring and connections are clean, sound and secure. The sender unit and the gauge cannot be repaired by the home mechanic, and therefore they must be renewed if proved faulty.

3   The wiring can be checked by connecting a substitute wire from the sender unit direct to the temperature gauge, running the engine (make sure no loose wires foul the fan) and observing the result. Alternatively a test lamp or electrical multi-meter can be used to check the continuity of the wires.

4   A suspect sender unit is best checked by substituting a new unit. The sender unit is located just in front of the thermostat housing at the top left-hand side of the cylinder block. Before removing it, partially drain the system as described in Section 2, then disconnect the supply lead and unscrew the unit (photo).

5   Refit the new sender unit using a reversal of the removal procedure, and then refill the cooling system as described in Section 4.

6   Details of removing and refitting the temperature gauge are contained in Chapter 10.

13 Fault diagnosis – cooling system

Symptom	Reason(s)
Overheating (check gauge for accuracy)	Low coolant level (due to leakage or neglect) Broken or slipping pump drivebelt Engine oil level low or incorrect grade Thermostat defective Fan clutch not operating correctly Coolant pump defective Internal or external clogging of radiator matrix Internal clogging of engine waterways Radiator pressure cap defective New engine not yet run-in (drive more slowly!) Brakes binding (see Chapter 8) Ignition timing retarded or automatic advance defective (see Chapter 4) Mixture too weak (see Chapter 3) Cylinder head gasket blown Cylinder head or liner(s) distorted or cracked
Overcooling (check gauge for accuracy)	Defective thermostat Fan clutch not operating correctly
External leakage	Overfilling (loss due to expansion) Loose or perished hoses Leaking coolant pump or thermostat gaskets Defective pressure cap Coolant pump seals defective Radiator matrix damaged Heater matrix damaged
Internal leakage	Blown head gasket (steam in exhaust and/or combustion gases in coolant) Head or liner(s) cracked or warped Inlet manifold cracked

Chapter 3 Fuel and exhaust systems

For modifications, and information applicable to later models, see Supplement at end of manual

Contents

Specifications

Air cleaner
Type .... Dry type, oiled expanded polyurethane foam element
Maker and model:
  GL and GR cars .... Lautrette L1322
  SR cars .... Peugeot 1104

Fuel pump
Type .... Mechanical engine-driven, pushrod operated

Fuel tank
Type and location .... Flat tank under rear floor
Capacity .... 9.46 gal (43 litres)

Fuel grade
All models .... Super grade 4-star petrol (97 RON)

Carburettor
GL and GR models .... Solex 34 PBISA5
SR models .... Solex 35 PBISA9

Carburettor specifications:

	34 PBISA5	35 PBISA9
Identification	PEU A110	PEU A202
Venturi	26	30
Main jet	130 to 135	150 to 160
Correction jet	150 to 170	150 to 170
Emulsion tube	01	12
Float bowl vent diameter	5	5
Idling jet	42 to 48	36 to 56
Idling air orifice	170 to 190	160 to 200
Bypass slot	4.5 x 0.6	4.5 x 0.6
Accelerator pump injector	40 to 50	30 to 50
Throttle opening for full stroke of pump	5.5 to 6.5	3 to 5
Uniform CO jet	25 to 35	20 to 40
Uniform CO air orifice	170 to 190	160 to 200
Ball type needle valve	1.5	1.5
Float weight (g)	5.7	5.7
Normal idling positon (NIP)	50'	30'
Positive opening (PO)	13°	12° 05'
Drill diameter for accelerator pump stroke adjustment (Section 9)	6 mm	4 mm

Idling speed
All models .... 900 to 950 rpm

Torque wrench settings

	lbf ft	kgf m
Fuel pump/timing case bolts	12.7	1.75

1 General description

The Peugeot 305 fuel system is conventional in layout and operation. The fuel tank is located at the rear of the car under the luggage compartment and between the rear wheels. Fuel is drawn from the tank by a mechanically operated pump located on the engine timing case under the distributor. The pump is operated by a pushrod activated by an eccentric cam on the oil pump/distributor driveshaft mechanism. The fuel pump incorporates a mesh filter.

One of two types of carburettor is fitted, depending on the engine models, but both are similar in most respects. The carburettor is a single barrel downdraught instrument incorporating a mechanical accelerator pump and manual choke. The carburettor body is warmed by hot coolant tapped from the engine cooling system. A mesh filter is fitted in the carburettor fuel inlet connection.

Air for the carburettor is drawn through an air filter with a renewable dry element. On SR models warmed air is admitted to the intake in cold conditions by an automatic control. On GL and GR models the control is manual.

2 Air filter element – removal and fitting

1   The air filter element, although described as a dry element, is in fact made of oil-moistened porous material. As air is drawn into the carburettor, dust and dirt adhere to the element which progressively becomes contaminated and must eventually be renewed. Under severe conditions in dusty atmospheres renewal must be more frequent than normal. The maker recommends that normal renewal should be at 20 000-mile (30 000-km) intervals and at 10 000-mile (15 000-km) intervals in severe conditions.

2   To remove the element, undo the air intake top cover retaining nut(s) – two on SR models and one on GL and GR models. Lift the cover taking care not to stress the hose connection (all models) and the automatic preheat control (SR models only) (photo).

3   Lift the old element out of the intake case and wipe the inside of the case and cover clean with fluff-free rag (photo).

4   Insert the new element and check that it is seated correctly (photo). Refit the cover, making sure that it is properly bedded down, and refit the retaining nut(s).

3 Fuel pump – removal, servicing and refitting

1   The fuel pump is located at the right-hand rear corner of the engine, being mounted on the timing case. Access is difficult because, on right-hand drive cars, the brake servo and master cylinder are mounted directly over the distributor which itself is located over the fuel pump (photos). The pump has an inlet and an outlet hose connection and it is secured to the timing case by two bolts. More than one type of pump has been fitted by the makers on these models but they all operate on the usual lever-actuated diaphragm principle. Although routine filter cleaning should present few problems, make sure that a servicing kit is available before completely dismantling a pump; it may be necessary to fit a new pump if the installed one is

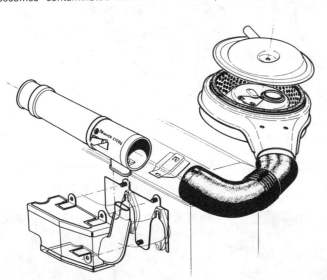

Fig. 3.1 The 1290 cc (XL5) engine air filter assembly with manual intake heat control (Sec 2)

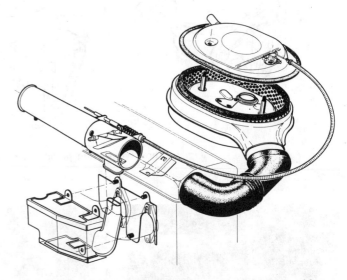

Fig. 3.2 The 1472 cc (XR5) engine air filter assembly with automatic intake heat control (Sec 2)

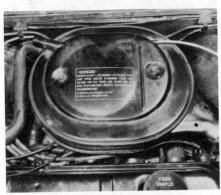

2.2 Undo the nuts to remove the cover ...

2.3 ... and, after removing the old element, clean the case ...

2.4 ... before fitting a new element

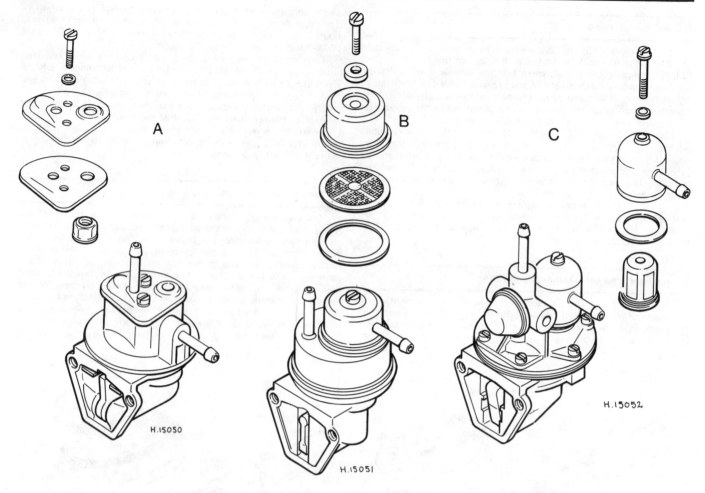

Fig. 3.3 Three types of fuel pump which have been fitted to the Peugeot 305 (Sec 3)

A   Sofabex 3201   B   AC   C   Guiot SY527C

3.1a Access to the fuel pump is difficult (ignition harness, etc, removed) ...

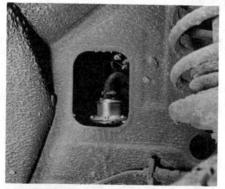

3.1b ... but there is an aperture in the right-hand wheel well

3.3 Remove the fuel pump cover ...

giving trouble and no servicing spares are obtainable.

2   To remove the pump, disconnect the inlet and outlet hoses and temporarily plug them to prevent loss of fuel or ingress of dirt. Unscrew the two retaining bolts and carefully lift the pump clear from the timing case. Remove the old gasket.

3   On the type of pump shown in the photographs the top cover is retained by two screws. Other models of pump may have only one or more than two screws. Remove the cover retaining screws and note that they have sealing washers under their heads. Remove the cover and the gasket underneath. The filter will be seen in the pump body (photo).

4   Take the filter out and wash it in clean fuel (photo). Don't use any cloth or tissue for filter cleaning, let the filter dry in air. Clean out the pump bowl with fuel; you may find some sediment in the bottom which must be removed. Again don't use rags for cleaning.

5   Further dismantling may not be possible on some types of pump. Even if it is, it should only be attempted if you have a repair kit. First mark the top and bottom halves of the pump for reassembly and then progressively loosen and remove the screws holding the two halves together. The diaphragm is connected to the operating mechanism beneath, and details will vary with different pumps. Note the sequence of assembly so that reassembly can be achieved in the same order.

3.4 .... to remove the pump filter

3.8a Make sure that the pump operating plunger is fitted before ...

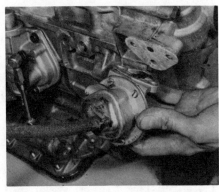

3.8b ... refitting the pump. Use a new gasket

6   Renew all defective parts; the kit will contain a variety of seals or gaskets which should automatically be fitted in place of the originals regardless of the fact that they may appear fit for further use.

7   Reassembly is the reverse of the dismantling sequence. Make sure that the upper and lower halves of the pump body are aligned and tighten the joint screws progressively and diagonally. Don't over-tighten the top cover screws.

8   Before refitting the pump check that the operating plunger is in position in the timing case and use a new gasket which must be of the same thickness as the original. Tighten the two securing bolts to the specified torque and make sure that the fuel hoses are connected to their correct pump connections (photos).

4 Fuel pump – testing

1   If the performance of the fuel pump is in doubt, first examine for fuel leaks and check that the fuel line connections are all sound.

2   Disconnect the fuel hose at the carburettor inlet connection and disconnect the high tension lead from the coil. Ensure that the tank contains fuel.

3   Direct the fuel feed hose into a suitable container and have an assistant operate the starter to crank the engine. A good spurt of fuel should be delivered on every second revolution of the engine. If not, check that the hose is not blocked. If that is clear the pump will need removal for examination or renewal.

5 Carburettor – general description

Figs. 3.4 and 3.5 are cross-sectional views of the two types of carburettor fitted to the Peugeot 305. The carburettor type is stamped on a plate (photo).

Both carburettors are single barrel downdraught instruments and they incorporate the following features:

(a) a cold start
(b) an idling circuit
(c) a uniform CO circuit
(d) a progression circuit
(e) a main circuit
(f) a diaphragm type accelerator pump

In addition the 34 PBISA9 carburettor fitted to SR models has an Econostat economiser.

Operation of the carburettors follows conventional practice. Fuel enters through a mesh filter and fills a chamber to a level which is controlled by a float operated valve.

During normal engine running above idling, the depression gener-ated in the venturi draws fuel through a main jet to an emulsifying tube located in the venturi where the air/fuel mixture is admitted to the main air stream. A conventional butterfly valve throttle controls the flow of the mixture.

At idling, due to inadequate depression at the venturi, an air/fuel mixture is delivered to the edge of the almost closed throttle butterfly where a greater depression exists. Mixture and volume control screws are provided to adjust the engine idling speed.

The Econostat on the 35 PBISA9 carburettor supplies fuel to an outlet above the venturi where, with an open throttle, the depression is large enough to cause the fuel to enter the airstream. At lower engine speeds with the throttle nearer the closed position this depression diminishes and no fuel flows. In this way the engine receives a weaker mixture at low engine speeds. Such a mixture at high engine speeds would cause overheating and possibly mechanical damage.

The choke flap incorporates a poppet valve which is lightly sprung closed. When the engine is being turned on the starter the poppet remains closed, accentuating the choke effect and thereby assisting starting. As soon as the engine is running the poppet opens to reduce the choke effect.

The diaphragm type accelerator pump ejects fuel directly into the venturi on each occasion that the throttle is opened. The pump recharges itself when the throttle is closed. This additional fuel helps to produce smooth acceleration as otherwise there would be a momentary weakening of the air/fuel mixture entering the engine due to the inertia of the fuel.

6 Carburettor – maintenance

1   Before blaming the carburettor for any shortcomings in engine performance, remember that there is no reason why the carburettor should lose tune and in fact what usually happens is that, as the engine gets older and less efficient, more or less fruitless attempts are made to restore performance by interfering with the carburettor. In those parts of the world where exhaust emission is regulated by law it is inadvisable and may be illegal to alter carburettor settings without monitoring exhaust emission levels using special equipment.

5.0 The type of carburettor is indicated on a data plate (arrowed)

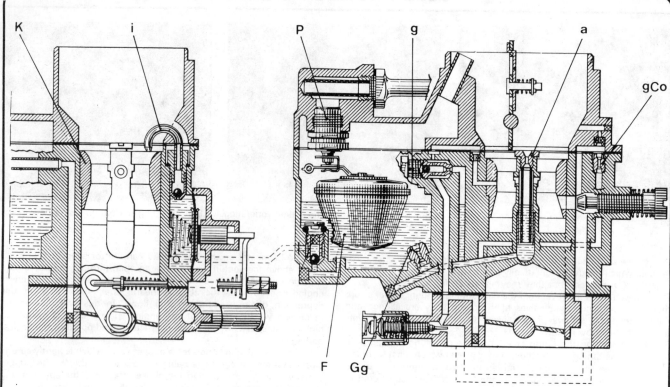

Fig. 3.4 Cross-sectional view of the Solex 34 PBISA5 (PEU A110) carburettor fitted to the 1290 cc (XL5) engine (Sec 5)

K	Venturi	g	Idling jet	F	Float
Gg	Main jet	i	Pump injector	gCO	Uniform CO jet
a	Corrector jet	P	Needle ball valve	Ce	Econostat orifice

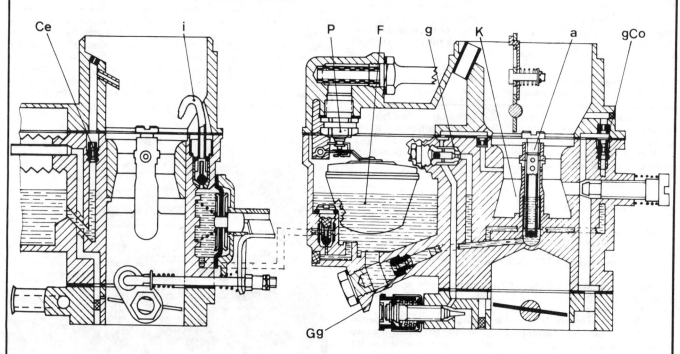

Fig. 3.5 Cross-sectional view of the Solex 35 PBISA9 (PEU A202) carburettor fitted to the 1472 cc (XR5) engine (Sec 5)

See Fig. 3.4 for key

2   The ultimate cause of most carburettor problems is wear in moving parts or dirt in the jets. The Solex carburettor has no continuously moving parts except for the float and the throttle spindle which makes it a very reliable device so long as dirt does not get in. A drop of oil on the various linkages and flap spindle will ensure that they last for years without trouble; in consequence carburettor overhaul should be no more frequent than major engine overhaul.

3   Routine carburettor maintenance consists only of periodic cleaning of the float chamber and jets and an occasional look at the small gauze filters fitted in the fuel inlet connection and on the accelerator pump inlet valve. These tasks can be undertaken with the carburettor installed on the engine. The jets can be identified and located by reference to the relevant illustrations. The gauze filters are also shown.

4   Before separating the top of the carburettor from the bottom, give the outside a good clean using paraffin or a proprietary cleaner and a stiff brush, afterwards drying with clean rag. It is well worth taking this extra trouble to reduce the risk of dirt getting into the carburettor.

5   After removing the jets clean them by washing in clean fuel and blowing air through them. Never use a piece of wire as the jet calibration can be easily altered.

6   The float can be removed after taking out the hinge pin. The float needle valve can then be unscrewed and washed in fuel. Clean any dirt out of the float chamber using clean fuel but don't use rag for drying. The fuel inlet filter gauze and the accelerator pump inlet valve gauze should both be washed in clean fuel and dried in air, again don't use rag to dry them. On refitting the float check, and if necessary adjust, the level setting as explained in Section 8. The accelerator pump stroke adjustment should also be checked, and if necessary adjusted, after reassembly as explained in Section 9.

7.5a Adjusting the carburettor volume control screw and ...

7   Carburettor – adjustments

1   Generally speaking unless the carburettor is obviously out of tune or is malfunctioning it is not advisable to tamper with it. In any case the only running adjustment that can be made is to the idling.

2   Correct adjustment can only be achieved provided that the engine is in generally good condition. The valve clearances must be correct and the ignition system must be in good condition and adjusted correctly.

3   An independent tachometer is necessary to make accurate adjustment and it should be connected to the engine in accordance with the maker's instructions. The air filter must be fitted. Run the engine until warmed as indicated by the engagement of the cooling fan.

4   If local regulations preclude adjustment other than to the volume control screw, adjust the idling speed to that listed in the Specifications.

5   Where it is not illegal to adjust on both the volume and the mixture screws, first adjust the volume control screw over the accelerator pump link (photo) to obtain the specified idling speed plus 50 rpm. Remove the tamperproof plug from the mixture screw situated under the accelerator pump link and turn the screw, either way, to achieve maximum rpm at that throttle setting (photo). Repeat the adjustments on the volume control screw and then the mixture screw until the maximum speed achieved after adjusting the mixture screw is 50 rpm above the specified idling speed. When this point is reached tighten the mixture screw slightly to reduce the idling speed to that specified.

7.5b ... the mixture screw (air cleaner removed for clarity)

8   Carburettor – float level setting

1   Incorrect fuel level in the carburettor will drastically affect engine performance and it is essential to maintain the correct level. This is easily done by adjusting the float which controls the needle valve. A special gauge is necessary but one can be made from scrap material quite simply by the home mechanic.

2   Refer to Fig. 3.6 and make up a gauge for the model of your carburettor to the size and shape indicated. It can be made out of thin sheet metal or plastic; material is not important but accuracy in sizes is critical, so take some care on this.

3   The float level should be checked before reassembling the carburettor after routine maintenance or when the level adjustment may be in doubt. Flooding of a carburettor is nearly always due to dirt

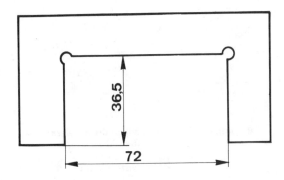

Fig. 3.6 Details of float level setting gauge. All dimensions in mm
(Sec 8)

in the needle valve or a punctured float. However, incorrect level adjustment can also be the culprit even though it is unlikely.

4　Apply the gauge to the inverted top of the carburettor, making sure that the sealing gasket is in position. The float should just contact the gauge with the needle valve closed, see Fig. 3.7.

5　If necessary adjust the position of the float by gently bending the float suspension arm. Do this carefully and check the adjustment with the gauge.

9　Carburettor – accelerator pump stroke and injector, checking and adjustment

1　After disturbance of the accelerator pump linkage, or if the performance of the pump is suspect, the pump stroke and the injector setting should be checked. Any adjustment found necessary can easily be made.

2　The pump stroke is set by using a gauge to position the throttle butterfly and then adjusting the pump linkage. The gauge can be an appropriately sized metric twist drill, but the shank must be in an unmarked condition. To make the check the carburettor must be inverted. Loosen the nut on the pump linkage rod between the throttle lever and the pump operating arm. Open the throttle and insert the drill shank between the edge of the flap and the intake bore. Lightly hold the flap in this position, turn the adjusting nut until it just contacts the pump operating arm and then tighten the locknut. Check the adjustment and then remove the drill from the carburettor barrel.

3　Fuel from the accelerator pump is delivered by an inverted U-tube nozzle in the carburettor bore. The setting of the nozzle should be checked and adjusted whenever the accelerator pump performance is suspect.

4　The carburettor should not be installed for this check as neat fuel would be injected into the manifold. For this reason position a suitable receptacle under the carburettor and, with the fuel hose connected, fill the float chamber. Open the throttle manually and observe the pattern of fuel spray as it is ejected into the carburettor bore. It should be midway between the edge of the throttle and the barrel wall when the throttle is open about 8 mm (0.315 in), see Fig. 3.9.

5　If correction is necessary, gently bend the injection nozzle to obtain the required direction of spray. Recheck after adjustment.

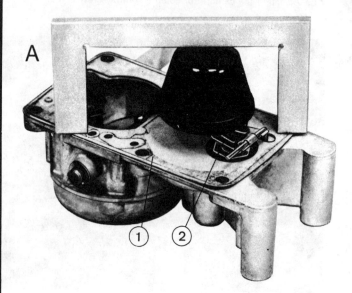

Fig. 3.7 Using the float level setting gauge (Sec 8)

1　Gasket must be in position
2　Adjust on float arm

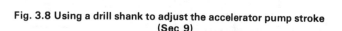

Fig. 3.8 Using a drill shank to adjust the accelerator pump stroke (Sec 9)

A　Adjustment nut

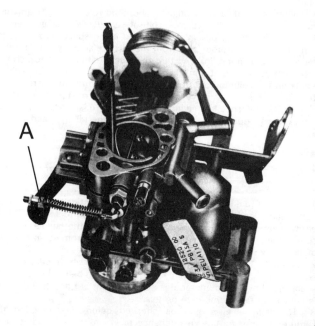

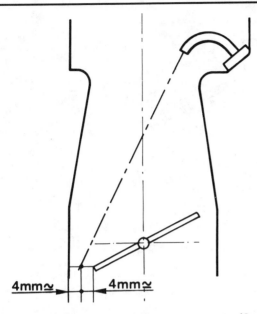

4mm≃ **4mm≃**

Fig. 3.9 Accelerator pump delivery spray pattern (Sec 9)

10 Carburettor – removal and refitting

1   Carburettor removal requires either partial draining of the cooling system or the clamping of the two coolant hoses connected to the carburettor to prevent loss of coolant. Refer to Chapter 2 for coolant draining procedures.

2   Remove the air cleaner by first removing the top cover, held by one or two nuts depending on model. Disconnect the breather hose and, on SR models, move the cover to one side taking care not to stress the preheater operating cable; on other models remove the cover from the car. Unscrew and remove the three bolts securing the air cleaner case to the carburettor. Lift the case off the carburettor, disconnect the air inlet connection and remove the air cleaner from the car.

3   Loosen the fuel feed hose connection and pull the hose off the carburettor inlet union. Temporarily plug the hose to prevent fuel loss and dirt ingress.

4   Pull the vacuum advance pipe which leads to the distributor free from its carburettor connection.

5   Undo the choke cable retainer and disconnect the cable from the carburettor control lever.

6   Disconnect the throttle cable from the spring-loaded drum and the bracket on the carburettor.

7   Undo and remove the two nuts securing the carburettor to the intake manifold and lift the carburettor off. Retrieve the old joint gasket and put a piece of cloth over the aperture in the manifold to prevent anything from falling in accidentally whilst the carburettor is removed.

8   Refitting the carburettor is the reverse of the removal procedure. Remove all traces of the old gasket and use a new one on installation. After fitting the carburettor reconnect the choke and throttle controls. Make sure that the choke is correctly adjusted. When the control is pushed fully in the flap should be fully open and there should be a small amount of possible additional movement on the control knob. Check that the flap closes when the control is pulled.

9   After reconnecting the two coolant hoses remove the clamps if these were used and in any case top up the cooling system.

10 Adjust the idle speed on completion as described in Section 7.

11 Carburettor – dismantling, overhaul and assembly

1   The carburettor should not normally need to be dismantled except for cleaning and checking the float level.

2   If the carburettor is to be dismantled, remember that it is a relatively delicate instrument and therefore requires careful handling. Use the correct tools for the job and do not interchange jets or clean them out with wire or any similar item which could damage them and interfere with their calibration.

3   Before dismantling the carburettor or any part of it, first clean the outside and prepare a clean work area. When taking anything mechanical apart, and this applies particularly to such components as carburettors, it is always sound policy to make sure that the individual parts are put back exactly where they came from, and even the same way round if it is possible to do otherwise, even though they may apear to be interchangeable. To help in this procedure mark or label items, put small parts in boxes or tins so that they don't get mixed up, and lay parts out in order of assembly on clean paper.

4   Identify the relevant illustrations for the carburettor being dismantled (Figs. 3.4, 3.5, 3.10 and 3.11). Remove the top of the carburettor by undoing the six retaining screws and separating the cover from the lower part. The float can be removed by pushing out the hinge pin and then the needle valve assembly can be unscrewed from the cover. Unscrew the fuel inlet connection and remove the gauze filter. Examine the filter for particles of foreign matter.

5   Remove the accelerator pump operating rod and then remove the cover by progressively undoing the four retaining screws, restraining it against the action of the spring under the diaphragm. Examine the diaphragm for splits or damage.

6   Remove the accelerator pump inlet valve cover located in the bottom of the float chamber, taking care not to lose the ball valve. Examine the filter for contamination.

7   Unscrew and remove the jets, checking them for dirt or blockage. Observe the caution mentioned in paragraph 2.

8   It should not be necessary to interfere with any adjusting screws but, if this is necessary, count the number of turns require to remove the screw so that it can be refitted in approximately the same position.

9   Do not disturb the choke flap and throttle butterfly valves or spindles. Their actuating mechanisms are external and normally require no attention unless excessively worn. If the spindles are worn in the carburettor body then serious consideration should be given to renewing the complete carburettor. Such wear is an indication that the carburettor is due for renewal and it would be false economy to refit the original instrument. Air leaks around worn spindles make it impossible to tune the carburettor correctly and poor performance and impaired economy will inevitably result.

10 The respective chambers, passages and jet seats can be brush cleaned using clean fuel and they should then be blown dry, if an air supply is available, or allowed to dry naturally. Don't use rag or cloth. Clean and blow through the jets in a similar manner.

11 Reassembly is the reverse of the dismantling procedure. Whenever possible use new washers, gaskets, or seals wherever fitted. During reassembly check and adjust the float level as described in Section 8, and set the accelerator pump stroke as described in Section 9. On completion of assembly check and, if necessary, adjust the accelerator pump discharge nozzle, also described in Section 9. Finally, after installation, adjust the idling as described in Section 7.

12 Accelerator cable – removal and refitting

1   Undo the nut and bolt clamping the inner cable of the accelerator control to the spring-loaded drum on the carburettor, remove the cable from the groove on the drum and pull the cable and its outer protective sheath from the anchor point on the carburettor bracket.

2   Working inside the car, detach the cable end fitting from the end of the accelerator foot pedal. Withdraw the cable assembly from the car by pulling it into the passenger compartment, at the same time feeding it through the bulkhead grommet.

3   Before fitting a new cable assembly lubricate the inner cable with engine oil.

4   Refitting an accelerator cable assembly is the reverse of the removal procedure. Before tightening the inner cable clamp bolt check that the inner cable is correctly located in the groove on the spring-loaded drum (photo). Tighten the clamp bolt and nut and check that the throttle is fully closed with the foot pedal free. If necessary readjust the inner cable in the clamp bolt and nut.

13 Choke cable – removal and refitting

1   Loosen the clamp bolt securing the inner cable to the choke flap operating link (photo).

2   Loosen the bolt securing the clamp plate which holds the outer sheath on the carburettor bracket. Detach the inner cable and outer

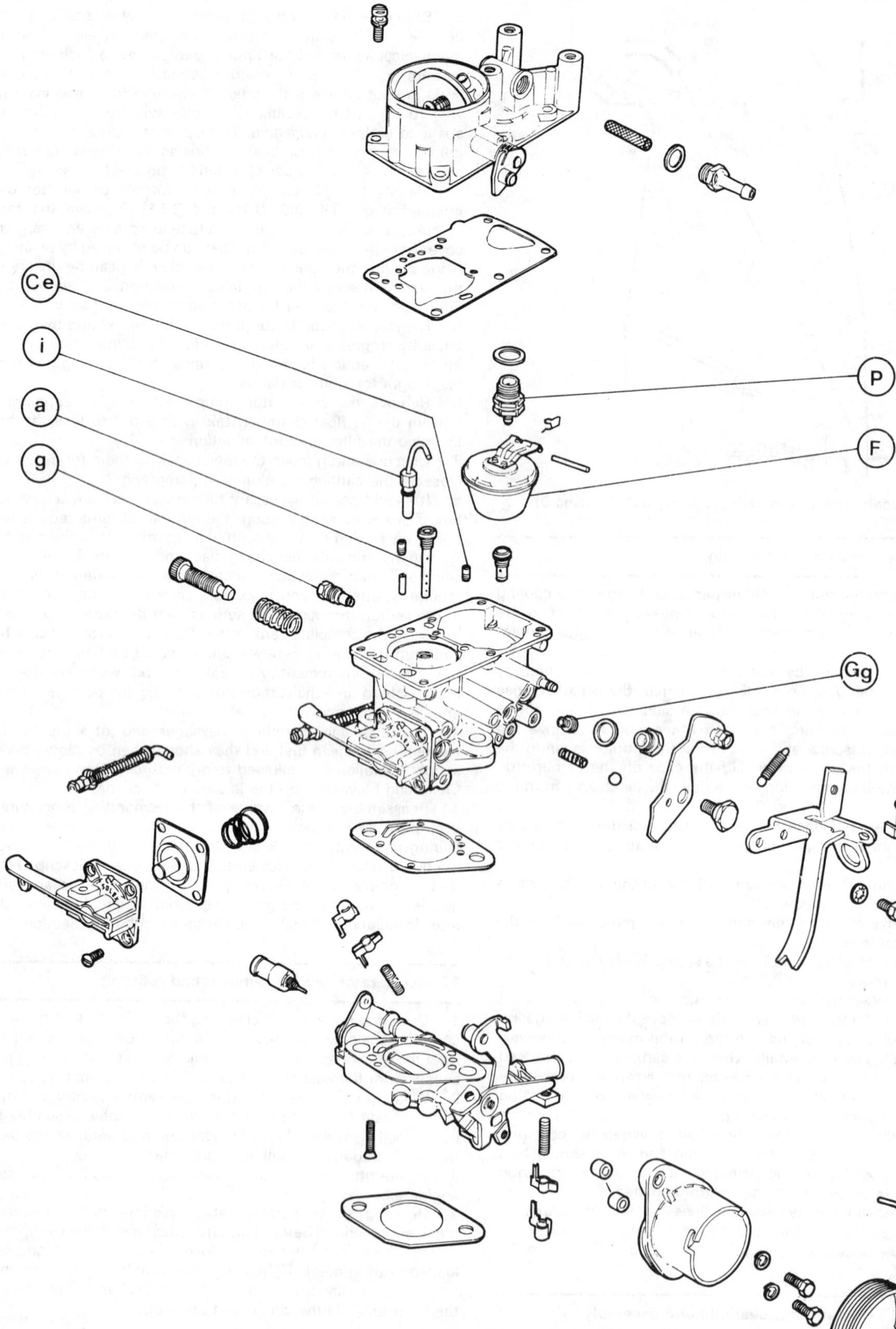

Fig. 3.10 Exploded view of the Solex 34 PBISA5 (PEU A110) carburettor (Sec 11)

See Fig. 3.4 for key

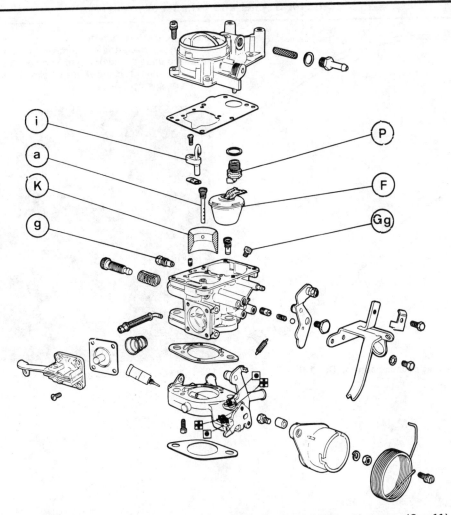

Fig. 3.11 Exploded view of the Solex 35 PBISA9 (PEU A202) carburettor (Sec 11)

See Fig. 3.4 for key

12.4 Accelerator cable must locate in groove (arrowed)

Fig. 3.12 Details of accelerator control (Sec 12)

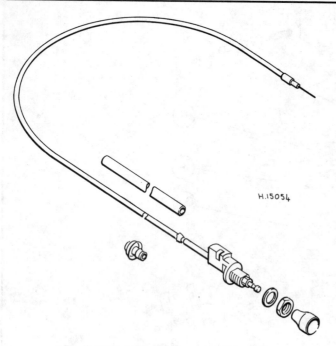

Fig. 3.13 Details of choke control (Sec 13)

sheath from the carburettor.

3   Working inside the car, remove the knob from the choke control cable and undo the control retaining nut. Push the control through the facia and then disconnect the choke warning light cable from the switch on the control.

13.1 Choke cable inner is secured by clamp bolt (arrowed)

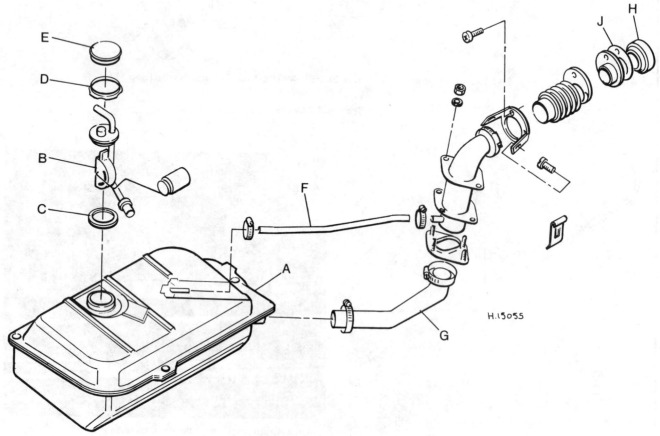

Fig. 3.14 Details of the fuel tank installation (Sec 14)

A	Fuel tank	D	Locking ring	G	Filler pipe
B	Fuel gauge float assembly	E	Boot floor plastic cap	H	Filler cap
C	Rubber gasket	F	Vent pipe	J	Gasket

4   Pull the control assembly into the car, working it through the rubber grommet in the bulkhead.

5   Refitting the choke control is the reverse of the removal procedure. When fitted, with the air cleaner removed check that the choke is fully open when the control knob is pushed home and closed when the knob is pulled. Check that the warning light is on when the choke is pulled.

14 Fuel tank – general

1   The fuel tank is located under the car floor between the rear wheels. Installation details are shown in Fig. 3.14.

2   If it is necessary to remove the tank, first siphon out as much fuel as possible. Access to the fuel feed and the fuel gauge transmitter is gained by removing the plastic cap in the boot floor. Disconnect all connections referring to the figure and photos for details and, after removing the tank attachment bolts, manoeuvre it off its support ledges and remove it from the car (photos).

3   Don't attempt to repair a tank unless it is completely empty of fuel and fuel fumes. This can only satisfactory be achieved by steam cleaning and it is best to leave this sort of repair to a specialist.

15 Inlet air heating system

1   To maintain engine performance in cold conditions, warm air is admitted to the air intake before entering the air cleaner. Air is pre-heated by a muff on the exhaust manifold and its intake is controlled manually on GL and GR models, or automatically on SR models.

2   The manual control consists of a lever on the air intake duct above the exhaust muff which can be moved to two positions, one marked HIVER (winter) and the other ETE (summer).

3   The automatic control is progressive and it uses a thermostat located in the air cleaner top cover to activate a valve in the air intake

duct above the exhaust muff via a connecting cable (photos). When the intake air is cold the wax in the thermostat contracts and the connecting cable moves the valve to reduce the intake of cold air and increase the flow of hot air. The reverse action takes place in warm conditions.

4   The system calls for no special maintenance but the manual control on GL and GR models must be moved to the appropriate position as the season demands.

16 Exhaust system – general

1   A four-piece exhaust system is fitted to the Peugeot 305. The system is similar on all models. It consists of a damping chamber on the exhaust manifold, a front pipe which is secured to the engine assembly, an intermediate pipe and a rear pipe. The system is made of aluminised sheet steel to resist the effects of corrosion. The front pipe is connected to the intermediate pipe by a spring-loaded coupling (not fitted on later models) which, whilst maintaining a gastight joint, absorbs engine movement. The intermediate and rear pipes are suspended beneath the car by flexible hangers and the rear pipe incorporates a silencer with soundproofing as well as a recirculating pipe which accelerates the gas flow by cooling.

2   Maintenance is limited to checking for gas leaks and repair by renewal. Whilst temporary repairs can be made with proprietary materials such as tape or paste, the only satisfactory repair is renewal of the system, or part system if the fault is limited to one area. However when one part of the system requires renewal it often follows that the whole lot is best renewed.

3   When removing the old system don't waste a lot of time trying to undo rusted and seized nuts, bolts or clamps. Cut them off. New ones will be required in any case if they are that bad.

4   When fitting the new system use an exhaust joint sealant when assembling pipe sections to ensure that the respective joints are free from leaks. Get the system into position but don't tighten anything up until everything is properly located. After checking that all is well you

14.2a Fuel filler neck passes through the boot into the right-hand rear wheel well

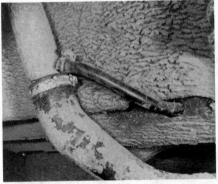

14.2b The tank vent pipe connection with the filler pipe in the wheel well

14.2c The fuel filler-to-tank connection

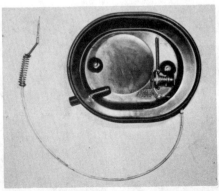

15.3a The air intake heating system control in the air cleaner cover and ...

15.3b ... the cable connection with the duct valve

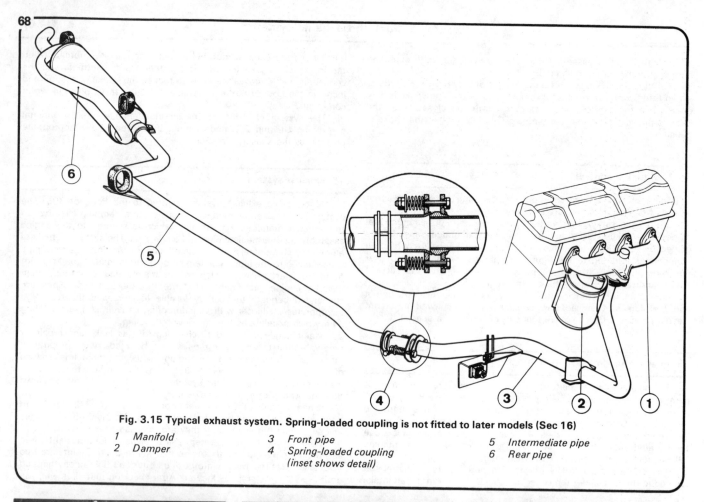

Fig. 3.15 Typical exhaust system. Spring-loaded coupling is not fitted to later models (Sec 16)

1	Manifold	3	Front pipe	5	Intermediate pipe
2	Damper	4	Spring-loaded coupling (inset shows detail)	6	Rear pipe

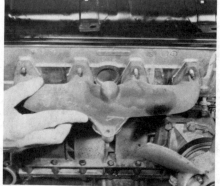

16.4a After fitting the manifold ...

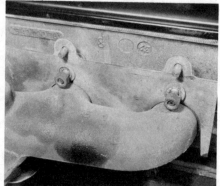

16.4b ... fit the heater muff backplate ...

16.4c ... and then the heater muff

16.4d The exhaust damper fitted to the manifold

16.4e The exhaust suspension at the front of the sump ...

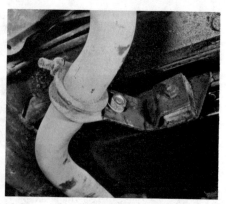

16.4f ... and on the bracket at the rear

16.4g The spring-loaded joint coupling

16.4h A flexible exhaust support

can then tighten the securing bolts or nuts. If the flexible hangers are breaking up or otherwise deteriorated they must be renewed, otherwise the system will vibrate leading to leaks or even fractures (photos).
5   If fitted, the spring-loaded joint coupling between the front and intermediate pipes should be tightened to compress the springs by 3 mm (0.118 in), that is, shorter by that amount than their free length. The coupling should be lubricated to prevent grating, using a special high temperature grease which can be obtained from a Peugeot agent.

17 Fault diagnosis – fuel and exhaust systems

Unsatisfactory engine performance and excessive fuel consumption are not necessarily the fault of the fuel or carburettor. In fact they more commonly occur as a result of ignition and timing faults. Before acting on the following it is necessary to check the ignition system first. Even though a fault may lie in the fuel system it will be difficult to trace unless the ignition is correct. The faults below, therefore, assume that this has been attended to first (where appropriate).

Symptom	Reason(s)
Excessive fuel consumption	Excessive use of throttle
	Short journeys (engine not warming up)
	Leakage
	Air cleaner blocked
	Choke control maladjusted
	Incorrect use of choke control
	Carburettor float level incorrect or needle valve defective
	Carburettor badly worn
	Excessive carbon build-up in cylinder head
	Engine badly worn
Difficult starting when cold	Choke control maladjusted
	Carburettor float level incorrect
	Air leaks at inlet manifold or carburettor
Difficult starting when hot	Air cleaner blocked
	Choke control maladjusted
	Carburettor float level incorrect or needle valve defective
	Vapour lock in fuel line (especially in hot weather or at high altitude)
Backfiring in exhaust system	Air leaks in manifold(s) or exhaust system
	Weak mixture
	Incorrect valve clearances or burnt exhaust valve(s)
	Incorrect valve timing (after rebuild)
	Incorrect ignition timing or other ignition fault
Spitting back in carburettor	Incorrect valve clearances or burnt inlet valve(s)
	Weak mixture
	Incorrect valve timing (after rebuild)
	Incorrect ignition timing or other ignition fault
Insufficient fuel delivery	Tank empty
	Fuel tank vent pipe blocked
	Fuel line blocked
	Leak on suction side of pump (air bubbles in delivered fuel)
	Pump defective or filter blocked
	Carburettor inlet union filter blocked

Chapter 4 Ignition system

For modifications, and information applicable to later models, see Supplement at end of manual

Contents

Specifications

General
System type	12 volt, negative earth, coil and contact breaker
Firing order	1-3-4-2 (No 1 cylinder is nearest the clutch)

Distributor
Type	Ducellier 6635 or Paris-Rhone DA4E519
Drive	Skew gear from crankshaft and offset dogs in driveshaft
Ignition advance	Centrifugal and vacuum-controlled
Advance curve	M89
Dwell angle	54° to 60° (60 to 66%)
Contact breaker points gap	0.40 mm (0.016 in)
Direction of rotation	Clockwise, looking down on distributor

Ignition timing
XL5 (118) engine, 8.8 compression ratio	8° BTDC static or idling
XR5 (142) engine, 9.2 compression ratio	10° BTDC static or idling

Spark plugs
Type	Champion BN9Y, AC 42LTS or equivalent
Gap	0.6 mm (0.024 in)

Torque wrench settings
	lbf ft	kgf m
Spark plugs	13	1.75

1 General description

In order that the engine may run correctly it is necessary for an electrical spark to ignite the fuel/air mixture in the combustion chamber at exactly the right moment in relation to engine speed and load.

Basically the ignition system functions as follows. Low tension voltage from the battery is fed to the ignition coil, where it is converted into high tension voltage. The high tension voltage is powerful enough to jump the spark plug gap in the cylinder many times a second under high compression pressure, providing that the ignition system is in good working order and that all adjustments are correct.

The ignition system comprises two individual circuits known as the low tension (LT) circuit and the high tension (HT) circuit.

The low tension circuit (sometimes known as the primary circuit) comprises the battery, lead to ignition switch, lead to the low tension or primary coil windings and the lead from the low tension coil windings to the contact breaker points and condenser in the distributor.

The high tension circuit (sometimes known as the secondary circuit) comprises the high tension or secondary coil winding, the heavily insulated ignition lead from the centre of the coil to the centre of the distributor cap, the rotor arm, the spark plug leads and the spark plugs.

The complete ignition system operation is as follows:

Low tension voltage from the battery is changed within the ignition coil to high tension voltage by the opening and closing of the contact breaker points in the low tension circuit. High tension voltage is then fed, via a contact in the centre of the distributor cap, to the rotor arm of the distributor. The rotor arm revolves inside the distributor cap, and each time it comes in line with one of the four metal segments in the cap, these being connected to the spark plug leads, the opening and closing of the contact breaker points causes the high tension voltage to build up, jump the gap from the rotor arm to the appropriate metal segment and so via the spark plug lead, to the spark plug where it finally jumps the gap between the two spark plug electrodes, one being earthed.

The ignition timing is advanced and retarded automatically to ensure the spark occurs at just the right instant for the particular load at the prevailing engine speed.

The ignition advance is controlled both mechanically and by a vacuum-operated system. The mechanical governor mechanism comprises two weights which move out under centrifugal force from the central distributor shaft as the engine speed rises. As they move outwards they rotate the cam relative to the distributor shaft, and so advance the spark. The weights are held in position by two light springs, and it is the tension of these springs which is largely responsible for correct spark advancement.

The vacuum control comprises a diaphragm, one side of which is connected, via a small bore tube, to the carburettor, and the other side to the contact breaker plate. Depression in the induction manifold and carburettor, which varies with engine speed and throttle opening, causes the diaphragm to move so moving the contact breaker plate and advancing or retarding the spark.

2 Contact breaker points – initial adjustment

1 To adjust the contact breaker points accurately, the use of a dwell meter is required and this is explained in the next Section. As many owners will not possess a dwell meter the following paragraphs describe adjusting the points with a feeler gauge. This will enable the car to be taken to a garage where the points can be accurately set with a dwell meter. Even if you have a dwell meter you will need to make an intitial adjustment of the contact breaker points following renewal or overhaul before you can tune with the meter.

2 First prise the distributor cap retaining clips away and lift the cap from the distributor. Clean the cap thoroughly with a clean dry cloth and check that the segments are not excessively burnt. Examine the cap closely for cracks. Burnt segments or cracks in the cap will require the cap to be renewed.

3 Check that the carbon brush in the roof of the cap moves in and out freely by depressing it once or twice and check that the brush is not broken or chipped.

4 Carefully lift the rotor arm off the cam and clean it with a clean dry cloth. Excessive burning of the brass distributor arm or cracks in the rotor moulding will require the rotor to be renewed.

5 Using a small screwdriver carefully prise the contact points open and examine them closely. If they are rough, pitted, worn or dirty it will be necessary to remove them for servicing or renewal as described in Section 4.

6 Assuming that the points are satisfactory, turn the crankshaft in the normal direction of rotation using a spanner on the pulley bolt, until the moving contact heel is positioned on the highest point of one of the cam lobes.

7 Using feeler gauges of the correct thickness (see Specifications) check the contact breaker gap. The feelers should slide between the points with a slight drag but without forcing the points wider apart. Take care not to contaminate the point faces with oil from the feeler gauge.

8 If adjustment is required, proceed according to the type of distributor as follows.

9 **Ducellier.** Use a 7 mm open-ended or box spanner on the adjusting nut protruding from the side of the distributor and turn to obtain the correct gap (photo).

10 **Paris-Rhone.** Insert a 3 mm Allen key in the hole in the plastic plug protruding from the side of the distributor and engage it with the recess in the fixed contact. Turn to obtain the correct gap.

11 After adjustment, turn the crankshaft until the heel of the moving contact is on the peak of the next cam lobe and check the gap again. Repeat on the other two lobes. Any variation indicates that the distributor spindle is bent and, if excessive, it must be renewed.

12 Refit the rotor arm and distributor cap and make sure that the clips are secure.

3 Dwell angle – adjustment

1 The dwell angle is the number of degrees that the cam rotates whilst the contact points are closed and this angle is measured with a dwell meter. The contact points are adjusted so that the dwell angle corresponds with the maker's specifications; a large gap produces a small dwell angle and vice versa.

2 To adjust the dwell angle a dwell meter is required and you should follow the instructions supplied with the meter. Note especially how to read the meter for a 4-cylinder engine as many meters can be used on 4, 6 or 8-cylinder engines. Also check that the meter can be used on negative earth circuits.

3 The procedure is broadly as follows. If necessary set the meter to zero. This is only possible if the meter has an adjusting screw on the needle pivot. Connect the red lead to the coil ignition switch connection and the black lead to earth. Disconnect the LT lead between the coil and the distributor. Get an assistant to turn the ignition key and crank the engine for a few seconds while you read the

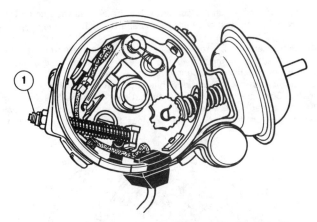

Fig. 4.1 Contact breaker gap adjustment on the Ducellier distributor – turn the nut, 1 (Sec 2)

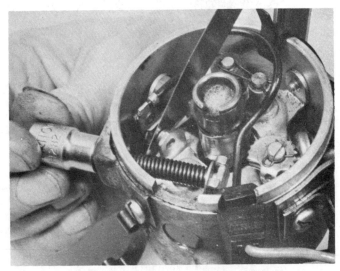

2.9 Adjusting the contact breaker gap (Ducellier distributor)

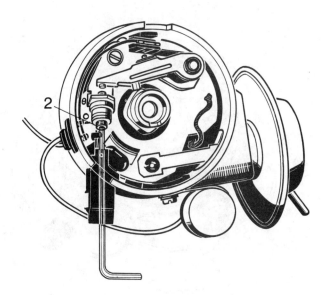

Fig. 4.2 Contact breaker gap adjustment on the Paris-Rhone distributor – use a 3 mm Allen key in the fixed contact recess, 2 (Sec 2)

meter. Turn the adjusting screw on the meter until the needle is set according to the maker's instructions and the meter is then ready for use.

4   After setting the meter remove the black lead from its earth connection and connect it to the LT lead between the coil and the distributor which was disconnected to zero the meter. Again get your assistant to crank the engine while you read the dwell angle on the meter. Compare your reading with that quoted in the Specifications.

5   If the reading is wrong you will have to adjust the contact breaker points gap as described in the previous Section. Remember that to

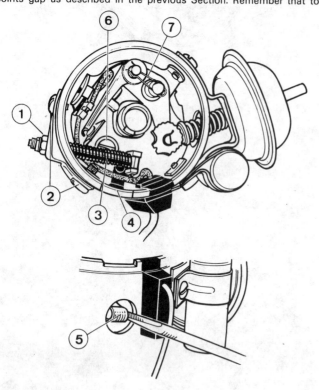

Fig. 4.3 Renewing the Ducellier contact breaker points. See text for key (Sec 4)

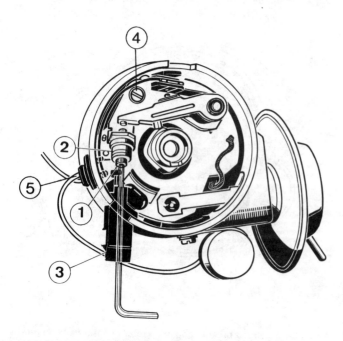

Fig. 4.4 Renewing the Paris-Rhone contact breaker points. See text for key (Sec 4)

reduce the dwell angle you must increase the gap and vice versa.

6   After adjusting the points recheck the dwell angle and when you are satisfied that it is correct, disconnect the meter and reconnect the LT lead between the coil and the distributor.

4   Contact breaker points – removal, servicing and refitting

1   If the contact breaker points are excessively burnt or pitted they must be removed for refacing or renewal.

2   To remove the points unclip the distributor cap and lift it away, then pull the rotor arm off the central cam.

3   **Ducellier model.** Refer to Fig. 4.3 and unscrew the adjuster nut (1). Remove the two screws (2) and then remove the adjustment stud (3) together with its spring. Slide the plastic plug (4) and LT wire out of the slot in the distributor case and prise out the retaining lug (5) next to it with a small screwdriver. Remove the retaining screw (6) and lift out the fixed contact. Carefully remove the spring clip (7) and withdraw the moving contact.

4   **Paris-Rhone model.** Refer to Fig. 4.4 and remove the retaining screw (4). Unfasten the spring clip (5) by sliding it up and remove the contact breaker assembly.

5   **All models.** Dress the face of each contact squarely on an oilstone, or with a special equalising file available from accessory shops, until all traces of pips and craters have been removed. After repeated dressing of the contact points, the tungsten tips will be reduced to the base metal and it will then be necessary to fit new points.

6   Refitting the contact breaker points is a reversal of the removal procedure, but the following additional information should be noted:

   (a) *Clean the points, even if they are new, with methylated spirit before assembly*

   (b) *Lightly lubricate the moving contact pivot and the cam lobes with petroleum jelly*

   (c) *When refitting the Paris-Rhone adjustable contact (1), see Fig. 4.4, make sure that it is centred in relation to its carrier (2)*

   (d) *Take care to reassemble all washers in the same sequence as originally installed, if necessary make written notes during dismantling to avoid mistakes*

   (e) *Adjust the contact points gap as described in Section 2 and check the dwell angle as described in Section 3*

5   Condenser – removal, testing and refitting

1   The condenser acts as a 'buffer' in the low tension circuit of the ignition system by absorbing the surges of current which are produced by the contact breaker points opening and closing. This greatly reduces the arcing at the points, and its action also assists in the rapid collapse of the magnetic field set up by the primary winding within the coil. Failure of the condenser will reduce the spark plug voltage in the high tension circuit, and if difficulty in starting the engine is experienced accompanied by 'missing' under load, the fault may well be in the condenser.

2   To remove the condenser, first unclip the distributor cap and remove it, then lift the rotor arm off the central cam.

3   **Ducellier model.** Disconnect the condenser lead by pulling its terminal our of the socket. Undo the condenser retaining screw and remove the condenser (photo).

4   **Paris-Rhone model.** Disconnect the LT cable from the distributor at the coil terminal and disconnect the spring clip (5), Fig. 4.4. Undo the screw holding the insulating block retaining plate, remove the plate and withdraw the insulating block from the distributor case. Undo the condenser retaining screw, taking care not to lose the distributor cap clip, and remove the condenser and leads assembly.

5   Without the use of specialist equipment the only sure way of diagnosing a faulty condenser is to renew it and note if there is any improvement. However, a simple test is to separate the points by hand with the ignition switched on; if this action is accompanied by a strong blue flash across the points, condenser failure is indicated (a **weak** flash is normal).

6   Refitting the condenser is a reversal of the removal procedure but tighten the retaining screw(s) securely.

5.3 Removing the condenser (Ducellier distributor)

6 Distributor – lubrication

1   Periodically the distributor should be lightly lubricated. Smear a little petroleum jelly or high melting-point grease on the lobes of the distributor cam to provide lubrication for the contact point heel.

2   Remove the rotor arm and apply two drops of engine oil into the cam recess. Apply a small drop of oil to the moving contact pivot.

3   Apply two or three drops of oil through the aperture between the baseplate and cam spindle to lubricate the governor weights.

4   Great care must be taken not to use too much lubricant and all surplus should be wiped up. Excessive oil or petroleum jelly may contaminate the contact points and cause ignition failure.

7 Distributor – removal and refitting

1   The distributor is located at the right-hand rear corner of the engine. On right-hand drive cars access to the distributor is complicated by the fact that the brake servo and master cylinder are located immediately above. Removal and refitting of the distributor will disturb the ignition timing and you must be sure of what you are doing if problems are to be avoided. With an installed engine it is best carefully to note the exact position of the rotor arm before removing the distributor, marking the position of the distributor relative to the timing case and then making sure that the crankshaft is not turned

after removing the distributor. It is then a simple matter to refit the distributor in its original position. If you cannot avoid moving the crankshaft while the distributor is removed, or if you are in the process of reassembling the engine or its timing mechanism after overhaul, then you will have to time the distributor from scratch on assembly.

2   Identify the spark plug leads so that they can be refitted to their original plugs, then carefully pull them off the plug terminals. Disconnect the HT lead from the coil and then unclip and remove the distributor cap and leads assembly.

3   Disconnect the coil-to-distributor LT lead at the coil terminal.

4   Disconnect the vacuum pipe from the vacuum capsule.

5   Turn the crankshaft with a spanner on the pulley bolt until the distributor rotor arm approaches the point where it faces No 2 segment in the distributor cap, then continue to turn the crankshaft until the notch in the pulley rim aligns with the first notch (in the direction of crankshaft rotation, ie clockwise looking at the pulley face) in the timing plate on the clutch housing.

6   Mark the distributor body and the timing case so that you can eventually refit the distributor in the same position, then unscrew and remove the single bolt and spring washer. Do not loosen the clamp bolt in the mounting plate.

7   Carefully lift the distributor up out of the timing case.

8   To refit the distributor where the crankshaft and timing mechanism have not been disturbed, first check that the notch in the crankshaft pulley does still line up with the first timing plate notch.

9   Turn the distributor spindle until the rotor arm is in alignment with the No 2 segment in the distributor cap. Check the dogs on the driving end of the distributor spindle for alignment with the off-centre slot in the engine drive; if all is well they should be in the same relative position. Insert the distributor and engage the drive dogs with their slot. Turn the distributor case – only very slight movement should be necessary – and align the marks made before removal. Fit and tighten the clamp plate retaining bolt and washer and finally check that the rotor arm is still aligned with the No 2 segment in the cap.

10   If the timing has been disturbed as a result of other work, a few extra precautions are necessary on assembly to ensure that the ignition timing can be accurately set.

11   The crankshaft must first be turned to the correct timing position but this is complicated by the fact that there are two notches in the crankshaft pulley rear flange at 180° to each other. In fact these are used to check any variation between the ignition timing of all four cylinders using a stroboscopic lamp with the engine running. The ignition is timed on No 2 cylinder and, to identify which of the two notches to use, first turn the crankshaft in the normal direction of rotation (clockwise looking at the pulley face) until No 2 cylinder is rising on the compression stroke. This can be recognised by removing the valve rocker cover and watching for both valves of No 2 cylinder to be closed, ie with clearance on both rockers. At this point one of the notches on the pulley will be approaching the timing plate. Turn the crankshaft until that notch aligns with the first notch in the timing plate. Check that No 2 cylinder is still on compression stroke.

12   The distributor can now be fitted by following the procedure in

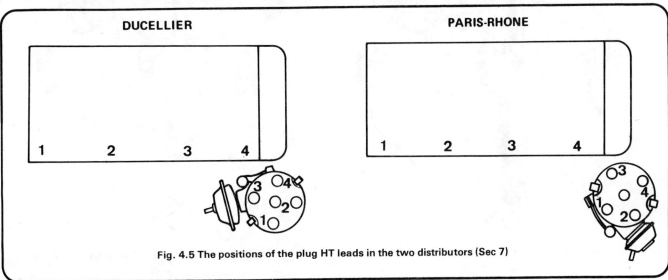

DUCELLIER   **PARIS-RHONE**

1   2   3   4   1   2   3   4

Fig. 4.5 The positions of the plug HT leads in the two distributors (Sec 7)

paragraph 9, disregarding references to alignment marks if these are not applicable.

13 After refitting the distributor check the ignition timing as described in Section 10, then tighten the clamp bolt and clamp plate retaining bolt. Refit the distributor cap and reconnect the spark plug leads and LT lead. Reconnect the HT lead to the coil and refit the vacuum pipe to the vacuum capsule. If the plug leads have been muddled refer to Fig. 4.5 for identification.

8 Distributor – overhaul

1 It has been found from practical experience that overhauling a distributor is not worthwhile even if all parts are available. The usual items needing attention are such parts as the distributor cap, rotor arm, contact breaker points and condenser. After these have been considered, there is not a great deal left to wear except the shaft assembly, bush and automatic advance system. If one of these parts is worn then it is reasonable to assume the remainder are so all in all it is best to obtain a guaranteed service exchange unit which could

work out cheaper than purchasing a complete set of individual parts. For the more ambitious, exploded views of the two types of distributor fitted to the Peugeot 305 are given. No problems should arise in stripping and rebuilding provided that the exact location of each part, however small, is noted.

2 The assembly sequence of the Ducellier distributor is shown (photos).

9 Timing plate – checking and adjusting

1 The ignition timing plate is bolted to the clutch housing adjacent to the crankcase pulley. After initial installation and adjustment a dab of paint is applied as a seal. If the plate has been moved during overhaul or on renewal of the clutch housing, or if you suspect the accuracy of setting, it can be checked and adjusted as follows.

2 An alignment tool is provisioned by Peugeot as a special tool but you can easily make one from a piece of rod 8 mm (0.315 in) diameter and about 130 mm (say 5 in) long.

3 Remove the plug in the timing case just above the cover over the

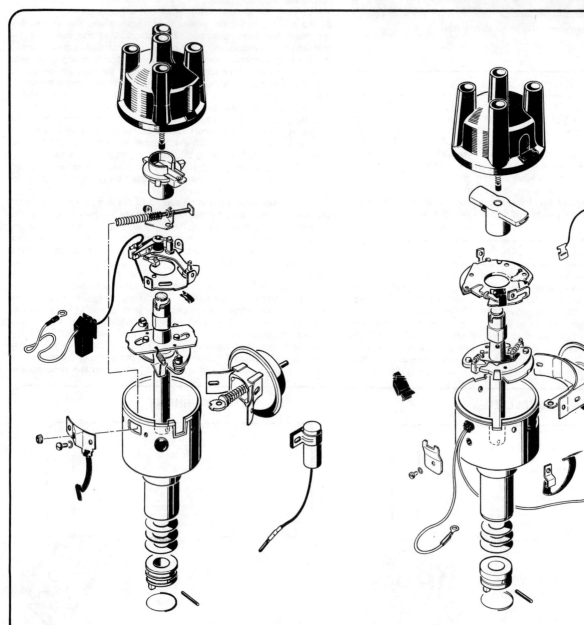

Fig. 4.6 Exploded view of the Ducellier distributor (Sec 8)   Fig. 4.7 Exploded view of the Paris-Rhone distributor (Sec 8)

Measuring plug gap. A feeler gauge of the correct size (see ignition system specifications) should have a slight 'drag' when slid between the electrodes. Adjust gap if necessary

Adjusting plug gap. The plug gap is adjusted by bending the earth electrode inwards, or outwards, as necessary until the correct clearance is obtained. Note the use of the correct tool

Normal. Grey-brown deposits, lightly coated core nose. Gap increasing by around 0.001 in (0.025 mm) per 1000 miles (1600 km). Plugs ideally suited to engine, and engine in good condition

Carbon fouling. Dry, black, sooty deposits. Will cause weak spark and eventually misfire. Fault: over-rich fuel mixture. Check: carburettor mixture settings, float level and jet sizes; choke operation and cleanliness of air filter. Plugs can be re-used after cleaning

Oil fouling. Wet, oily deposits. Will cause weak spark and eventually misfire. Fault: worn bores/piston rings or valve guides; sometimes occurs (temporarily) during running-in period. Plugs can be re-used after thorough cleaning

Overheating. Electrodes have glazed appearance, core nose very white – few deposits. Fault: plug overheating. Check: plug value, ignition timing, fuel octane rating (too low) and fuel mixture (too weak). Discard plugs and cure fault immediately

Electrode damage. Electrodes burned away; core nose has burned, glazed appearance. Fault: pre-ignition. Check: as for 'Overheating' but may be more severe. Discard plugs and remedy fault before piston or valve damage occurs

Split core nose (may appear initially as a crack). Damage is self-evident, but cracks will only show after cleaning. Fault: pre-ignition or wrong gap-setting technique. Check: ignition timing, cooling system, fuel octane rating (too low) and fuel mixture (too weak). Discard plugs, rectify fault immediately

8.2a Check that the counterweight mechanism is clean and lightly oiled then ...

8.2b ... fit the baseplate and

8.2c ... the insulated block

8.2d Secure the baseplate with a screw through spring clip

8.2e Connect the vacuum advance mechanism and ...

8.2f ... secure with a screw through a clip and into the baseplate

8.2g Make sure that the adjusting star wheel is aligned as before dismantling

8.2h Fit adjuster bracket to baseplate with stepped screw and wavy washer

8.2j Connect and secure adjuster

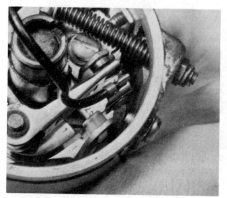

8.2k Fit contact moving point and lead with spring in insulated block ...

8.2l ... and secure with hairpin clip and insulated washer

8.2m Fit the plastic plug to the body

8.2n Fit the LT leads and block

9.3 Remove the plug (arrowed) in the timing case

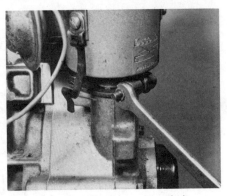

10.4 Loosen the distributor clamp bolt

end of the crankshaft (photo). Turn the crankshaft using a spanner on the pulley bolt to line up one of the notches in the pulley flange with the second notch in the timing plate, rotating the pulley in a clockwise direction looking at the pulley face. Push the rod partly into the timing case hole and rock the crankshaft slightly. If you are lucky the rod will enter a slot in the crankshaft web and lock the crankshaft in the TDC position for Nos 2 and 3 positions. If you are not lucky you will be 180° out so turn the crankshaft half a rev and try again aligning the other pulley notch with the timing plate. Do not lose the rod inside the timing case hole!

4   With the crankshaft locked in the TDC position you can now examine the timing plate for accuracy. If the pulley notch is not aligned precisely with the second plate notch (the first notch is the ignition timing mark which is 8° or 10° BTDC), slacken the retaining bolt slightly, reposition the plate accurately and tighten the bolt. When you are satisfied, clean off the old paint mark and apply a new one.

5   Remove the alignment rod and refit the blanking plug.

10 Ignition timing

1   After servicing the contact breaker or the distributor, or whenever the ignition timing has been disturbed or is suspect, the timing must be checked and if necessary adjusted. Correct ignition timing is vital for efficient engine operation. There are two ways of checking the timing, statically (with the engine at rest) or, and this method is more accurate, dynamically (with the engine running).

Static timing

2   Connect a 12 volt test lamp between the distributor LT lead and earth. Remove the distributor cap or the coil HT lead so that the engine cannot fire.

3   Switch on the ignition and use a spanner on the crankshaft pulley bolt to turn the crankshaft in the normal directin of rotation. The test lamp should light every time that one of the crankshaft pulley notches comes into line with the first notch on the timing plate.

4   If the lamp lights too early or too late, align the timing notches and slacken the distributor clamp bolt (photo). Rotate the distributor slightly so that the lamp is just lit. Tighten the clamp bolt, rotate the crankshaft further and check again.

5   When satisfied that the timing is correct, switch off the ignition, disconnect the test lamp and refit the distributor cap or coil HT lead.

Dynamic timing

6   Clean the timing plate and the crankshaft pulley rim, then mark the two pulley notches and the first timing plate notch with quick-drying paint. Typist's correction fluid is ideal for this application.

7   Disconnect and plug the distributor vacuum pipe. Connect a stroboscope timing light to the coil-to-distributor HT lead in accordance with the maker's instructions.

8   Start the engine and reduce the idling speed to 800 rpm. At greater engine speeds the centrifugal advance mechanism in the distributor will come into operation). Shine the timing light into the timing plate. If the timing is correct and the distributor in good order, the two pulley notches will appear as one and aligned with the first notch in the timing plate.

Fig. 4.8 Under the stroboscopic light this timing is a little late and needs advancing to align the pulley notch with the left-hand notch in the timing plate (Sec 10)

9   If the pulley notch appears to be out of alignment with the timing plate notch, slacken the distributor clamp bolt and turn the distributor slightly until the notches are aligned. Tighten the bolt and recheck.

10   If the pulley notch appears to be wide, or if two adjacent notches are visible, this is indicative of wear in the distributor or cam. Compensate for slight wear by turning the distributor to align the timing plate notch midway between the two pulley notches (Fig. 4.9).

11   To determine if the wear is excessive, turn the distributor to align the right-hand pulley notch with the right-hand edge of the timing plate. The other notch should not appear further away than the TDC notch; if it does, the distributor should be renewed. Restore correct timing after checking.

12   It is not possible for the home mechanic to check the operation of the centrifugal and vacuum advance mechanisms with any accuracy. However, under the stroboscope the pulley marks should be seen to advance as the engine speed is increased to a fast idle; the advance should increase further if the vacuum pipe is reconnected.

13   Tighten the clamp bolt on completion, disconnect the timing light and restore the idling speed to its normal value.

Timing from scratch

14   If the timing is lost completely, either during overhaul or as a result of moving the distributor too far during adjustment, remove the rocker cover and turn the crankshaft until No 2 piston is rising on the compression stroke (both valves closed, ie clearance on both rockers) and the timing marks are aligned. Slacken the distributor clamp bolts, remove the distributor cap and turn the distributor until the rotor arm is pointing towards the No 2 segment in the distributor cap. Refer to Fig. 4.5 if necessary. It should then be possible to proceed with the static timing procedure as described above.

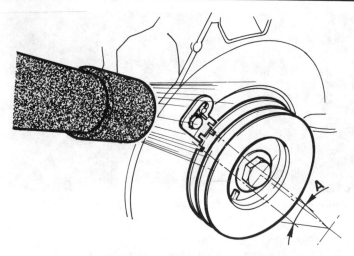

Fig. 4.9 With the stroboscopic light working on the coil lead, two notches will indicate some discrepancy in the firing of all four cylinders. If not excessive align the two notches (space A) equidistant each side of the timing mark (Sec 10)

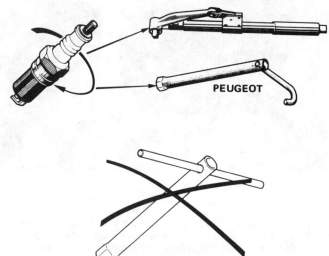

Fig. 4.11 Only use a torque wrench or the special Peugeot spanner to fit the spark plugs (Sec 11)

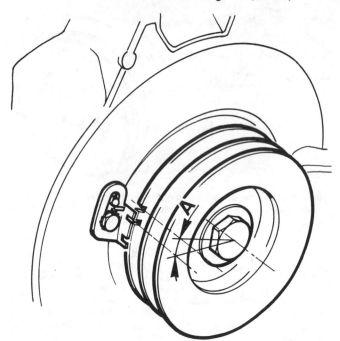

Fig. 4.10 To determine if the discrepancy is excessive align one pulley notch on the edge of the timing plate. The other notch in the pulley must not be more than the distance of the TDC notch in the timing plate away (distance A) (Sec 10)

11 Spark plugs and HT leads

1   The correct functioning of the spark plugs is vital for the correct running and efficiency of the engine.
2   At the intervals specified in Routine Maintenance the plugs should be removed, examined, cleaned, and if worn excessively, renewed. The condition of the spark plugs will also tell much about the overall condition of the engine.
3   If the insulator nose of the spark plug is clean and white, with no deposits, this is indicative of a weak mixture, or too hot a plug (a hot plug transfers heat away from the electrode slowly – a cold plug transfers it away quickly).
4   If the top and insulator nose are covered with hard black looking deposits, then this is indicative that the mixture is too rich. Should the plug be black and oily, then it is likely that the engine is fairly worn, as

well as the mixture being too rich.
5   If the insulator nose is covered with light tan to greyish brown deposits then the mixture is correct and it is likely that the engine is in good condition.
6   If there are any traces of long brown tapering stains on the outside of the white portion of the plug, then the plug will have to be renewed, as this shows that there is a faulty joint between the plug body and the insulator, and compression is being lost.
7   Plugs should ideally be cleaned by a sand blasting machine, which will free them from carbon more thoroughly than cleaning by hand. The machine will also test the condition of the plugs under compression. Any plug that fails to spark at the recommended pressure should be renewed.
8   The spark plug gap is of considerable importance, as, if it is too large or too small, the size of the spark and its efficiency will be seriously impaired. The spark plug gap should be set to the figure given in the Specifications at the beginning of this Chapter.
9   To set it, measure the gap with a feeler gauge, and then bend open, or close, the **outer** plug electrode until the correct gap is achieved. The centre electrode should **never** be bent as this may crack the insulation and cause plug failure if nothing worse.
10 Details of the approved types of spark plug are listed in the Specifications. These plugs all have a tapered seat to mate with taper faces in the cylinder head and they must *not* have plug washers fitted on installation. Furthermore, as they fit into a light alloy head they must not be overtightened. Ideally they should be tightened to the specified torque using a torque wrench with a long plug socket. Alternatively, use the special plug spanner provided by Peugeot which is clipped on top of the right-hand front wheel arch under the bonnet (photo). Make sure that the plug taper seats and the cylinder head mating faces are thoroughly clean when fitting the plugs. The plug leads from the distributor must be fitted to the correct plugs; if you are in doubt about which lead goes where, refer to Fig. 4.5 and trace each lead to its correct location.
11 The plug leads require no routine maintenance other than being kept clean and dry and being wiped over regularly with a clean dry cloth. When removing the plugs for servicing or renewal, remove the leads from the distributor cap, one at a time to avoid confusion, and make sure that no water has penetrated the connections. Remove any corrosion from the lead end fittings and wipe the distributor cap lead location clean before refitting each lead.
12 Apart from routine wear and tear, plugs suffer a slow fall off in performance and it is good practice to renew them at alternate routine servicings in order to maintain optimum engine performance. When fitting new plugs keep the old ones and, after having them cleaned, you can carry them in the car for emergency use or for when you want to have the fitted plugs cleaned.

11.10 The special spanner for the plugs is located on the right-hand front wheel well

12 Diagnostic test socket

1   The Peugeot 305 is fitted with a diagnostic test socket for electronic monitoring of engine performance and ignition system condition. Although this facility is of no use to the home mechanic it does enable a suitably equipped garage to make a quick assessment and with greater accuracy than the usual procedures.

2   The socket is located at the top left-hand end of the cylinder head rocker cover. The connections are shown in Fig. 4.12 and, with the appropriate equipment the following checks or adjustments can be made with the engine running.

(a)   Primary (LT) circuit condition
(b)   Condition of contact breaker points
(c)   Adjustment of contact breaker dwell angle
(d)   Setting of initial advance
(e)   Centrifugal and vacuum advance curves
(f)   Engine speed

3   If it becomes necessary to renew or disturb the TDC sensor, refer to the next Section for the procedure for adjusting the sensor air gap.

13 TDC sensor – removal, refitting and adjustment

1   The TDC sensor, which is part of the diagnostic test socket system (see above), is located in the bottom rear of the clutch housing. Its purpose is to generate a signal, each time a notch in the clutch assembly passes on rotation, to indicate TDC in the diagnostic test equipment. The sensor must be adjusted to provide the correct air gap whenever any of the following occurs:

(a)   The clutch mechanism is changed (this does not include routine clutch friction plate renewal)
(b)   The clutch housing is changed
(c)   The TDC sensor mounting bracket is moved in relation to the TDC sensor
(d)   In the event of any error in setting initial ignition advance using diagnostic equipment

2   To remove the TDC sensor, undo the hexagon-headed bolt securing the mounting bracket to the clutch housing and withdraw the sensor and its bracket. **Do not** disturb the cross-headed screw in the bracket. If the TDC sensor is removed in this way and none of the work listed in paragraph 1 has been undertaken, the sensor can be refitted without the need to adjust the air gap between the sensor and the clutch disc.

3   To renew the TDC sensor, undo the cross-headed clamp screw in the bracket and withdraw the sensor. Removing the sensor in this way will necessitate adjustment of the air gap.

4   To refit the TDC sensor and adjust the air gap proceed as follows. Assemble the bracket to the sensor but do not fully tighten the cross-headed clamp screw. Check that the notch in the clutch assembly is not aligned with the sensor location hole in the housing – if it is, move the crankshaft using a spanner on the pulley bolt. Bolt the bracket in position on the clutch housing and gently press the sensor into contact with the clutch assembly. Tighten the cross-headed screw and then unbolt and withdraw the bracket, containing the sensor, from clutch housing. Mark the position of the sensor in the bracket, loosen the cross-headed clamp screw and carefully withdraw the sensor 1 mm (0.040 in) from its marked position. Tighten the cross-headed clamp screw. Refit the bracket and sensor to the clutch housing and tighten the retaining bolt. There should now be a gap of 1 mm (0.040 in) between the end of the sensor and the clutch assembly (Fig. 4.13).

5   To fit a new sensor which has not previously been used, follow the procedure contained in the previous paragraph as far as tightening the cross-head screw but do not unbolt and remove the bracket as for a used sensor. No further action is required as far as adjusting the gap is concerned as new sensors are designed to be fitted in this way.

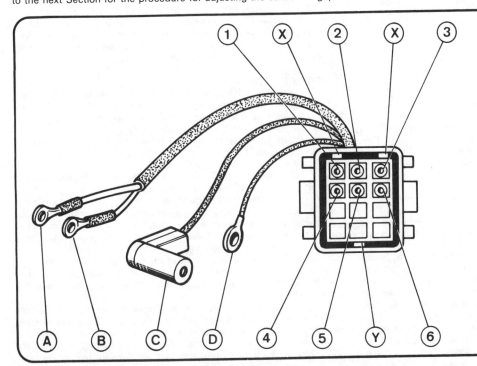

Fig. 4.12 Identification of the diagnostic test socket pins and connectors (Sec 12)

A   To coil contact breaker terminal – black lead, red sleeve
B   To coil + terminal – grey lead, blue sleeve
C   To TDC sensor
D   Earth lead (yellow)
X   Locating lugs
Y   Locating lug
1   TDC sensor signal (red)
2   Earth (yellow)
3   Contact breaker (black)
4   TDC sensor signal (white)
5   TDC sensor signal
6   Coil + (grey)

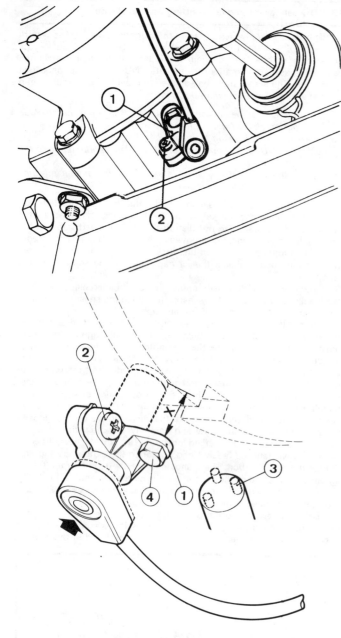

Fig. 4.13 Fitting the TDC sensor (Sec 13)

1	Mounting bracket	X	Depth of sensor when in
2	Clamp screw		contact with clutch –
3	Sensing pins		adjust to x minus 1 mm
4	Hexagon-headed bolt		(0.040 in)

14 Fault diagnosis – ignition system

1   By far the majority of breakdown and running troubles are caused by faults in the ignition system in the low tension or high tension circuit. There are two main symptoms indicating ignition faults. Either the engine will not start or fire, or the engine is difficult to start and misfires. If it is a regular misfire, ie the engine is only running on two or three cylinders, the fault is almost sure to be in the secondary, or high tension, circuit. If the misfiring is intermittent, the fault could be in either the high or low tension circuits. If the car stops suddenly, or will not start at all, it is likely that the fault is in the low tension circuit. Loss of power and overheating, apart from faulty carburation settings, are normally due to faults in the distributor or incorrect ignition timing.

Engine turns but will not start

2   If the engine fails to start and the car was running normally when it was last used, first check that there is fuel in the petrol tank. If the engine turns over normally on the starter motor and the battery is evidently well charged, then the fault may be in either the high or low tension circuits. First check the HT circuit.

3   One of the commonest reasons for bad starting is wet or damp spark plug leads and distributor. Remove the distributor cap. If condensation is visible internally, dry the cap with a rag and wipe over the leads. Refit the cap.

4   If the engine still fails to start, check that current is reaching the plugs, by disconnecting each plug lead in turn at the spark plug end, and holding the end of the cable about $\frac{3}{16}$ inch (5 mm) away from the cylinder block. Hold the lead with insulating material – a rubber glove, a dry cloth or insulated pliers – to avoid electric shocks. Have an assistant spin the engine on the starter motor.

5   Sparking between the end of the cable and the block should be fairly strong with a regular blue spark. If current is reaching the plugs, then remove them and clean and regap them to the specified gap. The engine should now start.

6   If there is no spark at the plug leads, take off the HT lead from the centre of the distributor cap and hold it to the block as before. Spin the engine on the starter once more. A rapid succession of blue sparks between the end of the lead and the block indicates that the coil is in order and that the distributor cap is cracked, the rotor arm faulty or the carbon brush in the top of the distributor cap is not making good contact with the spring on the rotor arm.

7   If there are no sparks from the end of the lead from the coil, check the connections at the coil end of the lead. If it is in order start checking the low tension circuit. First clean and gap the contact breaker points as described in Section 2 and check again for a spark from the coil HT lead. If there is still no spark, carry on with the checks below.

8   Use a 12 volt voltmeter or a 12 volt bulb and two lengths of wire. With the ignition switch on and the points open test between the low tension wire to the coil (it is marked +) and earth. No reading indicates a break in the supply from the ignition switch. Check the connections at the switch to see if any are loose. Refit them and the engine should run. A reading shows a faulty coil or condenser or broken lead between the coil and the distributor.

9   Take the condenser wire off the points assembly and with the points open, test between the moving point and earth. If there now is a reading, then the fault is in the condenser. Fit a new one and the fault is cleared.

10   With no reading from the moving point to earth, take a reading between earth and the negative (–) terminal of the coil. A reading here indicates a broken wire which must be renewed between the coil and distributor. No reading confirms that the coil has failed and must be renewed. Remember to connect the condenser wire to the points assembly. For these tests it is sufficient to separate the contact breaker points with a piece of paper.

Engine misfires

11   If the engine misfires regularly, run it at a fast idling speed. Pull off each of the plug caps in turn and listen to the note of the engine. Hold the plug cap in a dry cloth or with a rubber glove as additional protection against a shock from the HT supply.

12   No difference in engine running will be noticed when the lead from the defective circuit is removed. Removing the lead from one of the good cylinders will accentuate the misfire.

13   Remove the plug lead from the end of the defective plug and hold it about $\frac{3}{16}$ inch (5 mm) away from the block. Restart the engine. If the sparking is fairly strong and regular, the fault must lie in the spark plug.

14   The plug may be loose, the insulation may be cracked, or the points may have been burnt away, giving too wide a gap for the spark to jump. Worse still, one of the points may have broken off. Either renew the plug, or clean it, reset the gap, and then test it.

15   If there is no spark at the end of the plug lead, or if it is weak or intermittent, check the ignition lead from the distributor to the plug. If the insulation is cracked or perished, renew the lead. Check the connections at the distributor cap.

16   If there is still no spark, examine the distributor cap carefully for tracking. This can be recognised by a very thin black line running between two or more electrodes, or between an electrode and some other part of the distributor. These lines are paths which now conduct electricity across the cap, thus letting it run to earth. The only answer

is a new distributor cap.

17 Apart from the ignition timing being incorrect, other causes of misfiring have already been dealt with under the section dealing with the failure of the engine to start. To recap, these are that:

(a) *The coil may be faulty giving an intermediate misfire*
(b) *There may be a damaged wire or loose connection in the low tension circuit*
(c) *The condenser may be short circuiting*

(d) *There may be a mechanical fault in the distributor (broken driving spindle or contact breaker spring)*

18 If the ignition timing is too far retarded, it should be noted that the engine will tend to overheat, and there will be a quite noticeable drop is power. If the engine is overheating and the power is down, and the ignition timing is correct, then the carburettor should be checked, as it is likely that this is where the fault lies.

Chapter 5 Clutch

For modifications, and information applicable to later models, see Supplement at end of manual

Contents

Specifications

General

Type	Single dry plate, diaphragm spring
Actuation	Cable
Clutch disc outer diameter	200 mm (7.874 in)

Adjustment data

Clutch pedal travel	135 mm (5.315 in) minimum
Clutch pedal free play	10 mm (0.394 in) minimum

Overhaul data

Clutch housing gasket face permissible distortion:

Between two points more than 100 mm apart	0.10 mm (0.004 in) maximum
Between two points less than 100 mm apart	0.05 mm (0.002 in) maximum
Input pinion endfloat	0.25 to 0.40 mm (0.010 to 0.016 in)
Endfloat adjusting shim sizes	0.07, 0.15, 0.20, 0.25 and 0.50 mm
	(0.00276, 0.00591, 0.00787, 0.00984 and 0.01969 in)

Torque wrench settings

	lbf ft	kgf m
Clutch pedal pivot bolt nut	20	2.75
Clutch pressure plate-to-flywheel bolts......................	18	2.5
Clutch outer half case bolts.......................................	7.2	1.0
Crankshaft pulley bolt	65	9.0
Starter attachment bolts	25.3	3.5
Engine mounting left top bracket nuts	14.5	2.0
Alternator securing bolt	25.3	3.5
Jockey pulley bolts (size M7)	9.4	1.3
Lower jockey pulley pivot bolt	39.7	5.5
Oil drain plug	20	2.75
Clutch housing-to-engine bolts	9	1.25

1 General description

The clutch is a single dry plate diaphragm type located at the left-hand end of the engine. The complete assembly is bolted to the rear face of the flywheel.

The clutch disc or driven plate is splined to the input pinion of the gearbox train and is free to move between the faces of the flywheel and the pressure plate. The double friction lining on the outer portion of the disc is attached to the inner splined hub by means of six coil spring dampers which cushion the initial take-up of the drive.

The input pinion is located on the crankshaft, from which it is separated by a double row needle bearing. The clutch assembly is located outboard of the input pinion gear teeth which mesh with the gearbox primary shaft. Although oil sealing arrangements are more complicated, this arrangement allows the clutch to be removed or serviced without interfering with the geartrain.

The clutch mechanism is mounted on the end of the crankshaft to which it is mated by a polygon taper – one which has three faces to transmit the drive positively. A special tool is essential to separate the clutch from the crankshaft.

The pressure plate is actuated by a release bearing which slides on a locating sleeve and depresses the diaphragm centre fingers; this causes the annular plate to move away from the driven plate friction linings and drive from the clutch assembly to the input pinion ceases.

The release bearing is moved by the release arm which is actuated by a cable and spring return. The cable is connected at its other end to the clutch pedal.

On depressing the clutch pedal the cable, moving the release arm, causes the release bearing to bear on the diaphragm fingers. The periphery of the diaphragm lifts the pressure plate away from the driven plate which can then remain motionless while the clutch assembly spins round in. In this state no drive is transmitted by the input pinion to the gearbox.

On releasing the clutch pedal the reverse operations take place and, when the drive plate is squeezed between the pressure plate and the flywheel, drive is transmitted through the input pinion to the gearbox.

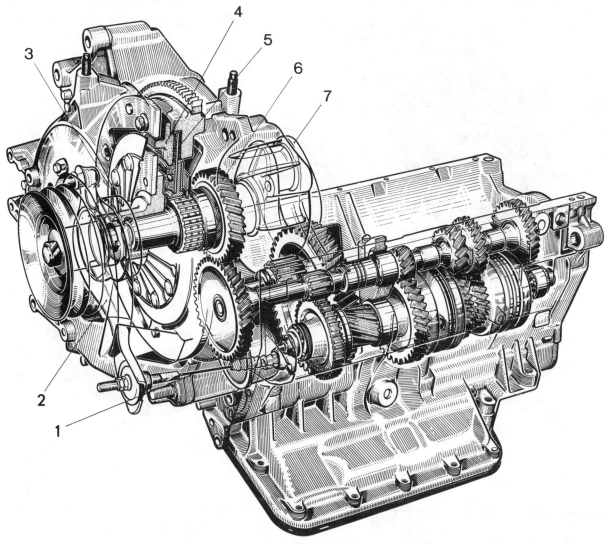

Fig. 5.1 The Peugeot 305 clutch assembly (Sec 1)

1	Operating cable	3	Thrust bearing	5	Friction disc	7	Crankshaft
2	Release fork	4	Pressure plate	6	Input pinion	

2 Clutch – adjustment

1   Although some free play in the clutch control is necessary to ensure that the release bearing is freed when the pedal is not depressed, excessive play could result in the driven plate not being freed when the pedal is depressed. For these reasons the control must be adjusted initially to establish the correct amount of free play and then, periodically, the control must be checked as wear in the system will increase the amount of play.

2   The makers recommend that the free play is checked every 10 000 miles (15 000 km) but it would be worthwhile making this check more frequently as it doesn't involve much work.

3   First check the pedal travel by measuring the distance through which it can be depressed from the normal up position to fully down. The minimum distance is given in the Specifications. With the clutch pedal in the normal up position, lift it upwards and measure the distance through which it moves, that is the amount of free play. The minimum distance is again given in the Specifications.

4   Adjustment, if required, is made at the engine end of the cable where the end fitting connects with the release arm (photo). Loosen the locknut on the threaded end fitting and turn the adjoining nut to obtain the required adjustment. Operate the foot pedal several times and then recheck the pedal travel and free play. If necessary readjust; when the correct adjustment is achieved tighten the end fitting

2.4 The clutch cable adjustable end fitting (arrowed)

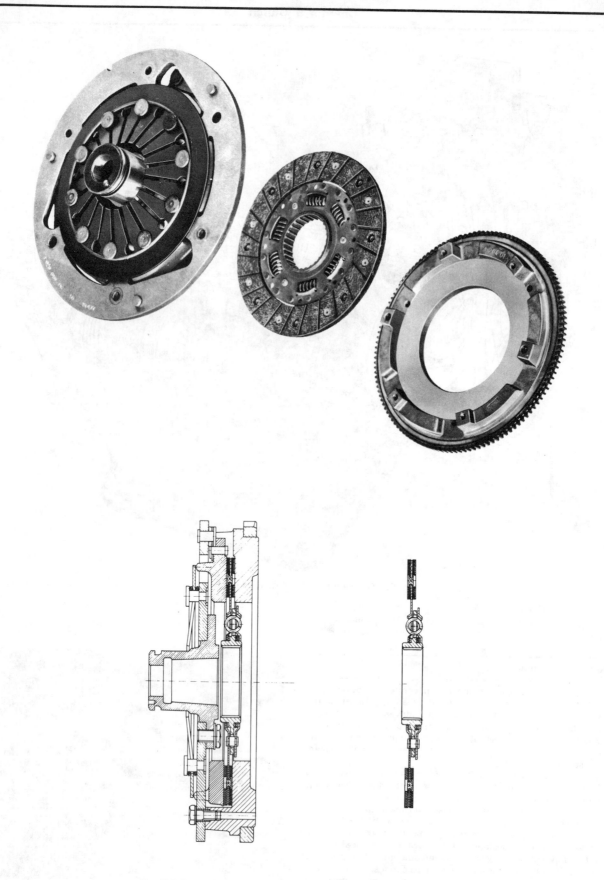

Fig. 5.2 Exploded and cross-sectional views of the clutch (Sec 1)

locknut. When using a spanner on the locknut or the adjusting nut, prevent the end fitting from turning with a spanner on the flats at its inner end. On completion recheck the clutch pedal operation.

3 Clutch cable – removal and refitting

Note: *Once a clutch cable has been removed it must not be refitted; a new cable must be used. It is not permissible to grease a cable as this is done on manufacture using a special grease which will not mix with the usual commercially available greases.*

1 Jack up the front of the car and support it on ramps or axle stands. Apply the handbrake.
2 Loosen the locknut and undo the adjusting nut on the engine end of the clutch cable. The clutch bearing release arm in which the cable end fitting fits is slotted and the cable, together with its washers and nuts, can be slid out of the release arm and the stop bracket.
3 Working inside the car, remove the carpet and sound proofing in

the vicinity of the clutch pedal to gain access to the pedal and its mounting.
4 Unhook the return spring from the pedal and unscrew and remove the pivot nut and bolt. Disconnect the cable end fitting from the pedal arm, see Fig. 5.4.
5 To disconnect the cable outer sheath from the bulkhead, turn the cable sheath end fitting through 90° after prising the locating pip in the flange out of its hole. By turning the end fitting, two retaining lugs are brought into alignment with clearance slots and the cable assembly can then be pulled forward into the engine bay. Remove the cable from the car.
6 Refitting a new cable is essentially the reverse of the removal procedure, but the following points should be noted.

(a) On assembly, grease the clutch pedal pivot and the cable end fitting on the pedal using a general purpose grease. Do not grease the cable in its outer sheath
(b) Fit a new Nylstop nut to the pedal pivot bolt and tighten to the specfied torque
(c) Reassemble the rubber washers, metal washers, and nuts on the cable engine end fitting in the same sequence as originally fitted. Lightly grease the domed adjusting nut where

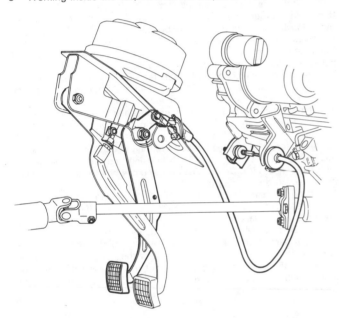

Fig. 5.3 The clutch control installation. LHD shown, RHD similar (Sec 3)

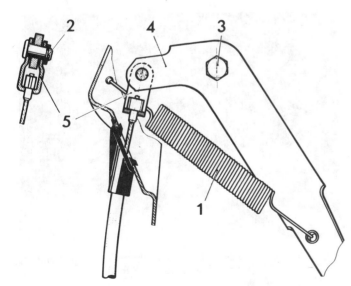

Fig. 5.4 The clutch pedal and cable attachment (Sec 3)

1 Return spring
2 Cable fitting pivot
3 Pedal pivot
4 Pedal arm
5 Cable end fitting

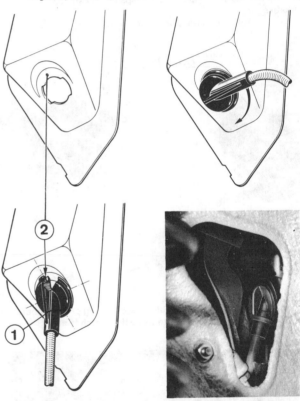

Fig. 5.5 The cable sheath attachment at the bulkhead (Sec 3)

1 Sheath end fitting
2 Locating pip

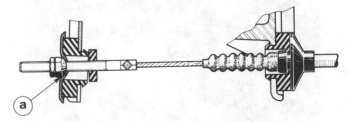

Fig. 5.6 Assembly details of the cable fittings at the engine end (Sec 3)

a Apply general purpose grease at this point only

it contacts the bearing release arm using a general purpose grease.

(d) On completion, adjust the clutch control as described in Section 2.

4   Clutch – removal

1   Separating the clutch assembly from the crankshaft requires the use of at least one special tool, Peugeot clutch hub extractor 8.0206 A. If the clutch removal is to be carried out with the engine in the car, crankshaft pulley dog 8.0206 HZ and ½ inch-to-23 mm adaptor 8.1403 B, or equivalent, will also be required. The extractor is needed to 'unstick' the clutch from the crankshaft taper; even with the engine removed from the car, separation is unlikely using a normal universal puller. With the engine in the car, access is very restricted and the pulley dog and the adaptor, in conjunction with a 24 mm socket spanner and 23 mm and 41 mm open-ended spanners, will be needed in order to remove the crankshaft pulley. If you cannot hire or borrow these tools it would be better to entrust the work to a Peugeot dealer.

2   First disconnect the battery earth terminal and then jack up the front end of the car. Support it on ramps or axle stands and apply the handbrake.

3   To save a lot of extra dismantling, locate the nut on one of the

clutch housing bolts under the cooling system thermostat, see Fig. 5.8, and wedge it in position with a pellet of modelling clay or similar material.

4   Remove the following components, in the order shown, referring if necessary to the relevant Chapters quoted:

(a)   *Air intake duct from the air filter case forwards (Chapter 3)*
(b)   *Alternator (Chapter 10)*
(c)   *The upper and lower pulley brackets carrying the cooling fan/pump drivebelt (Chapters 1 and 2)*
(d)   *The cooling fan/pump drivebelt (Chapter 2)*
(e)   *The alternator drivebelt (Chapter 10)*

5   Without draining the cooling system, undo the radiator mounting attachments (refer to Chapter 2) and move the radiator from its mounting towards the battery.

6   Support the left-hand end of the engine with a jack under the exhaust pipe mounting bracket.

7   Undo the alternator regulator mounting nuts, and without disconnecting the wires move the regulator to one side.

8   Undo the four nuts and washers securing the left-hand top engine mounting bracket and remove the bracket.

9   Using the special tool 8.0206 HZ to restrain the crankshaft from turning, undo the crankshaft pulley retaining bolt and remove the pulley and bolt. Refer to Fig. 5.11 for details.

10 Loosen the clutch control cable locknut and the adjusting nut. Slide the control cable end fitting out of the bearing release arm; there's no need to remove the nuts and washers.

11 Undo the clutch housing retaining bolts and remove the outer half housing case and the bearing release arm. Remove the clutch release bearing.

12 Undo the hexagon-headed bolt securing the TDC sensor bracket in the bottom of the inner half clutch housing and remove the bracket with the sensor in it. Do not disturb the cross-headed screw securing the sensor in the bracket (photo).

13 Using the special extractor 8.0206 HZ, remove the clutch assembly and flywheel from the crankshaft. The two half collars locate in the groove on the clutch spigot and they are held in place by the sleeve. Considerable torque will be needed, including the use of extension bars to unstick the clutch. The crankshaft can be restrained from turning by gagging the gear teeth of the flywheel if necessary.

14 When the assembly is freed, extract it from the car. Remember that it is heavy and take care not to drop it. Avoid damaging the cooling system hoses.

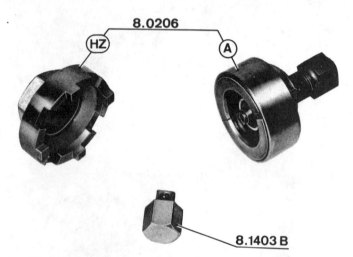

Fig. 5.7 The Peugeot special tools, showing part numbers, required to remove the clutch (Sec 4)

Fig. 5.8 Retain the nut, 1, with modelling clay (Sec 4)

Fig. 5.9 Move the radiator towards the battery without draining the cooling system (Sec 4)

Fig. 5.10 Support the left-hand end of the engine on a jack (Sec 4)

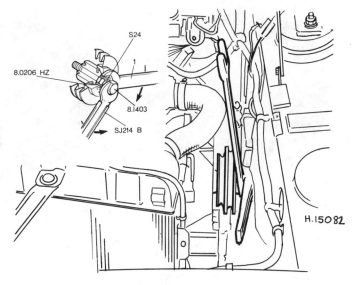

Fig. 5.11 Using the special tools to remove the crankshaft pulley (Sec 4)

1	*41 mm spanner*
S24	*24 mm socket*
SJ214	*Handle for 23 mm spanner*
8.0206 HZ	*Crankshaft pulley dog*
8.1403 B	*½ inch-to-23 mm adaptor*

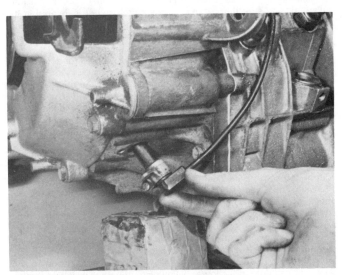

4.12 Removing the TDC sensor (engine on bench)

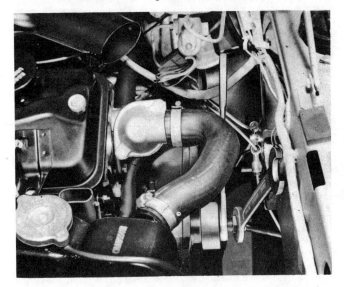

Fig. 5.12 Removing the clutch assembly with the special tools (Sec 4)

5 Clutch – inspection and renovation

1 With the clutch assembly on the bench, progressively loosen the six bolts securing the pressure plate mechanism to the flywheel/starter ring. Retrieve the three coil springs after separating the two halves of the assembly.

2 The clutch disc (driven plate) should be examined for wear or deterioration of the friction linings and the six damper springs. If the linings have worn to within 0.04 in (1.0 mm) of the rivet heads, or if they are contaminated with oil, the disc must be renewed. The cause of any oil contamination must be determined and rectified. The likelihood is that oil will have leaked past a defective seal in the inner half case or in the input pinion bore, see Section 7.

3 Examine the machined faces of the clutch pressure plate and the flywheel. These should be bright and smooth although occasional, shallow scores are acceptable. If the disc linings have worn excessively it is possible that the rivet heads have worn grooves in the machined faces. It is useless fitting a new disc to an assembly with scored faces hoping that the defect will be cured. Slip, juddering, and rapid wear

will soon occur requiring very early renewal. Where scoring is present it might be possible to have it machined out by an engineering works, but more likely new parts will be required.

4 If only light scoring is present on the machined faces and the assembly appears otherwise fit for use, rub the faces over lightly with emery cloth and clean them thoroughly with methylated spirit. Take care not to contaminate the cleaned surfaces with oily finger marks.

5 Dismantling of the pressure plate is not practicable for the home mechanic. If defects are found in either the pressure plate assembly or in the flywheel they must both be renewed as a matched pair. These parts are balanced together during manufacture and it is not permissible to renew one without the other.

6 Examine the gear teeth on the starter ring which is shrunk onto the flywheel. Look for localised wear as it is not uncommon for wear to be concentrated in one segment of the periphery. The starter ring can be changed as an independent part but this work is best left to a suitably

5.8a Place the flywheel face down and ...   5.8b ... then locate the clutch disc on it and,   5.8c ... fit the pressure plate
                                                     with the three coil springs in the flywheel ...

equipped garage or engineering works (see Chapter 1).

7   The clutch release thrust bearing which slides on the pressure plate spigot should be checked for wear by spinning it and observing whether there is any excessive wear or harshness present. Considering the amount of work involved in gaining access to the release bearing it is prudent to renew the bearing, especially if a new clutch disc (driven plate) has been fitted.

8   Reassemble the clutch assembly by first placing the flywheel face down on the bench. Locate the clutch disc on the face, note that this will fit in only one way with the plain side uppermost. Check that the two diametrically opposed locating dowels are in position in the flywheel and position the three springs in their locations. Place the pressure plate down on the flywheel, checking that the three springs enter their locations on the pressure plate. Fit the six assembly bolts and new wavy washers, but do not tighten at this stage as the clutch disc must be centralised on the crankshaft first (photos).

9   Although it is not really part of the clutch, examine the input pinion on the crankshaft, particularly the splines which mate with the clutch disc for wear or corrosion. These can lead to the fault of clutch spin. Removal and refitting of the input pinion are covered in Section 7.

6   Clutch – refitting

1   When refitting a clutch assembly which has been dismantled, it is necessary to centralise the clutch disc during a trial fit. If the assembly has not been dismantled. Ignore intervening paragraphs and proceed to paragraph 7.

2   The oil deflector plate on the input pinion must be removed prior to the clutch disc centering operation. Use a pair of circlip pliers to open the circlip on the pinion, remove the circlip and the oil deflector plate. Remove the old O-ring behind the plate.

3   Check that the six assembly bolts in the clutch mechanism are loose and offer the assembly up to the crankshaft, aligning the pin in the end of the clutch spigot with the mark on the end of the crankshaft. Push the assembly home and, with luck, it will go on. If not, the clutch disc needs slight realignment so remove the assembly, move the disc slightly and have another attempt. When it is home check that the clutch pin is still aligned with the mark on the crankshaft and temporarily fit the crankshaft pulley and bolt but only lightly nip the bolt – remember that the assembly has got to come off again (photos).

4   Progressively and evenly tighten the six clutch assembly bolts to the specified torque (photo).

5   Remove the clutch mechanism, if necessary using the special extractor to which reference is made in Section 4. Fit a new O-ring to the input pinion and fit the oil deflector so that its outer periphery is dished in towards the engine. Refit the retaining circlip, pressing the deflector in against the O-ring seal.

6   Thoroughly clean the tapered polygon seating for the clutch on the crankshaft and give it a light spray of Molykote 321 or equivalent, including the splines on the input pinion. Make sure that the Molykote does not come into contact with oil seals or their contacting surfaces.

7   Refit the clutch mechanism, after cleaning the mating faces in the bore, and align the pin on the clutch spigot with the crankshaft mark – at this stage just push the clutch into position (photo).

8   Load the groove in the clutch spigot with a good general purpose grease but don't overfill it, and then fit the clutch release thrust bearing (photos).

9   Lightly spray the working surfaces of the clutch release arm with Molykote 321 R or equivalent and apply a little graphited grease to the ball pivot in the outer half case. Fit the release arm in the case, making sure that the spring clips fit under the rubber cup (photo).

10   Fit the clutch case and tighten the six attachment bolts to the specified torque.

11   Clean and oil the threads on the crankshaft pulley bolt and fit the pulley, making sure that the pin on the clutch spigot is located in its hole in the pulley rear face. Tighten the pulley bolt to the specified torque, using the special tool 8.0206 HZ to restrain the crankshaft from turning if necessary (photos).

12   Refit the clutch control cable, referring to Section 3 for details, and adjust as described in Section 2.

13   Refit the TDC sensor in the clutch housing. If the original clutch has been refitted no adjustment will be necessary, but if new parts (apart from the clutch disc and release bearing) have been fitted, readjust the fit of the sensor as described in Chapter 4, Section 13.

14   Refit the starter motor using new wavy washers under the bolt heads and tighten the three bolts to the specified torque.

15   Refit the engine mounting bracket at the left-hand end of the engine and tighten the four nuts to the specified torque. Refit the voltage regulator to its location on the left-hand front wheel bay wall.

16   Refer to Chapter 10 for details and refit the alternator, its drivebelt, and tension the belt during the refitting. Tighten the alternator securing bolt to the specified torque and reconnect the wiring.

17   Refit the fixed and adjustable jockey pulleys for the cooling pump/fan drivebelt and tighten the bolts to the specified torque (photo). Refer to Chapter 2 for details for fitting and tensioning the drivebelt, and tighten the lower pulley pivot bolt to its specified torque.

18   Refit the remaining components in the reverse sequence to that of removal and, on completion, start the engine and run it up to maximum rpm very briefly a few times once it has warmed enough to engage the cooling fan.

19   Stop the engine, loosen the crankshaft pulley bolt and retighten it to its specified torque. It is important not to neglect this retorquing of the pulley bolt.

7   Input pinion and oil seals – removal and refitting

1   Oil contamination of the clutch disc will be due to one or more leaking seals on the input pinion. Renewing these seals will involve removal of the input pinion but this work, although requiring some care, is fairly straightforward and can be done with the engine installed in the car.

2   Refer to Section 4 and follow the procedure described for removing the clutch, but in this case drain the cooling system and remove the radiator, referring to Chapter 2 for details. In addition, drain the oil from the engine sump, referring to Chapter 1 for details, if necessary. Renew the oil drain plug sealing washer, refit and tighten the plug to its specified torque. When fitting the support jack under the left-hand side of the engine, lift the engine slightly. At the same time the engine must be moved forwards on the left-hand side by about 2.5 in (say 6 cm). This can be done using suitable wooden levers, but prop

6.3a Offer the assembly up to the crankshaft ...

6.3b ... making sure that the pin is adjacent to the crankshaft mark

6.3c Using the crankshaft pulley and retaining washer and bolt to hold the assembly in position ...

6.4 ... tighten the six bolts

6.7 After fitting the oil deflector refit the clutch assembly

6.8a Load the clutch spigot groove (arrowed) with grease and then ...

6.8b ... fit the release bearing

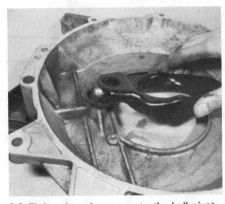
6.9 Fitting the release arm to the ball pivot

6.11a Fit the crankshaft pulley and ....

6.11b ... tighten the retaining bolt

6.17 Refitting the upper, fixed, pulley bracket

the engine forward so that it cannot move back during the job. Remove the starter without disconnecting the electrical connections and move it to one side.

3   After removing the clutch assembly, undo the bolts securing the inner half of the clutch housing to the engine and remove the housing. The input pinion will come off with the housing so remove it carefully. Cover the open end of the engine to prevent dirt or dust contamination and take the clutch housing and input pinion to a clean, wooden topped work bench for dismantling.

4   Using circlip pliers, open the circlip on the input pinion and remove it, then remove the oil deflector and O-ring seal. The input pinion can then be removed from the housing.

5   Clean the input pinion in paraffin and dry it thoroughly. Examine it for such defects as worn or deformed splines, damaged oil seal seat, chipped or worn gear teeth, scored or dented thrust faces, and seized or worn needle bearings.

6   Clean the clutch housing and examine it for damage. If the joint between the housing and the engine has leaked oil, check the gasket face for freedom from dents or scoring. Use a straight-edge and feeler gauges to check the flatness of the face. The maximum acceptable distortion is listed in the Specifications.

7   Lever the old oil seal out of the clutch housing and the one out of the bore in the input pinion.

8   If the input pinion thrust washer located on the engine block or the one in the clutch housing is worn or scored it should be renewed

(photos). However it will be necessary to check, and perhaps adjust the input pinion endfloat in this case. Similarly, if a new input pinion is going to be fitted, or if the clutch housing is going to be renewed, the endfloat must also be checked in these cases too. The endfloat is adjusted by shim washers located under the input pinion thrust washer in the clutch housing.

9   To check the endfloat, reassemble the input pinion into the clutch housing and refit the housing to the engine using at least six bolts tightened to 9 lbf ft (1.25 kgf m). If you have a dial test indicator (clock gauge), mount it with the spindle button resting on the input pinion outer face and with the spindle parallel with the crankshaft axis. Press the input pinion in against the thrust washer on the main bearing face, set the gauge to zero and then pull the pinion forward to butt against its thrust washer in the clutch housing. Note the amount of endfloat registered on the indicator. If you have no dial test indicator a vernier caliper with depth gauging facility can be used instead (photos). Compare your reading with the permitted tolerance quoted in the Specifications. If the endfloat is out it will be necessary to adjust the shim washers; these are available in various thicknesses as listed in the Specifications.

10   To renew the input pinion thrust washer or to adjust the shim washers beneath it, lever the thrust washer out of the case. Fit the correct shim washers to achieve the specified endfloat of the input pinion and reposition the thrust washer. When fitting the shims and washer make sure that they are perfectly clean and dry because any

7.8a The input pinion thrust washer (arrowed) in the engine block ...

7.8b ... and the one in the clutch housing

7.9a Fit the input pinion and ...

7.9b ... the clutch housing to measure pinion endfloat

dirt or grit here will upset the input pinion endfloat (photo).

11 Press firmly on the thrust washer and secure it with three punch marks spaced at 120° intervals to deform the housing slightly and retain the washer. Wipe the washer clean and lubricate it with clean engine oil (photo).

12 With the clutch housing engine side down on the bench and the input pinion removed from the housing, clean the oil seal recess in the housing. Lightly grease a new seal and carefully tap it into its recess, with the lip facing in towards the engine side of the housing. Fit the seal fully into the housing (photo).

13 Clean the oil seal recess in the input pinion, lightly grease a new seal and tap it into the pinion, with its lip down towards the gear end of the pinion, until it is fully home (photo).

14 The input pinion can now be fitted to the crankshaft. First wrap PVC adhesive tape over the step on the crankshaft to prevent damage to the input pinion internal seal lip as it is being fitted, and smear grease on the tape to assist fitting (photo). Lubricate the engine side thrust washer with clean engine oil. Grease the input pinion needle

bearing and carefully fit the pinion, easing the seal lip over the greased PVC tape (photo), then remove the tape.

15 Now wrap PVC tape on the input pinion to cover the splines on which the clutch disc seats and just overlap the shoulder of the bearing surface for the seal in the clutch housing. Again coat the tape with grease to aid fitting (photo). Check that all traces of the old gasket are removed and fit a new gasket to the engine face. Freely lubricate the pinion and transmission input shaft gear teeth with clean engine oil and also lubricate the thrust washer in the clutch housing.

16 Carefully fit the clutch housing to the engine, easing the lip of the seal over the greased tape on the input pinion (photo). Fit the twelve retaining bolts using new wavy washers and tighten them to the specified torque.

17 Peel back the PVC tape on the input pinion to uncover the O-ring location, but keeping the splines covered. Fit a new O-ring seal, then remove the tape from the pinion (photos).

18 Fit the oil deflector plate to the input pinion with its outer periphery dished towards the engine side of the clutch housing. Press

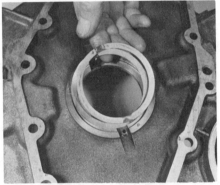
7.10 Fitting the shim washers and ...

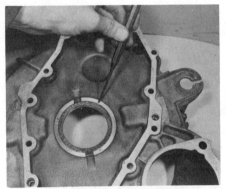
7.11 ... securing the thrust washer

7.12 Fitting a new oil seal to the clutch housing and ...

7.13 ... a new oil seal to the input pinion

7.14a Wrap plastic tape on the crankshaft step and grease it before ...

7.14b ... fitting the input pinion

7.15 Similarly wrap plastic tape on the input pinion and grease it before ...

7.16 ... fitting the clutch housing

7.17a Fit a new O-ring seal ...

7.17b ... and then remove the tape

7.18a Fit the oil deflector plate, dished side inwards and ...

7.18b ... secure it with the retaining circlip

the deflector down against the O-ring seal and fit the retaining circlip, making sure that it is bedded down in its recess in the input pinion (photos). Make sure that no remnants of PVC tape or grease remain on the input pinion splines or crankshaft polygon taper.

19 Where the clutch housing has been renewed, transfer the timing plate from the old housing to the new one and adjust its position as described in Chapter 4.

20 Continue to reassemble the clutch, housing, and ancillary components following the procedures already described in Sections 6 and 5, and by reversing the additional dismantling procedures in this Section. Refill the cooling system and top up the engine oil before attempting to run the engine and don't omit the retorquing of the pulley bolt after the initial engine run.

8   Fault diagnosis – clutch

Symptom	Reason(s)
Excessive pedal travel	Incorrect cable adjustment Excessive crankshaft endfloat (only on very worn engine)
Clutch will not disengage	Incorrect cable adjustment Clutch disc rusted onto splines (only after long disuse. Depressing pedal with gear engaged and turning engine on starter may free) Pressure plate damaged or misaligned Input pinion seized on crankshaft
Clutch slip (engine speed increases with no increase in road speed)	Incorrect cable adjustment Worn or contaminated friction linings Damaged or weak springs in pressure plate
Clutch judder	Engine/transmission mountings loose or worn Friction linings worn or contaminated Release mechanism worn Flywheel run-out
Squeal or rumble when pedal depressed	Release bearing worn or dry Pressure plate defective

Chapter 6 Transmission

For modifications, and information applicable to later models, see Supplement at end of manual

Contents

Specifications

General
Gearbox series	BB8 (406)
Number of gears	Four forward, one reverse
Type of gears	Helical, constant mesh
Synchromesh	All forward gears
Lubricant type/specification	Shares engine lubricant

Ratios (overall)
	GL and GR	SR
1st	0.0674	0.0737
2nd	0.1111	0.1274
3rd	0.1694	0.1874
4th	0.2495	0.2647
Reverse	0.0624	0.0716

Speedometer drive
	145 x 14 tyres	155 x 14 tyres
Worm, starts	8	8
Pinion, teeth	18	17
Identification colour	White	Yellow

Overhaul data
Differential bearings preload	0.2 mm (0.0079 in)
Secondary shaft shim sizes (between 1st gear driven pinion bush and roller bearing)	0.15, 0.20, 0.25 and 0.50 mm (0.0059, 0.0079, 0.0098 and 0.0197 in)
Secondary shaft spacer sizes (between 2nd gear driven pinion bush and 3rd gear driven pinion bush)	2.0 to 2.9 mm in steps of 0.05 mm (0.0787 to 0.1142 in in steps of 0.00197 in)

Torque wrench settings
	lbf ft	kgf m
Selector mechanism cover bolts (4)	7.2	1.0
Mainshaft centre bearing cap bolts (2)	16.3	2.25
Mainshaft ball-bearing retaining plate bolts (3)	7.2	1.0
Differential housing:		
8 mm dia short bolts (4)	14.5	2.0
10 mm dia long bolts (4)	28.9	4.0
Bearing cover bolts (4)	14.5	2.0
Oil sump screen bolts (3)	4.3	0.6
Sump cover bolts (13)	7.2	1.0
Sump drain plug (1)	19.9	2.75
Reversing light switch (1)	25.3	3.5
Transmission-to-engine bolts (14)	9.4	1.3
Oil pipe banjo bolts (2)	12.7	1.75
Dipstick tube (1)	18.1	2.5
Secondary shaft nut	37	5.0

1 General description

The Peugeot 305 is fitted with a four forward speed manual gearbox mounted transversely underneath and in-line with the engine. The transmission housing is cast in aluminium alloy and, besides the gearbox, also contains the differential and final drive units. Drive to the gearbox from the engine is via an input pinion located on the crankshaft between the cylinder block and the clutch; see Chapter 5 for details.

The gearbox has a conventional two-shaft, constant mesh layout. There are four pairs of gears, one for each forward speed. The gears on the primary shaft are fixed to the shaft, while those on the secondary shaft with which they mesh are floating, each being locked to the secondary shaft only when engaged by its synchromesh unit. The reverse idler gear is located on a separate shaft.

Each gear selector fork engages in a slot in the synchromesh unit; these are made to slide axially along the secondary shaft in order to engage the appropriate gear. The forks are pinned to selector shafts which are operated by levers from the manual control mechanism.

An integral gear on the secondary shaft is in constant mesh with the crownwheel gear on the differential unit which is located on the front of the gearbox. The differential incorporates the final drives and the assembly is mounted in taper roller bearings.

Although the transmission system employed is relatively simple, nevertheless a few words of warning must be stressed, before any inexperienced dismantlers start work, to make sure that they know what they are letting themselves in for.

First of all decide whether the fault you wish to repair is worth the time and effort involved. Secondly bear in mind that, if the transmission is well worn, then the cost of the necessary component parts could well exceed the cost of an exchange factory unit and, furthermore, you will get a guaranteed job without the bother of having to do it yourself. Thirdly, if you are intent on doing it yourself, make sure that you understand how the transmission works.

Special care must be taken during all dismantling and assembly operations to ensure that the housing is not overstressed or distorted in any way. When dismantled, check the cost and availability of the parts to be renewed and compare this against the cost of a replacement unit, which may not be much more expensive and therefore would be a better proposition.

On reassembly, take careful note of the tightening procedures and torque wrench settings of the relevant nuts and bolts. This is most important to prevent overtightening, distortion and oil leakage and also to ensure smooth, trouble-free running of the unit.

2   Transmission unit – removal

1   The transmission unit cannot be removed as a separate assembly from the car; the engine and transmission have to be removed first as a complete assembly. The procedure for this operation is given in Chapter 1.

2   With the engine/transmission unit removed, clean off all road dirt, oil, grease, etc, using a proprietary engine cleaner or paraffin. Wipe the unit dry with clean rag and then remove the following ancillary components, referring to the relevant Chapters for specific procedures if necessary:

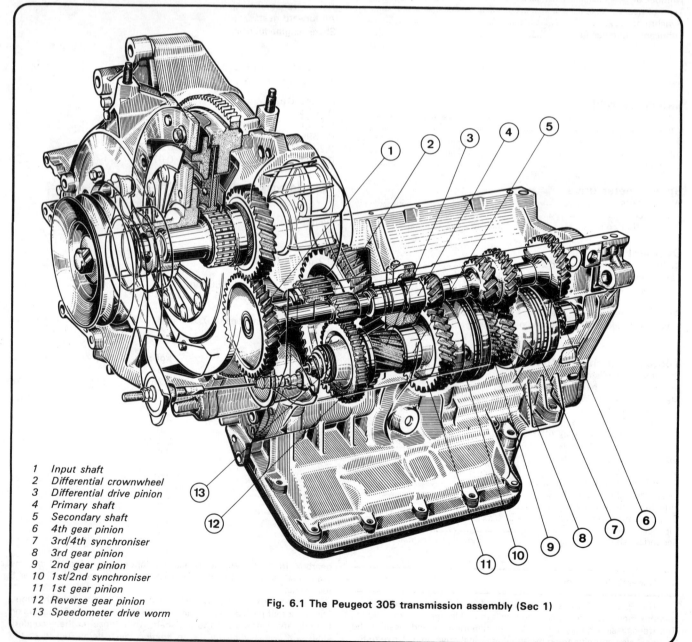

1   Input shaft
2   Differential crownwheel
3   Differential drive pinion
4   Primary shaft
5   Secondary shaft
6   4th gear pinion
7   3rd/4th synchroniser
8   3rd gear pinion
9   2nd gear pinion
10 1st/2nd synchroniser
11 1st gear pinion
12 Reverse gear pinion
13 Speedometer drive worm

Fig. 6.1 The Peugeot 305 transmission assembly (Sec 1)

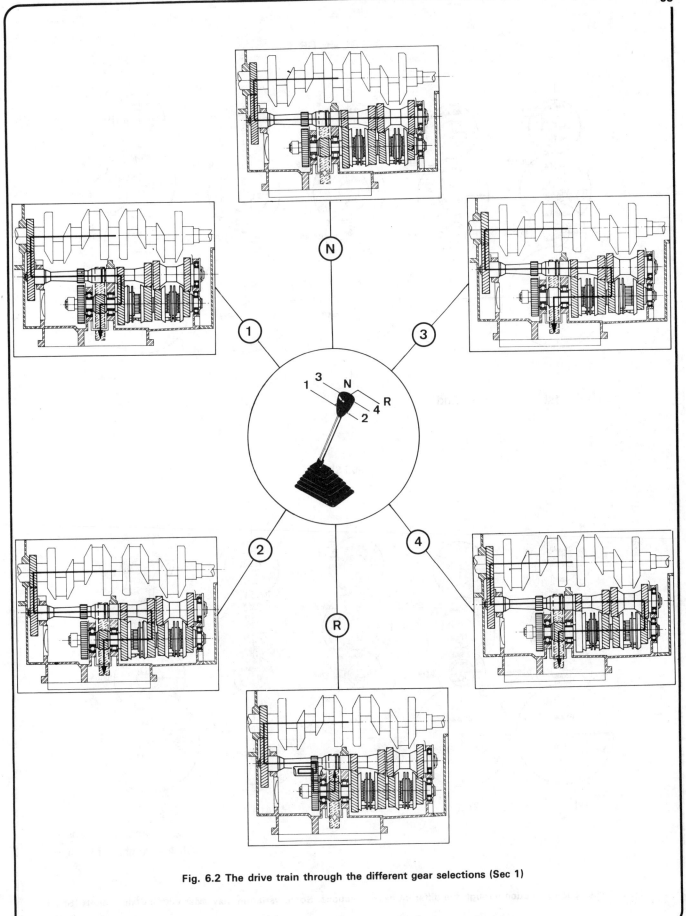

Fig. 6.2 The drive train through the different gear selections (Sec 1)

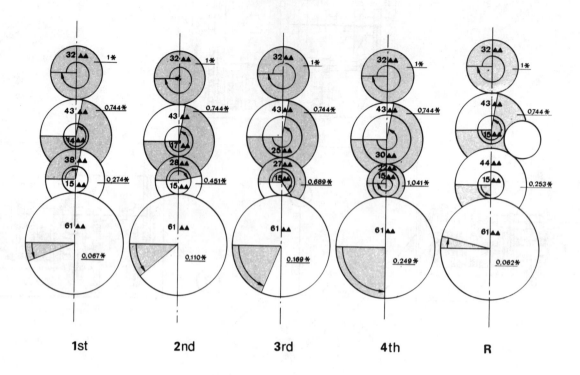

305 GL and GR

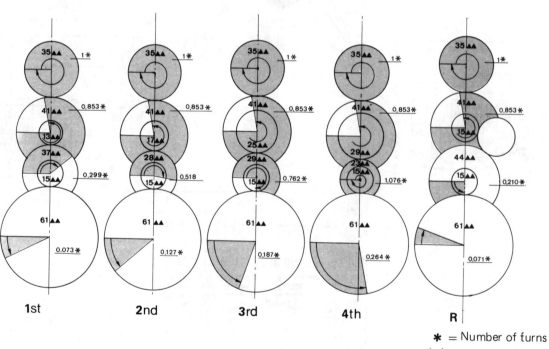

305 SR

* = Number of turns
▲▲ = Number of teeth

Fig. 6.3 The speed reduction through the different gear selections. Some variation may exist with certain models (Sec 1)

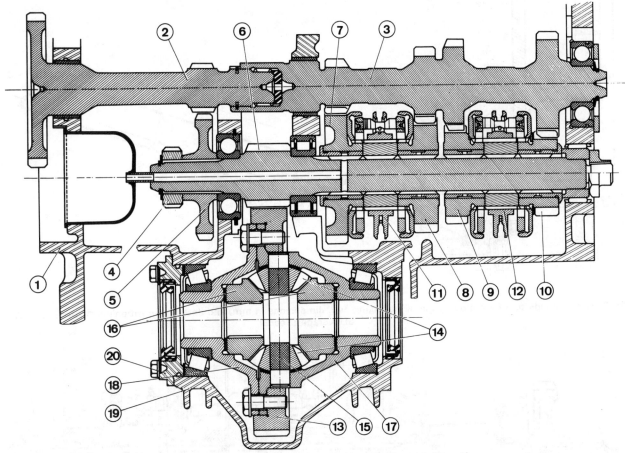

Fig. 6.4 Cross-sectional view of the transmission unit (Sec 1)

1	Gearbox housing	7	1st gear driven pinion	13	Differential crownwheel	18	Differential carrier,
2	Input shaft	8	2nd gear driven pinion	14	Planet gears		LH side
3	Primary shaft	9	3rd gear driven pinion	15	Planet gear spindles	19	Differential main housing
4	Speedometer drive pinion	10	4th gear driven pinion	16	Sun gears	20	Differential side cover
5	Reverse gear pinion	11	1st/2nd synchronizer	17	Differential carrier,		
6	Crownwheel	12	3rd/4th synchronizer		RH side		

(a) Alternator and mountings (Chapter 10)
(b) Starter motor (Chapter 10)
(c) Clutch and housing complete (Chapter 5)
(d) Distributor cover and spark plug leads
(e) Cylinder head cover
(f) Timing chain case (Chapter 1)
(g) Dipstick and tube

3   Unscrew and remove the gearbox-to-crankcase securing bolts
4   Support the engine and gearbox as the last bolts are removed and carefully separate the two units. Should they stick together, carefully lever them apart with a wooden lever.

3   Transmission unit – dismantling

1   Before proceeding with dismantling the transmission unit first read Section 1, if you have not already done so. It is assumed that the unit has already been removed from the car and separated from the engine. Don't attempt to dismantle it on the floor. The unit is not particularly heavy and you should work on it on a clean bench or table top. Later, on reassembly, you will need to renew all gaskets, but don't throw away the original gaskets as you dismantle the unit for they will act as a guide for the fitment of the new ones supplied in the gasket set. In addition to new gaskets you should also fit new lockwashers, circlips and roll pins on assembly but, again, keep the old ones as samples. If you have not already done so clean the outside of the unit free of all road dirt, grease or oil and avoid contaminating the interior. Start work with clean tools, clean hands and a plentiful supply of clean

rag. To simplify reassembly a methodical work routine is essential. Put parts in small containers, lay the parts out in order of assembly as they are removed, mark individual items, or make sketches as you proceed. In practice most people use a combination of these procedures.
2   First turn the unit over and remove the bolts and special washers securing the sump plate. If it has not already been removed you will first need to remove the three nuts securing the bracket for the exhaust pipe. Note that the three bolts are longer than the others and note their positions in the transmission case.
3   Remove the three bolts securing the gauze oil strainer, noting the rubber seal between the screen and the case.
4   Undo the four bolts securing the oil seal retainer plate at the clutch end of the differential final drive. Mark the plate and case so that they can be reassembled correctly, and carefully remove the plate, watching out for loose shim washers as it is removed. Keep all the shims together. The O-ring seal between the plate and case, and the drive oil seal in the plate, will both need renewal on assembly.
5   Undo the four large and the four smaller bolts securing the differential unit to the transmission case and remove the differential housing. It may be tight, due to the locating spigot, and may require gently tapping with a soft-faced hammer to free it. The differential unit can be lifted out of its half case, but take care to keep the taper bearing outer races with their relative bearings. It is not intended to cover the dismantling and overhaul of the differential unit in this manual. If there is any fault with the assembly, or if it is excessively worn, it should be renewed complete, or referred to a Peugeot agent.
6   Remove the nut and locking screw retaining the speedometer drive and remove the drive unit.
7   An oil collecting cup is fitted in the clutch end of the transmission

98

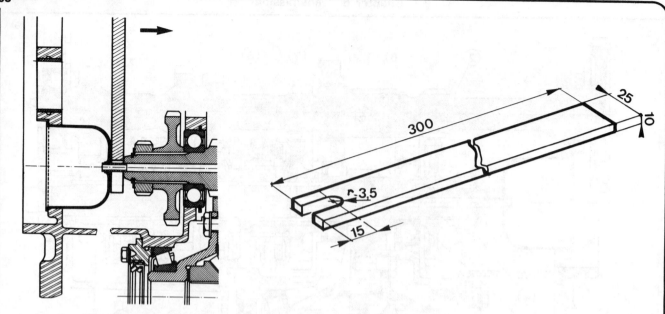

Fig. 6.5 Home-made tool for removing the oil collecting cup, dimensions in mm, and details of positioning. Arrow shows direction of leverage (Sec 3)

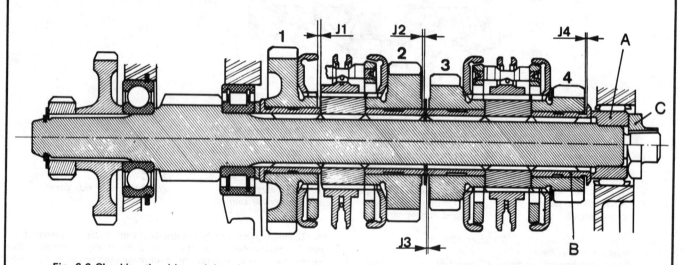

Fig. 6.6 Checking the driven pinion clearances, J1, J2, J3 and J4. Race A must contact bush B and nut C (Sec 3)

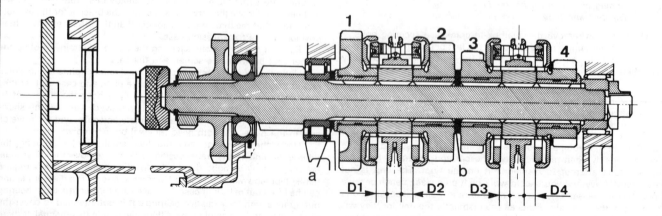

Fig. 6.7 Checking the centralising of the synchronisers. Spaces D1, D2, D3 and D4 should be equal; adjustment is made on shims 'a' and/or spacer washer 'b' (Sec 3)

case with a short connecting pipe entering the secondary shaft. This is to direct oil into the shaft to lubricate the 1st gear pinion through drilled passages. A special tool is required to remove the oil cup, but one can easily be fabricated following the details shown in Fig. 6.5. Use it as shown to lever the cup out of the case.

8 Engage reverse gear and then carefully drive out the roll pin securing the reverse selector fork to its shaft. Hold the reverse idler pinion engaged and change to 1st gear. The input, primary and secondary shafts are now locked and the nut on the timing end of the secondary shaft can be loosened. This nut must be renewed on reassembly. Fit the new nut now and tighten it very lightly, say 3 lbf ft (about 0.5 kgf m). This is to permit endfloat and clearance checks before removal of the secondary shaft later on.

9 Undo and remove the three bolts retaining the triangular plate which retains the primary shaft ball-bearing.

10 The bearing outer race has a groove for a special extractor and two slots are machined in the case to permit fitting the extractor claws. However, if you cannot get hold of a suitable extractor to remove the bearing it can still be removed by the following method. First remove the circlip and the dished washer behind it on the end of the primary shaft. Note that the outer rim of the dished washer is in contact with the ball-bearing inner race and the inner rim with the circlip. Tap the input shaft gently in towards the gear assembly and the ball-bearing on the far end of the primary shaft will be moved out slightly. Hold the bearing out with screwdriver blades in the retracting groove and have an assistant gently tap the primary shaft back into the case. Repeat the procedure, tapping first the input shaft in to move the bearing and then the primary shaft back to reposition it in the bearing inner race, and progressively you can work the bearing out of the case. Don't use excessive force and be satisfied with a little movement at a time.

11 With the bearing removed, disengage the reverse idler gear. Undo the two bolts securing the bearing cap over the primary shaft bearing in the middle of the case and remove the cap. Refit the roll pins to the case if they come out with the cap.

12 Squeeze the circlip in the input and primary shaft joint and separate the two shafts. Note that there is a rubber washer in the aperture in the primary shaft on which the end of the input shaft butts when assembled. This washer must be renewed on reassembly. Remove the two shafts from the case and set the gear selectors to the neutral position.

13 It is now necessary to make endfloat and clearance checks on the secondary shaft assembly to determine whether any worn parts must be renewed.

14 *Endfloat.* The easiest way to measure this is with a dial test indicator (clock gauge) mounted on the casing with its button resting on the end of the secondary shaft and the spindle parallel with the shaft axle. Move the shaft to its limit in each direction axially and measure the endfloat. Alternatively a depth gauge could be used, but as the maximum permissible endfloat is only 0.5 mm (0.020 in) considerable care is needed to get an accurate assessment of the condition of the shaft ball-bearing which is what controls the endfloat. If the endfloat is found to be excessive a new bearing and a new retaining circlip must be fitted. The endfloat must then be rechecked. If it is still outside the permissible limit the gearbox housing must be renewed and obviously this would be the time to think again about renewing the complete gearbox assembly.

15 *Clearances of driven pinions.* Each pinion on the secondary shaft has a working clearance to permit it to rotate on the pinion bush when it is not engaged to drive the shaft. Refer to Fig. 6.6 and first check that the inner race of the needle bearing (at the nut end of the shaft) is in positive contact with the 4th speed pinion bush and also that the retaining nut is in contact with the needle bearing inner race. Using feeler gauges measure the clearances J1, J2, J3 and J4 which should be between 0.2 and 0.35 mm (0.008 and 0.014 in). If the clearance is outside these limits the driven pinion bushes must be renewed.

16 The next essential check concerns the centralising of the synchronisers, but it is no use doing this until the endfloat and driven pinion clearances are within limits. However, if the gearbox housing has been renewed or if it is intended to renew the secondary shaft, selector forks, selector spindles or detent plungers, then the synchroniser centralising checks can be left until the gearbox is being reassembled.

17 When the selector forks are in the neutral position the synchroniser rings must be centred in relation to the synchroniser cones. This involves checking the distances marked D1, D2, D3 and D4 in Fig. 6.7 to ensure that they are equal when the parts in question are opened to the maximum. A special gauge is provided by Peugeot but the

distances can easily be checked with a made-up gauge of 9 mm (0.3543 in) width for insertion in the appropriate gaps.

18 Before making the checks the secondary shaft must be lightly loaded towards the nut end of the shaft. Again Peugeot provide a special tool, shown in the illustration, but a piece of wood with a wedge can be used instead. The special tool is only hand tightened to load the shaft (to the right in the illustration) so make sure that your arrangement conforms to this. Also check that all the selector forks and shafts are in their neutral positions as registered by the shaft detent plungers.

19 Insert the gauge between each synchroniser cone and the adjacent face of the synchroniser hub but don't use force. Ideally the gauge will enter all four positions but, if it doesn't, refer to Figs. 6.8 and 6.9 where the eight possible variations are shown together with the remedial action that will be required. Adjustment is made on the shims 'a' and the spacer washer 'b' shown in the illustration. At this stage in dismantling it will be enough to note the size of the required new items and fit them on assembly. A recheck will then be required to confirm that all is well

20 Remove the block and wedge used to load the secondary shaft, and engage 4th gear. Carefully drive out the roll pins from the 3rd/4th selector fork and the reverse idler pinion spindle. Remove the spindle and the idler pinion from the gearbox and reset the selectors to the neutral position.

21 Undo the banjo bolts securing the external oil pipe to the gearbox housing and remove the pipe, bolts and washers. Undo the four bolts securing the selector cover to the housing and carefully remove the cover, taking precautions to retain the detent balls and springs. Remove the springs and balls from the housing. Remove and discard the cover gasket.

22 Engage the reverse gear detent and rotate the selector upwards carefully. As you do this the detent ball will be ejected so be ready to prevent its loss; retrieve the spring. Drive out the roll pin connecting the detent to the reverse selector spindle and remove the detent followed by the spindle.

23 Engage 2nd gear and drive out the roll pin securing the 3rd/4th detent to its shaft. Drive out the roll pin securing the 1st/2nd selector fork to its shaft but leave the pin punch in the roll pin hole and set the fork to the neutral position. Turn the 3rd/4th selector spindle upwards a quarter of a turn to prevent the stop pin from falling out.

24 Now remove the two selector spindles, the 3rd/4th detent block, the two selector forks and the interlock plungers.

25 Remove the nut from the timing case end of the secondary shaft. From the other (clutch) end remove, in order, the circlip, dished washer, speedometer drive worm gear, shim, and the reverse gear driven pinion.

26 Working through the aperture normally locating the differential unit, spring open the circlip retaining the secondary shaft middle roller bearing outer race and, using a soft-faced hammer, tap the shaft towards the clutch end of the unit and remove it. Lift the synchroniser and gear assemblies out of the housing and take careful note of the washers and shims located in the assembly. Do not separate the synchronisers and hubs; these must be refitted in their original positions unless, of course, they are renewed.

27 This completes the normal dismantling of the transmission unit. Further dismantling such as the removal of the secondary shaft ball-bearing, or the removal of the input shaft bush from the transmission housing, will be dictated by the condition of parts. Do not disturb them unless there is good reason to do so. Note that, if the input shaft bush in the housing is renewed, it is essential to have the new bush fitted by a specialist engineering shop with in-line reaming equipment as the alignment of the bush bore with the other two bearings is critical.

4 Transmission unit – inspection

1 Having removed and dismantled the transmission unit, the various components should be thoroughly washed with a suitable solvent or with petrol and paraffin, and then wiped dry. Take care not to mix components or to lose identification of where they fit and which way round they should be fitted. Don't use hard scrapers or emery cloth to clean the housing mating faces as the surface must be kept perfectly flat and undamaged.

2 Inspect the transmission housing and the differential unit housing for cracks or damage, particularly near bearings or bushes. The transmission housing, differential housing and the mainshaft centre

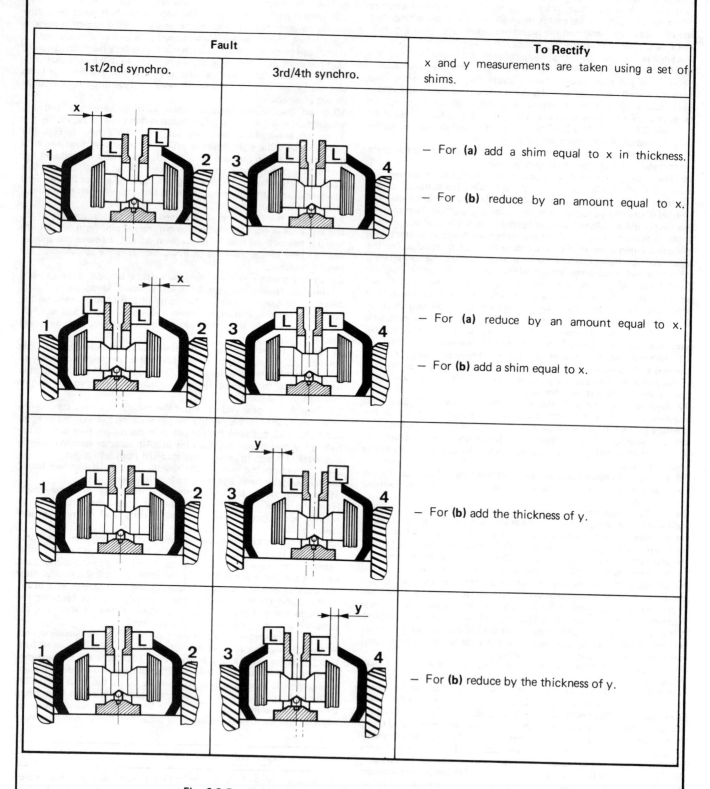

Fault		To Rectify
1st/2nd synchro.	3rd/4th synchro.	x and y measurements are taken using a set of shims.

Fig. 6.8 Rectifying unequal centralising of one synchroniser (Sec 3)

x   Discrepancy on 1st/2nd synchro unit
y   Discrepancy on 3rd/4th synchro unit
a   Adjusting shims, see Fig. 6.7

b   Spacer washer, see Fig. 6.7
L   Gauging tool

To Rectify content:

— For **(a)** add a shim equal to x in thickness.

— For **(b)** reduce by an amount equal to x.

— For **(a)** reduce by an amount equal to x.

— For **(b)** add a shim equal to x.

— For **(b)** add the thickness of y.

— For **(b)** reduce by the thickness of y.

Fault		To rectify	
1st/2nd synchro.	3rd/4th synchro.		
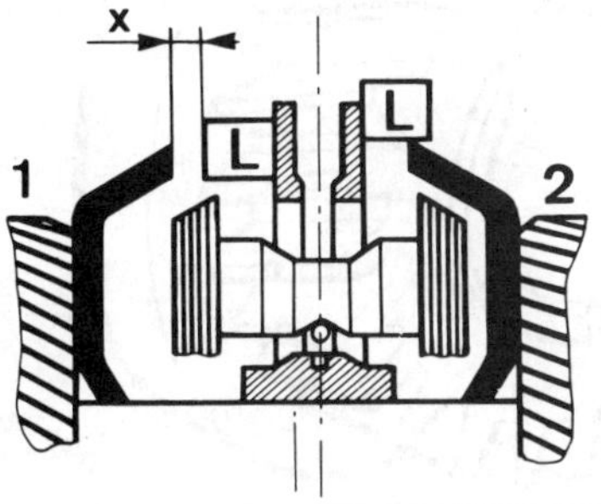	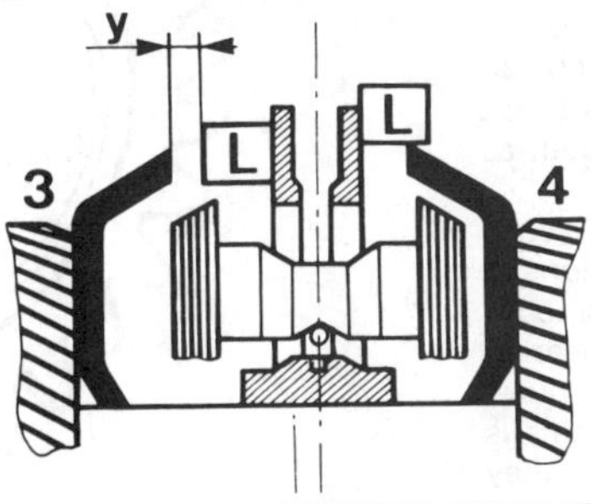	x = y	For **(a)** add thickness of x.
		x > y	For **(a)** add thickness of x. For **(b)** reduce by x - y.
		y > x	For **(a)** add thickness x. For **(b)** add y - x.
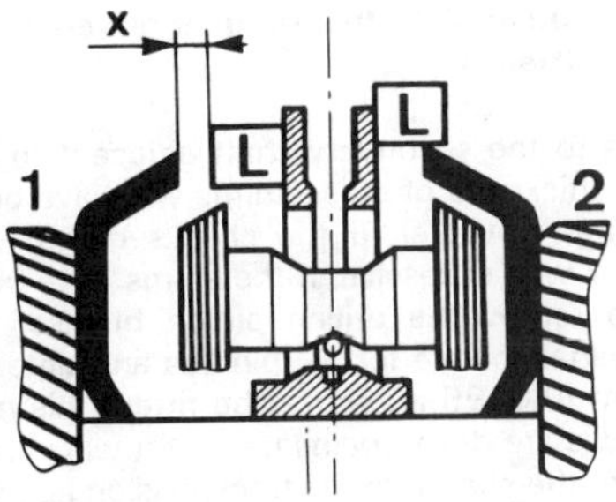	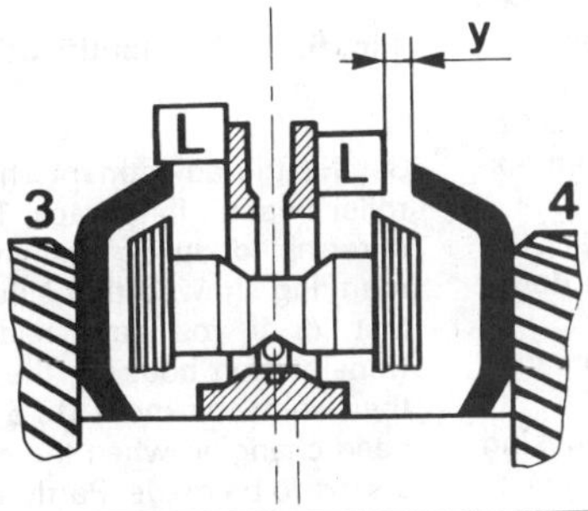	— For **(a)** add thickness x. — For **(b)** reduce by x + y.	
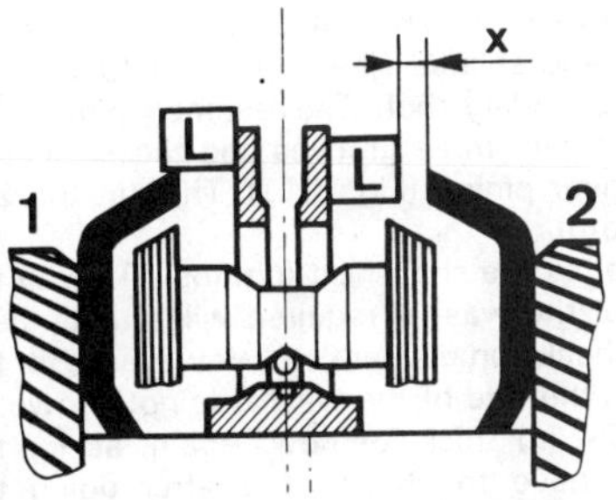	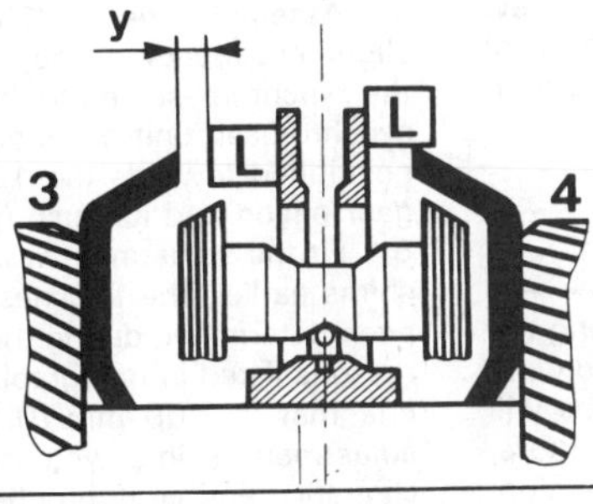	— For **(a)** reduce by thickness x. — For **(b)** add x + y.	
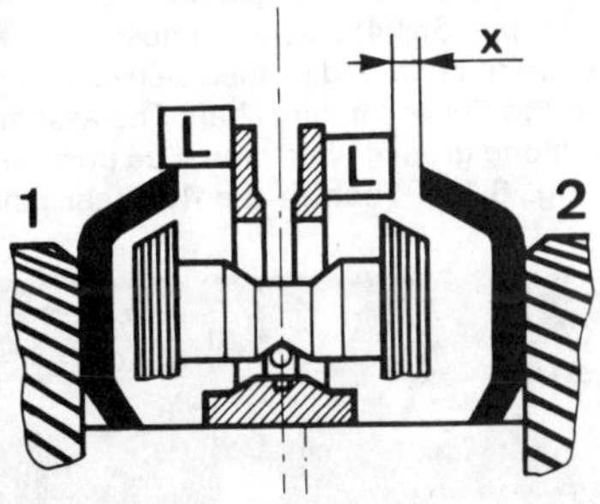	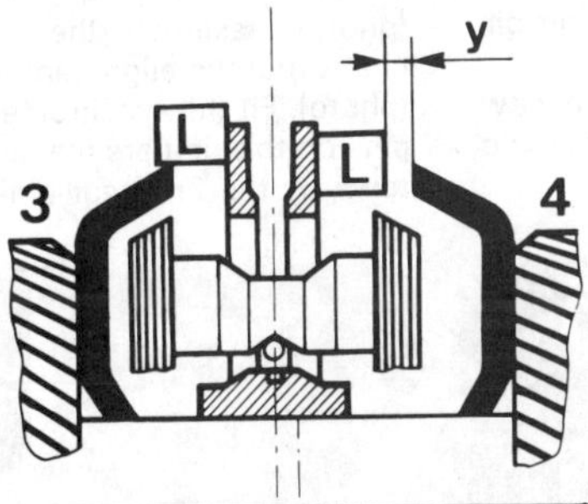	x = y	For **(a)** reduce thickness x.
		x > y	For **(a)** reduce thickness x. For **(b)** add x - y.
		y > x	For **(a)** reduce thickness x. For **(b)** reduce to y - x.

Fig. 6.9 Rectifying unequal centralising of both synchronisers. See Fig. 6.8 for key (sec 3)

bearing cap are all machined after assembly and none of these parts must be renewed separately.

3   Components requiring special attention will have been noted as a result of the performance of the transmission when installed in the car or will have been noted during dismantling.

4   Examine the teeth of all gears for signs of uneven or excessive wear or chipping. If you find a gear in a bad state have a close look at the gear it engages with – this may have to be renewed as well. All gears should run smoothly on their bushes or in their bearings with no sign of rocking or sloppiness. Do not be misled by a groove cut in the teeth of the 1st, 3rd and 4th gear driven pinions in the transmission unit fitted to SR model cars (see Fig. 6.10). This is merely an identification mark to differentiate between similar gears fitted to GL and GR models which, however, have a differing number of teeth as the gearbox ratios are different.

5   A not so obvious cause of noise and trouble is bearing wear. Wash and dry the bearings thoroughly and examine them closely for signs of scoring, pitted tracks or blueing. Rotate the races and feel for smooth movement with no grittiness or abnormal noise. A new ball bearing will show no perceptible axial movement between the inner and outer races. As the bearing wears some play will be evident but if this is excessive the bearing must be renewed. After examining bearings they should be lubricated with clean engine oil to prevent corrosion, and wrapped to avoid contamination with dust and dirt. Discard the two half shell bearings of the input shaft as it is a sound proposition to fit new shells on reassembly.

6   Carefully inspect the synchromesh units for excessive wear or damage. If weak or ineffective synchromesh action has been experienced, renew the units as complete assemblies.

7   Check the selector forks for wear in the areas which contact the synchromesh units. Any wear evident should be minimal; if in doubt renew the forks.

8   Inspect the selector shafts and detents for wear which can cause imprecise gear changing, and renew where necessary.

9   All remaining components such as the speedometer gears, locking plungers, springs, balls, and so on, should be inspected for signs of wear or damage and, where necessary, renewed.

10   It is now worth reviewing the total requirements needed to restore the transmission unit to full serviceability, not forgetting the new lockwashers, circlips, roll pins, seals and gaskets. Compare the cost with that of an overhauled or good condition secondhand unit as it may be more economical to go for one of these alternatives.

5   Transmission unit – reassembly

1   All components must be spotlessly clean before reassembling the transmission unit, the work surface must be clean and you should work with clean hands. Some precision checks are necessary and you will not get accurate results unless everything is spotless. Furthermore, unless the assembled unit is free of contamination on completion, early wear, noise, a short life or even mechanical failure can result. Lubricate individual parts as they are installed with clean engine oil, particularly the bearings and moving parts.

2   Position the transmission housing on the bench and fit a new circlip in the groove in the secondary shaft ball-bearing housing (photo).

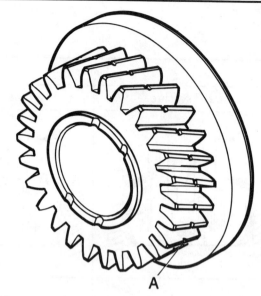

Fig. 6.10 The identification groove, A on the 4th gear driven pinion (Sec 4)

3   Fit the adjustment shims to the secondary shaft adjacent to the roller bearing inner race. The thickness of these shims will have been determined during dismantling. However, if the checks during dismantling showed that sideplay was excessive, if the shims have been lost, or if you have had to renew the driven pinion bushes, the transmission housing, the layshaft or the forks, spindles and detents, then shim thickness 0.75 mm (0.0295 in) should be fitted; this may need changing when the checks are done again later but it will enable a start to be made. Partly enter the shaft into the transmission housing and as it enters fit the 1st driven pinion and its bush to the shaft (photos).

4   Assemble the 1st/2nd synchromesh unit and check that the alignment marks on the hub and splined sleeve coincide (photo). Fit the synchromesh unit to the secondary shaft. The assembly pins on the synchromesh unit are marked with three grooves and these must be positioned towards the 1st gear pinion (Fig. 6.11). Then fit the 2nd gear pinion and its bush (photo).

5   Fit the adjustment washer to the shaft next (photos). As with the shims earlier, the thickness of the washer required will already have been determined during the checks on dismantling. However if, for the reasons listed in paragraph 3, the size of the washer is not known, fit one that is 2.60 mm (0.1024 in) thick for now. Again, as for the adjustment shims, you may have to change this after doing the clearance and centring checks as stated in paragraph 15.

6   After the adjusting washer, fit the 3rd gear pinion and its bush (photo). Assemble the cones to the 3rd/4th synchromesh unit and check that the alignment marks on the hub and splined sleeve coincide (photo). Fit the synchromesh unit to the secondary shaft. The assembly pins on this unit are marked with one groove which must be positioned towards the 3rd gear pinion (Fig. 6.12). Then fit the 4th gear pinion

5.2 Fit a new circlip in the secondary shaft ball-bearing housing

5.3a Enter the shaft into the housing and ...

5.3b ... fit the 1st driven pinion and its bush

5.4a Assemble the 1st/2nd synchromesh unit

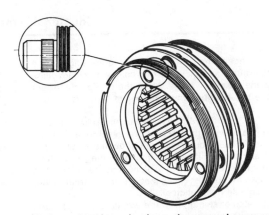

Fig. 6.11 The 1st/2nd synchroniser pins have three annular grooves (Sec 5)

5.4b Fit the synchro unit and 2nd gear pinion to the secondary shaft

5.5a The adjustment washer has two internal lugs which ...

5.5b ... locate in the shaft/grooves when fitted

5.6a Fit the third gear pinion and its bush to the secondary shaft

5.6b Assemble the 3rd/4th synchromesh unit ...

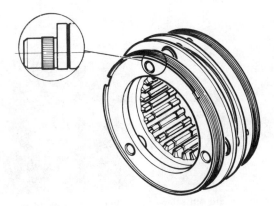

Fig. 6.12 The 3rd/4th synchroniser pins have a single annular groove (Sec 5)

5.6c ... and fit it with the 4th gear pinion to the shaft

and its bush (photo).

7   Gently tap the secondary shaft assembly into the housing. As the ball-bearing approaches its circlip, hold the ring open with circlip pliers and continue to tap the assembly home. Allow the circlip to contract into its groove in the ball-bearing outer race when they are aligned (photo).

8   Insert the 1st/2nd and 3rd/4th gear selector forks into the assembly, engaging them with their respective synchromesh units (photo). Insert the 1st/2nd selector fork spindle through the hole in the 3rd/4th selector fork and position it with the interlock plunger notch on the axis of the plunger hole. Fit an interlock plunger in the hole to rest on the 1st/2nd fork selector spindle; check that it is not protruding into the 3rd/4th selector spindle hole (photos).

9   Hold the 3rd/4th selector spindle with the two flats on it upwards and fit the stop pin in its hole, using a little grease to retain it in position (photo). Fit the spindle to the housing and, at the same time, to its selector block (photo). Rotate the spindle $\frac{1}{4}$ turn towards the selector mechanism cover. Fit new roll pins to the selector fork spindles, forks and selector block (photos).

10 Fit the second interlock plunger into its hole.

11 Fit the reverse gear pinion to the secondary shaft with the shallow boss in contact with the ball-bearing inner race, then fit the speedometer drive worm wheel (photos). These are secured by a dished spring washer and circlip, but first put the dished washer in position on the shaft with its outer rim in contact with the worm wheel and check that, when the circlip is fitted, the washer will be compressed slightly. If this is not the case a shim will have to be fitted between the reverse gear pinion and the speedometer drive worm wheel to ensure that the washer is compressed. When satisfactory, put the circlip on the bevelled end of the shaft and use a tubular drift to tap it into position in its groove (photos).

12 Fit the reverse selector spindle to its bearing location in the housing with the flats towards the selector mechanism cover and fit the selector fork when at full travel (photos). If the selector block has been removed, fit it to the spindle and secure with a new roll pin.

13 Turn the spindle so that the selector block points upwards and fit the spring and ball to their location in the block (photo). Compress the spring by lowering the block and move the selector to the neutral position.

14 Fit the three springs and balls to the spindle detents and check that the locating spigot (roll pin) is in position in the face on which the selector mechanism cover beds. Fit a new gasket and fit the cover using new washers under the heads of the four retaining bolts (photos). Tighten the bolts to the specified torque. Check the operation of the four forward gear selectors – do not operate the reverse gear – and make sure that the action is smooth and positive. Leave the selectors in the neutral position.

15 Fit the secondary shaft needle bearing inner race. Early models have a washer which must first be fitted, but later models have a recess counterbored in the race. This must be fitted to contact the 4th driven pinion bush (photo). Tap the race into position using a suitable tubular drift (such as a socket spanner) and fit a new retaining nut, but only tighten it lightly to (say) 3 lbf ft (about 0.5 kgf m) at this stage as the centring of the driven pinions on the secondary shaft must be checked. The procedure is described in Section 3, paragraphs 17 to 19 to which reference should be made. If, due to new parts for example, the centring check reveals the need for adjustment, the transmission assembly will have to be dismantled to have the appropriate shims and/or adjusting washer fitted to the secondary shaft assembly (photo).

16 When the centring of the pinions has been achieved satisfactorily, or if there is no need for adjustment, fit the reverse idler spindle and the idler pinion. Engage the reverse selector fork with the pinion as it is assembled and then fit a new roll pin to secure the spindle in the housing (photos).

17 Apply a light smear of sealer around the mating rim of the oil collector cup and fit it in its location in the housing. Tap it gently into position, making sure that the oil delivery spigot centres with the end of the secondary shaft (photo).

18 Fit a new O-ring to the speedometer drive assembly and smear lightly with grease. Fit the drive to the housing, meshing the worm and wheel, and align the locking screw holes. Fit the locking screw and its locknut, but do not tighten them until the power unit is installed in the car and the speedometer drive cable is fitted (photo).

5.7 Allow the circlip to contract into the outer race groove (arrowed)

5.8a Insert the two selector forks and ...

5.8b ... fit the selector spindle

5.8c An interlock plunger being fitted using a magnet

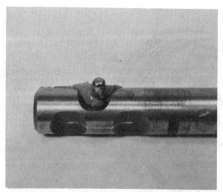
5.9a Fit the stop pin to the 3rd/4th selector spindle using grease to retain it in position

5.9b Fit the selector block as the spindle is installed

5.9c Fit new roll pins to the selector forks ...

5.9d ... and selector block

5.11a Fit the reverse gear pinion with its shallow boss towards the bearing, then ...

5.11b ... fit the speedometer drive worm wheel followed by ...

5.11c ... the dished washer with its outer rim contacting the worm wheel and ...

5.11d ... use a tubular drift to secure the circlip

5.12a Fit the reverse selector spindle ...

5.12b ... and the selector fork

5.13 Fit the spring and ball to the reverse selector block

5.14a Fitting one of the three detent balls using a magnet

5.14b Fit the three springs and then ...

5.14c ... fit the selector mechanism cover

5.15a The needle bearing inner race being fitted to the secondary shaft

5.15b Using a home-made gauge to check the centering of the driven pinions

5.16a Fitting the reverse idler pinion and selector fork followed by ...

5.16b ... the spindle and ...

5.16c ... a new roll pin to secure it

5.17 Fitting the oil collector cup

5.18 The speedometer drive being fitted

5.19a New half bearing shells being fitted to the mainshaft bearing

5.19b Fit a new circlip (arrowed) to the input shaft

5.20a Fit the mainshaft

5.20b Enter the input shaft into the housing and ...

5.20c ... when engaged with the mainshaft the circlip will expand into its groove

19 Fit new half bearing shells to the mainshaft bearing and cap (photo). Fit a new rubber washer in the mainshaft/input shaft coupling and fit a new circlip to the input shaft (photo). Check that the half bearing locating spigots are fitted in the main housing and lubricate the half bearing shells.

20 Place the mainshaft in the housing (photo) and enter the input shaft through its plain bearing, taking care not to damage the bearing surface (photo). With the notch in the mainshaft coupling upwards, engage the input shaft in the coupling. Compress the circlip on the input shaft and push the shaft into the coupling until the circlip expands into its groove in the mainshaft (photo).

21 Fit the bearing cap with the mark D towards the mainshaft (photo). Fit new plain washers to the two retaining bolts and tighten them to the specified torque (photo).

22 Fit the mainshaft ball-bearing to the housing and shaft, making sure that the extractor groove is towards the outside of the housing (photo). Tap the bearing home with a tubular drift on the inner race and make sure that it is fully seated. Fit a new dished washer and drift a new circlip over the bevelled end of the shaft. Compress the ring into

the shaft groove and check that its outside diameter does not exceed 22.6 mm (0.8898 in) (photos).

23 Engage 1st gear and also engage the reverse idler pinion in order to lock the gear train. Tighten the secondary shaft nut to its specified torque (photos).

24 Return the 1st gear to the neutral position then fit a new roll pin to the reverse gear selector fork and spindle (photo). Operate all gear selections, including reverse, and check that selection is smooth and positive both in engagement and disengagement.

25 Lock the secondary shaft nut by squeezing the skirt onto the shaft flats using a pair of self-grip pliers. Don't use a hammer to do this as the bearings or shaft could be damaged (photo).

26 Fit the mainshaft ball-bearing triangular retaining plate and tighten the three bolts to the specified torque load (photo).

27 Assemble the outer races to the differential taper bearings and place the assembly in its location in the transmission housing (photo). Coat the mating faces of the differential half-housing and the transmission housing with a sealing compound and assemble them (photo). Using new spring washers fit the four long and the four short

5.21a When fitting the bearing cap make sure that the D (arrowed) is towards the mainshaft, then ...

5.21b ... tighten the bolts to the correct torque

5.22a Fit the mainshaft ball-bearing with the extractor groove outwards, then ...

5.22b ... fit the dished washer and a new circlip

5.22c Measure the circlip to ensure that it is fully contracted

5.23a Engage 1st gear and the reverse idler pinion (both arrowed) to lock the gear train ...

5.23b ... and tighten the secondary shaft nut

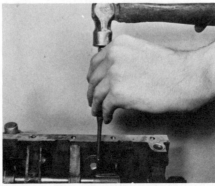
5.24 Fitting a new roll pin to the reverse gear selector fork and spindle

5.25 Lock the nut by squeezing the skirt into the shaft flats

5.26 Fit the bearing retainer plate and tighten the securing bolts

5.27a Place the differential assembly in the half bearings and ...

5.27b ... fit the differential half-housing

5.28a Fit the end cover after removing the oil seal and ...

5.28b ... lightly tighten the securing bolts

5.29a Measuring from the cover mounting face to the outer race face and ...

5.29b ... measuring from the cover inner face to the mounting flange face

5.30a Fitting the shims and the cover which has a new O-ring

5.30b Tighten the short bolts in the differential housing first ...

5.30c ... followed by the long bolts ...

5.30d ... and finally the cover bolts

5.31a Fit a new seal to both final drive apertures and ...

5.31b ... fill the space between the lips of the seal with grease

5.32a Fit a new seal to the sump screen and ...

5.32b ... then fit the screen to the bottom of the transmission unit

5.33a Use a new gasket and fit the sump cover ...

5.33b ... fitting the exhaust bracket at the same time

bolts but *do not* tighten them at this stage.

28 Check that the oil seal has been removed from the differential end cover and fit the cover to the differential housing, tightening the four retaining bolts only lightly to about 7 lbf ft (1 kgf m) (photos). Now lightly tighten the four smaller (8 mm dia.) bolts in the differential housing to 3 or 4 lbf ft (0.5 kgf m). When you have done this, undo the bolts in the end cover and remove the cover. Check that the outer race is bedded down on the rollers.

29 The taper bearings have to be slightly loaded when assembled and this condition is obtained by fitting shims under the end cover so that when it is bolted down a precise nip is achieved. To establish what size shims must be fitted, a couple of precision measurements must now be made. Use a depth gauge or a vernier gauge to measure the distance from the cover mounting face on the differential housing to the outer race face whilst lightly pressing the differential unit in (photo). Next measure the distance on the bearing cover from the face on the mounting flange to the face which would contact the outer race when assembled if it extended enough (photo). Subtract the second measurement from the first – this gives the space between the cover and the bearing race. Now add 0.2 mm (0.0079 in) to that figure to give the thickness of the shims which must be used to obtain the correct preloading.

30 Fit a new greased O-ring to the cover and coat the cover mating surface with a sealing compound. Position the correct adjustment shims on the bearing outer race and fit the cover to the differential housing (photo). Use new spring washers under the bolt heads and tighten the bolts in the differential unit to the specified torque in the following sequence (photos):

(a) 8 mm dia short bolts in half-housing
(b) 10 mm dia long bolts in half-housing
(c) Cover bolts

31 Lightly grease and fit a new double lip oil seal to both apertures in the differential drives (photo). Use a suitable drift and tap the seals in gently until they bottom on the flange in the apertures. Before the driveshafts are fitted on installing the power unit, the space between the two lips on each seal must be filled with grease (photo).

32 Fit a new rubber grommet to the oil sump screen (photo), and fit the screen to its location on the bottom of the transmission (photo). Tighten the three securing bolts to the specified torque.

33 Check that the mating faces of the transmission housing and the sump cover are clean and undamaged. Use a new gasket and fit the sump cover (photo). When fitting the bolts use the special lockplates and locate the three longer bolts on which the exhaust bracket is mounted in their correct holes, that is, the middle three on the rear edge (photo). Tighten the bolts to the correct torque. Fit a new sealing washer to the sump drain plug and tighten the plug to the specified torque.

34 The dipstick tube and the external oil pipe are best fitted after the transmission has been assembled to the engine, see the next Section for details.

6 Transmission-to-engine – reassembly

1 Refitting the transmission to the engine is a straightforward job. A total of fourteen bolts join the two assemblies in two flange joints. one on the front and one to the rear of the unit.

2 First check that the mating faces are clean and undamaged and then smear them with a jointing compound. Lower the engine onto the transmission housing, guiding the two locating dowels into their spigot holes (photo).

3 Fit the coil mounting bracket to the second and third bolts from the right on the rear flange joint (photo). The manifold support bracket fits to the centre bolt in the rear flange joint, but it can be left until the manifold is fitted or after installation of the power unit, whichever is more convenient.

4 Fit the retaining bolts and tighten them evenly and progressively to the specified torque.

5 If the transmission unit has just been overhauled the reversing light switch can be fitted and tightened to its specified torque (photos). Fit the external oil pipe using a new joint washer on each face of the banjos – four washers together. Make sure that everything is clean

6.2 Lowering the engine onto the transmission housing

6.3 Fit the coil mounting bracket. Note that the manifold support bracket bolt has been left until engine installation (arrow)

6.5a Using a new sealing washer, fit the reversing light switch and ...

6.5b ... tighten to the correct torque

6.5c Tightening the external oil pipe banjo bolts

6.6 The dipstick can be fitted at any convenient stage of assembly

before assembly and tighten the two banjo bolts to the specified torque (photo).

6   Apply thread locking compound to the dipstick tube threads and fit the tube to its location in the transmission housing. Tighten to the specified torque. If further assembly of the power unit remains to be done, eg starter assembly etc, the refitting of the dipstick tube can be left until after the other components have been fitted (photo).

7   If necessary, complete the reassembly of the power unit by reversing the dismantling sequence listed in Section 2.

7   Engine/transmission – installation

As the transmission can only be installed in the car as part of the assembled power unit the procedure is dealt with in Chapter 1 to which reference should be made.

8   Differential oil seals – removal and refitting

1   The differential oil seals can be renewed with the engine/transmission unit installed in the car, but the driveshafts will obviously have to be removed first. This procedure is contained in Chapter 7.

2   With the driveshafts withdrawn, lever out the old oil seals from the differential unit housing using a screwdriver. Take care not to damage the housing.

3   Clean out the seating before installing a new seal. Lightly grease the new seal to assist assembly and gently tap it into position, with the flat side outwards and using a suitable drift which will not damage the seal, until it beds on the limiting flange in the differential housing. Repeat for the other seal.

4   Pack the space between the two lips in each seal with grease before refitting the driveshafts. Clean the driveshafts before refitting and take great care not to damage the new seals as the shafts are being re-engaged with the differential.

9   Floor mounted gearchange – overhaul and adjustment

1   The floor mounted gearchange mechanism is illustrated in Fig. 6.13. Normally this mechanism gives no problems, and overhaul consists of checking the individual components for wear and/or damage, lubricating the balljoints and pivot and renewing them if necessary. Unless there has been gross neglect, or the car has covered a high mileage or suffered damage, it is unlikely that renewal will be necessary.

2   To adjust the linkage, or when renewing it, set the lengths of the adjustable rod or link to those shown in Fig. 6.15; check that the selection link length between centres is correct, Fig. 6.16.

3   On assembly lubricate all moving joints with the specified grease.

10   Fault diagnosis – transmission

Note: *It is sometimes difficult to decide whether it is worthwhile removing and dismantling the gearbox for a fault which may be nothing more than a minor irritant. Gearboxes which howl, or where the synchromesh can be 'beaten' by a quick gearchange, may continue to perform for a long time in this state. A worn gearbox usually needs a complete rebuild to eliminate noise because the various gears, if realigned on new bearings, will contined to howl when different wearing surfaces are presented to each other.*

The decision to overhaul therefore, must be considered with regard to time and money available, relative to the degree of noise or malfunction that the driver has to suffer.

Gearbox noisy in neutral

1   In neutral with the engine running the rotating parts are the input shaft, primary shaft, and the four gear pinions; all bearings in this train are plain bush, except at the timing case end of the primary shaft which is a ball-bearing. Noise can result from excessively worn gear teeth or bearings and worn circlips or dished washers. Examine the gearbox for these faults and rectify by renewal.

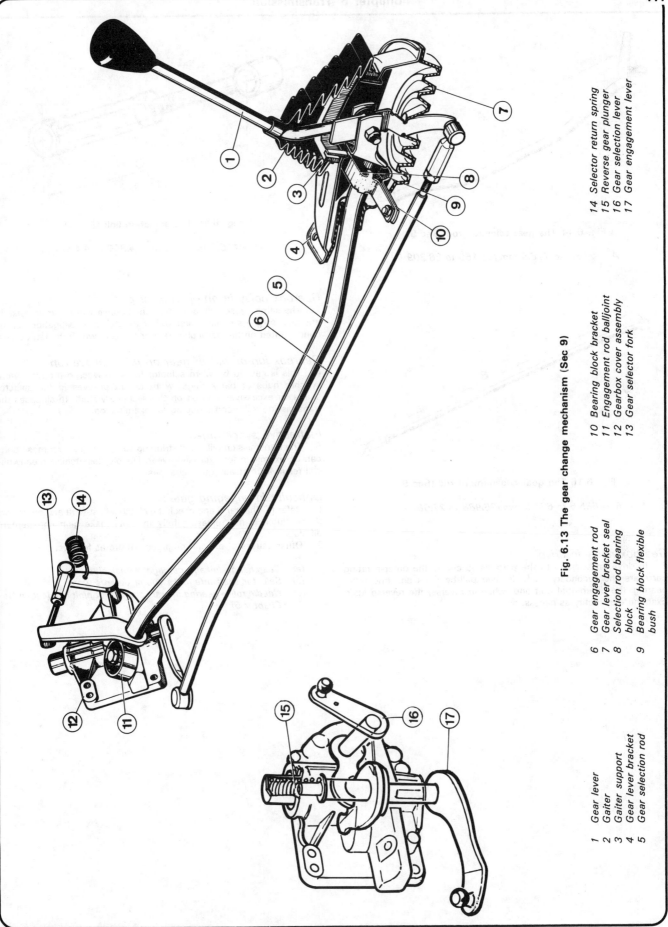

Fig. 6.13 The gear change mechanism (Sec 9)

1 Gear lever
2 Gaiter
3 Gaiter support
4 Gear lever bracket
5 Gear selection rod

6 Gear engagement rod
7 Gear lever bracket seal
8 Selection rod bearing block
9 Bearing block flexible bush

10 Bearing block bracket
11 Engagement rod balljoint
12 Gearbox cover assembly
13 Gear selector fork

14 Selector return spring
15 Reverse gear plunger
16 Gear selection lever
17 Gear engagement lever

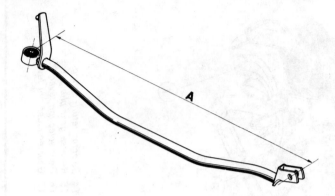

Fig. 6.14 The gear selection rod (Sec 9)

A = 715.5 to 716.5 mm (28.169 to 28.209 in)

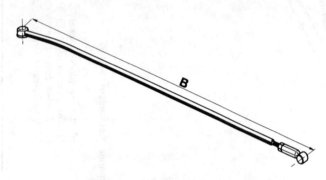

Fig. 6.15 The gear engagement rod (Sec 9)

B = 685.5 to 657.5 mm (26.988 to 27.067 in)

Gearbox noisy in drive
2   In drive, in addition to the parts listed above, the other rotating parts are the secondary shaft, its two ball-bearings and one roller bearing, the differential unit and (when in reverse) the reverse idler. Examine and rectify as necessary.

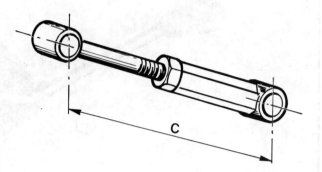

Fig. 6.16 The selection link (Sec 9)

C = 110.5 to 112.5 mm (4.350 to 4.429 in)

Gearbox noisy in one particular gear
3   The same causes already mentioned above will result in noise in any gear or gears when selected, but the defect investigation can be concentrated on the particular train or trains in which the fault exists.

Gearbox jumps out of gear on drive or overrun
4   This is caused by worn selector forks or synchro grooves; worn synchro hubs or baulk rings; worn detent grooves in the selector shafts, or excessive endfloat on the secondary shaft. In all cases the transmission will need stripping for examination.

Ineffective synchromesh
5   The transmission will need stripping so that the synchromesh units can be examined for excessive wear. Double declutching meanwhile will result in relatively quiet changes.

Difficulty in engaging gears
6   Refer to Chapter 5 and check the clutch adjustment and operation. If the clutch is not releasing fully this will make gear engagement difficult.
7   Other causes of difficult engagement are as follows:

   (a)   *Gearchange linkage damage or maladjusted*
   (b)   *Selector shaft interlocks and/or detents worn*
   (c)   *Needle roller bearing in crankshaft input pinion defective (see Chapter 5)*

Chapter 7 Driveshafts, hubs, wheels and tyres

For modifications, and information applicable to later models, see Supplement at end of manual

Contents

Specifications

Driveshafts .... Front wheel driveshafts each having two tripod constant velocity joints; inner end splines permit axial movement

Wheel hub bearings
Front .... Twin track ball-bearings
Rear .... Two tapered roller bearings
Lubricant type/specification .... Multi-purpose lithium-based grease (Duckhams LB 10)

Wheels
Type .... Pressed steel disc, 3-stud fixing or light alloy
Size .... $4\frac{1}{2}$J 14.3.45
Maximum permitted warp .... 1.5 mm (0.0591 in) on rim
Maximum permitted eccentricity .... 1.2 mm (0.0472 in) on bead seat

Tyres
Type .... Radial ply, tubeless

Sizes and pressures in bars (lbf/in²):	Front	Rear
145 x 14	1.8 (26)	2.1 (30.5)
155 x 14	1.9 (27.6)	2.1 (30.5)

Torque wrench settings

	lbf ft	kgf m
Oil sump drain plug	19.9	2.75
Balljoint pin clamp bolt	36.2	5
Driveshaft/hub nut	181	25
Wheel nuts or bolts:		
Pressed steel	43.4	6
Light alloy	63	8.5
Bump stop bolt	9.4	1.3
Track control arm inboard pivot nut	39.8	5.5
Anti-roll bar slotted nut:		
Minimum	43.4	6
Maximum	86.8	12
Rear hub retaining nut:		
Initial	21.7	3
Final	7.2	1

1 General description

The drive to the front wheels of the Peugeot 305 is transmitted directly from the final drive/differential unit on the front of the gearbox to the front wheel hubs by two driveshafts. Constant velocity universal joints are fitted near each end of the shafts to accommodate the steering and suspension angular movements. The inner ends of the shafts mate with the final drives with sliding splines which plunge to allow changes in length of the drives resulting from suspension and steering movements.

Little maintenance by the home mechanic is possible on the driveshafts. Even changing the rubber bellows is a specialised operation which is best entrusted to your Peugeot dealer.

The driveshafts are splined into the front wheel hubs. These run on double row ball-races located in the hub carrier at the bottom of each front shock absorber strut.

The rear wheel hubs run on conventional taper-roller bearings on stub axles in the rear trailing arms.

2 Driveshafts – removal and refitting

1 Position a suitable container under the engine oil drain plug in the sump cover, remove the plug and drain the engine oil. Clean around the plug hole, fit a new sealing washer to the plug, refit it and tighten to the specified torque. To avoid inadvertent starting of the engine before the oil is replenished, disconnect the battery earth cable.

2 Apply the handbrake and engage first gear. Remove one of the wheel nuts and remove the hub cap. Undo and remove the driveshaft nut and the washer under it. Slacken the other two wheelnuts.

3 Under the car clean off all road dirt, oil and grease from the areas at both ends of the driveshaft. When the driveshaft has been removed it is important not to contaminate the exposed bearings etc with dirt. The driveshaft must now be prevented from withdrawing from the final drive/differential unit during the early removal stages. Peugeot have a

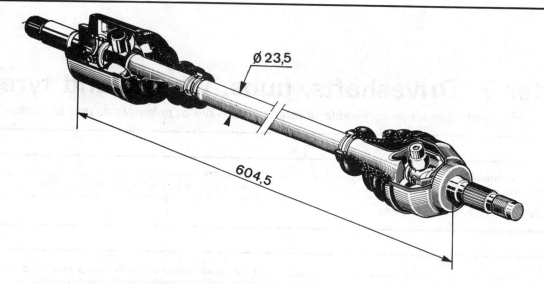

Fig. 7.1 Two similar driveshafts are fitted to the Peugeot 305. Dimensions in mm (Sec 1)

special tool to do this but a makeshift arrangement can be achieved with wire around the shaft and around protruding bolts in the differential case.

4   Undo the balljoint pin clamp nut over the outer end of the track control arm. Remove the split pin and remove the slotted nut, and washers, from the end of the anti-roll bar protruding through the track control arm. Remove the nut from the track control arm inner end pivot bolt. Undo and remove the rear bolt holding the bump stop over the inner end pivot bolt (photos).

5   Remove the clamp bolt from the track control arm outer end attachment, remove the bump stop from the inner end attachment and remove the inner end track control arm pivot bolt.

6   With a jack under the front jacking point (just behind the wheel arch), raise the front end of the car and support it on a stand or substantial blocks. Withdraw the inner end of the track control arm from its attachment bracket and position a block of wood 120 mm (4.7 in) thick under the front wheel. Lower the car onto its wheels and free the balljoint pin from its clamp. If necessary prise the clamp open carefully to release the pin (Fig. 7.2).

7   Raise the front end again and support the car on stands or blocks. Turn the wheel inwards at the front and disengage the track control arm from the anti-roll bar. Take care not to damage the rubber boot on the balljoint. Retrieve the spacer and washer from the anti-roll bar, noting which way they are fitted for reassembly.

8   Carefully move the shock absorber strut out sideways, easing the driveshaft splines out of the wheel hub.

9   Remove the makeshift wire retainer and, turning the wheel outwards at the front to the full extent, remove the driveshaft from the final drive/differential unit. Be prepared for a slight oil spillage on removal.

10 Lever out the oil seal in the final drive/differential unit, and also the

one in the wheel hub. Both seals must be renewed on refitting the driveshaft.

11 Lightly grease a new, double-lipped oil seal and carefully tap it into its recess in the final drive/differential unit with the side containing the spring facing into the unit. Make sure that the seal is abutting the internal shoulder in the unit case. Fill the space between the double lips with general-purpose grease. Similarly fit a new seal, of similar pattern, in the wheel hub, making sure that it abuts the bearing retaining ring. Again, fill the space between the lips with grease.

12 Check the driveshaft before fitting to make sure that it is free of obvious defects. Clean the splines at both ends and, at the wheel hub end only, give the splines a thin coat of Molykote 321R or a suitable alternative anti-friction agent.

13 Carefully fit the driveshaft to the final drive/differential unit and be sure not to damage the oil seal. Prevent the shaft from disengaging with wire, tying it back to the differential unit.

14 Insert the driveshaft into the wheel hub, again exercising caution to avoid damaging the oil seal. Fit the thrust washer and a new nut but don't tighten it yet.

15 Refit the spacer and washer to the anti-roll bar, observing the correct assembly as noted in paragraph 7. Then fit the track control arm to the end of the anti-roll bar. Take care not to damage the balljoint rubber boot.

16 Insert the balljoint pivot into its clamp on the hub assembly casting, then fit the clamp bolt with its head to the rear. Fit the washer and slotted nut to the anti-roll bar, leaving the nut loose for the moment.

17 Locate the bump stop on its bracket, fit a new plain washer to the bolt and fit the bolt with its head upwards. Put a second plain washer on the bolt and fit a new Nylstop nut, but don't tighten it yet.

2.4a The balljoint pin clamp bolt, A, the anti-roll bar slotted nut, B, and ...

2.4b ... the track control arm inner end pivot bolt and nut

2.4c The bump stop nut and bolt (arrowed)

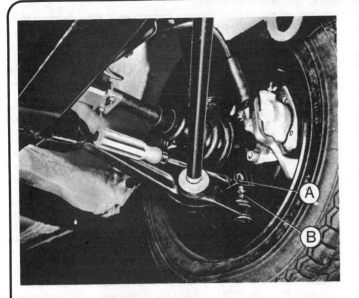

Fig. 7.2 Prise the clamp, A, open if necessary to remove the balljoint pin, B (Sec 2)

Fig. 7.3 With the car on stands, turn the front of the wheel in (Sec 2)

Fig. 7.4 When disengaging the track control arm from the anti-roll bar, take care not to damage the rubber boot, A, and retrieve the washer, B, and the spacer, C (Sec 2)

Fig. 7.5 Pivot the strut out, remove the shaft from the hub and then withdraw the shaft from the transmission (Sec 2)

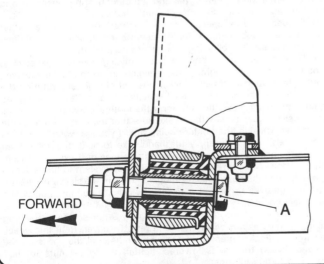

Fig. 7.6 Assembly details of the track control rod inner pivot and bump stop (Sec 2)

A   Bolt head to rear

FORWARD

18 Tighten the nut on the balljoint pin clamp bolt to the specified torque.

19 Lower the vehicle to the ground. It is now necessary to load the front end of the car so that the rubber bush hole in the inboard end of the track control arm aligns with the bolt holes in the arm's mounting bracket. Peugeot have a special tool to pull the car down on its springs whilst it is raised on a lift. If you can get hold of a set of spring compressors this could be your solution; it may be possible to compress the front springs sufficiently to achieve the right geometry. Failing that, if you have some well-developed friends perhaps they could be encouraged to add some weight, so to speak. With the track control arm lined up, fit the inboard pivot bolt with its head to the rear, fit a plain washer and a new Nylstop nut but don't tighten it. Unclamp the spring compressors or dismiss the heavy squad, as appropriate, and remove the wire retaining the driveshaft to the differential case.

20 Tighten the driveshaft nut to its specified torque and, with a suitable blunt punch, deform the rim on the nut into the groove in the shaft to lock it. Fit the wheel hub cap and the third wheel nut. Tighten all wheel nuts to their specified torque.

21 Release the handbrake and select neutral. Relax the suspension by rocking the car forwards and backwards slightly to allow the assembly to assume its normal position, then re-apply the handbrake.

22 Refit the spring compressors, or reload the front suspension, so that there is a gap of 50 mm (1.97 in) between the driveshafts and the wing valances. This is best set by using a block of wood on each side, cut to the dimension given, and interposing them between the shafts and the wing valances.

23 Tighten the track control arm inboard pivot bolt nut to its specified torque. Tighten the nut and bolt securing the bump stop to the specified torque.

24 Tighten the slotted nut on the anti-roll bar to its specified torque load. If the split pin hole doesn't line up with a slot in the nut tighten a little more until it does align, but don't exceed the maximum permitted torque specification. Fit a new 3 mm (7/64 in nearest equivalent) split pin to lock the nut, then remove the spring compressors or the front suspension load as applicable.

25 Check the front wheel toe-in, referring to Chapter 9.

26 Replenish the engine oil and reconnect the battery earth cable.

3 Driveshaft joints – maintenance

1 As has been stated earlier, there is little maintenance which can be done by the home mechanic on the driveshaft joints. Any attempt to dismantle them will be thwarted by the need for special equipment – particularly for reassembly.

2 In view of this it is recommended that work on the driveshafts is limited to removal, visual inspection, cleaning etc, and refitting only. Any repair or overhaul should be entrusted to a Peugeot garage.

3 Any leakage of grease from the joint protector or rubber boot must have immediate attention. Apart from the loss of the special lubricant, the risk of dirt contamination of the joint concerned demands prompt remedial action. Either take the car to a Peugeot garage or remove the shaft concerned and take that to the garage for expert attention.

4 Front wheel hub bearings – removal and refitting

1 The front hub bearings are twin track ball-races and removal for cleaning, inspection or replacement necessitates removing the wheel hub and brake disc.

2 The hub and disc unit will have to be separated from the strut assembly using a Peugeot special tool as it is not possible to use the usual sort of three or two-legged puller. As the same tool is used for extracting and inserting the bearings, as well as reassembling the hub and disc unit to the strut, it will be obvious that, either this tool must be borrowed or hired, or the job will have to be done by a Peugeot agent who will have the tool. As it is a simple matter to remove the absorber strut, and in any case removing the strut will make the job far easier, it is recommended that the strut is removed as explained in Chapter 9 and the assembly taken to the nearest Peugeot agent for servicing. The two oil seals will need renewing regardless of the condition of the bearings.

3 Reassembly is the reverse of the removal procedure. When tightening nuts and bolts, do so with the weight of the car on the suspension and tighten to the specified torque.

5 Rear wheel hub bearings – removal and refitting

1 Each rear wheel runs on a pair of taper-roller bearings which must be renewed as a complete pair on a hub if the need arises.

2 To remove a rear hub, first slacken the wheel nuts of the wheel concerned. Select first gear and chock the front wheels. Jack up the rear of the car and support it on stands or substantial blocks with the wheels free. Remove the wheel nuts and the wheel, then prise off the hub cover. Undo and remove the two countersunk screws retaining the brake drum and remove the drum. If difficulty arises removing the drum, refer to Section 7, Chapter 8. Take care not to spread any brake dust in the atmosphere or, in particular, inhale it as it is a health hazard. Clean out the dust. If grease or hydraulic fluid has contaminated the brake shoes they will have to be removed, as described in Chapter 8.

3 Undo the hub retaining nut and discard it as a new one is necessary on reassembly. Remove the thrust washer from the stub axle and remove the hub. Prise out the grease seal in the back of the hub and remove the O-ring seal from the cover locating spigot.

4 Remove the outer and inner bearings from the hub, if they have not already been removed, and identify them so that they can be refitted to their original position if they are fit for re-use. Clean the bearings and their tracks thoroughly. Examine them for signs of wear, overheating indicated by discolouration, pitting and any other damage. New bearings should be fitted if there is any evidence of deterioration or any doubt about their condition.

5 Only remove the bearing tracks if it is intended to renew them. Carefully drift them out using suitable drifts and supports for the hub. Clean the bearing track housings before fitting new tracks. A bearing and its outer track are matched components and they must be fitted together. Don't degrease new bearings before fitting them. The best way of fitting new bearings is with a large draw bolt and two thrust plates, or suitable large socket spanners if available. Make sure that the tracks are fully bedded in their locations.

6 After fitting the outer tracks, fit the inner bearing to the hub after greasing it thoroughly with general-purpose grease. Fit a new oil seal, with its lip facing in towards the hub and its outer face flush with the hub rim. Wipe off all surplus grease from the outside of the hub (photo).

7 Before refitting the hub, fit the outer bearing to the cleaned stub axle and ensure that it slides on easily. If it doesn't, use some emery cloth on the axle bearing surface cautiously to obtain a free fit. Make sure that all traces of emery dust are cleaned off afterwards (photo).

8 Try the new nut on the stub axle threads and screw it down to check that there is no abnormal resistance. If necessary deburr the grooves in the axle into which the rim of the nut is to be staked.

9 When all is satisfactory fit the hub and push it on until it is properly located. Put a minimum of 80g (2.8 oz) of general-purpose grease inside the hub bore. Then fit the greased outer bearing inner race and the flat safety washer. Fit the new nut (photos).

10 Peugeot use a special tool to tighten the nut in a rather complicated procedure. A fairly accurate result can be obtained without the tool by following this suggested procedure.

11 Fit the brake drum and its two retaining countersunk screws. Rotate the drum and tighten the retaining nut to the initial specified torque (see Specifications). Slacken the nut off and, still rotating the drum, tighten the nut to the final specified torque. Stop rotating the drum and do not move the nut. Apply the footbrake two or three times to adjust the rear brakes (but make sure that the brake drum on the other rear wheel is fitted before doing this, if you are working on both rear wheels), and then apply the handbrake to hold the brake drum during the next stage. Carefully note the position of the nut relative to the axle and *slacken* it through 30°. This is equivalent to half a flat on the nut. Keep the nut in this position and deform the sleeve on the nut into the grooves on the axle to lock it, using a suitable punch and hammer (photos).

12 If it has not already been done, fit a new O-ring seal to the bearing cover locating spigot on the hub and refit the cover. Refit the wheel, leaving the final tightening of the wheel nuts until the car is on the ground. When the car is lowered, tighten the wheel nuts to their specified torque (photos).

5.6 The oil seal in the rear wheel hub

5.7 The rear wheel stub axle (brake assembly removed)

5.9a After fitting the rear wheel hub ...

5.9b ... fit the outer bearing followed by ...

5.9c ... the safety washer

5.11a Tighten the nut as explained in the text

5.11b Punch the nut skirt into the axle grooves

5.12a With a new O-ring seal on the drum, fit the bearing cover

5.12b Tighten the wheel nuts

6   Wheels and tyres – general care and maintenance

Wheels and tyres should give no real problems in use provided that a close eye is kept on them with regard to excessive wear or damage. To this end, the following points should be noted.

Ensure that tyre pressures are checked regularly and maintained correctly. Checking should be carried out with the tyres cold and not immediately after the vehicle has been in use. If the pressures are checked with the tyres hot, an apparently high reading will be obtained owing to heat expansion. Under no circumstances should an attempt be made to reduce the pressures to the quoted cold reading in this instance, or effective underinflation will result.

Underinflation will cause overheating of the tyre owing to excessive flexing of the casing, and the tread will not sit correctly on the road surface. This will cause a consequent loss of adhesion and excessive wear, not to mention the danger of sudden tyre failure due to heat build-up.

Overinflation will cause rapid wear of the centre part of the tyre tread coupled with reduced adhesion, harsher ride, and the danger of shock damage occurring in the tyre casing.

Regularly check the tyres for damage in the form of cuts or bulges, especially in the sidewalls. Remove any nails or stones embedded in the tread before they penetrate the tyre to cause deflation. If removal of a nail *does* reveal that the tyre has been punctured, refit the nail so that its point of penetration is marked. Then immediately change the wheel and have the tyre repaired by a tyre dealer. Do *not* drive on a tyre in such a condition. In many cases a puncture can be simply repaired by the use of an inner tube of the correct size and type. If in any doubt as to the possible consequences of any damage found, consult your local tyre dealer for advice.

Periodically remove the wheels and clean any dirt or mud from the inside and outside surfaces. Examine the wheel rims for signs of rusting, corrosion or other damage. Light alloy wheels are easily damaged by 'kerbing' whilst parking, and similarly steel wheels may become dented or buckled. Renewal of the wheel is very often the only course of remedial action possible.

The balance of each wheel and tyre assembly should be maintained to avoid excessive wear, not only to the tyres but also to the steering and suspension components. Wheel imbalance is normally signified by vibration through the vehicle's bodyshell, although in many cases it is particularly noticeable through the steering wheel. Conversely, it should be noted that wear or damage in suspension or steering components may cause excessive tyre wear. Out-of-round or out-of-true tyres, damaged wheels and wheel bearing wear/maladjustment also fall into this category. Balancing will not usually cure vibration caused by such wear.

Wheel balancing may be carried out with the wheel either on or off the vehicle. If balanced on the vehicle, ensure that the wheel-to-hub relationship is marked in some way prior to subsequent wheel removal so that it may be refitted in its original position.

General tyre wear is influenced to a large degree by driving style – harsh braking and acceleration or fast cornering will all produce more rapid tyre wear. Interchanging of tyres may result in more even wear, but this should only be carried out where there is no mix of tyre types on the vehicle. However, it is worth bearing in mind that if this is completely effective, the added expense of replacing a complete set of tyres simultaneously is incurred, which may prove financially restrictive for many owners.

Front tyres may wear unevenly as a result of wheel misalignment. The front wheels should always be correctly aligned according to the settings specified by the vehicle manufacturer.

Legal restrictions apply to the mixing of tyre types on a vehicle. Basically this means that a vehicle must not have tyres of differing construction on the same axle. Although it is not recommended to mix tyre types between front axle and rear axle, the only legally permissible combination is crossply at the front and radial at the rear. When mixing radial ply tyres, textile braced radials must always go on the front axle, with steel braced radials at the rear. An obvious disadvantage of such mixing is the necessity to carry two spare tyres to avoid contravening the law in the event of a puncture.

In the UK, the Motor Vehicles Construction and Use Regulations apply to many aspects of tyre fitting and usage. It is suggested that a copy of these regulations is obtained from your local police if in doubt as to the current legal requirements with regard to tyre condition, minimum tread depth, etc.

7 Fault diagnosis – driveshafts

Symptom	Reason(s)
Knock or clunk when taking up drive	CV joints worn Splined couplings worn Front hub nuts loose or bearings worn
Vibration	Wheel nuts loose Wheels unbalanced (check for security of balance weights and accumulations of mud) CV joints or splined couplings worn
Metallic grating varying with road speed	CV joints worn Wheel bearings worn
Abnormal noise when turning	Differential unit defective CV joints worn Wheel bearings worn

Chapter 8 Braking system

For modifications, and information applicable to later models, see Supplement at end of manual

Contents

Specifications

General

Footbrake	Hydraulic dual circuit, discs front and drums rear, servo-assisted and self-adjusting
Handbrake	Mechanical, cable-operated to rear wheels only

Front disc brakes

Type	Single piston, Teves or DBA
Disc diameter	263 mm (10.3543 in)
Disc thickness:	
New	10 mm (0.3937 in)
Minimum, after machining both sides	9 mm (0.3543 in)
Minimum, renewal essential	8.5 mm (0.3346 in)
Maximum variation over disc	0.02 mm (0.0008 in)
Disc runout on hub, measured 24 mm (0.9449 in) from disc edge	0.07 mm (0.0028 in) max

Disc pads:	**Teves**	**DBA**
Type	NECTO 248 GG	NS 414
Size	44 x 75 mm	44 x 97.5 mm
	(1.7323 x 2.9528 in)	(1.7323 x 3.8386 in)
Minimum material thickness	2.5 mm (0.0984 in)	
Front wheel cylinder diameter	48 mm (1.8898 in)	

Rear drum brakes

Make	Girling or DBA
Drum internal diameter:	
New	228.6 mm (9.0000 in)
Maximum after machining	229.6 mm (9.0394 in)
Maximum difference between two drums on same axle ...	0.15 mm (0.0059 in)
Maximum ovality	0.10 mm (0.0039 in)
Maximum out-of-round, drum on hub	0.10 mm (0.0039 in)
Lining track width	47.5 mm (1.8701 in)
Shoe lining width	40 mm (1.5748 in)
Shoe linings	Ferodo 617
Rear wheel cylinder diameter:	
Girling	22 mm (0.8661 in)
DBA	23.8 mm (0.9370 in)

Master cylinder

Type	Tandem
Bore	19 mm (0.7480 in)

Servo unit

Type	Master-Vac
Diameter	150 mm (5.9055 in)

Brake fluid

Brake fluid	Hydraulic fluid to SAE J1703 (Duckhams Universal Brake and Clutch Fluid)

Torque wrench settings

	lbf ft	kgf m
Front caliper securing bolts	58	8
Bleed screw	9.0	1.25

1 General description

All Peugeot 305 models have a conventional modern brake system with disc brakes on the front wheels and drum brakes on the rear. The brakes are operated by a servo-assisted hydraulic system having a tandem master cylinder actuated by a suspended foot pedal. The dual circuit system incorporates a brake pressure regulator to prevent the rear wheels locking.

The rear brakes can be applied for parking purposes by means of a cable operated handbrake.

Various manufacturers supply system parts and in consequence there is a certain amount of variation in details in system components. In some cases the parts supplied by different makers are not interchangeable or may be interchangeable with qualification. For this reason care is needed when buying spares to get the right parts; it's best to take a sample with you, if possible.

2 Routine maintenance

1 All work undertaken on the braking system, including routine maintenance, must be to the highest standard. It is vitally important to maintain the integrity of the system and to use the right fasteners with correct locking devices where appropriate. Adjustments must be within specified limits where these apply and spare parts must be new or in faultless condition. Absolute cleanliness when assembling hydraulic components is essential. New seals and fresh hydraulic fluid must be used and any fluid drained or removed from the system must be discarded. Remember that your life and possibly the lives of others could depend on these points; if you are in any doubt at all concerning what to do or how to do it, get professional advice or have the job done by an expert.

2 If the brake system tell-tale warning light comes on and the handbrake is not applied, immediately check the level of the brake fluid (see below). If the level is satisfactory check the setting of the handbrake warning switch.

Every 5000 miles (7500 km) or six monthly

3 Thoroughly clean around the hydraulic fluid reservoir cap, remove the cap and check the fluid level. Some reservoirs are made of semi-transparent plastic and the fluid can be seen without removing the cap. Ho.vever, you should only rely on this check once you have satisfied yourself that an accurate indication of the fluid level is possible. If necessary top up with fresh fluid, but make allowances for the change in level that will occur when the cap, with its switch and float, is refitted. The level in the reservoir will rise to some extent due to displacement by the switch assembly. Check that the vent hole in the filler cap is clear. Any need for regular topping up must be viewed with suspicion and the whole hydraulic system inspected for signs of leaks. A *small*, slow fall in the level as the disc pads wear is normal.

Every 10 000 miles (15 000 km) or annually

4 Inspect the front disc pads for wear (see Section 5). The grooves in the pads should be visible, indicating that adequate pad material remains.

5 Remove the rubber inspection plugs in the rear brake backplates and inspect the shoe linings for wear. All four shoes will need renewing if the thickness of any one lining is below 2.5 mm (0.1 in) (photo).

6 Check the operation of the handbrake. The brakes should lock the wheels when the lever has been moved six to eight notches.

7 Check the clearance between the brake foot pedal and the floor when the brakes are applied, to make sure that the pedal is not bottoming.

Every 20 000 miles (30 000 km) or every 2 years

8 Remove the rear brake drums and carefully clean out the brake dust, **taking care not to inhale it or disperse it**. In addition to repeating the check for wear, inspect the shoe linings for contamination by grease from the bearings or fluid from the hydraulic system.

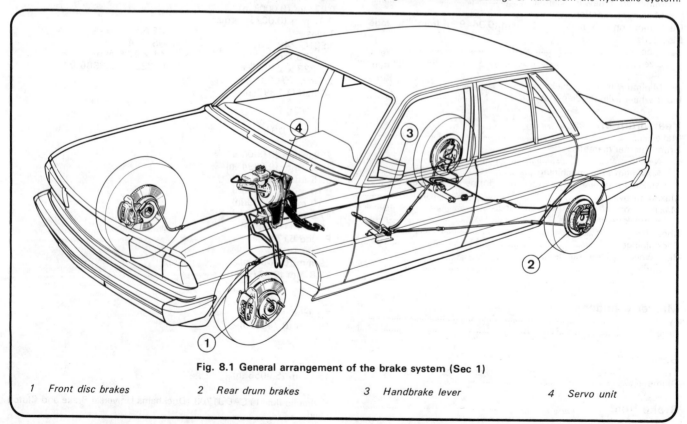

Fig. 8.1 General arrangement of the brake system (Sec 1)

1 *Front disc brakes*	2 *Rear drum brakes*	3 *Handbrake lever*	4 *Servo unit*

Renewal is essential if they are contaminated and all four shoes will need renewing even if only one is contaminated. If contamination is found, trace the source and take appropriate rectification action.

Every 30 000 miles (45 000 km) or every 2 years

9   Renew the brake fluid in the hydraulic system. Over a period of time the fluid degenerates as the inhibitors, which prevent corrosion and seal deterioration, decay. In addition the fluid absorbs moisture from the atmosphere which is why cans of fresh fluid must be kept tightly sealed. The moisture will affect both the boiling point and the freezing characteristics of the fluid. It is false economy not to change the fluid on a regular basis, and could even be dangerous.

3   Bleeding the hydraulic system

1   The system should need bleeding only when some part of it has been dismantled which would allow air into the fluid circuit, or if the reservoir level has been allowed to drop so far that air has entered the master cylinder. Removal of all air from the fluid circuit is essential if the brakes are to work efficiently and safely.
2   First check all the brake line unions and connections for possible leakage, then remove the reservoir filler cap and check that the fluid level is correct. Check that the vent hole in the cap is clear.
3   Precautions should be taken to protect the body paintwork from possible spillage of brake fluid as the fluid is an efficient paint stripper.
4   You will need a supply of fresh, non-aerated brake fluid of the correct specification; try to leave the tin undisturbed for 24 hours to release air that may be present. A clean glass jar and a length of rubber or plastic tube which will tightly fit the bleed nipples will be needed, as well as a spanner which will fit the bleed screws. Although special rigs for bleeding are available to enable the job to be done single-handed, the best and quickest way is with the help of an assistant to operate the brake pedal as required. Apart from opening and closing the bleed screws, the level in the reservoir must be constantly maintained as fluid is pumped out of the system. If you let the level fall, air will get in and defeat the whole object of the exercise. Discard all fluid removed from the system as it is not fit for re-use.
5   Before starting, depress the brake pedal a few times to exhaust any residual vacuum in the servo. Go round the bleed screws and give them all a thorough clean. Put about an inch (25 mm) of brake fluid in the glass jar.
6   Starting at the rear left-hand brake, fit the tubing onto the bleed nipple and immerse the other end in the fluid in the jar. Keep the open end of the tube immersed throughout the bleeding procedure. Un-screw the bleed screw for about half a turn and get your assistant to depress the brake pedal fully, then allow the pedal to return un-assisted. Pause for a few seconds and then repeat. To make sure no fluid re-enters the system from the jar it is best to close the bleed screw when the pedal is fully down and only open it as the pedal starts to be depressed. It is not essential to remove all the air from one brake

at a time. If the whole system is to be bled, attend to each wheel for three or four complete pedal strokes and then repeat the whole process. After every three or four pedal strokes replenish the reservoir with fresh fluid – don't reuse the fluid bled from the bleed screws. When no air bubbles can be seen in the jar when the pedal is being depressed tighten the bleed screw before releasing the pedal, remove the tube, wipe up any spilt fluid and fit the dust cap.
7   Continue until all four brakes have been completed. Test the system by depressing the foot pedal which should offer firm resistance with no suggestion of sponginess. The pedal must not go down under sustained pressure; if it does the seals in the master cylinder are probably leaking, requiring renewal of the seals or of the master cylinder itself if the bores are scored.
8   When the car is next taken onto the road, proceed with caution until you have tried the brakes and found them to be satisfactory.

4   Brake adjustments

Front disc brakes

1   The front disc brakes are fully self-adjusting in that, as the lining material of the brake pads wears, the pistons move towards the disc and hydraulic fluid will be drawn from the reservoir to compensate. No manual means of adjustment is provided but the brake pads must be inspected periodically for wear and the hydraulic reservoir level must be kept up.

Rear drum brakes

2   As with the front disc brakes, the rear drum brakes are self-adjusting and require no attention apart from periodical checks for wear and possible hydraulic system leaks or grease contamination. In order for the automatic adjuster to operate correctly, it is essential that the handbrake is not over-adjusted (refer to following paragraphs).

Handbrake adjustment

3   First raise the hand-lever until the third notch in the ratchet is engaged.
4   Jack up the rear of the car and support it with the wheels free, on axle stands or firmly based blocks. Chock the front wheels and engage a gear.
5   Adjust on the handbrake cable adjusters where the cables enter the car floor (photo). Loosen the locknuts and turn the adjusters until, on turning the wheels, the brakes can be felt just starting to bind. Readjust if necessary, so that the bar at the back of the handbrake assembly in the car is at right-angles to the fore-and-aft centre-line of the car, by loosening on one adjuster and tightening on the other. Recheck the wheels for binding, which should just be apparent on both sides. Then tighten the cable adjuster locknuts.
6   Check the operation of the handbrake by ensuring that both wheels lock when the hand lever is between the 6th and 8th notch and are free to rotate when it is released.
7   Lower the car to the ground.

2.5 Removing a rubber inspection plug from a rear brake backplate

4.5 One of the two adjusters for the handbrake cables

5   Disc pads – inspection and renewal

1   Before dismantling any part of the brakes they should be thoroughly cleaned. With a stiff brush remove as much road dirt as possible and finish off using hot water and a mild detergent (dish washing fluid will do). Do not use paraffin, petrol or other solvents which could cause deterioration of the friction pads or piston seals etc.

2   Use ramps to raise the front of the car, or jack it up and support it on stands. Do not work under a car supported only on the wheel changing jack. Apply the handbrake to prevent movement of the car.

3   Inspection of the front brake disc pads will require removal of the front wheels as the brake calipers are buried in the wheel wells. In addition the Teves type of caliper will require the pad spring removed as it covers the wear slots in the pads. Remove the roadwheels and, on Teves brakes, drive out the bottom pin retaining the disc pads and lift out the pad leaf spring. Each pad has a groove to indicate the remaining depth of friction material. When the groove is not apparent the pads have worn below their minimum permissible thickness and must be renewed. All four pads on the front brakes must be renewed when any one or more of them is worn or is renewed for some other reason.

4   To renew the pads, first remove the front wheels if they have not already been removed and then, using a clean syringe, remove some of the hydraulic fluid from the reservoir. When new pads are fitted the pistons must be moved back into the cylinders to accommodate the extra thickness and if fluid is not first removed from the system it might overflow with possible damage to the car's paintwork – apart from the mess it will cause. Discard the fluid removed as it is unsuitable for re-use in the system.

5   The two types of front calipers fitted to Peugeot 305 models are shown in Fig. 8.2 and, although they are interchangeable, it is essential that both calipers on the car are of the same type.

Teves brakes

6   To remove the pads first drive out the two retaining pins using, if necessary, a 3 mm (0.118 in) diameter pin punch, and remove the damping spring (photos).

7   Lever the caliper slide towards the centre of the car and remove the inner pad (photo). Then lever the slide back to remove the outer pad. Note that the outer pad has a recess in its backing plate to locate on a key in the caliper (photos).

8   Inspect the disc friction area. If it is badly scored, cracked or excessively worn, the disc will have to be renewed. Unfortunately removal of the disc from the suspension strut can only be undertaken by a Peugeot agent, see Chapter 9, Section 7. Worn discs can be resurfaced by a specialist garage if the wear is within limits.

9   If the pads are not worn out but have a black, shiny surface, before fitting them roughen the surface with a piece of emery cloth to remove the glaze, but don't overdo it. Pads must be refitted to their original positions.

10 Visually check the condition of the caliper, the hydraulic hose, and the cylinder assembly before fitting the pads. Look carefully for signs of fluid leaks and remove any corrosion and scale. Renew the retaining pins and spring if they are worn or corroded.

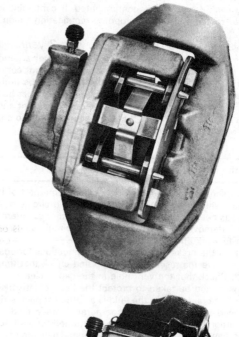

Fig. 8.2 The two types of front calipers fitted to the Peugeot 305 (Sec 5)

Upper: Teves (early models)
Lower: DBA 111 A (later models)

5.6a First remove the pad retaining pins ...

5.6b ... and the damping spring

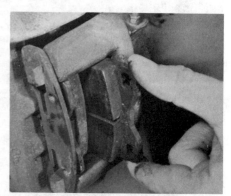

5.7a Removing the disc brake pads

5.7b The key in the caliper (arrowed) on which the outer pad sits

5.7c The back of the outer pad, left, has a recess for the caliper key

5.11 Use a piece of wood to push the piston, arrowed, back in the caliper

11 If new pads are to be fitted (remember that all four pads on the front brakes will have to be renewed) first remove some fluid from the brake reservoir as described in paragraph 4. With a piece of wood, or a similar blunt tool, push the piston back in the caliper cylinder (photo).

Check that the new pads are the right ones by comparing them and their markings with the originals.
12 Spray the pad backing plate backs with Permatex sound-deadening compound which can be obtained from a Peugeot agent, part No 9730.61. Make sure that none of this compound contaminates the pad friction material. The best way of doing this is to cut an aperture in a piece of cardboard into which the pad friction material will just fit, leaving the backing plate exposed. The card will mask the friction material when the back of the plate is sprayed. Allow the Permatex compound to dry. Check that no grease or oil contamination is present on the pads or the disc. If contaminated, pads must be discarded and the disc must be cleaned using methylated spirit on clean rag.
13 Refitting the pads is basically the reverse of the removal procedure. Fit the outer pad first, making sure that the key is located in its slot, then fit the inner pad followed by the spring and retainer pins.

DBA brakes
14 With a pair of long-nosed pliers, remove the clips from the keys and slide the keys out of their slots.
15 With the keys removed, the wheel cylinder can be removed from the caliper and, without disturbing the hose connection, swung to one side out of the way; make sure that the hose is not stressed.
16 Remove the old pads from the caliper and take careful note of the springs fitted to the top ends of the pads, especially how they fit and the way round they are fitted.
17 Refer to paragraphs 8 to 12 inclusive and follow the same procedures as far as they apply to DBA brakes. Examine the slides where the keys fit and remove any burrs with an oilstone, cleaning off any abrasive dust on completion.
18 Assemble the springs to the pads in the same way as originally

Fig. 8.3 Remove the clips, 1, from the keys ...

Fig. 8.4 ... and then slide the two keys, 2 and 3, out of the caliper (Sec 5, DBA brakes)

Fig. 8.5 Remove the cylinder, 1, from the caliper (Sec 5, DBA brakes)

noted in paragraph 16. The crossing wire must be over the pad recess, see Fig. 8.6.

19 Apply a fine film of Molykote 321R, or a suitable alternative dry anti-friction agent, to the pad keys and set aside to dry.

20 Hold the pair of pads face to face and, after checking that the springs are correctly fitted, assemble them to the caliper, springs to the top.

21 Refit the cylinder on the caliper and slide the keys home. Make sure that the wire springs locate *under* the slides on the cylinder. They must not be inserted between the keys and the slides.

22 Fit new clips to retain the keys in the slides.

All front brakes

23 Repeat the procedure on the other front brake assembly and then refit the roadwheels, tightening the wheel nuts to the specified torque.

24 Top up the brake fluid reservoir using fresh fluid and, with the engine running, apply the brakes several times to locate the pistons correctly. Top up the reservoir again on completion if necessary.

25 Remember that new pads need bedding in before they produce full efficiency, so exercise extra caution until they are fully effective.

6 Disc brake calipers – removal, overhaul and refitting

1 To prevent excessive loss of fluid when the front brake hoses are disconnected, remove the brake reservoir filler cap and seal off the filler neck with a piece of plastic sheeting large enough to accommodate the low level switch float in the cap. Refit the cap tightly Alternatively, if you can get hold of another filler cap of the right size, block off the vent hole in the cap and fit it to the reservoir, with a seal, in place of the correct filler cap.

2 Slacken the front wheel nuts, then jack up the front of the car and support it on stands or substantial blocks with the wheels free. Apply the handbrake and remove the front wheels.

3 Clean off all the road dirt from the brake units and then disconnect the hydraulic hose from the wheel cylinder of the first unit to be serviced. Plug the end of the hose to stop dirt getting in.

4 Refer to the previous Section and remove the disc pads.

5 Undo the two bolts securing the brake caliper unit to the wheel axle assembly (photo) and remove the unit.

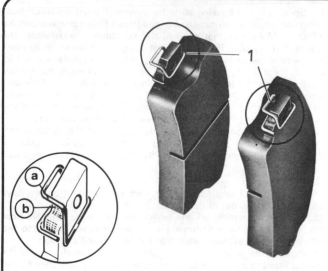

Fig. 8.6 Fit the pad springs, 1, as shown in the inset with the crosspiece, a, over the notch, b (Sec 5, DBA brakes)

Fig. 8.7 Fit the pads with the springs, 1, to the top (Sec 5, DBA brakes)

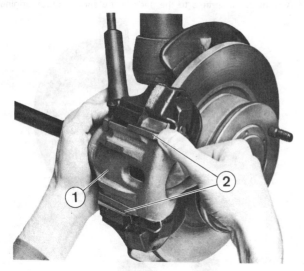

Fig. 8.8 Refitting the cylinder, 1, and the keys, 2 (Sec 5, DBA brakes)

Fig. 8.9 Ensure that the springs, 3, are under the slides and not between the keys and slides, then fit new clips, 4 (Sec 5, DBA brakes)

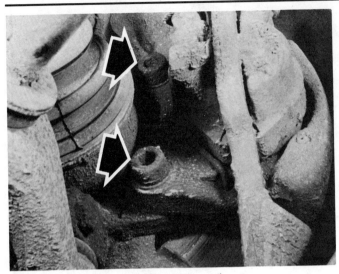

6.5 The two caliper retaining bolts (arrowed)

Teves brakes

6   With the unit on the bench, remove the cylinder from the caliper bracket.

7   Remove the rubber dust cover and extract the piston. This can be done by carefully blowing it out, using a low pressure air line or tyre pump applied to the brake hose connections. Take care to prevent the piston flying out by wrapping the assembly in rags. If the piston is seized in the bore it could be difficult to remove without causing some damage, but try soaking the assembly with penetrating fluid and leaving it to work. This may do the seal no good but it must be renewed in any case.

8   With the piston removed, extract and discard the seal from its groove in the cylinder bore. Clean all metal parts thoroughly in methylated spirit, but don't use any abrasive cleaning materials, and don't use a metal scraper which could scratch machined surfaces or the anti-corrosive finish.

9   Closely examine the piston sliding surface for scores, grooves, ridges, corrosion pits and similar wear and tear. If such damage exists the piston must be renewed; on no account attempt to polish out any blemish. Examine all the component parts of the brake assembly for obvious damage, renewing where necessary.

10 Soak the new cylinder seal in fresh hydraulic fluid and lubricate the cylinder bore and the piston with the same fluid. Carefully fit the seal into the cylinder groove and then fit the piston taking care not to damage the seal. Wipe the assembly dry with fluff-free rag and then fit the new rubber dust cover.

DBA brakes

11 Servicing the DBA brake calipers follows broadly the same procedure as that already covered for the Teves brakes in the previous paragraphs, to which reference should be made.

All brakes

12 Reassembly and refitting of the brake calipers is the reverse of the removal and dismantling sequences, but note the following points:

(a) *When fitting the caliper to the axle clean the threaded holes and the bolt threads thoroughly and coat the bolt threads with thread locking compound. Fit new washers to the bolts and tighten them to the specified torque*

(b) *Fit the brake pads as described in Section 5*

(c) *Remove the bleed screw and prime the wheel cylinder with fresh brake fluid, tipping the cylinder in all directions to release trapped air before installation. Refit the bleed screw.*

(d) *Fit a new copper gasket to the hose connector union and when the unit is fitted make sure that the hose is not twisted on reconnection. Check that the hose cannot foul any part of the car when the weight is on the wheels and steering is applied in both directions, lock to lock*

(e) *Remove the piece of plastic or the dummy filler cap from the reservoir and bleed the system as described in Section 3*

7   Rear brake drums – removal and refitting

1   With the weight of the car on the wheels, slacken the rear wheel retaining nuts.

2   Jack up the rear of the vehicle and support it on axle stands or substantial blocks with the wheels free. Do not work under a car supported only by the wheel changing jack. Chock the front wheels securely, engage a gear, and release the handbrake.

3   Undo the wheel nuts and remove the wheel. Undo and remove the two countersunk screws retaining the brake drum and remove the drum.

4   If the drum resists removal the likely cause is that the brake shoes need retracting. Prise out the plug in the backplate located in the bottom rear area of the plate and insert a screwdriver through the backplate hole. Apply pressure to the handbrake lever within the drum and push the lever sideways to permit retraction of the shoes. Refit the plug in the backplate.

5   With the drum off, carefully clean out the brake dust so as to disperse it as little as possible. *It is important not to spread the dust in the atmosphere or to inhale it* as there is a danger to health due to the asbestos content. An old paintbrush and a damp cloth are useful for cleaning the assembly but discard the cloth in a dustbin afterwards.

6   Examine the brake assembly for fluid leaks from the wheel cylinder, grease contamination or leakage from the hub bearings, deterioration of the rubber covers on the cylinder and the general condition of the moving parts. If there are signs of fluid or grease the source must be located and the fault rectified. If the brake linings are contaminated, all four linings on the rear wheels must be renewed. Inspect the linings for wear and if the thickness of the friction material is 2.5 mm (0.1 m) or lesss, or if it is estimated that it might be worn to that extent before the next servicing, the linings must be renewed. Refer to Chapter 7 for details of renewing the bearings and seals in the wheel hubs.

7   Before refitting the drum examine it for grooving, scores, cracks, corrosion or any other obvious damage. If the presence of ridges indicating wear by the shoes is seen, consideration should be given to having the drums skimmed out by a specialist workshop, providing that the wear is within limits and no other damage exists, see Section 10 for details.

8   Refitting the drums is a reversal of the removal procedure. Refit the wheels but leave the final tightening of the wheel nuts until the weight of the car is on the ground, then tighten to the specified torque. Depress the brake pedal several times to adjust the brake shoes and then adjust the handbrake as described in Section 4.

8   Rear brake shoes – removal, inspection and refitting

1   Remove the brake drums as described in the previous Section and clean the assemblies, observing the precautions mentioned concerning brake dust. Slacken the handbrake cable adjusters (see Section 4 for details).

2   Three different brake assemblies have been used on Peugeot 305 models and they are illustrated in Fig. 8.10. Although all are interchangeable it is essential that both rear brake assemblies on an axle are of the same type.

Girling brakes (early pattern)

3   Remove the self-adjusting lever spring and the self-adjusting lever, refer to Fig. 8.11. Note which way springs are fitted as it is possible to fit some the wrong way round on reassembly.

4   Unhook and remove the shoe return springs, (Fig. 8.12).

5   Remove the leading shoe retaining spring by turning the washer after depressing it to align the slot with the retaining pin, Fig. 8.13. Lift out the leading shoe and withdraw the automatic adjusting device.

6   Remove the trailing shoe retaining spring in the same way and lift out the trailing shoe. Unhook the handbrake cable and remove the shoe assembly.

7   Clean the assembly thoroughly and inspect for wear and damage. Check the condition of the rubber boots on the cylinder. Any defective parts must be renewed, using new fasteners where appropriate.

8   Brake shoes must be renewed in sets of four, that is, both rear brake assemblies complete. There are three different shoes in the set of four. The two leading shoes are identical and may be fitted to the left or right wheel assemblies. They have their linings riveted, with

Fig. 8.10 The three types of rear brake assemblies (Sec 8)

Top: *Girling, early pattern*
Centre: *Girling, later pattern*
Bottom: *DBA*

Fig. 8.11 Remove the spring, 1, and the self-adjusting lever, 2 (Sec 8)

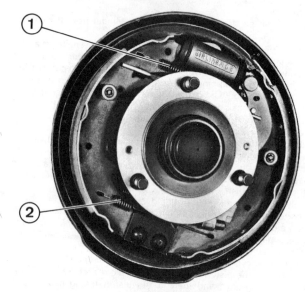

Fig. 8.12 Remove the shoe return springs, 1 and 2 (Sec 8)

Fig. 8.13 Remove the shoe retaining spring and washer, 1 (Sec 8)

rivets offset towards the bottom of the shoes. The two trailing shoes are handed by the different positions of the handbrake lever and they have their lining rivets offset towards the top of the shoe.

9 The horizontal links in the self-adjusting device are also handed and they can be identified by the fact that the link for the left-hand brakes is marked with an L and its ratchet wheel nut has no chamfered face. The right-hand link has no identifying letter but the ratchet wheel nut has a chamfered face towards the fork.

10 Before reassembling the shoes apply a little Molykote 321R or similar anti-friction agent to the handbrake lever pin on the trailing shoe, taking great care not to contaminate the shoe lining material.

11 Hook the end of the handbrake cable into the bottom fitting on the handbrake lever and fit the trailing shoe to the brake backplate. Fit the retaining pin, spring, and washer.

12 Fit the horizontal link of the self-adjusting device, making sure that you have got the correct one. Then fit the leading shoe, engaging it with the link. Fit the shoe retaining pin, spring and washer.

13 Fit the upper and lower shoe return springs making sure that they are the right way round.

14 The diameter across the two linings must now be adjusted to 227.7 mm (8.965 in) and the easy way to do this is to make a simple gauge out of a piece of scrap metal or sheet plastic with a gap of that dimension. Adjust the ratchet wheel nut on the self-adjuster horizontal link to set the linings to fit the gauge.

15 Refit the self-adjusting lever and its spring.

Girling brakes (later pattern)

16 These brakes are similar to the early pattern but they have a different, improved self-adjusting mechanism.

17 The dismantling and reassembling procedure can follow that already described in paragraphs 3 to 15 inclusive, but note that on these brakes the self-adjuster horizontal links have a left-hand thread on the left-hand link and a right-hand thread on the right-hand link. Before installing the links run the ratchet wheel nuts up to the stops on the links, but don't tighten them. The reassembly sequence is shown (photos). Note that the hub is removed for clarity, and the assembly built up off the backplate for the same reason. Assembly can be done on the backplate with the hub in position.

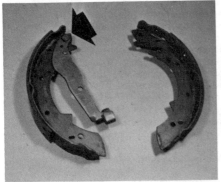

8.17a Sparingly lubricate the handbrake lever pin (arrowed) with Molykote 321 R before assembling the brakes. Girling later pattern shown

8.17b Fit the brake shoe top return spring

8.17c Then fit the horizontal link of the self-adjusting mechanism ...

8.17d ... to both shoes

8.17e Fit the self-adjuster ratchet ...

8.17f ... and its return spring

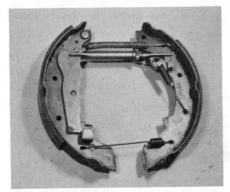

8.17g Then fit the brake shoe bottom return spring

8.17h Check that the brake backplate is clean and lightly lubricate the points where the shoes rub with Molykote 321 R

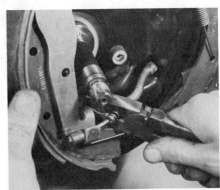

8.17j Fit the shoes to the backplate, engaging the handbrake cable in its lever

8.17k Engage the shoes with the cylinder pistons and, after bedding the assembly down ...

8.17m ... fit the shoe retaining springs, pins and washers

8.18 Use a locally made gauge to check the diameter across the shoe linings

18 On completion of assembly the diameter across the linings must be adjusted to 227.7 mm (8.965 in) using the ratchet wheel nuts on the horizontal links (photo).

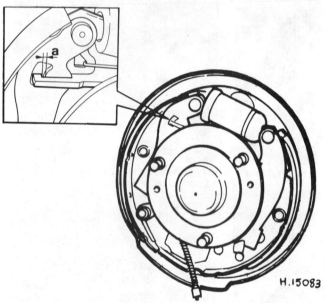

Fig. 8.14 Check the clearance (a) between the horizontal link and the lever (Sec 8)

DBA brakes

19 After removing the drum, remove the shoe return spring located under the wheel cylinder and then check the clearance between the horizontal link and the brake shoe lever which should be 0.6 to 0.8 mm (0.024 to 0.032 in) see Fig. 8.14. If the clearance is outside this tolerance the worn or damaged parts must be renewed.

20 Remove the brake shoe retaining springs. This can be done using a bolt or an Allen key which will just fit in the conical springs. Push the bolt or key to extend the spring and unhook it from its anchorage. Repeat the procedure on the other shoe. These springs are prone to corrosion and must be renewed on reassembly.

21 Unhook the handbrake cable from the bottom of the handbrake lever, move the other lever towards the hub to disengage the ratchet and then disconnect the horizontal link from it. Allow the ratchet lever to return to its original position and remove the shoe assembly from the backplate.

22 Clean the assembly thoroughly and inspect for wear and damage. Check the condition of the rubber boots on the wheel cylinder. Any defective parts must be renewed, using new fasteners where appropriate.

23 Brake shoes must be renewed in sets of four, that is, both rear brake assemblies complete. There are three different shoes in the set of four. The two trailing shoes are identical and may be fitted to the left or right wheel assemblies. They have their lining rivets offset towards the top of the shoe and they have no pivot pin in the bottom end – only the hole for a pin. The leading shoes have their lining rivets offset towards the bottom of the shoes and the right-hand assembly shoe has a pin protruding to the right, viewed with the lining away from you and the pin at the bottom. The left-hand shoe has the pin protruding to the left when viewed in the same fashion.

24 Providing that it is in good condition, transfer the adjuster lever to the outer face of the new leading shoe using a new clip (Fig. 8.15). Then transfer the ratchet and spring, securing them with a new retaining circlip (Fig. 8.16).

25 Similarly transfer the handbrake lever to the outer face of the new trailing shoe and lock it in place with a new clip (Fig. 8.17).

26 Fit the horizontal link to the trailing shoe with the curved edges facing upwards, and attach the spring on the back (Fig. 8.18). Note that the horizontal links are handed for left and right-hand assemblies.

27 Attach the bottom spring to the two shoes so that it lies underneath the shoes (Fig. 8.19). Offer the assembly to the backplate,

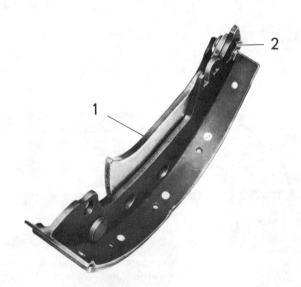

Fig. 8.15 Transfer the adjuster lever, 1, to the shoe using a new clip, 2 (Sec 8)

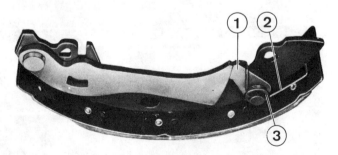

Fig. 8.16 Fit the ratchet, 1, the spring, 2, and a new circlip, 3 (Sec 8)

Fig. 8.17 Fit the handbrake lever, 1, and secure with a new clip, 2 (Sec 8)

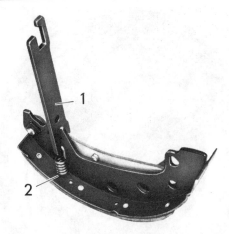

Fig. 8.18 Fit the horizontal link, 1, and attach the spring, 2 (Sec 8)

Fig. 8.19 Attach the bottom spring so that it is under the shoes (Sec 8)

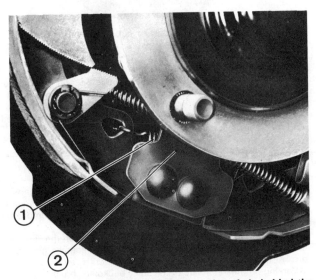

Fig. 8.20 Make sure that the bottom spring, 1, is behind the bracket, 2 (Sec 8)

Fig. 8.21 Push the lever, 1, towards the hub and connect the horizontal link, 2 (Sec 8)

making sure that the bottom spring lies behind the bottom bracket (Fig. 8.20). Push the adjusting lever towards the hub and connect the horizontal link. Work the assembly into position on the backplate until the upper ends of the shoes rest on the wheel cylinder pistons. Then, using a pair of long-nosed pliers, refit the upper spring. Push the adjusting lever fully forwards against the brake shoe.

28 Lever the handbrake lever forwards and connect the cable to the bottom end.

29 Fit new shoe retaining springs using a long bolt or an Allen key to hook them into their anchorages with their anchor lugs horizontal (Fig. 8.23).

30 Adjust the diameter across the two linings to 227.7 mm (8.965 in) by moving the adjusting lever notch by notch towards the hub (Fig. 8.24).

Fig. 8.22 Fit the spring, 1, and push the adjuster lever, 2, towards the shoe (Sec 8)

Fig. 8.23 Connect the handbrake cable, 1, and fit the shoe retaining springs, 2 (Sec 8)

Fig. 8.24 Adjust the lining diameter by moving the lever A (Sec 8)

All rear brakes

31 Give the assembly a final visual check to make sure that all is well, then refit the drums and wheels as described in Section 7 and adjust the handbrake as described in Section 4. As already mentioned for the front brake disc pads, new brake shoes need bedding in before they produce full braking efficiency and you should exercise extra care in driving until they are fully effective.

9 Rear wheel cylinders – removal, overhaul and refitting

1 Jack up the rear of the car and support it on axle stands or substantial blocks. Never work under a car supported only on a wheel changing jack. Chock the front wheels and engage a gear. Remove the brake drum as described in Section 7.
2 Remove the hydraulic reservoir filler cap and seal off the filler neck as described in Section 6, paragraph 1. This will minimise the loss of fluid from the system when the hose connection is undone.
3 Working on the inner side of the brake backplate, brush off all road dirt and clean around the hydraulic hose connection, the bleed screw and the two bolts which secure the wheel cylinder to the backplate (photo).

4 Carefully undo the hydraulic line connection to the wheel cylinder, and cover the pipe open end to stop dirt getting in.
5 Unscrew and remove the two wheel cylinder retaining bolts. Unclip the upper shoe return spring and, prising the brake shoes apart at the top, remove the wheel cylinder.
5 If the cylinder has been leaking and the brake linings are contaminated with fluid they must be renewed on *both* rear wheels. This procedure is described in Section 8.
7 Clean off the outside of the cylinder using methylated spirit and take it to a clean work area for dismantling.
8 Pull the rubber boots off each end of the cylinder and carefully extract the pistons, seal cups, and spring. Take careful note of the sequence of assembly of the individual parts and which way round they are fitted.
9 Inspect the cylinder bore carefully for any signs of grooving, scores, corrosion or similar damage. If any damage is present the cylinder must be renewed.
10 Providing that the cylinder is serviceable, clean it thoroughly with methylated spirit – don't use any abrasive material and don't use metal scrapers which could damage the cylinder bore. When clean, wipe the cylinder dry with clean, non-fluffy rag.
11 Sort out the new seals in the repair kit by matching them with the originals and immerse them in clean hydraulic fluid before assembly.

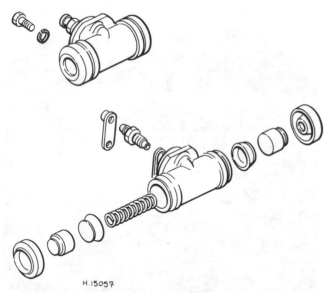

Fig. 8.25 Exploded view of a typical rear brake wheel cylinder (Girling) (Sec 9)

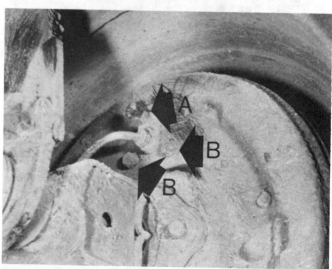

9.3 The bleed screw, A (with dust cap fitted) on a rear brake backplate and, B, the bolts retaining the wheel cylinder

12 Lubricate the cylinder with clean hydraulic fluid and assemble the spring, pistons and cup seals. Take care not to damage the seals as you fit them into the cylinder. Fit the rubber boots and then wipe the assembly dry with clean rag.

13 Reassembly of the wheel cylinder to the brake backplate is the reverse of the dismantling procedure, but note the following:

(a) *Take care not to cross-thread the brake pipe union when reconnecting it to the wheel cylinder*

(b) *Refit the brake drum following the procedure described in Section 7*

(c) *Bleed the brake hydraulic system and top up the reservoir remembering to remove the piece of polythene or the dummy filler cap as appropriate. See Section 3 for the procedure for bleeding*

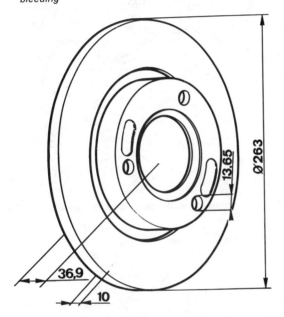

Fig. 8.26 The front disc dimensions in mm (Sec 10)

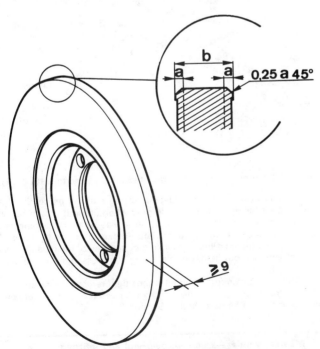

Fig. 8.27 When the disc is reground the amount of material removed, a, must be the same on both sides in relation to the original thickness, b. Minimum thickness after machining is shown in mm (Sec 10)

10 Discs and drums – repair by machining

1 Worn discs or drums, providing that the wear has not exceeded the maximum permissible limits and that the components are otherwise fit for use, can be machined to provide an extended lease of life. This work will have to be done by a specialist workshop but it may be cheaper than fitting new items.

Discs

2 First examine the disc for signs of any damage which necessitates renewal. Heavy corrosion, pitting, deep grooves and cracks are the sort of thing which can only be rectified by fitting a replacement disc. If the disc appears sound take a series of micrometer readings to determine its thickness. The minimum thickness after machining is given in the Specifications. There must be enough metal on the disc to enable it to be machined and remove the defects. After refacing on a machine the disc can continue in use until its thickness is reduced to the minimum specified and then, regardless of its condition, it must be renewed. Another point to note is that the machining process must maintain the original centre-line of the disc which means that the same amount of metal must be removed from each face; if only one face was resurfaced, the centre-line would be offset, resulting in alignment problems with the disc pads. See Figs. 8.26 and 8.27 and Specifications for dimensional limits for the discs.

Drums

3 As with the brake discs, the brake drums must first be examined for damage which would necessitate renewal such as heavy corrosion, pitting, deep grooves, cracks and excessive ovality. An internal micrometer should be used to take a series of diametrical measurements across the drum lining track. The difference between the largest and smallest diameter indicates the maximum ovality of the drum which must not exceed that specified. The maximum diameter to which the drums can be skimmed out is also given in the Specifications and, as with the discs, there must be enough metal available to be machined out and remove the defects. Also note that the two drums on the same axle must be machined to within 0.15 mm (0.0059 in) of the same internal diameter. See Fig. 8.29 for dimensional limits for the drums.

11 Hydraulic fluid pipes – inspection and renewal

1 Periodically, and certainly well in advance of the DoE (MoT) test, if due, all brake pipes, connections and unions should be carefully examined.

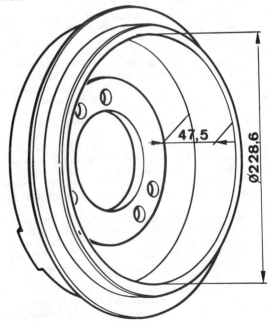

Fig. 8.28 The rear drum dimensions in mm (Sec 10)

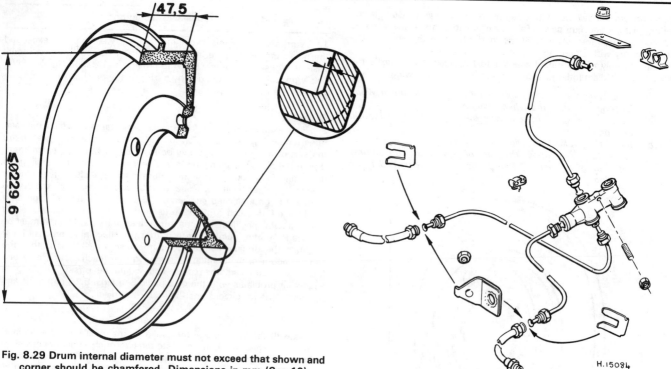

Fig. 8.29 Drum internal diameter must not exceed that shown and corner should be chamfered. Dimensions in mm (Sec 10)

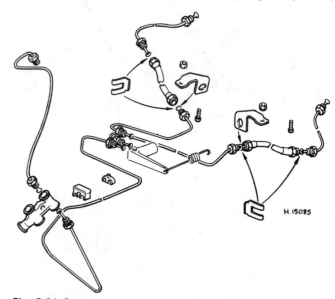

Fig. 8.30 Components in the front brakes pipe system (Sec 11)

2   First examine all the unions for signs of leaks. Then look at the flexible hoses. Later cars have armoured hoses so check that the wire armouring is not broken as it could then endanger the hose itself. Look for chafing, splits and cracks in the rubber, and of course leaks. This is only a preliminary examination of the hoses as exterior condition does not necessarily indicate interior condition which will be considered later.

3   The rigid pipes must be examined equally carefully. They must be brushed clean and inspected for signs of dents or other impact damage, chafing against the structure and corrosion pits. Slight surface corrosion is not necessarily important but deep pitting could lead to leaks and, where present, the piping must be renewed; this is a certain cause for failure of the test. Corrosion and damage to the piping is most likely to occur in those areas under the car body and along the rear suspension arms where the pipes are exposed to the full force of road and weather conditions.

4   If a hydraulic union has to be undone, say to renew a hose, seal the hydraulic reservoir filler neck as described in Section 6, paragraph 1. This will minimise the loss of fluid when the union is undone.

5   Rigid pipe removal is usually straightforward once the unions are undone, but these can give trouble on old cars. The best sort of spanner for the job is a split ring spanner which is like a ring spanner but has a gap in it to permit fitting over the piping. In the absence of this tool a pair of self-gripping pliers is a good alternative. To avoid twisting the pipe, especially when fitting new piping, use two spanners or grips, one to turn the union and the other to hold the fitting to which it is attached.

6   Flexible hoses are always fitted to a rigid support bracket where they join a rigid pipe and the bracket is attached to the structure or rear suspension arm as appropriate. Again use two tools when undoing or connecting the unions and, in cases of difficulty due to corrosion or seizure, give the joint a prolonged soak with penetrating fluid beforehand.

7   Once the flexible hose is removed it can be examined internally. Blow the hose through with air to clear it of fluid and look down the bore, holding the hose straight with a good light at the other end. Any signs of restrictions in the bore such as wrinkles, blisters, flaking of the lining or similar defects indicate that the lining is breaking up and the hose must be renewed.

8   Rigid pipes which need renewal can sometimes be purchased made up, but the more usual procedure is to get the pipe you want made up by a garage with the necessary equipment. Clearly it is best if you can supply the original pipe as a pattern as then there will be a better chance of getting a good fit when the new one is installed.

Fig. 8.31 Components in the rear brakes pipe system (Sec 11)

9   Refitting of the pipes is a reversal of the removal procedure. Be careful about bending the new rigid pipe when fitting it. Acute bends should have been made by the garage on a pipe bending machine and you should only attempt smooth, large-radiused bends by hand in order to avoid the possibility of kinking or collapse of the pipe. Always clean a new pipe out before fitting, using compressed air or hydraulic fluid.

10 With the pipes refitted and all unions tight remove the plastic seal from the reservoir filler, or the dummy filler cap if one was used, and bleed the system as described in Section 3.

12 Master cylinder – removal, overhaul and refitting

1   Internal fluid leakage past the seals of the master cylinder will be indicated if the brake pedal slowly moves towards the floor when pressure is applied and there are no leaks in an otherwise satisfactory

system. The seals themselves may be defective or the master cylinder bore may be worn or grooved. In either case the unit will need removing, dismantling and inspecting before the fault can be rectified. The master cylinder is bolted to the front of the brake vacuum servo unit and carries the hydraulic reservoir on top (photo). A repair kit containing all the necessary replaceable items can be obtained from a Peugeot agent.

2   Remember that hydraulic fluid is harmful to paintwork. Try to avoid spillage but if this occurs mop it up immediately. Spread a sheet of plastic and some rags under the master cylinder before undoing unions.

3   Remove the reservoir filler cap and, with a clean syringe, empty the reservoir. Discard the fluid removed as it is unsuitable for re-use.

4   Disconnect the hydraulic pipe connections on the unit and carefully push the pipes out of the way sufficiently to permit removal of the unit. Cover the open ends to prevent dirt from getting in.

5   Remove the two nuts and spring washers securing the master

cylinder to the servo unit and remove it, wrapped in rags to contain any fluid spillage. Remove the reservoir from the master cylinder and discard the two rubber grommets which must be renewed.

6   As the master cylinder is dismantled take careful note of the sequence of assembly of the various parts and also which way round they are fitted. In many cases a quick sketch will prove more reliable than memory. Depress the piston visible in the cylinder bore and remove the piston stop. Still depressing the piston, remove the circlip in the end of the bore and remove the piston assembly. If necessary the pistons can be removed by air pressure but restrain the parts from flying out with a piece of rag wrapped round the unit.

7   Clean all metal parts in methylated spirit – never use any abrasive when cleaning hydraulic system fittings and don't use metal scrapers which could score machined surfaces.

8   Sort out the new seals in the repair kit by matching them carefully with the old ones before discarding the old ones. Immerse the new seals in fresh brake fluid before reassembly.

9   Closely inspect all the metal parts for wear, corrosion and obvious damage. Any sign of scoring in the master cylinder bore, however slight, will require renewal, and it is clearly more sensible to renew the whole assembly as a unit if this is necessary.

10   Reassembly is the reverse of the dismantling procedure. Meticulous cleanliness is vital in this work. Wash your hands before starting; wipe all metal components clean, and dry them with fluff-free rag or absorbent kitchen paper. Freely lubricate all parts with clean hydraulic fluid before reassembly. On completion wipe the unit dry before refitting the reservoir using new rubber grommets.

11   Refitting the master cylinder in the car is the reverse of the removal sequence. When refitted, and with the pipe connections remade, fill the reservoir with fresh hydraulic fluid and bleed the system as described in Section 3.

12   Test the brakes on the next run out, choosing a quiet straight stretch of road and, initially, at low speed. Always check that there is nothing behind before braking.

13 Vacuum servo unit – removal and refitting

1   Slacken the clip securing the vacuum hose to the servo unit and carefully remove the hose from the valve fitting.

2   Undo and remove the two nuts securing the master cylinder to the servo unit and very carefully ease the master cylinder forward to disengage it from the servo unit studs. If you can do this it will save having to disconnect the hydraulic pipelines with the attendant penalty of having to bleed the system. If you find, because of your installation, that you cannot achieve this quick procedure then the master cylinder will have to be removed as described in the previous Section.

3   Remove the spring clip retaining the pivot pin to the foot pedal-to-servo unit pushrod joint and remove the pivot pin.

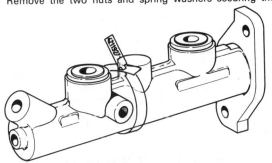

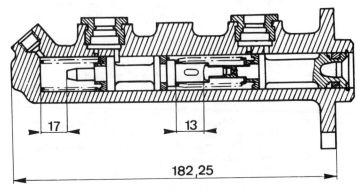

Fig. 8.32 The brake master cylinder. Dimensions in mm (Sec 12)

12.1 The master cylinder, with brake fluid reservoir on top, is bolted to the servo unit

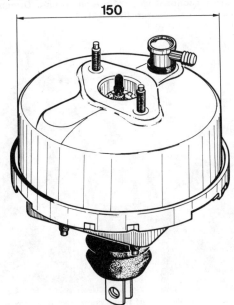

Fig. 8.33 The brake vacuum servo unit. Dimensions in mm (Sec 13)

4   Undo and remove the four nuts securing the servo unit to the bulkhead and retrieve the four washers. Remove the servo unit from the car.
5   Refitting the servo unit is the reverse of the removal procedure. If the master cylinder had to be removed it will be necessary to bleed the hydraulic system as described in Section 3.

14 Vacuum servo unit – overhaul

1   It is rare for a servo unit to develop an internal fault and when it is worn out after a long life, renewal of the complete unit is the best remedy.
2   Should a fault develop in the unit it should be noticed by the additional effort needed to operate the brakes, but if the fault is progressive it may not be noticed. If you suspect a fault, have the unit checked by your Peugeot agent who will have the necessary equipment to service the unit. The only work feasible on the servo unit for the home mechanic consists of renewing the air filter which is advisable every two years, and renewing the one-way valve which may remedy malfunction if this occurs. First make sure that the new parts can be obtained however.

Air filter renewal
3   The servo unit can remain in position for a filter change. The air filter is located around the input rod and is covered by the rubber boot on the rear wall of the unit.

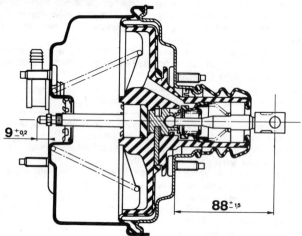

Fig. 8.34 Cross-sectional view of the servo unit. Dimensions in mm (Sec 14)

4   Remove the clip retaining the pivot pin connecting the input rod to the brake pedal and remove the pin. Remove the rubber boot and the filter retainer. The old filter can then be extracted with a hooked tool and discarded.
5   As the filter will not pass over the input rod end fitting, make a diagonal cut along the axis with a sharp knife so that the filter can be opened and fitted onto the input rod. Fit the filter, retainer and boot. Refit the pivot pin and secure with a new clip.

Renewing the one-way valve
6   Loosen the clip and detach the vacuum hose from the one-way valve on the forward face of the unit. The valve can then be extracted by pulling and twisting it from the sealing grommet. It would be worthwhile fitting a new grommet; if it is perished or cracked, renewal is essential. Refit the components in the reverse order. A little hydraulic fluid can be used as a rubber lubricant to aid reassembly.

15 Brake compensator – general

1   A brake compensator is fitted in the rear brake hydraulic system and it is located under the car floor just forward of the rear suspension. Its purpose is to maintain equal braking effect on the front and rear wheels and prevent the rear brakes from locking up.
2   If you find that, on applying the brakes, the effect is mainly on the front wheels and that it is impossible to lock the rear brakes without using the handbrake or, alternatively, if you find that the rear brakes invariably lock under heavy braking, it is likely that the compensator is defective.
3   Early models were fitted with an adjustable load-sensitive compensator, but on later cars this was replaced by a non-adjustable compensator (photo). In both cases a Peugeot agent will have to test the component if its performance is in doubt as pressure test equipment is necessary. No attempt must be made to dismantle either unit.
4   Renewal of a brake compensator is a straightforward removal and refitting procedure following by bleeding of the hydraulic system. The early type of compensator should be adjusted as follows, after refitting.
5   Check that the rear tyre pressures are as specified.
6   Load the rear end of the car until the distance between the centre of the stub axle and the bottom of the top edge of the wheel arch is between 305 and 315 mm (12.0 and 12.4 in).
7   Refer to Fig. 8.35. Peugeot use a special tool, part number 8.0803 P, shown in the figure, to set the compensator, but it is only a block of metal 9 mm (0.3543 in) thick with a slot into which the spring link fits when the block is positioned as shown. This setting block can be made of any suitable scrap metal or plastic. Put the block into position

15.3 The non-adjustable type of brake compensator (arrowed)

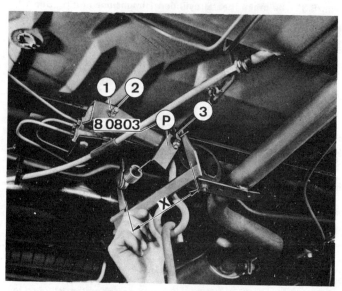

Fig. 8.35 Adjusting the early type of brake compensator. See text for details (Sec 15)

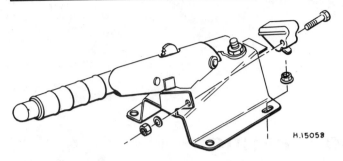

H.15058

Fig. 8.36 The handbrake lever assembly (Sec 16)

and slacken the locknut (1 in Fig. 8.35). Adjust the screw (2) so that the overall distance X is 223.5 mm (8.7992 in). *On no account must the stop block (3) be adjusted or altered in any way.* Hold the adjusting screw and tighten the locknut. If the stop block is adjusted or altered, resetting will have to be done by a Peugeot agent as pressure measurements of the front and rear brake systems are necessary.

8   Since the non-adjustable compensator was introduced the earlier model has been taken out of production. If you have an early model and suspect a defect, have it checked by a Peugeot agent. If a new compensator is needed, the non-adjustable type can be fitted providing that the crossmember has a brake compensator bracket on it; a new brake pipe is required with the new compensator.

16 Handbrake system – general

Handbrake lever – removal and refitting

1   Chock the front wheels and engage a gear. Raise the rear of the car and support it on stands or firm blocks. Release the handbrake.
2   Slacken the rear brake cable adjusters where they emerge from the car floor.
3   Working in the car, undo and remove the securing nuts and bolts and release the brake cables from the handbrake equalising bar.
4   DIsconnect the handbrake warning light switch, and remove the handbrake lever from the car.
5   Refitting is the reverse of the removal sequence. On completion adjust the cables as described in Section 4.

Handbrake cables – removal and refitting

6   Follow the procedures in paragraphs 1 to 3 above and, referring to Section 7, remove the brake drums and disconnect the cables from the shoe operating levers.
7   Withdraw the cable assemblies from the car by pulling them out of their front end locations and from the rear brake backplates.
8   Refitting is the reverse of the removal procedure but, before refitting a cable assembly, lubricate the inner cable in its sheath with a general purpose grease. Leave the end fitting which fits into the brake shoe lever dry.
9   On completion adjust the cables as described in Section 4.

17 Fault diagnosis – braking system

Symptom	Reason(s)
Excessive brake pedal travel	Friction linings excessively worn Automatic adjusters seized Disc run-out excessive Hydraulic system defect
Brakes pull to one side	Tyre pressures incorrect Friction linings contaminated on one side Piston or wheel cylinder seized on one side Pads or shoes renewed on one side only Steering or suspension fault
Judder felt through brake pedal and/or steering wheel on braking	Front wheels unbalanced or wheel nuts loose Disc pads excessively worn Disc run-out excessive Disc(s) scored or grooved Caliper mounting bolts loose Brake drum(s) distorted or scored Backplate attachment bolts loose Steering or suspension fault
Brakes binding	Seized hydraulic pistons Handbrake incorrectly adjusted or cable seized Automatic adjusters seized or defective Master cylinder defective
Brake pedal appears spongy or soggy	Air in hydraulic system Master cylinder defective
Excessive effort required to stop vehicle	Servo malfunction Friction linings worn, contaminated or incorrect grade Brake shoes incorrectly fitted New linings not yet bedded in Leakage in one brake circuit
Brake pedal travels to floor with little resistance	Leak in hydraulic system Master cylinder seals defective

Chapter 9 Suspension and steering

For modifications, and information applicable to later models, see Supplement at end of manual

Contents

Specifications

Suspension – general

Front suspension	Independent, coil springs and MacPherson struts with anti-roll bar
Rear suspension	Independent single pivot trailing arms with coil springs, shock absorber struts and anti-roll bar.
Shock absorbers	Peugeot telescopic double-acting hydraulic

Front wheel alignment

Toe-in	2 to 4 mm (0.0787 to 0.1575 in)
Camber *	0° 05' to 1° 35'
Castor *	0° 10' to 1° 10'
Swivel pin tilt	11° 30' to 12° 30'

* Non-adjustable

Dimensions

Wheelbase	2.62 m (8 ft 7.15 in)
Track:	
Front	1.37 m (4 ft 5.94 in)
Rear	1.322 m (4 ft 4.05 in)
Ground clearance (fully laden):	
GL	0.125 m (4.9 in)
GR	0.123 m (4.8 in)
SR	0.120 m (4.7 in)

Steering

Type	Rack-and-pinion
Ratio	20.1 : 1
Turning circle (wall to wall)	10.85 m (35 ft 7.17 in) diameter
Steering wheel turns (lock to lock)	3.6

Torque wrench settings

	lbf ft	kgf m
Front suspension		
Track control arm balljoint pin clamp bolt	36.2	5
Track control arm inboard pivot nut	39.8	5.5
Bump stop bolt	9.4	1.3
Anti-roll bar:		
Slotted nuts:		
Minimum	43.4	6
Maximum	86.8	12
Centre mounting/structure bolts	12.7	1.75
Centre mounting clamp bolts	25.3	3.5
Outer mounting bracket bolts	32.5	4.5
Shock absorber:		
Top mounting bolts	7.2	1
Shaft nut	32.5	4.5

Rear suspension

Shock absorber mountings bolts:		
Top	7.2	1
Bottom	32.5	4.5
Crossmember attachment nuts	21.7	3
Trailing arm spindle shaft nuts (inner and outer)	86.8	12
Anti-roll bar bolts	25.3	3.5

Steering

Rack attachment bolts	28.9	4
Flexible coupling nuts	16.3	2.25
Coupling clamp bolt	10.8	1.5
Track rod locknuts (early and later types)	32.5	4.5
Track rod balljoint pin nuts	25.3	3.5
Wheel nuts	43.4	6

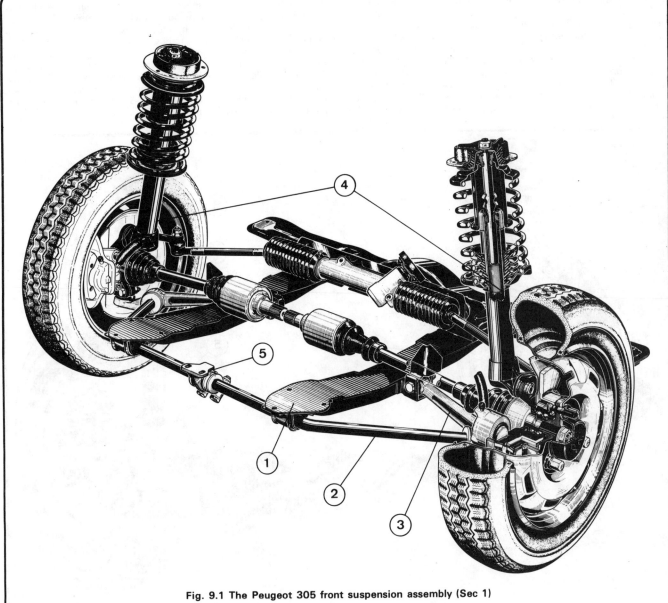

Fig. 9.1 The Peugeot 305 front suspension assembly (Sec 1)

1   Front subframe
2   Anti-roll bar
3   Track control arm
4   Shock absorber strut
    and axle assembly
5   Anti-roll bar centre
    mounting

1 General description

The Peugeot 305 has independent suspension at the front and rear. At the front, MacPherson struts incorporate telescopic double-acting hydraulic shock absorbers and coil springs. The struts are located at the top end in the inner wing top structure. At their bottom ends the struts are located by the track control arms and the anti-roll bar. The front wheel bearings locate in the lower part of the MacPherson strut which also incorporates the brake mountings, the track control arm mounting, and the steering arm.

The rear axle comprises two independent trailing arms which carry the rear wheel stub axles. Telescopic shock absorbers and coil springs control vertical movements of the wheels and independent wheel movement is limited by an anti-roll bar.

A rack-and-pinion steering unit is fitted and it is located at the bottom of the engine bay bulkhead behind the transmission unit.

The majority of the work on the suspension and steering systems which is within the scope of the home mechanic is limited to inspection, removal and refitting procedures as special tools are necessary for overhaul. These are also required in some removal/refit sequences but suggested alternatives, where possible, will help you overcome this problem. Before starting a job read through the instructions and be sure that your tools and facilities will be adequate.

All work undertaken on the steering mechanism must be to the highest standard. It is vitally important to maintain the integrity of the system. Always use the right fasteners with correct locking devices and renew them where indicated. Any adjustments must be within the specified limits and spare parts must be in new or faultless condition. Your life, and that of others, could depend on these points and if you are in any doubt concerning what to do or how to do it you should get professional advice or have the job done by a skilled expert.

2 Routine maintenance

1   Although the maintenance of the suspension and steering components has been reduced to a minimum it does not mean that it can be ignored completely. A periodic manual and visual check should be made.
2   Inspect the suspension joints and their attachments, including rubber bushes, for security, excessive play or deterioration.
3   Check the steering components and connections for signs of wear and for security.
4   Inspect the shock absorbers for looseness in their mountings and their rubber bushes for security and deterioration. Look for fluid leakage and, if evident, renew *both* shock absorbers on that axle.
5   Check the tightness of the steering rack attachment bolts, but don't exceed their specified torque. Check the joints for signs of excessive wear and the rack rubber gaiters for splits or leakage. Examine the steering shaft lower flexible joint for wear and fraying.
6   The manufacturers require the above maintenance to be carried out every 30 000 miles (45 000 km) but it would pay to do it more frequently, say every 10 000 miles (15 000 km) or even earlier, particularly on the older car.

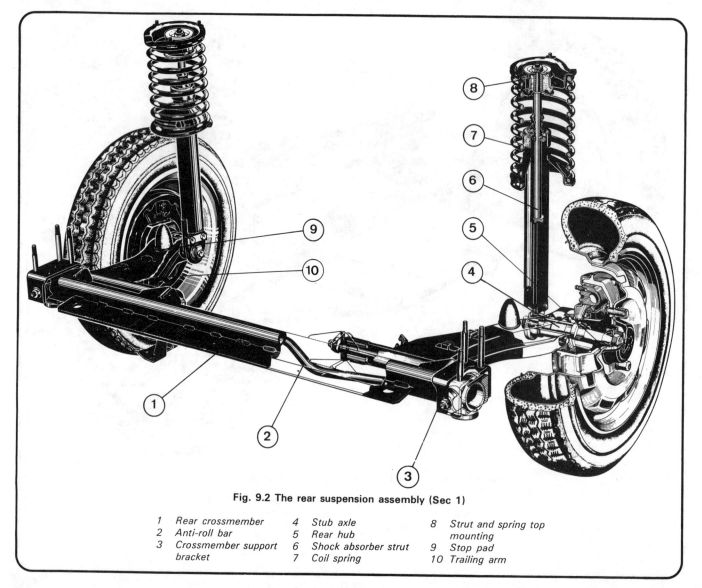

Fig. 9.2 The rear suspension assembly (Sec 1)

1	Rear crossmember	4	Stub axle	8	Strut and spring top
2	Anti-roll bar	5	Rear hub		mounting
3	Crossmember support	6	Shock absorber strut	9	Stop pad
	bracket	7	Coil spring	10	Trailing arm

3   Suspension and steering – testing and examination

1   Because of the construction of these vehicles the suspension cannot be considered in isolation from the steering and vice versa. The safety of the car depends to a very large extent on the steering and suspension and this is the reason why the compulsory test required for cars three years old or more pays special attention to the condition of these systems.

2   Any parts which are badly worn, weak or broken must be renewed immediately. Take great care checking the following items. The first list is of those parts which are particularly prone to wear with usage, and the second list is of special check points of those parts which tend to work loose. Check for wear:

   (a)   *Track control arm balljoints*
   (b)   *Track control arm rubber bushes*
   (c)   *Shock absorbers and mounting bushes*
   (d)   *Steering track rod balljoints and inner joints*
   (e)   *Rack-and-pinion*
   (f)   *Steering column bush*
   (g)   *Front and rear hub bearings*
   (h)   *Rear trailing arm bushes*
   (j)   *Anti-roll bar bushes*

All these points can be tested by physically moving the components concerned either by hand or by cautious use of a tyre lever or large screwdriver to see what degree of movement exists. Check for security:

   (k)   *Anti-roll bar*
   (m)   *Steering rack mounting bolts*
   (n)   *Steering rack-to-column coupling*
   (p)   *Shock absorber struts top and bottom mounting*
   (q)   *Rear trailing arms*

These checks represent only the minimum requirements. When making them be on the alert for *any* abnormality as different methods of use generate different types of wear and tear on the systems.

4   Front anti-roll bar – removal and refitting

1   The front anti-roll bar can be removed and refitted without the need for special tools, although they are used by Peugeot agents, but if the anti-roll bar centre mounting assembly is dismantled a special tool is essential to reset it. Removal of the anti-roll bar to renew rubber mountings or to renew other suspension parts will require the front of the car to be raised on axle stands or ramps or for the car to be positioned over a pit or on a lift. The car will require lifting and lowering at the front end at various stages during the removal and refitting procedure in order to line parts up or relieve weight or spring loads. Make sure that the car is stable when lifted and keep the handbrake applied.

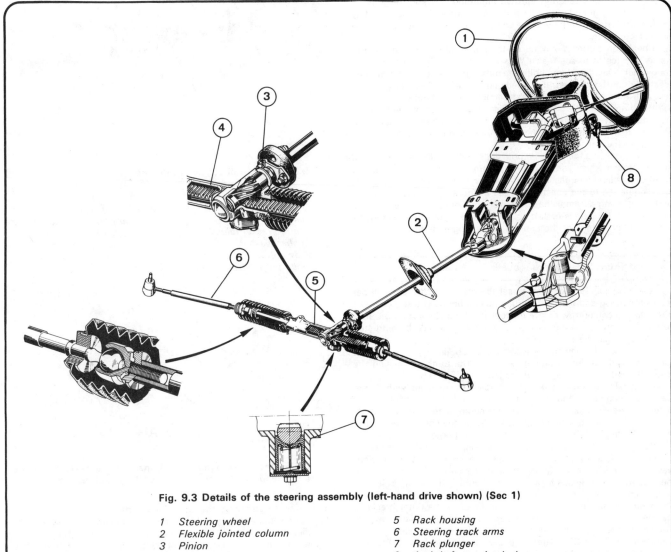

Fig. 9.3 Details of the steering assembly (left-hand drive shown) (Sec 1)

   1   *Steering wheel*
   2   *Flexible jointed column*
   3   *Pinion*
   4   *Rack*
   5   *Rack housing*
   6   *Steering track arms*
   7   *Rack plunger*
   8   *Anti-theft steering lock*

4.2 Undo the two mounting bolts (arrowed) but do not disturb the clamp bolts

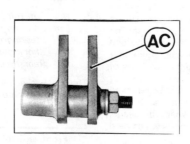

Fig. 9.4 The special tool 8.0903 AC for setting the preload of the anti-roll bar centre mounting (Sec 5)

5.3 One of the front anti-roll bar outer mountings

2   The preliminary stages are covered in Chapter 7, Section 2, paragraphs 2 to 7 inclusive, to which reference should be made. First though, remove the two bolts securing the centre mounting of the anti-roll bar (photo). Don't disturb the two nuts and bolts in the two clamps on the bar itself as these have to be specially set.
3   After removing the track control arm on the first side, remove the split pin, nut and washer from the end of the anti-roll bar on the other side and lower the car onto its wheels.
4   Undo the bolts securing the two mountings holding the anti-roll bar, raise the front end of the car and remove the anti-roll bar by tilting the free end. Retrieve the washer and spacer from the end of the bar just disconnected.
5   Check the centre mounting on the bar carefully for distortion or cracks and test it to see that it does not rotate easily. If it appears in good order, leave the clamp bolts and nuts tightened and the mounting assembly can be re-used. If it needs repair, renewal or refitting to a new anti-roll bar, refer to the next Section for overhaul details.
6   Refitting the anti-roll bar is basically a reversal of the removal procedure, but also refer to the procedure described in Chapter 7, Section 2, as alignment of the track control arm will require front loading on the car.
7   Before refitting the bar, coat both ends of it with Kluber Proba 270 Altemp grease which can be obtained from a Peugeot agent (part No 9730.67). Follow the reassembly procedure, leaving the bolts and nuts to be tightened to the specified torque at the stages indicated. If the centre mounting assembly has been disturbed or renewed, refer to the next Section for details of setting the preload before the bolts in the two outer mountings of the anti-roll bar are tightened.

5   Front anti-roll bar centre mounting – overhaul

1   A special tool is necessary to set the preload of the anti-roll bar centre mounting and before disturbing the mounting you should make sure that you can borrow or hire the tool. It is Peugeot part No 8.0903, item AC. If you cannot get hold of one the work should be entrusted to a Peugeot garage.
2   A repair kit of renewable washers can be obtained from a Peugeot agent to overhaul the mounting assembly. The parts comprising the assembly and their arrangement are shown in Fig. 9.5.
3   Removal and refitting of the anti-roll bar are dealt with in the previous Section, although complete removal in this case is not necessary. As soon as one end is free the centre mounting clamp bolts can be undone and the old components slid off the end of the bar. The outer mounting will have to be removed first (photo).
4   Reassemble the parts, carefully observing the correct sequence, on the bar. Make sure that the aluminium bracket is put on the right way round and use new Nylstop nuts on the two clamp bolts, fitting the bolts with their heads forwards. Don't tighten the clamp bolts and nuts at this stage.
5   If new rubber mountings are being fitted in the outer brackets, make sure that the heels on the flat surface of the rubbers are towards the rear. Grease their bores liberally and fill the internal recess in each using Kluber Proba 270 Altemp grease, obtainable from a Peugeot agent. Leave the bracket bolts untightened at this stage.
6   Fit the special tool, part No 8.0903 item AC, to engage the two clamps on the centre mounting. Hand tighten the nut on the tool

Fig. 9.5 The anti-roll bar centre mounting, exploded view (Sec 5)

1   Clamp bolts
2   Anti-roll bar
3   Clamp
4   Centre bracket (aluminium)
5   Rubber washer
6   Grey polyamide washer and white polyacetate washer
7   Rubber bush
8   White polyacetate washer and grey polyamide washer
9   Rubber washer
10 Clamp
11 Plain washers and Nylstop nuts

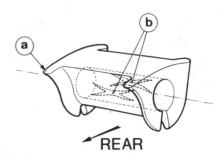

Fig. 9.6 Fit the outer rubber mountings with the heels (a) towards the rear and fill the recesses (b) with special grease (Sec 5)

sufficiently to compress the assembled parts.
7   Tighten the securing bolts in the outer mounting brackets to the specified torque. Check that the clamps in the centre mounting are aligned as shown in Fig. 9.7 and, with the special tool nut hand tightened, mark the position of the nut. From that position tighten the nut one complete turn. Then tighten the two clamp bolts and nuts to the specified torque.

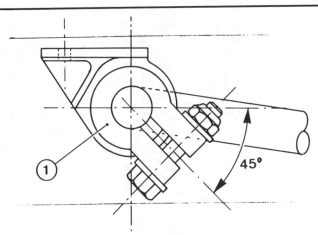

Fig. 9.7 Align the clamps (1) on the bar as shown (Sec 5)

Fig. 9.9 Tighten the nut (a) one full turn, then tighten the clamp bolts (1) and nuts (Sec 5)

Fig. 9.8 Hand tighten the nut on the special tool and mark its position (a) (Sec 5)

Fig. 9.10 Tighten the centre mounting bracket attachment bolts (Sec 5)

8   Remove the special tool and tighten the two bolts securing the centre mounting bracket to the structure to the specified torque.
9   Finally check the front wheel alignment, referring to Section 13.

6   Front suspension strut – removal and refitting

1   Raise the front end of the car and support it on axle stands or blocks. Check that the handbrake is firmly applied.
2   Most of the dismantling work is described in Chapter 7, Section 2, paragraphs 2 to 7, to which reference should be made. In addition you will need to remove the brake caliper and disconnect the steering arm from the track rod.
3   Refer to Chapter 8, Section 6, for details of removing the brake caliper. However, in this case it is not necessary to interfere with the hydraulic system. Don't disconnect the hydraulic hose, but swing the assembly to one side and support it on wire from a convenient point on the structure or engine. Take care not to stress the flexible hose as the assembly is heavy.
4   Disconnect the steering track rod balljoint by removing the nut and using a balljoint separator to extract the pin from the hub assembly.
5   Support the bottom of the suspension strut on wooden blocks to take the weight and remove the three securing bolts in the top attachment (photo). Carefully remove the strut from the car.
6   Refitting a strut is a straightfoward reversal of the removal procedure. When the strut is in position support it on blocks, fit a new locking plate to the top attachment, fit and tighten the three bolts to the specified torque and bend up the locking tabs. Check that the shock absorber shaft nut on the top of the strut is tightened to the correct torque; the slotted spindle must be restrained with a screwdriver during this check

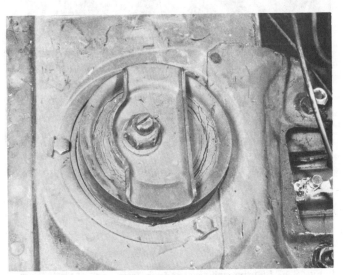

6.5 The front suspension strut top attachment bolts

142

Fig. 9.11 Remove the rear suspension strut top attachment nuts and washers (Sec 8)

8.3 The rear shock absorber bottom attachment bolts (arrowed)

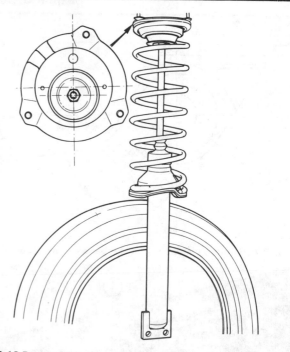

Fig. 9.13 Position the eccentric offset (arrowed) outwards towards the wheel (Sec 8)

Fig. 9.14 Use a spanner to align the strut (Sec 8)

Fig. 9.12 Pull the trailing arm down (arrowed) and remove the strut assembly (Sec 8)

Fig. 9.15 Tighten the bolts and bend up the lockplate (Sec 8)

7 Complete the reassembly by reversing the remainder of the removal sequence.

7 Front suspension strut – overhaul

Removal and refitting of a suspension spring on the front suspension strut and overhaul of the strut itself, including brake disc renewal, require the use of a number of special tools. Where either of these operations is necessary it is considered that the work should be undertaken by a Peugeot dealer who will have the necessary equipment.

8 Rear suspension strut – removal and refitting

1 Working inside the car, remove the rear seat back and squab, and remove the shelf to gain access to the top attachment nuts of the rear suspension strut. Undo and remove the three nuts and discard the old washers, as new ones must be fitted on reassembly.
2 Jack up the rear end of the car and support it on stands or blocks located just forward of the trailing arms on each side. Chock the front wheels and engage a gear.
3 Hold the shock absorber body and remove the two bolts securing it to the trailing arm attachment (photo).
4 Pull the trailing arm downwards and, at the same time, withdraw the suspension strut from the car.
5 Refitting a strut is largely the reverse of the removal procedure. On installing the strut in the car, position the maximum offset in the eccentricity of the upper mounting towards the wheel, see Fig. 9.13. Fit new washers to the three studs, fit and tighten the nuts to the specified torque.
6 Check that the bottom of the suspension strut aligns with its attachment on the trailing arm. If not, use an adjustable spanner or self-grip pliers to turn the strut into alignment. Lift the trailing arm and fit the front bolt with a new locking plate under its head.
7 Align the rear holes and fit the rear bolt. Run both bolts down but not tight,
8 Repeat the operations on the other strut and then lower the car to the ground. Tighten the two bolts on each strut to the specified torque and bend up the locking plate to lock them.

9 Rear suspension strut – overhaul

As with the front suspension struts, due to the need for a range of special tools, any work on the rear suspension struts other than removal and refitting should be undertaken by a Peugeot dealer who will have the required equipment.

10 Rear axle complete – removal and refitting

1 Although it is not possible for the home mechanic to renew the rubber bushes in the rear suspension, because of the number and variety of special tools needed, he should be able to remove the complete rear axle or a single trailing arm, if required, using an average

tool kit. Removal and refitting of a trailing arm is dealt with in the next Section, but it should be noted that both arms should receive similar servicing to maintain vehicle stability and it might be easier to remove the complete assembly for overhaul by a Peugeot agent.
2 Preferably place the vehicle over a pit or on a ramp, but if neither is available jack the rear of the vehicle up and support it, with the rear axle free, on stands or blocks. Chock the front wheels and engage a gear.
3 Refer to Chapter 8 and seal the brake reservoir. Disconnect the brake hydraulic pipeline at the most suitable point, forward of the axle assembly, depending on the car; this varies with the type of brake compensator installed. Where necessary unclip the pipeline from the structure to permit removal of the assembly. Seal the open ends of the pipelines to prevent dirt ingress.
4 Remove the rear section of the exhaust system, disconnecting it at the spring-loaded joint, where this is fitted.
5 Inside the vehicle remove the cover over the handbrake assembly and remove the handbrake bracket from the floor. Slacken the cable adjusters and disconnect the cables from the handbrake.
6 Still inside the car, remove the rear seat to gain access to the rear crossmember securing nuts. Remove the three nuts and washers at each side.
7 Underneath the car pull the handbrake cables through their locations in the floor. Jack up the vehicle and position a wooden block 120 mm (4.73 in) thick under each rear wheel. Lower the car onto these blocks to free the three studs in each end of the crossmember.
8 Carefully raise the rear end of the vehicle, *keeping the rear wheels in contact with the blocks,* and fully extend the rear springs. Bend back the tabs and undo and remove the two bolts in the bottom end of each suspension strut securing it to the trailing arm attachments.
9 Remove the blocks from under the wheels and, raising the rear end to clear, remove the rear axle assembly to the rear. Make sure that the car is left in a stable condition on its supports.
10 Refitting the rear axle assembly is a straightforward reversal of the removal procedure, but the following points will need attention:

   (a) *Use six new Nylstop nuts and plain washers on the three studs at each end of the rear crossmember, tightening them to the specified torque*
   (b) *Tighten the four bolts securing the two suspension struts to the trailing arm fittings, after fitting new locking plates, to the specified torque with the vehicle on its wheels*
   (c) *Refer to Chapter 8 to adjust the handbrake cables and bleed the hydraulic system*
   (d) *When reassembling the exhaust system tighten the nuts and bolts in the spring joint (where fitted) to compress the spring by 3 mm (0.1181 in) and then tighten the locknuts*

11 Rear axle trailing arm – removal and refitting

1 Refer to the previous Section regarding the prospect of removing the complete rear axle assembly if this is more profitable. If not, prepare the car in the same way as that described. The hydraulic pipeline can be disconnected at the hose junction of the arm to be removed, and the exhaust pipe only has to be removed if the left-hand trailing arm is to be removed. A special extractor is used by Peugeot to remove the trailing arm spindle shaft and this should be borrowed

11.2a The trailing arm spindle inner nut (arrowed)

11.2b The rear anti-roll bar retaining bolts on the right-hand side

Fig. 9.16 Tap down the studs securing the crossmember (Sec 11)

Fig. 9.17 Remove the brake hose bracket (1) and the spindle inner nut (2) (Sec 11)

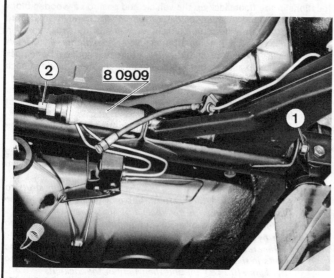

8 0909

Fig. 9.18 With the special extractor 8.0909 fitted, loosen the spindle outer nut (1) and tighten the inner nut (2) (Sec 11)

Fig. 9.19 Remove the two strut attachment bolts (1) (Sec 11)

11.4 The jacking point (arrowed) in front of a rear wheel

11.5 The trailing arm spindle outer nut

or hired to simplify the work; its part number is 8.0909. In addition a thin, open-ended spanner which can be used with a torque wrench is required to loosen or tighten the trailing arm spindle outer nut, metric size 22 mm.

2 Prepare the car, following the procedure in the previous Section, to the stage where the hydraulic pipe is disconnected, the handbrake cable is disconnected inside the car and, on models with the early type brake compensator, the spring is unhooked from its rear anchorage (don't disturb the adjustments on this type of compensator). Loosen the inner end nut on the trailing arm spindle shaft and remove the anti-roll bar securing bolts (photos).

3 Remove the rear seat, and undo and remove the three nuts and washers securing the crossmember to the underside of the floor. Tap the studs, with a soft-faced hammer or with a piece of wood interposed, to dislodge the crossmember. Pull the handbrake cable through its location in the floor.

4 Remove the brake hose bracket adjacent to the inner end of the trailing arm and remove the spindle shaft inner nut. Remove the rear wheel and rest the brake backplate on a block of wood 120 mm (4.72 in) thick with the car on a 250 mm (9.84 in) tall block located under

the jacking point just forward of the wheel well (photo).

5 Slacken the outer nut on the trailing arm spindle shaft as far as possible, using the thin spanner (photo). Fit the special extractor to the inner end of the spindle shaft and tighten the extractor nut to draw the shaft in towards the centre of the car to the limit of the outer nut on the spindle shaft. Now remove the outer nut and continue to withdraw the spindle shaft until it is free (Fig. 9.18).

6 Bend up the locktabs on the two bolts securing the bottom end of the suspension shock absorber strut to the attachment on the trailing arm. Undo and remove the bolts and remove the trailing arm from the car.

7 To refit the trailing arm, support the car on the 250 mm (9.84 in) tall block of wood under the jacking point just forward of the wheel arch and locate the front of the trailing arm between its attachments in the crossmember. Rest the brake backplate on the 120 mm (4.72 in) block of wood.

8 Engage the spindle shaft through the trailing arm and its attachments but leave it protruding at the inner end 42 mm (1.65 in).

9 Fit a new Nylstop nut to the outer end of the spindle shaft, and fit a new plain washer and Nylstop nut to the inner end but just run the nut on without tightening. Refit the brake hose attachment bracket.

10 Using a new locking plate, fit the two bolts securing the bottom end of the suspension shock absorber strut to the attachments on the trailing arm but do not tighten them just yet.

11 If necessary lift the rear end of the car to engage the three attachment studs with the holes in the car floor and fit three new plain washers and three new Nylstop nuts. Tighten the nuts to the specified torque.

12 Now the rear end of the car must be loaded to compress the rear suspension so that the distance between the centre of the stub axle on the trailing arm and the edge of the wheel arch above it is between 305 and 315 mm (12.0 and 12.4 in).

13 Give the trailing arm spindle shaft a tap with a soft-faced hammer to unstick it and tighten the outer nut to its specified torque. Then slacken it off one quarter of a turn.

14 Run the inner nut up until it contacts the bracket face and then tighten it to its specified torque.

15 Tighten the two bolts at the bottom of the suspension shock absorber strut to the specified torque and bend up the locking plate to lock the heads.

16 Refit the brake hose using a new fastener.

17 Refit the anti-roll bar securing bolts and plates using new lockwashers, and tighten the bolts to the specified torque.

18 Remove the load from the rear of the car and raise the rear to refit the rear wheel. Tighten the wheel nuts to the specified torque.

19 Refit the handbrake cable, and continue to restore all fittings to their original position following the reverse of the removal sequence. Refer to Chapter 8 for adjustment of the handbrake, bleeding of the

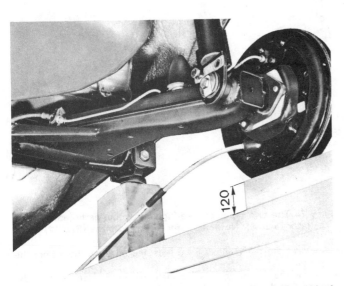

Fig. 9.20 On refitting the trailing arm support the car on a block with another block 120 mm thick under the brake backplate (Sec 11)

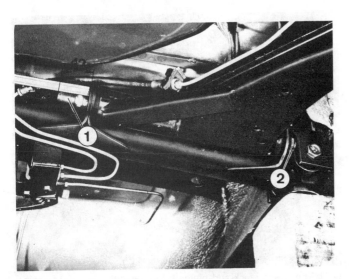

Fig. 9.21 Leave the inner end of the spindle (1) protruding and fit a nut (2) on the outer end (Sec 11)

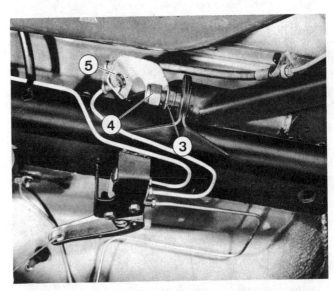

Fig. 9.22 Fit a plain washer (3) and a nut (4) on the inner end and refit the brake hose bracket (5) (Sec 11)

Fig. 9.23 Load the car to achieve the indicated dimension. Peugeot use a setting gauge (1) but this is not essential (Sec 11)

hydraulic system and, on vehicles fitted with the early type compensator, adjustment of the brake pressure compensator.

12 Steering rack-and-pinion – removal and refitting

1   Two standards of steering rack-and-pinion assemblies have been fitted to the Peugeot 305, and the principal difference concerns the track rods and their end fittings. The early assembly has the balljoints on the outer ends of the track rods integral with the rods (photo). Adjustment of the front wheel toe-in is made on the inner joints of the rods, inside the rubber gaiters. The later assembly has the balljoints separated from the rods but screwed into them and secured with a locknut on each. Toe-in adjustment is made by loosening the locknuts and rotating the track rods on the balljoint screw threads. Although the complete assemblies, including balljoints, are interchangeable, individual parts of the assemblies are not. The rack-and-pinion assembly itself is located behind the engine (photo).

2   To remove the steering rack-and-pinion, first slacken the front wheel nuts and jack up the front of the car. Support it on stands or blocks located at each end of the subframe. Remove the roadwheels.

3   Disconnect the balljoints at the ends of the steering track rods. On the early assembly use a balljoint separator; on the later, loosen the

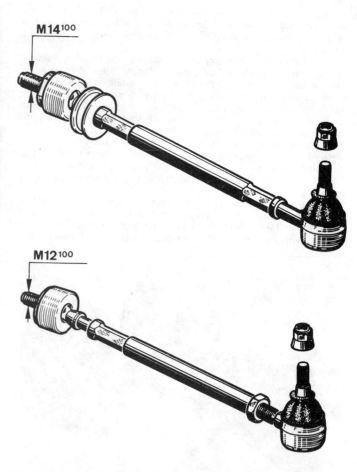

Fig. 9.24 The two types of steering track rods, early (above) and later (below). Numbers refer to thread sizes (Sec 12)

locknuts at the outer ends of the rods and unscrew them from the balljoints.

4   Inside the car under the facia shelf, loosen the clamp bolt at the lower end of the steering column flexible joint.

5   Just above the steering rack-and-pinion assembly remove the two upward-facing nuts on the flexible coupling and disconnect the steering column from the coupling.

6   Working under the car, undo and remove the two bolts securing

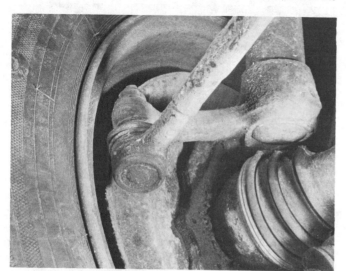

12.1a The early pattern of steering track rod

12.1b The steering rack-and-pinion is located at the rear of the engine subframe (engine removed for clarity)

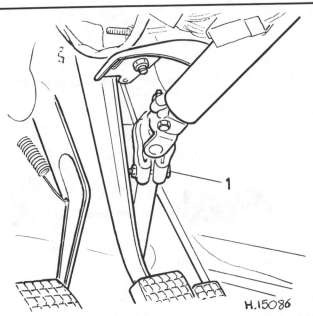

Fig. 9.25 Loosen the lower clamp bolt (1) in the flexible joint. LHD shown (Sec 12)

Fig. 9.26 Remove the two upward-facing nuts on the flexible coupling (1). LHD shown (Sec 12)

Fig. 9.27 Remove the two bolts (1) securing the rack assembly. LHD shown (Sec 12)

Fig. 9.28 Extract the steering rack and pinion assembly. LHD shown. (Sec 12)

the steering rack-and-pinion assembly to the structure.

7   Carefully extract the steering rack-and-pinion assembly to the right (on right-hand drive cars).

8   Repair or overhaul of the assembly should be entrusted to a Peugeot dealer who will have the necessary special tools. Inspect the condition of the flexible coupling and, if there is any doubt about it, fit a new one. Use new self-locking nuts if you do this and tighten them to the specified torque. Similarly renew the rubber gaiters if they look tatty or perished. If they were split or leaking grease however, have the assembly checked by a Peugeot dealer as the inner joints may have been contaminated with road dirt. When renewing the gaiters make sure that the wire clips are properly fitted as shown in Fig. 9.30 and locate the 'ears' of the clips so that they point downwards when the assembly is installed (photo). Clean the attachment bolt and bolt hole threads.

9   Before refitting the steering rack-and-pinion assembly set the steering wheel to the straight-ahead position and similarly set the rack to the corresponding position as shown in Fig. 9.31.

10 Insert the steering rack-and-pinion assembly into its location from the right-hand side of the car (for right-hand drive). Coat the threads

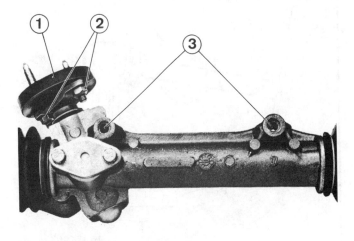

Fig. 9.29 If the flexible coupling (1) is renewed, renew the self-locking nuts (2). Clean the bolt holes (3). LHD shown. (Sec 12)

1

48

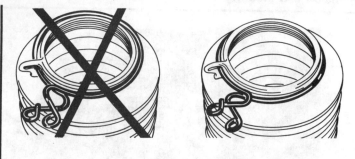

Fig. 9.30 The wrong and right way to fit the gaiter clip (Sec 12)

Fig. 9.31 The steering rack set to the straight-ahead position (Sec 12)

12.8 Arrange the steering gaiter clips to point downwards

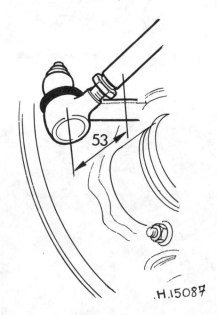

Fig. 9.32 Preset the steering track arms, dimension in mm (Sec 12)

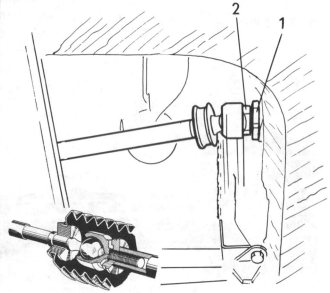

Fig. 9.33 Adjust toe-in on the early pattern steering track rod (1) after loosening the locknut (2) (Sec 13)

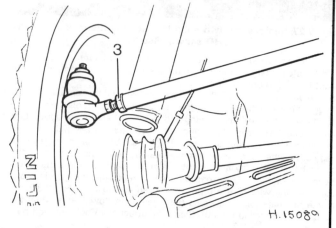

Fig. 9.34 On the later pattern steering track rod loosen the locknut (3) to permit rotating the rod to adjust toe-in (Sec 13)

of the two attachment bolts with thread locking compound and fit new washers. Fit the bolts and tighten them to the specified torque.

11 Assemble the bottom end of the steering column to the flexible coupling using two new self-locking nuts and tighten them to the specified torque.

12 Engage the steering column anti-theft lock. Move the steering wheel up and down to its limits and position it midway. Tighten the clamp bolt in the lower flexible joint under the facia to its specified torque.

13 Connect the outer ends of the track rods to the steering arms. On the early models fit the balljoint pivot pins to the arms and, using new self-locking nuts, tighten them to the specified torque. On the later models rotate the track rods to engage the threads of the balljoints and preset the lengths to 53 mm (2.0866 in) as shown in Fig. 9.32.

14 Fit the two front roadwheels, lower the car to the ground and tighten the wheel nuts to the specified torque.

15 Adjust the front wheel toe-in, referring to the next Section for information.

13 Front wheel alignment

1 Accurate front wheel alignment is essential to provide good steering characteristics and maximum tyre life. Much of the alignment accuracy depends on design geometry and the only adjustment available is for the front wheel toe-in.

2 Checking and adjusting toe-in requires accurate equipment not normally available to the home mechanic and it is recommended that the work is done by a properly equipped garage.

3 If the track rod settings have been disturbed, as a result of work on the steering rack-and-pinion assembly for example, an approximate adjustment can be made to enable the car to be taken to a garage for an accurate measurement and readjustment, as required, to be made.

4 The toe-in is the difference between the distances across the car measured at the front rim of the wheels and the rear rim of the wheels at hub centre height. A gauge can be made up with an adjustable pointer at one end to compare these distances when the wheels are in the straight-ahead position. The toe-in should be 3 to 4 mm (0.1181 in to 0.1575 in).

5 If adjustment is necessary (and remember that with only a small error the car can still be safely taken to the garage for an accurate check) proceed as follows.

6 *Early models, with no locknuts at the balljoint ends of the track rods.* Release the gaiter clip at the inner end of the track rod to permit moving the gaiter back and exposing the inner joint on the track rod. Slacken the locknut (see Fig. 9.33) and turn the inner balljoint socket to alter the length of the track rod. A half turn will alter the toe-in at the wheel rim by 0.65 mm (0.0256 in). If more than half a turn is necessary, the adjustment must be shared equally between both track rods to maintain turning lock angles. Hold the balljoint socket steady and tighten the locknut to its specified torque. When the toe-in is set, reposition the gaiters and their clips. See the previous Section concerning the correct fitment of the gaiter clips.

7 *Later models, with locknuts at the balljoint ends of the track rods.* With the locknuts loose, turn the track rods on the balljoint threads to alter the track rod lengths. A half turn of a rod will alter the toe-in on the related wheel rim by 1mm (0.0394 in) at the rim. Again, if more than half a turn is necessary to produce the correct toe-in, the adjustment must be equally shared on both track rods. Tighten the locknuts, with the bottom face of the balljoints horizontal, to the specified torque.

8 It is emphasised that this adjustment, in the absence of accurate alignment checking equipment, must be regarded as purely temporary and the car should be taken to a properly equipped garage for precise checks and adjustments to be made at the first opportunity. The same applies if accident or kerb-impact damage is thought to have affected the steering geometry.

14 Fault diagnosis – suspension and steering

Before diagnosing faults from the chart below, be sure that trouble is not due to:

    (a) Binding brakes
    (b) Incorrect tyre pressures
    (c) Inappropriate tyre combinations
    (d) Unbalanced wheels or loose wheel nuts
    (e) Accident damage

Symptom	Reason/s
Vehicle pulls to one side	Wheel alignment incorrect Steering or front suspension components excessively worn or distorted
Pitching and/or rolling on corners, over bumps and during braking	Shock absorber(s) defective – test by bouncing car at each corner. Poor shock absorber will allow oscillation Suspension struts or anti-roll bar mountings loose or deteriorated
Excessively stiff steering	Front wheel alignment incorrect Steering column misaligned or binding Front suspension unit(s) defective Rack-and-pinion unit unlubricated or defective
Excessive play at steering wheel	Steering balljoints worn Front suspension swivel joints worn Rack-and-pinion unit worn
Wheel wobble and vibration	Front suspension units loose or defective Shock absorber(s) defective Steering balljoints or front suspension swivel joints worn
Car sags at one corner	Coil spring broken or defective Suspension unit loose or defective Shock absorber(s) defective
Excessive or uneven tyre wear	Front wheel alignment incorrect Suspension unit(s) loose or defective Shock absorber(s) defective

Chapter 10 Electrical system

For modifications, and information applicable to later models, see Supplement at end oι manual

Contents

Specifications

Battery

Type	Lead acid
Voltage	12
Terminal earthed	Negative
Capacity:	
Europe	45 Amp-hours
Cold climate	60 Amp-hours

Alternator

	Paris-Rhone	Sev-Marchal
Maker		
Type No	A12R12	71210602
Power	500W	500W
Output at 14V	30A	35A
Corresponding speed (warm) rpm	3000	5000
Rotor resistance, ohms	5.5	5.5
Maximum speed, rpm	12 000	12 000
Drive ratio	1.89:1	1.89:1

Voltage regulator

Type no:	
Ducellier	8371
Paris-Rhone	AYB 2 119
Sev-Marchal	727 11 302

Starter motor

	Paris-Rhone	Ducellier
Maker		
Type No	D8 E 144	532 011A
Lock torque (kgf m)	1.20	1.15
Corresponding current (amps)	410	400
Maximum output under load (kw)	1.05	0.92
Corresponding current (amps)	200	220
Corresponding torque (kgf m)	1.05	0.9
Direction of rotation (view on pinion)	Anti-clockwise	Anti-clockwise
Number of pinion teeth	9	9

Light bulbs (typical)

	Wattage
Sidelights	5
Headlights	45/40
Direction indicators	21
Reversing light	21
Stoplights	21
Foglights	21
Rear number plate lights	5
Interior lights (festoon)	4
Boot light (festoon)	4

Fuses

	Rating (amps)
1 (at front)	Not used
2	5
3	10
4	15
5	15
6	10
7 (at rear)	5

Torque wrench settings

	lbf ft	kgf m
Starter motor bolts	25.32	3.5
Alternator securing bolt	25.32	3.5

1 General description

The electrical system consists of three major components: (1) the battery, (2) the alternator and its regulator, and (3) the starter. In addition the remaining electrical equipment can be divided into three further groups: (1) the lighting system, (2) auxiliary components and (3) instruments and warning light circuits.

The battery supplies a steady amount of current for the starting, ignition, lighting and electrical circuits, and provides a reserve of power when the current consumed by the electrical equipment exceeds that being produced by the alternator.

The alternator generates electricity in order to maintain the battery in its optimum charged state, and also to ensure that the electrical circuits are supplied with the correct current to enable the auxiliary components to function. A regulator is incorporated into the alternator circuit and effectively controls the output to match the requirements of the electrical system and battery.

The starter motor turns the engine with a pinion which engages with the flywheel ring gear. Due to the amount of currect required by the starter, it is necessary to use a separate circuit direct to the battery incorporating special cable.

When recharging the battery it is important to disconnect the terminal leads from the battery, otherwise serious damage can occur to the alternator internal diodes. In addition there may be other semiconductor devices and accessories fitted to the vehicle which could also be damaged.

The electrical system has a negative earth and it is important to check that such items as radios and extra electrical items are connected correctly.

In emergencies it is in order to connect another battery with the aid of 'jumper' leads, but connect the positive terminals first followed by the negative terminals, and remove them in the reverse order.

2 Battery – removal and refitting

1 The battery is located in the engine compartment next to the radiator and access is gained to it by lifting the bonnet.

2 To remove the battery disconnect the negative (earth) terminal, coloured green, first. Unscrew the thumb nut and ease the cable off the battery post, then similarly disconnect the positive terminal, coloured red.

3 Bend the terminal leads away from the battery, and unscrew and remove the battery clamp bolt which retains the battery to the tray (photo).

4 Lift out the battery carefully to avoid spilling electrolyte on the body paintwork.

5 Refitting the battery is a reversal of the removal procedure but, before reconnecting the terminals, clean off any corrosion present and smear them with petroleum jelly.

2.3 The battery clamp bracket and bolt

3 Battery – maintenance and inspection

1 Normal weekly battery maintenance consists of checking the electrolyte level of each cell to ensure that the separators are covered by 10 mm (0.4 in) of electrolyte. If the level has fallen, top up the battery using only purified water. Do not overfill; if a battery is overfilled or any electrolyte spilled, immediately wipe away the excess as electrolyte attacks and corrodes any metal it comes into contact with very rapidly.

2 As well as keeping the terminals clean and covered with petroleum jelly, the top of the battery, and especially the top of the cells, should be kept clean and dry. This helps prevent corrosion and ensures that the battery does not become partially discharged by leakage through dampness and dirt.

3 Once every three months remove the battery and inspect the battery securing bolts, the battery clamp plate, tray, and battery leads for corrosion (white fluffy deposits on the metal which are brittle to touch). If any corrosion is found, clean off the deposits with ammonia and paint over the clean metal with an anti-rust/anti-acid paint.

4 At the same time inspect the battery case for cracks. If a crack is found, clean and plug it with one of the proprietary compounds marketed for this purpose. If leakage through the crack has been excessive then it will be necessary to refill the appropriate cell with fresh electrolyte as detailed later. Cracks are frequently caused to the

top of the battery case by pouring in purified water in the middle of winter *after* instead of *before* a run. This gives the water no chance to mix with the electrolyte and so the former freezes and splits the battery case.

5   If topping up the battery becomes excessive and the case has been inspected for cracks that could cause leakage, but none are found, the battery is being overcharged and the voltage regulator will have to be checked.

6   Every three months check the specific gravity with a hydrometer to determine the state of charge and the condition of the electrolyte. There should be very little variation between the different cells and if a variation in excess of 0.025 is present, it will be due to either:

(a)   *Loss of electrolyte from the battery caused by spillage or a leak resulting in a drop in the specific gravity of the electrolyte. The deficiency was probably made up with purified water instead of fresh electrolyte*

(b)   *An internal short circuit caused by buckling of the plates or a similar malady pointing to the likelihood of total battery failure in the near future*

7   The specific gravity of the electrolyte for fully charged and fully discharged batteries at different temperatures of the electrolyte is given below.

Specific gravity – battery fully charged	Electrolyte temperature	Specific gravity – battery fully discharged
1.259	43°C (110°F)	1.089
1.263	38°C (100°F)	1.093
1.267	32°C (90°F)	1.097
1.271	27°C (80°F)	1.101
1.275	21°C (70°F)	1.105
1.279	16°C (60°F)	1.109
1.283	10°C (50°F)	1.113
1.287	4°C (40°F)	1.117
1.295	–7°C (20°F)	1.126
1.303	–18°C (0°F)	1.133
1.311	–29°C (–20°F)	1.142

4   Battery – electrolyte replenishment

1   If the battery is in a fully charged state and one of the cells maintains a specific gravity reading which is 0.025 or more lower than the others, and a check of each cell has been made with a voltmeter to check for short circuits (a four to seven second test should give a steady reading of between 1.2 to 1.8 volts), then it is likely that electrolyte has been lost from the cell which shows the low reading.

2   Top up the cell with a solution of 1 part sulphuric acid to 2.5 parts of water. If the cell is already fully topped up, draw some electrolyte out of it with a pipette or you can use a hydrometer as a syringe.

3   When mixing the sulphuric acid and water **never add water to sulphuric acid** – always pour the acid slowly into the water in a glass container. **If water is added to sulphuric acid it will explode.**

4   Continue to top up the cell with the freshly made electrolyte and then recharge the battery and check the hydrometer readings.

5   Battery – charging

1   In normal use the battery should be kept charged by the alternator. Except in extremely adverse conditions a regular need to charge the battery from an external source suggests that the battery or alternator is faulty, or that a short-circuit is draining the battery.

2   Charging from an external source may be useful to temporarily revive a flagging battery. A battery which is not in use should be given a refresher charge every six to eight weeks.

3   Disconnect the battery from the car's electrical system, and preferably remove it completely, before connecting a mains charger.

4   As a rule of thumb, the charging rate (in amps) should not exceed one-tenth of the battery capacity (in amp-hours), or one-fiftieth of the rapid discharge rate to -18°. This suggests a rate of between three and six amps, which is about the output of most domestic battery chargers.

5   Connect the charger to the battery, observing correct polarity (+ to + and – to –), then switch on the mains. Switch off the mains **before**

disconnecting the charger. Ensure adequate ventilation during charging.

6   Rapid or 'boost' charging should be avoided except under expertly supervised conditions. With the sealed type of battery there is a risk of explosion due to rapid build-up of gas during charging. Any battery can be ruined by overheating caused by over-fast charging.

6   Alternator – general description

The alternator generates alternating current (AC) which is rectified by diodes into direct current (DC) and is the current needed for charging the battery.

The main advantage of the alternator lies in its ability to provide a high charge at low revolutions. Driving slowly in heavy traffic with a dynamo invariably means no charge is reaching the battery. In similar conditions even with the heater, wiper, lights and perhaps radio switched on the alternator will ensure a charge reaches the battery.

The alternator is of the rotating field ventilated design and comprises principally a laminated stator on which is wound the output winding: a rotor carrying the field windings – each end of the rotor shaft runs in ball race bearings which are lubricated for life.

The rotor is belt-driven from the engine through a pulley keyed to the rotor shaft. A fan adjacent to the pulley draws air through the unit. This fan forms an integral part of the alternator specification. It has been designed to provide adequate airflow with minimum noise, and to withstand the high stresses associated with the maximum speed. Rotation is clockwise when viewed from the drive end.   The regulator is set during manufacture and requires no further attention. However, should its operation be faulty it must be renewed as a complete unit.

7   Alternator – maintenance

1   The equipment has been designed for the minimum amount of maintenance, the only items subject to wear being the field brushes and the rotor bearings.

2   The brushes should be examined after about 75 000 miles (120 000 km) usage, and renewed as necessary. The bearings are pre-packed with grease for life during manufacture and should not require further attention.

3   Every 5000 miles (7500 km) examine the condition of the alternator drivebelt. If it is frayed, cracked or stretched it should be renewed. If satisfactory, check for correct tension. Renewing and tensioning the drivebelt are explained in Sections 10 and 11.

4   Every 5000 miles (7500 km) clean the exterior of the alternator with paraffin-moistened rag, particularly around the ventilating holes at the opposite end to the fan. Also check the wiring connections on the alternator and on the regulator, located on the left front wheel bulkhead, for tightness and security.

8   Alternator – special precautions

1   Disconnect the battery terminals whenever the battery is being charged in the car as the alternator rectifying diodes could otherwise be damaged.

2   To avoid damaging the alternator the alternator/battery connections must be complete whenever the engine is run.

3   Never earth the wire number 8, marked EXC (field exciter), on the alternator or the regulator.

9   Alternator – removal and refitting

1   Open the bonnet and disconnect the negative battery terminal followed by the positive battery terminal.

2   Note the location of the alternator supply wires, then disconnect them from the rear cover (photo).

3   Loosen the adjustment and pivot bolts, swivel the alternator towards the engine and remove the drivebelt from the pulley (photo).

4   Support the alternator and unscrew and remove the adjustment and pivot bolts; the alternator can then be carefully lifted from the vehicle.

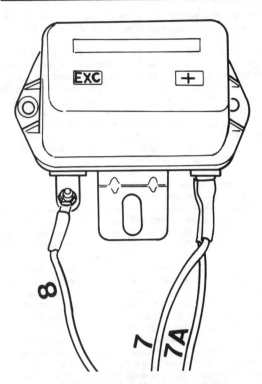

Fig. 10.1 The connections to the voltage regulator. For lead identification refer to wiring diagram (Sec 8)

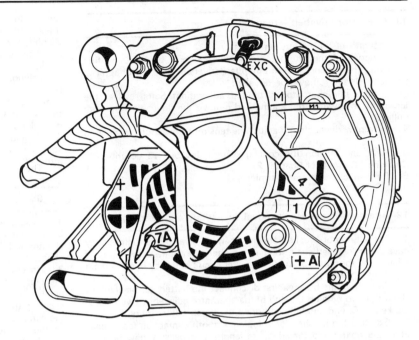

Fig. 10.2 The alternator connections (Sec 9)

9.2 The connections on the alternator rear cover.

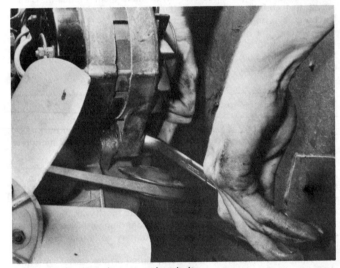

9.3 Loosening the alternator pivot bolts

5   Refitting the alternator is a reversal of the removal procedure but the alternator wiring should be connected and the nuts tightened before the battery is reconnected.
6   Refer to the next Section and adjust the drivebelt tension.

10 Alternator drivebelt – tension adjustment

1   Correct tensioning of the alternator drivebelt will ensure that it has a long and useful life. If the belt is loose, alternator performance will be affected and possibly the battery could be discharged. If the belt is too tight it will cause unnecessary alternator bearing wear. In either case the belt itself will suffer and its life will be shortened.
2   The drivebelt is tensioned by pivoting the alternator out and securing it when the belt is correctly tensioned.

3   To adjust the drivebelt tension first check that it is correctly located in both pulleys. Make two marks on the outer face of the slack belt 100 mm apart (work in metric units for this adjustment) and lightly tighten the pivot bolts and the adjusting link bolts.
4   Pivot the alternator outwards to tighten the drivebelt. You can use a lever to help achieve this but it must be a wooden one and it must be used only at the pulley end of the alternator. Levering on the case or at the end opposite to the drive pulley can easily cause expensive damage.
5   Tighten the belt until the marks on it have stretched to between 101.5 and 102 mm for a new belt, or to between 101.8 and 102.8 mm for a used belt. Then tighten all the alternator mounting and adjusting link bolts to the specified torque. A rough and ready adjustment of the tension can be made by tightening the belt until you can depress it by finger pressure at a point midway between the two pulleys for about $\frac{1}{2}$ in (say 13 mm), but you will probably get a better belt life by using the measured distance technique which is the Peugeot recommended procedure.

11 Alternator drivebelt – renewal

1 Disconnect the battery terminals.
2 Renewal of the alternator drivebelt can only be done by first removing the cooling system pump/fan drivebelt. Refer to Chapter 2, Section 10, and remove the drivebelt.
3 Loosen the alternator pivot and adjustment bolts, swivel the alternator in towards the engine and remove the drivebelt from both pulleys.
4 Fit a new drivebelt and adjust the tension as described in Section 10.
5 Refit and tension the cooling system drivebelt as described in Sections 10 and 9 of Chapter 2.
6 Reconnect the battery terminals.

12 Alternator brushes – removal, inspection and refitting

1 The alternator brushes are not likely to give trouble unless they have been installed for a long time, when they may show signs of wear. They form part of the field exciter circuit and they bear on plain slip rings on the rotor.
2 To remove the brushes first disconnect the battery terminal leads. Undo the two nuts on the end of the alternator adjacent to wire No 8, marked EXC, and carefully withdraw the brush holder (photo).
3 Examine the brushes for chipping, smooth contact surfaces, easy fit in the holder and for adequate length. If necessary new brushes should be fitted if they can be obtained but, if not, the alternator should be removed for servicing by a specialist servicing agency. If the brushes do not slide freely in the holders they can be eased slightly with a smooth file but be careful not to make them a loose fit. Clean off all dust and dirt with a petrol-damped soft lint-free rag and wipe the brush slip rings clean.
4 Refitting the brushes is the reverse of the removal procedure, taking care not to damage them when reinserting them in their locations. Make sure that the alternator and battery connections are complete before starting the engine.

13 Starter motor – general description

The starter motor is located on the clutch housing under the intake manifold and is of the pre-engaged type, having a solenoid mounted on top (photo).

The starting circuit is initially energised when the ignition switch key is turned to the starting position; at this stage current flows through the solenoid coil and the magnetic field produced causes the solenoid plunger to move. Movement of the plunger operates a lever arm which, in turn, slides the starter pinion into mesh with the flywheel ring gear. At the end of its travel the solenoid plunger bridges internal electrical contacts which then direct full battery current to the starter motor causing it to rotate.

When the engine starts, a one-way clutch on the starter armature shaft allows the pinion to spin on the shaft and be driven by the flywheel, thus avoiding damage to the starter which could occur if it was driven by the engine. As soon as the starter key is released, the solenoid coil is de-energised and a spring returns the solenoid plunger to the rest position. At the same time the lever arm disengages the starter pinion from the flywheel ring gear. As the solenoid plunger returns under the spring load, the electrical contacts are opened and the starter motor is de-energised.

14 Starter motor – testing on engine

1 If the starter motor fails to operate then check the condition of the battery by turning on the headlamps. If they glow brightly for several seconds and then gradually dim, the battery is in a discharged condition.
2 If the headlamps glow brightly and it is obvious that the battery is in good condition, then check the tightness of the battery wiring connections (and in particular the earth lead from the battery terminal to its connection on the bodyframe). If the positive terminal on the battery becomes hot when an attempt is made to work the starter, this is a sure sign of a poor connection on the battery terminal. To rectify,

remove the terminal, clean the contact surfaces and reconnect. Check the solenoid and starter connection for tightness, and check the wiring visibility for damage.
3 If the starter motor is still inoperative listen for a loud click when the ignition key is turned to the start position. If no click is heard, either the solenoid or its electrical supply is at fault. Disconnect the supply lead, No 46, from the solenoid and, with a voltmeter or a 12V bulb connected to the lead and to a good earth on the engine, again switch to start, and check that current flows. If it does then the solenoid is defective but if not, a fault in the supply must be located.
4 Should the battery be fully charged, the wiring intact, and the solenoid working, failure of the starter motor will necessitate its removal from the vehicle for examination.

15 Starter motor – removal and refitting

1 Disconnect the battery earth terminal cable.
2 Access to the starter is difficult and it will pay to remove the air cleaner and, if you still have difficulty in reaching the terminals on the starter solenoid, the intake manifold as well (Chapter 3).
3 Unscrew and remove the nut securing the heavy supply cable on the starter solenoid terminal and remove the cable and the thinner, positive lead mounted with it. Unscrew and remove the small nut securing the ignition switch cable to the solenoid terminal and remove the cable. Leave the terminal nut securing the feed to the starter motor on the remaining terminal done up (photo).
4 Unscrew and remove the three retaining bolts securing the motor to the clutch housing and carefully remove the starter from the engine (photo). Take care to avoid damaging the flywheel ring gear.
5 Refitting the starter motor is the reverse of the removal procedure. Tighten the retaining bolts to the specified torque.

16 Starter motor – dismantling and reassembly

1 Unscrew and remove the solenoid terminal-to-starter cable securing nut and remove the cable; slip the nut back on the terminal for security and as a reminder of the correct terminal to reconnect the cable to (photo).
2 Unscrew and remove the two nuts on the solenoid through-bolts. Remove the solenoid and the two bolts; the armature will remain with the starter motor assembly. Remove the solenoid spring (photos).
3 The horizontal plastic fulcrum pin on which the solenoid lever pivots is eccentrically mounted to provide adjustment of the pinion depth of mesh on engagement. As it is important to maintain its position on reassembly, carefully mark the head of the fulcrum pin and the adjacent casing. Then drive out the central metal pin followed by the plastic fulcrum pin (photos).
4 Note that the starter motor body is located to the pinion end casting by a tongue and slot. Undo and remove the two bolts securing the starter to the end casting. Remove the packing piece between the casting and the starter and carefully remove the end casting, leaving the solenoid-operated lever meshed with the armature collar. Then remove the lever from the collar (photos).
5 Carefully prise off the dust cap on the brush endplate which protects the end of the armature. Hold the pinion end of the armature spindle in a vice, using soft metal packing between the jaws of the vice and the spindle to prevent marking the spindle, and undo the bolt in the brush end of the armature spindle. *This bolt has a left-hand thread.* Take careful note of the washers and locking plate under the bolt head and their relative positions as they must be reassembled in the same sequence (photo).
6 Note that the brushplate is located to the motor case by a tongue and slot. Carefully lift the brushplate off the armature and case. Take careful note of the shim and wavy washers on the armature spindle at the brushplate end as, again, these must be reassembled in the same sequence. Do not attempt to separate the brushplate from the motor case; it is retained by the field cable (photos).
7 The brushes can now be examined for wear, chipping and freedom in their housings (photo). Clean off any carbon dust with a rag lightly moistened with petrol. If the brushes stick in their housings they can be eased with a smooth file but don't make them a loose fit.
8 Remove the armature from the starter case (photo). Clean the armature with a petrol-dampened rag and examine the commutator segments. If they appear glazed or dirty wrap a piece of glass paper,

12.2 Withdraw the holder to inspect the alternator brushes

13.0 The starter motor is underneath the starter solenoid, arrowed. (Intake manifold removed for clarity)

15.3 Undoing the starter supply cable terminal

15.4 The three starter retaining bolts (arrowed), loosened

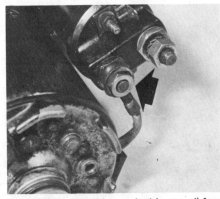

16.1 The supply cable terminal (arrowed) from the solenoid to the starter motor

16.2a Remove the solenoid ...

16.2b ... and the spring

16.3a Drive out the steel pin ...

16.3b ... followed by the plastic eccentric fulcrum

16.4a Remove the two through-bolts ...

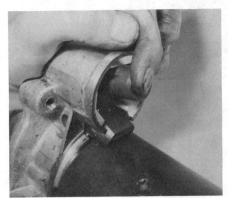

16.4b ... and then retrieve the packing piece between the end casting and armature case

16.4c Carefully remove the end casting

16.4d ... and the solenoid-operated plastic lever

16.5 The bolt in the brush end of the armature spindle has a left-handed thread

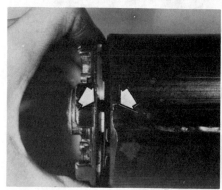

16.6a Note the locating tongue on the case which fits the slot on the brushplate (arrows)

16.6b Carefully note the shims and washers on the armature shaft

16.7 Examine the brushes ...

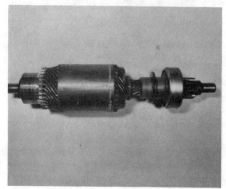

16.8 ... and the armature

not emery cloth, round the commutator and lightly clean them up.

9　Heavily grooved segments, signs of electrical arcing or such damage as a bent armature spindle or obvious overheating will require the attention of a specialist repair agency and even, perhaps, a new motor. Such repair work is outside the scope of this manual.

10　Reassembly of the starter is essentially the reverse of the dismantling procedure. It is important to reassemble shim washers in their original positions and make sure that the locating tongues and slots, mentioned during the dismantling procedure, are mated correctly on assembly. The solenoid lever fulcrum pin must also be refitted in its original position.

17.1 The fuse panel is located on the left-hand wing valance

17　Fuses

1　The fuse panel is located under a removable cover in the front left-hand wing valance; open the bonnet for access (photo).

2　There are seven positions for fuses in the panel which are numbered from front to rear. The first position is not used and the second position only used if rear fog lights are fitted. The remaining fuses, Nos 3 to 7, are allocated as follows, but variations may exist depending on the car:

Fuse No	Rating	Services
2	5A	Rear fog lights (where fitted)
3	10A	Reversing lights
		Electro-magnetic cooling fan
		Stoplights
4	15A	Car heater
		Windscreen wipers and washer
		Direction indicators
		Instrument panel tell-tale warning lamps
		Fuel gauge
		Water temperature indicator
		Front window winders (where fitted)
		Supplementary accessories
5	15A	Heated rear window
6	10A	Clock (continuous feed)
		Cigarette lighter
		Courtesy lights
		Horns
		Hazard warning lights
7	5A	Front and rear sidelights, boot and tell-tale
		Instrument panel lighting
		Rear number plate lights

3　The fuses are identified in the wiring circuit diagrams at the end of this Chapter by the key F1, F2, F3, etc.

Since start of series

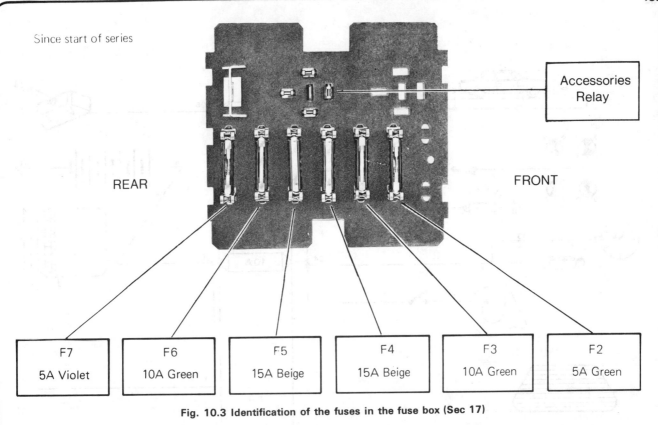

F7	F6	F5	F4	F3	F2
5A Violet	10A Green	15A Beige	15A Beige	10A Green	5A Green

REAR   FRONT

Accessories Relay

Fig. 10.3 Identification of the fuses in the fuse box (Sec 17)

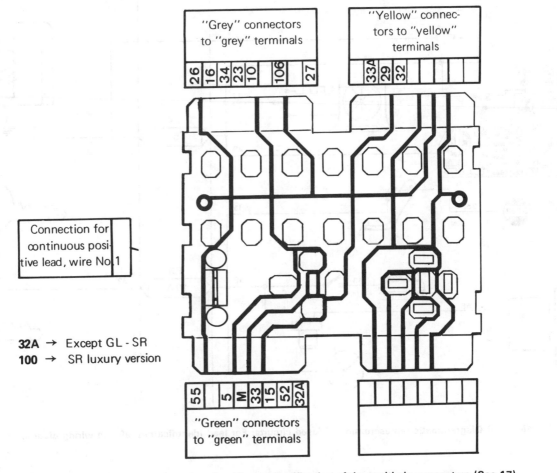

"Grey" connectors to "grey" terminals: 26 16 34 23 10 106 27

"Yellow" connectors to "yellow" terminals: 33A 29 32

Connection for continuous positive lead, wire No.1

32A → Except GL - SR
100 → SR luxury version

"Green" connectors to "green" terminals: 55 5 M 33 15 52 32A

Fig. 10.4 The printed circuit under the fuse board and identification of the multi-pin connectors (Sec 17)

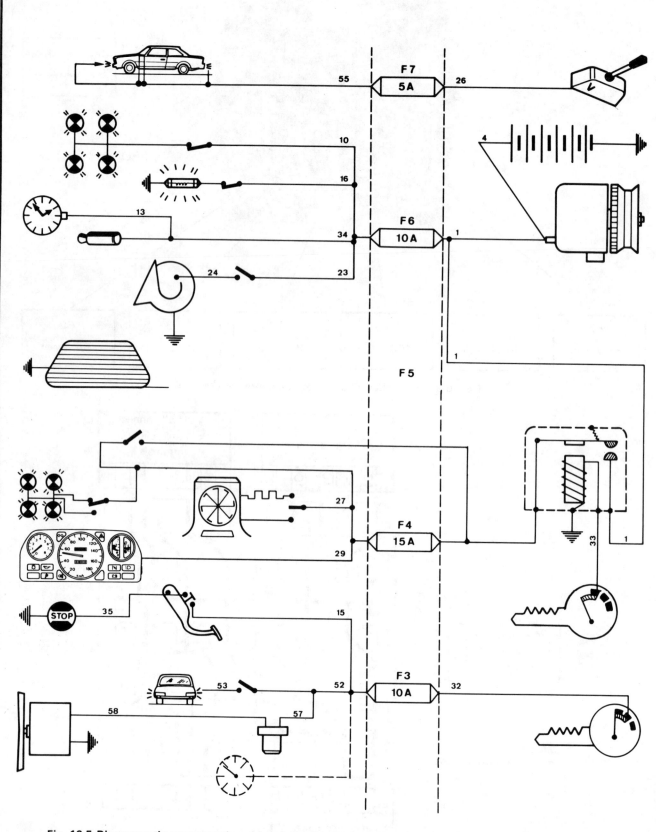

Fig. 10.5 Diagrammatic representation of fused circuits. For lead identification refer to wiring diagram (Sec 17)

18 Headlamps – removal, bulb renewal, and refitting

1   Disconnect the battery earth terminal.
2   Lift the spring-retained catch at the top of the headlamp unit to release the headlamp and pull the top forwards. Lift the headlamp unit out of its bottom locating sockets (photos).
3   To remove the bulb first disconnect the terminal connector from the back of the bulb. Lift the two springs retaining the bulb in the headlamp and remove the bulb by easing it out of its location (photos).
4   Refit the new bulb following the reverse procedure but make sure that the locating notch in the bulb flange is mated with that in the headlamp (photo). If halogen bulbs are used take care not to touch the glass with your fingers – use the protective sleeve supplied with the bulb. If by accident the glass is touched, clean it using alcohol (methylated spirit). Some bulb mountings can be adjusted for left or right-hand drive traffic. Check that the slider clip on the headlamp fitting, if applicable, is moved to the correct position.
5   Refitting the headlamp unit is the reverse of the removal procedure and provided that the adjustment screws have not been disturbed, it will not be necessary to adjust the headlamp alignment.

19 Headlamps – alignment

1   Accurate alignment of the headlamps is essential for your own safety and that of other road users. Alignment is best done by a garage with the necessary optical alignment equipment; the job is quick and inexpensive.
2   Temporary adjustment can be made, if this should be necessary, using the adjustment screws provided at each headlamp. At the centre top is a single screw for vertical adjustment of the beam (photo) and down at each lower corner, accessible from the engine compartment, are two finger knobs for left/right adjustment (photo). Adjust the beams so that, with dipped beam selected, each beam shines straight ahead and slightly below the horizontal. Have the beams properly adjusted at the first opportunity.

18.2a Lift the spring-retained catch ...

18.2b ... and lift the headlamp out of its bottom locating sockets

18.3a Disconnecting the bulb connector

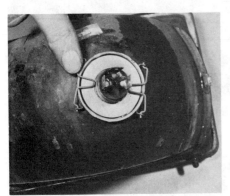

18.3b Lift the springs to ...

18.3c ... remove the bulb

18.4 Align the locating tongue and slot on refitting the bulb

19.2a The headlight beam vertical adjustment screw and ...

19.2b ... the horizontal adjustment knob (battery removed for clarity)

3   A further adjustment is provided to permit lowering the headlamp beams when the car is heavily loaded. This loading causes the tail end to settle with the result that, even with dipped beams selected, the headlamps shine upwards causing annoyance and possibly danger to oncoming drivers. This can be corrected by using the rocking lever behind each headlamp top retaining clip. With the right-hand side of the lever (viewed from the driver's position) pressed down, the lamp is in the normal load position. When the left-hand side of the lever is depressed, the headlamp is rocked slightly down to the heavy load position (photo).

20 Rear light clusters – bulb renewal

1   Access to the bulbs in the rear light clusters is gained from inside the boot. All the bulbs in each cluster are mounted on a printed circuit board which can be easily removed for bulb renewal.
2   To remove the printed circuit board, squeeze the two catches and slide the board towards the centre of the car slightly to release the retaining lugs and lift the board away. To remove the board completely, if this is necessary, disconnect the multi-pin connector at the outside edge (photos).
3   Each bulb rating is marked on the board adjacent to the appropriate bulb holder. All bulbs are single filament, bayonet fitting with the exception of one festoon type bulb in the right-hand cluster used to illuminate the boot interior. Note that there is no separate switch for this bulb – the boot interior light is on whenever the sidelights are switched on.
4   Refitting of the printed circuit boards is the reverse of the removal procedure. Check the operation of the lights on completion.

21 Front sidelights and direction indicators – bulb renewal

1   The front sidelight and direction indicator bulbs are located under a removable plastic lens on each side of the car.
2   To renew a defective bulb, unscrew the top and bottom retaining screws in the plastic lens and separate the lens from its mounting. Unclip the bulb holder to expose the two bulbs. Each is a single filament, bayonet fitting type, removed by depressing, twisting anti-clockwise and withdrawing. Refitting is the reverse procedure (photos).
3   When refitting the lens take care not to overtighten the screws or the plastic material may crack. Check the operation of the lights on completion.

Note: *Direction indicator system failure which cannot be cured by bulb renewal may be due to a fault with the direction indicator flasher unit. This is shown in Fig. 11.7 on page 186.*

22 Rear number plate lamp bulbs – removal and refitting

1   Two lamps illuminate the rear number plate and access to their bulbs is gained from inside the boot lid.
2   Each bulb is mounted in a holder. To renew a bulb, withdraw the holder from its mounting. Each bulb is a single filament bayonet fitting type and can be removed from the holder by depressing, turning anti-clockwise and withdrawing (photo).
3   Fit the new bulb, following the reverse sequence to that for removal, and test the operation of the lights on completion.

23 Interior lamp bulb – removal and refitting.

1   The two interior lamps are mounted on the left and right-hand sides of the roof lining. To renew a bulb, first remove the lamp lens by gently prising it out of its mounting with a blunt knife, taking care not to mark or damage the roof lining.
2   The festoon type bulb is removed by easing it out of its two spring clips.
3   Refitting the bulb and lens is a reversal of the removal procedure, but make sure that the bulb is firmly held in its clips; if necessary gently bend the clips inwards slightly to increase security. Test the lamp on completion.

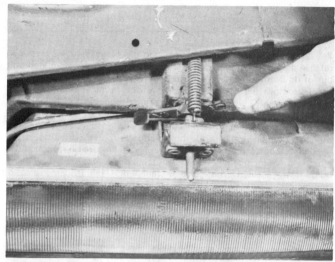

19.3 The headlamp beam load adjustment lever

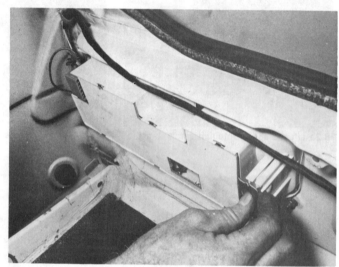

20.2a Slide the rear lights printed circuit board inboard ...

20.2b ... to remove it from ...

20.2c ... the lights assembly

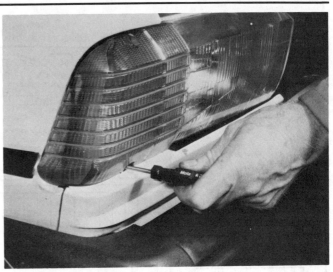

21.2a Remove the retaining screws to ...

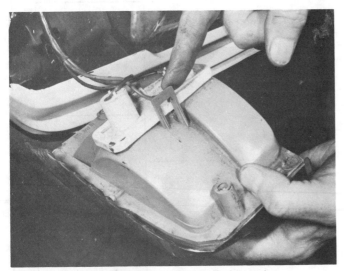

21.2b ... release the sidelights assembly. Lift the catch to ...

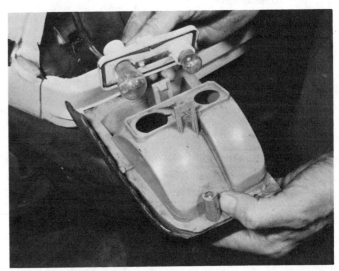

21.2c ... release the bulb holder

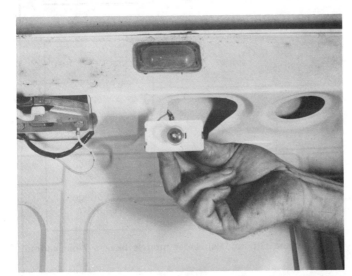

22.2 One of the two rear number plate bulb holders in the boot lid

24 Instrument panel – removal and refitting

1   Disconnect the battery earth terminal.

2   Remove the instrument panel bezel, that is, its surrounding frame, by lifting it at the bottom, pulling towards you and removing it from the panel (photo).

3   To release the instrument panel use a small screwdriver or similar tool inserted between the top of the panel and the facia to lift the top catch and let the top of the panel come towards you. Then lift the bottom of the panel out of the bottom retaining catch (photo). Movement of the panel will be limited by the connections on its rear; take care not to overstress them.

4   Disconnect the speedometer drive by squeezing the sides of the end fitting and pulling it out of the back of the speedometer. You may find that access is difficult; this can be improved by releasing the speedometer drive at the gearbox, refer to Chapter 1 for details, and then sliding the drive up towards the instrument panel to permit more movement of the panel.

5   Disconnect the electrical multi-pin connectors and remove the instrument panel as an assembly (photo).

6   Dismantling of the instrument panel should be limited to essential requirements. Take care not to mark the instrument faces or to leave finger marks on the inside of the 'glass'. The odometer reset knob can be gently pulled off its spindle but take care not to lose the washer,

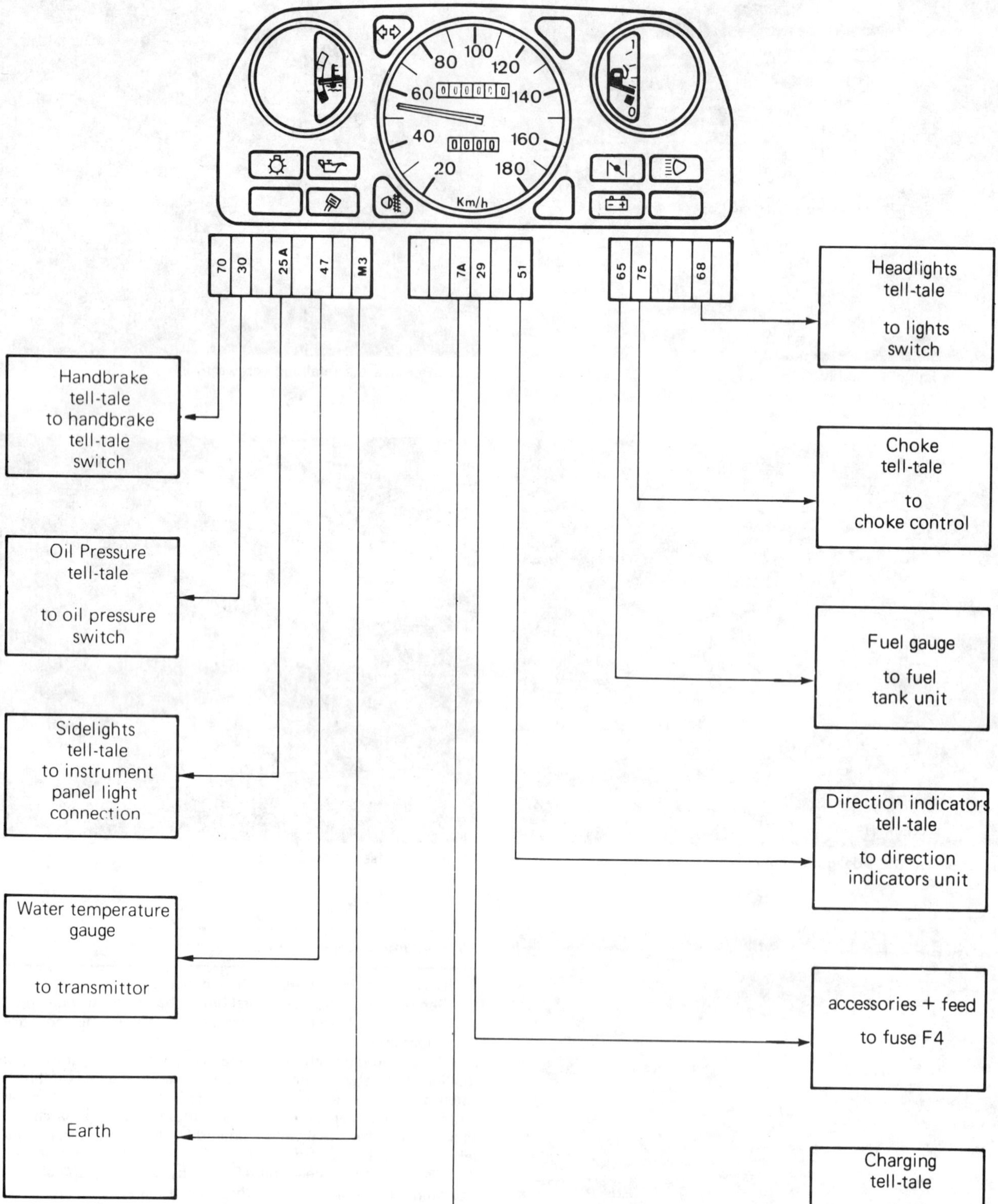

Fig. 10.6 Identification of the instrument panel multi-connector circuits (GL and GR models). Later models have a 7-pin central connector (Sec 24)

163

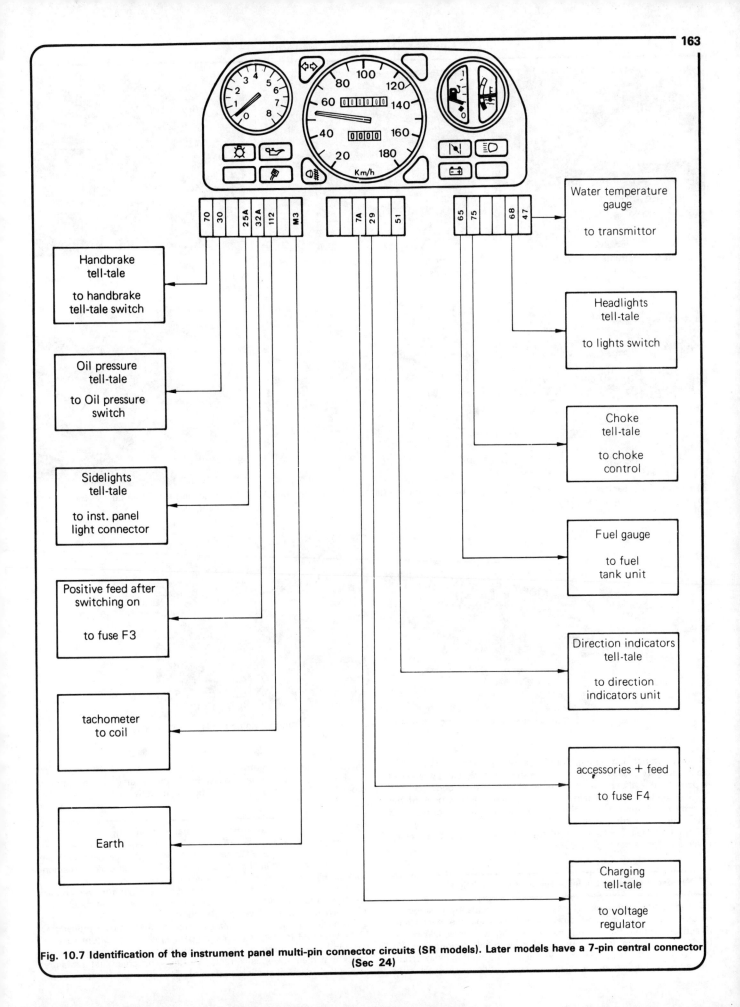

Fig. 10.7 Identification of the instrument panel multi-pin connector circuits (SR models). Later models have a 7-pin central connector (Sec 24)

24.2 Lift the instrument panel bezel at the bottom to remove it

24.3 Lift the bottom of the panel out of the bottom catch

24.5 The speedometer drive cable and the multi-pin connectors behind the instrument panel

24.6a Note the sequence of assembling the parts of the odometer reset knob

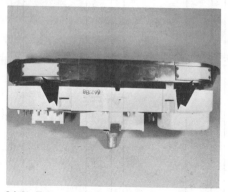

24.6b Two catches (arrowed) retain the panel front to the body

24.7 Renewing a tell-tale bulb in the instrument panel

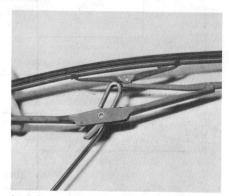

25.2 Removing a wiper blade from the arm

26.2 The wiper arm retaining nut is under the hinged cap

rubber grommet and spring. Note their sequence of installation for reassembly. Two catches at the top of the assembly can be released to permit removal of the front of the panel from its main body (photos).

7   Illuminating and tell-tale bulbs are retained in the back of the assembly. To remove a bulb give a partial turn anti-clockwise and withdraw it from the panel (photo).

8   Refitting bulbs, reassembly of the panel and its refitting are the reverse of the removal procedures.

25 Windscreen wiper blades – removal and refitting

1   The windscreen wiper blades should be frequently checked for deterioration and as soon as they fail to wipe the windscreen effectively without leaving smears they should be renewed. Wipe the blades clean with a damp cloth occasionally to help prolong their life.

2   To remove a blade assembly, lift the wiper arm off the windscreen and squeeze the clip in the assembly hinge fitting (photo). Slide the blade assembly off its arm.

3   Refitting a wiper blade assembly is the reverse of the removal procedure. Ensure that the clip is fitting correctly.

26 Windscreen wiper arms – removal and refitting

1   Before removing a wiper arm, turn the windscreen wiper switch on and off to ensure that the arms are in their normal parked position parallel with the bottom edge of the windscreen.

2   Lift the hinged cap at the bottom end of the wiper arm and remove the arm retaining nut. Lift the arm fully to release its catch and withdraw it from the drive spindle (photo).

3   Refitting a wiper arm is the reverse of the removal procedure. Make sure that the wiper blades are parallel with the bottom edge of the windscreen on refitting and operate the wipers on completion to check that their sweep is correct. (Wet the windscreen first if it is dry to avoid damage to the wiper blades.)

27 Windscreen wiper mechanism – fault diagnosis and rectification

1   Should the windscreen wipers fail or work very slowly, check the electrical connector to the motor for security and check the wiring for breakage, loss of insulation which could cause a short-circuit, and for adequate earthing. If all appears in order, check the motor current consumption by connecting an ammeter into the circuit and turning on the wiper switch. Current flow should not exceed 5 amps. The ignition switch and wiper switch must be on, of course.

2   If no current is available at the motor, check fuse No 4 by switching on the heater fan (ignition on) which will confirm the fuse as fit or otherwise. If satisfactory use a 12 volt test lamp and, by reference to the wiring diagrams, trace the current supply from the fuse to the motor connection.

3   Should the wiper motor take a very high current, check the wiper arms and linkages for free movement; if in order the motor will have to be removed for further investigations. Similarly if the motor takes a very low current and the battery is fully charged, the motor will have to be removed.

28 Windscreen wiper mechanism – removal and refitting

1   Disconnect the battery earth terminal and remove the windscreen wiper arms as described in Section 26.

2   Remove the four clips and the centrally located cross-head screw securing the black plastic grille on the scuttle air intake. Remove the gauze insect screen and pull off the two plastic supply pipes to the screen washers. Remove the plastic grille (photos).

3   Remove the two bolts securing the central water deflector panel over the heater fan and remove the panel. Place a piece of clean rag over the heater fan to prevent any loose article from falling into the fan assembly (photo).

4   Remove the water shield from each drive spindle. Undo and remove the two retaining nuts and retrieve the seal washers and thin washers from each spindle (photo).

5   Undo and remove the stepped bolt and lockwasher securing the mechanism in the car, unplug the electrical connector and remove the cable from the clips securing it to the assembly. Carefully manoeuvre the mechanism from the car (photos).

6   If it is necessary to remove the motor from the linkage mechanism, first note the aligned position of the motor spindle with the operating arm so that they can be reassembled in the same relative positions. To remove the motor assembly, undo and remove the spindle nut and then remove the three retaining bolts securing the assembly to the mounting plate (photo).

Fig. 10.8 The four clips (arrowed) securing the plastic grille (Sec 28)

28.2a The central, cross-headed screw in the plastic grille

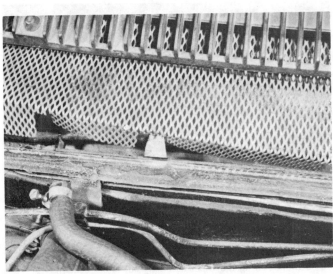

28.2b Removing the gauze screen

28.2c Remove the plastic supply pipes (arrowed) from each screen washer

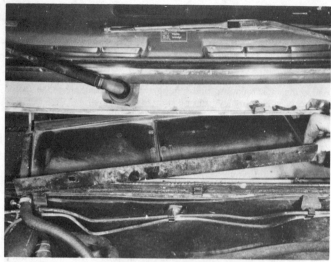

28.3 Removing the water deflector panel

28.4 Removing the spindle retaining nuts and washers

7   Refitting the motor assembly to the linkage mechanism is essentially the reverse of the removal procedure. Similarly, refitting the wiper mechanism to the car is also the reverse of the removal procedure, but the following points should be noted:

(a)   Lubricate all moving parts sparingly before installation
(b)   Fit the thin washer to the wiper arm drive spindles first, followed by the thick one and then the retaining nut. Tuck the washers under the bottom edge of the windscreen rubber seal, and tighten the nuts (photo)
(c)   Clip up the cable to prevent it becoming trapped in the moving mechanism when the wipers are operated. Don't forget to reconnect the connector
(d)   Fit the water deflector over the heater fan with the sponge side downwards, after removing the temporary cover

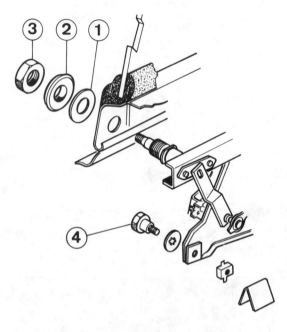

Fig. 10.9 Details of the windscreen wiper mechanism attachments
(Sec 28)

1   Thin plain washer   3   Retaining nut
2   Seal washer   4   Stepped bolt

28.5a Remove the stepped bolt and unplug the connector above it

28.5b Manoeuvring the wiper assembly out of its location

28.6 If the motor is to be removed, undo the drive spindle nut and the three attachment bolts

28.7a Tuck the washers under the windscreen seal

28.7b Connect the washer supply hoses and fit them in their locating clips, arrowed

28.7c Tuck the rear edge of the plastic grille under the windscreen seal

29.1a The windscreen washer pump and reservoir are located behind the right-hand headlamp and ...

29.1b ... the reservoir filler cap is in the top of the right-hand wing valance

(e) Before refitting the black plastic grille, reconnect the windscreen washer hoses and locate them in their securing clips (photo)

(f) When refitting the grille, tuck its rear edge under the bottom edge of the windscreen rubber seal and secure with one screw and four clips (photo)

(g) On completion check the operation of the wipers

29 Windscreen washer unit – general

1 The windscreen washer unit is operated by an electric pump which draws fluid from a reservoir tank and directs it to two nozzles which spray the fluid onto the windscreen. Operation is obtained by pressing the lights/wiper switch control arm in towards the steering wheel with the ignition switched on. The reservoir is located behind the right-hand headlamp unit and the pump is just in front of the reservoir. Access to both is by removal of the headlamp, refer to Section 18 for details, but the reservoir can be filled by opening the bonnet and then removing the plastic cover in the top of the right-hand wheel bay structure (photos).

2 Malfunction is usually due to blocked spray nozzles. If the pump can be heard running and, with fluid in the reservoir, there is no spray from the nozzles, they should be cleared with a piece of thin wire or a pin. Other causes of failure to spray are blocked, kinked or disconnected pipes. In winter failure may be due to water freezing in the pipes or in the reservoir; use of a proprietary windscreen washer antifreeze (see below) will prevent this problem.

3 Should the pump fail to run when switched on, and the wipers confirm that power is available, gain access to the pump and unplug the electrical connection. Connect a 12V test bulb across wire No 87 and the earth wire M23 and check for power availability. If the bulb lights then the pump motor must be renewed. If the bulb fails to light, trace the circuit back, using the wiring diagrams and the test bulb, until the cause of the failure is located.

Note: *Never use standard cooling system antifreeze in the washer system as the car paintwork could be damaged and, in any case, the*

windscreen will not be cleaned. Special windscreen washer additives to aid windscreen cleaning and to prevent freezing in winter are available from most garages and accessory shops.

30 Horns – fault diagnosis and rectification

1 Twin horns are mounted behind the front bumper adjacent to the right-hand headlamp and are accessible with the grille removed.

2 If the horn fails to operate disconnect the supply lead, wire No 24 and, using a 12V test lamp, check that power is available. If not, trace the cause using the wiring diagrams and the test lamp.

3 If the horns fail to operate with a confirmed power supply, check that they have a good earth to the structure. If this is sound then the defect must be in the horns although it is unlikely for both to fail at the same time.

4 Substitution of a known satisfactory horn will confirm the circuit. Defective horns will have to be renewed as they are not adjustable or repairable.

31 Radios and tape players – fitting (general)

A radio or tape player is an expensive item to buy and will only give its best performance if fitted properly. It is useless to expect concert hall performance from a unit that is suspended from the dash panel on string with its speaker resting on the back seat or parcel shelf! If you do not wish to do the installation yourself there are many in-car entertainment specialists who can do the fitting for you.

Make sure the unit purchased is of the same polarity as the car and ensure that units with adjustable polarity are correctly set before commencing installation.

It is difficult to give specific information with regard to fitting, as final positioning of the speakers and aerial is entirely a matter of personal preference. However, the following paragraphs give guidelines to follow, which are relevant to all installations.

Radios

Most radios are a standardised size of 7 inches wide, by 2 inches deep – this ensures that they will fit into the radio aperture provided in most cars. The Peugeot 305 is equipped to accept a radio in the console in front of the gearchange lever, but your radio might need an adaptor mounting plate for it to be fitted. It would be best to consult a dealer in this respect if you are in any doubt. The set must be securely fitted and properly earthed.

Use the radio manufacturer's instructions when wiring the radio into the car's electrical system. The power supply should come from an accessories feed, that is, one which is energised when the ignition switch is turned to the A position. Fuse No 4 supplies this circuit but it is rated at 15 amps and, to provide adequate protection for the radio, you must fit an in-line fuse in the power supply lead rated at the value recommended by the set manufacturer, usually about 2 amps.

The type of aerial used, and its fitted position, is a matter of personal preference. In general the taller the aerial, the better the reception. It is best to fit a fully retractable aerial – especially if a mechanical car-wash is used or if you live in an area where cars tend to be vandalised. In this respect electric aerials which are raised and lowered automatically when switching the radio on or off are convenient, but are more likely to give trouble than the manual type.

When choosing a site for the aerial the following points should be considered:

(a) *The aerial lead should be as short as possible – this means that the aerial should be mounted at the front of the car*

(b) *The aerial must be mounted as far away from the distributor and HT leads as possible*

(c) *The part of the aerial which protrudes beneath the mounting point must not foul the roadwheels, or anything else*

(d) *If possible the aerial should be positioned so that the coaxial lead does not have to be routed through the engine compartment*

(e) *The plane of the panel on which the aerial is mounted should not be so steeply angled that the aerial cannot be mounted vertically (in relation to the 'end-on' aspect of the car). Most aerials have a small amount of adjustment available*

Having decided on a mounting position, a relatively large hole will have to be made in the panel. The exact size of the hole will depend upon the specific aerial being fitted, although, generally, the hole required is of $\frac{3}{4}$ inch (19 mm) diameter. Try to get hold of a tank-cutter of the relevant diameter as this is the best tool for making holes in sheet metal. This tool needs a small diameter pilot hole drilled through the panel through which the tool clamping bolt is inserted. To avoid slipping with the drill and scratching the car finish, stick a piece of adhesive plastic tape over the spot you wish to drill and drill through the tape – it can be removed after you have made the hole. You can also cut the hole by drilling a hole and filing to size with a round or half-round file, but this takes longer and requires more energy. When the hole has been made the raw edges should be de-burred with a smooth file and then treated with an anti-corrosion preparation to prevent rusting.

Fit the aerial according to the manufacturer's instructions. If the aerial is very tall, or if it protrudes beneath the mounting panel for some way, it is worth considering fitting a stay between the aerial and the vehicle under the panel. This stay or brace can be made up from slotted metal strip available in most accessory shops. The stay must be securely bolted or screwed in place for it to be of any use. For best reception it is advisable to fit an earth lead between the aerial and the vehicle frame – this is essential if you have made a good job of anti-corrosion treatment when making the hole as the aerial will be insulated from earth.

It will probably be necessary to drill one or two holes through bodywork panels in order to feed the aerial lead into the interior of the car. Where this is the case ensure that the holes are fitted with rubber grommets to protect the cable, and to stop possible entry of water.

The Peugeot-installed radio available as an optional extra on the 305 has a roof-mounted aerial located in the centre front end of the roof with the aerial lead running down the windscreen pillar to the radio console.

The speaker is located in the middle of the facia in a housing which, when no speaker is fitted, is masked by a plastic grille. Fitting the speaker is just a matter of removing the grille from the aperture and screwing or bolting the speaker in place. Take great care not to damage the speaker diaphragm when doing this.

However, if you aim to fit stereo equipment, the two speakers will probably be 'pod' types which are best located on the shelf behind the rear seat. The pods can be secured to the mounting panel with self-tapping screws.

When connecting a rear-mounted speaker to the radio, the wires should be routed through the vehicle beneath the carpets or floor mats – preferably the middle, or along the side of the floorpan, where they will not be trodden on by passengers. Make the relevant connections as directed by the radio manufacturer.

By now you will have several yards of additional wiring in the car, use PVC tape to secure this wiring out of harm's way. Do not leave electrical leads dangling. Ensure that all new electrical connections are properly made (wires twisted together will not do) and completely secure.

The radio should now be working, but before you pack away your tools it will be necessary to 'trim' the radio to the aerial. If specific instructions are not provided by the radio manufacturer, proceed as follows. Find a station with a low signal strength on the medium-wave band, slowly turn the trim screw of the radio in, or out, until the loudest reception of the selected station is obtained – the set is then trimmed to the aerial.

Tape players

Fitting instructions for both cartridge and cassette stereo tape players are the same and in general the same rules apply as when fitting a radio. Tape players are not usually prone to electrical interference like radio – although it can occur – so positioning is not so critical. If possible the player should be mounted on an 'even-keel'. Also, it must be possible for a driver wearing a seat belt to reach the unit in order to change or turn over tapes.

For the best results from speakers designed to be recessed into a panel, mount them so that the back of the speaker protrudes into an enclosed chamber within the car (eg door interiors or the boot cavity).

To fit recessed type speakers in the front doors first check that there is sufficient room to mount a speaker in each door without them fouling the latch or window winding mechanism. Hold the speaker against the skin of the door, and draw a line around the periphery of the speaker. With the speaker removed draw a second 'cutting' line, within the first, to allow enough room for the entry of the speaker back, but at the same time providing a broad seat for the speaker flange. When you are sure that the cutting line is correct, drill a series of holes around its periphery. Pass a hacksaw blade through one of the holes and then cut through the metal between the holes until the centre section of the panel falls out.

De-burr the edges of the hole and then paint the raw metal to prevent corrosion. Cut a corresponding hole in the door trim panel – ensuring that it will be completely covered by the speaker grille. Now drill a hole in the door edge and a corresponding hole in the door surround. These holes are to feed the speaker leads through – so fit grommets. Pass the speaker leads through the door trim, door skin and out through the holes in the side of the door and door surround. Refit the door trim panel and then secure the speaker to the door using self-tapping screws. Note: If the speaker is fitted with a shield to prevent water dripping on it, ensure that this shield is at the top.

Pod type speakers can be fastened to the shelf behind the rear seat, or anywhere else offering a corresponding mounting point on each side of the car. If the pod speakers are mounted on each side of the shelf behind the rear seat, it is a good idea to drill several large diameter holes through to the boot cavity beneath each speaker – this will improve the sound reproduction. Pod speakers sometimes offer a better reproduction quality if they face the rear window – which then acts as a reflector – so it is worthwhile to do a little experimenting before finally fixing the speaker.

32 Radios and tape players – suppression of interference (general)

To eliminate buzzes and other unwanted noises, costs very little and is not as difficult as sometimes thought. With a modicum of common sense and patience and following the instructions in the following paragraphs, interference can be virtually eliminated.

The first cause for concern is the generator. The noise this makes over the radio is like an electric mixer and the noise speeds up when you rev up (if you wish to prove the point, you can remove the drivebelt and try it). The remedy for this is simple; connect a $1.0\,\mu F - 3.0\,\mu F$ capacitor between earth, probably the bolt that holds down the generator base, and the *large* terminal on the alternator to which are connected wires 1 and 4. This is most important for if you connect it to the small terminal, you will probably damage the generator permanently (see Fig. 10.10).

A second common cause of electrical interference is the ignition system. Here a $1.0\,\mu F$ capacitor must be connected between earth and the 'SW' or '+' terminal on the coil (see Fig. 10.11). This may stop the tick-tick-tick sound that comes over the speaker. Next comes the spark itself.

The Peugeot 305 is fitted with suppressed ignition plug leads and you should get no interference from that source, but if the leads have been renewed at some time with non-standard leads this may not apply.

There are several ways of curing interference from the ignition HT system. One is to use carbon film HT lead but these have a tendency to snap inside and you don't know why you are firing on only half your cylinders. So the second, and more successful method is to use resistive spark plug caps (see Fig. 10.12) of about 10 000 ohm to 15 000 ohm resistance. If, due to lack of room, these cannot be used, an alternative is to use 'in-line' suppressors (Fig. 10.12) – if the interference is not too bad, you may get away with only one suppressor in the coil-to-distributor line. If the interference does continue (a 'clacking' noise) then doctor all HT leads.

At this stage it is advisable to check that the radio is well earthed, also the aerial, and to see that the aerial plug is pushed well into the set and that the radio is properly trimmed (see preceding Section). In addition, check that the wire which supplies the power to the set is as

short as possible and does not wander all over the car.

At this point the more usual causes of interference have been suppressed. If the problem still exists, a look at the causes of interference may help to pinpoint the component generating the stray electrical discharges.

The radio picks up electromagnetic waves in the air; now some are made by radio stations and other broadcasters and some, not wanted, are made by the car. The home made signals are produced by stray electrical discharges floating around the car. Common producers of these signals are electric motors; ie, the windscreen wipers, electric screen washers, electric window winders, heater fan or an electric aerial if fitted. Other sources of interference are flashing turn signals, and instruments. The remedy for these cases is shown in Fig. 10.13 for an electric motor whose interference is not too bad and Fig. 10.14 for instrument suppression. Turn signals are not normally suppressed. In recent years, radio manufacturers have included in the line (live) of the radio, in addition to the fuse, an 'in-line' choke. If your installation lacks one of these, put one in as shown in Fig. 10.15.

All the foregoing components are available from radio shops or accessory shops. For a transistor radio, a 2A choke should be adequate. If you have an electric clock fitted this can be suppressed by connecting a $0.5\,\mu F$ capacitor directly across it as shown for a motor in Fig. 10.13.

If, after all this, you are still experiencing radio interference, first assess how bad it is, for the human ear can filter out unobtrusive unwanted noises quite easily. But if you are still adamant about eradicating the noise, then continue.

As a first step, a few 'experts' seem to favour a screen between the radio and the engine. This is OK as far as it goes, literally! – for the whole set is screened and if interference can get past that then a small

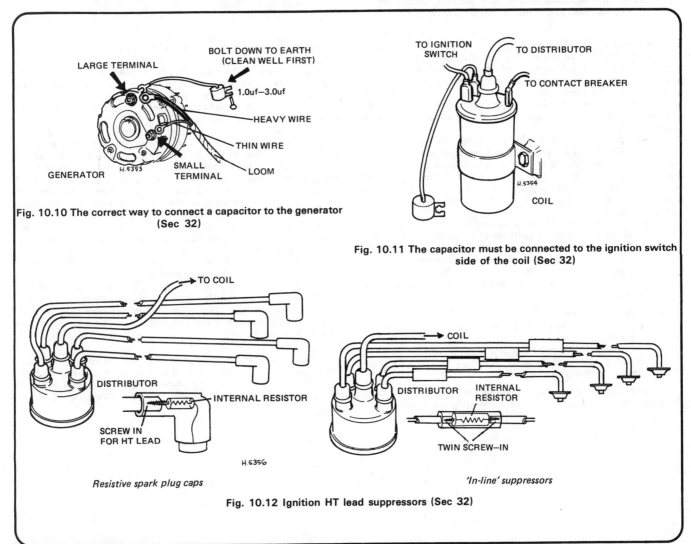

Fig. 10.10 The correct way to connect a capacitor to the generator (Sec 32)

Fig. 10.11 The capacitor must be connected to the ignition switch side of the coil (Sec 32)

Resistive spark plug caps

'In-line' suppressors

Fig. 10.12 Ignition HT lead suppressors (Sec 32)

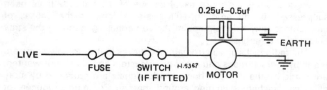

Fig. 10.13 Correct method of suppressing
electric motors (Sec 32)

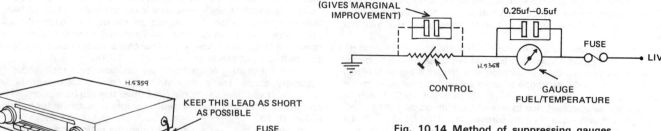

Fig. 10.14 Method of suppressing gauges
and their control units (Sec 32)

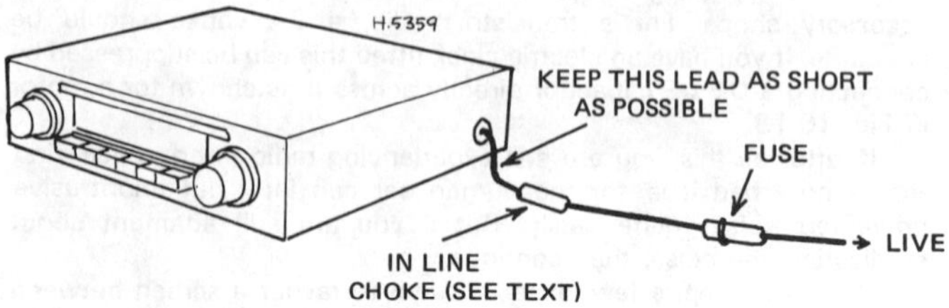

KEEP THIS LEAD AS SHORT
AS POSSIBLE

Fig. 10.15 An in-line choke should be fitted into the live supply
lead as close to the unit as possible (Sec 32)

piece of aluminium is not going to stop it.

A more sensible way of screening is to discover if interference is coming down the wires. First, take the live lead; interference can get between the set and the choke (hence the reason for keeping the wires short). One remedy here is to screen the wire and this is done by buying screened wire and fitting that. The loudspeaker lead could be screened also to prevent 'pick-up' getting back to the radio – although this is unlikely.

Without doubt, the worst source of radio interference comes from the ignition HT leads, even if they have been suppressed. The ideal way of suppressing these is to slide screening tubes over the leads themselves. As this is impractical, we can place an aluminium shield over the majority of the lead areas. In a vee- or twin-cam engine, this is relatively easy but for a straight engine the results are not particularly good.

Now for the really impossible cases, here are a few tips to try out. Where metal comes into contact with metal, an electrical disturbance is caused which is why good clean connections are essential. To remove interference due to overlapping or butting panels you must bridge the join with a wide braided earth strap. The most common moving parts that could create noise and should be strapped are, in order of importance:

a) *Silencer-to-frame*
b) *Exhaust pipe-to-engine block and frame*
c) *Air cleaner-to-frame*
d) *Front and rear bumpers-to-frame*
e) *Steering column-to-frame*
f) *Bonnet or boot lids-to-frame*

These faults are most pronounced when (1) the engine is idling, (2) labouring under load. Although the moving parts are already

connected with nuts, bolts, etc, these do tend to rust and corrode, thus creating a high resistance interference source.

If you have a 'ragged' sounding pulse when mobile, this could be wheel or tyre static. This can be cured by buying some anti-static powder and sprinkling it liberally inside the tyres.

If the interference takes the shape of a high pitched screeching noise that changes its note when the car is in motion and only comes now and then, this could be related to the aerial, especially if it is of the telescopic or whip type. This source can be cured quite simply by pushing a small rubber ball on top of the aerial (yes, really!) as this breaks the electric field before it can form; but it would be much better to buy yourself a new aerial of a reputable brand. If, on the other hand, you are getting a loud rushing sound every time you brake, then this is brake static. This effect is most prominent on hot dry days and is cured only by fitting a special kit, which is quite expensive.

In conclusion, it is pointed out that it is relatively easy, and therefore cheap, to eliminate 95 per cent of all noises, but to eliminate the final 5 per cent is time and money consuming. It is up to the individual to decide if it is worth it. Please remember also, that you will not get concert hall performance from a cheap radio.

Finally at the beginning of this Section are mentioned tape players; these are not usually affected by interference but in a very bad case, the best remedies are the first three suggestions plus using a 3 – 5 amp choke in the 'live' line and in incurable cases screen the live and speaker wires.

Note: *If your car is fitted with electronic ignition, then it is not recommended that either the spark plug resistors or the ignition coil capacitor be fitted as these may damage the system. Most electronic ignition units have built-in suppression and should, therefore, not cause interference.*

33 Fault diagnosis – electrical system

Symptom	Reason(s)
Starter motor fails to turn engine	Battery discharged Battery connections loose or corroded Starter motor connections, or earth straps, loose or broken Solenoid wiring loose or broken Ignition/starter switch defective Solenoid defective Starter motor defective
Starter motor turns engine slowly	Battery discharged Battery connections loose or corroded Starter motor connections, or earth straps, loose or damaged Starter motor defective
Starter motor spins without turning engine	Pinion actuating lever maladjusted Starter pinion or ring gear damaged
Starter motor noisy or rough on engagement	Mounting bolts loose Starter pinion or ring gear damaged
Battery will not hold charge	Battery connections loose or corroded Electrolyte level low Alternator drivebelt slack Alternator connections loose Short-circuit draining battery (isolate battery and see if charge retained) Battery defective internally Alternator or voltage regulator defective
Ignition (no-charge) warning light stays on with engine running	Alternator drivebelt slack or broken Alternator or voltage regulator defective
Ignition (no-charge) warning light fails to come on	Light bulb blown Bulb holder or printed circuit damaged Wiring disconnected or broken Alternator or voltage regulator defective
Fuel and/or temperature gauges give no reading	Wiring disconnected or broken No 4 fuse blown (other systems on that fuse will also fail) Gauge or sender unit faulty (earth wire at sender with ignition on – full gauge reading indicates defective sender, no reading indicates defective gauge or wiring)
Fuel or temperature gauges read maximum continuously	Lead shorting to earth Sender unit defective
Lights fail to come on	Bulb(s) blown Fuse blown (check other circuits on same fuse) Wiring disconnected or broken Earth fixing loose or corroded Switch defective
Lights very dim	Battery discharged Connections or earth mounting loose or corroded Incorrect wattage bulb fitted Bulb decayed with age Reflector or glass tarnished or dirty (if applicable)
Direction indicators fail to work	Bulb blown (failure, or excessively rapid operation, on one side only) Flasher unit disconnected, defective or inadequately earthed (failure on both sides) Direction indicator switch defective
Electrical component failure – general	Fuse blown (check other components served by same fuse) Wire broken or disconnected Multi-pin connector unplugged or pin(s) corroded Switch defective Earth return defective (wire broken, component mounting loose or corroded)

For windscreen wiper or horn faults refer to Sections 27 or 30 respectively

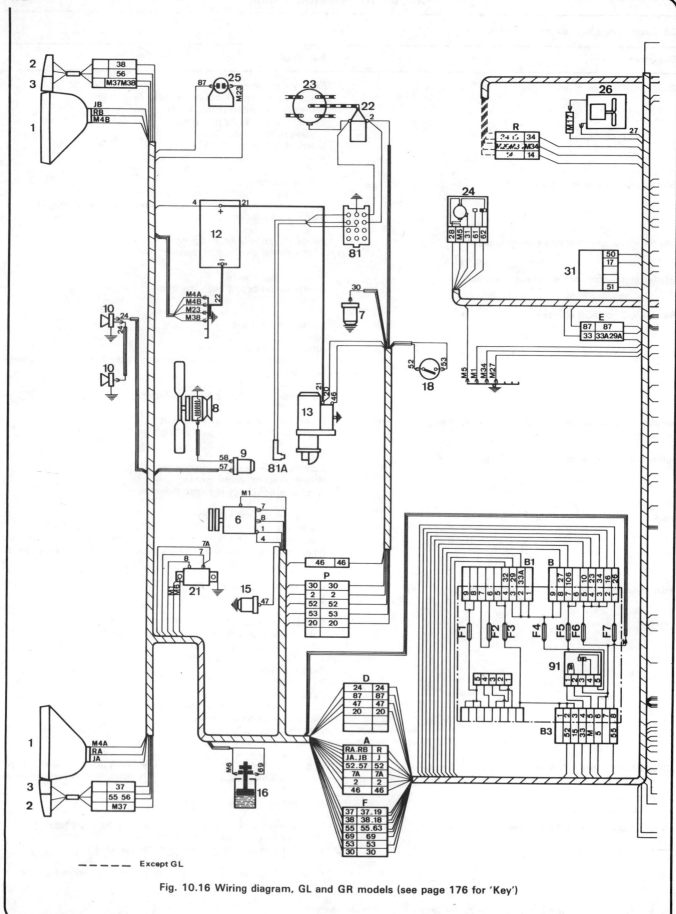

Fig. 10.16 Wiring diagram, GL and GR models (see page 176 for 'Key')

- - - - - Except GL

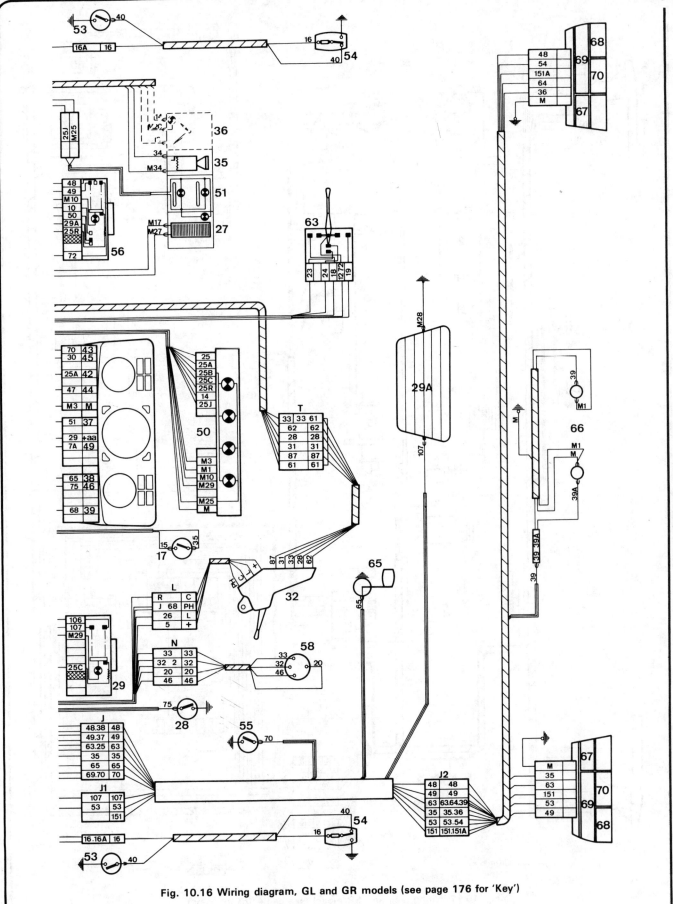

Fig. 10.16 Wiring diagram, GL and GR models (see page 176 for 'Key')

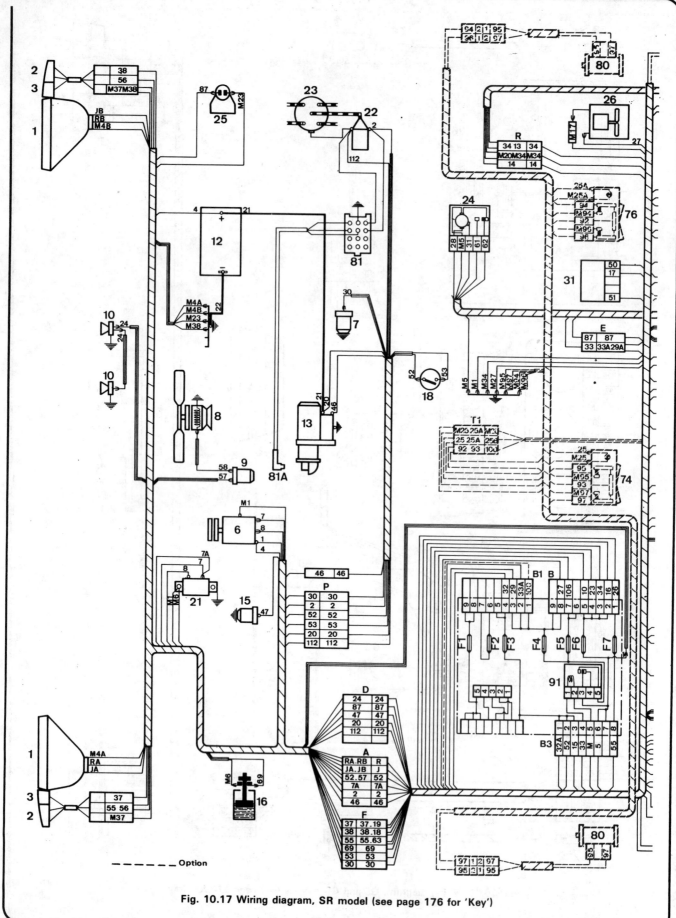

Fig. 10.17 Wiring diagram, SR model (see page 176 for 'Key')

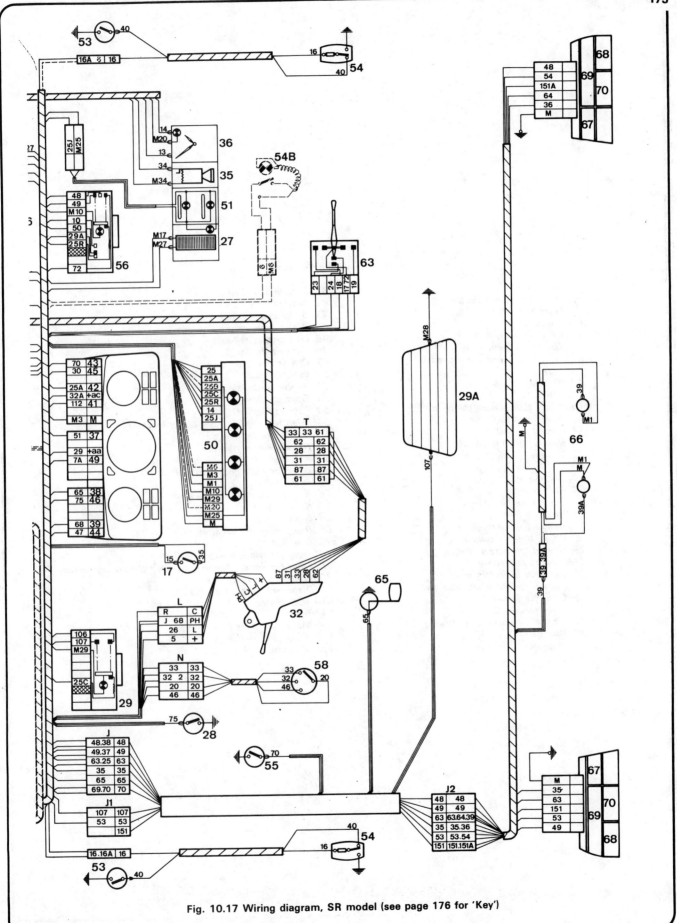

Fig. 10.17 Wiring diagram, SR model (see page 176 for 'Key')

Key to wiring diagram

1 Headlight
2 Front direction indicator
3 Front sidelight
6 Alternator
7 Oil pressure switch
8 Electro-magnetic fan
9 Electro-magnetic fan thermostat
10 Horn
12 Battery
13 Starter
15 Water temperature transmitter
16 Brake fluid reservoir
17 Stoplights switch
18 Reversing lights switch
21 Voltage regulator
22 Coil
23 Distributor
24 Screen wiper
25 Screen washer pump
26 Heater blower
27 Heater blower rheostat
28 Choke tell-tale switch
29 Heated rear screen switch
29A Heated rear screen
31 Direction indicators unit
32 Lights – screen wash/wipe switch
35 Cigarette lighter
36 Clock (except GL)
37 Direction indicators tell-tale
38 Fuel gauge
39 Main beam tell-tale

41 Tachometer (SR)
42 Sidelights tell-tale
43 Brakes system tell-tale
44 Water temperature indicator
45 Oil pressure tell-tale
46 Choke tell-tale
47 Charge indicator
50 Facia lighting
51 Heater controls lighting
53 Front door switch
54 Courtesy light
54B Map reading light (SR luxury version)
55 Handbrake tell-tale switch
56 Hazard warning switch
58 Anti-theft/ignition switch
63 Direction indicators/horn switch
65 Fuel tank unit
66 Rear number plate lighting
67 Reversing lights
68 Stoplights
69 Rear direction indicators
70 Rear lights
74 Front LH window winder switch ⎫
76 Front RH window winder switch ⎬ SR Luxury version
80 Window winder motor ⎭
81 Diagnostic take-off socket
81A TDC sensor
91 Relay
+aa Accessories feed
+ac Feed after switching on
+p Continuous feed

Chapter 11 Bodywork and fittings

For modifications, and information applicable to later models, see Supplement at end of manual

Contents

1 General description

The structure of the Peugeot 305 is based on the monocoque principle of a welded shell built up of a variety of preformed parts. The design is a direct result of trials with the Peugeot Experimental Safety Vehicle (VSS) resulting in a rigid, non-collapsible compartment for the occupants which is protected at front and rear by impact-absorbing structures. Side impact protection is achieved with a heavily ribbed and reinforced floor, anti-jamming doors with special safety locks and a protected fuel tank. The bonnet attachments are specially arranged to prevent rearward movement in the event of a collision.

Extensive anti-corrosive treatment by dipping and plating structural components is augmented by sprayed-on anti-chipping compounds and the injection of wax/tar compounds inside box sections.

As a result the 305 is a leading example of the typically robust product with built-in long life that has come to be expected from the Peugeot stable.

2 Maintenance – bodywork and underframe

1 The general condition of a car's bodywork is the thing that significantly affects it value. Maintenance is easy but needs to be regular. Neglect, particularly after minor damage, can lead quickly to further deterioration and costly repair bills. It is important also to keep watch on those parts of the car not immediately visible, for instance the underside, inside all the wheel arches and the lower part of the engine compartment.

2 The basic maintenance routine for the bodywork is washing – preferably with a lot of water, from a hose. This will remove all the loose solids which may have stuck to the car. It is important to flush these off in such a way as to prevent grit from scratching the finish. The wheel arches and underframe need washing in the same way to remove any accumulated mud which will retain moisture and tend to encourage rust. Paradoxically enough, the best time to clean the underframe and wheel arches is in wet weather when the mud is thoroughly wet and soft. In very wet weather the underframe is usually cleaned of large accumulations automatically and this is a good time for inspection.

3 Periodically, it is a good idea to have the whole of the underframe of the car steam cleaned, engine compartment included, so that a thorough inspection can be carried out to see what minor repairs and renovations are necessary. Steam cleaning is available at many garages and is necessary for removal of the accumulation of oily grime which sometimes is allowed to become thick in certain areas. If steam cleaning facilities are not available, there are one or two excellent grease solvents available which can be brush applied. The dirt can then be simply hosed off.

4 After washing paintwork, wipe off with a chamois leather to give an unspotted clear finish. A coat of clear protective wax polish will give

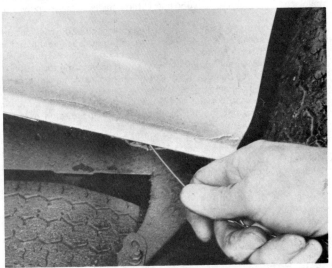

2.4 Use a piece of wire to check that the body and door drains are clear

added protection against chemical pollutants in the air. If the paintwork sheen has dulled or oxidised, use a cleaner/polisher combination to restore the brilliance of the shine. This requires a little effort, but such dulling is usually caused because regular washing has been neglected. Always check that the door and ventilator opening drain holes and pipes are completely clear so that water can be drained out (photo). Bright work should be treated in the same way as paintwork. Windscreens and windows can be kept clear of the smeary film which often appears, by adding a little ammonia to the water. If they are scratched, a good rub with a proprietary metal polish will often clear them. Never use any form of wax or other body or chromium polish on glass.

3 Maintenance – upholstery and carpets

1 Mats and carpets should be brushed or vacuum cleaned regularly to keep them free of grit. If they are badly stained remove them from the car for scrubbing or sponging and make quite sure they are dry before refitting. Seats and interior trim panels can be kept clean by a wipe over with a damp cloth. If they do become stained (which can be more apparent on light coloured upholstery) use a little liquid detergent and a soft nail brush to scour the grime out of the grain of the material. Do not forget to keep the head lining clean in the same way as the upholstery. When using liquid cleaners inside the car do not

over-wet the surfaces being cleaned. Excessive damp could get into the seams and padded interior causing stains, offensive odours or even rot. If the inside of the car gets wet accidentally it is worthwhile taking some trouble to dry it out properly, particularly where carpets are involved. *Do not leave oil or electric heaters inside the car for this purpose.*

4 Minor body damage – repair

The photographic sequences on pages 182 and 183 illustrate the operations detailed in the following sub-sections.

Repair of minor scratches in the vehicle's bodywork

If the scratch is very superficial, and does not penetrate to the metal of the bodywork, repair is very simple. Lightly rub the area of the scratch with a paintwork renovator, or a very fine cutting paste, to remove loose paint from the scratch and to clear the surrounding bodywork of wax polish. Rinse the area with clean water.

Apply touch-up paint to the scratch using a thin paint brush; continue to apply thin layers of paint until the surface of the paint in the scratch is level with the surrounding paintwork. Allow the new paint at least two weeks to harden: then blend it into the surrounding paintwork by rubbing the paintwork, in the scratch area, with a paintwork renovator or a very fine cutting paste. Finally, apply wax polish.

Where the scratch has penetrated right through to the metal of the bodywork, causing the metal to rust, a different repair technique is required. Remove any loose rust from the bottom of the scratch with a penknife, then apply rust inhibiting paint to prevent the formation of rust in the future. Using a rubber or nylon applicator fill the scratch with bodystopper paste. If required, this paste can be mixed with cellulose thinners to provide a very thin paste which is ideal for filling narrow scratches. Before the stopper-paste in the scratch hardens, wrap a piece of smooth cotton rag around the top of a finger. Dip the finger in cellulose thinners and then quickly sweep it across the surface of the stopper-paste in the scratch; this will ensure that the surface of the stopper-paste is slightly hollowed. The scratch can now be painted over as described earlier in this Section.

Repair of dents in the vehicle's bodywork

When deep denting of the vehicle's bodywork has taken place, the first task is to pull the dent out, until the affected bodywork almost attains its original shape. There is little point in trying to restore the original shape completely, as the metal in the damaged area will have stretched on impact and cannot be reshaped fully to its original contour. It is better to bring the level of the dent up to a point which is about $\frac{1}{8}$ in (3 mm) below the level of the surrounding bodywork. In cases where the dent is very shallow anyway, it is not worth trying to pull it out at all. If the underside of the dent is accessible, it can be hammered out gently from behind, using a mallet with a wooden or plastic head. Whilst doing this, hold a suitable block of wood firmly against the outside of the panel to absorb the impact from the hammer blows and thus prevent a large area of the bodywork from being 'belled-out'.

Should the dent be in a section of the bodywork which has double skin or some other factor making it inaccessible from behind, a different technique is called for. Drill several small holes through the metal inside the area – particularly in the deeper section. Then screw long self-tapping screws into the holes just sufficiently for them to gain a good purchase in the metal. Now the dent can be pulled out by pulling on the protruding heads of the screws with a pair of pliers.

The next stage of the repair is the removal of the paint from the damaged area, and from an inch or so of the surrounding 'sound' bodywork. This is accomplished most easily by using a wire brush or abrasive pad on a power drill, although it can be done just as effectively by hand using sheets of abrasive paper. To complete the preparation for filling, score the surface of the bare metal with a screwdriver or the tang of a file, or alternatively, drill small holes in the affected area. This will provide a really good 'key' for the filler paste.

To complete the repair see the Section on filling and re-spraying.

Repair of rust holes or gashes in the vehicle's bodywork

Remove all paint from the affected area and from an inch or so of the surrounding 'sound' bodywork, using an abrasive pad or a wire brush on a power drill. If these are not available a few sheets of abrasive paper will do the job just as effectively. With the paint removed you will be able to gauge the severity of the corrosion and therefore decide whether to renew the whole panel (if this is possible) or to repair the affected area. New body panels are not as expensive as most people think and it is often quicker and more satisfactory to fit a new panel than to attempt to repair large areas of corrosion.

Remove all fittings from the affected area except those which will act as a guide to the original shape of the damaged bodywork (eg headlamp shells etc). Then, using tin snips or a hacksaw blade, remove all loose metal and any other metal badly affected by corrosion. Hammer the edges of the hole inwards in order to create a slight depression for the filler paste.

Wire brush the affected area to remove the powdery rust from the surface of the remaining metal. Paint the affected area with rust inhibiting paint; if the back of the rusted area is accessible treat this also.

Before filling can take place it will be necessary to block the hole in some way. This can be achieved by the use of Zinc gauze or Aluminium tape.

Zinc gauze is probably the best material to use for a large hole. Cut a piece to the approximate size and shape of the hole to be filled, then position it in the hole so that its edges are below the level of the surrounding bodywork. It can be retained in position by several blobs of filler paste around its periphery.

Aluminium tape should be used for small or very narrow holes. Pull a piece off the roll and trim it to the approximate size and shape required, then pull off the backing paper (if used) and stick the tape over the hole; it can be overlapped if the thickness of one piece is insufficient. Burnish down the edges of the tape with the handle of a screwdriver or similar, to ensure that the tape is securely attached to the metal underneath.

Bodywork repairs – filling and re-spraying

Before using this Section, see the Sections on dent, deep scratch, rust holes and gash repairs.

Many types of bodyfiller are available, but generally speaking those proprietary kits which contain a tin of filler paste and a tube of resin hardener are best for this type of repair. A wide, flexible plastic or nylon applicator will be found invaluable for imparting a smooth and well contoured finish to the surface of the filler.

Mix up a little filler on a clean piece of card or board – measure the hardener carefully (follow the maker's instructions on the pack) otherwise the filler will set too rapidly or too slowly.

Using the applicator apply the filler paste to the prepared area; draw the applicator across the surface of the filler to achieve the correct contour and to level the filler surface. As soon as a contour that approximates the correct one is achieved, stop working the paste – if you carry on too long the paste will become sticky and begin to 'pick up' on the applicator. Continue to add thin layers of filler paste at twenty-minute intervals until the level of the filler is just proud of the surrounding bodywork.

Once the filler has hardened, excess can be removed using a metal plane or file. From then on, progressively finer grades of sandpaper should be used, starting with a 40 grade production paper and finishing with 400 grade wet-and-dry paper. Always wrap the abrasive paper around a flat rubber, cork, or wooden block – otherwise the surface of the filler will not be completely flat. During the smoothing of the filler surface the wet-and-dry paper should be periodically rinsed in water. This will ensure that a very smooth finish is imparted to the filler at the final stage.

At this stage the 'repair area' should be surrounded by a ring of bare metal, which in turn should be encircled by the finely 'feathered' edge of the good paintwork. Rinse the repair area with clean water, until all of the dust produced by the rubbing-down operation has gone.

Spray the whole repair area with a light coat of primer – this will show up any imperfections in the surface of the filler. Repair these imperfections with fresh filler paste or bodystopper, and once more smooth the surface with abrasive paper. If bodystopper is used, it can be mixed with cellulose thinners to form a really thin paste which is ideal for filling small holes. Repeat this spray and repair procedure until you are satisfied that the surface of the filler, and the feathered edge of the paintwork are perfect. Clean the repair area with clean water and allow to dry fully.

The repair area is now ready for final spraying. Paint spraying must be carried out in warm, dry, windless and dust free atmosphere. This condition can be created artificially if you have access to a large indoor working area, but if you are forced to work in the open, you will have to pick your day very carefully. If you are working indoors, dousing the floor in the work area with water will help to settle the dust which would otherwise be in the atmosphere. If the repair area is confined to one body panel, mask off the surrounding panels; this will help to minimise the effects of a slight mis-match in paint colours. Bodywork fittings (eg chrome strips, door handles etc) will also need to be masked off. Use genuine masking tape and several thicknesses of newspaper for the masking operations.

Before commencing to spray, agitate the aerosol can thoroughly, then spray a test area (an old tin, or similar) until the technique is mastered. Cover the repair area with a thick coat of primer; the thickness should be built up using several thin layers of paint rather than one thick one. Using 400 grade wet-and-dry paper, rub down the surface of the primer until it is really smooth. While doing this, the work area should be thoroughly doused with water, and the wet-and-dry paper periodically rinsed in water. Allow to dry before spraying on more paint.

Spray on the top coat, again building up the thickness by using several thin layers of paint. Start spraying in the centre of the repair area and then, using a circular motion, work outwards until the whole repair area and about 2 inches of the surrounding original paintwork is covered. Remove all masking material 10 to 15 minutes after spraying on the final coat of paint.

Allow the new paint at least two weeks to harden, then, using a paintwork renovator or a very fine cutting paste, blend the edges of the paint into the existing paintwork. Finally, apply wax polish.

5   Major body damage – repair

1   If damage is limited to the major replaceable components, namely doors, boot lid, bonnet, front wings, or bumpers, repair is a simple matter of renewing the component(s) concerned. However it is more likely that major body damage will involve the basic unit structure. In this case repairs must be undertaken by a properly equipped body repair shop with hydraulic straightening facilities and welding equipment.
2   Extensive damage to the body may distort the structure and in this case precision alignment checking equipment will be necessary to measure the degree and location of the distortion and to check the structure after repair. As a distorted chassis can result in unstable and even dangerous handling characteristics, as well as excessive wear to tyres and suspension or steering components, it is imperative that remedial work is only undertaken by specialists.

6   Hinges, door catches and locks – maintenance

1   Periodically oil the hinges of the bonnet, the boot lid and the doors with a drop or two of light oil. A good time to do this is just after washing the car, especially if a detergent wash has been used.
2   Oil the bonnet release mechanism and catches at the same time.
3   Do not overlubricate door latches and strikers as it is only too easy to stain clothing. A non-staining lubricant for these areas can be obtained from accessory shops if you have a problem in this area but

normally, minimal lubrication, wiping off all surplus, suffices.

7   Bonnet – removal and refitting

1   Open the bonnet and prop it on its stay.
2   Mark round the hinges at the rear of the bonnet to show their correct location and thus facilitate reassembly. Undo and remove the upper hinge bolt and nut securing the stay to the bonnet and hold the bonnet up with the aid of an assistant (photos).
3   Undo and remove the bolts securing the hinges to the bonnet and carefully remove the bonnet. Park it in a safe place where it can't get damaged, knocked down or blown down.
4   Refitting is simply a reverse of the removal procedure, making sure that the hinges align with the marks made on removal. Check the fit of the closed bonnet and oil the hinges, stay pivots and catches on completion (photos).

8   Doors – removal and refitting

1   Both front and rear doors can be removed in the same manner. First open the door to be removed and support it underneath, but don't lift it.
2   The upper and lower hinge pins have plastic caps in their ends. When the caps are removed, a special Peugeot tool can be fitted to remove the pins but, in the absence of the tool, the pins can be carefully drifted out although this is more difficult. Remove the roll pin in the door stay before removing the hinge pins.
3   Refitting the door is a direct reversal of the removal procedure. Use new hinge pins if the old ones are worn and lubricate them before assembly. Check the door for closing and alignment on completion.
4   Adjustment of door fit is made on the door half of the hinges, which are bolted into the door by two bolts each (photo). Before disturbing the hinge bolts scribe a line round the hinge brackets to act as datum for subsequent reference.
5   The door latch is secured by two countersunk bolts (photo) and a special male six-pointed screwdriver bit to fit a socket wrench is needed to adjust the latch position.

9   Door trim panel – removal and refitting

1   Removal and refitting of a door trim panel is a similar procedure for all four doors. The procedure for the SR front left door is shown in the photographs.
2   First unscrew the door lock knob (photo).
3   Carefully prise out the trim surround of the door latch release lever and remove it (photo).
4   Press back the plastic washer behind the window winding handle and, with a hooked tool made of wire, pull the retaining clip free from the handle. Remove the handle and washer (photo).
5   Undo and remove the cross-head screw securing the front of the armrest/door pull and then remove the two screws under the armrest. Remove the armrest (photos).
6   Use a screwdriver with a wide blade, or a similar tool such as a blunt knife, and carefully insert it between the trim panel and the door.

7.2a Mark the bonnet hinges before dismantling to facilitate reassembly

7.2b Disconnect the upper hinge bolt when removing the bonnet

7.4a Lubricate the bonnet catches and ...

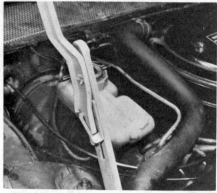
7.4b ... don't neglect the stay centre hinge

8.4 The top hinge bolts inside the door

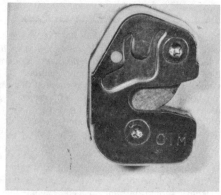
8.5 A special screwdriver bit is needed to fit the door latch bolts

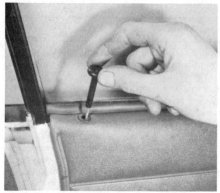
9.2 Unscrew the door lock knob and ...

9.3 ... prise out the trim round the door release lever

9.4 Removing the window winding handle

9.5a Undo the armrest/door pull front screw and ...

9.5b ... after undoing the two securing screws in the armrest remove it

9.6 One of the plastic clips retaining the trim panel

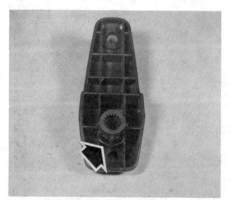
9.7 Before fitting the window winder handle, engage the retaining clip (arrowed)

10.3 Slide the door latch release lever mechanism forward to disengage it from the door

10.4 Removing the window seals

Apply leverage to prise the plastic clips retaining the trim panel to the door, and work round the panel until all clips are removed and the panel can be taken off the door (photo).

7   Refitting is a simple reversal of the removal procedure. Engage the trim panel clips by pressing them into their retainers. When refitting the window winder handle first fit the retaining clip to the handle (photo), fit the washer to the spindle and then fit the handle. Check its position, which should be clear of the seat occupant's knees when the door is shut and the window is wound fully up.

10 Door window – removal and refitting

1   Despite minor differences between the front and rear door window installations, the removal and refitting procedure is similar for all. The front left door window installation which is described here can be adapted for the others.

2   First remove the trim panel as described in the previous Section.

3   Undo the cross-head screw at the front edge of the door latch release lever mechanism, slide the mechanism forward to disengage it from the door, then disconnect the operating rod and remove the mechanism (photo).

4   Wind the window down and, after prising out the front triangular plastic trim, prise the window seals out of their clips in the door and remove them (photo).

5   Undo the bolts in the bottom of the door edge tracks at the front and rear bottom corners of the door (photos).

6   Wind the window partly up and loosen the five nuts securing the winding mechanism in the door (photo).

7   Support the window, remove the nuts securing the winding mechanism, disengage the winder roller from the window bottom track and, still supporting the window, extract the winder mechanism (photos).

8   Tilt the window rear edge upwards and remove it from the door, taking care not to jam it or apply bending loads to it (photo).

9   Clean and examine the winder mechanism for wear. As individual spare parts are not likely to be available for repairs, renewal of the complete assembly is the only feasible remedy. Lubricate all moving parts before refitting (photo).

10 Refitting the window and winder mechanism is a reversal of the removal procedure. Make sure that the window seals are bedded down and secure in their retaining clips when fitted. Check the window operation before refitting the door trim panel and fittings.

11 Door lock cylinder – removal and refitting

1   The front door lock cylinder is retained by a sliding clip and renewal is a simple task (photo).

2   First remove the door trim panel as described in Section 9 and wind the window fully up. This will give access to the sliding clip (photo).

3   Slide the lock cylinder retaining clip out of its location to release the cylinder and remove the cylinder from the door (photo).

4   Refitting is the reverse of the removal procedure and presents no problems, provided that the locating lugs on the door are engaged with the recess in the lock cylinder before fitting the retaining clip.

12 Facia panel – removal and refitting

1   Removal and refitting the facia panel is not a difficult job although it is complex, involving a large number of disconnections and fastener removals. A methodical work procedure is necessary and careful note should be taken of such details as cable runs, location and length of fastening screws and bolts, earth connections, fitting details of individual parts and so on. Written notes and sketches are well worth making, particularly if there is likely to be a time gap between removal and refitting. Peugeot go to great lengths sound-proofing their cars and much effort is expended preventing rattles and buzzes which can arise inside the car especially behind the facia. Retrieve all pieces of foam, mastic, rubber and similar materials for re-use on refitting so that these unwanted noises can be avoided.

2   Due to variations between models, and progressive modifications resulting from improvements, it is not possible to give a detailed procedure to cover all possibilities but the broad procedure which

10.5a Undo the bottom front ...

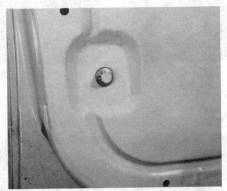
10.5b ... and rear bolts securing the edge tracks

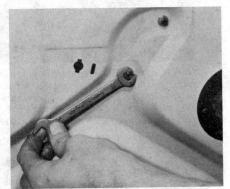
10.6 Loosening the winding mechanism securing nuts

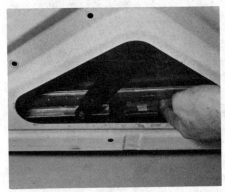
10.7a Disengage the winder roller from the window bottom track ...

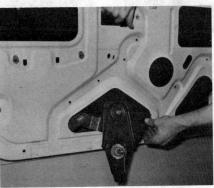
10.7b ... and remove the winder mechanism

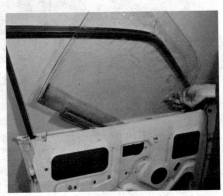
10.8 Tilt the window to remove it

This sequence of photographs deals with the repair of the dent and paintwork damage shown in this photo. The procedure will be similar for the repair of a hole. It should be noted that the procedures given here are simplified – more explicit instructions will be found in the text

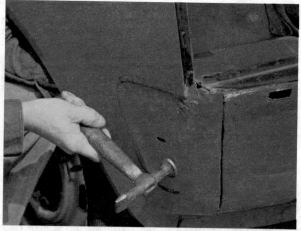

In the case of a dent the first job – after removing surrounding trim – is to hammer out the dent where access is possible. This will minimise filling. Here, the large dent having been hammered out, the damaged area is being made slightly concave

Now all paint must be removed from the damaged area, by rubbing with coarse abrasive paper. Alternatively, a wire brush or abrasive pad can be used in a power drill. Where the repair area meets good paintwork, the edge of the paintwork should be 'feathered', using a finer grade of abrasive paper

In the case of a hole caused by rusting, all damaged sheet-metal should be cut away before proceeding to this stage. Here, the damaged area is being treated with rust remover and inhibitor before being filled

Mix the body filler according to its manufacturer's instructions. In the case of corrosion damage, it will be necessary to block off any large holes before filling – this can be done with aluminium or plastic mesh, or aluminium tape. Make sure the area is absolutely clean before ...

... applying the filler. Filler should be applied with a flexible applicator, as shown, for best results; the wooden spatula being used for confined areas. Apply thin layers of filler at 20-minute intervals, until the surface of the filler is slightly proud of the surrounding bodywork

Initial shaping can be done with a Surform plane or Dreadnought file. Then, using progressively finer grades of wet-and-dry paper, wrapped around a sanding block, and copious amounts of clean water, rub down the filler until really smooth and flat. Again, feather the edges of adjoining paintwork

The whole repair area can now be sprayed or brush-painted with primer. If spraying, ensure adjoining areas are protected from over-spray. Note that at least one inch of the surrounding sound paintwork should be coated with primer. Primer has a 'thick' consistency, so will find small imperfections

Again, using plenty of water, rub down the primer with a fine grade wet-and-dry paper (400 grade is probably best) until it is really smooth and well blended into the surrounding paintwork. Any remaining imperfections can now be filled by carefully applied knifing stopper paste

When the stopper has hardened, rub down the repair area again before applying the final coat of primer. Before rubbing down this last coat of primer, ensure the repair area is blemish-free – use more stopper if necessary. To ensure that the surface of the primer is really smooth use some finishing compound

The top coat can now be applied. When working out of doors, pick a dry, warm and wind-free day. Ensure surrounding areas are protected from over-spray. Agitate the aerosol thoroughly, then spray the centre of the repair area, working outwards with a circular motion. Apply the paint as several thin coats

After a period of about two weeks, which the paint needs to harden fully, the surface of the repaired area can be 'cut' with a mild cutting compound prior to wax polishing. When carrying out bodywork repairs, remember that the quality of the finished job is proportional to the time and effort expended

10.9 Clean and examine the winder mechanism

11.1 The door key cylinder, right, is retained by a sliding clip, left

11.2 Remove the panel trim to get to the door lock cylinder clip, arrowed

11.3 Remove the door lock cylinder after removing the clip

follows can, with common sense, be adapted for any of the 305 models. Where necessary refer to other Chapters for details. Note also that the illustration sequence (Figs. 11.2 to 11.12 inclusive) shows a left-hand drive car; due allowance must be made for this on RHD models.

3   First disconnect the battery earth lead and then undo the fuse box retaining fasteners and remove the carburettor air filter. Disconnect the choke control and outer cover from the carburettor.

4   Disconnect the multi-pin connectors under the fuse box and also those for the headlights and engine wiring looms (Fig. 11.1).

5   Inside the vehicle, remove the shelf under the facia. Remove the casing round the steering column and undo the lower bolts at each side of the footwells. Remove the passenger's shelf.

6   Remove the screws holding the heater cover and remove the cover. Unplug the hazard warning flasher unit connector (Figs. 11.3 and 11.4).

7   Undo six screws and remove the glove compartment (Fig. 11.5).

8   Disconnect the heater controls from the heater unit, refer to Section 16. Disconnect the multi-pin connectors in the looms supplying the facia.

9   Remove the turn indicator flasher unit on the bracket near the steering column bottom bracket. Loosen the two nuts in the bottom bracket of the steering column and remove the two nuts in the top bracket. Disconnect the multi-pin connectors supplying the steering column (Figs. 11.7, 11.8 and 11.9).

10   Disconnect the stoplight switch on the brake pedal bracket and disconnect three earthing leads. Unfasten the wiring loom and free the leads to the steering column and the bulkhead (Fig. 11.10).

11   Disconnect the speedometer drive cable by giving it a sharp pull from the instrument panel forwards.

12   Lever out the plastic grille in the centre top of the facia. Remove the central retaining screw, working through the top central hole in the facia left by removing the grille. Remove the facia retaining nut behind the steering column and, after removing the two side retaining screws, remove the facia from the car (Figs. 11.11 and 11.12).

13   Refitting the facia is the reverse of the removal procedure and, provided that due note was taken as recommended in paragraph 1 during the removal, no problems should arise. Tighten the steering column retaining nuts to a torque of 1 kgf m (7.2 lbf ft) after refitting and refer to Section 16 for refitting the heater. On completion check the operation of all accessories and circuits disturbed during the process.

Fig. 11.1 Disconnect the multi-pin connectors under the fusebox (Sec 12)

Fig. 11.2 Remove the shelf, 1, the steering column casing, 2, and the bolts 3 (Sec 12)

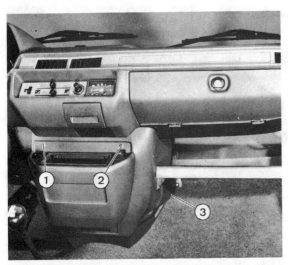

Fig. 11.3 Remove the heater cover screws, 1, 2 and 3 (Sec 12)

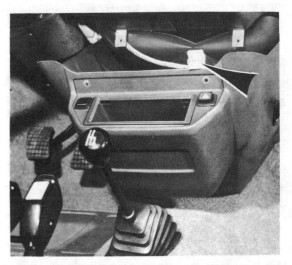

Fig. 11.4 Remove the cover and disconnect the hazard warning flasher (arrowed) (Sec 12)

Fig. 11.5 Undo the screws (arrowed) and remove the glove compartment (Sec 12)

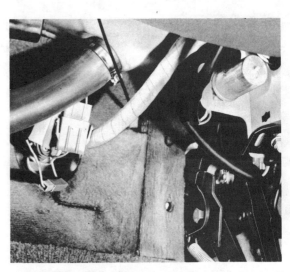

Fig. 11.6 Disconnect the multi-pin connectors under the facia (Sec 12)

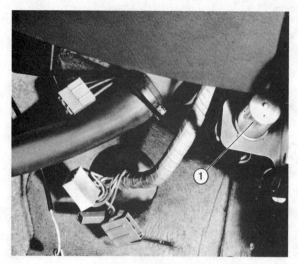

Fig. 11.7 Remove the turn indicator flasher unit, 1 (Sec 12)

Fig. 11.8 Loosen the bottom two nuts, 1, and remove the top two nuts, 2, securing the steering column (Sec 12)

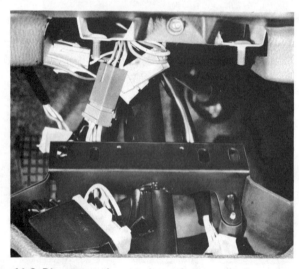

Fig. 11.9 Disconnect the steering column multi-pin connectors (Sec 12)

Fig. 11.10 Disconnect the stoplight switch (arrowed) (Sec 12)

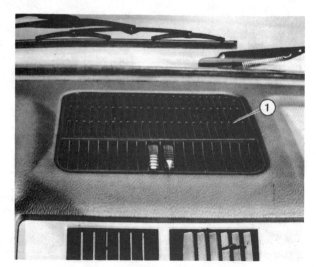

Fig. 11.11 Remove the grille, 1 (Sec 12)

Fig. 11.12 Undo and remove the nut and screws (arrowed) to remove the facia (Sec 12)

13 Radiator front grille – removal and refitting

1 The plastic grille in front of the radiator is retained by two turn-button clips.
2 To remove the grille, raise the bonnet and support it on its prop. Turn the two buttons securing the top of the grille to release them and lift the grille out of its bottom locations (photo).
3 Refitting the grille is the reverse of the removal procedure.

14 Windscreen – removal and refitting

1 If you are unfortunate enough to have a windscreen shatter or should you wish to renew your existing windscreen, fitting a replacement is one job that is best left for the specialist windscreen fitters. For the owner who wishes to do the job himself the following procedure can be used.
2 Cover the bonnet, the facia and the front seats with plastic sheeting to prevent accidental damage and then remove the windscreen wiper blades and arms as described in Chapter 10, Section 26.
3 If the screen has shattered remove the remaining crystals of glass from the rubber weatherstrip surround and clean out all visible glass crystals from the facia, ducts, floor and so on. Remove the weatherstrip from the car.
4 Remove the metal trim strip from the weatherstrip surround. This is in three sections with three joints. Slide the top centre joint to one side and carefully ease the strip out of the rubber moulding taking care not to bend or kink it. Work round to the bottom corner joint and remove the section from the car. Repeat the procedure on the other side section and then remove the bottom piece (photos).
5 If the screen is intact it must now be pressed out of the mounting flange and you will need the help of an assistant. Sit in the left-hand seat, to provide more freedom, and with a cloth pad interposed, put your feet on one corner of the screen and exert a progressive pressure. At the same time your assistant, working outside, should prise the screen and seal out of the car flange aperture using wide-bladed, blunt tools. Work progressively, and don't rush the job, until the top and side edges are free and then the panel and weatherstrip can be removed from the car.
6 Check the aperture flange in the car to ensure that is free from buckles and dents and that all traces of hardened sealer are removed from both sides of the flange. Clean and examine the weatherstrip and if it is damaged, perished or hardened, renew it.
7 Using a suitable sealer, obtainable from windscreen specialists or motor accessory shops, fill the weatherstrip inner groove and assemble the weatherstrip to the windscreen, remembering that the groove for the metal trim strip must be outside.
8 You will now need a length of stout cord, such as washing line, sufficiently long to wrap around the outer groove of the weatherstrip and overlap by a metre (say a yard). Fit the rope into the groove so that the ends overlap at the bottom centre.
9 Locate the windscreen and weatherstrip assembly on the bottom flange of the aperture and make sure that the rope ends are inside the car. Soapy water can be used to lubricate the rubber weatherstrip as it is fitted to the flange.
10 With your assistant outside pressing on the panel, start pulling on one end of the cord to lift the weatherstrip over the flange. Work round the panel until halfway is reached and then start on the other end of the rope and work round until the rope is free and the weatherstrip fitted over the flange. Where necessary ease any ill-fitting area of rubber into place with a screwdriver.
11 A suitable sealant should now be applied between the weatherstrip and the outside of the car. This can be obtained in containers with a nozzle which permits extruding the sealant under the rubber lip. Apply the sealant all round the weatherstrip.
12 Refit the trim strip, starting with the bottom piece, and use a screwdriver to prise open the groove in the weatherstrip as the trim strip is pressed into place. Fit the side/top pieces and slide the top joint into position. Clean off all surplus sealant from the windsceeen, weatherstrip and car body and then refit the windscreen wiper arms and blades.
13 With a new windscreen the mounting support for the rear view mirror must now be fitted. A new support block will be needed and Peugeot supply a two-part adhesive to stick it to the glass. The expense of buying this adhesive just to do this one job would be out of all proportion and you can probably get just as good a result using a suitable alternative adhesive. The support should be stuck to the glass according to the dimensions shown in Fig. 11.13. Fit the rear view mirror to the support and secure with the support plastic clip.

15 Front and rear bumpers – removal and refitting

1 To remove a bumper, undo and remove the end attachment bolts inside the wheel well (front) or inside the boot (rear). Undo and remove the main attachment bolts and remove the bumper from the car.
2 Refitting the bumper is the reverse of the removal procedure.

16 Car heater – removal and refitting

1 First disconnect the battery earth lead.
2 Remove the shelves under the facia and at each side of the heater. Remove the screws retaining the heater cover and remove the cover after disconnecting the hazard warning switch.
3 Disconnect the three controls from the heater, and disconnect the electrical connection to the fan motor (Fig. 11.14).
4 Remove the lower bracket to which the heater cover secures (Fig. 11.15).
5 If two hose clamps are available, fit these to the inlet and outlet hoses on the side of the heater. Clamps can be made from two strips of metal with nuts and bolts to tighten the two strips onto the hose. Another pair of strips are needed for the other hose. Alternatively a pair of self-grip pliers can be clamped on each hose if these are available. Failing all else the cooling system will have to be drained, refer to Chapter 2 (Fig. 11.16).
6 After clamping the two hoses, or draining the system, disconnect the hoses from the heater matrix. Be prepared for a small spillage of coolant which should be retained in a suitable container.
7 Undo and remove the bolt at the bottom and the two nuts at the

13.2 Turn the grille retaining buttons to disengage them

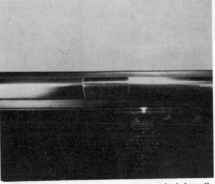
14.4a Slide the windscreen trim strip joint clip to one side to remove the strip

14.4b The trim strip bottom corner joint

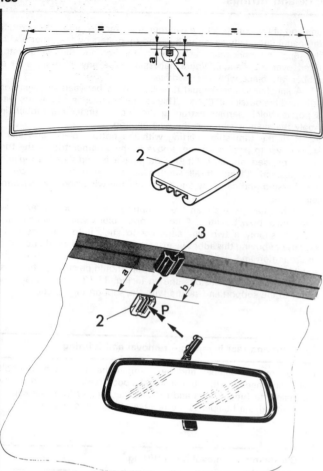

Fig. 11.13 Fitting the rear view mirror to the windscreen (Sec 14)

1   Clean this area with methylated spirit before applying
    adhesive
2   Support bracket
3   Plastic clip
P   Apply pressure for one minute after fixing with adhesive

a = 60 mm
b = 50 mm

Fig. 11.15 Remove the lower bracket (arrowed) to which the cover
secures (Sec 16)

Fig. 11.16 Avoid draining the cooling system by fitting hose
clamps (Sec 16)

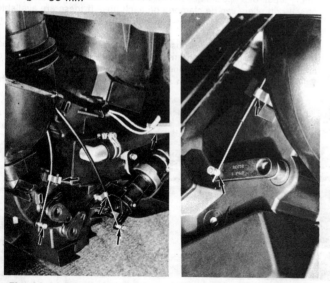

Fig. 11.14 Disconnect the heater controls (arrowed) (Sec 16)

Fig. 11.17 Remove the two top nuts (one arrowed, left) and the
bottom (arrowed, right) (Sec 16)

Fig. 11.18 Remove the matrix retaining bolt (1) to ...

Fig. 11.19 ... enable the matrix to be slid out of the heater case
(Sec 17)

top which retain the heater and remove the assembly from the car (Fig. 11.17).

8   Refitting the heater is the reverse of the removal procedure. On completion, top up the cooling system with the heater switched to maximum heat (red spot), referring if necessary to Chapter 2 for details of this procedure. Run the engine until the system is warm (fan engaged) and check for leaks. Top up after allowing the system to cool.

17 Car heater matrix – removal and refitting

1   The heater matrix can be removed on its own if required although there is not much saving in work compared with removing the heater as described in the previous Section.

2   Follow the procedure contained in the previous Section, but with the following differences:

   (a)   Leave the controls connected except for the valve control
   (b)   Leave the cover bracket installed
   (c)   Leave the fan motor connected

3   After the coolant hoses have been disconnected from the matrix, remove the matrix retaining bolt in the left-hand side of the heater case and slide the matrix out of the case to the right (Figs. 11.18 and 11.19).

4   Refitting the matrix is a reverse of the removal procedure, but refer to paragraph 8 of the previous Section for details of the work necessary to complete the job.

18 Sliding roof – general

1   A sliding roof panel is available as a factory-fitted extra on some 305 models. Details of the installation are shown in Fig. 11.20.

2   Maintenance of the sliding roof panel is confined to checking the condition and security of the moving parts. Grease the shoes and slides occasionally with Kluber Proba PN 9730.67 grease.

3   If trouble is experienced with noise from the area of the roof panel, first check that the moving parts are not worn or loose. If the shoe fixing spigots are a sloppy fit they can be bound with PTFE tape (this tape is used for sealing plumbing joints and is available from hardware shops). Ensure that there is tension in the cable when the roof panel is shut.

4   If troubles with noise persist, refer the matter to your Peugeot dealer who will be able to advise you further.

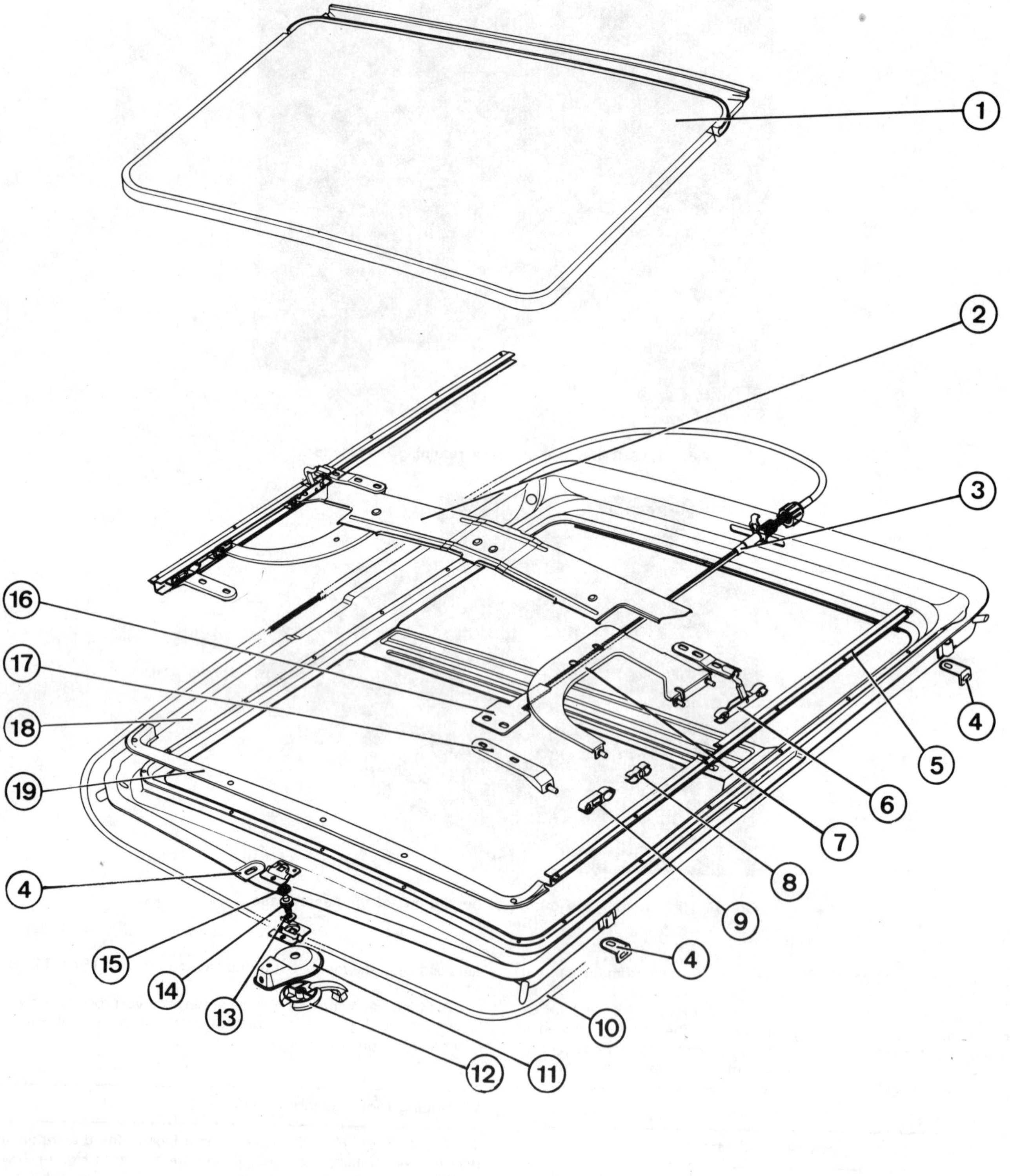

Fig. 11.20 The sliding sun roof installation (optional extra fitting) (Sec 18)

1	Sliding panel	6	Shoe with lifting arm
2	Centre sliding crossmember	7	Lateral sliding member
3	Cable guide tube	8	Intermediate shoe
4	Frame fixing brackets	9	Front shoe
5	Lateral rail	10	Cable plastic sheath

11	Drive mechanism housing	16	Notched type operating cable
12	Operating crank	17	Front shoe fixing
13	Distance piece	18	Frame
14	Drive pinion assembly	19	Front bright trim
15	Distance piece		

Peugeot 305 SR Estate

Chapter 12 Supplement:
Revisions and information on later models

Contents

1 Introduction

This supplement contains information which is additional to, or a revision of, material in the preceding Chapters. Although most of the material relates to additions to the range of engines and transmissions available, some items apply retrospectively to the appropriate models from the start of production.

The Sections in the Supplement follow the same order as the Chapters to which they relate. The Specifications are all grouped together for convenience, but they follow Chapter order.

It is recommended that before any particular operation is undertaken, reference be made to the appropriate Section(s) of the Supplement. In this way any changes to procedure or components can be noted before referring to the main Chapters.

Vehicle identification numbers (later models)

The location and interpretation of the various identification numbers on later models are shown in Fig. 12.1.

The engine identification plate for XU Series engines is included in Fig. 12.2. XU5S engines have the identification code 1CT or 171, XU51C engines have B1A, and XY95 engines have 159. The engine serial number is stamped on the identification plate, or on a separate plate next to it.

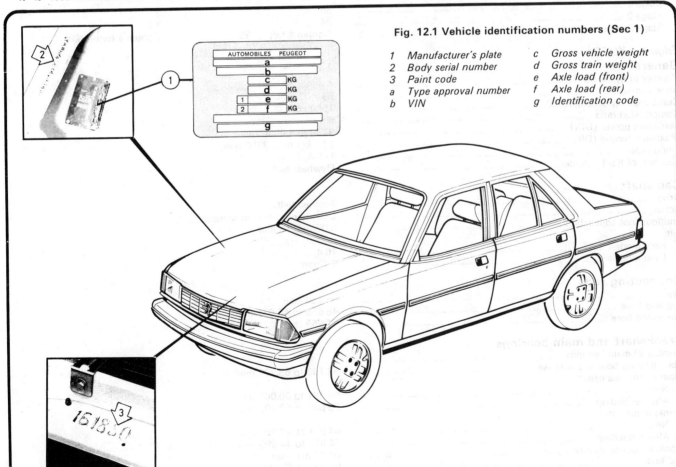

Fig. 12.1 Vehicle identification numbers (Sec 1)

1 Manufacturer's plate
2 Body serial number
3 Paint code
a Type approval number
b VIN
c Gross vehicle weight
d Gross train weight
e Axle load (front)
f Axle load (rear)
g Identification code

2 Specifications

The Specifications below are supplementary to, or revisions of those at the beginning of the preceding Chapters.

Engine – XR5A
General
As for XR5 (Chapter 1) except for the following:

Maximum power (DIN)	74 bhp at 5500 rpm
Maximum torque (DIN)	12.3 kgf m at 2500 rpm

Engine – XR5S
General
As for XR5 (Chapter 1) except for the following:

Maximum power (DIN):	
Fan disengaged	89 bhp at 6000 rpm
Fan engaged	86 bhp at 5800 rpm
Maximum torque (DIN):	
Fan disengaged	12.7 kgf m at 3000 rpm
Fan engaged	12.4 kgf m at 3000 rpm

Torque wrench settings

	lbf ft	kgf m
Main bearing cap side bolts	17	2.3

Engine – XL/XR (1984 on)
Cylinder liners

Base seal thickness (new type):	
Red or one tag	0.116 to 0.134 mm
Grey or two tags	0.136 to 0.154 mm
Blue or three tags	0.166 to 0.194 mm

Torque wrench settings

	lbf ft	kgf m
Cylinder head bolts (with new liner seals):		
Stage 1	36	5
Stage 2	54	7.5
Stage 3 (see text)	Tighten a further 35°	Tighten a further 35°

Engine – XU5S
General

Number of cylinders	4
Bore x stroke	83 x 73 mm
Cubic capacity	1580 cc
Compression ratio	9.5 : 1
Maximum power (DIN)	94 bhp at 6000 rpm
Maximum torque (DIN)	13.7 kgf m at 3750 rpm
Firing order	1-3-4-2
Location of No 1 cylinder	Flywheel end

Camshaft

Drive	Toothed belt
Action	Directly onto bucket tappets
Endfloat (not adjustable)	0.07 to 0.16 mm
Lift:	
Early models	10.4
Later models	9.7 mm

Connecting rods

Type	Forged steel
Big-end bore	48.655 to 48.671 mm
Small-end bore	21.959 to 21.971 mm

Crankshaft and main bearings

Number of main bearings	5
Main bearing bore in crankcase	63.708 to 63.727 mm
Main journal diameter:	
New	59.981 to 60.000 mm
After regrinding	59.681 to 59.700 mm
Crankpin diameter:	
New	44.971 to 44.990 mm
After regrinding	44.671 to 44.690 mm
Crankpin journal ovality	0.007 mm max
Endfloat	0.07 to 0.27 mm
Thrust washer thicknesses available	2.30, 2.35, 2.40, 2.45 and 2.50 mm

Cylinder liners
Type .... Wet, removable, matched to piston
Protrusion from block:
    Hexagon head bolts .... 0.08 to 0.15 mm
    Torx head bolts .... 0.03 to 0.10 mm

Pistons
Type .... Aluminium alloy with three compression rings and one scraper
matched to liner

Coding marks:
    For gudgeon pin .... Figure 1 (blue), 2 (white) or 3 (red)
    For liner .... One, two or three slashes

Gudgeon pins
Nominal diameter .... 20 mm
Coding mark .... Coloured paint (see piston specs)
Fit .... Clearance in piston, interference in connecting rod

Cylinder head
Material .... Aluminium alloy
Warp limit .... 0.05 mm
Valve guide bore .... 7.978 to 8.000 mm
Number of camshaft bearings 5

Valves
Head diameter:
    Inlet .... 40 mm
    Exhaust .... 32 mm (early models), 32.95 (later models)
Stem diameter:
    Inlet .... 7.965 to 7.980 mm
    Exhaust .... 7.945 to 7.960 mm
Length:
    Inlet .... 107.39 to 107.59 mm
    Exhaust .... 106.82 to 107.02 mm

Valve clearances (cold)
Inlet .... 0.20 ± 0.05 mm
Exhaust .... 0.40 ± 0.05 mm
Adjustment method .... Shims between tappet and valve stem

Valve springs
Identification:
    Early type (high lift camshaft) .... Blue marking
    Later type (reduced lift camshaft) .... Black marking

Valve timing
Notional clearance .... 1 mm
Inlet opens .... TDC
Inlet closes .... 37° BTDC
Exhaust opens .... 35° BBDC
Exhaust closes .... 2° ATDC

Lubrication system
Type .... Wet sump, pressure feed and splash
Filter type .... Full flow, disposable cartridge
Sump capacity .... 4.5 litres approx.
Pressure .... 3.5 bars at 4000 rpm
Warning light sender operates at .... 0.44 to 0.58 bar
Oil pump drive .... Chain from crankshaft
Lubricant type/specification .... Multigrade engine oil, viscosity SAE 10W/40, to API SF/CC
(Duckhams QXR, Hypergrade, or 10W/40 Motor Oil)

Torque wrench settings

	lbf ft	kgf m
Camshaft cover bolts	7	1.0
Camshaft bearing caps	11	1.5
Camshaft sprocket bolt	58	8.0
Crankshaft pulley bolt	80	11.0
Sump bolts	15	2.0
Main bearing cap nuts and bolts	36	5.0
Main bearing cap side bolts	18	2.5
Big-end cap nuts	36	5.0
Flywheel bolts (renew bolts and use thread locking compound)	36	5.0
Cylinder head bolts (hexagon head):		
Stage 1	43	6.0
Stage 2 (after slackening)	15	2.0
Stage 3	One third of a turn (120°) further	

Torque wrench settings (continued)	lbf ft	kgf m
Cylinder head bolts (Torx head):		
Stage 1	44	6.0
Stage 2 (after slackening)	15 + 300°	2.0 + 300°
Distributor/fuel pump/thermostat housing	11	1.5
Spark plugs	13	1.8
Engine mounting bracket bolts:		
M8	25	3.5
M10	33	4.5
Oil pump-to-block bolts	15	2.0
Oil seal carrier plate bolts	11	1.5
Camshaft drivebelt tensioner nuts	11	1.5
Coolant outlet housing bolt	15	2.0
Oil pressure switch	18	2.5
Alternator pivot bolt	29	4.0
Alternator strap bolt	15	2.0
Engine-to-transmission bolts	33	4.5
Starter motor bolts	25	3.5
Inlet manifold nuts	15	2.0
Exhaust manifold nuts	15	2.0
Coolant pump securing bolts	11	1.5

Engine – XU51C
General
As for XU5S except for the following:

Compression ratio	9.35 : 1
Maximum power (DIN)	80 bhp at 5600 rpm
Maximum torque (DIN)	13.5 kgf m at 2800 rpm

Engine – XU9S
General
As for XU5S except for the following:

Bore x stroke	83 x 88 mm
Cubic capacity	1905 cc
Compression ratio	9.3 : 1
Maximum power (DIN)	105 bhp at 5600 rpm
Maximum torque (DIN)	16.5 kgf m @ 3000 rpm
Crankpin diameter	50 mm nominal

Cooling system – XU engines
System type
Pressurised, sealed with expansion tank, pump and fan assisted

Capacity (including heater)
6.7 litres approx

Pump drive
From camshaft drivebelt

Thermostat

Commences opening	79°C
Open by 7.5 mm at	94°C

Fan

Drive	Electric motor, controlled by thermoswitch(es)
Thermoswitch – XU5 (except auto):	
Cuts in at	85° to 95°C
Cuts out at	75° to 85°C
Thermoswitch – XU5 auto and XU9:	
Low speed cuts in at	84°C
Low speed cuts out at	79°C
High speed cuts in at	89°C
High speed cuts out at	85°C

Temperature warning switch

Operating temperature	105°C

Torque wrench settings	lbf ft	kgf m
Coolant pump bolts	7	1.0
Thermostat elbow nuts	11	1.5

Fuel and exhaust systems
General

Carburettor types:	
XL5 engine (later models)	Solex 34 PBISA 14 A 254, 254/1 or 254/2
XL5 engine (code SB)	Weber 34 IBP 1/100, 100-1 or 100-2
XR5 and XR5A engines (later models)	Solex 35 PBISA 14 A 283, 34 PBISA 16 320
XR5S engine	Solex 32-35 TACIC A 179/1
XU5S engine (manual transmission)	Solex 32-34 CISAC Type Z

XU5S engine (automatic transmission)	Weber 32/34 DRTC4 100
XU51C engine	Weber 36 TLP 1/100
XU9S engine	Solex 34/34 CISAC Type Z

Adjustment data*

Idle speed:	
XU engines (manual gearbox)	750 rpm
XR5 (142) and XR5A (142C) engines, from No 8 980 001	700 rpm
All other models	900 rpm
CO emission at idle:	
34 PBISA 5, 35 PBISA 9	2 ± 0.5%
All other models	1.5 ± 0.5%

Refer also to owner's handbook or under-bonnet sticker

Carburettor – Solex 34 PBISA

	34 PBISA 14	34 PBISA 16
Choke tube	26 mm	27 mm
Main jet	135 ± 2.5	132 ± 5
Air correction jet	160 ± 10	150 ± 20
Emulsion tube	12	E2
Idle jet	43 ± 5	43 ± 5
Idle air orifice	2.5 ± 0.2 mm	2.5 ± 0.2 mm
Accelerator pump injector	40 ± 5	40 ± 5
Uniform CO jet	30 ± 5	–
Uniform CO air orifice	180 ± 10	–
Needle valve	1.5 mm	1.5 mm
Float weight	5.7 g	5.7 g
Normal idling position (NIP)	0°50'	9°15'
Positive throttle opening (PTO)	12°30'	20°20'
Drill diameter for accelerator pump adjustment	2.5 ± 0.5 mm	3.6 mm

Carburettor – Solex 35 PBISA 14

Choke tube	30 mm
Main jet	150 ± 2.5
Air correction jet	160 ± 10
Emulsion tube	12
Idle jet	45 ± 5
Idle air orifice	2.5 ± 0.2 mm
Accelerator pump injector	40 ± 10
Uniform CO jet	30 ± 5
Uniform CO air orifice	180 ± 10
Needle valve	1.5 mm
Float weight	5.7 g
Normal idling position (NIP)	30'
Positive throttle opening (PTO)	11°45'
Drill diameter for accelerator pump adjustment	4.0 ± 0.6 mm

Carburettor – Weber 34 IBP

Choke tube	27 mm
Main jet	144.5 ± 2.5
Air correction jet	180 ± 10
Emulsion tube	F6
Idle jet	47 ± 5
Idle air orifice	155 ± 10
Accelerator pump injector	45 ± 5
Needle valve	1.5 mm
Float weight	11g
Positive throttle opening (PTO)	21°30'
Drill diameter for accelerator pump adjustment	5 ± 0.5 mm
Float level	See text (Section 9)

Carburettor – Weber 36 TLP

Choke tube	28 mm
Main jet	$142 ^{+3}_{-2}$
Idle fuel jet	$46 ^{+3}_{-2}$
Idle air jet	125 ± 10
Air correction jet	155 ± 10
Emulsion tube	F80
Accelerator pump injector	50
Econostat fuel jet	65 to 80
Positive throttle opening (PTO)	19°30'
Needle valve	1.5 mm
Float level (gasket fitted)	32 mm

Carburettor – Solex 32-35 TACIC

	1st barrel	2nd barrel
Choke tube	24 mm	26 mm
Main jet	117.5 ± 5	122.5 ± 5
Air correction jet	155 ± 10	160 ± 10
Emulsion tube	18	2P1
Idle jet	40 ± 5	60 ± 5
Idle air orifice	160 ± 10	160 ± 20
Accelerator pump injector	40 ± 10	35 ± 10
Uniform CO jet	30 ± 5	–
Uniform CO air orifice	80 ± 20	–
Needle valve	1.5 mm	1.5 mm
Float weight	Not known	Not known
Normal idling position (NIP)	8°20'	8°30'
Float level (gasket in place)	41 mm	

Carburettor – Solex 32-34 CISAC (Type Z)

	1st barrel	2nd barrel
Choke tube	24 mm	26 mm
Main jet	140	120
Air correction jet	200	155
Emulsion tube	23	18
Idle jet	42	–
Idle air orifice	180	–
Progression fuel jet	–	70
Progression air jet	–	150
Enrichener calibration	70	–
Econostat calibration	–	70
Accelerator pump injector	40	35
Normal idling position (NIP)	11° (preset)	9°
Choke opening after starting (COAS)	6 ± 0.5 mm	
Needle valve	1.8 mm	
Float level (gasket in place)	33.5 ± 1 mm	
Accelerator pump jet arm	Centreline of throttle plates	
Positive throttle opening (PTO) speed	3600 ± 50 rpm (fan not operating)	

Carburettor – Solex 34/34 CISAC (Type Z)

	1st barrel	2nd barrel
Choke tube	25 mm	27 mm
Main jet	115 ± 15	122.5 ± 15
Air correction jet	145 ± 20	160
Emulsion tube	27	ZC
Idle jet	42 ± 10	–
Progression fuel jet	–	90
Progression air jet	–	145 ± 20
Enrichener calibration	50 ± 20	–
Econostat calibration	–	70 ± 20
Accelerator pump injector	40 ± 20	55 ± 20
Normal idling position (NIP)	11° (preset)	9°
Choke opening after starting (COAS)	6 ± 0.5 mm	
Needle valve	1.8 mm	
Float level (gasket in place)	33.5 ± 1 mm	
Accelerator pump jet arm	Centreline of throttle plates	
Positive throttle opening (PTO) speed	3600 ± 50 rpm (fan not operating)	

Carburettor – Weber 32/34 DRTC4 100

	1st barrel	2nd barrel
Choke tube	24 mm	26 mm
Main jet	105 ± 5	112 ± 5
Air correction jet	165 ± 20	160 ± 20
Emulsion tube	F27	F27
Idle jet	45 ± 5	–
Bypass jet	–	70
Accelerator pump injector	50	–
Econostat fuel jet	–	60
Normal idling position (NIP)	10°00'	12°15'
Positive throttle opening (PTO)	20°50'	–
Needle valve	1.75 mm	
Float level (gasket in place)	7.50 ± 0.25 mm	

Ignition system

HT lead resistance (all models)

Specific resistance by make:

Electrifil Bougicord 400	1400 ohms per metre
Electrifil Bougicord 403, Cavis B403 and Gregoire et Barilleau 22351 B	5600 ohms per metre

Individual lead resistance at 1400 ohms per metre:

	Length (mm)	Resistance (ohms)
Coil	220	308
No 1	565	791
No 2	480	672
No 3	350	490

No 4	275	385
Individual lead resistance at 5600 ohms per metre:		
Coil	220	1232
No 1	530	2968
No 2	445	2492
No 3	315	1764
No 4	250	1400

Electronic (breakerless) system

Distributor:	
Make	Ducellier, Bosch or Marelli
Pulse generator resistance	990 to 1210 ohms
Coil:	
Make	Ducellier or Bosch
Primary resistance	0.85 ohms
Secondary resistance	6000 ohms
Module make	Ducellier or Bosch

Spark plugs (later models)

Make and type:	
XL and XR engines	Champion S281YC, Bosch H7DC, or equivalent
XU engines	Champion S279YC, Bosch H6DC, or equivalent
Electrode gap (all models)	0.6 mm

Ignition timing – later models

Static or at idle speed:	
XR5A	8° BTDC
XR5S	10° BTDC
XU5S and XU51C	10° BTDC
XU9S	10° BTDC

Clutch (XU engines)
General

Type	Single dry plate, diaphragm spring pressure plate
Actuation	Cable

Adjustment

Pedal travel	135 mm

Torque wrench setting

	lbf ft	**kgf m**
Pressure plate-to-flywheel bolts	18	2.5

Manual transmission (with XU engine)
General

Maker's designation	BE1/5
Number of speeds	Five forward and one reverse

Lubrication

Lubricant type/specification:	
Up to 1986	Multigrade engine oil, viscosity SAE 10W/40, to API SF/CC (Duckhams QXR, Hypergrade, or 10W/40 Motor Oil)
1987 on with filler/level plug	Gear oil, viscosity SAE 75W/80 (Duckhams Hypoid PT 75W/80W)
Capacity:	
Without filler/level plug (up to 1986)	2.0 litres (3.5 pints)
With filler/level plug (1987 on)	1.8 litres (3.25 pints)

Ratios (typical) up to December 1986

1st	3.308 : 1
2nd	1.882 : 1
3rd	1.360 : 1
4th	1.069 : 1
5th	0.865 : 1
Reverse	3.333 : 1

Ratios (Jan 1987 on)

1st	3.250 : 1
2nd	1.850 : 1
3rd	1.360 : 1
4th	1.069 : 1
5th	0.865 : 1
Reverse	3.333 : 1

Torque wrench settings	lbf ft	kgf m
Rear cover bolts (use thread locking compound)	9	1.2
Input and output shaft nuts	40	5.5
Rear bearing retainer bolts	11	1.5
Selector rod backplate bolt	11	1.5
End casing-to-main casing bolts	9	1.2
Reverse idler spindle bolt	15	2.1
Selector shaft spring bracket	11	1.5
Reverse selector spindle nut	15	2.1
Breather	11	1.5
Reversing lamp switch	18	2.5
Drain plug (gearbox)	7	1.0
Drain plug (final drive)	22	3.0
Speedometer pinion adaptor	9	1.2
Final drive extension housing bolts	11	1.5
Crownwheel securing bolts	48	6.6
Final drive half housing bolts, 10 mm	30	4.1
Final drive half housing bolts, 7 mm	9	1.2
Clutch release bearing guide tube bolts	9	1.2
Mounting stud nut	25	3.5

Automatic transmission
General

Type	ZF 4 HP14
Number of speeds	Four forward, one reverse

Lubrication

Lubricant type/specification	Dexron II type ATF (Duckhams D-Matic)
Lubricant capacity:	
From dry	6.2 litres approx
Drain and refill	2.4 litres approx
Final drive lubrication	Integral with transmission

Ratios (typical)

1st	2.806 : 1
2nd	1.593 : 1
3rd	1.163 : 1
4th	0.859 : 1
Reverse	3.289 : 1

Torque wrench settings	lbf ft	kgf m
Starter inhibitor/reversing light switch	30	4.2
Fluid cooler bolt	37	5.1
Dipstick/filler tube nut	33	4.6
Sump bolts	7	1.0
End cover bolts	7	1.0
Selector cable bracket	22	3.0
Selector lever nut	22	3.0
Torque converter bottom shield bolts	7	1.0
Torque converter-to-driveplate bolts	26	3.6
Transmission-to-engine bolts	33	4.6
Transmission mounting:		
To transmission	26	3.6
To frame	13	1.8

Driveshafts (XU engine)

Torque wrench settings	lbf ft	kgf m
Driveshaft retaining nut	192	26.5
Driveshaft bearing retaining nuts	13	1.75

Rear hubs (1983 on)

Torque wrench setting	lbf ft	kgf m
Rear hub nut	199	27.5

Wheels and tyres

Tyre pressures in bar (lbf/in²)*	Front	Rear
Saloons:		
GR/SR (155 SR 14)	1.7 (25)	2.0 (29)
SR (170/65 TR 365)	1.7 (25)	1.9 (28)
GT (165/70 SR 14 or 170/65 TR 365)	1.9 (28)	2.0 (29)
GTX (185/60 HR 14):		
Normal running	1.9 (28)	2.0 (29)
High speed running	2.0 (29)	2.2 (33)
Automatic (155 SR 14)	1.8 (26)	2.0 (29)
S5 (165/70 14)	1.9 (28)	2.0 (29)

Estates:

GT (155 SR 14):		
Unladen	1.8 (26)	2.2 (33)
Fully laden	1.8 (26)	2.7 (40)
GTX (165/70 HR 14) and Auto (155 SR 14):		
Unladen	1.8 (26)	2.2 (33)
Fully laden	1.8 (26)	2.6 (38)
S5 (165/70 14):		
Unladen	1.8 (26)	2.1 (30)
Fully laden	1.8 (26)	2.6 (38)
Other models (155 SR 14):		
Unladen	1.7 (25)	2.1 (31)
Fully laden	1.7 (25)	2.6 (38)

Consult owner's handbook or driver's door striker for latest information

Torque wrench setting

	lbf ft	kgf m
Wheel nuts or bolts:		
Steel or alloy wheels	63	8.5

Braking system (1983 on)

Brake discs

Thickness, ventilated:	
New	20.4 mm
Minimum after machining	18.5 mm
Wear limit	18.0 mm

Torque wrench setting

	lbf ft	kgf m
Caliper securing bolts	87	12

Steering (1983 on, XU engined vehicles)

Power-assisted steering – general

Fluid type/specification	Dexron II type ATF (Duckhams D-Matic)
Fluid capacity (from dry)	0.5 litres approx

Torque wrench settings*

	lbf ft	kgf m
Steering gear-to-crossmember bolts	33	4.6
Flexible coupling pinch-bolt	15	2.1
Flexible coupling flange bolts	18	2.5
Track rod balljoint pin nuts	26	3.6
Track rod balljoint locknuts	33	4.6
Rack damper cover screws	9	1.3

These apply both to manual and to power-assisted versions

Suspension (1983 on)

Front suspension geometry

Camber	0°25' ± 30'*
Caster	1°45' ± 30'*
Toe-in:	
XL and XR engines, up to No 9 030 081	3 ± 1 mm
XL and XR engines, from No 9 030 082, and all XU engines	4 ± 1 mm
Steering axis inclination	9°20' ± 30'
Track	1420 mm (55.9 in)

* Non-adjustable

Rear suspension geometry

Camber:	
Saloon	−1°00' ± 30'
Estate and Van	−0°10' ± 10'
Toe-in:	
Saloon	4.3 ± 2 mm
Estate (except GT/GTX)	0.8 ± 2 mm
Estate (GT/GTX)	1.7 ± 2 mm
Van	0.8 ± 2 mm
Track	1349 mm (53.1 in)

Torque wrench settings

	lbf ft	kgf m
Front suspension:		
Stub axle clamp nut and bolt	40	5.5
Lower arm balljoint nut	22	3.0
Lower arm pivot bolt (front)	58	8.0
Lower arm pivot nut (rear)	33	4.5
Lower arm yoke bolts	33	4.5
Anti-roll bar link-to-lower arm bolt	58	8.0
Anti-roll bar collar and clamp nuts and bolts	18	2.5

	lbf ft	kgf m
Shock absorber shaft nut	33	4.5
Strut top mounting nuts	7	1.0
Rear suspension (Estate):		
Shock absorber nut	13	1.8
Suspension arm pivot nut and bolt	94	13
Anti-roll bar mountings	47	6.5
Rear axle-to-body nuts:		
Front (two each side)	20	2.8
Rear (one each side)	9	1.3

Electrical system
Alternator (later models)
Separate regulator type:

	SEV	Bosch	Ducellier
Make	SEV	Bosch	Ducellier
Type No	716 35 202	0120400937	513 010 A
Power	500W	500W	500W
Output at 14V	35A	30A	30A
Corresponding speed (warm)	5000 rpm	4000 rpm	4000 rpm
Rotor resistance	5 to 6 ohms	5 to 6 ohms	5 to 6 ohms

Integral regulator type:

	Ducellier	Paris-Rhone
Make	Ducellier	Paris-Rhone
Type No	514 007	A 12 R 44
Power	500W	500W
Output at 13.5V	33A	33A
Corresponding speed (warm)	4000 rpm	4000 rpm
Rotor resistance	3.7 ohms	4.1 to 5.1 ohms
Regulated voltage	13.8 to 14.8	13.8 to 14.8

Alternator drivebelt (XU engine)
Type	Ribbed
Tension (using 'Krikit' tensioner tool):	
New belt	60 kg/span*
Used belt	40 kg/span*

* In the absence of the tensioner tool, adjust belt to give a deflection of 6 mm at centre of longest run

Fuses (1983 on) – typical

Fuse No	Rating (A)	Circuits protected
1	10	Windscreen wash/wipe, heated rear window switch, stop-lamps, tachometer, radio
2	15	Gauges, warning lights, direction indicators, heater blower
3	20	Heated rear window element, horn
4	7.5	Electric cooling fan
5	15	Clock, cigarette lighter, interior lamps
6	10	RH side and tail lamps, instrument panel and switch illumination, number plate lamp
7	7.5	LH side and tail lamps
8	7.5	Rear foglamps
9	20	Electric window winders
10	15	Electric sunroof
11	10	Central door locking
12	15	Hazard warning flasher
13	7.5	Reversing lamps, alternator
14	7.5	Spare
15	7.5	Radio (alternative fitment)

Torque wrench settings
	lbf ft	kgf m
Alternator mountings (XU engine):		
Pivot	29	4.0
Strap	15	2.0
Starter motor mounting bolts (XU engine)	25	3.5

Dimensions, weights and capacities
Overall dimensions (1983 on)
	Saloon	Estate
Length	4.263 m	4.283 m
Width	1.636 m	1.636 m
Height	1.410 m	1.425 m
Wheelbase	2.621 m	2.621 m
Front track	1.420 m	1.420 m
Rear track	1.349 m	1.349 m

Weights (1983 on)
	Saloon	Estate
Kerb weight (approx:		
GL, GR	930 kg	985 kg
SR	945 kg	1000 kg
GT	975 kg	1000 kg
GTX	975 kg	1030 kg
Automatic	1005 kg	1060 kg

Towing limits (subject to local restrictions):
  Unbraked trailer:

GL	445 kg	490 kg
GR	465 kg	495 kg
SR	470 kg	500 kg
GT	485 kg	500 kg
GTX	500 kg	500 kg

  Braked trailer (subject to gross train weight):

Basic Saloon	1000 kg	–
All other models	1050 kg	1050 kg
Roof rack load limit	75 kg	100 kg

Capacities (1983 on)

Engine oil (XU engine)	4.5 litres approx
Coolant (XU engine)	6.7 litres
Fuel tank:	
Saloon	56 litres
Estate	50 litres
Manual transmission (BE1)	2.0 litres
Up to 1986 without level/filler plug	2 litres
1987 on with level/filler plug	1.8 litres
Automatic transmission:	
From dry	6.2 litres
Drain and refill	2.4 litres
Screen washer reservoir:	
Saloon	1.5 litres
Estate	3.0 litres

3 Routine maintenance

Maintenance intervals

1 For the 1985 model year the service intervals laid down by the manufacturer have been extended from 5000 to 6000 miles; the time interval (six months) remains unchanged.

2 The DIY mechanic may prefer to follow the old service intervals. High-mileage vehicles, or those which are used under adverse conditions, should in any case be serviced more frequently.

3 On models with electronic (breakerless) ignition, periodic checking of the ignition timing is not necessary.

4 Regular checking of the engine valve clearances is not specified for 1985 and 1986 models.

5 On all models, the time interval for maintenance tasks should be followed when the specified mileage is not covered in that time. This is because many fluids and lubricants deteriorate with time as well as with use.

Additional maintenance tasks

6 Every 5000 or 6000 miles (as applicable):
Check automatic transmission fluid level
Check power steering fluid level

7 Every 20 000 or 24 000 miles
Renew manual transmission lubrication (BE1 gearbox up to 1986)
Renew automatic transmission fluid

8 Every 36 000 miles – Nov 1986 on
Consequent upon the introduction of a new transmission oil (production fill) the transmission is now 'filled for life', but checking the oil level and topping up is still required at 36 000 mile intervals. Refer to Section 12 of this supplement for details of level plug. This new oil should be used for topping up and is available from your dealer (refer to Specifications at beginning of this Supplement)

4 Engine modifications (XL/XR Series)

Liner seal changes

1 During 1984 the cylinder liner base seals were changed from paper to steel construction. The liners themselves were also modified. See Specifications for seal thickness identification.

2 New liners and seals may be fitted to old engines, but new seals may not be fitted to old liners (or vice versa). With the new seals the following cylinder head tightening procedure must be observed.

3 Refer to Chapter 1, Section 35. Make sure that the cylinder head bolts are category 10.9, then tighten in the order shown in Fig. 1.19 to the Stage 1 torque specified at the beginning of this Supplement.

4 Tighten the bolts in the same order to the Stage 2 specified torque.

5 Start the engine and run it up to operating temperature. Stop the engine and tighten each bolt by a further 35°. The valve clearances should be adjusted after this.

6 There is no need for subsequent retightening of the cylinder head bolts after the first thousand miles.

Main bearing cap side bolts (XR5S)

7 For greater rigidity, the centre main bearing cap on the XR5S engine is secured by two side bolts in addition to the normal securing bolts.

8 When removing the crankshaft, remove the side bolts before attempting to remove the centre main bearing cap.

9 When refitting the crankshaft, first tighten the ten main bearing cap bolts to the specified torque, then tighten the two side bolts to their specified torque.

Timing cover sealing (all models)

10 On some models, a timing cover gasket was not used in production; RTV jointing compound was used instead. On these models a different size O-ring is used between the block and the timing cover.

11 When refitting such a timing cover, either use RTV jointing compound and renew the O-ring with one of the appropriate size, or use a normal gasket and O-ring.

12 The O-rings may be identified by their internal diameter: 12 mm when used with a gasket, and 14 mm without.

5 Engine minor work (XU Series)

General description

1 The XU Series engine fitted to GT, GTX and later GR and SR models is similar to the XL and XR units in having four wet liner cylinders, a five-bearing crankshaft and an overhead camshaft.

2 Camshaft drive is by toothed belt. The belt is tensioned by a spring-loaded wheel and also drives the coolant pump. The camshaft operates directly on bucket tappets (cam followers); valve clearance adjustment is by shims inserted between the tappet and the valve stem. The distributor is driven directly from the tail of the camshaft.

3 The oil pump is located in the sump and is chain driven from the crankshaft.

4 The engine and transmission are mounted in line instead of integrally; this improves access to many components.

204

1 Air cleaner
2 Dipstick (engine/transmission oil)
3 Fuse box
4 Oil filler cap
5 Diagnostic socket
6 Air intake temperature control mechanism
7 Screen washer motor
8 Headlight load adjuster (remote type)
9 Radiator cap
10 Battery
11 Throttle cable
12 Choke cable
13 Ignition module and coil
14 Brake fluid reservoir cap and warning switch
15 Breather pipe

Underbonnet view of SR Estate showing location of components related to Routine Maintenance

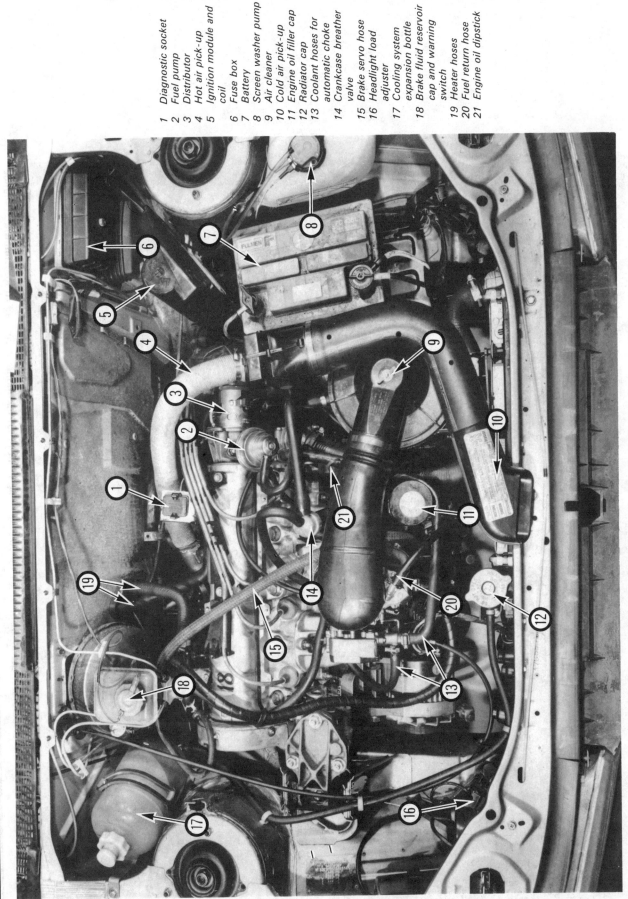

1 Diagnostic socket
2 Fuel pump
3 Distributor
4 Hot air pick-up
5 Ignition module and coil
6 Fuse box
7 Battery
8 Screen washer pump
9 Air cleaner
10 Cold air pick-up
11 Engine oil filler cap
12 Radiator cap
13 Coolant hoses for automatic choke
14 Crankcase breather valve
15 Brake servo hose
16 Headlight load adjuster
17 Cooling system expansion bottle
18 Brake fluid reservoir cap and warning switch
19 Heater hoses
20 Fuel return hose
21 Engine oil dipstick

Underbonnet view of GT Saloon showing location of components related to Routine Maintenance

1 Gearchange rods
2 Exhaust coupling
3 Fuel flow and return lines
4 Brake hydraulic line
5 Track rod ends
6 Driveshaft gaiters
7 Anti-roll bar links
8 Radiator bottom hose
9 Engine bottom mounting
10 Driveshaft intermediate bearing
11 Engine oil drain plug
12 Final drive drain plug
13 Speedometer cable

Underside view of front of GT Saloon showing location of components related to Routine Maintenance

Fig. 12.2 Cut away view of XU Series engine. Inset shows identification plate (Secs 1 and 5)

Major operations possible with engine installed

5   The following items can be removed and refitted with the engine in the car:

(a)   Cylinder head
(b)   Camshaft drivebelt and camshaft
(c)   Sump and oil pump
(d)   Clutch and flywheel (after removal of transmission)

6   Since the sump and cylinder head can be removed *in situ*, it is in theory possible to renew the pistons, liners and big-end bearings without removing the engine. Such work is not recommended, however, since it can be performed more easily with the engine on a bench.

Major operation requiring engine removal

7   The engine must be removed for the following operation:

Removal of crankshaft and main bearings

Valve clearance checking

8   Remove the distributor cap and HT leads. Unbolt and remove the camshaft cover, trying not to damage the gasket.
9   Prepare to rotate the engine, either by jacking up one front wheel and turning the wheel with 4th or 5th gear engaged, or with a spanner on the crankshaft pulley bolt. The engine will be easier to rotate if the spark plugs are first removed.
10 Have ready a pencil and paper to record the measured clearances.
11 Turn the engine until the cam lobe nearest the pulley end is pointing vertically upwards. Use feeler gauges to measure the clearance between the base of the cam and the tappet (photo). Record the clearance.
12 Repeat the measurement for the other seven valves, turning the engine as necessary so that the cam lobe in question is always vertically upwards.
13 Calculate the difference between each measured clearance and the desired value (see Specifications). Note that the value for inlet valves is different from that for exhaust. Counting from either end of the engine, the valve sequence is:

Exhaust – Inlet – Inlet – Exhaust – Exhaust – Inlet – Inlet – Exhaust

5.11 Measuring a valve clearance

14 If any clearance measured is outside the specified tolerance, adjustment must be carried out as described below.
15 If all clearances are within tolerance, refit the camshaft cover, using a new gasket if necessary. Note the copper washer under the bolt at the timing belt end (photo).

Valve clearance adjustment

16 Remove the camshaft as described later in this Section.
17 Lift off a tappet and its shim. Be careful that the shim does not fall out of the tappet. Clean the shim and measure its thickness with a micrometer (photos).

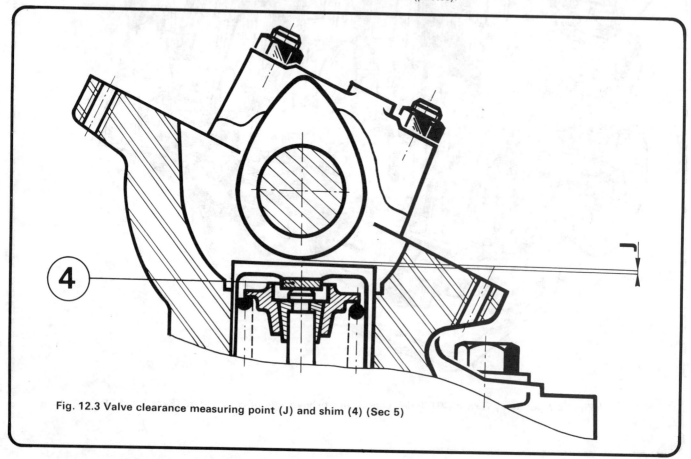

Fig. 12.3 Valve clearance measuring point (J) and shim (4) (Sec 5)

5.15 Camshaft cover bolt and copper washer (arrowed)

5.17A Removing a tappet (cam follower)

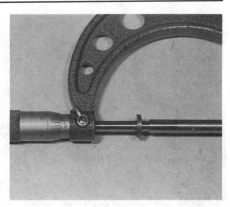

5.17B Measuring the thickness of a shim

18 Refer to the clearance recorded for the valve concerned. If the clearance was larger than specified, a thicker shim must be fitted; if the clearance was too small, a thinner shim must be fitted.

Sample calculation – clearance too large:
    Desired clearance (A) 0.20 mm.
    Measured clearance (B) 0.28 mm.
    Difference (B-A) = 0.08 mm.
    Original shim thickness 2.62 mm.
    Required shim thickness 2.62 + 0.08 = 2.70 mm.

Sample calculation – clearance too small:
    Desired clearance (A) 0.40 mm.
    Measured clearance (B) 0.23 mm.
    Difference (B-A) = 0.17 mm.
    Original shim thickness 2.86 mm.
    Required shim thickness 2.86 – 0.17 = 2.69 mm.

19 Shims are available in thicknesses from 1.650 to 4.000 mm, in steps of 0.025 mm in the middle of the range and at the ends in steps of 0.075 mm. Clean new shims before measuring or fitting them.
20 Repeat the operations on the other tappets and shims, keeping each tappet identified so that it can be refitted in the same position.
21 When reassembling, oil the shim and fit it on the valve stem, then oil the tappet and lower it smoothly into position. If the tappet is raised at any stage the shim may be dislodged.
22 When all the tappets are in position with their shims, refit the camshaft. Check the valve clearances before refitting the camshaft drivebelt in case a mistake has been made and the camshaft has to be removed again. (Make sure that the pistons are at mid-stroke – paragraph 29 – and turn the camshaft by means of its sprocket to check the clearances.)
23 Should noise from the tappets (cam followers) be evident when the engine is hot, it may be possible to eliminate it by resetting the valve clearances to their minimum specified tolerance.
24 Later models are fitted with a modified camshaft bearing cap lubrication pipe to overcome this problem of tappet noise transmission. The modified pipe may be fitted to earlier models.

Camshaft drivebelt removal and refitting (engine fitted)
25 Disconnect the battery earth lead.

26 Remove the alternator drivebelt.
27 Remove the inner shield from the right-hand wheel arch and wedge the radiator bottom hose under the sump. Move the expansion bottle out of the way without disconnecting it (photo).
28 Remove the shield from the camshaft sprocket.
29 Turn the crankshaft until the dowel hole in the pulley is about 12 o'clock and the hole in the camshaft sprocket is at about 7 o'clock. In this position a 10 mm rod should pass through each hole and into the timing recess behind. Verify this and then remove the rods (photo).
30 Remove the clutch/torque converter bottom shield. Have an assistant jam the starter ring gear while the crankshaft pulley bolt is undone. This bolt is very tight. **Do not** jam the pulley by means of the timing dowel; damage will result. Remove the bolt and washer.
31 Check that the 10mm rod will enter the timing holes; adjust the crankshaft position if necessary by means of the starter ring gear. Remove the crankshaft pulley, retrieving the Woodruff key if it is loose.
32 Remove the plastic covers from the front of the camshaft drivebelt. Note the location of the various bolts.
33 Slacken the two nuts on the front of the drivebelt tensioner and the single nut at the rear. Use a spanner on the square end of the tensioner cam spindle to turn the cam to the horizontal position and so compress the tensioner spring. Tighten the cam locknut (photo).
34 Remove the camshaft drivebelt, taking care not to kink it or contaminate it with oil if it is to be re-used.
35 Commence refitting by positioning the belt on the crankshaft sprocket, then refitting the pulley and verifying the correct position of the crankshaft by means of the rod. (Observe the arrows on the belt showing the direction of rotation, and the timing lines which align with marks on the crankshaft and camshaft sprocket(s) (photo).)
36 Fit the belt to the camshaft sprocket, round the tensioner and to the coolant pump sprocket.
37 Release the tensioner cam locknut and turn the cam downwards to release the spring. Tighten the locknut and the tensioner front nuts (photo).
38 Remove the timing rods and turn the crankshaft through two full turns in the normal direction of rotation. Turn the crankshaft further to bring No. 1 piston to TDC on the firing stroke.

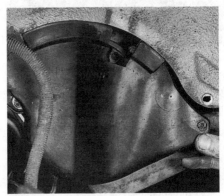

5.27 Removing right-hand wheelarch shield

5.29 Sprocket and pulley aligned using twist drills

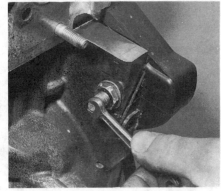

5.33 Turning the tensioner cam spindle

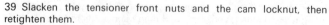

5.35 Timing belt and camshaft sprocket marks aligned (arrowed)

5.37 Timing belt tensioner front nuts

39 Slacken the tensioner front nuts and the cam locknut, then retighten them.
40 Turn the crankshaft further and make sure that the timing rods can still be inserted. If not, remove the drivebelt and start again.
41 If the old belt has been refitted, proceed to paragraph 45. If a new belt has been fitted, proceed as follows.
42 Tighten the crankshaft pulley bolt to the specified torque, then refit and tension the alternator drivebelt. Temporarily refit the camshaft sprocket cover.
43 Run the engine up to operating temperature, indicated by the cooling fan operating, then stop the engine and allow it to cool for at least two hours.
44 Rotate the crankshaft to the TDC position, No 1 cylinder firing, then slacken and retighten the tensioner nuts once more. Remove the alternator drivebelt.
45 Remove the crankshaft pulley. Refit and secure the plastic covers, then refit the pulley and tighten its bolt to the specified torque. Refit and tension the alternator drivebelt.
46 Check the ignition timing and adjust if necessary.

Camshaft removal and refitting (engine fitted)
47 Remove the camshaft drivebelt as previously described.
48 Remove the camshaft cover. For ease of access, remove the

distributor cap and HT leads also.
49 Remove the distributor and the fuel pump from the thermostat housing.
50 Remove the camshaft lubrication manifold.
51 Lock the camshaft sprocket (eg with a timing dowel) and remove the sprocket retaining bolt. Remove the sprocket and the cover plate behind it. Remove the thrust plate (photos).
52 Progressively slacken the camshaft bearing cap securing nuts and make identifying marks if necessary, then remove the caps. Be prepared for the camshaft to spring upwards. Remove the camshaft.
53 Commence refitting by making sure that the crankshaft is in the correct (dowelled) position – if not, move it to this position to avoid possible piston/valve contact.
54 Refit the camshaft, then oil and fit its bearing caps. Tighten the cap nuts progressively to the specified torque. Refit and secure the thrust plate.
55 Fit a new oil seal to the sprocket end of the camshaft.
56 Refit the sprocket rear cover plate, locate it correctly with a 10mm rod and tighten its fastenings (photo). Fit the camshaft sprocket, dowel it and tighten its securing bolt to the specified torque.
57 Refit the fuel pump, the distributor and the lubrication manifold.
58 Refit the camshaft cover, the HT leads and the distributor cap.
59 Refit the camshaft drivebelt.

5.51A Removing the camshaft thrust plate screw

5.51B Removing the camshaft thrust plate

5.56 Locating the cover plate using a 10 mm twist drill

5.62 Slackening the engine lower mounting nut

5.68A Removing the coolant pipe from the pump inlet housing

5.68B Removing the diagnostic socket. Note the earth lead

5.72 Cylinder liners clamped with washers and bolts

5.73 Cylinder block dowel held in raised position

Cylinder head removal and refitting (engine fitted)

60 Remove the camshaft drivebelt as previously described.
61 Drain the cooling system.
62 Slacken, but do not remove, the engine lower mounting rubber centre nut and bolt (photo).
63 Remove the air cleaner, its pipes and trunking, and the crankcase breather and its pipes.
64 Remove the nut which secures the engine right-hand mounting rubber.
65 Carefully raise the engine 6 to 8 cm (say 3 inches) using a hoist or a well-protected jack. Remove the two bolts which secure the right-hand mounting bracket to the cylinder head, then lower the engine back into position.
66 Disconnect the fuel, coolant and vacuum pipes from the cylinder head, carburettor and manifold. Take careful note of the connections, or make matching marks, for use when refitting. Also disconnect the throttle cable and the electrical leads.
67 Disconnect the exhaust downpipes at the manifold flange.
68 Remove the coolant pipe from the pump inlet housing. Also remove the diagnostic socket from its bracket and unbolt the oil filler pipe from the inlet manifold (photos).
69 Remove the camshaft cover, at the same time removing the distributor cap and HT leads.
70 Slacken the cylinder head bolts in the reverse sequence to that used when tightening (Fig. 12.4). Remove the bolts.
71 Remove the cylinder head, using a couple of bars through two of the bolt holes and 'rocking' it towards the front of the car. Remove the gasket and recover any loose dowels. Do not lift the head as this would disturb the cylinder liner seals which would require the removal of the engine to rectify.
72 Fit cylinder liner clamps, or large washers secured with nuts and bolts, to keep the liners in position (photo). *If the liners are disturbed the engine will have to be removed for new seals to be fitted.*
73 Commence refitting by fitting the dowels to the cylinder block. Keep the flywheel end dowel raised by inserting a 5mm punch or large nail through the hole on the front of the block (photo). Remove the liner clamps.

74 Fit a new gasket, dry, with the tab at the flywheel end. Lower the cylinder head into position, making sure that it mates with the dowels. Remove the punch or nail.
75 Fit the cylinder head bolts, their threads clean and lightly oiled. Remember to fit the spacer to the bolt above the coolant pump.
76 Progressively tighten the bolts in the order shown in Fig. 12.4 to the Stage 1 specified torque.
77 Raise the engine slightly and refit the two bolts which secure the right-hand mounting bracket to the cylinder head. Tighten these bolts and slacken the one which holds the same bracket to the engine block. Lower the engine and tighten the right-hand mounting nut and the lower mounting rubber nut and bolt.
78 Slacken cylinder head bolt No 1, then immediately retighten it to the Stage 2 specified torque. Tighten further by the angle specified for Stage 3. Repeat for all the bolts, following the tightening sequence.
79 Check the valve clearances and adjust if necessary.
80 Refit the remaining components in the reverse order of removal.
81 Refill and bleed the cooling system (Section 8).
82 Start the engine and warm it up until the cooling fan cuts in, then

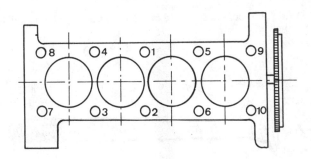

Fig. 12.4 Cylinder head bolt tightening sequence (Sec 5)

switch off and allow it to cool for at least two hours.
83 Retighten the cylinder head bolts as described in paragraph 76, then recheck the valve clearances.
84 If a new camshaft drivebelt has been fitted, retension it as described in paragraph 42.
85 Tighten the engine mounting bracket bolt.

Crankcase ventilation system modification
86 In cold weather it is possible for the engine oil filler cap to blow off after starting up. This is caused by water vapour freezing in the breather wire mesh, giving rise to pressure build-up when the engine runs.

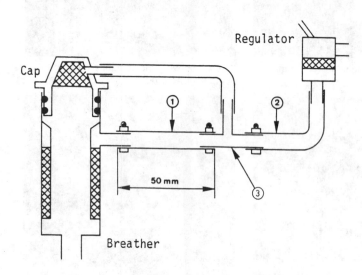

Fig. 12.5 Crankcase ventilation system modification (Sec 5)

1 Hose   2 Hose   3 Tee-piece

87 To cure this problem, a new type of oil filler cap with a hose connecting stub must be obtained. Cut the hose between the breather and the regulator, shorten the cut ends and insert a T-piece. Connect the spare arm of the T-piece to the new oil filler cap.
88 Keep the crankcase ventilation hoses clean and unblocked to avoid further problems.

Cylinder head bolts modifications
(XU Series – December 1986 on)
89 As from December 1986, Torx type (55) socket-headed bolts are used to secure the cylinder head.
90 In addition, thicker (8.0 mm) bolt washers are used and cylinder liner height is reduced by 0.05 mm to provide a modified protrusion of between 0.03 mm and 0.10 mm.
91 The tightening procedure to be used on engines using this type of bolt is given in the Specifications section of this Supplement. Before fitting the bolts, smear their threads and under their heads with Molybdenum type grease. The tightening sequence is as shown in Fig. 12.4.
92 Once tightened, the Torx type cylinder head bolts will not require further tightening.

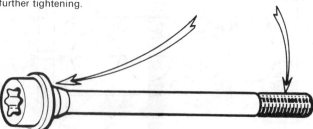

Fig. 12.6 Torx type cylinder head bolt (Sec 5)

Grease application points (arrowed)

6 Engine removal and dismantling (XU Series)

Removal with transmission
1 The method described and recommended is to remove the engine and transmission together from below the vehicle. If preferred it is possible to remove the transmission first (Section 12 of this Supplement) and then remove the engine from above, but this is not recommended as it involves considerable extra work.
2 Unless a commercial vehicle hoist is to be used, lifting tackle will be required to raise the front of the car far enough to permit the engine and transmission to be withdrawn from underneath.
3 Drain the engine oil, transmission oil and coolant. Refit the drain plugs on completion.
4 Remove the battery and its tray.
5 Remove the air cleaner and its trunking.
6 Disconnect the radiator top and bottom hoses. It is advisable to remove the radiator; disconnect the wires from the temperature switch and low level sender first.
7 Disconnect the throttle cable from the carburettor (photo).
8 Disconnect and plug the fuel return hose from the carburettor and the fuel supply hose from the pump. Be prepared for fuel spillage.
9 Disconnect the brake servo vacuum hose.
10 Disconnect and plug the heater hoses.
11 Unbolt the HT lead bracket from the camshaft cover. Remove the distributor cap, HT leads and bracket together.
12 Release the distributor LT connector clamp plate and unplug the connector. Loosely refit the clamp plate.
13 Free the diagnostic socket from its bracket and disconnect its earth lead.
14 Remove the TDC sensor (secured by a clamp bolt) from the flywheel housing (photo).
15 On models with power steering remove the fluid reservoir from the front panel and hook it onto the alternator. Disconnect and plug the pipes at the power steering valve; tie the pipes up near the distributor. Plug the pipe unions on the valve.
16 Disconnect the speedometer cable at the transmission (photo).
17 On manual transmission models, disconnect the clutch cable and the reversing light switch wires.
18 On automatic transmission models, disconnect the coolant hoses from the transmission fluid cooler. Disconnect the gearshift cable and the reversing light/starter inhibitor switch wires.
19 On all models, disconnect the leads from the two coolant switches on the inlet manifold. Note the wire colours for correct refitting.
20 Disconnect the alternator cables.
21 Disconnect the oil pressure switch wire.
22 Disconnect the earth lead from the transmission case.
23 Disconnect the exhaust downpipes at the manifold flange.
24 On manual transmission models, release the gearchange linkage balljoints by pressing them apart with a tyre lever or large screwdriver.

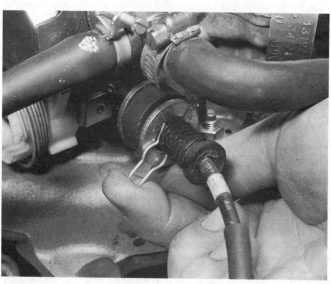

6.7 Throttle cable securing clip

6.14 Removing TDC sensor

6.16 Speedometer cable securing rubber peg (arrowed)

Also disconnect the reverse stop cable, when applicable (later models only).

25 Separate the driveshafts from the final drive housing by releasing the anti-roll bar lower links, the stub axle and steering balljoints on each side. Also release the intermediate bearing by slackening its retaining nuts and turning the retaining bolts through half a turn (180°). Free the left-hand driveshaft by pulling the hub outwards, then fit a tool to retain the differential side gears (Section 12, paragraph 20 of this Supplement). Similarly free the right-hand driveshaft.

26 If sufficient movement of the hubs cannot be obtained to withdraw the driveshafts from the final drive housing, the driveshafts will have to be removed. Refer to Section 12, paragraphs 12 to 21 of this Supplement.

27 Unbolt and remove the engine bottom mounting bracket.

28 Support the engine using lifting tackle attached to the two lifting eyes. Depending on the lifting tackle it may be necessary to remove the bonnet.

29 Take the weight of the engine/transmission unit and unbolt the top mountings (one on each side). Be prepared for the unit to take up a new position as the mountings are released.

30 Lower the engine/transmission unit out of the engine bay, paying attention to see that nothing is trapped or damaged.

31 Raise the front of the car and withdraw the unit from underneath.

Separation from transmission

32 Remove the starter motor, which is secured by three Allen bolts and a mounting bracket (photos).

33 Remove the remaining engine-to-transmission bolts.

34 Support the engine and pull the transmission away from it. Do not allow the weight of the transmission to hang on the input shaft. Recover any loose dowels.

Engine dismantling

35 Remove the ancillary components still on the engine:

(a) Alternator and drivebelt
(b) Oil filler and breather pipes (note connections)
(c) Inlet manifold and carburettor
(d) Clutch (Section 11)
(e) Oil filter (be prepared for spillage)
(f) Coolant manifold and hoses (note connections)
(g) Oil pressure switch
(h) Power steering pump (when fitted)

36 The exhaust manifold may be removed now, or it can be left in place to serve as a handle until the head is removed.

37 Unbolt and remove the crankshaft pulley. Jam the flywheel teeth when undoing the pulley bolt to stop the crankshaft rotating.

6.32A Unscrewing a starter motor bolt using an Allen key

6.32B Starter motor mounting bracket

38 Remove the camshaft drivebelt covers, noting the location of the various sizes of bolt.

39 Unbolt and remove the camshaft cover.

40 Rotate the crankshaft by means of the flywheel until a 10 mm diameter rod can be passed through the hole in the camshaft sprocket and into the timing recess. The pistons are now at mid-stroke so piston/valve contact cannot occur.

41 Release the camshaft drivebelt tensioner by slackening its nuts (two at the front and one behind the front plate) and using the square end of the cam spindle to bring the cam into a horizontal position.

42 Remove the camshaft drivebelt, taking care not to kink it and noting its direction of travel if it is to be re-used.

43 Unbolt and remove the camshaft drivebelt tensioner.

44 Remove the belt side covers and the crankshaft sprocket. Recover the Woodruff key.

45 Unbolt and remove the camshaft sprocket. Restrain the sprocket from turning if necessary using the 10 mm diameter rod inserted through the timing hole in the sprocket (photo).

46 Unbolt and remove the engine mounting bracket, the camshaft sprocket backplate and the coolant pump.

47 Slacken the ten cylinder head bolts, working in the reverse sequence of that used when tightening (Fig. 12.4). Remove the bolts and washers, noting the spacer under the No 8 bolt (directly above the coolant pump) (photo).

48 Remove the cylinder head. If it seems to be stuck, use a couple of metal rods in two of the bolt holes to rock it free. Do not attempt to

hammer or lever it off. Retrieve the two locating dowels if they are loose.

49 Fit liner clamps if it is not proposed to remove the pistons and liners. See Section 5, paragraph 72. Invert the engine.

50 Unbolt and remove the flywheel. It is dowelled so it can only be refitted one way.

51 Remove the suction drain pipe from the side of the sump (photo).

52 Unbolt and remove the sump. Note the location of the three Allen-headed bolts (photo).

53 Retrieve the bolts which secure the oil pump, noting the special centring bolt at the rear.

54 Unbolt and remove the oil seal carrier plate.

55 Lower the oil pump into the engine so that its chain can be removed. Withdraw the pump and recover the spacer, the dowels and the chain.

56 Pull the oil pump sprocket off the crankshaft and recover the Woodruff key.

57 Unbolt the connecting rod caps and push the pistons out through the tops of the liners. (If it is intended to re-use the pistons, it is prudent to remove the wear ridge at the top of the liner bores first, using a ridge reamer or scraper.) Make identification marks on the pistons, rods and caps so that they can be refitted in their original positions.

58 Remove the bolts from main bearing caps 1, 2, 4 and 5. Also remove the two nuts and the two side bolts from the centre cap. Make alignment marks on the bearing caps and remove them. Keep the

6.45 Camshaft sprocket locked against rotation using a twist drill

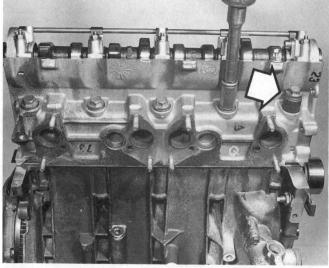

6.47 Unscrewing cylinder head bolts. Note location of spacer (arrowed)

6.51 Removing the oil suction drainpipe

6.52 Allen type socket-headed sump bolts

bearing shells with their caps if they are to be re-used. Recover the thrust washer segments from either side of No 2 bearing cap.
59 Remove the oil seal from the flywheel end of the crankshaft.
60 Lift the crankshaft out of the crankcase. Recover the upper half main bearing shells and the other two thrust washer segments.
61 Make alignment marks on the cylinder liners if they are to be re-used, then release the liner clamps and remove the liners. Dismantling of the engine is now complete.

Cylinder head dismantling
62 If not already done, remove the distributor, the fuel pump and the spark plugs. Also remove the manifolds and their gaskets.
63 Unbolt and remove the coolant outlet housing. Do not overlook the recessed securing screw in the end (photo). Remove the thermostat elbow from the housing and withdraw the thermostat.
64 Lift out the camshaft lubrication manifold (photo).
65 Unbolt and remove the camshaft thrust plate.
66 Progressively slacken the camshaft bearing cap nuts. Remove the caps – be prepared for the camshaft to spring upwards. Remove the oil seal from the sprocket end, then remove the camshaft (photo).
67 Remove the tappets and shims, identifying their locations if they are to be re-used.
68 Extract the oil filter gauze from the oilway (photo).
69 Use a universal type valve spring compressor to compress a valve spring. Remove the collets, carefully release the compressor and

extract the valve and spring. Repeat for the other seven valves.
70 Using long-nosed pliers, carefully remove the valve stem oil seals from their locations in the head. Dismantling of the cylinder head is now complete.

Cylinder head refinishing
71 The makers state that no machining of the cylinder head surface is permitted. A warped head must therefore be renewed.
72 Factory exchange cylinder heads may have had 0.2 mm machined off the mating face. These heads are identified by the letter 'R' stamped on a boss at the distributor end of the head. A gasket 0.2 mm thicker than normal must be used with such a head; the thicker gasket is identified by a cut-out in the tab at the clutch end.

Engine components examination and renovation (general)
73 Refer to Chapter 1, Sections 20 to 24 and 30.
74 Renew the camshaft drivebelt as a matter of course unless it is in perfect condition and is known to have covered only a nominal mileage. Renew the sprockets if they are damaged.
75 Inspect the camshaft lobes and bearing journals for wear and damage; if evident, renewal is probably necessary. Also inspect the bearing surfaces in the cylinder head and bearing caps.
76 Clean the camshaft lubrication manifold with solvent and then

6.63 Removing recessed screw from coolant outlet housing

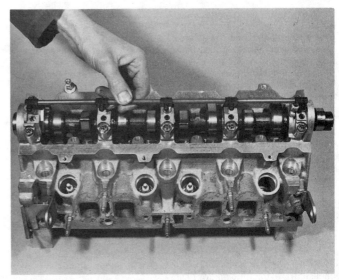

6.64 Lifting out the camshaft lubrication manifold

6.66 Removing the camshaft

6.68 Oil filter gauze partially removed from cylinder head

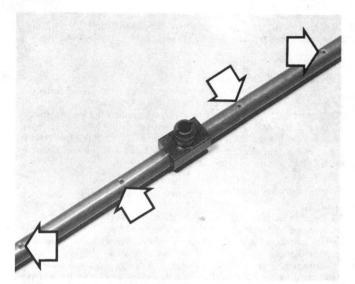

6.76 Ensure all of the lubrication manifold oil holes (arrowed) are clear

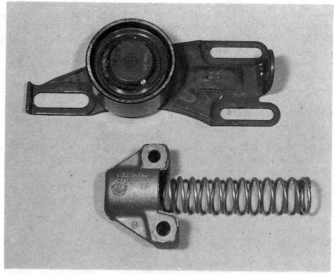

6.80 Timing belt tensioner components

blow through it with compressed air. All the holes must be clear (photo).
77 Inspect the tappets for wear and scuffing; renew them as necessary. New tappets **must** be fitted if the camshaft is renewed; it is also advisable to renew the valve springs.
78 If the starter ring gear is damaged a new one should be fitted by a Peugeot dealer or automobile engineer. Damage to the clutch mating face of the flywheel, if not severe, may be removed by machining but again this is a specialist job.
79 Inspect the manifolds as described in Chapter 1, Section 29, ignoring the references to connecting hoses.
80 The camsaft drivebelt tensioner should be examined for roughness of the wheel bearing and wear or distortion of the spring.
Renew as necessary – the wheel, bearing and backplate must be renewed as an assembly (photo).

Crankshaft spigot bush deletion
81 Later XU engines have no spigot bush in the crankshaft tail; the diameter of the gearbox input shaft is correspondingly increased.
82 If fitting a new style crankshaft to mate with an old style input shaft, obtain and insert a spigot bush.
83 If the reverse situation applies (new input shaft and old crankshaft), extract the spigot bush.

Oil pump dismantling, inspection and reassembly
84 Remove the six bolts which hold the two halves of the oil pump together. Separate the halves, being prepared for the release of the relief valve spring and plunger (photo).
85 Inspect the rotors and their housing for wear and damage. No wear limits are published for this pump; any visible wear on the moving parts

suggest that renewal is necessary. With the exception of the relief valve spring and plunger, individual components are not available (photos).
86 Lubricate the pump components well before reassembly. Bolt the two halves together being careful not to trap the spring.
87 If the pump is to be renewed it is wise to renew the chain and the crankshaft sprocket also.

Cylinder liner protrusion check
88 Liner protrusion is determined by the dimensions of the block and liners and is not adjustable. Nevertheless it should be checked as follows.
89 Make sure that the liners and their seats in the block are clean. Fit the liners without their seals, observing the marks made during dismantling if the old liners are being refitted.
90 Using a straight-edge and feeler blades, or for preference a dial gauge, measure the protrusion of each liner above the block and the relative difference in protrusion between adjacent liners. Desired values are given in the Specifications.
91 New liners can be rotated half a turn (180°), and/or fitted in a different position in the block, to bring protrusion within tolerance. Old liners which will not produce the desired results are best scrapped. Consult a Peugeot dealer for advice.
92 When the liners are correctly positioned, mark each one so that it may be refitted in the same position, then remove the liners from the block.

Oil leak from gallery plugs
93 If oil has been leaking from any of the oil gallery plugs in the cylinder block, remove the plugs, clean them, coat them with sealant and refit them.

6.84 Separating the two halves of the oil pump

6.85A Inspect the oil pump gears for wear

6.85B Oil pump relief valve spring and plunger

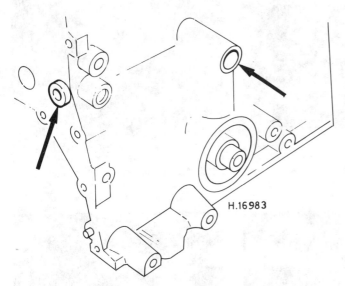

Fig. 12.7 Oil gallery plugs (arrowed) (Sec 6)

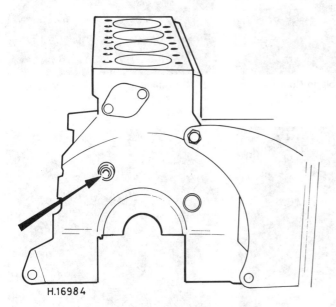

Fig. 12.8 Oil gallery plug (arrowed) (Sec 6)

7 Engine reassembly and refitting (XU Series)

Cylinder head reasembly

1 Fit new valve stem oil seals, then fit the valves, springs and collets. Oil the valve stems liberally; a smear of grease will hold the collets in position while the spring is compressed. The valve springs can be fitted either way up.
2 Lubricate the tappet bores. Secure each shim to its valve stem with a dab of grease and carefully fit the tappets. If new components have been fitted so that the valve clearances are unknown, fit the thinnest possible shims to all valves.
3 Fit the camshaft to the head and oil its lobes and journals. Fit the bearing caps, making sure that the middle ones are the right way round. Progressively tighten the bearing cap nuts to the specified torque.
4 Fit the camshaft thrust plate and tighten its securing bolt.
5 Press the lubrication manifold into position.
6 Fit a new filter gauze in the oilway.

7.3 Tightening the camshaft bearing nuts

7 Fit the coolant outlet housing, using a new gasket. Fit the thermostat and its elbow to the housing, again with a new gasket.
8 Fit the inlet and exhaust manifold, using new gaskets, and tighten their fastenings to the specified torque.
9 Fit and secure the fuel pump (new gasket) and the distributor. If alignment marks were not made when dismantling, set the distributor in mid-slot. The drive is offset so it can only be fitted one way.
10 Fit the carburettor and its heat insulator.
11 Fit a new oil seal to the sprocket end of the camshaft, using a piece of tube to drive it home.
12 If valve clearance adjustment is to be carried out now, temporarily fit the camshaft sprocket and stand the cylinder head on wooden blocks so that open valves do not strike the work surface.

Engine reassembly

13 Refer to Chapter 1, Sections 31 and 32. (Disregard the reference to the O-ring at the clutch end of the block.)
14 Position the block for access to the bottom end and fit the main bearing upper shells. Also fit the thrust washer segments to No 2 bearing, grooved sides outwards (photo); retain them with a smear of grease. Note that the recommended placement of grooved (G) and plain (P) bearing shells varies according to model:

Early models (up to Serial No 9 207 534)

Bearing No	1	2	3	4	5
Top	P	G	P	G	P
Bottom	P	P	P	P	P

Later models (from Serial No 9 207 535)

Bearing No	1	2	3	4	5
Top	G	P	P	P	G
Bottom	G	P	P	G	G

15 Oil the bearing shells and lower the crankshaft into position, taking care not to dislodge the thrust washer segments (photo). Inject some oil into the crankshaft oilways.
16 Fit the side seals to No 1 main bearing cap. Carefully fit the cap with its bearing shell; lubricate the shell, the sides of the cap and the locating surfaces in the block. There is a risk of displacing or distorting the side seals as the cap is fitted, so protect them with a couple of feeler blades or thin strips of tin which can be withdrawn rearwards after fitting the cap (photos).
17 Fit the shells to the other main bearing caps, lubricate them and fit the caps. Fit the thrust washer segments, grooved side outwards, to No 2 cap. Observe the mating marks when dismantling; the lug on each bearing cap points towards the timing sprockets.
18 Fit the main bearing cap nuts and bolts and tighten them to the specified torque. Tighten the side bolts on No 3 cap last (photo).
19 Check the protrusion of No 1 cap side seals above the sump mating face; it should be 2 mm. Trim off any excess.
20 Check the crankshaft endfloat as described in Chapter 1, Section 33, paragraph 8.

7.14 Fitting crankshaft thrust washer upper segment

7.15 Fitting the crankshaft

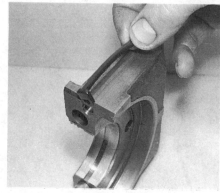
7.16A Fitting a side seal to No 1 main bearing cap

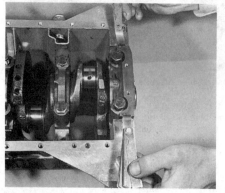
7.16B Protecting the side seals with feeler gauge blades

7.18 Tightening a side bolt on No 3 main bearing

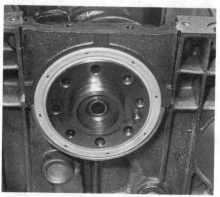
7.21 Crankshaft oil seal fitted at flywheel end

7.22 Piston crown directional arrow (towards camshaft sprocket)

B = Liner grade   2 = Gudgeon pin grade

7.23A Fitting the oil pump drive sprocket

7.23B Locating oil pump drive chain over crankshaft sprocket

7.24A Fitting the oil pump (engage the chain first)

7.24B Sliding in the oil pump spacer

7.25 Location of oil pump special bolt

21 Fit a new oil seal, lips inwards and lubricated, to the flywheel end of the crankshaft. Drive it into place with a piece of tube (photo).
22 Fit new O-ring seals to the cylinder liners, then fit the pistons and liners as described in Chapter 1, Section 34, paragraphs 7 and 8. Fit the big-end caps as described in paragraphs 9 and 10 of the same Section (photo).
23 Fit the Woodruff key and oil pump drive sprocket to the crankshaft nose. Fit the chain over the sprocket (photos).
24 Make sure that the locating dowel is in position, then engage the oil pump sprocket in the chain and offer the pump to the block. Engage the pump on the dowel, then lift it up far enough to slide the L-shaped spacer in underneath it (photos).
25 Fit the oil pump securing bolts, remembering that the special centring bolt is nearest the flywheel, and tighten them to the specified torque. Generously lubricate the pump and the chain (photo).
26 Refit the pulley oil seal carrier plate, using silicone jointing compound on the block mating faces. Fit a new oil seal, lubricated lips inwards, and drive it home with a piece of tube.
27 Fit the sump, using a new gasket, and tighten its securing bolts progressively to the specified torque. Remember the correct location of the three Allen-headed bolts.
28 Refit the suction drain pipe, using a new O-ring. Do not overtighten the securing nuts – 0.5 kgf m (say 3.5 lbf ft) is the maximum allowed.

7.40 Fitting the engine mounting bracket

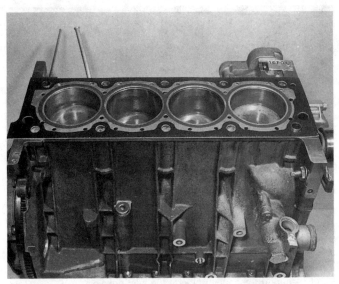
7.33 Cylinder head gasket correctly fitted

29 Fit the flywheel to the crankshaft flange and secure with new bolts, using thread locking compound. Tighten the bolts progressively to the specified torque.
30 Fit the clutch disc and pressure plate as described in Section 11.
31 Position the engine for access to the cylinder head face. Rotate the crankshaft to bring the pistons to mid-stroke (none at TDC), then remove the liner clamps.
32 Check that the head mating surface is clean and that the two locating dowels are present. Place a 5 mm diameter rod in the hole beneath the dowel at the flywheel end to stop the dowel being displaced downwards.
33 Fit a new cylinder head gasket, dry, with the protruding tab at the flywheel end (photo).
34 Lower the assembled cylinder head into position, making sure that it engages with the dowels.
35 Fit the cylinder head bolts, with their threads clean and lightly oiled. Remember to fit the spacer to the bolt above the coolant pump.
36 Tighten the cylinder head bolts progressively in the order shown in Fig. 12.2 to the Stage 1 specified torque.
37 Slacken bolt No 1 and then retighten it to the Stage 2 specified torque. Tighten the bolt further through the angle specified for Stage 3. Repeat this operation on the other bolts in sequence.

38 Fit the camshaft sprocket backplate, using a 10 mm rod through the timing hole to locate it precisely before tightening its securing bolts.
39 Fit the camshaft sprocket, washer and bolt. Use the 10 mm rod to lock the sprocket in the correct position and tighten the bolt to the specified torque. Remove the rod.
40 Fit the engine mounting bracket and tighten its bolts (photo).
41 Fit and secure the coolant pump, using a new gasket. Tighten the bolts to the specified torque.
42 Fit the covers around the coolant pump, noting the location of the various special bolts (Fig. 12.9).
43 Fit the Woodruff key and crankshaft sprocket.
44 Fit the camshaft drivebelt tensioner, but leave the nuts slack. Compress the spring by locking the cam in the horizontal position.
45 Temporarily fit the crankshaft pulley, its washer and bolt; lightly tighten the bolt. Carefully turn the crankshaft until a 10 mm rod will pass through the timing hole in the pulley and into the timing recess. If piston/valve contact occurs, back off and try again with the camshaft in a slightly different position. **Do not** try to force the crankshaft if a piston contacts a valve.
46 Use the 10 mm rod to position the camshaft sprocket, then remove the crankshaft pulley and fit the camshaft drivebelt. Be careful not to kink the belt as it is fitted, and observe the arrows showing the correct direction of rotation. The two white stripes on the belt should align with the timing marks on the sprockets.
47 Withdraw the timing rod. Tension the belt by turning the tensioner cam so that it points downwards and secure it with its locknut. Tighten the two nuts at the front of the tensioner.
48 Turn the crankshaft through two full turns in the normal direction of rotation; rotate it further to bring No 1 and 4 pistons to TDC with the valves on No 1 cylinder open.
49 Slacken the two nuts and the cam locknut on the drivebelt tensioner, then retighten them.
50 Temporarily refit the crankshaft pulley, rotate the crankshaft and check that the timing rods can be inserted simultaneously in the crankshaft pulley and camshaft sprocket holes. If not, remove the belt and try again. Remove the pulley.
51 Fit the drivebelt covers in the sequence shown in Fig. 12.10. (Note however that they will have to be removed to retension the drivebelt if a new one has been fitted.)
52 Fit the crankshaft pulley, washer and bolt, making sure that the Woodruff key is still in position. Jam the starter ring gear teeth and tighten the bolt to the specified torque.
53 Refit the camshaft cover, noting the copper washer at the sprocket end bolt, and using a new gasket.
54 Refit the ancillary components listed below; it may be preferable to

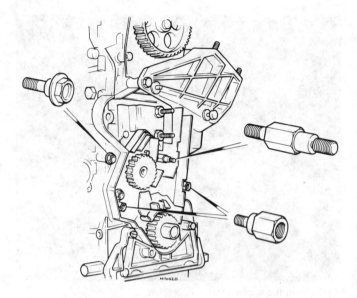

Fig. 12.9 Timing belt cover special bolts (Sec 7)

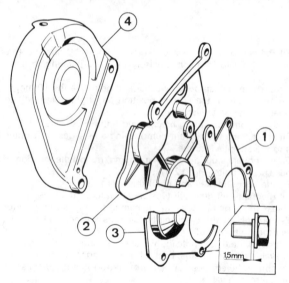

Fig. 12.10 Timing cover component fitting sequence (Sec 7)

7.54A Fitting oil filler and breather pipes

7.54B Securing the coolant pipe to the inlet housing

7.60 Driveshaft oil seal protector

leave delicate items such as the alternator and distributor until after the engine is refitted:

   (a) *Oil filler/breather pipe (photo)*
   (b) *Oil pressure switch*
   (c) *Coolant inlet housing and pipe (photo)*
   (d) *Spark plugs, distributor and HT leads*
   (e) *Alternator and drivebelt*

55 Fit a new oil filter with its sealing ring well lubricated; tighten by hand only.

Engine and transmission reassembly
56 Check that the clutch release components are correctly fitted in the gearbox and that the pressure plate and disc are fitted to the flywheel. (On automatic transmission models, check that the torque converter is properly located.)
57 Smear a little anti-seize compound on the nose and splines of the transmission input shaft, then offer the transmission to the engine. Do not allow the weight of the transmission to hang on the input shaft. If the input shaft does not wish to pass the clutch, it is possible that the clutch disc is not centred. Check also that the transmission input shaft is compatible with the spigot recess in the crankshaft (Section 6, paragraphs 81 to 83).

58 Engage the engine-to-transmission dowels and loosely fit the bolts. Also fit the starter motor, which is secured by three Allen bolts and a bracket. Tighten the bolts to the specified torque.
59 On manual transmission models, fit the clutch cable guide and pivot brackets.

Engine and transmission refitting
60 Fit the driveshaft oil seal protector to the right-hand side of the final drive unit (photo).
61 Raise and support the front of the vehicle and position the engine/transmission unit under the engine bay.
62 Attach lifting tackle to the unit and raise it into position, taking care not to foul cables, pipes etc. Engage the left-hand mounting stud in its location and fit the nut to it, then secure the right-hand top mounting.
63 Make sure that the right-hand driveshaft bearing carrier is in position, then fit the right-hand driveshaft to the final drive. Secure the bearing carrier and remove the oil seal protector.
64 Remove the differential side gear retaining tool and fit the left-hand driveshaft.
65 Fit and tighten the engine bottom mounting.
66 Remake the suspension and steering connections, using new nuts on the balljoints.
67 Refit the exhaust downpipes to the manifold flange, using a new gasket. Tighten the nuts.
68 Refit the right-hand wing inner panel and the radiator bottom hose, which is clipped to the panel for support.
69 Refit the wheels and lower the car. Refit the ancillary components, controls and associated hoses, wires etc., referring to the appropriate Sections for guidance. There are many clips and brackets whose location or function may not be evident if careful notes were not made when removing; make sure that they are all refitted!
70 When reconnecting the hoses to the inlet manifold, note that the servo vacuum take-off is at the front and towards the left-hand side. The coolant hose is connected to the front centre tapping and the breather hose to the rear centre tapping. Note also the carburettor connections (photo).

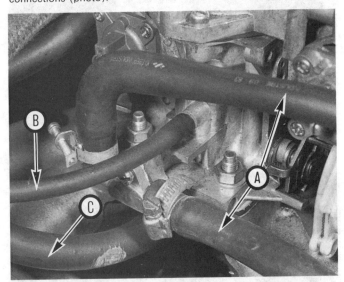

7.70 Some of the carburettor and inlet manifold hose connections

A   Coolant (to carburettor flange)   C   Crankcase ventilation
B   Distributor   (to manifold)

71 If the engine right-hand mounting was dismantled, check its movement and if necessary add or remove shims to achieve the clearances shown in Fig. 12.11. (Later models have a different type of mounting, without shims, and no adjustment is necessary.)
72 Replenish the engine oil and transmission oil (remember to measure the transmission oil in advance). Refill the cooling system and (where appropriate) the power steering reservoir.

Initial start-up after overhaul
73 Refer to Chapter 1, Section 44, paragraphs 1 to 7.
74 Allow the engine to cool for at least two hours. Loosen the bolt which secures the engine right-hand mounting bracket to the block,

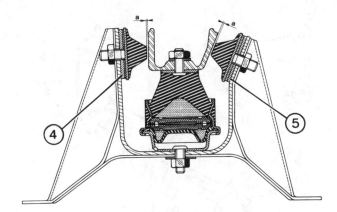

Fig. 12.11 Engine right-hand mounting (early type) (Sec 7)

a   1.0 mm (0.04 in)   4   Shims   5   Shims

then retighten the cylinder head bolts as described in paragraph 37. Tighten the mounting bracket bolt on completion. No subsequent retightening is necessary.
75 Recheck the valve clearances.
76 If a new camshaft drivebelt was fitted, retension it as described in Section 5, paragraphs 44 and 45.

8 Cooling system

Description (XU engine)
1   The cooling system differs from that fitted to XL and XR engines in three main features:

(a) It is sealed (the radiator vents into an expansion bottle, not to atmosphere)
(b) The coolant pump is driven by the camshaft drivebelt
(c) The radiator cooling fan is driven by an electric motor

2   Other minor differences will be found in hose routing and in the position of the thermostat. Except as noted in this Section, the procedures in Chapter 2 apply.

Low coolant level sensor (general)
3   The low coolant level sensor fitted to some later models is mounted in the radiator side tank. The sensor consists of a float, a magnet and a reed switch.
4   No repair is possible to the sensor; if it malfunctions it must be renewed. Drain the cooling system, remove the old sensor (bayonet fitting) and fit the new one (photo).

8.4 Fitting the low coolant level sensor

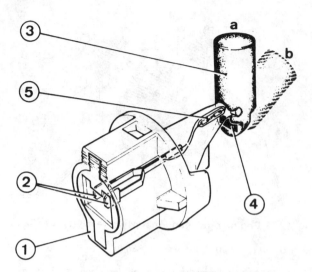

Fig. 12.12 Low coolant level sensor (Sec 8)

a Normal position	3 Float
b Low position	4 Magnet
1 Body	5 Reed switch
2 Terminals	

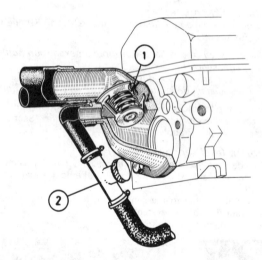

Fig. 12.13 Thermostat jiggle pin (1) and cooling system bleed valve (2) (Sec 8)

5   Do not attempt to remove or refit a coolant level sensor while the radiator is full or is in other than its normal upright position. Damage to the sensor and/or the radiator side tank may result.

Cooling system filling (pre-1983)
6   If problems are experienced with air locks when refilling the cooling system, fit a bleed valve (obtainable from a Peugeot dealer) in the small hose which runs from the thermostat housing to the heater return. At the same time check that the thermostat has a 'jiggle pin' (Fig. 12.13).
7   With the valve open, fill the cooling system until the level of coolant is about 5 cm (2 in) from the filler neck. When coolant, free of air bubbles, emerges from the bleed valve, close it.
8   Refit the radiator cap and run the engine up to operating temperature. Allow it to cool and then top up the coolant if necessary.

Cooling system draining (XU engine)
9   Proceed as described in Chapter 2, Section 2, but also remove the

cap from the expansion bottle and the drain plug (located just above the driveshaft intermediate bearing) from the engine.

Cooling system filling (XU engine)
10   Have the heater control at 'hot', open the two bleed valves (photos) and remove the caps from the radiator and the expansion bottle. Close the drain tap and refit the drain plug. (On automatic transmission models, and on all 1986 and later models, there are three bleed valves – see Fig. 12.81.)
11   Fill the system via the radiator orifice until the radiator is full, then fit its cap. Continue to fill via the expansion bottle until the correct level is indicated. Tighten the bleed valves when coolant, free of air bubbles, emerges from them.
12   Fit the expansion bottle cap, then start the engine and run it to operating temperature (indicated by the radiator fan operating). Run the engine for a further 5 minutes, then switch it off and allow it to cool for at least two hours.
13   Check the level in the expansion bottle and top up if necessary.

Coolant pump removal and refitting (XU engine)
14   Drain the cooling system.
15   Remove the camshaft drivebelt (Section 5).
16   Remove the camshaft drivebelt tensioner (three nuts).

8.10A Cooling system bleed valve (arrowed) on inlet side

8.10B Cooling system bleed valve (arrowed) on thermostat

8.18 Removing the coolant pump

8.22 Radiator cooling fan electrical connection

8.23 Removing the cooling fan

17 Remove the plastic shield, noting the locations of the different types of bolt.
18 Remove the five bolts which secure the coolant pump. Remove the pump and recover the gasket (photo).
19 The pump cannot be repaired; if defective it must be renewed.
20 Refit in the reverse order of removal. Use a new gasket and tighten the securing bolts to the specified torque.

Cooling fan removal and refitting (XU engine)
21 Remove the front grille (Chapter 11, Section 13).
22 Extract the fan harness electrical connector from the junction box on the right-hand inner wing. Separate the connector and draw the harness up to the fan (photo).
23 Remove the two bolts which secure the top of the fan mounting. Tip the fan forwards and free it from the lower mounting pegs (photo).
24 If wished, the fan can be pulled from the motor spindle after removing the circlip. The motor can be separated from the mounting after removing the three nuts and bolts. No spare parts for the motor are available.
25 Refit in the reverse order of removal. Check for correct operation of the fan on completion.

Radiator removal and refitting (XU engine)
26 Drain the cooling system.
27 Disconnect the top and bottom hoses from the radiator. Also disconnect the electrical leads from the thermoswitch and the low level sensor, and the expansion bottle hose.
28 Unbolt and remove the radiator top mounting. Pull the radiator towards the engine slightly and carefully lift it out.
29 Refit in the reverse order of removal. Refill and bleed the cooling system on completion.

Cooling system hose clips (all models)
30 The hose clips fitted in production are 'one-shot' devices, which are tightened by pulling the free end of the clip through a loop which grips the rack formed on the clip.
31 To release such a clip, either lever up the loop with a screwdriver or cut it off with side cutters.
32 Even if the clip is released without cutting it, successful re-use is unlikely. Use proprietary worm drive clips on reassembly.

9 Fuel and exhaust systems

Air cleaner element renewal (XU engine)
1 Remove the hot and cold air trunking together with the temperature control unit.
2 Undo the wing nut and remove the air cleaner lid. Extract the element (photo).
3 Wipe clean inside the housing, then fit the new element. Observe any directional markings on the element.
4 Refit and secure the lid, then refit the temperature control unit and trunking.

Oil contamination of air cleaner element (pre-1983)
5 Should contamination of the air cleaner element with engine oil occur, remove the rocker cover and inspect the breather baffle. If the baffle is of the 'trellis' type, substitute a 'pan scrubber' type, obtainable from a Peugeot dealer.

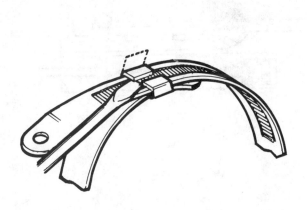
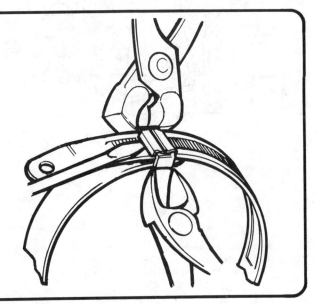
Fig. 12.14 Releasing production type hose clips (Sec 8)

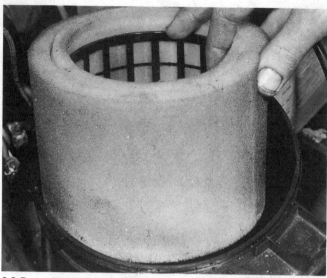

9.2 Removing the air cleaner element

Carburettor descriptions (later models)

Solex 34 PBISA 14 or 16 and 35 PBISA 14

6   These carburettors are, for practical purposes, identical to the 34 PBISA 9 described in Chapter 3. Details of different jet sizes, etc, will be found in the Specifications; small differences in adjustment procedures are noted later in this Section.

Weber 34 IBP

7   This carburettor is fitted to some XL5 engines as an alternative to the Solex 34 PBISA 14, which it closely resembles.
8   Except as noted in this Section, adjustment and overhaul procedures are as described in Chapter 3.

Weber 36 TLP

9   This carburettor is fitted to the 'low tune' version of the XU5 engine. It is a single barrel downdraught instrument with a manual choke. A vacuum unloader opens the choke flap a small amount as soon as the engine starts.
10 Idle adjustment is as described in Chapter 3, Section 7. Refer to Figs. 12.17 and 12.18 for the locations of the idle speed and mixture adjusting screws. (In Chapter 3 the idle speed adjusting screw is called the volume control screw, because it controls the volume of mixture flowing through the idle bypass circuit.)
11 Overhaul is basically as described in Chapter 3, Section 11. Other adjustments are described later in this Section.

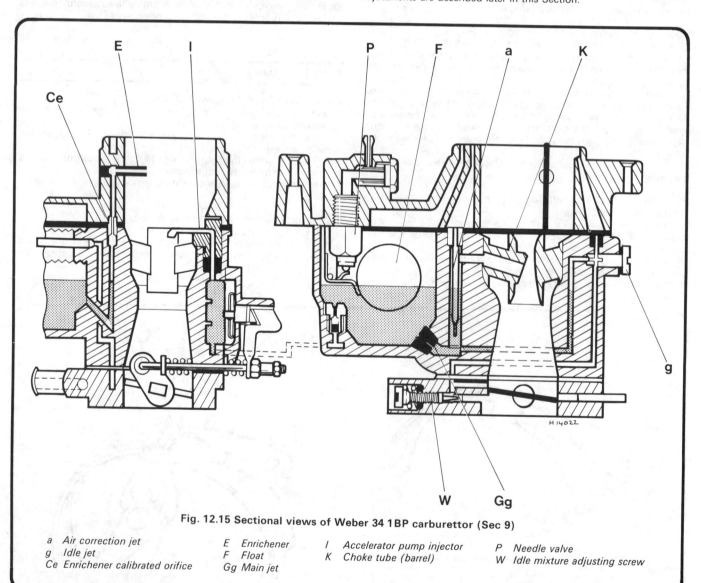

Fig. 12.15 Sectional views of Weber 34 1BP carburettor (Sec 9)

a Air correction jet	E Enrichener	I Accelerator pump injector	P Needle valve
g Idle jet	F Float	K Choke tube (barrel)	W Idle mixture adjusting screw
Ce Enrichener calibrated orifice	Gg Main jet		

**Fig. 12.16 Exploded view of Weber 34 1BP carburettor
(Sec 9)**

a   Air correction jet
g   Idle jet
i   Accelerator pump injector
F   Float
Gg Main jet
K   Choke tube (barrel)
P   Needle valve
W   Idle mixture adjustment
    screw
Z   Idle speed adjustment screw

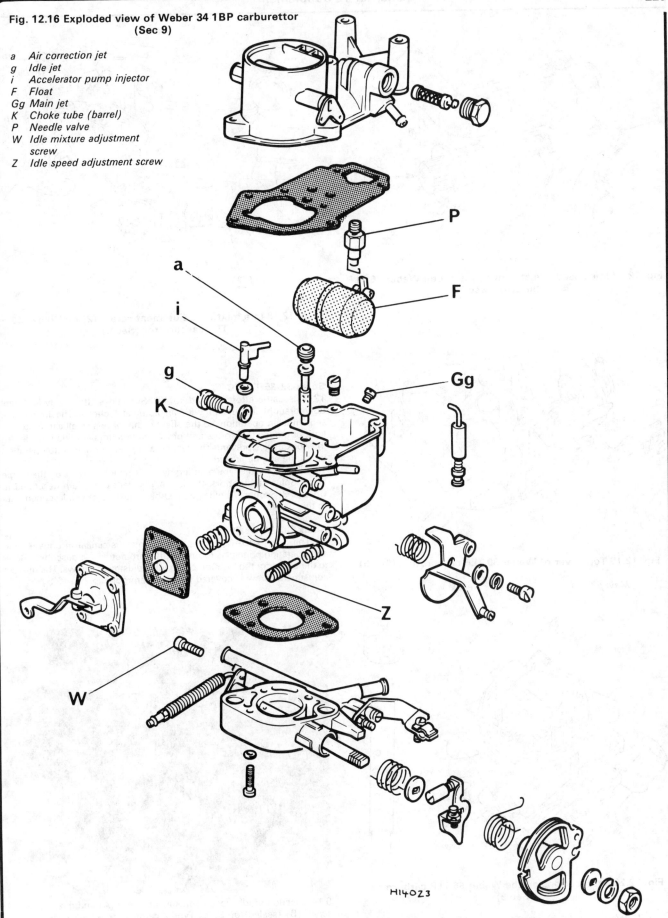

H14023

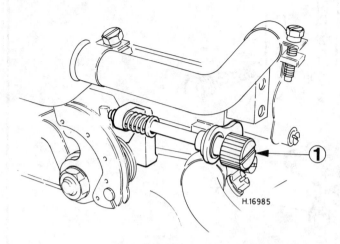

Fig. 12.17 Idle speed adjustment screw (1) on Weber 36 TLP carburettor (Sec 9)

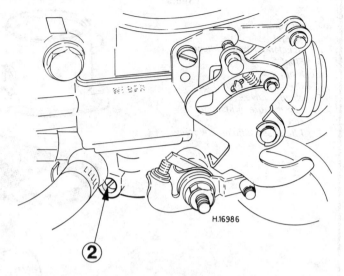

Fig. 12.18 Idle mixture adjustment screw (2) on Weber 36 TLP carburettor (Sec 9)

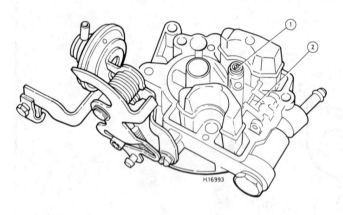

Fig. 12.19 Top cover of Weber 36 TLP carburettor (Sec 9)

1   Main jet   2   Needle valve (fuel inlet)

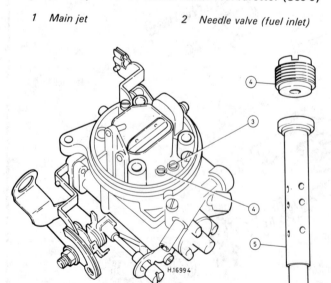

Fig. 12.20 Jet locations on the Weber 36 TLP carburettor (Sec 9)

3   Idle jet   4   Air correction jet   5   Emulsion tube

Solex 32-35 TACIC

12 This carburettor is fitted to XR5S engines. It is a twin barrel downdraught instrument with an automatic choke. The barrels are sequential in operation, so the effect is that of one small carburettor at light or moderate throttle, and of two carburettors at wide throttle. An interlock device prevents the second barrel from coming into operation when the engine is cold.

13 Since the same type of idling bypass circuit is used as on the single barrel Solex carburettors, the idle adjustment procedure described in Chapter 3, Section 7 holds good. Other adjustments are described later in this Section.

Solex CISAC or Z1

14 The Solex CISAC or Type Z carburettor is similar in construction and operating principles to the TACIC carburettor just described. Refer to the photo for the location of the idle adjustment screws. The mixture adjustment screw is covered by a tamperproof cap.

9.14 Location of idle speed adjustment screw (A) and mixture screw (B) (sealed) on Solex Type Z carburettor

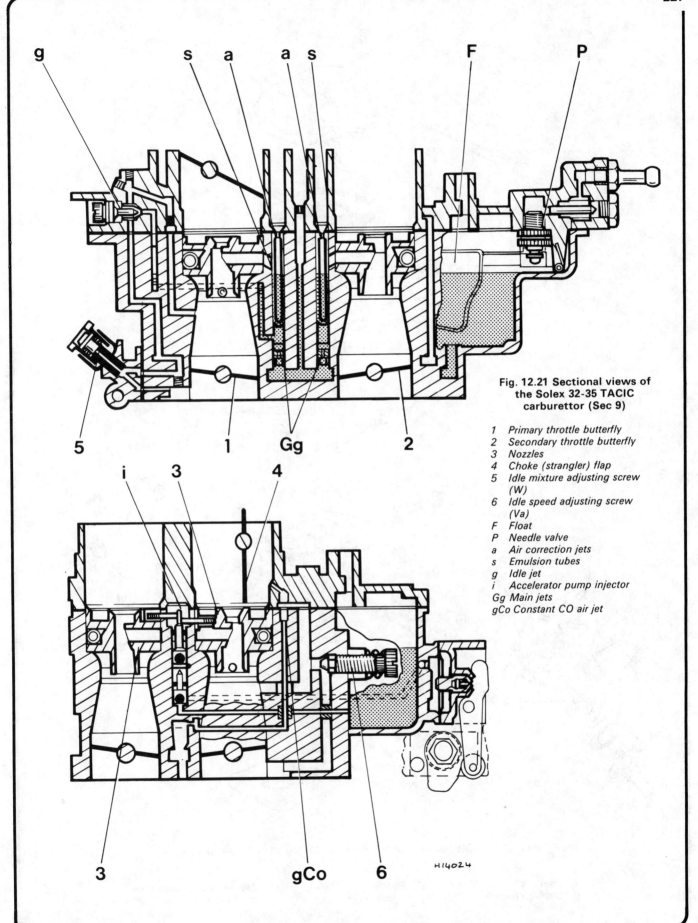

Fig. 12.21 Sectional views of the Solex 32-35 TACIC carburettor (Sec 9)

1 Primary throttle butterfly
2 Secondary throttle butterfly
3 Nozzles
4 Choke (strangler) flap
5 Idle mixture adjusting screw (W)
6 Idle speed adjusting screw (Va)
F Float
P Needle valve
a Air correction jets
s Emulsion tubes
g Idle jet
i Accelerator pump injector
Gg Main jets
gCo Constant CO air jet

H14024

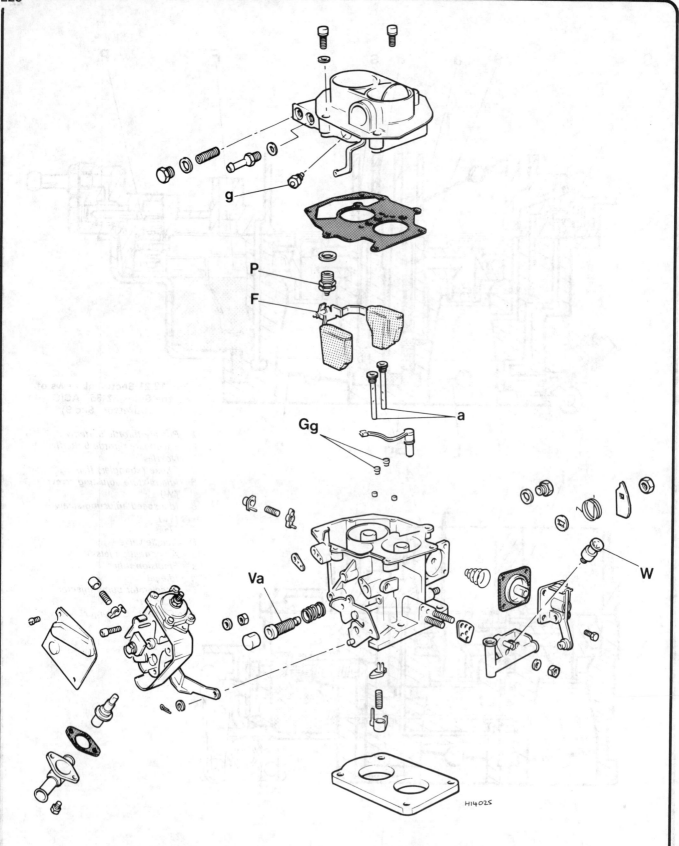

Fig. 12.22 Exploded view of the Solex 32-35 TACIC carburettor (Sec 9)

Gg	Main jets	F	Float	Va	Idle speed adjusting screw
a	Emulsion tubes	P	Needle valve	W	Idle mixture adjusting screw
g	Idle jet				

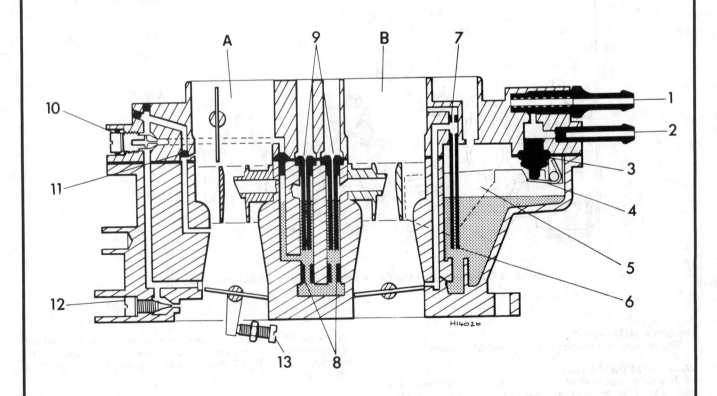

Fig. 12.23 Sectional views of
Solex CISAC and Type Z
carburettor (Sec 9)

A   Primary barrel
B   Secondary barrel
1   Fuel inlet
2   Fuel return
3   Needle valve
4   Float level adjusting tab
5   Float
6   Progression fuel jet
7   Progression air jet
8   Main jets
9   Air correction jets
10   Idle jet
11   Idle air calibration
12   Idle mixture adjustment
     screw
13   Idle speed adjustment screw
14   Accelerator pump cam
15   Accelerator pump
16   Accelerator pump injectors
17   Power enricher
18   Enrichener calibration
19   Enrichener valve
21   Econostat

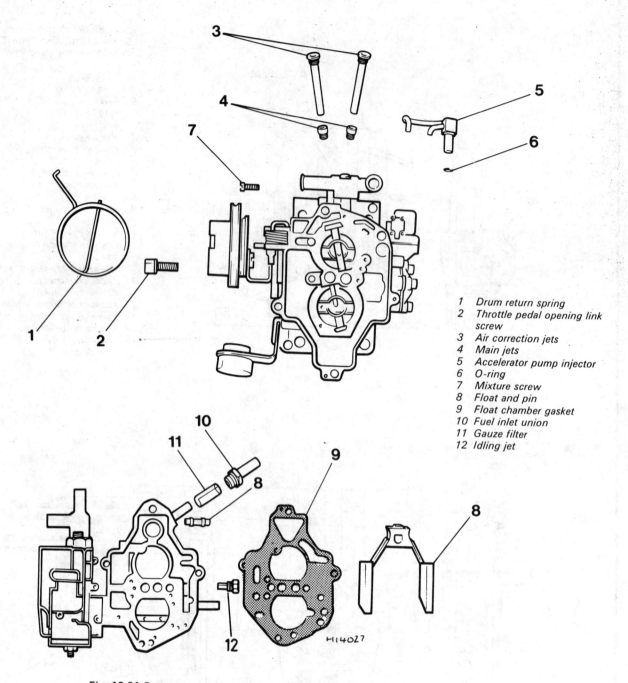

1   Drum return spring
2   Throttle pedal opening link
    screw
3   Air correction jets
4   Main jets
5   Accelerator pump injector
6   O-ring
7   Mixture screw
8   Float and pin
9   Float chamber gasket
10 Fuel inlet union
11 Gauze filter
12 Idling jet

Fig. 12.24 Components of the Solex CISAC (Type Z) carburettor (Sec 9)

The Solex 34/34 Type Z1
  This carburettor is fitted to later Auto and GTX models.

Weber 32/34 DRTC4 100
15 This carburettor is similar to the TACIC and CISAC instruments; additionally, it has an electrically-operated 'anti-dieseling' valve which interrupts the idle circuit when the ignition is switched off.
16 Idle adjustment is as described in Chapter 3, Section 7. Refer to Fig. 12.26 for the locations of the adjusting screws.

Carburettor float level setting (Solex)
17 It may be found that the float hinge is made of plastic, in which case adjustment by bending the hinge should not be attempted. Adjust by adding or removing washers under the needle valve.

18 For the 32-35 TACIC carburettor, the dimensions of the float level setting gauge (Chapter 3, Fig. 3.6) are 80 mm across the arms and 41 mm deep. For the Type Z the dimensions are 70 mm across and 33.5 mm deep.

Carburettor float level setting (Weber)
34 IBP and 32/34 DRTC4 100
19 The float level is checked by removing the float chamber cover and holding it vertically with the float hanging downwards. With the gasket in position and the float arm just resting against the needle valve ball, a drill shank of 7.5 ± 0.5 mm diameter should be a snug fit between the float and the gasket. (Do not measure from the seam on the float.) Adjust by carefully bending the float arm.

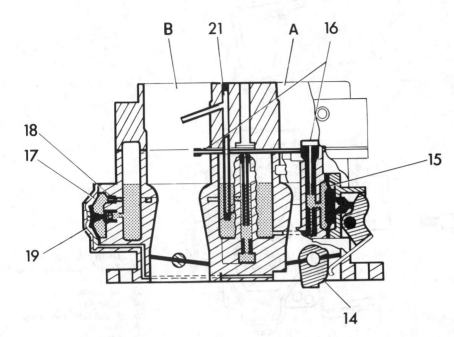

Fig. 12.23 Sectional views of
Solex CISAC and Type Z
carburettor (Sec 9)

A   Primary barrel
B   Secondary barrel
1   Fuel inlet
2   Fuel return
3   Needle valve
4   Float level adjusting tab
5   Float
6   Progression fuel jet
7   Progression air jet
8   Main jets
9   Air correction jets
10 Idle jet
11 Idle air calibration
12 Idle mixture adjustment
    screw
13 Idle speed adjustment screw
14 Accelerator pump cam
15 Accelerator pump
16 Accelerator pump injectors
17 Power enrichener
18 Enrichener calibration
19 Enrichener valve
21 Econostat

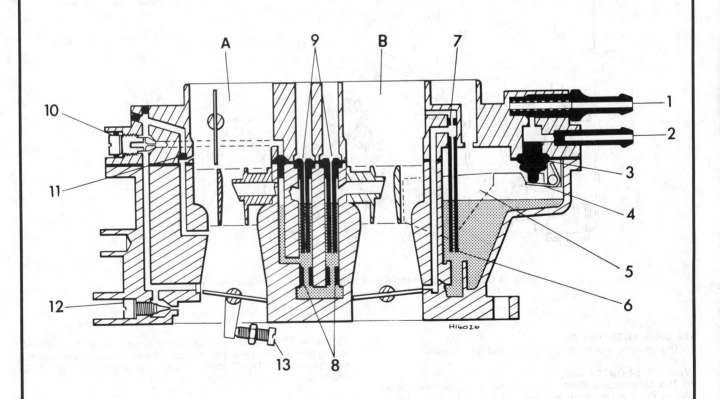

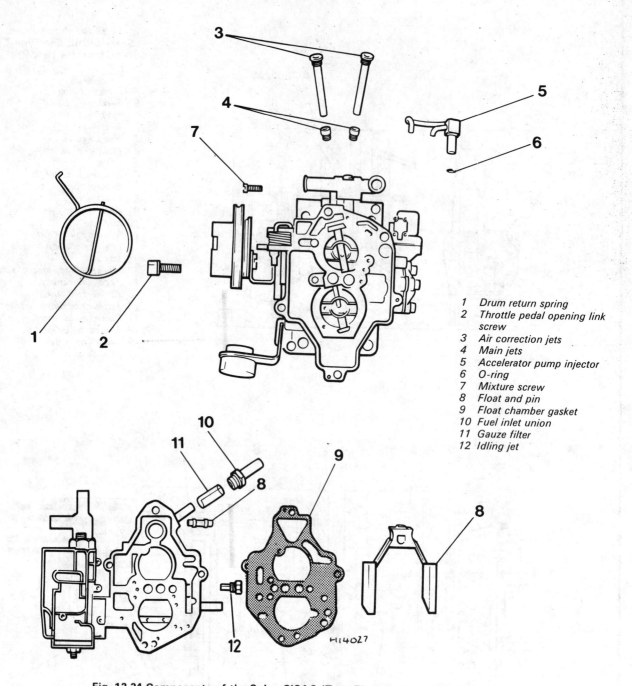

1   Drum return spring
2   Throttle pedal opening link
    screw
3   Air correction jets
4   Main jets
5   Accelerator pump injector
6   O-ring
7   Mixture screw
8   Float and pin
9   Float chamber gasket
10 Fuel inlet union
11 Gauze filter
12 Idling jet

Fig. 12.24 Components of the Solex CISAC (Type Z) carburettor (Sec 9)

The Solex 34/34 Type Z1
This carburettor is fitted to later Auto and GTX models.

Weber 32/34 DRTC4 100
15 This carburettor is similar to the TACIC and CISAC instruments; additionally, it has an electrically-operated 'anti-dieseling' valve which interrupts the idle circuit when the ignition is switched off.
16 Idle adjustment is as described in Chapter 3, Section 7. Refer to Fig. 12.26 for the locations of the adjusting screws.

Carburettor float level setting (Solex)
17 It may be found that the float hinge is made of plastic, in which case adjustment by bending the hinge should not be attempted. Adjust by adding or removing washers under the needle valve.

18 For the 32-35 TACIC carburettor, the dimensions of the float level setting gauge (Chapter 3, Fig. 3.6) are 80 mm across the arms and 41 mm deep. For the Type Z the dimensions are 70 mm across and 33.5 mm deep.

Carburettor float level setting (Weber)
34 IBP and 32/34 DRTC4 100
19 The float level is checked by removing the float chamber cover and holding it vertically with the float hanging downwards. With the gasket in position and the float arm just resting against the needle valve ball, a drill shank of 7.5 ± 0.5 mm diameter should be a snug fit between the float and the gasket. (Do not measure from the seam on the float.) Adjust by carefully bending the float arm.

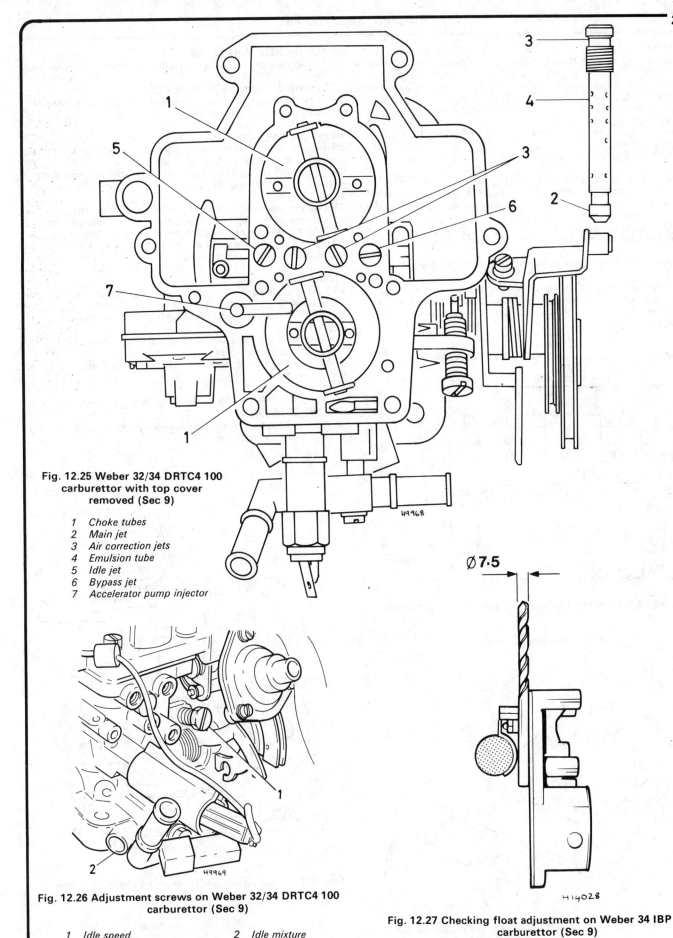

Fig. 12.25 Weber 32/34 DRTC4 100
carburettor with top cover
removed (Sec 9)

1   Choke tubes
2   Main jet
3   Air correction jets
4   Emulsion tube
5   Idle jet
6   Bypass jet
7   Accelerator pump injector

∅ 7·5

Fig. 12.26 Adjustment screws on Weber 32/34 DRTC4 100
carburettor (Sec 9)

1   Idle speed   2   Idle mixture

Fig. 12.27 Checking float adjustment on Weber 34 IBP
carburettor (Sec 9)

36 TLP

20 Make up a float level setting gauge to the dimensions shown in Fig. 12.28.

21 Remove the float chamber cover. Check that the gasket is in good condition and that it is securely fitted to the core.

22 Hold the cover vertically with the float hanging downwards. Offer the setting gauge to the floats; they should just contact the gauge. Adjust if necessary by carefully bending the float tongue and connecting bars.

23 Refit the float chamber cover.

Carburettor accelerator pump adjustment (Solex PBISA)

24 Refer to Chapter 3, Section 9, but check the Specifications at the beginning of this Supplement for the correct drill/gauge size for stroke adjustment on later models.

25 The nozzle aim for 34 PBISA 14 and 35 PBISA 14 carburettors should be to the centre of the throttle plate, **not** as shown in Fig. 3.9.

Carburettor accelerator pump adjustment (Weber)

34 IBP

26 Only the pump stroke is adjustable on this carburettor. Refer to the first two paragraphs of Section 9 in Chapter 3 for the procedures, and to the Specifications at the beginning of this Supplement for the drill/gauge size.

36 TLP and 32/34 DRTC4 100

27 The accelerator pump is set in production on these carburettors.

Choke adjustments (Weber 36 TLP)

28 These are not routine adjustments, but should be performed if difficult cold starting is experienced.

Choke opening after starting

29 Remove the air inlet from the top of the carburettor. Pull the choke control knob out fully to close the choke flap.

30 Disconnect the vacuum pipe from the choke unloader vacuum capsule. Connect a hand vacuum pump (or a modified bicycle pump) to the capsule.

31 Apply vacuum (400 mm Hg approx) to the capsule. The choke flap should open far enough to admit a drill shank or rod of 5 mm diameter.

32 Adjust if necessary by means of the screw on the vacuum capsule.

33 Disconnect the vacuum pump, remake the original vacuum connection and close the choke flap.

Mechanical opening

34 Having adjusted the vacuum capsule as just described, move the choke opening roller into the recess of the cam as shown in Fig. 12.31.

35 Check that the choke flap opening just admits a drill shank or rod of 8 mm diameter.

36 Adjustment is carried out by turning the nut shown (Fig. 12.32) after removing the carburettor.

37 When adjustment is complete, refit the carburettor (if removed) and the air inlet.

Carburettor dismantling and reassembly (Solex 32-35 TACIC)

38 Refer to Chapter 3, Section 11 for general advice on dismantling, and Fig. 12.22 for specific details.

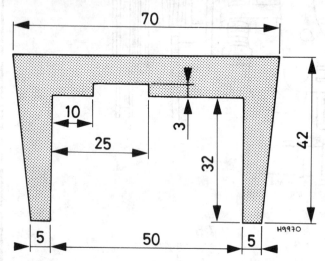

Fig. 12.28 Float setting gauge for Weber 36 TLP carburettor (Sec 9)

Dimensions in mm

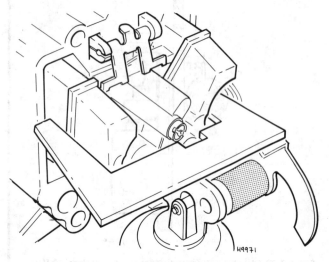

Fig. 12.29 Checking float adjustment on Weber 36 TLP carburettor (Sec 9)

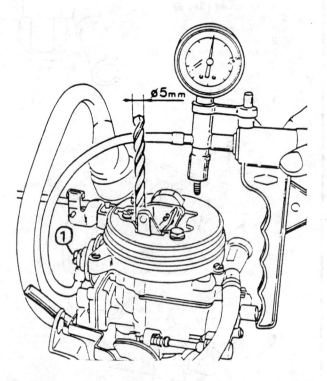

Fig. 12.30 Choke opening after starting check on Weber 36 TLP (Sec 9)

1   Adjusting screw

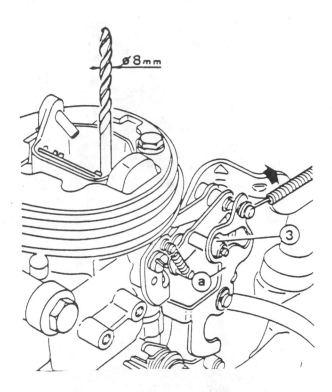

Fig. 12.31 Choke mechanical opening check on Weber 36
TLP (Sec 9)

a Cam	*3 Roller*

39 Do not dismantle the automatic choke mechanism more than
necessary. The wax expansion capsule can be renewed after removing
the end cover and gasket; renew the gasket on reassembly (photos).
40 Before reassembling, check the float level as previously described.
Use new gaskets throughout, and a new O-ring on the progression
circuit.
41 Before fitting the carburettor, checks should be made on the
normal idling position (NIP) of the throttle butterflies. Precision
measuring equipment is required for these checks, which should
therefore be done by a Peugeot dealer or carburettor specialist.

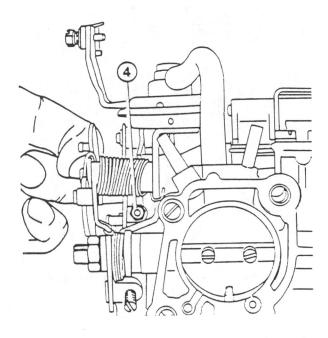

Fig. 12.32 Choke mechanical opening adjustment nut (4) on
Weber 36 TLP (Sec 9)

Carburettor automatic choke adjustment
(Solex 32-35 TACIC)
42 Peugeot tool No 8.0143 will be needed in order to carry out these
adjustments. A tachometer will also be required.

Choke opening after starting (COAS)
43 Run the engine up to operating temperature. Remove the air
cleaner adaptor from the top of the carburettor, also remove the cover
from the automatic choke mechanism.
44 With the engine idling, place the hole in tool 8.0143 over the
pivoting roller and move the gauge so that it abuts the choke housing.
In this position the choke flap should just allow the passage of a 5 mm
diamter rod or drill shank.
45 If adjustment is necessary, act on the locknut and adjusting screw
on the top of the choke housing. When the adjustment is correct,
tighten the locknut and remove the rod or drill and choke adjusting
tool.

9.39A Removing automatic choke end cover

9.39B Removing automatic choke expansion capsule

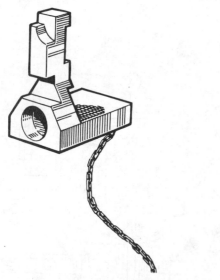

Fig. 12.33 Automatic choke setting gauge (Part no 8.0143) (Sec 9)

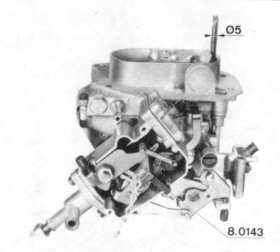

Fig. 12.34 Checking choke opening after starting on Solex 32-35 TACIC carburettor (Sec 9)

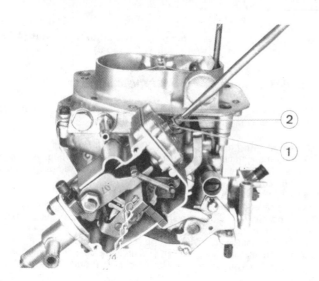

Fig. 12.35 Adjusting choke opening after starting on Solex 32-35 TACIC carburettor (Sec 9)

1   Locknut   2   Adjusting screw

Fig. 12.36 Adjusting automatic choke roller clearance on Solex 32-35 TACIC carburettor (Sec 9)

1   Screw   2   Nut   x = 2.0 mm (0.08 in)

Positive throttle opening

46 With the engine running and the idle speed and COAS adjusted, measure the clearance between the pivoting roller and the casing as shown (Fig. 12.36). If adjustment is necessary, act on the adjusting screw and nut shown in the illustration.

47 Place tool 8.0143 on the choke housing (Fig. 12.37) and tighten the adjusting screw until the pivoting roller enters the notch on the tool. From this position, remove the tool and tighten the screw a further one complete turn.

48 Remove the spring which connects the roller to the lever. Lift the lever until it makes contact, without forcing it; in this position the engine speed should be 3300 ± 50 rpm (fan disengaged).

49 If adjustment is necessary, turn the PTO screw (Fig 12.38) clockwise to increase the speed, anti-clockwise to reduce it.

50 Refit the spring, the choke cover and the air cleaner adaptor on completion.

Fig. 12.37 Automatic choke roller entering notch on setting gauge on Solex 32-35 TACIC carburettor (Sec 9)

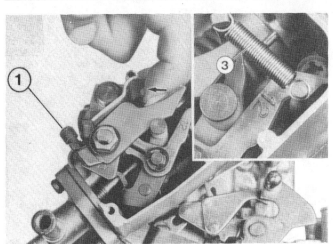

Fig. 12.38 PTO speed adjustment on Solex 32-35 TACIC carburettor. Finger lifting lever (arrowed) (Sec 9)

1   Adjustment screw   3   Spring

Carburettor dismantling and reassembly (Solex Type Z)

51 Refer to the paragraphs dealing with the 32-35 TACIC carburettor; the same remarks apply. Details of construction are given in the photos.

Carburettor automatic choke adjustment (Solex Type Z)

52 Refer to the paragraphs dealing with the 32-35 TACIC carburettor, but note the following differences:

(a) The tool required is No 8.0143 ZZ
(b) The COAS gap is different (see Specifications)
(c) The PTO speed is different (see Specifications)

Carburettor dismantling and reassembly (Weber 32/34 DRTC4 100)

53 It is not recommended that this carburettor be dismantled, except so far as to permit cleaning or renewal of jets, diaphragms, etc. Special angular measuring equipment is needed to set the throttle butterfly normal idling position (NIP) and positive throttle opening (PTO) after complete dismantling.

Carburettor automatic choke adjustments (Weber 32/34 DRTC4 100)

54 Peugeot tool 8.0145 F will be needed for these adjustments. A tachometer will also be required.

Cam position

55 With the engine running, position tool 8.0145 F as shown in Fig. 12.39. A rod or drill shank of 8.5 mm diameter should just pass between the cam and the roller. Turn the cam adjusting screw if necessary to correct the gap.

Choke opening after starting (COAS)

56 With the engine running and the special tool in the same position (Fig. 12.39) check that the choke flap will just admit a rod or drill shank of 5.5 mm diameter.
57 Adjust if necessary by means of the screw shown in Fig. 12.41.

Positive throttle opening (PTO)

58 Check the fit of the nose of the special tool between the lever and the flange (Fig. 12.42). If the tool is tight or slack, turn the lever adjusting screw until the fit is snug.
59 Reposition the tool as shown in Fig. 12.43 and use the tachometer to measure engine speed; it should be 3200 ± 50 rpm (engine warmed up, fan not engaged).
60 If adjustment is necessary, turn the PTO adjustment screw until the speed is correct. Remove the tool, accelerate the engine a couple of times, then refit the tool and check that the speed is still correct.
61 Stop the engine, remove the special tool and disconnect the tachometer.

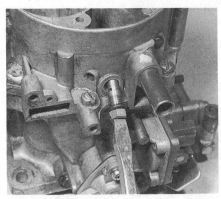

9.51A Removing the idle jet from Solex Type Z carburettor

9.51B Removing the cover securing screw and spacer on Solex Type Z carburettor

9.51C Removing enrichener cover, spring and diaphragm from Solex Type Z carburettor

9.51D Location of enrichener valves on Solex Type Z carburettor

9.51E Removing accelerator pump discharge tubes from Solex Type Z carburettor

9.51F Removing an emulsion tube from Solex Type Z carburettor. Main jets are beneath emulsion tube

Fig. 12.39 Cam position adjustment on Weber 32/34 DRTC4 100 carburettor (Sec 9)

| 1 Cam | 2 Roller | 3 Adjusting screw |

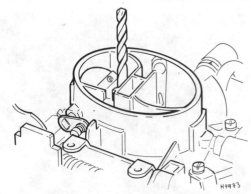

Fig. 12.40 Checking choke opening after starting on Weber 32/34 DRTC4 100 carburettor (Sec 9)

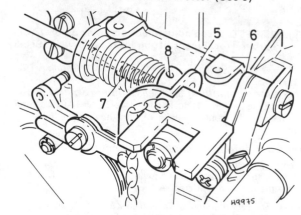

Fig. 12.42 PTO lever adjustment on Weber 32/34 DRTC4 100 carburettor (Sec 9)

| 5 Lever | 7 Adjusting screw |
| 6 Flange | 8 Access to nut |

Fig. 12.41 Choke opening adjusting screw (4) on Weber 32/34 DRTC4 100 carburettor (Sec 9)

Unleaded fuel

62 Vehicles equipped with the XU55 engine may be operated on unleaded fuel (95 RON) provided the ignition timing is retarded by 2°.
63 All other engines should be operated on leaded fuel (97 RON) otherwise valve seat damage may occur.

10 Ignition system

Electronic (breakerless) system description and precautions

1 The electronic ignition system fitted to later models relies on the distributor to produce an electrical pulse at each firing point; the pulse is produced by magnetic induction and is amplified by the ignition module which supplies LT current to the coil. HT voltage is generated and distributed in the traditional fashion.
2 Electronic ignition systems are normally very reliable because the effects of contact breaker wear have been eliminated and therefore the system does no go 'off tune'.
3 Take care not to damage the module or the distributor by applying wrong polarity or excessive voltage (eg by using a 'boost' charger with the battery connected). *Take extra care to avoid receiving personal*

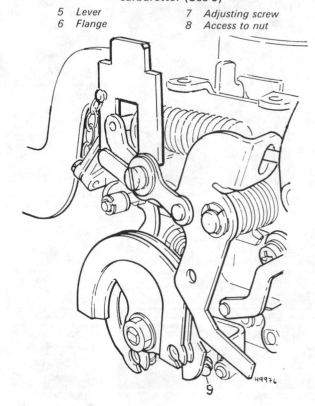

Fig. 12.43 PTO speed adjustment screw (9) on Weber 32/34 DRTC4 100 carburettor (Sec 9)

electric shocks from the system; considerably higher voltages may be present than in a conventional system.

Electronic (breakerless) system maintenance

4   Routine maintenance is limited to the periodic cleaning and renewal of the spark plugs. At the same intervals the HT leads, coil tower and distributor cap should be cleaned and inspected. Occasionally check the inside of the distributor cap and rotor arm for burning or cracks, and at the same time apply a little light oil to the centrifugal advance mechanism.

5   Check that the coil HT lead is routed away from the control module as shown (Fig. 12.44). If the HT lead is too close to the module or distributor LT leads, misfiring (and possibly erratic tachometer readings) may result.

Breakerless distributor removal and refitting

6   Unclip and remove the distributor cap, peeling back the 'rubber glove' protector. Make an alignment mark between the distributor mounting flange and the fuel pump/thermostat housing.

7   Release the securing plate and disconnect the LT lead (photos).

8   Remove the two securing nuts and withdraw the distributor (photo).

9   Refit in the reverse order of removal. The distributor drive is offset so there is no possibility of incorrect assembly. Use the alignment marks if refitting the old distributor; if fitting a new unit, set it to the middle of the travel allowed by the slotted holes.

10   Check the ignition timing and adjust if necessary.

Breakerless distributor dismantling and reassembly

11   Before commencing dismantling, check that spares are in fact available. If the mechanical components of the distributor are worn it will be necessary to renew the complete distributor.

Ducellier

12   Commence dismantling by removing the screws which hold together the upper and lower halves of the body. The lugs are offset to guarantee correct reassembly. Separate the body sections.

13   The pick-up coil and vacuum unit can now be removed from the upper body section – note into which hole the vacuum unit link engages. The rotor and centrifugal advance weights can be removed after extracting the circlip from the shaft; the drive dog is secured to the shaft by a pin.

14   Reassemble in the reverse order to dismantling.

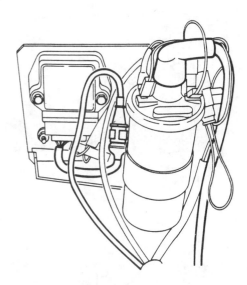

Fig. 12.44 Coil HT lead routed away from ignition module (Sec 10)

10.7A Releasing the securing plate

10.7B Unplugging the LT connector

10.8 Removing the distributor

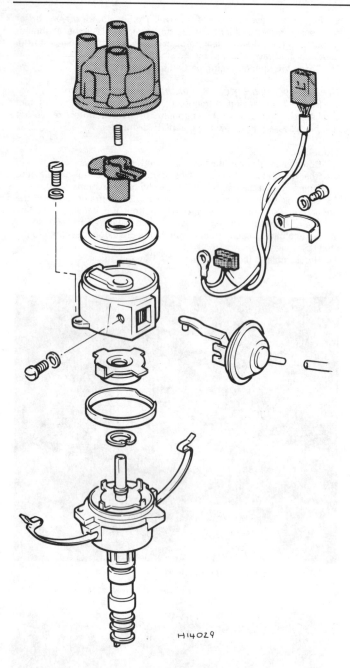

Fig. 12.45 Exploded view of Ducellier breakerless
distributor (Sec 10)

Bosch/Marelli
15 The procedure is similar to that just described, but the distributor
body is in one piece (photos). Remove the top plate and extract the
shaft circlip.

Electronic (breakerless) system ignition timing
16 Static timing as described in Chapter 4 is not possible with
electronic ignition. There is a reference mark on the rim of the
distributor body corresponding to the rotor tip position when No 1
cylinder is firing – this mark can be used for an initial setting when
timing from scratch (photo).

17 Dynamic timing is carried out using a strobe connected to No 1 HT
lead (some strobes will also require an external power source – refer to
the maker's instructions). The timing marks on XU Series engines are
on the flywheel rim and flywheel housing; once their location is known
they can be viewed without any dismantling (photo).

18 Disconnect and plug the vacuum pipe when checking the timing at
idle speed.

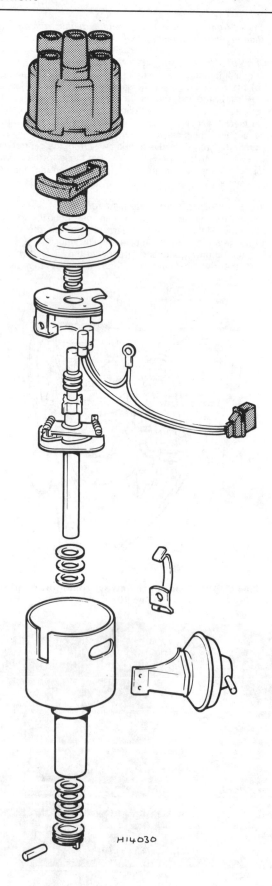

Fig. 12.46 Exploded view of Marelli breakerless distributor
(Sec 10)

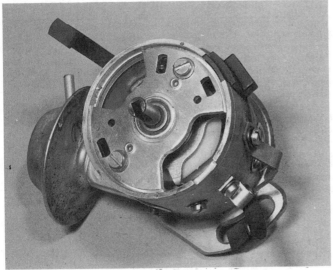

10.15A Location of top plate and fixing screws (Bosch/Marelli)

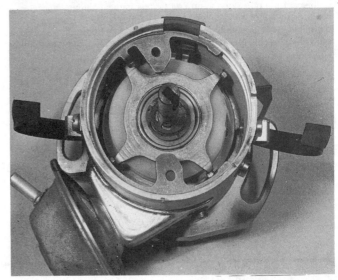

10.15B Location of distributor shaft circlip (Bosch/Marelli)

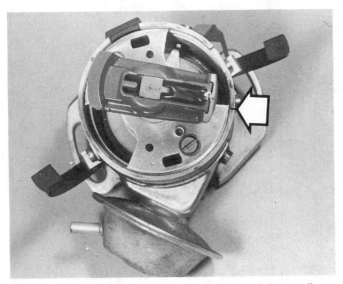

10.16 Tip of rotor arm aligned with rim reference mark (arrowed)

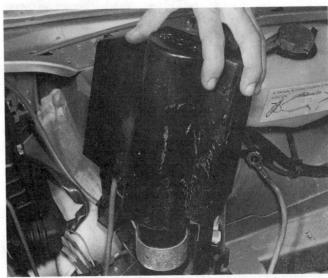

10.19 Removing the cover from the ignition coil and module

Electronic ignition module removal and refitting
19 Remove the cover from the coil and the module (photo).
20 Disconnect the wiring harness from the ignition module.
21 Undo the two securing screws and remove the module from its mounting plate.
22 Refit in the reverse order of removal.

Remotely-controlled door locks
23 On later GTX models, the door locks are controlled by a remote controller instead of the normal ignition key (see also Section 19).

Breakerless ignition system fault diagnosis
24 If an ignition system fault is suspected, check (by connecting a strobe lamp) whether HT voltage is present at the coil-to-distributor lead. If so, the fault lies in the HT distribution system – refer to Chapter 4, Section 14.
25 Check the routing of the coil HT lead – see paragraph 5 of this Section.
26 If a multi-meter is available, check the resistance of the distributor pulse generator coil and the ignition coil windings. (Switch off the ignition and disconnect the unit in question first). The desired resistance values are given in the Specifications.

10.17 Timing marks on XU Series engine

27 Inspect the pulse generator coil for mechanical damage and check the rotor-to-stator gap, which should be equal at all four lobes. Mechanical damage calls for renewal of the distributor. (On distributors with a top bearing plate, the rotor gap may vary when the plate is removed.)

28 With a multi-meter or low wattage 12 volt bulb, check the voltage at the points shown in Fig. 12.47 with the ignition on. The desired results are as follows:

U (across the battery) = 11 volts minimum.
U1 (coil '+' terminal) = battery voltage. If not, the coil feed wire is broken.
U2 (across coil LT terminals) = O volts. If a voltage is present, either the module is defective or the lead from the coil to the module is earthed.
U3 (module terminal 15) = battery voltage. A zero reading indicates a break in the wire from connector to the module.
U4 (module terminal 16) = battery voltage. A zero reading means that the wire from the coil to the module is broken.

29 Any further fault finding must be done by substitution of known good units.

11 Clutch (XU engine)

Clutch removal, inspection and refitting
1 Remove the gearbox as described in Section 12.
2 Make alignment marks on the clutch pressure plate and the flywheel, then progressively slacken the six bolts which secure the pressure plate. Remove the bolts, the pressure plate and the clutch disc (driven plate).
3 Examine the components as described in Chapter 5, Section 5, but disregard paragraphs 5 and 9. The pressure plate cannot be overhauled at home, but it can be renewed independently of the flywheel. The flywheel can be refaced within specifed limits but again this is specialist work.
4 Commence refitting by offering the clutch disc to the flywheel, making sure it is the right way round. It will only fit one way. Retain the disc in position by inserting a centring mandrel. Various proprietary centring tools are available, or alternatively, one can be made from a piece of dowel or bar built up with tape (photo).

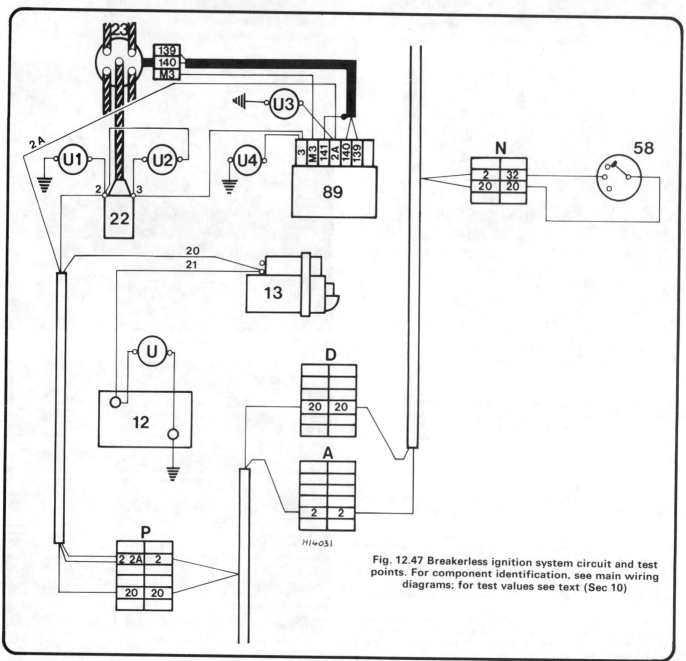

Fig. 12.47 Breakerless ignition system circuit and test points. For component identification, see main wiring diagrams; for test values see text (Sec 10)

11.4 Centring clutch driven plate using an alignment tool

11.7 Tightening clutch pressure plate bolts. Note tool jamming starter ring gear teeth

5 Fit the pressure plate, observing the alignment marks made when dismantling if the old plate is being refitted. Insert the six bolts and just nip them up so that the clutch disc is lightly gripped.
6 Make sure that the clutch disc is accurately centred, either by visual inspection or by inserting an old gearbox input shaft. If the disc is not centred it will not be possible to refit the gearbox.
7 With the centring mandrel in position, tighten the pressure plate securing bolts progressively to the specified torque. Remove the centring mandrel (photo).
8 Refit the gearbox on completion.

Clutch release mechanism removal and refitting
9 Remove the gearbox as described in Section 12.
10 The clutch release bearing may be removed by freeing its spring clips from the release fork (photo).
11 The clutch release fork can be pulled or levered off its balljoint. Renew the pivot bush as follows.
12 Drill out the rivets which secure the old bush. Remove the bush and discard it.
13 Position the new bush on the fork and pass its rivets through the holes. Heat the rivets with a cigarette lighter or a low powered blowlamp, then peen over their heads while they are still hot.
14 Lightly coat the bush with grease, then refit the release fork. Press it onto the balljoint unitil it snaps home.
15 Renewal of the release fork balljoint is covered in Section 13, paragraphs 36 and 126.

12 Manual transmission (Type BE1)

General description
1 The BE1/5 gearbox fitted to models with XU Series engines is quite different from the BB8 gearbox fitted to earlier models. One significant difference is the separation of engine and gearbox lubricants.
2 The gearbox has five forward gears, all with synchromesh, and one reverse. As is common practice in five-speed units, the 5th gear components are on the far side of an intermediate plate which carries one pair of shaft bearings.
3 The differential (final drive) unit is contained in its own housing which is bolted to the gearbox casing. The gearbox and differential share the same lubricant.
4 A four-speed version of the BE1 gearbox is fitted in some territories. It is very similar to the five-speed version apart from the absence of the 5th gear components

Routine maintenance (up to October 1986)
5 The only regular maintenance required is to change the lubricant.

11.10 Removing the clutch release bearing

There is no provision for checking the oil level in the gearbox or in the final drive unit. The oil must therefore be drained completely and the transmission be refilled with a known quantity of oil.
6 Apart from the regular oil change at the specified intervals (Section 3), the oil should be changed in a new or reconditioned unit after the first 1000 to 1500 miles, and in any unit after detection and rectification of an oil leak.
7 When draining the transmission oil, note that there are two drain plugs, one for the gearbox and one for the final drive. Both plugs must be removed.
8 When refitting the transmission with oil, do so through the filler plug orifice (photo). Remember to measure out the quantity of oil required beforehand.

Routine maintenance (November 1986 on)
9 As from October 1986, a combined final drive/gearbox level/filler plug is fitted to enable the transmission oil level to be checked and any topping up carried out. Only one drain plug is provided and this is located in the final drive casing through which the common gearbox/final drive oil is drained.

Removal and refitting
The BE1 transmission can be removed independently of the engine. Read through the procedure first to see what is involved.

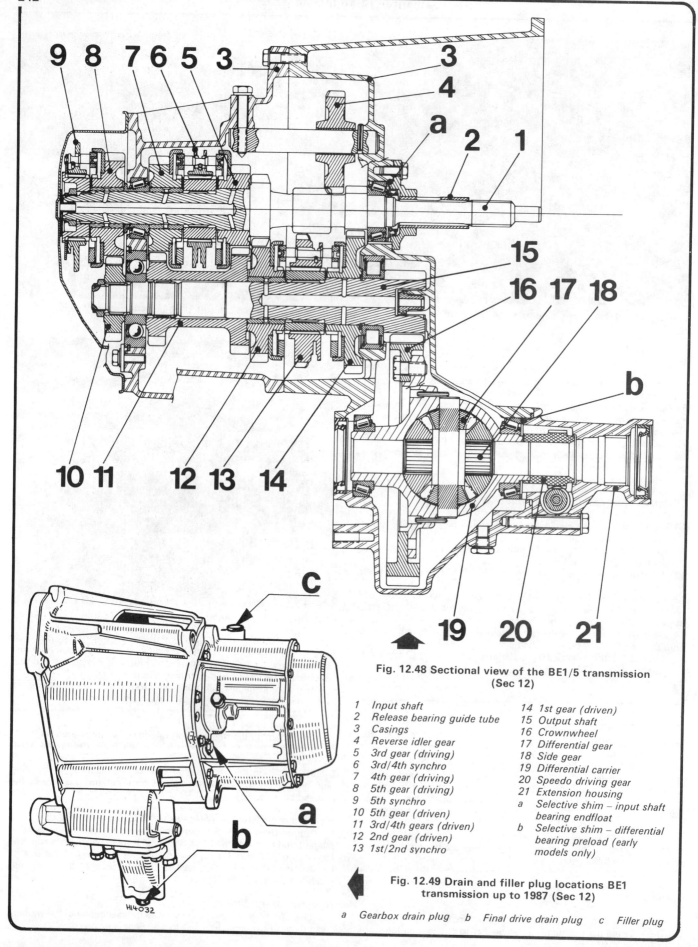

Fig. 12.48 Sectional view of the BE1/5 transmission
(Sec 12)

1	Input shaft	14	1st gear (driven)
2	Release bearing guide tube	15	Output shaft
3	Casings	16	Crownwheel
4	Reverse idler gear	17	Differential gear
5	3rd gear (driving)	18	Side gear
6	3rd/4th synchro	19	Differential carrier
7	4th gear (driving)	20	Speedo driving gear
8	5th gear (driving)	21	Extension housing
9	5th synchro	a	Selective shim – input shaft
10	5th gear (driven)		bearing endfloat
11	3rd/4th gears (driven)	b	Selective shim – differential
12	2nd gear (driven)		bearing preload (early
13	1st/2nd synchro		models only)

Fig. 12.49 Drain and filler plug locations BE1
transmission up to 1987 (Sec 12)

a   Gearbox drain plug   b   Final drive drain plug   c   Filler plug

H14032

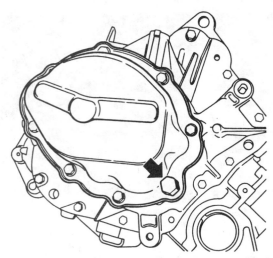

Fig. 12.50 Filler/level plug on later type transmission (Sec 12)

10 Remove the battery and its tray.

11 Remove the bonnet (Chapter 11, Section 7).

12 Slacken the front wheel bolts, then remove one bolt and (if fitted) the centre trim and hub cap. Remove the locking components and slacken the driveshaft retaining nut (photo). This nut is very tight. Remove the nut and the washer. Repeat the operations on the opposite wheel, and securely support the front of the car. Remove the front wheels.

13 If wheels without a centre hole are fitted, they will have to be removed to get at the driveshaft nuts. In this case a metal bar, suitably drilled, should be bolted to the hub and used to prevent the hub rotating when the driveshaft nut is being undone. Take care not to pull the car off its supports.

14 Drain the transmission oil by removing the gearbox and the final drive drain plugs. Refit the plugs when draining is complete. On later

models only one drain plug is fitted and this is located in the final drive casing.

15 Release the right-hand driveshaft bearing by slackening the two retaining nuts and turning each retaining bolt through half a turn (180°) (photo).

16 Undo the stub axle balljoint nuts and separate the balljoint (one on each side) using a proprietary balljoint splitter. Remove the balljoint nuts. Also release the steering balljoints and the anti-roll bar lower links (photos).

17 Separate the left-hand suspension arm from the balljoint shank by levering the arm downwards. Be careful not to damage the balljoint rubber boot (photo).

18 Free the left-hand driveshaft from the hub by pivoting the hub outwards. If the driveshaft is a very tight fit in the hub, it may be necessary to remove the brake disc and caliper in order to fit an extractor and push the shaft from the hub. **Do not** attempt to drive the shaft through by striking it. **Note: Never** move the car on its wheels without the driveshafts fitted.

19 Withdraw the left-hand driveshaft from the final drive housing.

20 Retain the differential side gears in position by fitting Peugeot tools 8.0317 M and 8.0317 N. *If this is not done, the side gears may fall into the differential housing.* In the absence of the special tools, it is possible to improvise using a length of wooden dowel, of 1 inch diameter, ground down slightly at one end to enter the splines in the side gear (photo).

21 Free the right-hand driveshaft by repeating paragraphs 17 to 19 on the right-hand side.

22 Remove the air cleaner and its trunking.

23 Remove the starter motor.

24 Disconnect the clutch cable at the transmission end. Recover the pushrod from the bellcrank (photo).

25 On models with power steering, unbolt the steering pump with its mounting and place them on the engine. There is no need to disconnect the pipes from the pump.

26 Separate the gearchange linkage at the gearbox end (photo).

27 Remove the cover plate from the bottom of the clutch housing.

28 Disconnect the reversing lamp switch and the speedometer cable.

29 Fit lifting tackle to the eye on top of the transmission and take its weight.

12.8 Filling the transmission with oil (up to Oct 1986)

12.12 Location of driveshaft nut lock and clip

12.15 Unscrewing one of the driveshaft bearing retaining nuts

12.16A Unscrewing a stub axle balljoint nut

12.16B Anti-roll bar lower link

12.17 Separating the suspension arm from the balljoint

12.20 Using a wooden dowel (arrowed) to retain the differential side gears

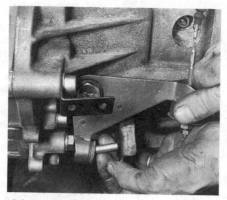

12.24 Location of clutch bellcrank and push-rod

12.26 Separating a gearchange linkage balljoint

30 Remove the nut from the transmission mounting stud.
31 Lower the hoist until the engine and transmission take up a stable position (hoist rope neither taut nor slack).
32 Remove the four transmission-to-engine bolts.
33 Pull the gearbox away from the engine until the input shaft is clear of the clutch, then lower the gearbox through the engine compartment and withdraw it from below.

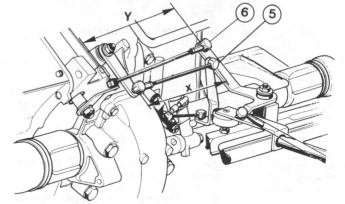

Fig. 12.52 Gearchange linkage adjustment – selector and engagement rods (Sec 12)

| 5 | Selector rod | X = 122 mm |
| 6 | Engagement rod | Y = 250 mm |

and compare them with the values given in Fig. 12.52. Adjust if necessary by slackening the locknut and screwing the rod in or out of the threaded portion of the end fitting. (The balljoints must be disconnected to do this.)
37 Inside the car, release the gear lever gaiter and slide it up the gear lever. Engage 2nd gear and let go of the lever.
38 Measure the gap between the plastic cam and the stop in the gear lever housing. If the gap is not as given in Fig. 12.53 remove the spring

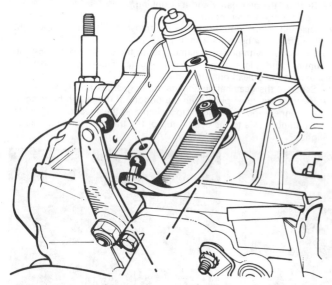

Fig. 12.51 Gearchange levers in neutral mode on BE1 transmission (Sec 12)

34 Refit in the reverse order to removal, noting the following points:

(a) Apply a smear of molybdenum grease to the gearbox input shaft
(b) Make sure that the gearchange levers are in the neutral position (Fig. 12.51)
(c) Use the oil seal protector (supplied with new oil seals) when fitting the right-hand driveshaft
(d) Tighten all fastenings to the specified torque; use new nuts on the stub axle balljoints. Make sure the drain plugs are tight
(e) Refill the transmission with the specified grade and quantity of oil
(f) Check the operation of the gearchange linkage and adjust if necessary, as follows

Gearchange linkage adjustment
Early models (without reverse stop cable)
35 With the gearbox in neutral, check that the gearchange levers on the gearbox are in the correct position (Fig. 12.51). There are no master splines so it is easy to put the levers in the wrong position after dismantling.
36 Measure the lengths of the engagement rod and the selection rod

12.38 Location of gearlever stop and cam

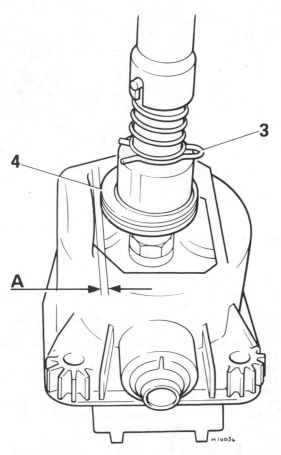

Fig. 12.53 Gear lever adjustment on models without reverse stop cable (Sec 12)

A = 4.5 mm   3   Spring clip   4   Cam

clip and lift the cam off its splines. Reposition the cam to obtain the correct clearance and secure with the spring clip. Apply a smear of grease to the side of the cam where it rubs against the stop (photo).

39 If, after this adjustment, it is still difficult to engage 1st and 2nd gears, measure the travel of the gear lever towards the 1st/2nd plane as follows.

40 Place the gear lever in neutral, then move it gently to the left until the commencement of resistance is felt.

41 Position a ruler against the gear knob with the zero marking aligned with the $1/2$ mark on the knob.

42 Push the gear lever as far as possible to the left without moving the ruler and note the distance travelled by the knob. Repeat the operation two or three times. The desired travel is 38 ± 2 mm.

43 If necessary, reposition the plastic cam as previously described to achieve the desired travel.

44 If the cam is positioned to give maximum lever travel, but the specified value has not been reached, lengthen the selection rod by 6 mm, then repeat the adjustment.

45 If the cam is positioned to give minimum lever travel, but the specified value is exceeded, shorten the selection rod by 6 mm, then repeat the adjustment.

46 Whatever adjustments have been carried out, check the engagement of all gears. Make sure that reverse gear cannot be engaged without lifting the collar on the gear lever.

47 Refit and secure the gear lever when adjustment is complete.

Later models (with reverse stop cable)
48 During 1985 the old gearchange linkage was dropped in favour of a new type. The new linkage can be identified by the use of a cable for releasing the reverse stop.

49 No adjustments are required to the reverse stop cable. Adjustment of the engagement and selection rods is as described in paragraph 36.

Selector and engagement levers (Feb 1987 on)
50 As from February 1987, the selector and engagement levers are secured to their shafts by roll pins instead of locating splines and a nut.

Fig. 12.54 Gearchange linkage for later models with reverse stop cable (Sec 12)

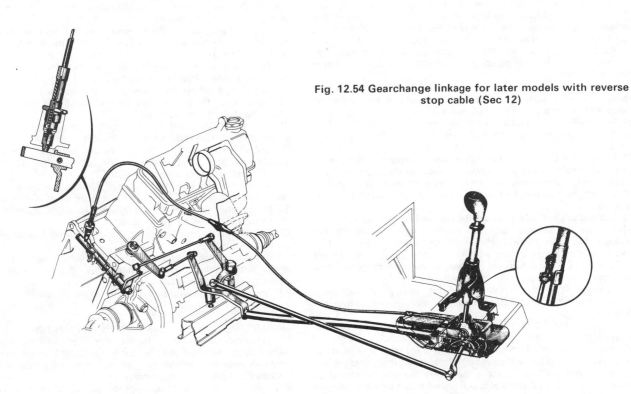

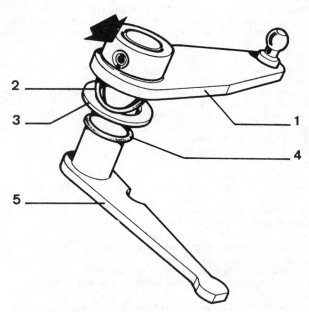

Fig. 12.55 Later type selector lever with roll pin (Sec 12)

1 *Lever*	3 *Washer*	5 *Finger*
2 *Spring*	4 *O-ring*	

Dismantling into major assemblies (five-speed)

51 Refer to Chapter 6, Section 3, paragraph 1. The same remarks apply here.

52 Remove the eight bolts and washers which secure the end cover. Remove the cover (photo).

53 Make alignment marks between the 5th gear synchro hub and its sliding sleeve.

54 Engage 5th gear, then drive out the 5 mm roll pin which secures 5th gear selector fork to the selector rod (photo).

55 Hold 5th gear selector fork in the engaged position and return the gear selector to neutral so that the selector rod moves through the fork.

56 Engage any other gear to lock up the shafts, then unscrew and remove the 28 mm nut from the end of the input shaft. If the nut is staked in position it may be necessary to relieve the staking (photo).

57 Remove the 5th gear synchro hub, sliding sleeve and selector fork from the input shaft. Be prepared for the ejection of the detent ball from the selector fork.

58 Refit the 5th gear sliding sleeve and hub and engage 5th gear again. Relieve the staking from the input shaft nut and remove the nut. Remove the sliding sleeve and hub again (photo).

59 Remove from the input shaft, the 5th gear, its bush and the spacer.

60 Remove the two bolts and washers which secure the output shaft rear bearing.

61 Remove the circlip from the output shaft bearing by prising up its ends. The circlip should be renewed anyway, so do not be afraid of breaking it. Raise the output shaft if the circlip is jammed in its groove.

62 Extract the securing bolt and remove the selector rod lockplate (photo).

63 Remove the bolt which retains the reverse idler gear spindle.

64 Remove the thirteen bolts and washers which secure the end casing to the main casing. Withdraw the end casing: it is located by dowels, and may need striking with a wooden or plastic mallet to free it. Do not use a metal hammer, nor lever in between the joint faces. Note the location of the clutch cable bracket.

65 Remove the selector arm and spring from the gear selector shaft. Remove the circlip and washer, push the shaft in and recover the O-ring (photo).

66 Drive out the roll pins which secure the selector finger and the interlock bracket to the selector shaft.

67 Inspect the cover which protects the end of the selector shaft. If it is tapered, proceed to the next paragraph. If it is cylindrical, use pliers or a self-gripping wrench to extract it, then press the gear selector shaft towards the cover so that the circlip and washer can be extracted from the end of the shaft. These components are not fitted to earlier models;

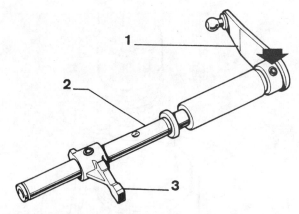

Fig. 12.56 Later type engagement lever with roll pin (Sec 12)

1 *Lever*	2 *Shaft*	3 *Finger*

there are associated changes in the shaft itself, the main casing and 5th gear selector fork (photos).

68 Pull the selector shaft out of the gearbox. From inside the gearbox recover, as they are freed from the shaft, the selector finger, the interlock bracket, the spring and its cup washers. Notice which way round the washers are fitted.

69 Screw the reverse idler spindle retaining bolt back into the spindle and use it as a lever to extract the spindle. Remove the reverse idler gear itself (photo).

70 Remove the swarf-collecting magnet from the casing (photo).

71 Carefully lift out the two geartrains with their shafts, the selector forks and the selector rods.

72 Remove the spring support bracket from inside the main casing.

73 If not already removed, drive out the selector shaft end cover, using a drift with a diameter no greater than 14 mm.

74 Extract the lubrication jet, using a wire hook.

75 Unscrew and remove the reversing lamp switch.

76 Remove the nut and washer which secure the reverse selector fork spindle. Remove the spindle and the selector fork. Recover the detent plunger and springs (photos).

77 Unscrew and remove the breather from the main casing (photo). (On models with a reverse stop cable, the cable bracket takes the place of the breather.)

78 Turning to the clutch housing, remove the clutch release bearing (if not already done). Pull off the release fork.

79 Unbolt and remove the release bearing guide tube.

80 From behind the tube remove the endfloat shim and the outer track of the input shaft front bearing.

81 To remove the final drive unit, first unbolt and remove the speedometer pinion and its adaptor (photo).

82 Unbolt and remove the extension housing. Recover the speedometer driving gear and the bearing preload shim (photos). (On later models the preload shim is deleted.)

83 Unbolt the final drive half housing. Remove the half housing and final drive unit. Note the location of the gearchange pivot bracket.

84 Identify the final drive bearing outer tracks; if they are to be re-used they must be refitted on the same sides.

85 Remove the selector lever from the main casing. It is retained by a circlip and a washer.

86 If it is a wished to remove the clutch release lever balljoint, do so with a slide hammer having a suitable claw. (A new gearbox will not necessarily be fitted with a balljoint.)

87 The gearbox is now dismantled into its major assemblies.

Dismantling into major assemblies (four-speed)

88 As mentioned previously, the four-speed and five-speed gearboxes differ only in respect of the 5th gear and associated components. The only difference in the dismantling procedure is in the method used to slacken the input and output shaft nuts.

89 The nuts can be slackened with the gearbox in the vehicle. To do so, engage a gear and apply the handbrake. Remove the end cover and

12.52 Removing gearbox end cover

12.54 Fifth gear selector fork roll pin (arrowed)

12.56 Unscrewing input shaft nut

12.58 Unscrewing output shaft nut

12.62 Unscrewing selector rod lockplate bolt

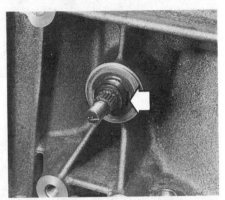

12.65 Location of circlip (arrowed) securing gear selector shaft

12.67A Location of gear selector shaft cover

12.67B Selector shaft circlip and washer (arrowed) exposed for removal

12.69 Removing reverse idler spindle

12.70 Removing swarf collecting magnet

12.76A Location of reverse selector fork

12.76B Removing detent plunger and spring

12.77 Removing the breather

12.81 Removing the speedometer pinion

12.82A Removing the final drive extension housing

12.82B Removing the speedometer drive gear

slacken the nuts on the input and output shafts. (The input shaft nut is combined with an oil thrower.) Refit the cover and proceed to remove the gearbox.

90 With the gearbox out of the vehicle, the best way to lock the shafts is to engage a gear and immobilise the input shaft with a clutch disc to which a metal bar has been welded (Fig. 12.58). It is unwise to attempt to grip the input shaft splines with any other tool, as damage may be caused.

91 With the input and output shaft nuts slackened, proceed as described for the five-speed box, making appropriate allowances.

Examination and renovation

92 Refer to Chapter 6, Section 4 for a general guide to examination of gearbox components.

93 Circlips, roll pins, gaskets, oil seals and locking devices should all be renewed as a matter of course. Prise out the old oil seal from the clutch release bearing guide tube, but do not fit the new seal until so instructed during reassembly. Renew the input and output shaft nuts.

94 If a new input shaft or differential bearings are to be fitted, a selection of preload shims may be required. Read through the relevant procedures before starting work.

Input shaft dismantling and reassembly

95 Remove the 3rd and 4th gear components from the input shaft by

supporting the assembly under the 3rd gear and pressing or driving the shaft through. Protect the end of the shaft. Once the rear bearing is free, the other components can be removed from the shaft in order: 4th gear and its bush, 3rd/4th synchro sleeve and hub and 3rd gear (photos).

96 Mark the synchro sleeve and hub relative to each other and to show which side faces 4th gear.

97 Remove the front bearing from the shaft, preferably using a press or a bearing puller. As a last resort it may be possible to support the bearing and drive the shaft through it: be sure to protect the end of the shaft if this is done.

98 Once the input shaft bearings have been removed, they must be renewed. Press the rear bearing outer track from the end casing and press in the new track, making sure it enters squarely.

99 Before commencing reassembly, make sure that the input shaft is free from burrs and wear marks. Lubricate all parts as they are fitted.

100 Fit a new front bearing to the shaft, using a suitable tube to press or drive it home.

101 Fit 3rd gear, 3rd/4th synchro hub and sleeve, 4th gear and its bush. Take care not to get 3rd and 4th gears mixed up as they are very similar in appearance (4th gear has more teeth). If the original synchro components are being refitted, observe the mating marks made during dismantling.

102 Fit a new rear bearing to the shaft, again using a piece of tube.

103 The input shaft is now reassembled.

249

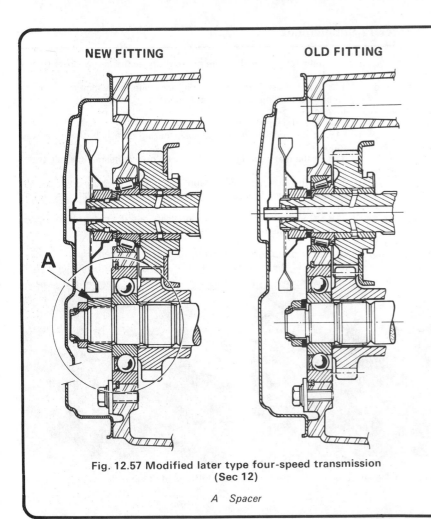

NEW FITTING   OLD FITTING

Fig. 12.57 Modified later type four-speed transmission
(Sec 12)

A Spacer

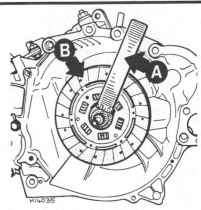

Fig. 12.58 Home-made tool used to
lock input shaft (Sec 12)

A Metal bar   B Old clutch driven plate

12.95A Removing from the input shaft; the
rear bearing ...

12.95B ... 4th speed gear ...

12.95C ... 4th speed gear bush ...

12.95D ... 3rd/4th synchro sleeve ...

12.95E ... synchro hub ...

12.95F ... and 3rd speed gear

12.95G Input shaft stripped except for front
bearing

Output shaft dismantling and reassembly

104 Remove 5th gear (when applicable) and the rear bearing from the output shaft. Use a puller or bearing extractor if they are a tight fit on the shaft (photo).

105 Remove 3rd/4th gear assembly, 2nd gear and its bush (photos).

106 Make alignment marks between the 1st/2nd syncrho hub and sleeve, then remove them from the shaft (photos).

107 Remove 1st gear and the half washers (early models) or needle thrust bearing and circlip (later models) (photos).

108 Press or drive the shaft out of the pinion end bearing, protecting the end of the shaft.

109 Before commencing reassembly, make sure that the shaft is free from burrs or wear marks. Lubricate all parts as they are fitted.

110 Fit the pinion end bearing to the shaft, using a piece of tube to drive or press it home. On later models, fit a new circlip.

111 Fit the half washers above the bearing, using a smear of grease to hold them in position. On later models, fit the needle thrust bearing instead.

112 Refit 1st gear, taking care not to dislodge the half washers (when fitted).

113 Refit the 1st/2nd synchro unit, observing the mating marks made when dismantling. The chamfer on the external teeth must face towards 1st gear.

114 Fit 2nd gear and its bush.

115 Fit the 3rd/4th gear assembly, making sure it is the right way round.

116 Fit the rear bearing, with the circlip groove nearest the tail of the shaft.

117 Fit the 5th gear, when applicable, with its boss towards the bearing. On early four-speed models fit the washer; on later models fit the spacer.

118 Fit a new nut to the output shaft but do not tighten it yet. Assembly of the output shaft is now complete.

Selector mechanism dismantling and reassembly

119 One of the unusual features of this gearbox is that the detent

12.104 Removing from the output shaft; the rear bearing ...

12.105A ... 3rd/4th speed gears ...

12.105B ... 2nd speed gear ...

12.105C ... and 2nd speed gear bush

12.106A Removing 1st/2nd synchro sleeve ...

12.106B ... and 1st/2nd synchro hub

12.107A Removing 1st speed gear ...

12.107B ... 1st speed gear needle thrust bearing ...

12.107C ... and bearing circlip (arrowed)

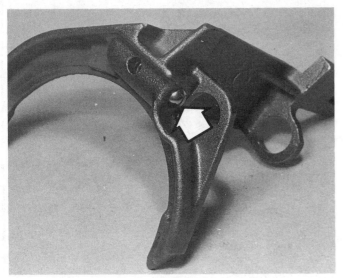

12.119 Gear selector fork showing captive detent ball and spring (arrowed)

springs and balls are located in the forks (photo). If a spring is weak, the whole fork must be renewed. (This does not apply to the 5th gear fork.)

120 Rotate the 1st/2nd and 3rd/4th selector rod to disengage the detent slots from the balls, then remove the rod from the forks.

121 Where applicable, remove 5th gear selector rod from the 1st/2nd fork.

122 Examine the forks and rods for wear or damage and renew as necessary.

123 Commence reassembly by inserting 5th gear selector rod into the 1st/2nd fork.

124 Offer the 3rd/4th fork to the 1st/2nd fork so that their holes and selector fingers align.

125 Insert the 1st/2nd and 3rd/4th selector rod, positioning the locking slot as shown (Fig. 12.61). Bring all the selector finger slots into line to position the selectors in neutral (photo).

126 Note that the selector mechanism has been modified on later models. Early and late components are not interchangeable.

Differential dismantling and reassembly

127 Unbolt the crownwheel from the differential housing.

128 Remove the side gears by pushing them round inside the housing until they can be removed (photo). (On later models with a side gear centralising ring, this may not be possible until after the differential gears have been removed.)

129 Drive out the roll pins which secure the differential gear spindle. Remove the spindle, the differential gears and their washers (photo). Note the different types of gear and washer (Fig. 12.65).

130 Use a press or bearing extractor to remove the bearings.

131 Examine all parts for wear or damage, and renew as necessary. Lubricate all parts as they are assembled.

132 Fit the bearings using a piece of tube to press or drive them home.

133 Fit the spindle with the differential gears and washers. Secure the spindle with new roll pins, which should be driven in until they are centrally located in their holes (photo).

134 Fit the side gears, one at a time, and work them into their proper positions. Retain them in this position using tool 8.0317 M or equivalent (see Section 12, paragraph 20 of this Supplement), inserted from the crownwheel side (photo). (This will not be necessary when a centralising ring is fitted.)

135 Fit the crownwheel with its chamfer towards the differential housing. Secure with the bolts, tightening them in diagonal sequence to the specified torque.

Reassembly of major units (five-speed)

136 Commence reassembly by fitting the selector lever into the main casing. Make sure that the locating dowel is in position on the final drive housing mating face.

137 Apply jointing compound to the mating face, then fit the

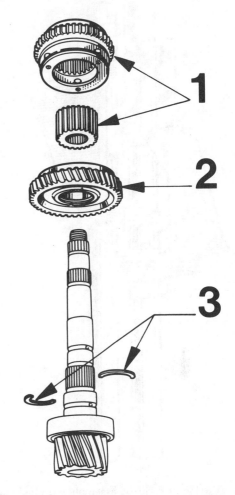

Fig. 12.59 Details of early type output shaft (Sec 12)

1 1st/2nd synchro   2 1st speed gear   3 Half washers

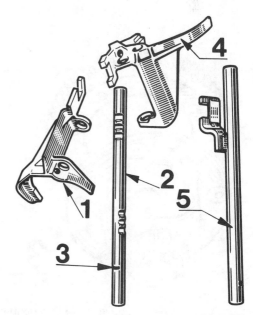

Fig. 12.60 Selector forks and rods (Sec 12)

1 3rd/4th fork   4 1st/2nd fork
2 1st/2nd and 3rd/4th rod   5 5th selector rod
3 Locking slot

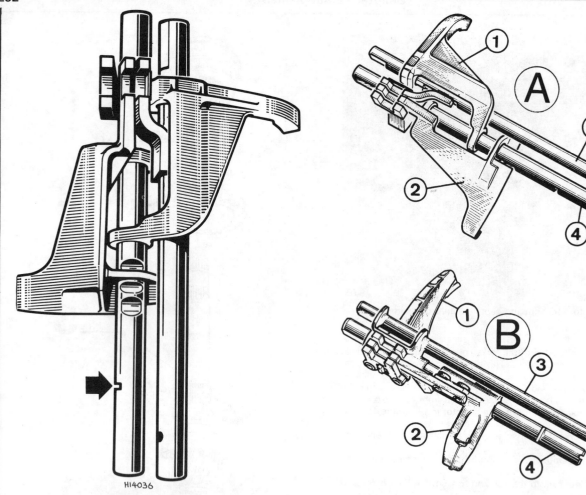

Fig. 12.61 Selector fork/rod assembly with locking slot (arrowed) correctly positioned (Sec 12)

Fig. 12.62 Early and later types of selector fork/rod assemblies (Sec 12)

A   Early
B   Later
1   1st/2nd fork
2   3rd/4th fork
3   5th selector rod
4   1st/2nd and 3rd/4th rod

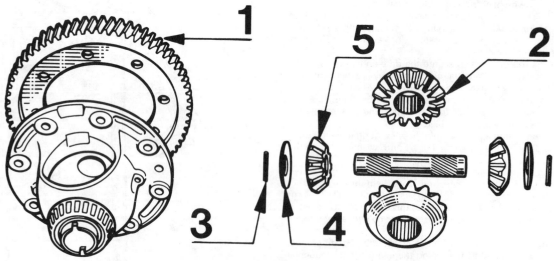

Fig. 12.63 Differential and final drive components (Sec 12)

1   Crownwheel
2   Side gear
3   Roll pin
4   Washer
5   Planet gear

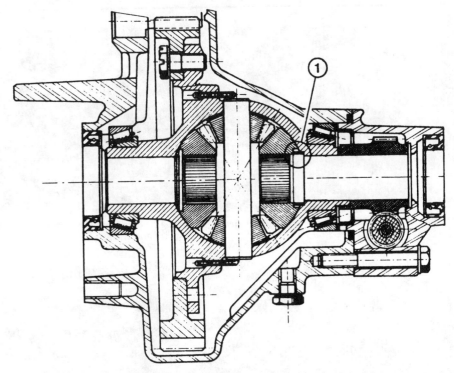

EARLY ASSEMBLY	LATER ASSEMBLY

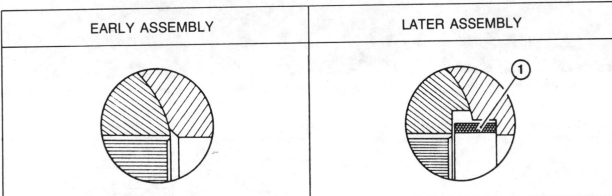

Fig. 12.64 Sectional view of final drive showing later modification (Sec 12)

1   Centralising ring

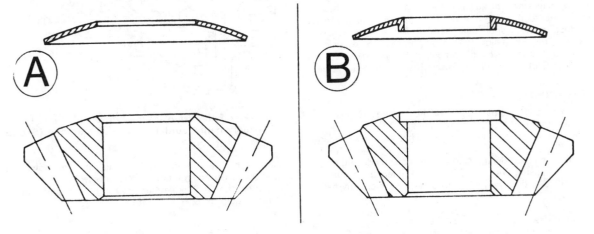

Fig. 12.65 Early and later types of differential gears and washers (Sec 12)

A   Early   B   Later

12.125 Selector rods and forks positioned in neutral mode

12.128 Removing a differential side gear

12.129 Removing the differential spindle, gears and washers

12.133 Spindle roll pin correctly located

12.134 Side gear retaining tool in position (arrowed)

12.137 Differential unit in position. Note locating dowel (arrowed)

differential assembly with its bearing tracks (photo).
138 Fit the final drive half housing and the extension housing, but only tighten their securing bolts finger tight at this stage.
139 Fit a new oil seal, lips well greased, to the other side of the final drive housing from the extension.

Early models (with preload adjustment shim)
140 Remove the extension housing. Fit a preload shim 2.2 mm thick to the bearing outer track and refit the extension housing (without its O-ring). Rotate the crownwheel while tightening the extension housing bolts until the crownwheel *just* starts to drag. This operation seats the bearings.
141 Remove the extension housing and the preload shim. With an accurate depth gauge, measure the distance from the final drive housing joint face to the bearing outer track. Call this dimension A. Similarly measure the protrusion of the spigot on the extension housing above the joint face. Call this dimension B (photos).
142 The thickness S of preload shim required is determined by the formula:

$$S = (A - B) + .010 \text{ mm}$$

The extra 0.10 mm is the preload factor for the bearings. Shims are available in thicknesses of 1.1 to 2.2 mm in steps of 0.1 mm.
143 Tighten the final drive half housing securing bolts to the specified torque.
144 Fit the preload shim just determined, the speedometer driving gear and the extension housing with a new O-ring. Tighten the securing bolts to the specified torque (photo). Make sure that the crownwheel is still free to rotate.

Later models (without preload adjustment shim)
145 Models which do not require a preload shim can be identified by the length of the extension housing shoulder (Fig. 12.66). If the shoulder is 10 mm long, no shim is required. When a shim is fitted the shoulder is 8.65 mm long.
146 Fit the speedometer driving gear (if removed). Fit the extension

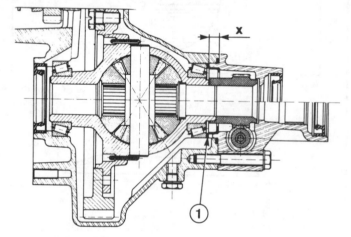
Fig. 12.66 Final drive assembly preload shim (1) is only fitted when shoulder (X) is 8.65 mm long (Sec 12)

housing with a new O-ring. Tighten the extension bolts a little at a time, at the same time rotating the crownwheel to seat the bearings.
147 Tighten the final drive half housing bolts and the extension housing bolts to the specified torque.

All models
148 Refit and secure the speedometer pinion and adaptor. Fit a new oil seal, lips well greased, into the extension housing. Also fit a new selector shaft oil seal in the main casing.
149 From the clutch housing side, fit the clutch release bearing guide

tube. Do not use a gasket under the guide tube flange, and only tighten the bolts finger tight. Invert the casing and fit an endfloat shim (any size) and the input bearing outer track (photos).

150 Fit the gear selector shaft spring bracket and tighten its securing bolts to the specified torque.

151 If removed, fit the two locating dowels in the main casing mating face.

152 Fit and tighten the breather (when applicable). Refit the lubrication jet (photo).

153 Fit the reverse detent spring and plunger. Depress the plunger and fit the reverse selector fork and its spindle. Tighten the spindle securing nut to the specified torque.

154 Fit the reversing lamp switch using a new copper washer. Tighten it to the specified torque (photo).

155 Assemble the geartrains and the selector forks and rods. Offer the whole assembly to the gearcase (photo).

156 Fit the reverse idler spindle and gear, with the chamfer towards the rear of the gearbox. Make sure the pin in the shaft is correctly located.

157 Refit the swarf-collecting magnet.

158 Insert the spring and washers into the bracket (photo).

159 Enter the selector shaft into the casing, passing it through the compressed spring and washers inside the casing. Also engage the shaft with the selector finger and the interlock bracket. It may be helpful to keep the finger and the bracket together with a short length of rod (maximum diameter 14 mm) which can be withdrawn as the selector shaft enters (photo).

160 Make sure that the flat on the shaft and the roll pin hole are correctly orientated (Fig. 12.67). Secure the selector finger and the interlock bracket with two new roll pins. The slots in the roll pins should be 180° away from each other and in line with the longitudinal axis of the shaft (photo).

161 On later models, fit the washer and a new circlip to the cover end of the shaft.

162 On all models, refit the selector shaft cover if it was removed.

163 To the lever end of the selector shaft fit a new O-ring, a washer and a new circlip.

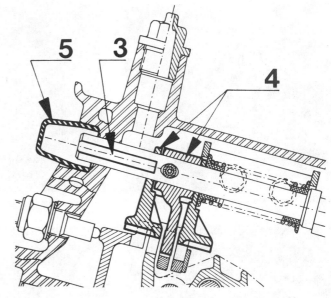

Fig. 12.67 Selector shaft fitting details (Sec 12)

3 *Flat on shaft*   4 *Selector finger and interlock bracket*
5 *Cover (early type)*

164 Apply jointing compound to the main casing/end casing mating face. Fit the end casing, making sure that the input and output shafts and the selector rods pass through their respective holes. Fit the thirteen securing bolts and tighten them progressively to the specified torque; remember to fit the clutch cable bracket (photo).

12.141A Measuring distance between joint face and bearing outer track

12.141B Measuring spigot protrusion

12.144 Fitting preload shim

12.149A Fitting input shaft endfloat shim ...

12.149B ... and front bearing outer track

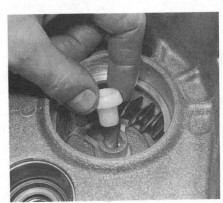

12.152 Fitting the lubrication jet

12.154 Fitting reversing lamp switch

12.155 Fitting geartrains and selector mechanism

12.158 Selector shaft spring and washers compressed in bracket

12.159 Fitting the selector shaft

12.160 One of the selector finger/interlock bracket roll pins fitted

12.164 Tightening a clutch cable bracket bolt

165 Fit the reverse idler spindle bolt, using a new washer. Tighten the bolt to the specified torque.

166 Fit the drain plug(s) using a new washer(s), and tighten to the specified torque.

167 Fit the selector rod lockplate. Secure it with its bolt and washer, tightening the bolt to the specified torque.

168 Fit the output shaft bearing circlip, making sure it is properly located in the groove.

169 Fit the output shaft rear bearing retaining washers and bolts. Tighen the bolts to the specified torque.

170 Fit the spacer (shoulder towards the bearing), 5th gear bush and 5th gear to the input shaft. Also fit the sliding sleeve and hub, but not the selector fork (photos).

171 Lock up the geartrains by engaging 5th gear with the sliding sleeve and any other gear with the selector shaft. Fit the output shaft nut and tighten it to the specified torque, then lock it by staking its skirt into the groove.

172 Remove the 5th gear sliding sleeve and hub, then refit them with the selector fork. If the original components are being refitted, observe the mating marks made when dismantling. As the fork is being lowered into position, insert the detent ball into its hole. Alternatively, extract the roll pin and insert the detent ball and spring from the other end (photos).

173 Engage two gears again, then fit the input shaft nut and tighten it to the specified torque. Lock the nut by staking.

174 Secure the 5th gear selector fork to its rod with a new roll pin.

175 Coat the mating faces with jointing compound, then refit the rear cover. Use thread locking compound on the securing bolts and tighten them to the specified torque.

176 Turn the clutch housing and remove the release bearing guide tube. If a new release lever balljoint is to be fitted, do so now: put thread locking compound on its splines and drive it in.

177 Refit the clutch release bearing guide tube with an endfloat shim 2.4 mm thick and without a gasket. Insert the retaining bolts and tighten them progressively, at the same time rotating the input shaft. Stop tightening when the shaft *just* starts to drag: the bearings are then correctly seated.

178 Remove the guide tube and the shim. Using a depth gauge, accurately measure the distance from the bearing outer track to the joint face on the casing. Call this dimension C. Similarly measure the protrusion of the spigot on the guide tube flange above the joint face. Call this dimension D (photos).

179 The thickness T of endfloat shim required is given by the formula:

$$T = (C - D) + 0.03 \text{ mm}$$

The extra 0.03 mm provides the correct amount of endfloat and allows for the thickness of the gasket which will be fitted. Shims are available in thicknesses from 0.7 to 32.4 mm in steps of 0.1 mm.

180 Fit a new oil seal, lips well greased, to the guide tube.

181 Fit the endfloat shim (of calculated thickness), a new gasket and the guide tube. Secure with the bolts and tighten them to the specified torque (photo).

182 Refit the clutch release fork and release bearing (see Section 11).

183 If not already done, refit the gearchange levers, making sure that they are in the correct position (Fig. 12.51). Also refit the clutch bellcrank (if removed) and the gearchange pivot bracket (photos).

184 Reassembly of the transmission is now complete. Do not refill it with oil until the driveshafts have been engaged.

Reassembly of major units (four-speed)

185 The only difference in reassembling the four-speed box, apart from the obvious absence of 5th gear components, lies in the method of locking the geartrains when tightening the input and output shaft nuts.

186 Refer to paragraphs 89 or 90 and use one of the methods described there. Remember to stake the nuts after tightening.

Manual transmission fault diagnosis

187 Refer to Chapter 6, Section 10, but consider the following additional points.

Gearbox noisy – check oil level and grade
Difficult engagement of reverse – clutch plate sticking on input shaft splines
Knocking noise in 1st gear – reverse selector fork worn

12.170A Fitting 5th speed gear spacer to input shaft ...

12.170B ... 5th speed gear bush ...

12.170C ... and 5th speed gear

12.172A Fitting detent ball and spring

12.172B Detent ball and spring secured with roll pin

12.178A Measuring distance between joint face and bearing outer track

12.178B Measuring spigot protrusion

12.181 Fitting input shaft endfloat shim

12.183A Fitting gearchange lever spring

12.183B Tightening clutch bellcrank pivot bolt

12.183C Fitting the gearchange pivot bracket. Note lockwashers under fixing nuts.

13 Automatic transmission (type ZF 4 HP14)

General description

1   The automatic transmission has four forward speeds and one reverse. In the interests of fuel economy the torque converter is completely bypassed in top (4th) and partially bypassed in 3rd; this reduces losses due to torque converter slip.

2   Gearchanging is automatic in use, the transmission responding to changes in speed and load. The usual 'kickdown' facility is provided for enhanced acceleration when the throttle is depressed fully.

3   Instead of the customary oil cooler mounted in the radiator, cooling is by means of a coolant/oil heat exchanger mounted on the side of the transmission.

Routine maintenance

4   At the specified intervals, or at the first sign of malfunction, the fluid level should be checked using the dipstick. The transmission should be hot (after at least half an hour's driving) and the selector in 'P', with the engine idling, when checking the level. Top up if necessary, via the dipstick tube using a clean funnel and a clean flexible tube (Fig. 12.69). Scrupulous cleanliness is essential when dealing with the automatic transmission.

5   If topping up is frequently necessary, inspect the transmission for leaks.

6   Also at the specified intervals, drain the transmission and final drive. **Caution:** *the transmission fluid may be very hot.* Refit the drain plugs and refill the transmission with the specified quantity of fresh ATF.

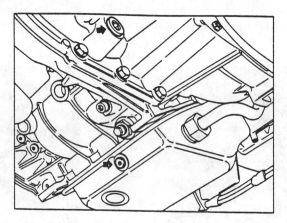

Fig. 12.70 Automatic transmission and final drive drain plugs (arrowed) (Sec 13)

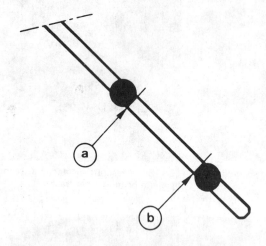

Fig. 12.68 Automatic transmission dipstick marking (Sec 13)

a   Maximum   b   Minimum

Precautions

7   If it is necessary to tow a vehicle with automatic transmission, the towing speed must be restricted to 30 mph and the distance to 30 miles. If these conditions cannot be met, or if transmission damage is the reason for seeking a tow, the vehicle must be transported on a trailer.

Fluid filter renewal

8   If routine changing of the transmission fluid has been neglected or if the fluid has become contaminated, then the gauze filter should be changed in the following way.

9   Drain the fluid as previously described and unscrew the dipstick guide tube union nut.

10   Extract the screws and withdraw the sump pan. Clean the interior of the pan and the magnet.

11   The filter is now exposed and it can be removed after unscrewing its nine fixing bolts.

12   Peel away the joint gasket from the valve block and discard it together with the O-ring seal.

13   Discard the old filter gauze and fit the new one into its frame. Locate a new O-ring and joint gasket and offer the filter assembly to the underside of the valve block.

14   Insert the nine fixing bolts noting very carefully the different locations according to their lengths and their individual torque settings using Fig. 12.73 in conjunction with the following table.

15   Fit the sump pan using a new gasket and tighten the fixing screws progressively to the specified torque.

16   Refill the transmission as previously described.

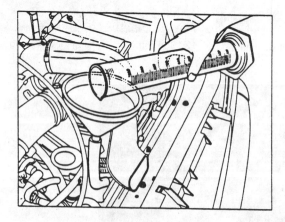

Fig. 12.69 Filling the automatic transmission (Sec 13)

Bolt	X (mm)	Y (mm)	Torque	
			lbf ft	Nm
7	80	12	6	8
8	80	10	4	6
9	70	12	6	8
10	65	10	4	6
11	60	10	6	4

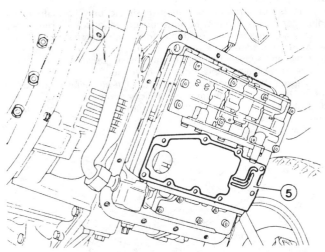

Fig. 12.71 Automatic transmission sump pan removed (Sec 13)

5   Filter casing

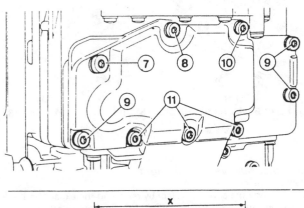

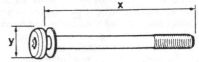

Fig. 12.73 Filter casing bolt identification (see text) (Sec 13)

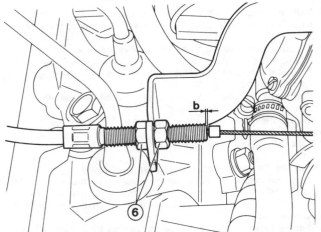

Fig. 12.75 Adjusting the kickdown cable – second stage (Sec 13)

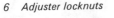

b = 0.5 mm maximum   6   Adjuster locknuts

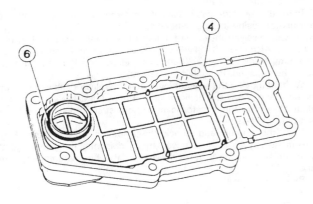

Fig. 12.72 Filter casing (4) and O-ring (6) (Sec 13)

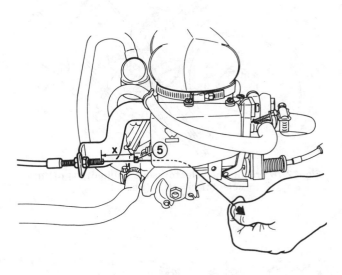

Fig. 12.74 Adjusting the kickdown cable – first stage (Sec 13)

X = 39.0 mm   5   Crimped stop

Kickdown cable adjustment

17 Before attempting to adjust the kickdown cable, the idle speed must be correct and the throttle cable must be correctly adjusted.

18 Disconnect the kickdown cable from the drum on the carburettor. Pull the cable inner until resistance is felt (beginning of kickdown) and measure the distance from the crimped stop to the cable adjuster (Fig. 12.74). It should be 39 mm (1.52 in). Release and re-crimp the stop if necessary to achieve this.

19 Reconnect the kickdown cable to the drum. With the throttle pedal released, there should be a small clearance (0.5 mm maximum) between the stop and the adjuster (Fig. 12.75). Release the adjuster locknuts and turn the adjuster if necessary to achieve this.

Kickdown cable renewal

20 Renewal of the cable entails the removal of the transmission sump and valve block. The home mechanic is advised to delegate the work to a Peugeot dealer or other competent specialist.

Selector linkage adjustment

21 Remove the air cleaner.
22 Prise the selector cable balljoint off the selector lever on the transmission, using an open-ended spanner.
23 Move the selector lever on the transmission into position 'P' (fully forwards). Also select 'P' inside the car. Confirm that 'P' is engaged by attempting to move the car (handbrake released) – the parking pawl should be engaged. Reapply the handbrake.
24 Without moving the selector lever, pull the selector cable to take up any slack and screw the balljoint up or down the cable end until the balljoint fits onto the selector lever without strain. Press the balljoint back onto the lever.
25 Start the engine and check the selection of all gears. Fine adjustment may be made if necessary by disconnecting the balljoint again and unscrewing it up or down the cable by one complete turn only.
26 Refit the air cleaner.

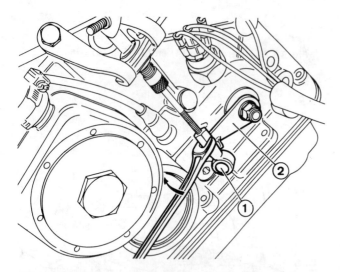

Fig. 12.76 Prising the selector cable balljoint (1) off the selector lever (2) (Sec 13)

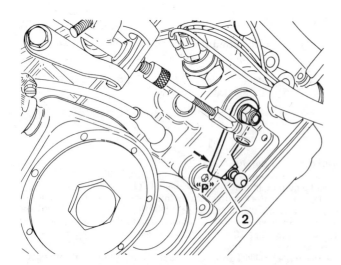

Fig. 12.77 Selector lever (2) in 'P' position (Sec 13)

Brake band adjustment

27 This is not a routine operation. It should only be performed if adjustment is suspected of being incorrect (denoted by engine speed variations during third to fourth and fourth to third changes), or after removal of the adjusting screw to rectify a leak.
28 Raise and support the front of the vehicle. Locate the brake band adjuster (near the transmission sump drain plug).
29 Slacken the adjuster locknut. Tighten the adjusting screw to 1.0 kgf m (7 lbf ft), then unscrew it by exactly two turns.
30 Tighten the locknut without disturbing the position of the adjusting screw.
31 Lower the vehicle.

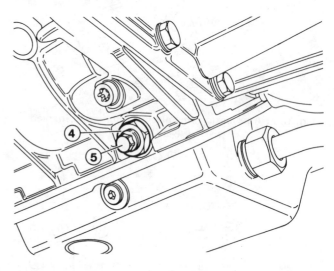

Fig. 12.78 Brake band adjuster (5) and locknut (4) (Sec 13)

Fluid cooler removal and refitting

32 Remove the air cleaner.
33 Depressurize the cooling system by removing the expansion bottle cap. Take precautions against scalding if the coolant is hot.
34 Clamp the coolant hoses near the fluid cooler and disconnect them from the cooler stubs. Be prepared for coolant spillage.
35 Clean around the cooler-to-transmission joint. Remove the cooler centre bolt, swivel the cooler so that the stubs point upwards and remove it from the transmission. Take great care to keep coolant and dirt out of the transmission.
36 When refitting, use new gaskets on the cooler, lubricated with clean ATF. Also renew the sealing ring under the head of the centre bolt.
37 Refit the cooler with its side face parallel with the converter housing-to-transmission joint. Tighten the centre bolt to the specified torque.
38 Reconnect the coolant hoses and remove the hose clamps.
39 Top up the cooling system as described in Section 8, paragraphs 10 to 13 of this Supplement. Note that there are three bleed valves on automatic transmission models (Fig. 12.81).
40 Check the transmission fluid level as described earlier in this Section, and top up if necessary.
41 Inspect the cooler for leaks of coolant or ATF when the engine is running.
42 Refit the air cleaner on completion.

Automatic transmission removal and refitting

43 If the transmission is being removed for repair, make sure before starting work that the repairer does not wish to examine the transmission *in situ*. Some faults cannot be diagnosed with the transmission removed.
44 Prepare for removal as described in Section 12, paragraphs 10 to 19 and 21 to 23 of this Supplement.
45 Release the dipstick/filler tube from the sump by undoing the tube nut. Remove the tube (its bracket is secured by one of the starter motor bolts).

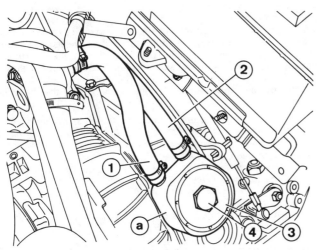

Fig. 12.79 Automatic transmission fluid cooler (3). Face (a) must be parallel with torque converter housing joint (Sec 13)

1   Coolant hose   2   Coolant hose   4   Centre bolt

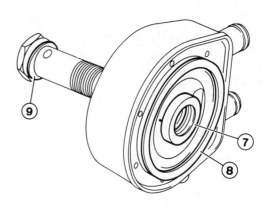

Fig. 12.80 Fluid cooler gaskets (7 and 8) and sealing ring (9) (Sec 13)

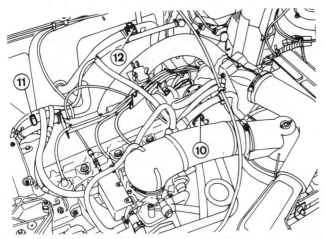

Fig. 12.81 Coolant bleed valves (10, 11 & 12) on automatic transmission models (Sec 13)

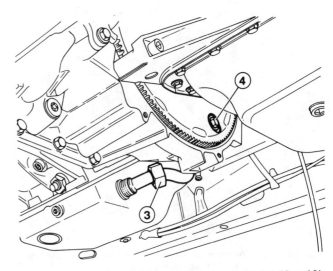

Fig. 12.82 Torque converter to driveplate bolt (4) (Sec 13)

3   Dipstick tube union nut

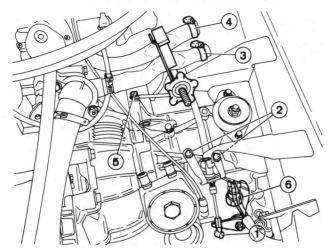

Fig. 12.83 Automatic transmission disconnection points (Sec 13)

1   Selector cable   4   Coolant hose   6   Starter inhibitor/reversing
2   Cable bracket   5   Earth strap   light switch
3   Coolant hose

46 Remove the torque converter bottom shield. Remove the three converter-to-driveplate bolts, turning the crankshaft to bring each bolt into view.
47 Disconnect the selector cable balljoint (paragraph 22). Unbolt the bracket and move the selector cable aside.
48 Clamp the coolant hoses and disconnect them from the transmission fluid cooler. Be prepared for coolant spillage.
49 Unbolt the earth strap(s) from the transmission. Also disconnect the starter inhibitor/reversing light switch.
50 Disconnect the kickdown cable at the carburettor end.
51 Disconnect the speedometer cable from the transmission by withdrawing its retaining plug.
52 Remove the bolt which secures the TDC sensor bracket.
53 Support the engine, either with lifting tackle from above or with a jack and wooden blocks from below. Take the weight of the engine and remove the left-hand engine/transmission mounting. Lower the engine until it takes up a stable position, then raise it slightly to ease the strain on the remaining mountings.
54 Attach lifting tackle to the eye on the top of the transmission. Take the weight of the transmission and remove the remaining transmission-to-engine bolts.

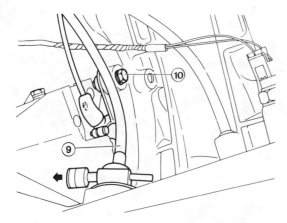

Fig. 12.84 Speedo drive cable retainer (arrowed) (Sec 13)

9   Cable   10 TDC sensor bracket bolt

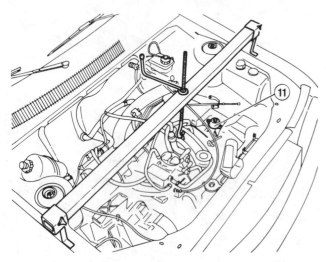

Fig. 12.85 Engine supported ready for removal of automatic transmission (Sec 13)

11 Left-hand mounting

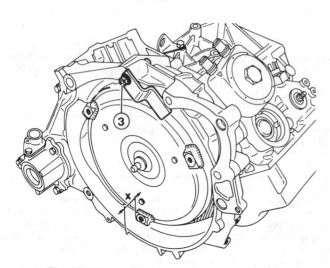

Fig. 12.86 Torque converter retainer (3) (Sec 13)

X = minimum of 7.0 mm

55 Draw the transmission away from the engine, lower it to the ground and remove it from under the car. Make sure that the torque converter stays in engagement with the oil pump during this operation; restrain it if necessary using an angled piece of metal secured through one of the transmission-to-engine bolt holes. The torque converter is properly engaged when dimension 'x' (Fig. 12.86) is greater than 7 mm.

56 Refit by reversing the removal operations, noting the following points:

(a) Apply a smear of grease to the crankshaft spigot bush
(b) Fit new driveshaft oil seals to the final drive unit; use the oil seal protector (supplied with new oil seals) when fitting the right-hand driveshaft
(c) Tighten all fastenings to the specified torque: use new nuts on the stub axle balljoints
(d) Refill the transmission with fluid and top up the cooling system
(e) Adjust the kickdown cable and the selector linkage as described earlier in this Section

Torque converter oil seal renewal

57 Remove the transmission as described previously. Remove the torque converter retaining tool (if used).
58 Remove the torque converter by screwing two long M8 X 125 bolts into its exposed face and using the bolts as handles. Be prepared for considerable ATF spillage.
59 Lubricate the oil seal housing with a little clean ATF, then extract the oil seal with a suitable hooked tool.
60 Lubricate the new seal with clean ATF. Fit the new seal, lips facing inwards, and set it with a piece of tube so that its outer face is flush with the housing.
61 Refit the converter, being careful not to damage the oil seal. Rotate the converter back and forth until its lugs engage with the oil pump. Remove the two long bolts.
62 Refit the transmission.

Starter inhibitor/reversing light switch (general)

63 The starter inhibitor/reversing light switch is located just above the selector lever. The switch interrupts the starter motor circuit in all positions except 'P' and 'N', and activates the reversing lights in position 'R'.
64 If the switch malfunctions, it must be renewed (repair is not possible). Disconnect the wiring from the old switch, unscrew it and remove it. Screw the new switch into position and reconnect the wiring. There is no provision for adjustment.
65 If water and road salt contaminate the switch and its connections, malfunction may result. Protect the switch by fitting a protective rubber boot (available from Peugeot dealers) and by smearing the switch terminals with silicone grease or petroleum jelly.

Automatic transmission fault diagnosis

66 At the first sign of transmission malfunction, check the fluid level as described at the beginning of this Section.
67 Where the fault is related to kickdown or to gear selection, check

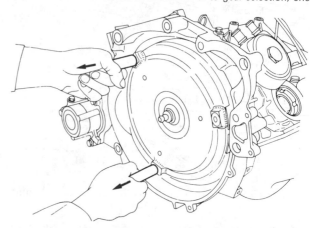

Fig. 12.87 Withdrawing the torque converter (Sec 13)

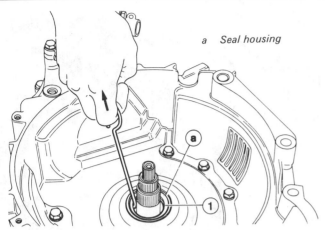

a   Seal housing

**Fig. 12.88 Hooking out the torque converter oil seal (1)
(Sec 13)**

the adjustment of the kickdown cable and the selector linkage respectively.
68 Brake band adjustment may be attempted when the fault consists of engine speed variations during third to fourth and fourth to third changes.
69 Any further fault diagnosis should be performed by a Peugeot dealer or transmission specialist.

14 Driveshafts (XU engined vehicles)

Removal and refitting

1 Refer to Section 12, paragraphs 12 to 21 of this Supplement, for the removal procedure. There is no need to drain the transmission if arrangements are made to catch any oil spilt when the driveshafts are withdrawn.
2 It is emphasized that if any attempt is made to move the car on its wheels without the driveshafts fitted, there is a danger that the front wheel bearings will collapse.
3 Refit in the reverse order of removal. When new final drive oil seals have been fitted, use the oil seal protector supplied with the seals when fitting the right-hand driveshaft. Tighten all fastenings to the specified torque using new nuts on the steering and suspension balljoints.
4 Top up the transmission to make good any oil loss.

Intermediate bearing renewal

5 Remove the right-hand driveshaft.
6 Unbolt and remove the engine mounting/intermediate bearing carrier. If the bearing did not come away with the driveshaft, press the bearing and its sealing ring out of the carrier (photo).
7 Fit the new bearing and sealing ring, refit the carrier and the driveshaft. Tighten all fastenings to the specified torque, using new nuts on the steering and suspension balljoints.

15 Hubs and bearings

Front hub removal and refitting (1983 on)

1 Fit the damper retaining cables 8.0903 AF, or equivalent, to the suspension strut on the side concerned. Refer to Section 17, paragraph 32 of this Supplement for further details.
2 Slacken the three nuts which retain the top of the strut.
3 Remove the driveshaft nut (see Section 12, paragraph 12 or 13 of this Supplement).
4 Raise and securely support the front of the car. Remove the roadwheel, the brake caliper and the brake disc. Tie the brake caliper up so that the hydraulic hose is not strained.
5 Clamp the driveshaft, using tool 8.0615 H or equivalent, so that it is not pulled out of the final drive.
6 Disconnect the anti-roll bar lower link.
7 Remove the nut and bolt which clamp the stub axle to the strut (photo).
8 Spread the clamp using a quarter inch square drive key (photo). Push the stub axle downwards to free it from the strut and pivot it

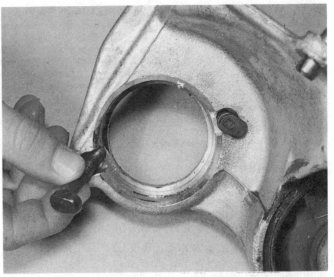

14.6 Driveshaft intermediate bearing carrier (removed) showing location of special bolts

15.7 Tightening stub axle carrier-to-strut clamp bolt

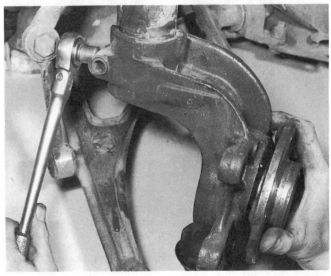

15.8 Prising open clamp jaws

outwards to free it from the driveshaft.

9 Should the driveshaft be an interference fit in the hub, use a puller or bearing extractor to prise it out. **Do not** attempt to drive the shaft out of the hub.

10 To remove the hub and bearing from the stub axle *in situ* requires a formidable number of special tools. The DIY mechanic is therefore recommended to remove the stub axle complete (by disconnecting the balljoints) and take it to a Peugeot dealer or auto engineering specialist to have the hub removed.

11 Renewal of the hub bearing itself also requires many special tools. This job too is therefore best done professionally. Once the hub has been separated from the stub axle, the bearing **must** be renewed. Note that larger bearings and associated components are fitted to later models, beginning during 1985.

12 Refit in the reverse order of removal. Use new nuts on the balljoints (if disturbed) and driveshaft; tighten all fastening to the specified torque. Make sure the strut is properly located – see Section 17, paragraph 41.

Rear-wheel bearings removal and refitting
Pre-1983 models

13 Proceed as described in Chapter 7, Section 5, but note that on Estate models there is a 'V' profile seal on the brake backplate; this seal must be renewed once it has been disturbed.

1983 and later models

14 Raise and securely support the rear of the vehicle. Remove the roadwheel and the brake drum on the side concerned.

15 Remove the hub grease cap. Undo the hub nut – it is very tight. It may be helpful to relieve the staking. Remove the washer from under the nut (photo).

16 Remove the hub from the stub axle. A heavy duty puller will almost certainly be required.

17 Use a drift or chisel to knock the seal locating cup back towards the centre of the vehicle. Fit the puller to the bearing inner track left behind on the stub axle and draw it off the axle.

18 Lever the seal locating cup at the positions shown (Fig. 12.89) and remove it.

Fig. 12.89 Removing seal locating cup (1) by levering at points (a) and (b) (Sec 15)

19 The seal locating cup, stub axle nut and grease cap should be renewed in any event once they have been disturbed. The hub and bearings are only available as a complete asssembly: do not try to separate them.

20 Commence reassembly by fitting a new seal locating cup. The makers specify the use of tool 8.0530 D for this purpose, but with care a tube of suitable diameter can be used instead. Do not press the cup on too far.

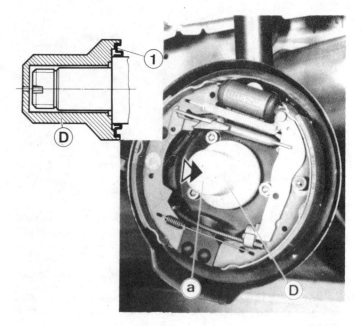

Fig. 12.90 Fitting a seal locating cup (Sec 15)

1 Cup	a Striking point	D Fitting tool

21 Put a light smear of oil or grease on the stub axle, taking care not to contaminate the brake shoes.

22 Place the bearing inner track on the stub axle. Force it down the stub axle by screwing on a new nut. Tap the nut gently with a mallet, rotating the nut at the same time, to get it started; after two or three turns the mallet can be discarded and the nut can be tightened with a spanner.

23 On Estate and Van versions the stub axle may rotate as the nut is tightened. In this case jam it with a 19 mm Allen key inserted from behind.

24 When the nut has reached the limit of its travel, unscrew it, fit a thick washer between the nut and the bearing track and force the track further down the axle by screwing up the nut again. Repeat this process with more washers until the track is nearly home.

25 Remove the nut and washers, offer the hub/bearing assembly to the stub axle and complete the location of the inner track by striking the hub with a mallet. Use a socket or tube to apply the load to the inner track.

15.15 Rear hub nut staked in position

26 Fit the washer and a new nut. Tighten the nut to the specified torque, then stake its skirt into the groove.
27 Refit the grease cap (photo), the brake drum and the roadwheel. Lower the car to the ground and tighten the wheel bolts to the specified torque.

16 Braking system

Brake bleeding (all models)

1 The use of pressure bleeding equipment is recommended for all models. Proprietary kits are available which use air from the spare tyre as the pressure source.
2 On models with a load-sensitive compensator, the weight of the vehicle must be on its wheels when the rear brakes are bled. If this is not possible, temporarily open the compensator by binding its arm with string or wire. Remember to remove the binding when bleeding is complete. Refer to Chapter 9, Section 15.

Disc pads removal and refitting (1983 on)

3 Slacken the front wheel nuts or bolts, raise and securely support the front of the vehicle and remove the front wheels. Disconnect the pad wear warning light wires (photo).
4 If necessary, remove some fluid from the brake hydraulic reservoir, using an old poultry baster or battery hydrometer. If this is not done there is a risk of fluid spillage during subsequent operations.
5 Remove the spring clip which secures the caliper sliding key. Extract the key, pulling it outwards from the caliper (photos).
6 Use a large tyre lever or similar to lever the caliper cylinder towards the disc, using the shock absorber leg as a fulcrum. When sufficient movement has occurred, extract the outer pad.

7 Push the caliper back towards the centreline and remove the inner pad (photo).
8 Inspect the caliper for fluid leaks and check that the cylinder slides freely. Inspect the disc for wear and damage.
9 If the groove which bisects the pad friction linings is no longer visible, they must be renewed. All four pads must be renewed even if only one has worn to the specified limit.
10 Clean in and around the caliper with an old dry paintbrush and a damp cloth, *taking car not to inhale the dust or disperse it into the atmosphere.*
11 Push the piston fully home, using a flat bar applied squarely across the piston face.
12 Coat the caliper lower slide with disc brake anti-seize compound. Fit the inner and outer pads, moving the caliper and cylinder as necessary. Reconnect the warning light wire.
13 Push the pads downwards and secure them with the key. Lock the key in place with a new retaining clip.
14 Repeat the operations on the opposite brake unit, then refit the roadwheels and lower the car to the ground. Tighten the wheel nuts or bolts to the specified torque.
15 Top up the brake fluid reservoir, then apply the brake pedal a number of times with the engine running to bring the pads up to the disc. Recheck the brake fluid level and top up further if necessary.
16 Exercise restraint in braking for the first few hundred miles to allow the new pads to bed in. New pads of Peugeot manufacture have a thin abrasive coating on the friction surface to remove minor imperfections from the discs. Follow the maker's instructions for bedding in such pads.

Caliper modifications (later models)

17 From VIN 9 352 397, the lugs on the caliper anti-rotation plate have been deleted. This is because it was possible for the lugs to jam in

15.27 Refitting the grease cap

16.3 Disc pad wear warning lamp wire connector

16.5A Caliper key spring clip (arrowed)

16.5B Extracting caliper sliding key

16.7 Removing a disc pad

the sleeves and restrict the sliding action of the caliper, causing uneven pad wear.

18 Earlier calipers may be modified if wished by grinding the lugs off the plate.

19 From VIN 9 457 811, the sealing between the caliper and the sleeves was improved. Prior to this, excessive clearance in some cases was causing brake chatter when reversing.

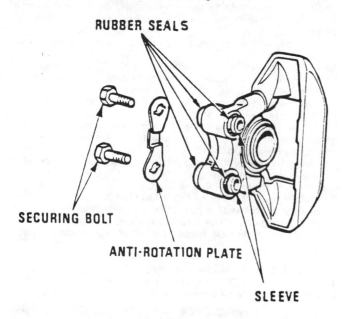

Fig. 12.91 Brake caliper anti-rotation plate (Sec 16)

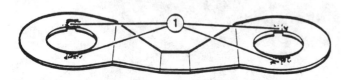

Fig. 12.92 Anti-rotation plate lugs (1) (Sec 16)

16.26 Removing a brake disc securing screw

20 Earlier calipers may be modified if wished using a sleeve renewal kit obtainable from a Peugeot dealer. The kit contains two sleeves, four sleeve seals, special grease for the sleeves and thread-locking compound for the caliper bolts.

21 When renewing the caliper sleeves, take the opportunity to grind the lugs off the anti-rotation plate if necessary.

Rear brake shoes removal and refitting (Teves)

22 The Teves rear brakes closely resemble the later type Girling brakes described in Chapter 8, Section 8, to which reference should be made. Note the following points concerning component identification.

23 The trailing shoes are identified by the letters 'L' and 'R' engraved upon them, and by the position of the handbrake lever. The leading shoes are identified by the position of the lever which engages with the self-adjusting strut.

24 The self-adjusting struts are identified by their rollers – the left-hand side roller carries a chamfer, the right-hand side does not. The plungers are also coded: left-hand side plungers are white, right-hand side plungers are yellow.

Brake disc removal and refitting (1983 on)

25 Raise and securely support the front of the vehicle. Remove the roadwheel and the brake pads on the side in question.

26 Remove the two screws which hold the disc to the hub. The disc can now be removed (photo).

27 Refit in the reverse order of removal.

Brake discs (GTX models)

28 The front brake discs on these models are of the ventilated type. Operations for removal and refitting and checking for distortion are as for solid discs.

Brake compensator adjustment (Estate models)

29 The brake compensator fitted to Estate models is of the adjustable load-sensitive type described in Chapter 8.

Models with XL or XR engine

30 To adjust the compensator, first raise and securely support the rear of the vehicle. Check that the suspension arm stops are present and in good condition: renew them if not.

31 Fit a slotted metal block of 5 mm thickness between the spring adjuster and the control lever.

32 Act on the control lever adjuster or on the spring adjuster itself until the metal block is a firm sliding fit.

33 Remove the metal block and lower the vehicle to the ground.

Models with XU engine

34 Pressure testing equipment is needed to adjust this type of compensator; the work must therefore be done by a Peugeot dealer.

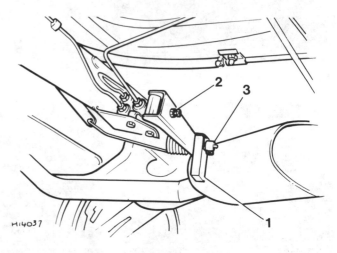

Fig. 12.93 Estate brake compensator (pressure regulator) – except XU engined versions (Sec 16)

1   Metal block   2   Control lever adjuster   3   Spring adjuster

17 Suspension and steering

Front suspension strut cartridge fitting (up to 1983)

1   The front suspension strut on earlier models is integral with the hub carrier and to reduce the expense of renewal, sealed cartridges became available after October 1987 to effect an economical repair. The repair procedure is described in the following paragraphs.
2   Raise the front of the car and support securely on axle stands.
3   Remove the roadwheel.
4   Have an assistant apply the footbrake pedal hard and unscrew the driveshaft hub nut.
5   Unbolt and tie the brake caliper up out of the way.
6   Disconnect the steering track rod from the steering arm on the hub carrier.
7   Disconnect the lower suspension arm from the body.
8   Unscrew the nut from the end of the anti-roll bar at its connection with the suspension lower arm.
9   Disconnect the strut upper mounting from the turret within the engine compartment. On no account unscrew the centre spindle nut at this stage.
10 Withdraw the hub carrier from the end of the driveshaft. If the splined end of the driveshaft is tight in the hub, use the centre screw of a three-legged puller to press it out.
11 With the strut removed, compress the coil spring using a proprietary coil spring compressor making sure that it is not likely to slip.
12 Unscrew the spindle top nut and take off the mounting components. The end of the spindle may be slotted or have a hexagon socket in which to engage a tool to prevent the spindle turning when the nut is unscrewed. Carefully remove the compressed coil spring.
13 Unscrew the gland nut and withdraw and discard the original piston/rod assembly, and tip out any hydraulic fluid from the strut tube.
14 Fit the new cartridge into the strut tube, tighten the gland nut to the specified torque of 87 lbf ft (12 kgf m).
15 Fit the coil spring, still compressed, then the top mounting components and tighten the spindle nut to the specified torque. Gently release the coil spring compressor.
16 Refit the strut to the car, tighten all fixings to specified torque (see Specifications Chapters 8 and 9). Apply thread locking fluid to the threads on the end of the driveshaft before fitting a new nut and staking it in position. Also apply thread locking fluid to the caliper fixing bolts.
17 On completion, apply the footbrake hard two or three times to bring the disc pads into full adjustment.

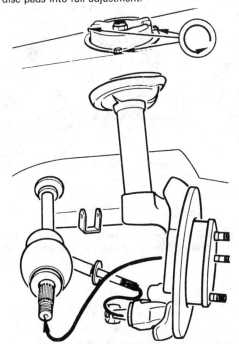

Fig. 12.94 Front strut disconnected (Sec 17)

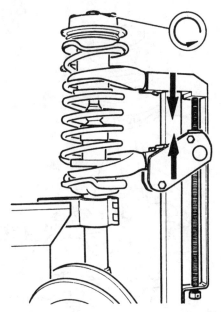

Fig. 12.95 Coil spring compressed (Sec 17)

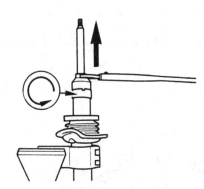

Fig. 12.96 Strut gland nut (Sec 17)

Front suspension description (1983 on)

18 The front suspension on later models is similar to that described in Chapter 8, but the track control arms have been replaced by 'wishbone' lower suspension arms. There are unsequential modifications to the anti-roll bar and its attachments, the front stub axles, suspension struts and the front subframe itself. The anti-roll bar also varies according to engine type.
19 Refer to the Specifications for the torque wrench settings which apply to the new components.

Front anti-roll bar centralising (XU engined vehicles)

20 This operation must be carried out after disturbing the anti-roll bar mountings, or after renewal of a suspension arm, a stub axle or the front subframe.
21 Remove the brake pads as described in the previous Section.
22 Refit the roadwheels and lower the vehicle; push the vehicle back and forth several times, working the steering wheel and bouncing the suspension, to settle the suspension components. (Do not touch the brake pedal, or the caliper pistons may be ejected.)
23 Turn the steering wheel onto full lock. Move the left-hand brake caliper as far as possible towards the anti-roll bar and check that some clearance exists between the bleed screw and the anti-roll bar link bolt. Turn the steering wheel to full right lock and repeat the check on the right-hand side.
24 If the bleed screws do not touch the link bolts on either side, centralisation is satisfactory – proceed to paragraph 29. If the screws

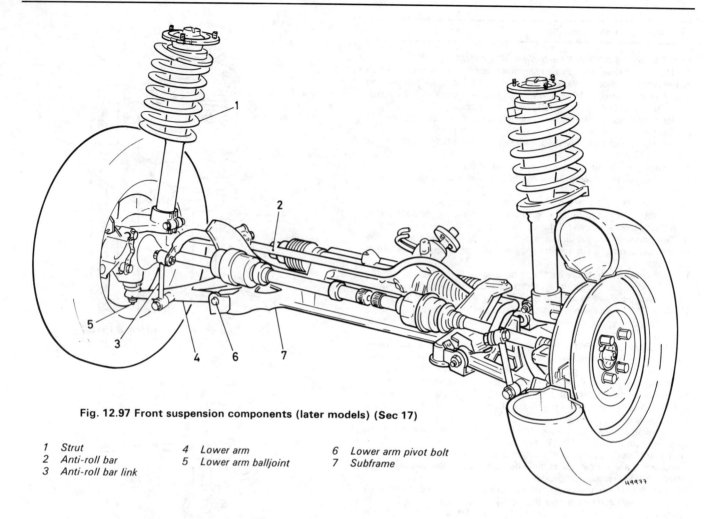

Fig. 12.97 Front suspension components (later models) (Sec 17)

1 Strut
2 Anti-roll bar
3 Anti-roll bar link
4 Lower arm
5 Lower arm balljoint
6 Lower arm pivot bolt
7 Subframe

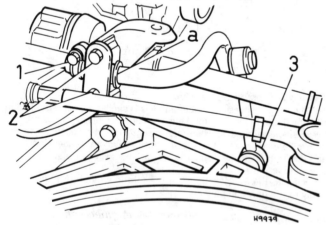

Fig. 12.98 Centralising the anti-roll bar (Sec 17)

a Reference line
1 Collar
2 Clamp bolts
3 Link bolts

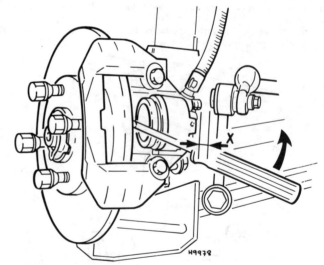

Fig. 12.99 Checking the clearance (X) between the caliper bleed screw and the anti-roll bar link bolt (Sec 17)

touch on both sides, the anti-roll bar is distorted and must be renewed. If the screw on one side only touches, proceed as follows.
25 Scribe or paint a line on the anti-roll bar next to one of the clamps so that the amount of movement can be judged.
26 Slacken the anti-roll bar collar and clamp nuts and bolts on both sides. Also slacken the link-to-lower arm bolts.
27 Move the anti-roll bar away from the side where screw contact was occurring. Tighten the nuts and bolts to the specified torque in the

following order:

(a) Collar bolts
(b) Clamp nuts and bolts
(c) Link-to-lower arm bolts

28 Repeat the check in paragraph 6.
29 Raise the vehicle and remove the front roadwheels. Refit the brake pads as described in Section 16.

30 Refit the roadwheels and lower the vehicle. Tighten the wheel nuts or bolts. Operate the brake pedal several times to bring the pads up to the discs.
31 Check the brake fluid level and top up if necessary.

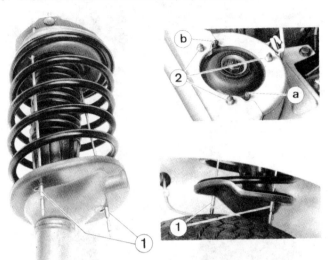

Fig. 12.100 Front suspension strut showing damper retaining cables (Sec 17)

1	Cable lower ends	a	Cable top end
2	Strut mounting nuts	b	Cable top end

Front suspension strut removal and refitting (1983 on)

32 The makers call up various special tools for this operation, among them damper retaining cables (tool No 8.0903 AF). It was found that a strut in good condition can safely be removed and refitted without using retaining cables. Damage or corrosion occurring at the spring lower seat could result in a dangerous situation if the cables were not used. Satisfy yourself that the strut is in good condition before deciding to dispense with the cables. **Severe injury could result from the uncontrolled release of the spring.**
33 Pass the damper retaining cables (if used) through the holes at the top of the strut. Hook the second weight on each cable into the slots in the spring lower seat.
34 Slacken the three nuts which secure the top of the strut, but do not remove them yet.
35 Slacken the front wheel nuts or bolts, raise and securely support the front of the vehicle and remove the roadwheel.
36 Secure the driveshaft, using tool No. 8.0615 H or equivalent, so that it will not be pulled out of the final drive.
37 Disconnect the anti-roll bar lower link.
38 Remove the nut and bolt which clamp the stub axle to the strut.
39 Spread the clamp using a quarter inch square drive key. Move the stub axle assembly off the bottom of the strut, taking care not to strain the brake hydraulic hose.
40 Remove the three nuts and washers from the top of the strut. The strut can now be removed from the vehicle. Take care not to dislodge the retaining cables.
41 Refit in the reverse order of removal, noting the following points:

(a) Use new self-locking nuts to secure the top of the strut and on the stub axle clamp
(b) Tighten all fastenings to the specified torque with the weight of the vehicle on its wheels
(c) If the strut does not enter the stub axle clamp fully, slacken the clamp nut after lowering the vehicle and then retighten it when the correct position has been assumed.
(d) If a new strut has been fitted, tighten the shaft nut to the specified torque, then secure it by staking. Hold the shaft stationary when tightening the nut.

Front suspension strut overhaul (1983 on)

42 As with the earlier type of strut, dismantling and reassembly are best left to a Peugeot dealer who will have the necessary tools and expertise.

43 The experienced DIY mechanic who has access to a substantial spring compressor may contemplate renewing the spring or the shock absorber. A fastening kit should be obtained, as well as the item to be renewed. **Take great care when dealing with the compressed spring.**
44 Final tightening of the shock absorber shaft nut should take place when the strut has been refitted to the vehicle.

Front suspension lower arm removal and refitting (1983 on)

45 Fit the damper retaining cables (paragraph 32).
46 Slacken the wheel nuts or bolts. Raise and support the front of the vehicle and remove the front roadwheel on the side concerned.
47 Remove the anti-roll bar link-to-lower arm bolt.
48 Slacken the lower arm balljoint nut. Use a proprietary separator tool to break the taper, then remove the nut and free the balljoint pin from the stub axle.
49 Remove the lower arm pivot bolt (at the front) and the two yoke bolts (at the rear). Remove the lower arm from the vehicle.
50 If the arm bushes are to be renewed, clamp the arm in a vice and remove the pivot nut and washer. The yoke can now be removed from the arm.

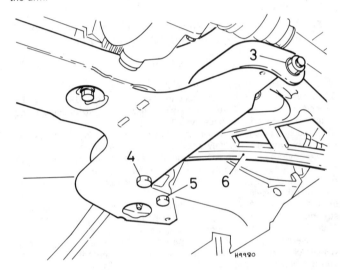

Fig. 12.101 Suspension lower arm attachment (Sec 17)

3	Pivot bolt	5	Yoke bolt
4	Yoke bolt	6	Lower arm

51 Bush renewal is best left to a Peugeot dealer or other specialist having the necessary press tools. At a pinch, a vice, suitable tubes and liquid soap may suffice.
52 Before refitting the arm, the yoke must be aligned with the arm as follows.
53 Fit the yoke to the arm. Secure it with the washer and nut, but do not tighten the nut yet.
54 Place the arm and yoke on a flat surface. Temporarily pass a 12 mm diameter bolt or rod through the front bush and place a block 23 mm thick under the bolt. Clamp the yoke so that it is flat against the surface (Fig. 12.102).
55 Hold the arm and tighten the pivot nut to the specified torque. Remove the clamp from the yoke and check that its edge is still in contact with the surface.
56 Refit the lower arm to the vehicle. Engage the balljoint pin and insert the pivot bolt and yoke bolts. Note that the balljoint pin must not be lubricated, but neither must it be de-greased with solvent.
57 Tighten the pivot bolt and the yoke bolts to the specified torque.
58 Tighten the balljoint nut to the specified torque.
59 Reconnect the anti-roll bar link and tighten its bolt to the specified torque.
60 Refit the roadwheel, lower the vehicle and tighten the wheel nuts or bolts.
61 Remove the damper retaining cables.

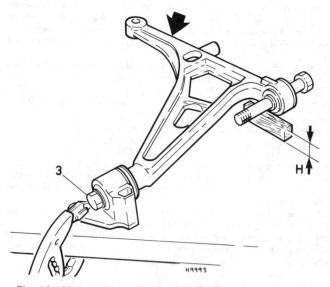

Fig. 12.102 Aligning yoke to suspension lower arm. With
arm depressed (arrowed) tighten nut (3) (Sec 17)

H = 23.0 mm

Rear suspension unit removal and refitting (Estate/Van)

62 A special spring compressor (Peugeot tool No 8.0912) will be
needed for this task. Other 'universal' compressors are unlikely to be
usable in the confined space available.

63 Prise the plastic cover off the shock absorber rod. Hold the rod
stationary with an Allen key and unscrew the nut (photo).

64 Remove the cup and spacer from the shock absorber rod, then refit
the nut by a few turns only. Remove the rebound stop (photo).

65 Compress the spring slightly, acting on the thrust cups rather than
on the spring itself.

66 Free the shock absorber balljoint from the suspension arm by
striking the balljoint smartly with a hammer and a brass or copper drift.
There is a hole in the suspension arm for this purpose.

67 Raise and securely support the rear of the vehicle with the rear
wheels clear of the ground. Remove the spare wheel if necessary to
improve access.

68 Free the balljoint from the suspension arm, taking care not to
damage the rubber boot. Compress the spring further if necessary.
Release the compressor and remove it when the balljoint is free.

69 Remove the shock absorber nut, then remove the suspension unit
from the car. Retrieve the half collars, which will probably fall out;
these are matched to the particular spring and **must not** be
interchanged from side to side.

Fig. 12.103 Components of Estate rear suspension unit
(Sec 17)

1	Half collars	6	Spacer
2	Spring lower seat	7	Collars retained with rubber
3	Washer		band
4	Gaiter	8	Straight coil end of spring
5	Washer		

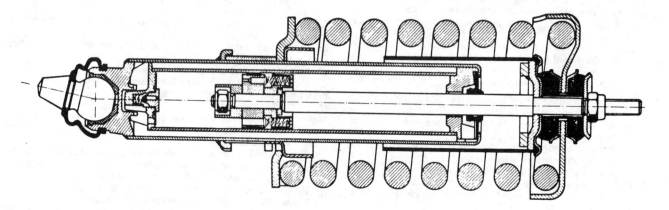

Fig. 12.104 Sectional view of Estate rear suspension unit (Sec 17)

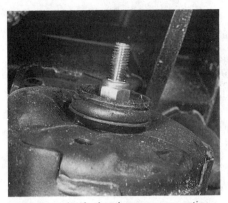

17.63 Rear shock absorber upper mounting (Estate)

17.64 Rear suspension rebound stop (Estate)

17.81 Rear suspension arm pivot bolt (Estate)

70 The unit may now be dismantled and components renewed as necessary. Remember to fit the new half collars if a new spring is being fitted. Renew the shock absorber nut also.

71 Prepare the unit for refitting by assembling all components on the shock absorber. Retain the half collars in place with a stout rubber band. Note that the straight coil end of the spring is to be fitted against the lower cup. Pull the shock absorber rod out as far as it will go.

72 Commence refitting by offering the unit to its housing. Refer to Fig. 12.105 for correct orientation. Fit the top mounting components, but only tighten the nut finger tight at this stage. Remember to hold the shock absorber rod stationary while tightening the nut.

73 Carefully compress the spring far enough to be able to insert the balljoint into the hole in the suspension arm. Release the spring slowly, making sure that the balljoint location is satisfactory. Remove the spring compressor.

74 Lower the vehicle so that its weight is on its wheels. Refit the rebound stops.

75 Tighten the shock absorber rod nut to the specified torque, holding the rod stationary. Refit the plastic cap.

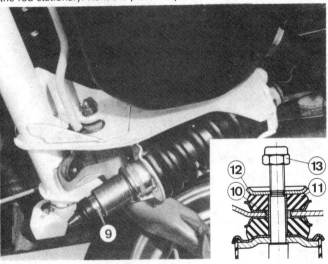

Fig. 12.105 Fitting Estate rear suspension unit (Sec 17)

9   Identification mark   11   Rubber spacer   13   Nut
10 Ring   12   Washer

Rear suspension arm removal and refitting (Estate/Van)

76 Working inside the car, remove the handbrake lever surround. Disconnect the handbrake cable on the side to be worked on.

77 Remove the rear suspension unit as just described.

78 Lower the rear of the vehicle onto its wheels until it is possible to remove the rear anti-roll bar clamp on the side concerned. Free the handbrake cable and remove the suspension arm nut on the side concerned.

79 Raise the rear of the vehicle again and support it securely. Remove the roadwheel on the side concerned.

80 Remove the handbrake cable clips. Disconnect the brake flexible hydraulic hose; plug or clamp the hose to minimize fluid loss. Take precautions to keep dirt out of open hydraulic lines. Also remove the brake union clip.

81 Pull the handbrake cable clear. Support the suspension arm and withdraw the pivot bolt (photo). The arm can then be removed from the crossmember.

82 Refit in the reverse order of removal, noting the following points:

    (a)   Use new brake union and handbrake cable clips
    (b)   Use a new self-locking nut on the suspension arm pivot bolt; tighten it to the specified torque with the rear of the vehicle still raised
    (c)   Adjust the handbrake and bleed the brake hydraulic system on completion

Rear suspension arm overhaul (Estate/Van)

83 The taper bearings and their seals can be renewed if they are worn, but the operation is best left to a Peugeot dealer. Several special tools and precision measuring equipment are required.

84 If the arm is bent or otherwise damaged it should be renewed.

Power-assisted steering (general)

85 Power-assisted steering is available on certain models. The power assistance is derived from a pump driven by the alternator drivebelt.

86 Maintenance consists of checking the drivebelt tension and condition (Section 18, paragraphs 5 to 7 of this Supplement) and checking the fluid level. The fluid reservoir is mounted on the front rail under the bonnet. The three level markings on the reservoir are:

MIN   –   *minimum level when cold*
COLD   –   *normal level when cold*
HOT   –   *maximum level when hot*

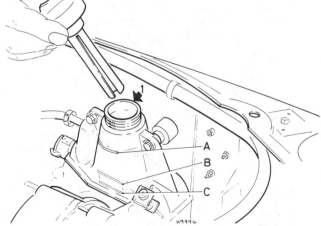

Fig. 12.106 Power steering fluid reservoir (1) showing level marks (Sec 17)

A   Hot maximum   B   Cold maximum   C   Minimum

87 Topping up should only be done with clean fluid of the correct type (see Specifications). Regular need for topping up can only be due to a leak, which should be rectified. If the pump is run dry it will be damaged; disconnect the drivebelt rather than let this happen.

Power-assisted steering system bleeding
88 If the fluid level falls so low that air enters the pump, or after components have been renewed, the system should be bled as follows.
89 Top the reservoir up with the specified fluid.
90 Start the engine and allow it to idle. Turn the steering wheel from lock to lock two or three times. Do not hold the steering wheel on full lock.
91 Stop the engine and check the reservoir fluid level; top up if necessary. Inspect the power steering unions for leaks.

Power-assisted steering pump removal and refitting
92 Disconnect the battery negative lead.
93 Remove the alternator and the alternator/steering pump drivebelt.
94 Unbolt the tensioner bracket from the steering pump.
95 Place a container below the pump. Disconnect the fluid pipes from the pump and allow the fluid to drain.
96 Remove the three mounting bolts and lift out the pump.
97 Refit by reversing the removal operations. Tension the drivebelt as described in Section 18.
98 Before running the engine, pour approximately 0.3 litre (0.53 pint) of fluid into the reservoir. Slowly move the steering wheel from lock to lock a couple of times.
99 Bleed the system as described earlier in this Section.

Steering rack and pinion removal and refitting (XU engined vehicles)
100 This procedure is based on the maker's instructions, which apply to LHD vehicles. Appropriate allowances must be made for RHD.
101 There is no specific procedure for removing the power-assisted steering gear from petrol-engined vehicles.
102 Slacken the front wheel nuts or bolts. Raise and support the front of the vehicle and remove the front roadwheels.
103 Remove the track rod end balljoint nuts. Separate the balljoints from the steering arms using a proprietary balljoint separator.
104 Remove the gearshift swivel pin (Fig. 12.108).
105 Remove the hairpin clip and release the gear selector rod from its balljoint (Fig. 12.109).
106 Separate the column flexible coupling by removing the two nuts which secure it to the pinion flange. Push the coupling and column upwards slightly.
107 Remove the two steering gear-to-crossmember bolts.
108 Remove the rack-and-pinion assembly from the right-hand side of the vehicle, being careful not to damage the bellows.
109 Refit by reversing the removal operations, noting the following points:

(a) Preset both track rods to the dimension shown in Fig. 12.110.
(b) Apply a smear of molybdenum-based grease to the gear-change balljoints
(c) Tighten all fastenings to the specified torque. Use new nuts to secure the flexible coupling and the track rod end balljoints
(d) Have the front wheel alignment checked on completion

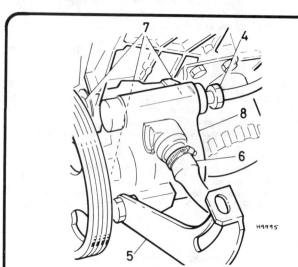

Fig. 12.107 Removing the power steering pump (8) (Sec 17)

4   Fluid pipe union   6   Fluid hose
5   Tensioner bracket   7   Mounting bolts

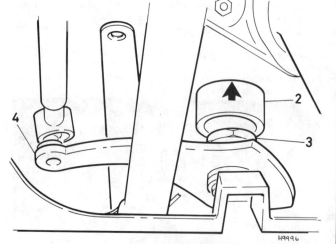

Fig. 12.108 Gearshift cap (2), pin (3) and swivel (4) (Sec 17)

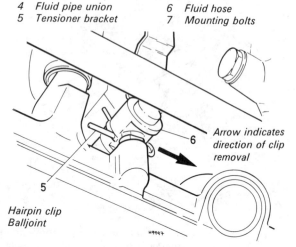

Arrow indicates direction of clip removal

5   Hairpin clip
6   Balljoint

Fig. 12.109 Gear selector rod attachment (Sec 17)

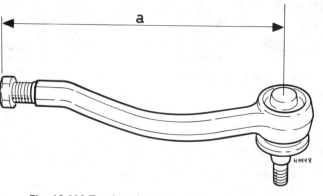

Fig. 12.110 Track rod setting dimension (Sec 17)

a   190.0 mm

18 Electrical system

Low-maintenance battery (all models)

1   A low-maintenance battery is fitted to later models as original equipment, and may well be supplied as a replacement for an older type.

2   If the battery has provision for checking the electrolyte level, this should be done annually (or as directed on the battery case). Even if the battery is claimed to be 'maintenance-free' it is wise to check the level occasionally.

3   The battery terminals and clamps must be kept clean and free of corrosion on all types of battery.

Alternator removal and refitting (XU engine)

4   Refer to Chapter 10, Section 9, but note that because the pivot bolt cannot be withdrawn completely, the front fixing is slotted (photo).

Alternator drivebelt tension adjustment (XU engine)

5   The ribbed drivebelt used on this engine runs under greater tension than the conventional V-belt. For this reason a positive tensioning arrangement is employed (photo).

6   Slacken the alternator pivot bolt and the adjusting strap pivot bolt. Screw the adjuster bolt in or out to achieve the desired tension, then tighten the pivot bolts.

7   The correct belt tension is given in the Specifications. In the absence of the proper tensioning gauge, set the belt so that it can be deflected approximately a quarter of an inch (say 6 mm) under firm thumb pressure.

Alternator with integral regulator brush renewal

8   There are so many different types of alternator fitted that it is not practical to describe the procedure for each one in detail. This procedure applies to the Paris-Rhone 750W alternator; detail differences will be found with other makes.

9   Remove the alternator from the vehicle.

10 Remove the rear shield: some force may be needed to prise it off (photo).

11 Remove the two screws which secure the regulator/brush holder assembly. Disconnect the regulator lead from the spade terminal and slide the assembly out (photos).

12 Unsolder the old brushes and solder on the new ones. Have this done professionally if you lack skill in soldering.

13 Clean the slip rings with a solvent-moistened cloth. Inspect them for excessive wear or damage which may cause early brush failure.

14 Refit and secure the regulator/brush holder and the rear shield, then refit the alternator to the vehicle.

Alternator testing fitted to vehicle (all models)

15 Should it appear that the alternator is not charging the battery, check first that the drivebelt is intact and in good condition and that its tension is correct. Also check the condition and security of the alternator electrical connections and the battery leads.

16 Accurate assessment of alternator output requires special equipment and a degree of skill. A rough idea of whether output is adequate can be gained by using a voltmeter (range 0 to 15 or 0 to 20 volts) as follows.

17 Connect the voltmeter across the battery terminals. Switch on the headlights and note the voltage reading; it should be between 12 and 13 volts.

18 Start the engine and run it at a fast idle (approx 1500 rpm). Read the voltmeter: it should indicate 13 to 14 volts.

19 With the engine still running at a fast idle, switch on as many electrical appliances as possible (heated rear windows, heater blower etc). The voltage at the battery should be maintained at 13 to 14 volts. Increase the engine speed slightly if necessary to keep the voltage up.

18.4 Alternator front bracket and pivot bolt

18.5 Adjusting the alternator drivebelt tension

18.10 Removing the alternator rear shield

18.11A Disconnecting the alternator voltage regulator lead

18.11B Alternator regulator/brush holder assembly removed

20 If alternator output is low or zero, check the brushes. If the brushes are OK, seek expert advice.
21 Occasionally the condition may arise where the alternator output is excessive. Clues to this condition are constantly blowing bulbs; brightness of lights varying considerably with engine speed; overheating of alternator and battery, possibly with steam or fumes coming from the battery. This condition is almost certainly due to a defective voltage regulator, but expert advice should be sought.

Headlamp unit removal and refitting (1983 on)
22 Remove the front grille.
23 Release the retaining spring from the rear of the headlamp unit and rotate the securing lever towards the centre of the car. Pull the headlamp unit outwards to free it from its fixing stub (photos).
24 Refit in the reverse order of removal.

Headlamp beam alignment (1983 on)
25 The location of the adjusting screws is shown in Fig. 12.111.
26 Except on models with remote control of beam aim, a load compensator is fitted at the back of each headlamp unit. The centre ('O') position is for average loading; position 'V' (vide) raises the aim for light loading, and position (C) (charge) lowers the aim for heavy loading.

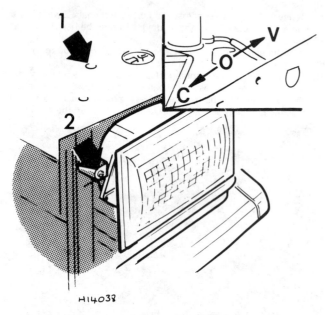

H14038

Fig. 12.111 Headlamp beam adjusting screws – later models (Sec 18)

1 Vertical adjustment
2 Horizontal adjustment
C Laden
O Normal
V Empty

Headlamp load adjuster description and overhaul (Estate)
27 When fitted, the headlamp load adjuster enables the headlamp beam to be altered from the driving seat. The system operates by hydraulic pressure; malfunction of the control or of either actuator means that the complete system must be renewed.
28 The headlamp actuators can be removed after unbolting their brackets and extracting the securing clips (photo). To remove the control itself, release the right-hand lower panel, prise off the control knob and remove the two securing screws. Displace the bulkhead grommet and feed the hydraulic pipes through the bulkhead.
29 After refitting, have the headlamps adjusted with no load on board and the load adjuster set to the highest possible beam alignment.

Dim-dip lighting operation
30 All models manufactured from late 1986 are fitted with a dim-dip lighting system, which essentially prevents the vehicle from being driven with the sidelights alone switched on.
31 When the ignition is switched on with the sidelights also switched on, a relay is energised, closing the internal contacts and supplying current to the dipped beam circuit via the resistor. This causes the dip filaments in the headlamps to be illuminated at one-sixth dipped beam brightness. The relay winding is earthed through the headlamp main beam filaments so that the relay is de-energised when the main beam is switched on.

Front sidelight/direction indicators bulb renewal (1983 on)
32 Remove the headlamp unit on the side concerned.
33 Depress the clip or clips which secure the front light unit and remove it (photos).
34 Extract the bulbholder and renew the bulb. Refit the bulbholder, the light unit and the headlamp.

Side repeater lamps description
35 These are fitted to later models to operate in conjunction with the direction indicator circuit.
36 The lamps are a press fit in the front wings and in the event of bulb failure, the lamp is supplied as a complete assembly.

Rear light cluster bulb renewal (Saloon – 1983 on)
37 The rear light bulbs are mounted on a printed circuit board similar to that shown in Chapter 10, Section 20, but the board is released by depressing the lugs at each end (photo).

Rear light cluster bulb renewal (Estate)
38 Open the tailgate and remove the single securing screw from the top of the cluster (photo).
39 Pull the cluster outwards and upwards. Unclip the printed circuit board to gain access to the bulbs.
40 Refit in the reverse order of removal.

Number plate light bulb renewal (Estate)
41 If the light unit is mounted in the bumper, prise it out to gain access to the bulb.

18.23A Headlamp retaining spring

18.23B Headlamp securing lever

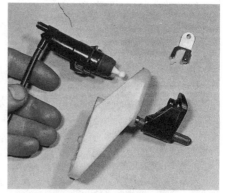

18.28 Headlamp load adjuster, bracket and clip

42 If the light unit is mounted on the tailgate, remove the two securing screws and extract the unit. Separate the lens from the bulbholder, extract the old bulb and fit a new one (photo).
43 Refit in the reverse order of removal.

Map reading light bulb renewal
44 Carefully prise the light from its location (photo).
45 Extract the festoon bulb and press in a new one. Make sure the bulb is well gripped by the spring contacts.
46 Press the light back into place.

Rear window wiper motor removal and refitting (Estate)
47 Disconnect the battery earth lead.
48 Remove the wiper arm, then remove the spindle nut and washers.
49 Open the tailgate and remove the trim panel by tugging or prising it free. Try not to break the securing clips.
50 Remove the two bolts which secure the wiper motor. Disconnect the electrical leads and remove the motor (photo).
51 No spare parts are available for repair of the wiper motor; if defective it must be renewed. Check first that the relay is not at fault (photo).
52 Refit in the reverse order of removal.

Rear window washer jet removal and refitting (Estate)
53 Carefully pull or prise the jet from its location, taking care not to damage the paintwork. Pull the jet off the elbow connector (photo). Put a clothes peg on the hose to stop it falling back into the tailgate.
54 Refit in the reverse order of removal.

Instrument panel removal and refitting (1983 on)
55 Disconnect the battery earth lead.
56 Remove the four screws which secure the instrument panel surround. Remove the surround.
57 Release the instrument panel from the two clips which secure its lower edge. Carefully draw the panel forwards until it is possible to disconnect the speedometer cable and the multi-plugs.
58 Refit in the reverse order of removal. Refer to Fig. 12.112 for details of multi-plug identification. When connecting the speedometer cable push it home until it clicks into place.

Oil level warning system description (1985 models)
59 An engine oil level warning system is fitted to 1985 model year vehicles. The components of the system are a level sensor in the sump, a warning light in the instrument cluster and an electronic control unit mounted under the facia.

18.33A Front parking lamp securing clip

18.33B Front parking/indicator lamp unit withdrawn

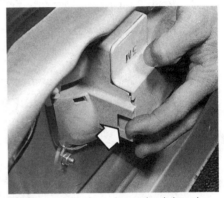
18.37 Location of rear lamp circuit board retaining lug (arrowed) (Saloon)

18.38 Removing rear lamp cluster fixing screw (Estate)

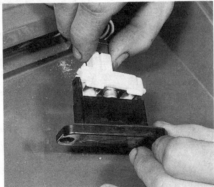
18.42 Removing rear number plate lamp (Estate)

18.44 Removing the map reading lamp

18.50 Location of rear wiper motor fixing bolts (arrowed) on Estate

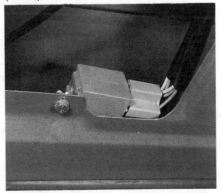
18.51 Location of rear wiper motor relay (Estate)

18.53 Removing rear window washer jet (Estate)

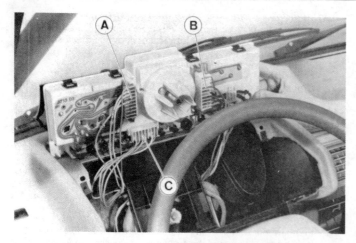

Fig. 12.112 Instrument panel multi-plugs (Sec 18)

A   Green (9-way)   B   White (10-way)   C   White (8-way)

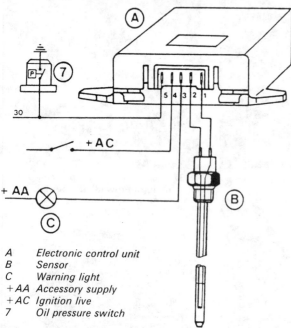

A   Electronic control unit
B   Sensor
C   Warning light
+AA   Accessory supply
+AC   Ignition live
7   Oil pressure switch

**Fig. 12.113 Circuit diagram for oil level warning system
(Sec 18)**

60 When the ignition is switched on, an electric current is passed
through the level sensor. The resistance change in the sensor caused
by the heating effect of the current varies according to the depth of
immersion of the sensor in the oil. The electronic control unit measures
the sensor resistance change and determines whether or not the oil
level is low.
61 Normal oil level is signalled by the warning light illuminating for
two seconds when the ignition is switched on, then going out. Low oil
level is indicated if the light flashes after the first two seconds.
62 The system does not operate when the engine is running. This is
achieved by earthing the control unit through the oil pressure warning
light switch (Some late 1984 models may not be so wired, but can be
modified – consult a Peugeot dealer).
63 False warnings may result if the vehicle is parked on a slope, or if
the engine is stopped and re-started before the oil has had time to
return to the sump. To stop the light flashing in such cases, park on
level ground and stop the engine for a few seconds.

Heater blower rheostat removal and refitting (pre-1983)
64 Disconnect the battery earth lead.
65 Pull the knobs off the heater slide controls.

66 Remove the cigarette lighter element. Extract the lighter body by
twisting it until a stop is reached, then pulling it out. Disconnect the
electrical leads from the lighter.
67 Remove the cigarette lighter mounting ring, then pull out the
heater control panel.
68 Withdraw the blower rheostat and disconnect its leads.
69 Refit in the reverse order of removal. When refitting the cigarette
lighter body, note that the groove in the body lines up with the notch in
the mounting ring.

Heater blower rheostat removal and refitting (1983 on)
70 Disconnect the battery earth lead.
71 Remove the lower half of the steering column cowl, which is
secured by five screws. Remove the two screws so exposed to free the
heater control panel side finisher; free the finisher on the passenger
side by removing the two screws which are accessible from inside the
glovebox.
72 Remove the two central air vents by carefully pushing them from
above and behind. Also remove the ashtray and coin box.
73 Remove the four screws from around the clock aperture (Fig.
12.114). Pull off the control knobs and remove the front part of the
heater control panel.
74 Remove the three screws which secure the top of the heater control
panel. Tilt the panel forwards and disengage the two lower retaining
lugs (photos).
75 Free the rheostat wires from the multi-plug, using a small
screwdriver. Remove the rheostat.
76 Refitting is a reversal of the removal procedure.

**Fig. 12.114 Screws (4) around clock aperture securing
instrument panel (Sec 18)**

*Heater blower control box description and testing
(1983 on)*
77 On later models the heater blower rheostat does not carry blower
motor current; it simply passes a signal to a control box, consisting of a
power transistor and a heat sink. The control box is located on the
left-hand front wing valance.
78 To test the control box in the event of blower motor malfunction,
first refer to Fig. 12.115, to identify the control box terminals.
79 With the ignition switched on, disconnect wire M27C from the
control box. Connect control box terminal M27C to earth. If the blower
motor now operates, there is a fault either in the rheostat or in wire
M27C. If the motor does not operate, proceed as follows.
80 Disconnect wire M27B from the control box and connect the wire
to earth. If the blower motor now operates, the control box is defective;
if not, there is a fault in the motor or its wiring. Do not forget to check
the fuse.
81 Remake the original connections on completion.

Fuse and relay details (1983 on)
82 The fuse/relay panel is considerably more complex on later models.
Refer to Figs. 12.116 and 12.117 for details of the connectors.

277

18.74A Removing heater control panel screw from air vent aperture

18.74B Rear view of heater control panel

Fig. 12.115 Heater control box terminal identification (Sec 18)

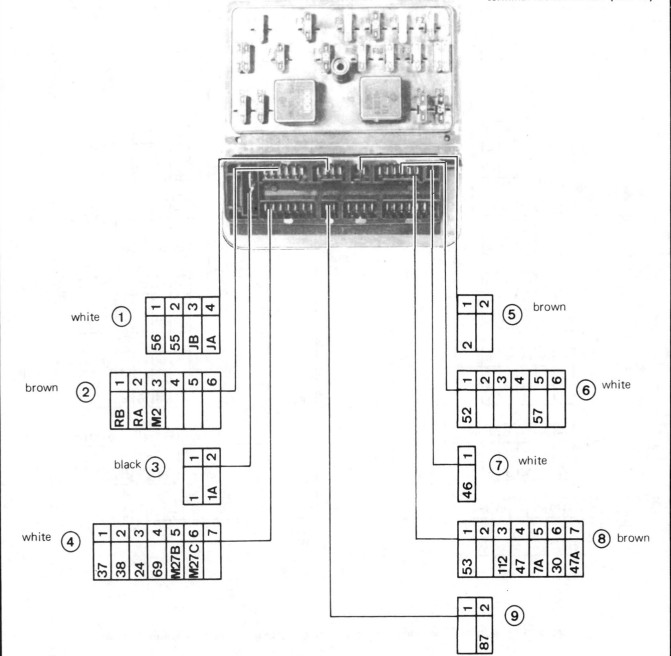

Fig. 12.116 Fuse/relay panel front connectors. Refer also to main wiring diagram (Sec 18)

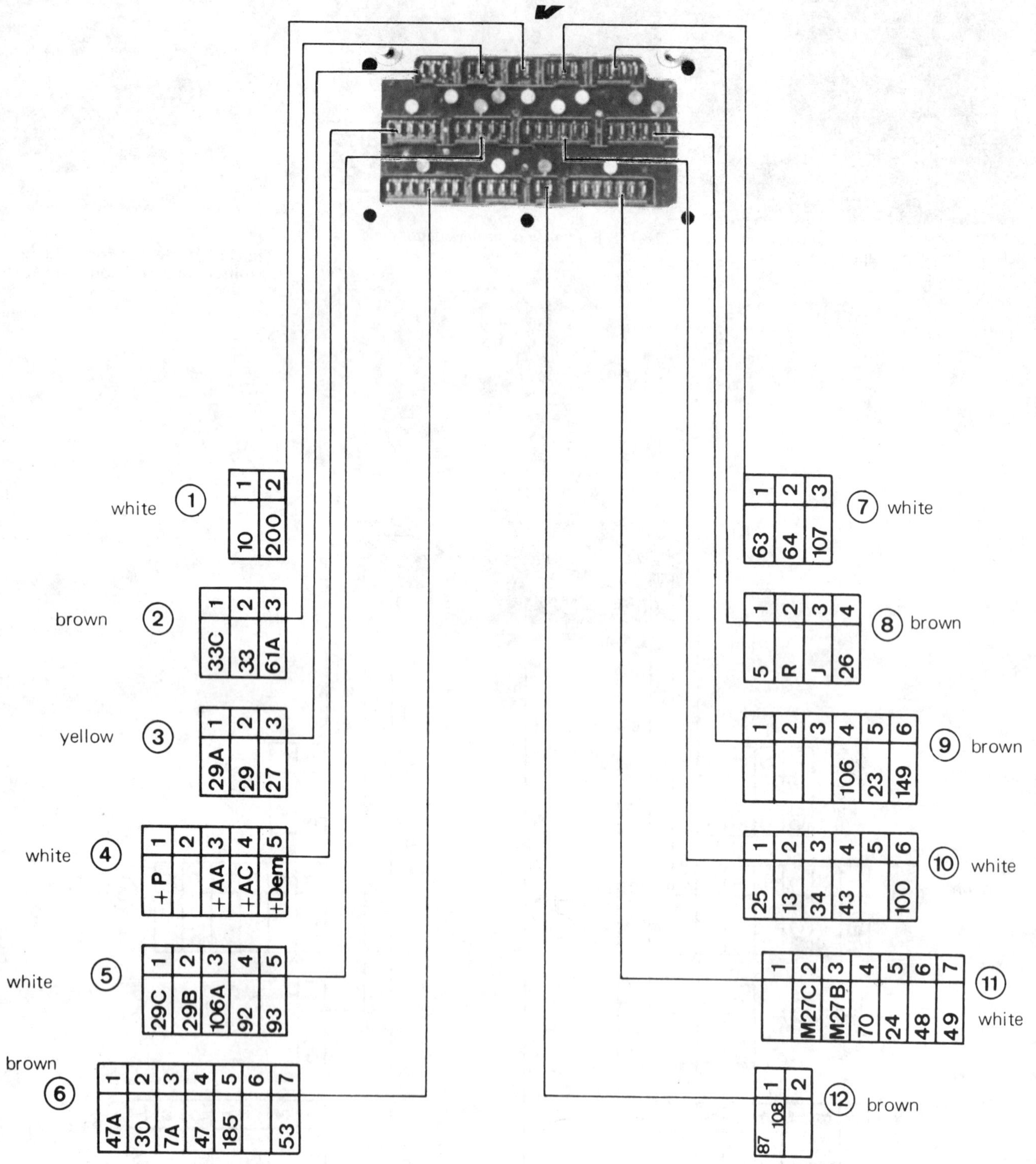

Fig. 12.117 Fuse/relay panel rear connectors. Refer also to main wiring diagram (Sec 18)

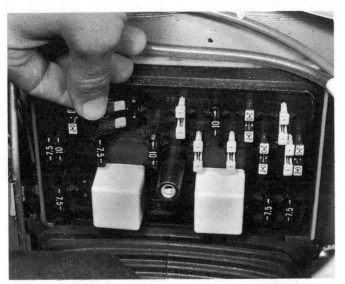

18.83 Removing blade fuse from later type of fuse panel

83 Fuse functions are given in the Specifications. The fuses themselves are of the blade type (photo). An intact fuse has a wire link visible in its centre section; a blown fuse does not.
84 The two relays on the board supply the accessories and the heated rear window.

Central door locking system description
85 Fitted to some models from 1981, the central door locking system uses electro-mechanical lock units to actuate all door locks by

imitating the position of the driver's door lock. Manual locking and unlocking is still possible in case of electrical failure.
86 Access to the lock solenoids and wiring is obtained after removal of the door trim panels.
87 A further development of the central locking system allows the driver to lock or unlock all doors using an infra-red transmitter (remote control PLIP) held in the hand. The transmitter gives out a coded signal which is recognised by a receiver in the car.

Electrically-operated windows description
88 Operation of the front door windows on some later models is by means of electric motors, controlled by two switches in the centre console.
89 Access to the winding mechanism is as described in Chapter 11, Section 10.

Electrically-operated sunroof (1985 on)
90 This is fitted as standard to GTX models and is available as an option on other versions.

Radio interference from front brake calipers
91 On pre-1986 models it is possible for 'white noise' or 'hash' type radio interference to be generated in the front brakes, especially when driving on damp or salted roads. The interference is passed into the electrical system via the pad wear warning wires.
92 The interference may be reduced by earthing the calipers or the strut piston rods. Later DBA calipers have a 5 mm diameter hole in the anti-rotation plate for the attachment of an earth strap; Girling calipers have a blind tapped hole next to the hydraulic hose connection, which will accept a screw of 5 mm diameter, 0.8 mm pitch and 10 mm maximum length, for the same purpose.
93 Do not attempt to drill holes or otherwise modify calipers in order to attach earth straps. If necessary consult a Peugeot dealer.
94 On GTX models with DBA calipers, the earth strap should be secured by a mud deflector retaining bolt.

1 Control box
2 Master actuator
3 Driver's door lock
4 Link rod
5 Slave actuators
6 Passenger's door lock

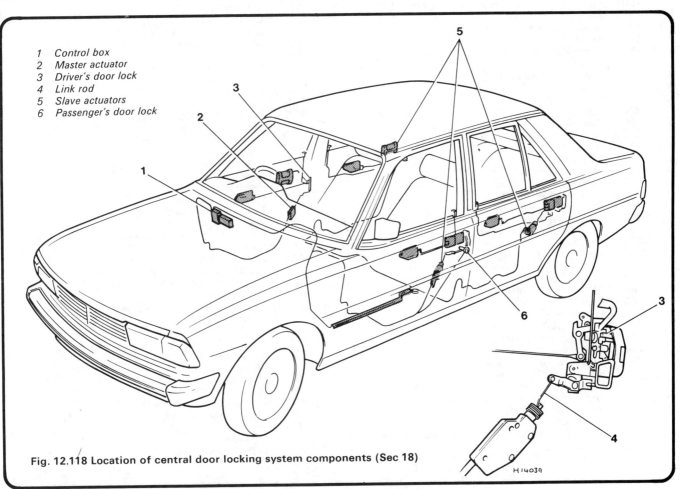

Fig. 12.118 Location of central door locking system components (Sec 18)

Key to all wiring diagrams. Not all items are fitted to every model

1	Headlight	32A	Windscreen wiper/windscreen washer switch
2	Front direction indicator	32B	Lighting/direction indicator/horn control switch
3	Front sidelight	33	Headlight flasher relay
4	Direction indicator repeater	34	Sidelights
5	Starter relay	35	Cigar lighter, front
5A	Neutral safety relay	35A	Cigar lighter, rear
6	Alternator	35B	Illumination, cigar lighter
7	Oil pressure switch	36	Clock
7A	Oil level indicator	37	Direction indicator repeater light
7B	Control box, oil level indicator	38	Fuel gauge
7C	Checking diode, oil level indicator	38A	Warning light, low fuel level
8	Electro-magnetic fan or electric fan	39	Main beam warning light
8A	Disengaging fan relay	39A	Dip beam warning light
8B	Air conditioning electric fan	40	Hazard warning light
8C	Electric fan relay	41	Rev counter
8D	Diodes	42	Sidelight warning light
9	Temperature switch, fan clutch or electric fan	43	Brake safety warning light
9A	Temperature switch, fan clutch, cooling system	43A	Brake safety warning light checking diode
9B	Temperature switch, fan clutch, lube system	44	Coolant temperature gauge
9C	Sender unit, oil temperature gauge	45	Oil pressure warning light
10	Horn	45A	Warning light, oil temperature
11	Headlight relay	45B	Warning light, oil pressure and temperature
12	Battery	46	Choke warning light
12A	Battery cut-out	47	Oil and water warning light
13	Starter motor	48	Preheater warning light
14	Brake pads	49	Charge/discharge warning light
15	Sender unit, coolant temperature	50	Instrument panel lighting
15A	Switch, coolant temperature	50A	Gearchange gate light
15B	Coolant temperature warning light switch or coolant temperature warning light	50B	Rheostat, gearchange gate light
15C	Resistor, coolant temperature gauge	50C	Switch lighting
15D	Checking diode, coolant temperature warning light	51	Heater lighting
15E	Switch, coolant level	51A	Console lighting
16	Brake fluid reservoir	51B	Console lighting rheostat
17	Stop switch	52	Glove compartment light
18	Reversing light switch	52A	Glove compartment light switch
19	Starter safety cut-out	53	Front door switch
20	Idling cut-out or carburettor resistance	53A	Rear door switch
21	Regulator	54	Interior lighting
22	Coil	54A	Light under facia panel
22A	Coil relay	54B	Map reading light
22B	Coil resistor	54C	Illumination, courtesy mirror
22C	Coil resistor relay	55	Handbrake switch
23	Distributor	56	Hazard warning light switch
23A	Pulse generator	57	Sun roof switch
24	Windscreen wiper	57A	Sun roof motor
24A	Windscreen wiper relay	57E	Locking relay, sun roof
24B	Windscreen wiper timer	58	Steering lock
24C	Rear window wiper	58B	Ignition switch light
24D	Windscreen wiper unit	59	Preheat – starter switch
25	Windscreen washer pump	59A	Preheater plugs
25A	Rear window washer pump	60	Pump cut-out motor or solenoid valve
26	Heating/ventilation fan, front	61	Preheater warning light switch
26A	Rear heating/ventilation fan	62	Preheater relay
26B	Heating/ventilation fan switch	63	Direction indicator and horn control
26C	Air conditioning blower	64	Boot or rear compartment lighting
26D	Relay, air conditioning blower	64A	Boot lid or tailgate switch
27	Heating/ventilation switch or rheostat	65	Fuel gauge tank unit with or without low fuel warning
27A	Rheostat resistor or heating/ventilation fan resistor	65A	External tank unit resistor
27B	Rear heating/ventilation switch	65B	Rheostat, fuel gauge
27C	Air conditioning control unit	66	Number plate light
28	Choke warning light switch	67	Reversing lights
29	Heated rear window switch	68	Stop light
29A	Heated rear window	68A	Stop/tail lamp (twin filament)
30	Windscreen wiper/windscreen washer switch	68B	Stop/tail lamp (twin filament)
30A	Rear window wiper/washer switch	69	Rear direction indicator
31	Direction indicator flasher unit	70	Tail lamp
32	Lighting – windscreen wiper/windscreen washer switch	71	Tailgate switch
		72	Door mounted light

Key to all wiring diagrams (continued). Not all items are fitted to every model

73	Left-hand relay window winder switch		118	Control pressure regulator
73A	Locking relay, LH rear window winder		119	Additional air control
74	Window winder switch, LH front		120	Sensor plate switch
74A	Locking relay, LH front window winder		121	Cold starting injector
75	Interlock, rear window winder		122	Thermal time switch
76	Window winder switch, RH front		123	Speed regulator switch
76A	Locking relay, RH front window winder		123A	Speed regulator electronic unit
77	Window winder switch, RH rear		123B	Speed regulator servo
77A	Locking relay, RH rear window winder		123C	Speed regulator safety switch
78	Left-hand window rear switch		123D	Speed regulator disengagement switch
79	Right-hand window winder rear switch		123E	Speed regulator pick-up
80	Window winder motor		123F	Speed regulator fuse
80A	Window winder relay		123G	Safety relay speed regulator
81	Diagnostic socket		123H	Vacuum capsule
81A	TDC sensor, diagnostic socket		123I	Safety relay
82	Door lock switch		123J	Main switch, speed regulator
83	Control box, central door locking		125	Radio connection
83A	Actuator, door lock		125D	Radio speaker, front RH
83B	Actuator, fuel filler flap		125G	Radio speaker, front LH
86	Fuel pump		125AD	Radio speaker, rear RH
86A	Primary fuel pump		125AG	Radio speaker, rear LH
87	Solenoid valve		125E	Connector, radio speaker
87A	Solenoid valve control switch		129	Speed sensor
88	Ignition pick-up		142	Tachymetric relay, fuel cut-off on over-run
89	Electronic unit or amplifier module		142A	Relay, fuel injection cut-off on over-run
90	Rear foglights		142B	Control unit, for delay of fuel injection cut-off
90A	Rear foglight switch		150	Warning light, economy
90B	Rear foglight warning light		150A	Vacuum pick-up
91	Relay		151	Switch, water detector
91B	Tachymetric relay		151A	Warning light, water detector switch
91C	Accessory relay		152	Connector, front fog lamps
91D	Heated rear window relay		152A	Switch, front fog lamps
92	Connecting terminal		152B	Relay, front fog lamps
92A	Connection board		170	Relay ignition system
93	Services connection board		171	Calculator, ignition advance
93A	Fusebox No 1		172	Control unit, knock detector
93B	Fusebox No 2		172A	Knock detector
94	Conductive tailgate stay		173	Warning light, LED, knock detector
95	Brake servo vacuum switch		174	Relay, capsule venting
96	Brake pedal travel switch		175	Electronic relay
97	Headlight washer/wiper switch		180	Relay, fuel injection system
98	Headlight washer pump		181	Calculator, fuel injection system
99	Headlight wiper motor		182	Air flow sensor
99A	Headlight wiper relay		183	Injector
100	Pressure drop indicator		184	Throttle switch unit
101	Tachograph		185	Temperature sensor, engine
102	Flasher light		190	Sensor, fuel pressure
102A	Flasher light switch		191	Sensor, turbocharger excess pressure
103	Centre interior light		192	Gauge, turbocharger pressure
103A	Centre interior light switch		195	100 mbar switch – turbo fuel load control, turbo injection intercooler
104	Feed warning light		196	Switch, advance curve selector
104A	Feed warning light switch		197	Resistor, full load circuit (turbo injection intercooler)
105	Air fan		200	Control unit, voice synthesizer
105A	Air fan switch		200A	Filter
106	Warning bell		201	Test button, voice synthesizer
106A	Warning bell switch		210	Trip computer
107	Electrical plug		211	Display control
108	Compressor clutch		212	Fuel flow sensor
108A	Compressor clutch switch		213	Digital display
108B	Relay, compressor clutch		M	Earth
109	Thermostat		+P	Supply from the battery
109A	Protection diode, thermostat		+aa	Accessory supply
110	Constant pressure unit		+ac	Supply from the ignition switch
111	Idling speed compensation solenoid valve			
111A	Air conditioning shut off pressure switch			

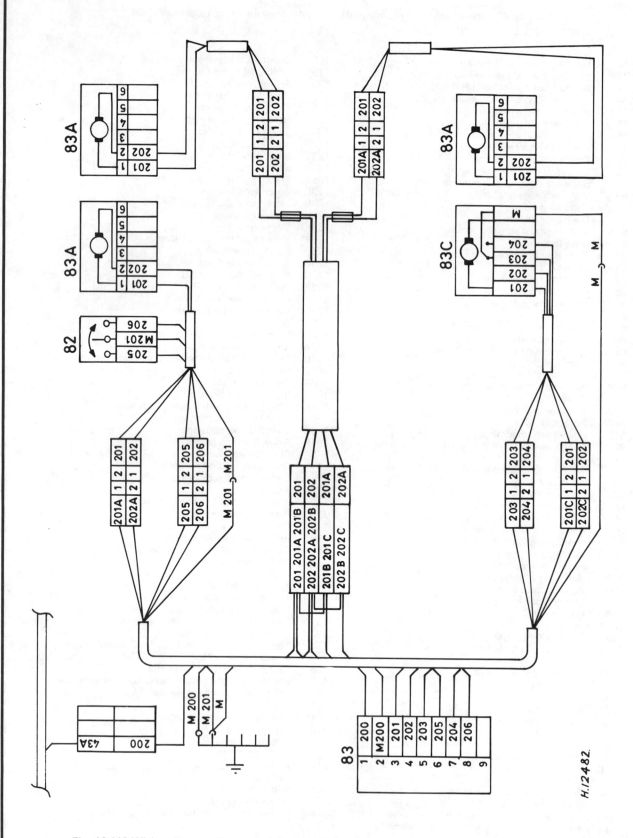

Fig. 12.119 Wiring diagram for central door locking system (typical). For key see pages 280 and 281

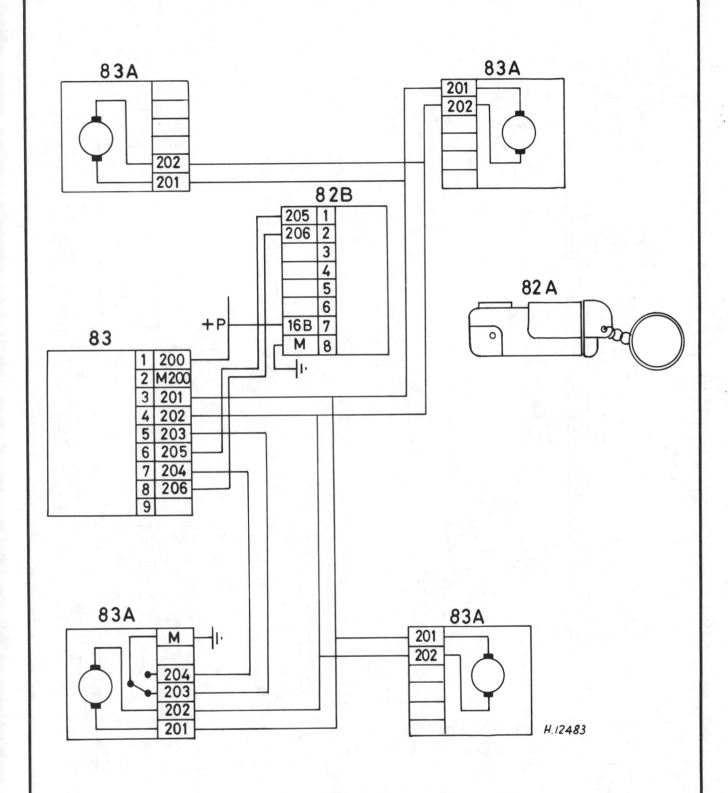

Fig. 12.120 Wiring diagram for central door locking system with keyless locking and unlocking

82	Door lock switch	83	Control box
82A	Infra-red transmitter	83A	Slave actuators
82B	Infra-red receiver	83C	Master actuator

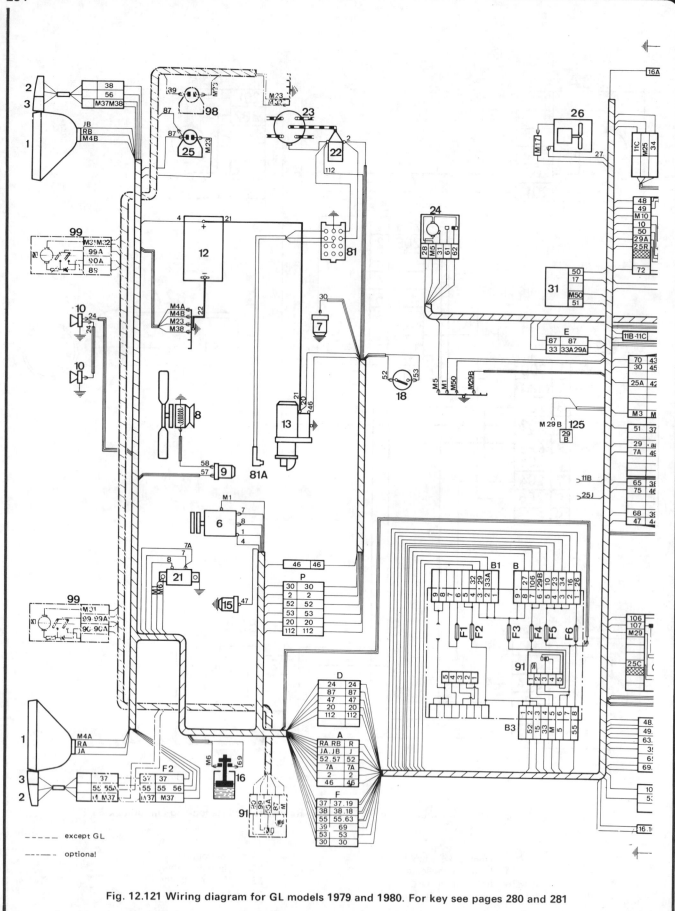

Fig. 12.121 Wiring diagram for GL models 1979 and 1980. For key see pages 280 and 281

- - - - - except GL

- - - - - optional

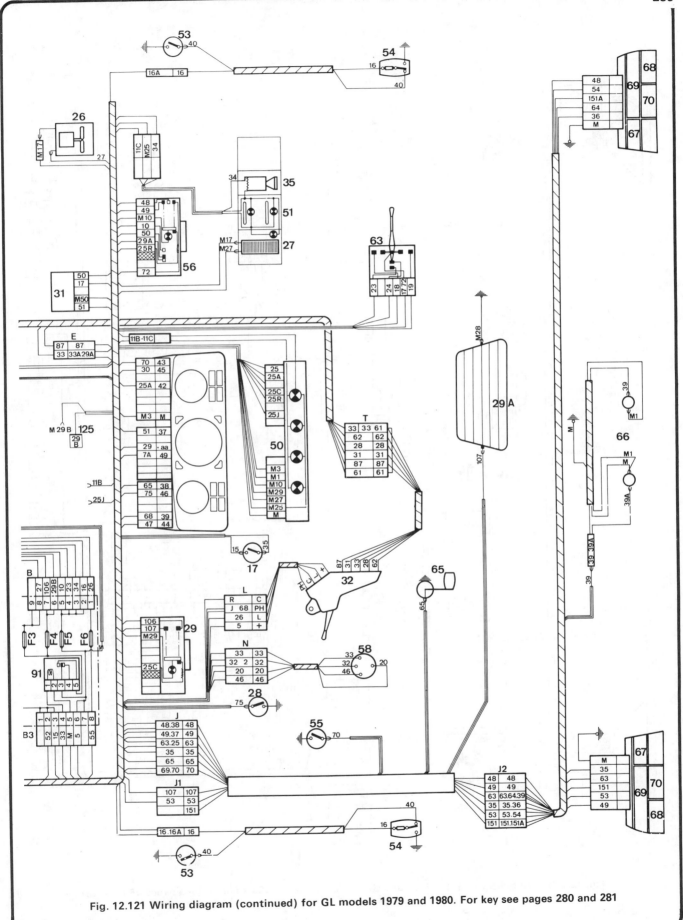

Fig. 12.121 Wiring diagram (continued) for GL models 1979 and 1980. For key see pages 280 and 281

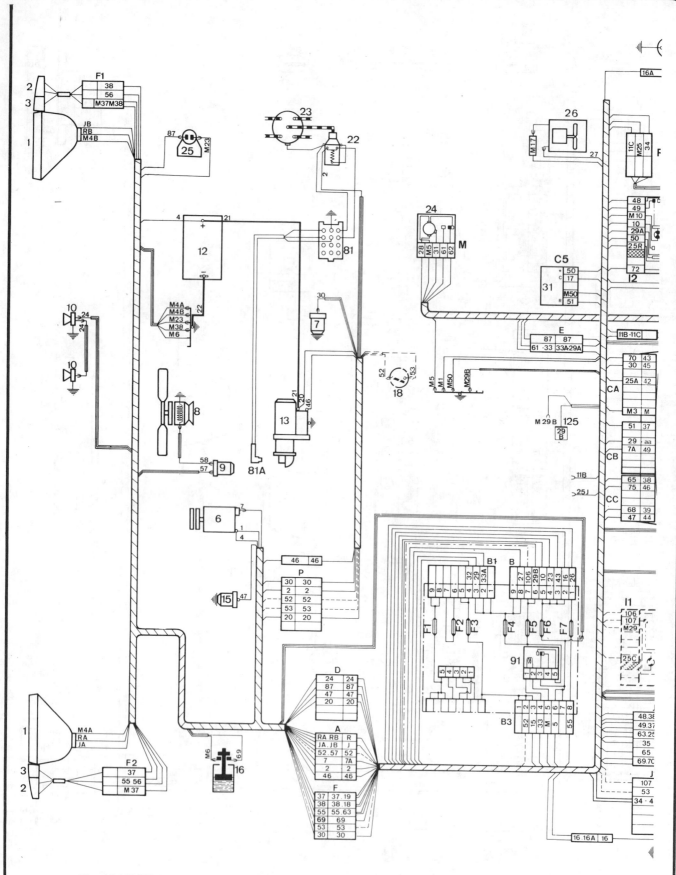

Fig. 12.122 Wiring diagram for Saloon and GL models 1980 and 1981. For key see pages 280 and 281

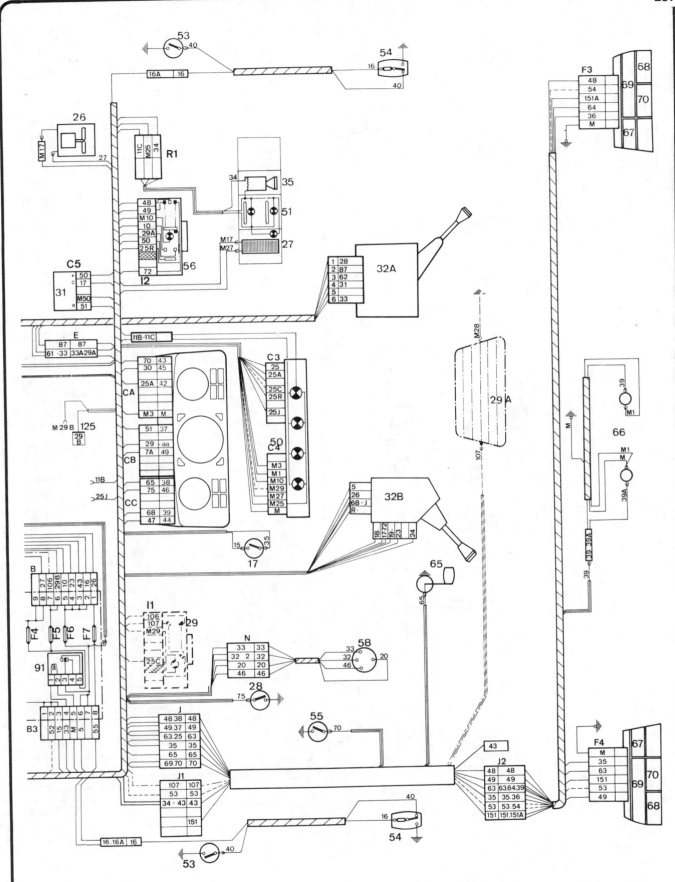

Fig. 12.122 Wiring diagram (continued) for Saloon and GL models 1980 and 1981. For key see pages 280 and 281

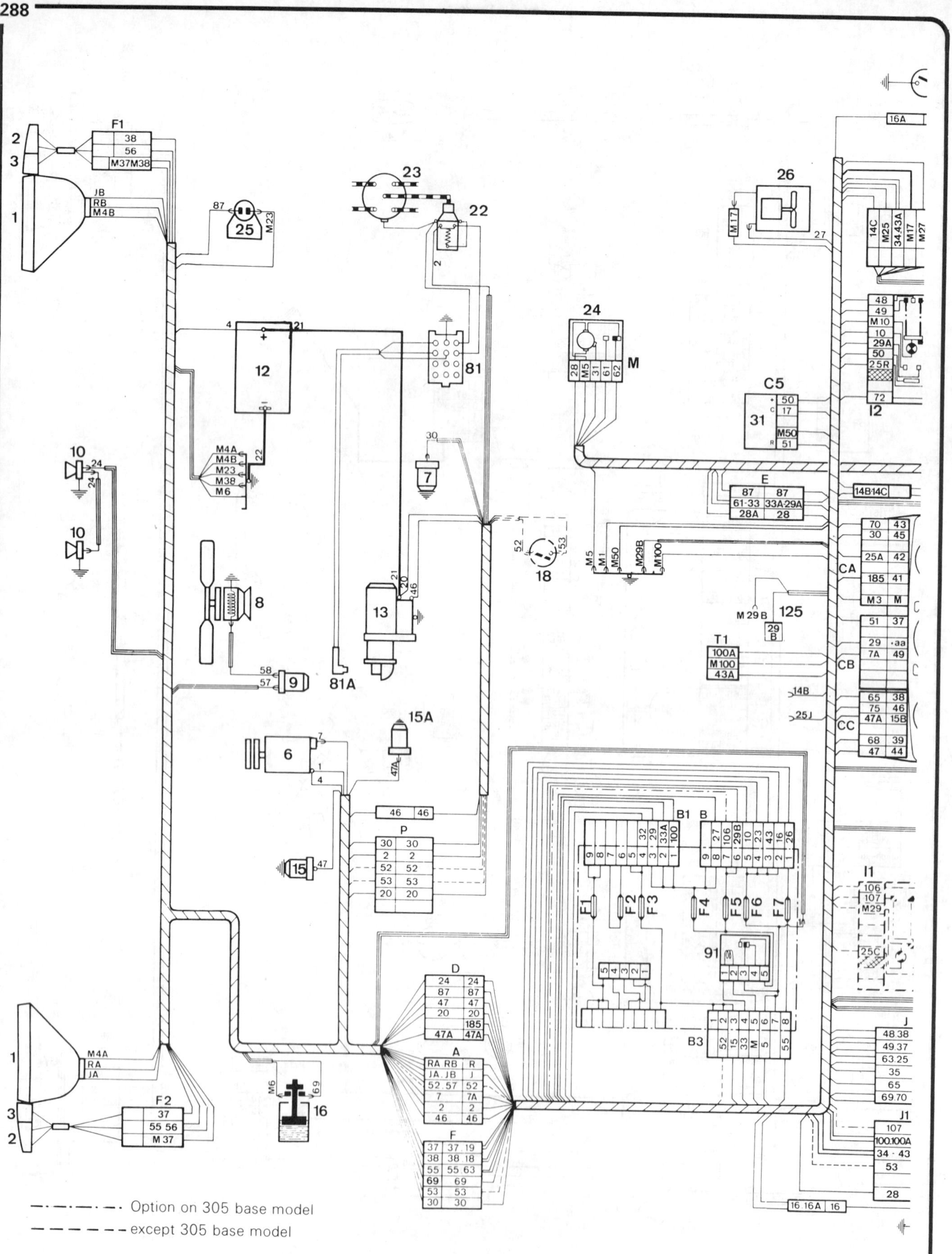

Fig. 12.123 Wiring diagram for Saloon and GL models 1981 on. For key see pages 280 and 281

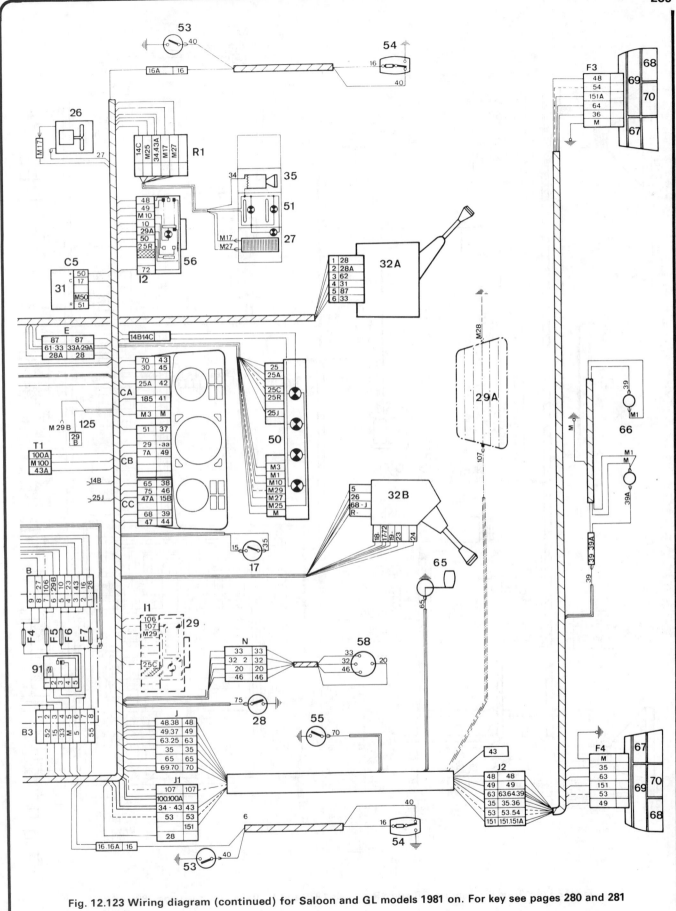

Fig. 12.123 Wiring diagram (continued) for Saloon and GL models 1981 on. For key see pages 280 and 281

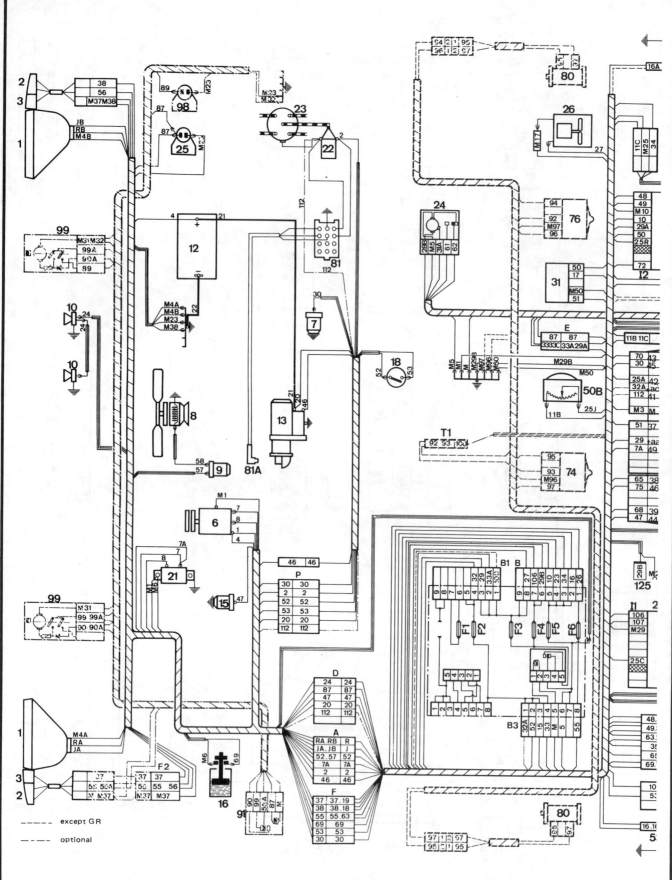

Fig. 12.124 Wiring diagram for GR and SR models 1979 and 1980. For key see page 280 and 281

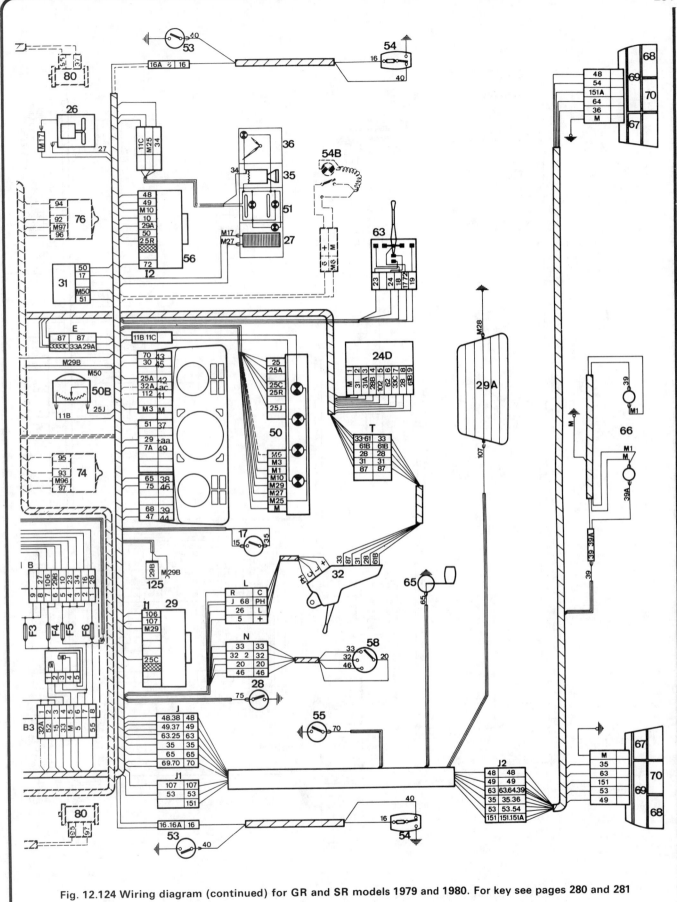

Fig. 12.124 Wiring diagram (continued) for GR and SR models 1979 and 1980. For key see pages 280 and 281

291

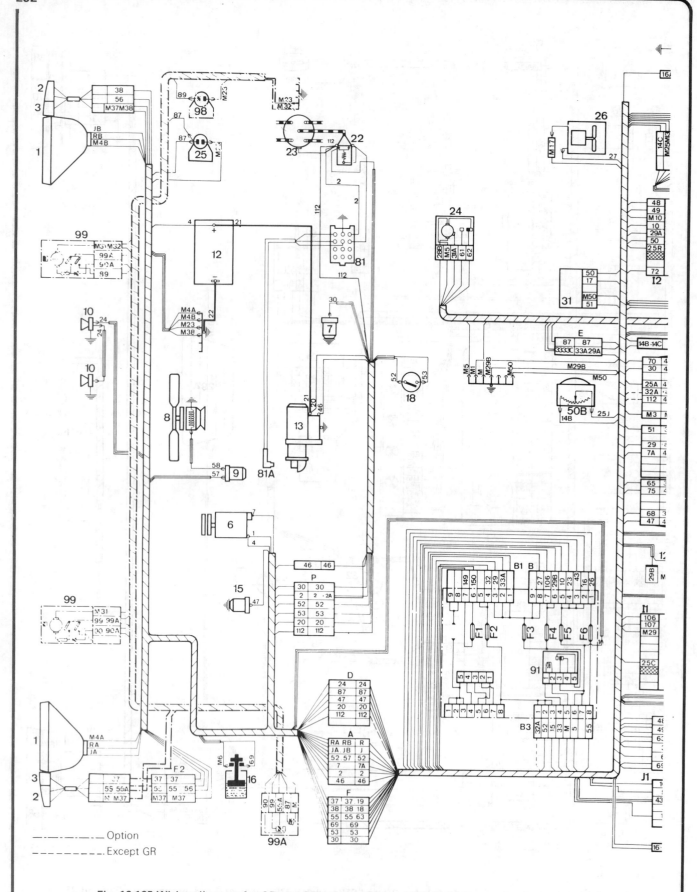

Fig. 12.125 Wiring diagram for GR and SR models 1980 to 1982. For key see pages 280 and 281

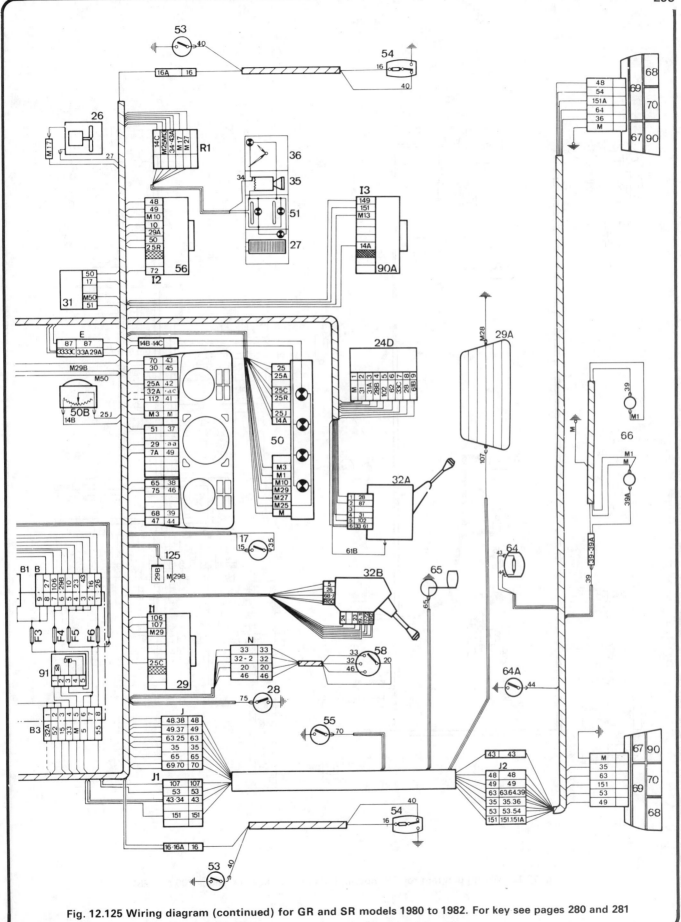

Fig. 12.125 Wiring diagram (continued) for GR and SR models 1980 to 1982. For key see pages 280 and 281

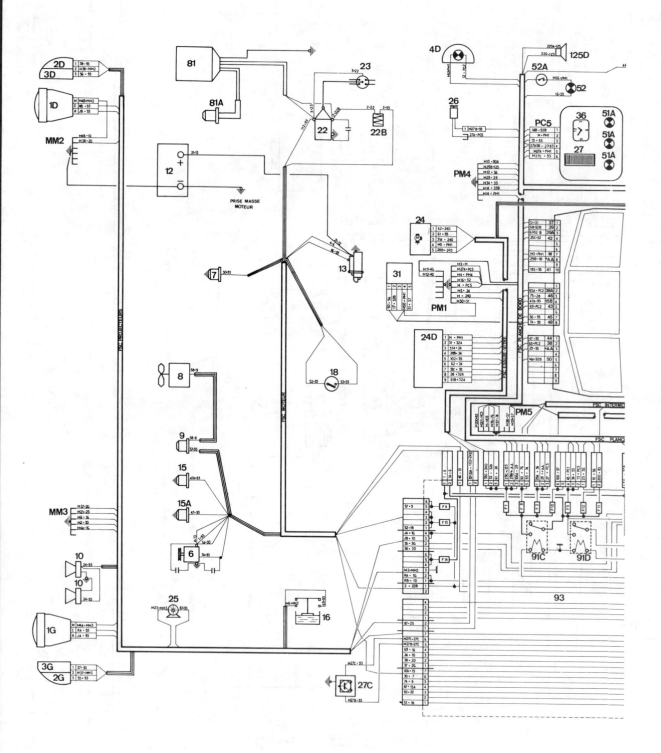

Fig. 12.126 Wiring diagram for SR models 1983 on. For key see pages 280 and 281

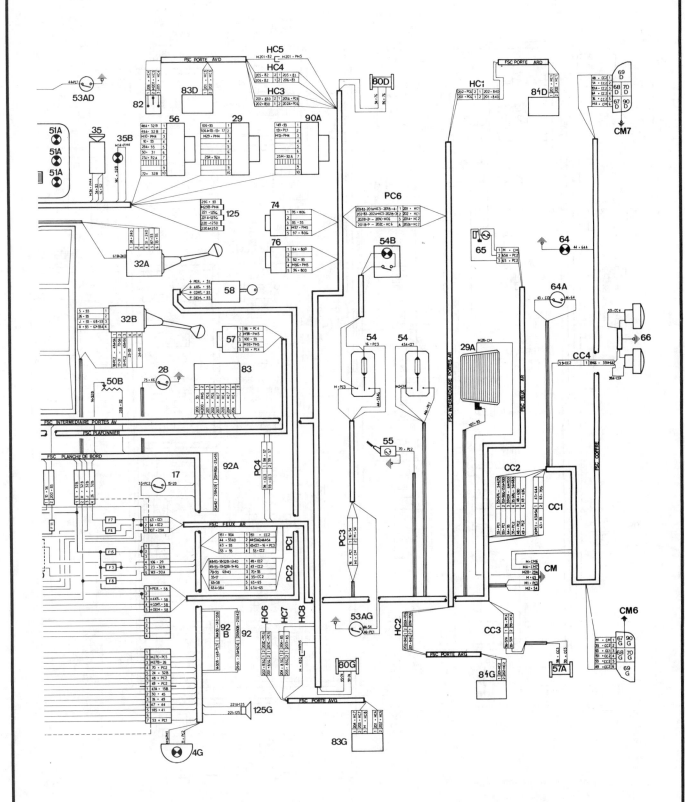

Fig. 12.126 Wiring diagram (continued) for SR models 1983 on. For key see pages 280 and 281

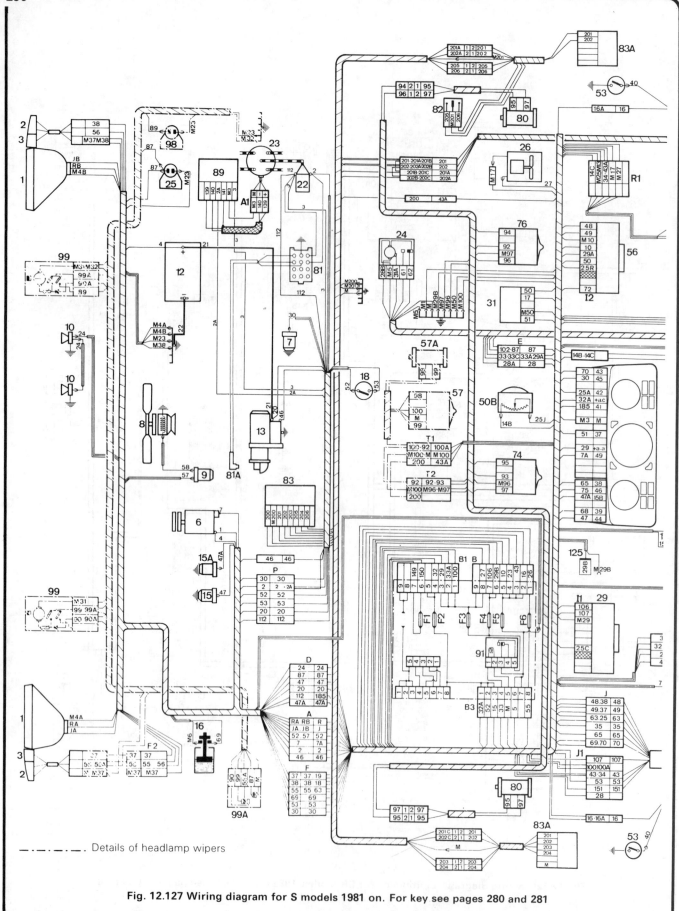

_.___.___.___ Details of headlamp wipers

Fig. 12.127 Wiring diagram for S models 1981 on. For key see pages 280 and 281

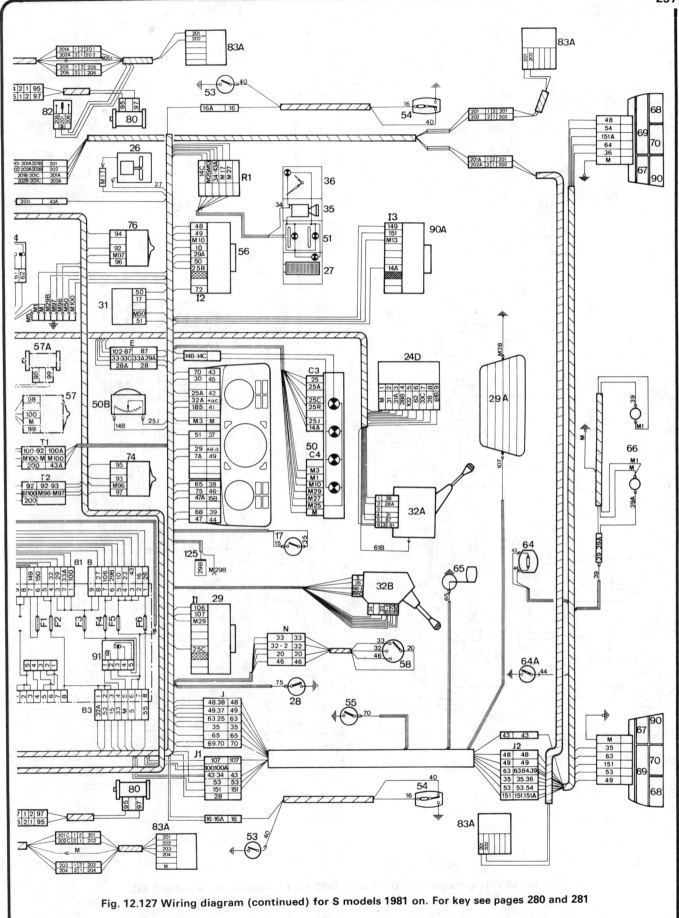

Fig. 12.127 Wiring diagram (continued) for S models 1981 on. For key see pages 280 and 281

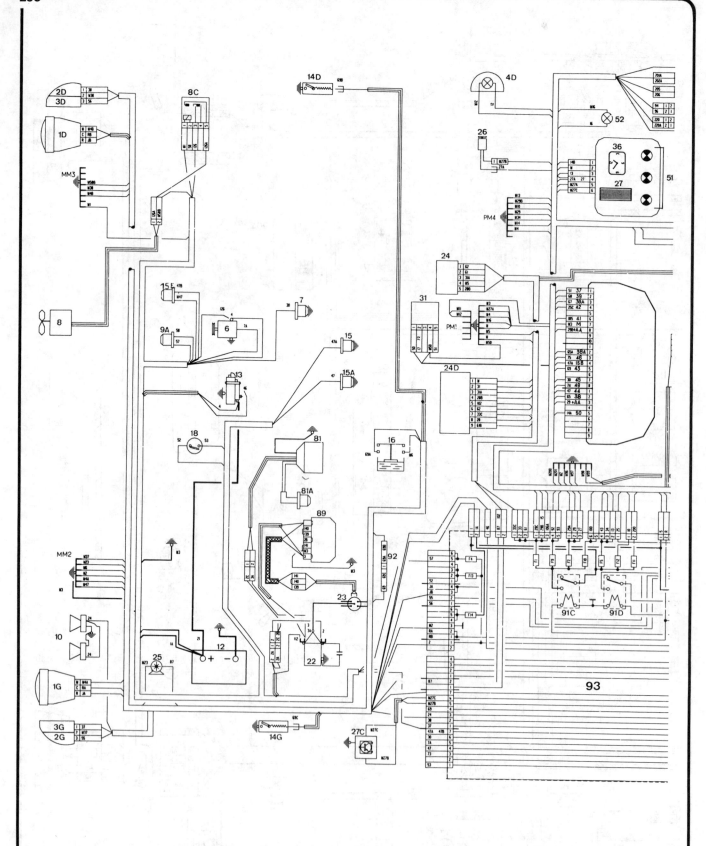

Fig. 12.128 Wiring diagram for GT models 1983 on. For key see pages 280 and 281

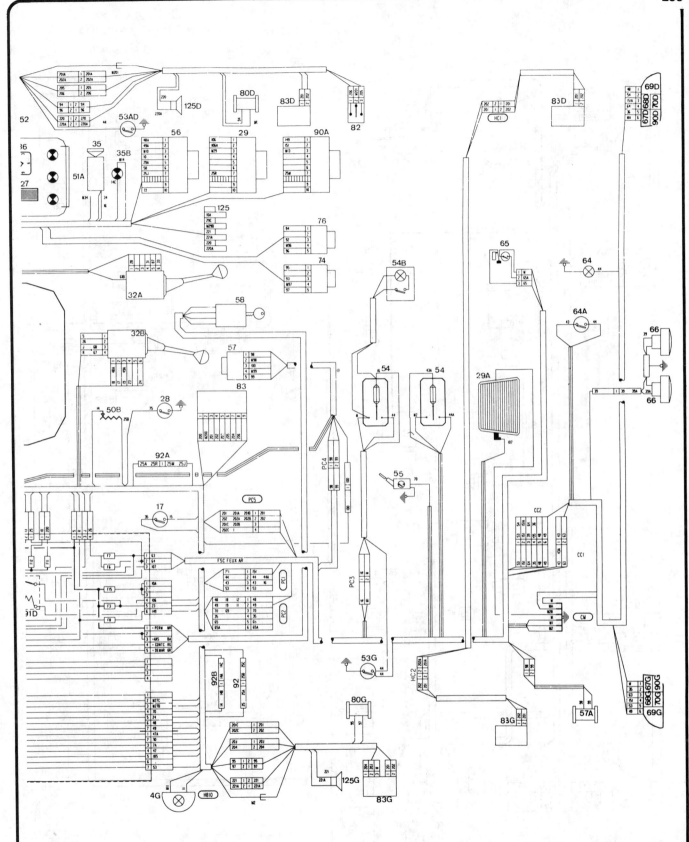

Fig. 12.128 Wiring diagram (continued) for GT models 1983 on. For key see pages 280 and 281

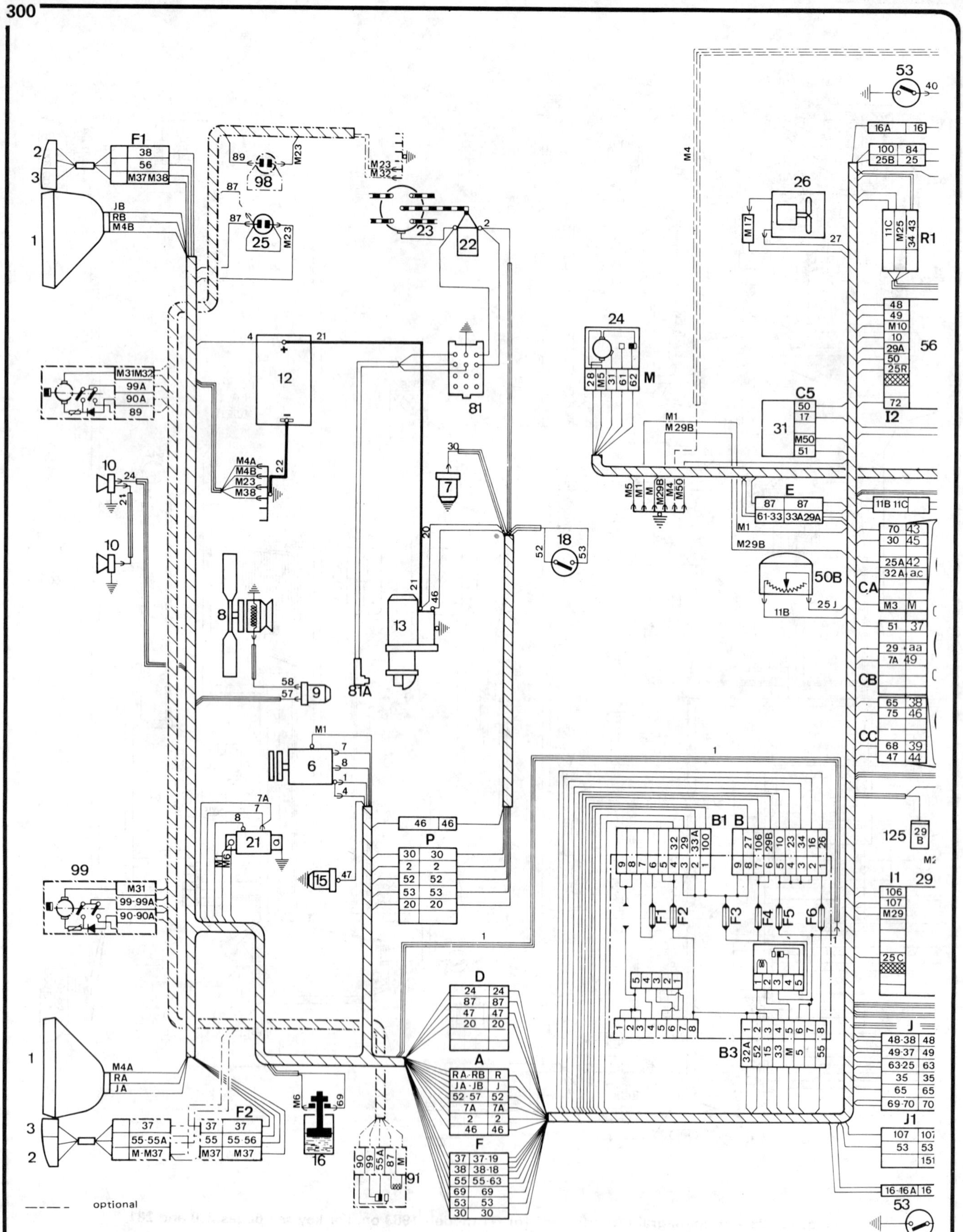

Fig. 12.129 Wiring diagram for Estate and Van models up to 1981. For key see pages 280 and 281

optional

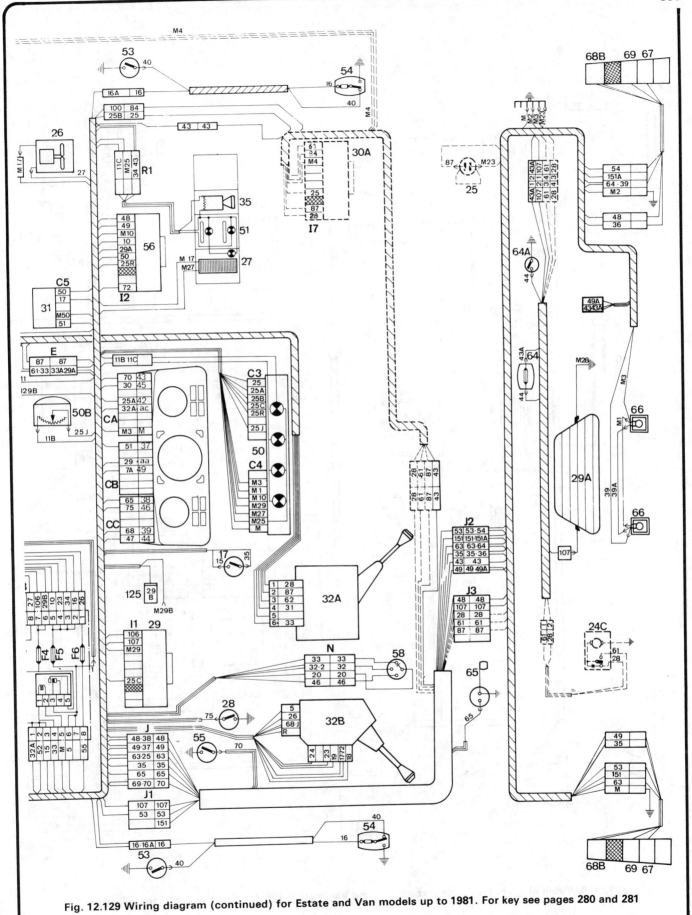

Fig. 12.129 Wiring diagram (continued) for Estate and Van models up to 1981. For key see pages 280 and 281

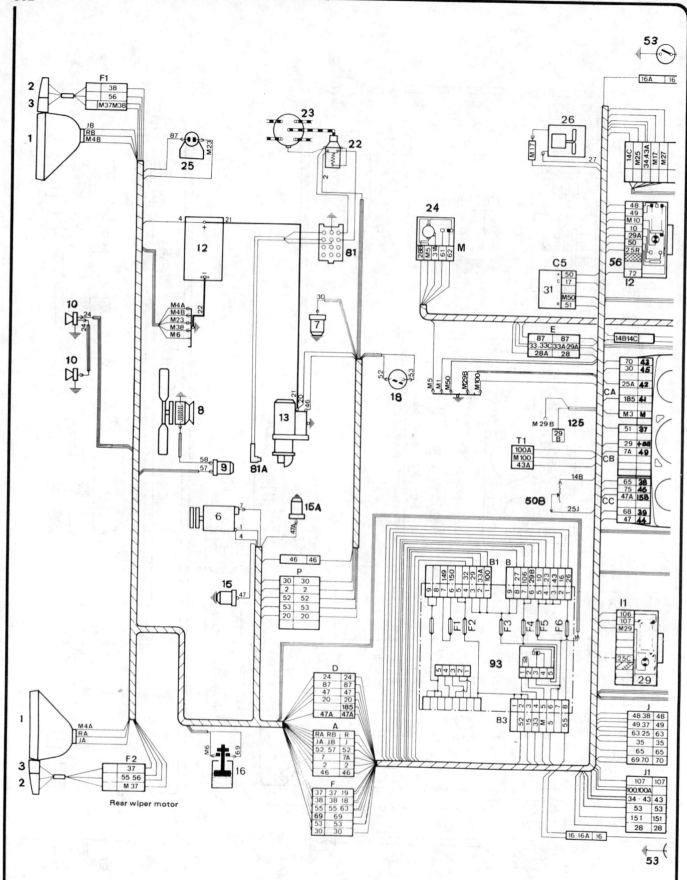

Rear wiper motor

Fig. 12.130 Wiring diagram for Estate (except SR) and Van models 1981 on. For key see pages 280 and 281

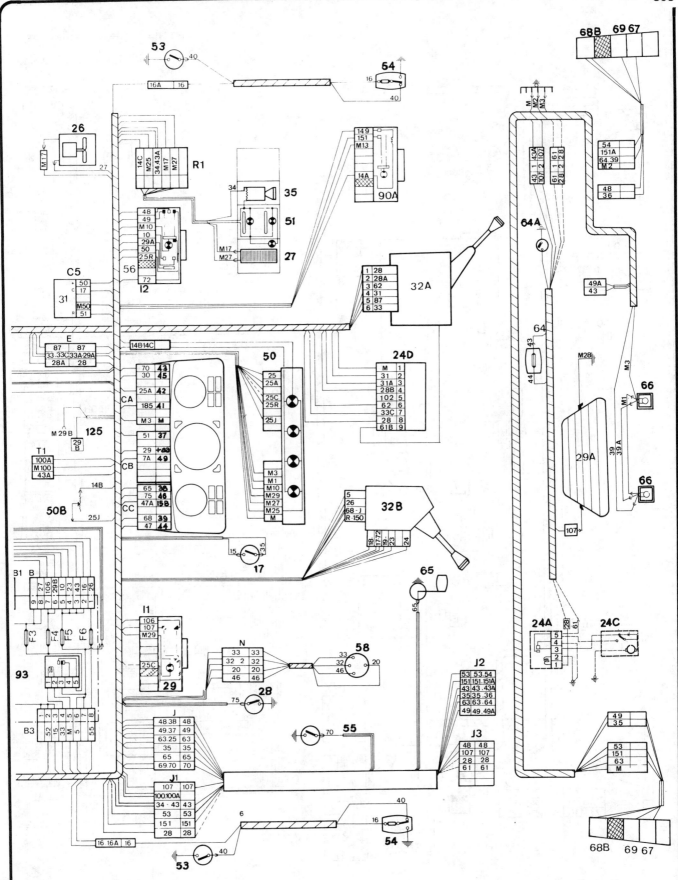

Fig. 12.130 Wiring diagram (continued) for Estate (except SR) and Van models 1981 on. For key see pages 280 and 281

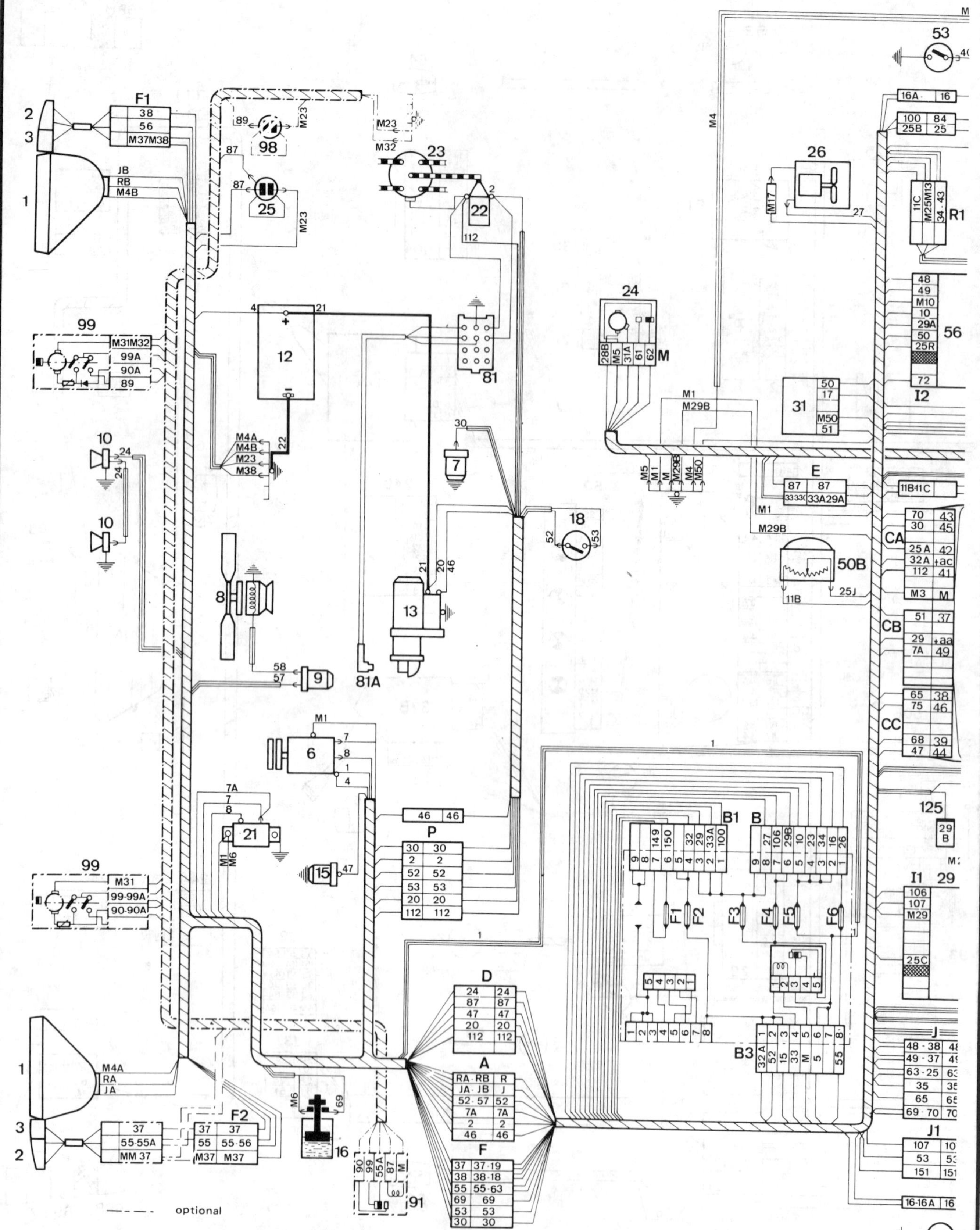

Fig. 12.131 Wiring diagram for GL and GR models 1986. For key see pages 280 and 281

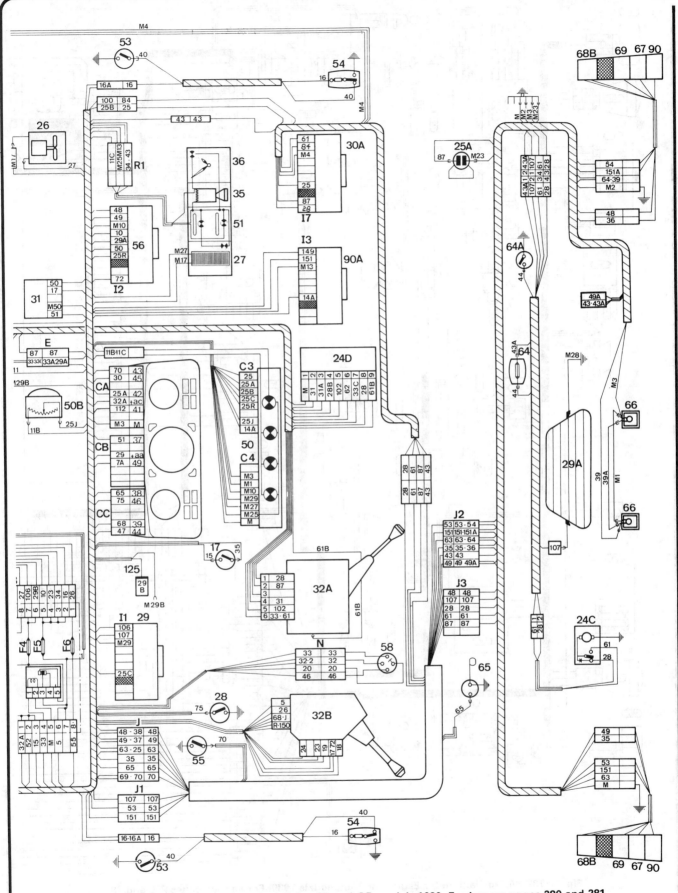

Fig. 12.131 Wiring diagram (continued) for GL and GR models 1986. For key see pages 280 and 281

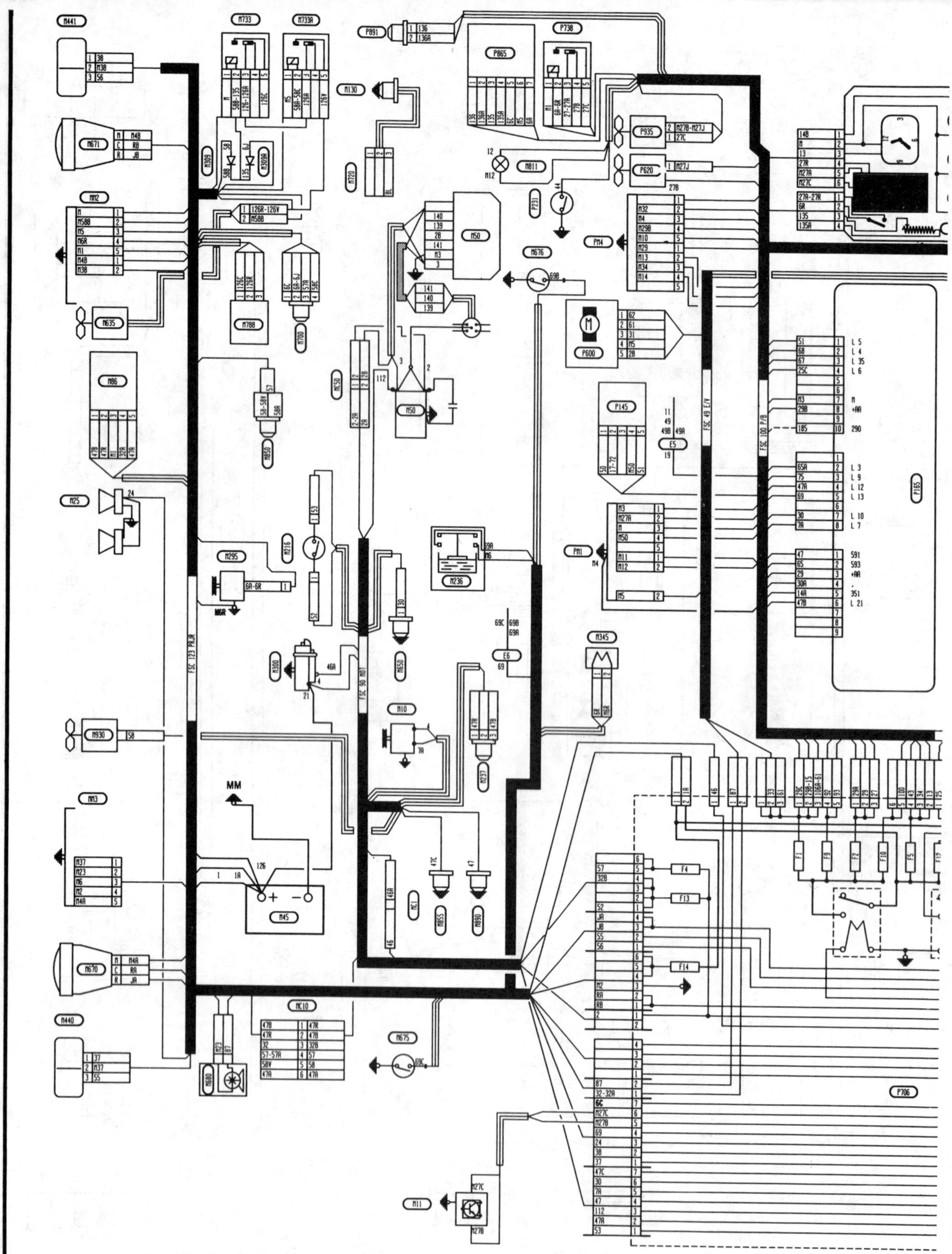

Fig. 12.132 Wiring diagram for Estate and Van models 1986. For key see pages 280 and 281

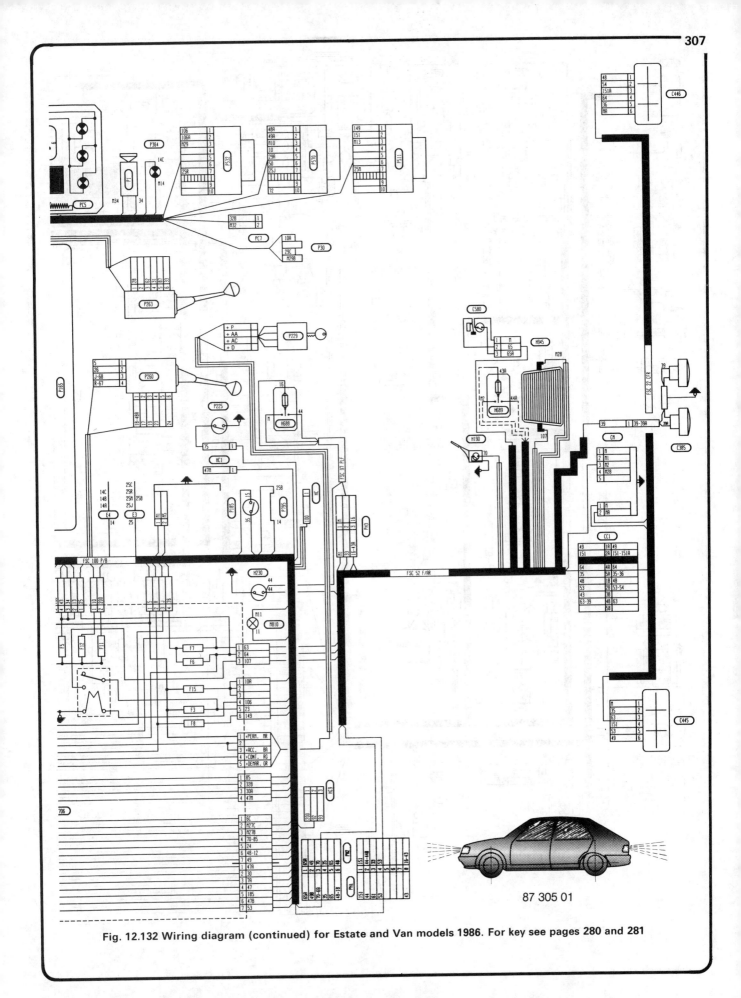

Fig. 12.132 Wiring diagram (continued) for Estate and Van models 1986. For key see pages 280 and 281

87 305 01

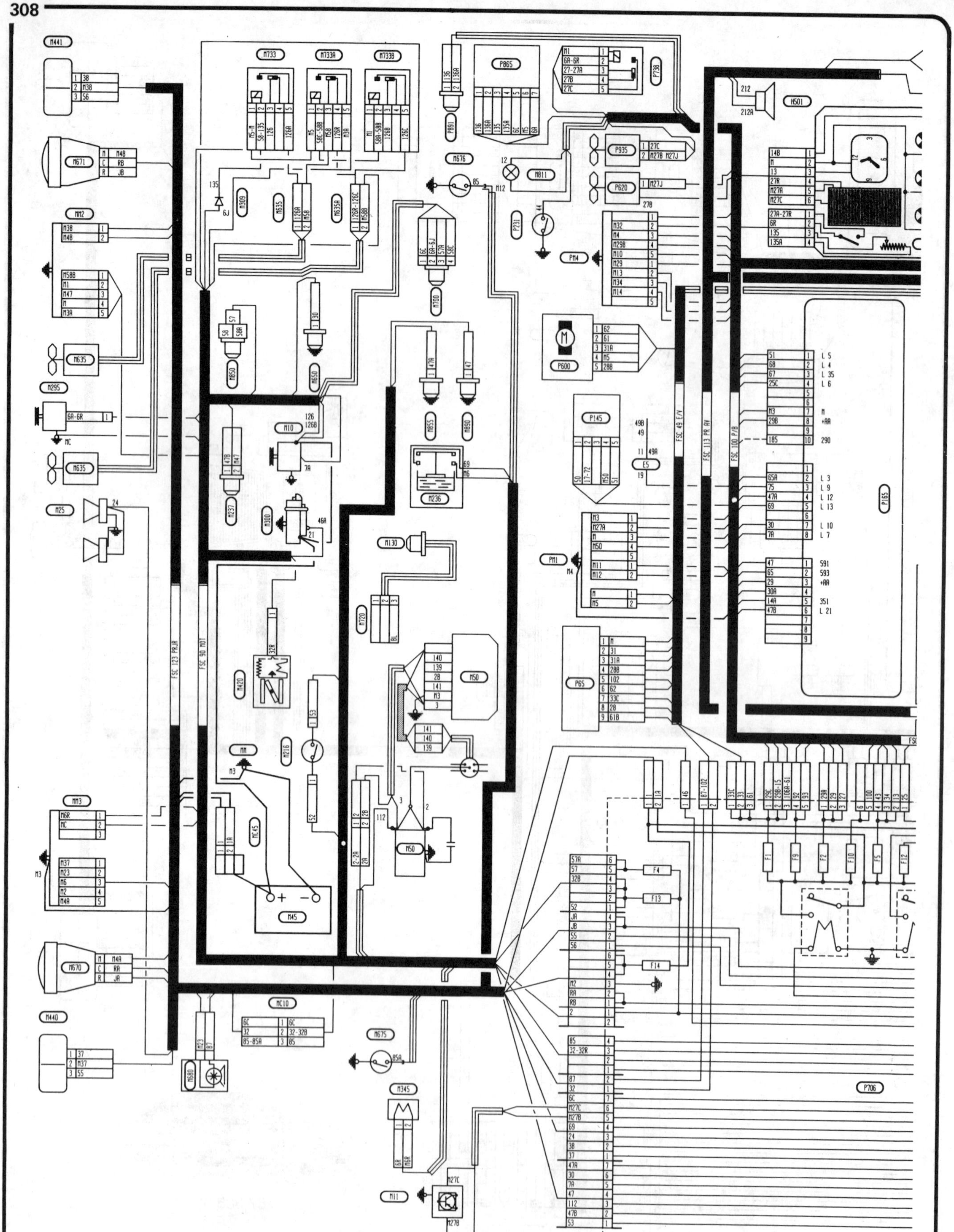

Fig. 12.133 Wiring diagram for GL and GR models 1986. For key see pages 280 and 281

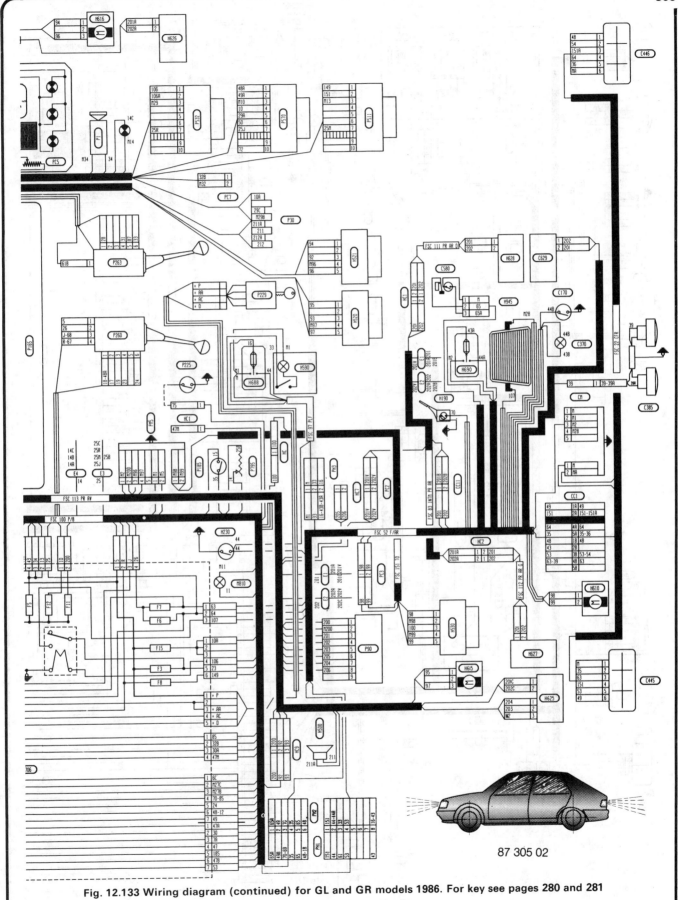

87 305 02

Fig. 12.133 Wiring diagram (continued) for GL and GR models 1986. For key see pages 280 and 281

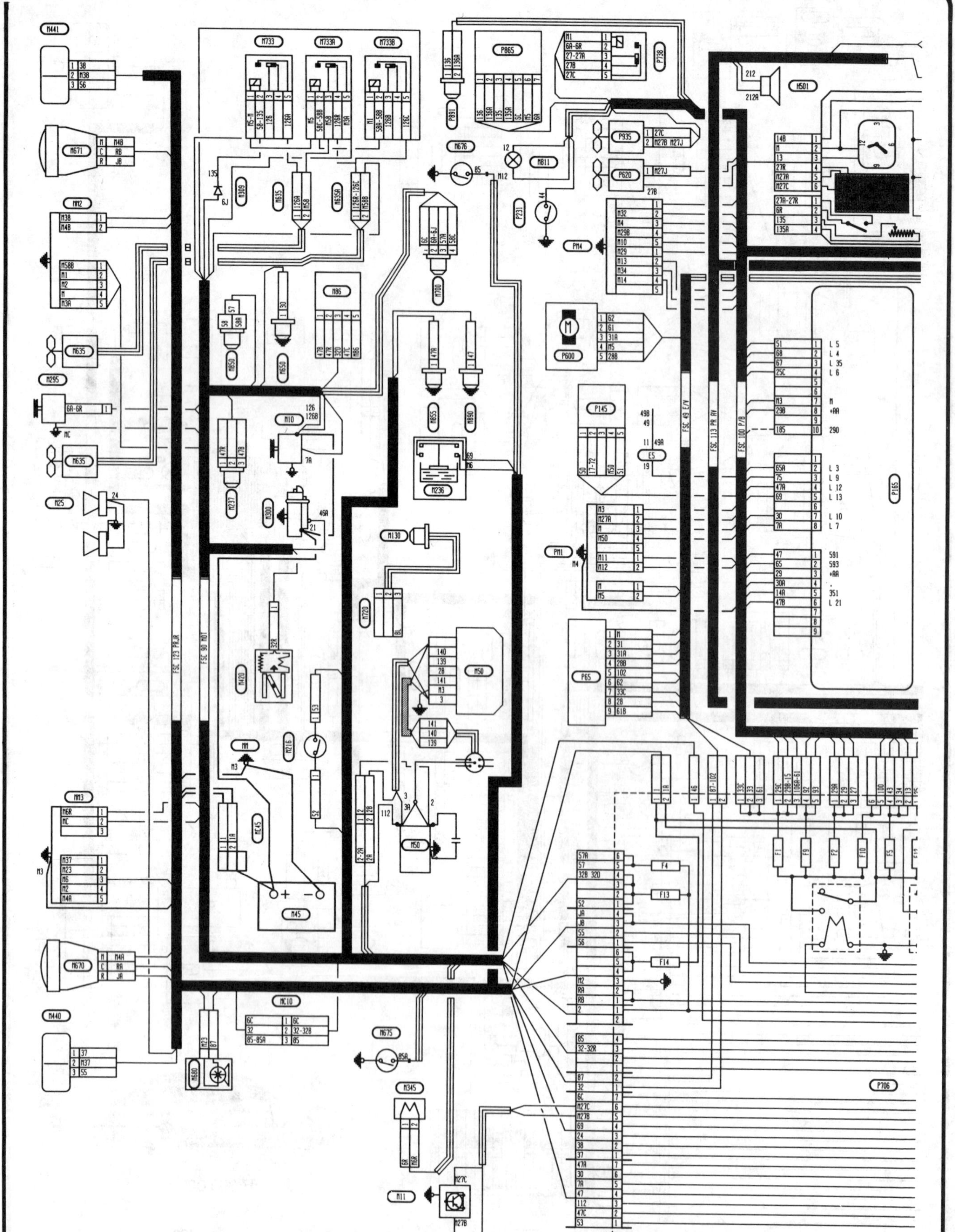

Fig. 12.134 Wiring diagram for GL and GR models 1987. For key see pages 280 and 281

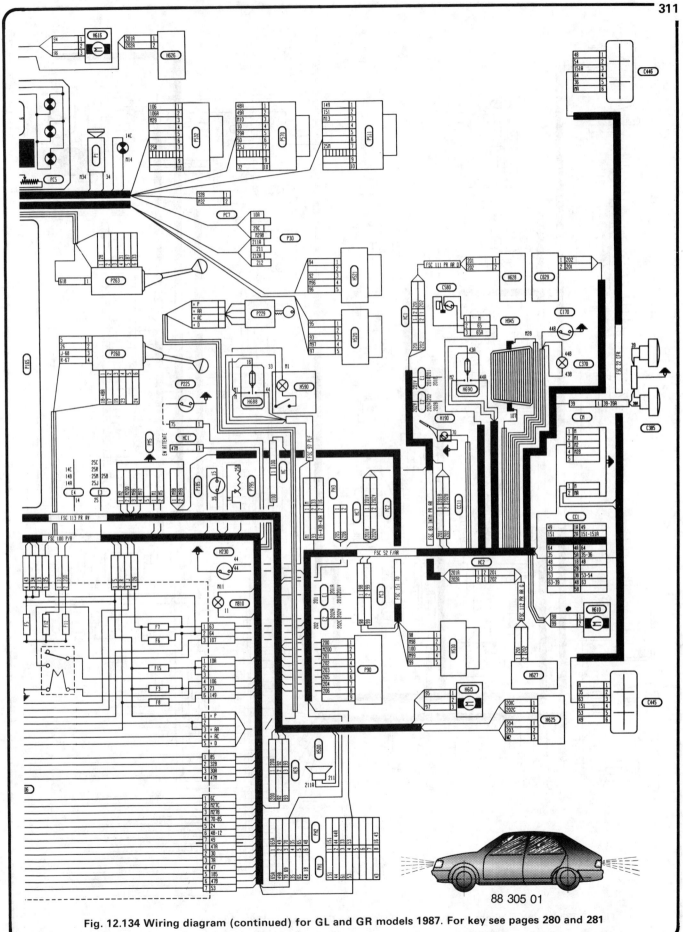

88 305 01

Fig. 12.134 Wiring diagram (continued) for GL and GR models 1987. For key see pages 280 and 281

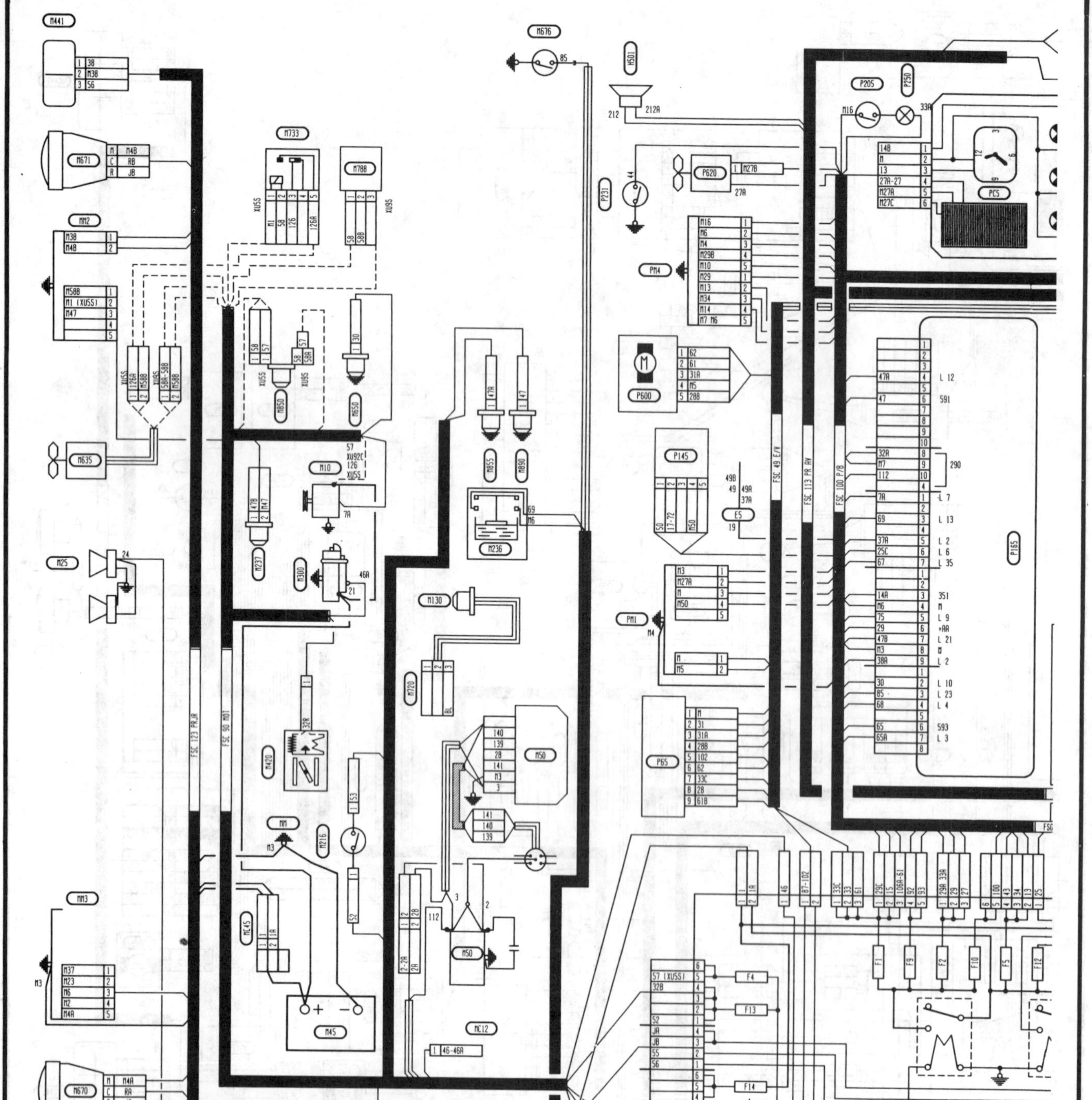

Fig. 12.135 Wiring diagram for Automatic Estate and GTX models 1986. For key see pages 280 and 281

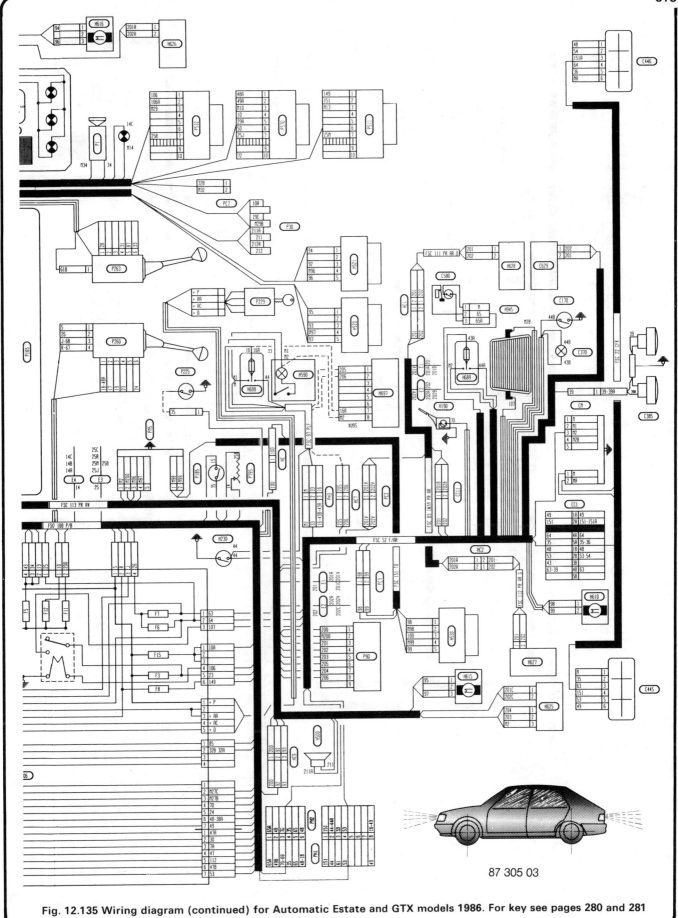

87 305 03

Fig. 12.135 Wiring diagram (continued) for Automatic Estate and GTX models 1986. For key see pages 280 and 281

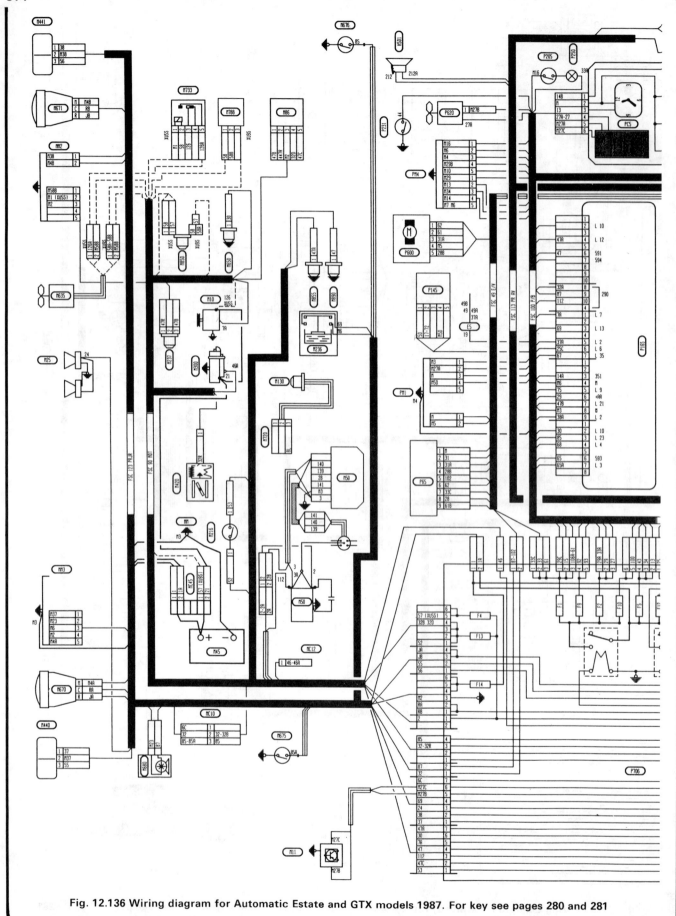

314

Fig. 12.136 Wiring diagram for Automatic Estate and GTX models 1987. For key see pages 280 and 281

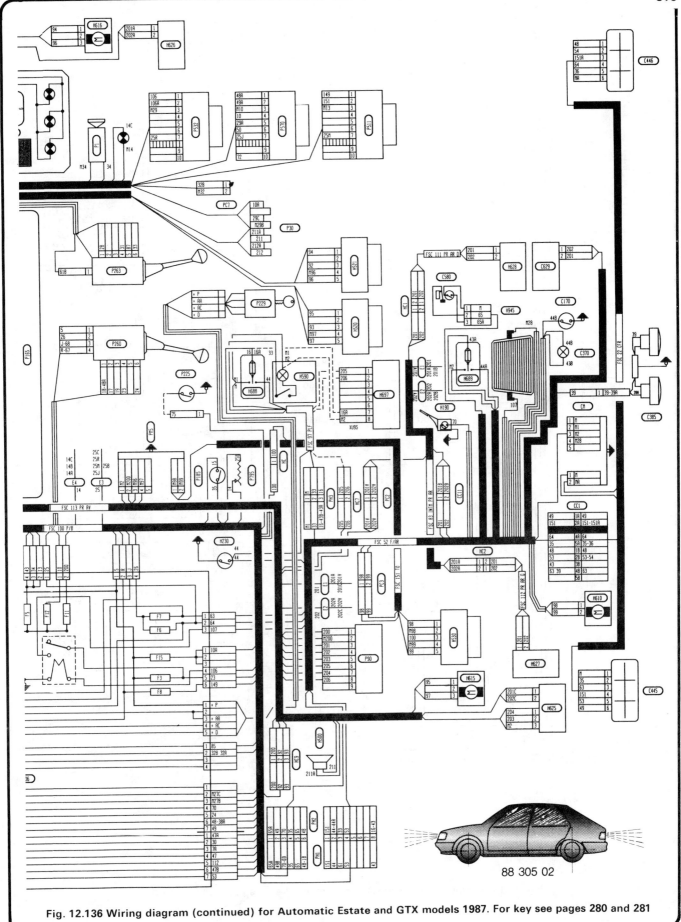

88 305 02

Fig. 12.136 Wiring diagram (continued) for Automatic Estate and GTX models 1987. For key see pages 280 and 281

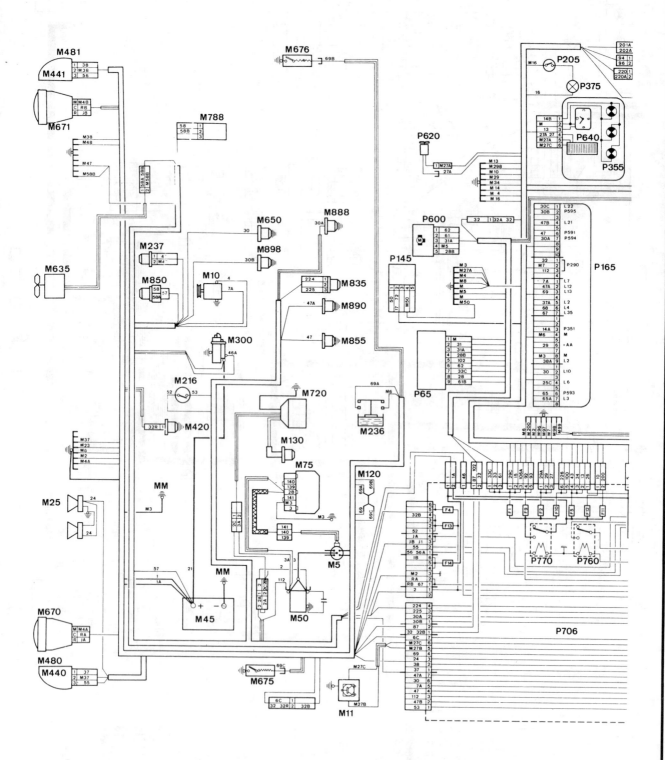

Fig. 12.137 Wiring diagram for GTX models. For key see pages 280 and 281

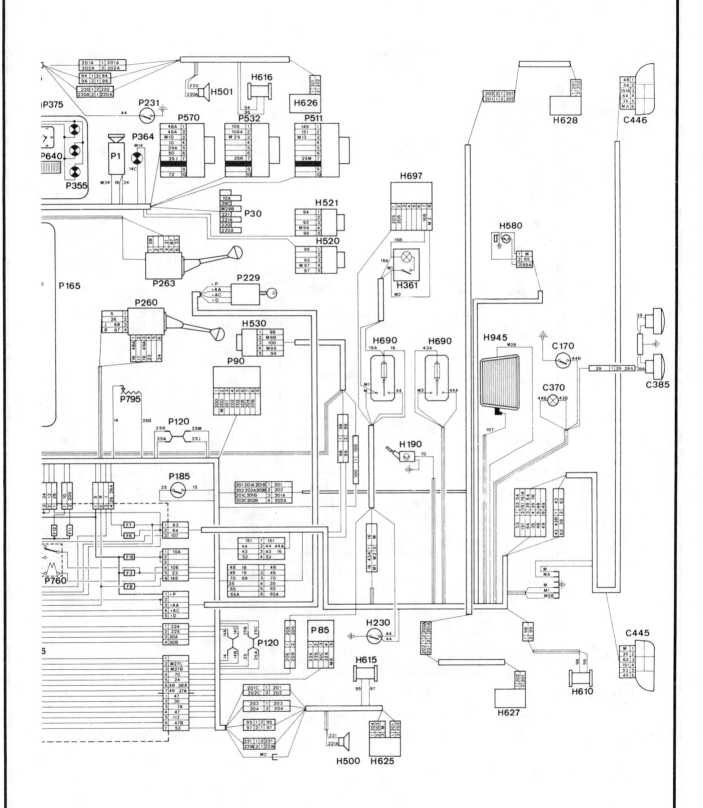

Fig. 12.137 Wiring diagram (continued) for GTX models. For key see pages 280 and 281

317

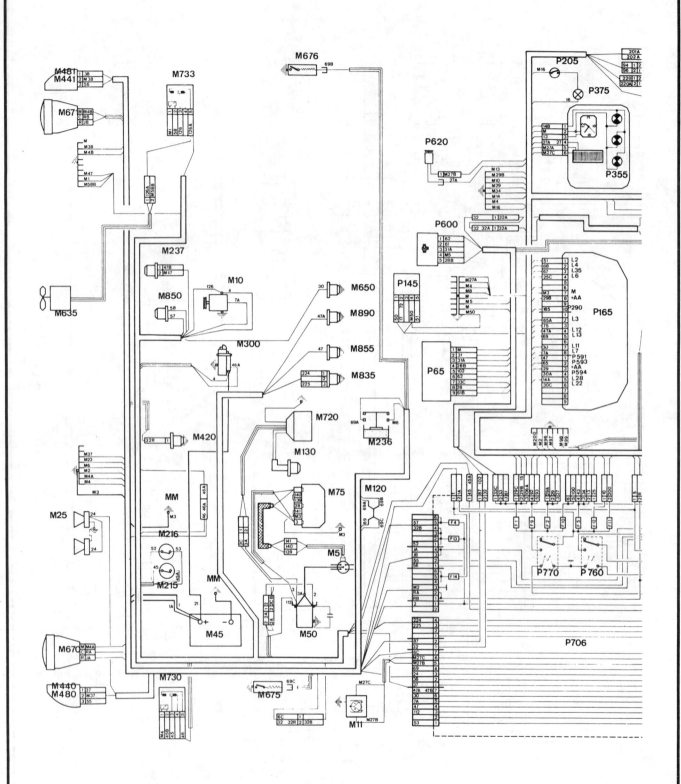

Fig. 12.138 Wiring diagram for GT Automatic model. For key see pages 280 and 281

319

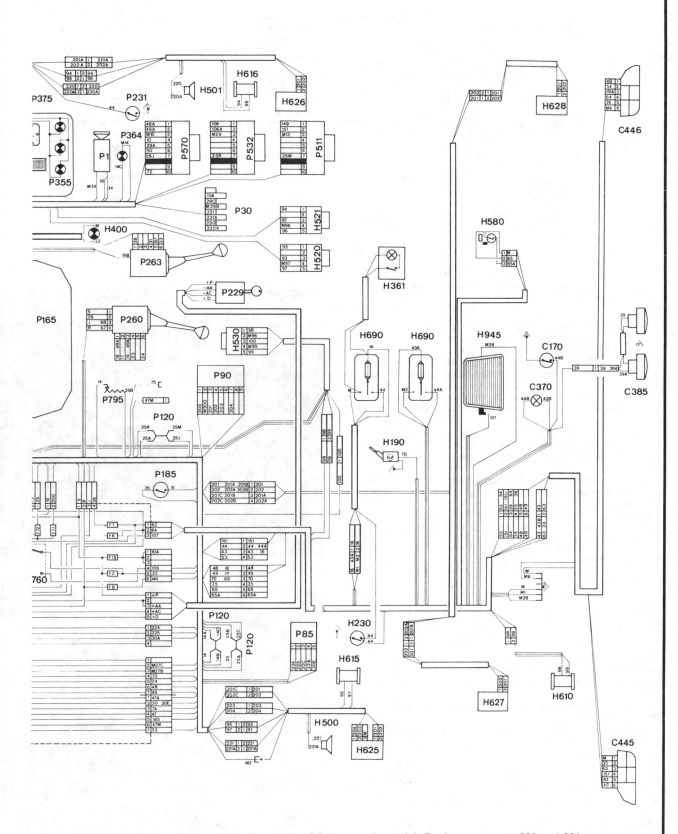

Fig. 12.138 Wiring diagram (continued) for GT Automatic model. For key see pages 280 and 281

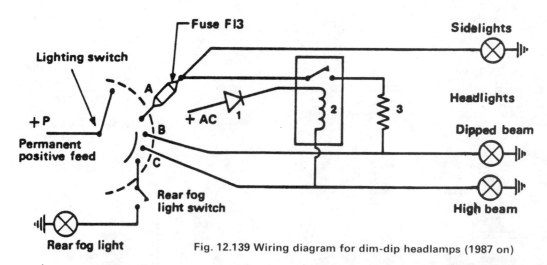

Fig. 12.139 Wiring diagram for dim-dip headlamps (1987 on)

A   Sidelight/dim-dip supply   1   Blocking diode   3   Dropping resistor
B   Normal dipped beam supply   2   Relay   +   AC Ignition-controlled supply
C   Main beam supply

19 Bodywork and fittings

Heater removal and refitting (1983 on)

1   Disconnect the battery earth lead.
2   Remove the trim from around the gearlever by pulling the trim plate rearwards. Lift the plate and gaiter up the gearlever to gain access to the two screws which retain the rear of the centre console. Remove the screws.
3   Remove the two screws (one each side) which secure the front of the console. Remove the console, noting and disconnecting the eletrical leads.
4   Release the heater control panel as described in Section 18, paragraphs 70 to 74 of this Supplement. Also remove the driver's cubby hole (five screws) disconnecting the rheostat wires as it is removed.
5   Clamp the coolant hoses at the matrix pipe stubs and disconnect the hoses. Be prepared for some coolant spillage. Disconnect the control cable from the matrix valve.
6   Disconnect the vacuum pipes from the control flap actuators. The pipes are coloured, and both the control and the actuators are marked as follows to identify the pipes:

   J (jaune) – yellow
   N (noir) – black
   R (rouge) – red
   V (vert) – green

7   Remove the heater ducting and disconnect the blower motor supply leads. Also disconnect the bunch of green leads from their common connector on the left-hand side. It does not matter which lead goes to which tag.
8   Remove the console securing bracket from the bottom of the heater, then remove the bolt at the bottom so exposed.
9   Remove the two nuts (one on each side) which secure the top of the heater.
10 Unclip or disconnect any remaining wires, cables or pipes, then manoeuvre the heater unit clear.
11 The matrix or actuators can now be removed if wished (photo).
12 Refit in the reverse order of removal. Top up and bleed the cooling system on completion.

Boot lid stay removal and refitting (Saloon)

13 Free the right-hand rear door aperture sealing strip where it passes the quarter panel. Remove the rear seat backrest and the quarter panel trim.
14 Raise the boot lid and prop it in the fully open position.
15 Release the balljoints, top and bottom, by undoing the safety clips. Unsnap the balljoints and remove the stay.
16 Refit in the reverse order of removal. Remember to engage the balljoint safety clips before refitting the quarter panel trim.

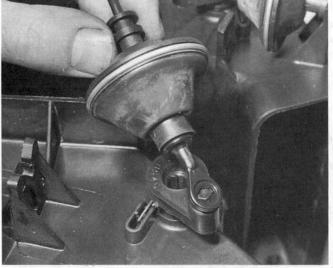

19.11 Removing heater flap vacuum actuator

Fig. 12.140 Access to boot lid stay from inside car (Sec 19)

1   Sealing strip

Tailgate removal and refitting (Estate)

17 Disconnect the battery earth lead.

18 Open the access flap on the left-hand side of the luggage area. Extract and separate the wire connectors which supply the tailgate harness (photo). Tie a piece of string to the tailgate harness and draw it out of the aperture at the top of the frame. Untie the string and leave it in position for refitting.

19 Disconnect the window washer water pipe (when fitted) (photo).

20 Slacken, but do not remove, the tailgate hinge bolts.

21 Have an assistant support the tailgate. Release the strut balljoints by pulling out their tabs, then remove the struts (photo). Remove the hinge bolts and lift away the tailgate.

22 Refit in the reverse order of removal. Adjust the buffers on the strut mountings and the catch release rod as necessary to achieve satisfactory opening and closing (photo).

Glovebox catch repair (pre-1983)

23 If the glovebox catch is broken, it can be repaired with a reinforcement plate made up to the dimensions shown (Fig. 12.141). The material to be used is mild steel sheet 2 mm thick.

24 With the reinforcement plate in position on the catch support, the side holes can be drilled in the plastic by using a bent pointed rod, 5 mm in diameter, heated in a gas flame.

25 Secure the reinforcement plate with nuts and bolts at the side.

Internally adjustable door mirror removal and refitting

26 Remove the cover plate from around the mirror handle.

27 Undo the three Allen screws and remove the mirror (photo).

28 Refit in the reverse order of removal.

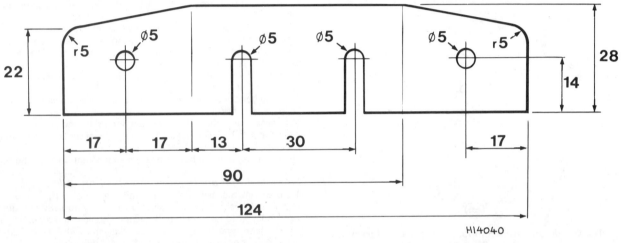

H14040

Fig. 12.141 Glovebox catch repair plate – dimensions in mm (Sec 19)

19.18 Location of tailgate wiring connectors

19.19 Disconnecting the tailgate glass washer pipe

19.21 Tailgate strut balljoint removed showing locking tab

19.22 Tailgate catch adjustment bolt (arrowed)

19.27 Exterior rear view mirror cover plate removed showing screw hole locations

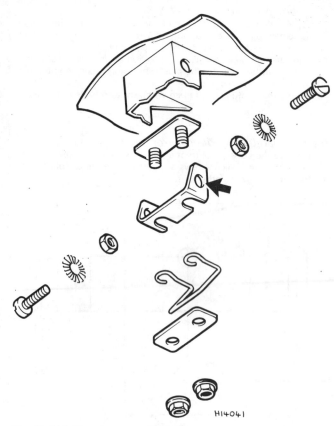

Fig. 12.142 Glovebox catch components showing (arrowed)
position of repair plate (Sec 19)

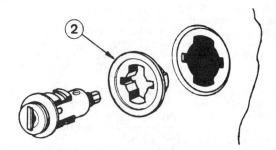

Fig. 12.143 Adaptor piece (2) for fitting old locks to new
doors (Sec 19)

41 Rear seat belts may be of static or inertia reel type depending upon model.
42 Rear seat belts may be fitted to earlier models which do not have them as standard equipment, by utilising the tapped anchorage points which are located in the floor pan beneath the seat cushion and behind the trim of the rear quarter panels.
43 Periodically check the belts for fraying or other damage. If evident, renew the belt.
44 If the belts become dirty, wipe them with a damp cloth using a little liquid detergent only.
45 Check the tightness of the anchor bolts and, if they are ever disconnected, make quite sure that the original sequence for fitting the washers, bushes and anchor plate is retained.
46 **Never** modify the belt or alter its attachment point to the body.

Front seat belt anchorages modification (all models)
47 The front seat belt inertia reel units are secured by four bolts and shakeproof washers on models up to 1985. During 1985 the four bolts were reduced to two, each bolt having a conical and a plain washer.
48 The later type bolts are stronger than the earlier type. Early type bolts **must not** be used on a two-bolt mounting.
49 If an early type mounting is disturbed, new type bolts should be used on reassembly.

Plastic components
With the use of more and more plastic body components by the vehicle manufacturers (eg bumpers, spoilers, and in some cases major body panels), rectification of more serious damage to such items has become a matter of either entrusting repair work to a specialist in this field, or renewing complete components. Repair of such damage by the DIY owner is not really feasible owing to the cost of the equipment and materials required for affecting such repairs. The basic technique involves making a groove along the line of the crack in the plastic using a rotary burr in a power drill. The damaged part is then welded back together by using a hot air gun to heat up and fuse a plastic filler rod into the groove. Any excess plastic is then removed and the area rubbed down to a smooth finish. It is important that a filler rod of the correct plastic is used, as body components can be made of a variety of different types (eg polycarbonate, ABS, polypropylene).
Damage of a less serious nature (abrasions, minor cracks etc) can be repaired by the DIY owner using a two-part epoxy filler repair material. Once mixed in equal proportions, this is used in similar fashion to the bodywork filler used on metal panels. The filler is usually cured in twenty to thirty minutes, ready for sanding and painting.
If the owner is renewed a complete component himself, or if he has repaired it with epoxy filler, he will be left with the problem of finding a suitable paint for finishing which is compatible with the type of plastic used. At one time the use of a universal paint was not possible owing to the complex range of plastics encountered in body component applications. Standard paints, generally speaking, will not bond to plastic or rubber satisfactorily. However, it is now possible to obtain a plastic body parts finishing kit which consists of a pre-primer treatment, a primer and coloured top coat. Full instructions are normally supplied with a kit, but basically the method of use is to first apply the pre-primer to the component concerned and allow it to dry for up to 30 minutes. Then the primer is applied and left to dry for about an hour before finally applying the special coloured top coat. The result is a correctly coloured component where the paint will flex with the plastic or rubber, a property that standard paint does not normally possess.

Doors and locks compatibility (all models)
29 During 1985 the door lock barrel diameter was increased. New doors have holes to fit the larger barrels; old lock barrels can be transferred to new doors by using an adaptor piece obtainable from a Peugeot dealer.

Seats removal and refitting
Front
30 The tubular seat frames are secured to the slides by studs and nuts. The slides are fixed to the floor with socket-headed screws.
31 To remove the seat push it fully forward and remove the slide rear screws, then push the seat fully to the rear and remove the slide front screws.
32 The seat can then be lifted out through the door opening.

Rear (Saloon)
33 Remove the screw from the front face of the seat cushion and remove the cushion.
34 Release the seat back lower fixings and lift and remove the seat back.
35 Where a centre arm rest is fitted, this is simply unbolted from its pivot arms.

Rear (Estate)
36 The seat cushions and the seat backs are removed by unbolting their side pivot assemblies.
37 The refitting procedure for all seats is a reversal of removal.

Front seat headrests
38 The front seat headrests are secured by spring clips which engage in the headrest pillars.
39 To adjust the position of the headrests or to remove them, simply give a sharp pull upwards to disengage the clips from the pillar notches.

Seat belts description and maintenance
40 Inertia reel type front seat belts are fitted to all models.

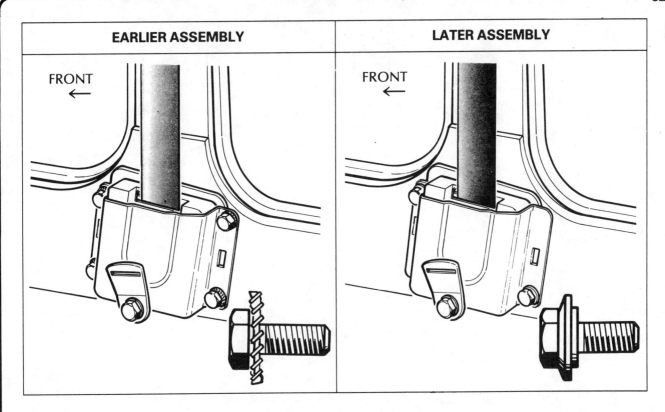

EARLIER ASSEMBLY	LATER ASSEMBLY
FRONT ←	FRONT ←

Fig. 12.144 Old and new type seat belt anchorages (Sec 19)

General repair procedures

Whenever servicing, repair or overhaul work is carried out on the car or its components, it is necessary to observe the following procedures and instructions. This will assist in carrying out the operation efficiently and to a professional standard of workmanship.

Joint mating faces and gaskets

Where a gasket is used between the mating faces of two components, ensure that it is renewed on reassembly, and fit it dry unless otherwise stated in the repair procedure. Make sure that the mating faces are clean and dry with all traces of old gasket removed. When cleaning a joint face, use a tool which is not likely to score or damage the face, and remove any burrs or nicks with an oilstone or fine file.

Make sure that tapped holes are cleaned with a pipe cleaner, and keep them free of jointing compound if this is being used unless specifically instructed otherwise.

Ensure that all orifices, channels or pipes are clear and blow through them, preferably using compressed air.

Oil seals

Whenever an oil seal is removed from its working location, either individually or as part of an assembly, it should be renewed.

The very fine sealing lip of the seal is easily damaged and will not seal if the surface it contacts is not completely clean and free from scratches, nicks or grooves. If the original sealing surface of the component cannot be restored, the component should be renewed.

Protect the lips of the seal from any surface which may damage them in the course of fitting. Use tape or a conical sleeve where possible. Lubricate the seal lips with oil before fitting and, on dual lipped seals, fill the space between the lips with grease.

Unless otherwise stated, oil seals must be fitted with their sealing lips toward the lubricant to be sealed.

Use a tubular drift or block of wood of the appropriate size to install the seal and, if the seal housing is shouldered, drive the seal down to the shoulder. If the seal housing is unshouldered, the seal should be fitted with its face flush with the housing top face.

Screw threads and fastenings

Always ensure that a blind tapped hole is completely free from oil, grease, water or other fluid before installing the bolt or stud. Failure to do this could cause the housing to crack due to the hydraulic action of the bolt or stud as it is screwed in.

When tightening a castellated nut to accept a split pin, tighten the nut to the specified torque, where applicable, and then tighten further to the next split pin hole. Never slacken the nut to align a split pin hole unless stated in the repair procedure.

When checking or retightening a nut or bolt to a specified torque setting, slacken the nut or bolt by a quarter of a turn, and then retighten to the specified setting.

Locknuts, locktabs and washers

Any fastening which will rotate against a component or housing in the course of tightening should always have a washer between it and the relevant component or housing.

Spring or split washers should always be renewed when they are used to lock a critical component such as a big-end bearing retaining nut or bolt.

Locktabs which are folded over to retain a nut or bolt should always be renewed.

Self-locking nuts can be reused in non-critical areas, providing resistance can be felt when the locking portion passes over the bolt or stud thread.

Split pins must always be replaced with new ones of the correct size for the hole.

Special tools

Some repair procedures in this manual entail the use of special tools such as a press, two or three-legged pullers, spring compressors etc. Wherever possible, suitable readily available alternatives to the manufacturer's special tools are described, and are shown in use. In some instances, where no alternative is possible, it has been necessary to resort to the use of a manufacturer's tool and this has been done for reasons of safety as well as the efficient completion of the repair operation. Unless you are highly skilled and have a thorough understanding of the procedure described, never attempt to bypass the use of any special tool when the procedure described specifies its use. Not only is there a very great risk of personal injury, but expensive damage could be caused to the components involved.

Conversion factors

Length (distance)

Inches (in)	X	25.4	= Millimetres (mm)	X 0.0394	= Inches (in)
Feet (ft)	X	0.305	= Metres (m)	X 3.281	= Feet (ft)
Miles	X	1.609	= Kilometres (km)	X 0.621	= Miles

Volume (capacity)

Cubic inches (cu in; in³)	X	16.387	= Cubic centimetres (cc; cm³)	X 0.061	= Cubic inches (cu in; in³)
Imperial pints (Imp pt)	X	0.568	= Litres (l)	X 1.76	= Imperial pints (Imp pt)
Imperial quarts (Imp qt)	X	1.137	= Litres (l)	X 0.88	= Imperial quarts (Imp qt)
Imperial quarts (Imp qt)	X	1.201	= US quarts (US qt)	X 0.833	= Imperial quarts (Imp qt)
US quarts (US qt)	X	0.946	= Litres (l)	X 1.057	= US quarts (US qt)
Imperial gallons (Imp gal)	X	4.546	= Litres (l)	X 0.22	= Imperial gallons (Imp gal)
Imperial gallons (Imp gal)	X	1.201	= US gallons (US gal)	X 0.833	= Imperial gallons (Imp gal)
US gallons (US gal)	X	3.785	= Litres (l)	X 0.264	= US gallons (US gal)

Mass (weight)

Ounces (oz)	X	28.35	= Grams (g)	X 0.035	= Ounces (oz)
Pounds (lb)	X	0.454	= Kilograms (kg)	X 2.205	= Pounds (lb)

Force

Ounces-force (ozf; oz)	X	0.278	= Newtons (N)	X 3.6	= Ounces-force (ozf; oz)
Pounds-force (lbf; lb)	X	4.448	= Newtons (N)	X 0.225	= Pounds-force (lbf; lb)
Newtons (N)	X	0.1	= Kilograms-force (kgf; kg)	X 9.81	= Newtons (N)

Pressure

Pounds-force per square inch (psi; lbf/in²; lb/in²)	X	0.070	= Kilograms-force per square centimetre (kgf/cm²; kg/cm²)	X 14.223	= Pounds-force per square inch (psi; lbf/in²; lb/in²)
Pounds-force per square inch (psi; lbf/in²; lb/in²)	X	0.068	= Atmospheres (atm)	X 14.696	= Pounds-force per square inch (psi; lbf/in²; lb/in²)
Pounds-force per square inch (psi; lbf/in²; lb/in²)	X	0.069	= Bars	X 14.5	= Pounds-force per square inch (psi; lbf/in²; lb/in²)
Pounds-force per square inch (psi; lbf/in²; lb/in²)	X	6.895	= Kilopascals (kPa)	X 0.145	= Pounds-force per square inch (psi; lbf/in²; lb/in²)
Kilopascals (kPa)	X	0.01	= Kilograms-force per square centimetre (kgf/cm²; kg/cm²)	X 98.1	= Kilopascals (kPa)
Millibar (mbar)	X	100	= Pascals (Pa)	X 0.01	= Millibar (mbar)
Millibar (mbar)	X	0.0145	= Pounds-force per square inch (psi; lbf/in²; lb/in²)	X 68.947	= Millibar (mbar)
Millibar (mbar)	X	0.75	= Millimetres of mercury (mmHg)	X 1.333	= Millibar (mbar)
Millibar (mbar)	X	0.401	= Inches of water (inH$_2$O)	X 2.491	= Millibar (mbar)
Millimetres of mercury (mmHg)	X	0.535	= Inches of water (inH$_2$O)	X 1.868	= Millimetres of mercury (mmHg)
Inches of water (inH$_2$O)	X	0.036	= Pounds-force per square inch (psi; lbf/in²; lb/in²)	X 27.68	= Inches of water (inH$_2$O)

Torque (moment of force)

Pounds-force inches (lbf in; lb in)	X	1.152	= Kilograms-force centimetre (kgf cm; kg cm)	X 0.868	= Pounds-force inches (lbf in; lb in)
Pounds-force inches (lbf in; lb in)	X	0.113	= Newton metres (Nm)	X 8.85	= Pounds-force inches (lbf in; lb in)
Pounds-force inches (lbf in; lb in)	X	0.083	= Pounds-force feet (lbf ft; lb ft)	X 12	= Pounds-force inches (lbf in; lb in)
Pounds-force feet (lbf ft; lb ft)	X	0.138	= Kilograms-force metres (kgf m; kg m)	X 7.233	= Pounds-force feet (lbf ft; lb ft)
Pounds-force feet (lbf ft; lb ft)	X	1.356	= Newton metres (Nm)	X 0.738	= Pounds-force feet (lbf ft; lb ft)
Newton metres (Nm)	X	0.102	= Kilograms-force metres (kgf m; kg m)	X 9.804	= Newton metres (Nm)

Power

Horsepower (hp)	X	745.7	= Watts (W)	X 0.0013	= Horsepower (hp)

Velocity (speed)

Miles per hour (miles/hr; mph)	X	1.609	= Kilometres per hour (km/hr; kph)	X 0.621	= Miles per hour (miles/hr; mph)

Fuel consumption*

Miles per gallon, Imperial (mpg)	X	0.354	= Kilometres per litre (km/l)	X 2.825	= Miles per gallon, Imperial (mpg)
Miles per gallon, US (mpg)	X	0.425	= Kilometres per litre (km/l)	X 2.352	= Miles per gallon, US (mpg)

Temperature

Degrees Fahrenheit = (°C x 1.8) + 32   Degrees Celsius (Degrees Centigrade; °C) = (°F - 32) x 0.56

*It is common practice to convert from miles per gallon (mpg) to litres/100 kilometres (l/100km), where mpg (Imperial) x l/100 km = 282 and mpg (US) x l/100 km = 235

Index

Printed by
J H Haynes & Co Ltd
Sparkford Nr Yeovil
Somerset BA22 7JJ England